THE WORLD ALMANAC®
ATLAS OF THE WORLD

Maps created by

MapQuest.com, Inc.

D1119735

MAPQUEST.COM™   WORLD ALMANAC BOOKS

PRIMEDIA Reference Inc. Staff

Director of Editorial Production
Andrea J. Pitluk

Director–Purchasing and Production
Edward A. Thomas

Deputy Editor
William A. McGeveran, Jr.

Senior Editor   **Associate Editors**
Lori Wiesenfeld   Beth R. Ellis
                 Mark S. O'Malley

Vice President & Editorial Director
Robert Famighetti

MapQuest.com, Inc. Staff

Project Manager   Keith Winters

Project Coordinator
(Encyclopedia map set)   Nancy Hamme
Associate Project Coordinator
(Encyclopedia map set)   Andrew DeWitt

Project Coordinator
(Atlas)   Andrew Green
Associate Project Coordinator
(Atlas)   Matt Tharp

Layout & Design
Jeannine Schonta, Andy Skinner

Research & Compilation
Marley Amstutz, Laura Hartwig, Bill Truninger

Research Librarian   Luis Freile

GIS
John Fix, Mark Leitzell, Brad Sauder, Dave Folk,
Larry Meyers

Cartographers
Zach Davis, Brian Goudreau, Kendall Marten,
Todd Martin, Jeff Martz, Tara Petrilli, Justin
Morrill, Tracey Morrill, Linda Peters, Hylon
Plumb, Robert Rizzutti

Editors
Robert Harding, Dana Wolf

Production Support
Shawna Roberts

Imagesetting/Proofing
Chris Gruber, Fred Hofferth

Copyright © 2000
MapQuest.com, Inc.

ISBN 0-88687-855-1 (Paperback)
ISBN 0-88687-856-X (Hardcover)

Printed and manufactured in the
United States of America

TABLE OF CONTENTS

The WORLD in the 21st CENTURY

4 WORLD

6 ASIA and OCEANIA

8 Japan
9 North Korea, South Korea, Taiwan
10 China
11 Vietnam, Laos, Cambodia, Mongolia
12 Thailand, Burma (Myanmar), Philippines
13 Indonesia, Brunei, Singapore, Malaysia
14 Australia
15 Papua New Guinea, New Zealand,
     Federated States of Micronesia
16 Marshall Is., Nauru, Solomon Is., Tuvalu
17 Kiribati, Fiji, Palau, Tonga
18 Vanuatu, New Caledonia &
     Dependencies, Samoa, American Samoa
19 Nepal, Maldives, Bhutan, Sri Lanka
20 India
21 Bangladesh, Pakistan
22 Afghanistan, Iran, Turkmenistan
23 Kazakhstan, Uzbekistan, Kyrgyzstan,
     Tajikistan
24 Iraq, Kuwait, Saudi Arabia
25 Bahrain, Qatar,
     United Arab Emirates, Yemen, Oman
26 Lebanon, Israel, Jordan
27 Turkey, Cyprus, Syria

28 EUROPE

30 Great Britain & Northern Ireland
31 Republic of Ireland
32 Denmark, Netherlands
33 Belgium, Liechtenstein, Luxembourg
34 France
35 Monaco, Switzerland
36 Portugal, Malta, Gibraltar, Andorra
37 Spain
38 Italy
39 Austria, Vatican City, San Marino
40 Germany
41 Poland
42 Czech Republic, Slovakia
43 Hungary, Romania
44 Russia
45 Armenia, Georgia, Azerbaijan
46 Estonia, Latvia, Lithuania
47 Belarus, Ukraine
48 Slovenia, Croatia,
     Bosnia & Hercegovina,
     F.Y.R. Macedonia
49 Albania, Yugoslavia
50 Moldova, Bulgaria
51 Greece
52 Iceland, Norway
53 Sweden, Finland

54 AFRICA

56 Egypt, Libya
57 Algeria, Tunisia, Morocco
58 Western Sahara, Cape Verde,
     Mali, Mauritania
59 Chad, Niger, Sudan
60 Eritrea, Djibouti, Ethiopia, Somalia
61 Kenya, Uganda, Rwanda, Burundi
62 Senegal, The Gambia, Guinea,
     Guinea-Bissau
63 Sierra Leone, Côte d'Ivoire,
     São Tomé & Príncipe, Liberia
64 Ghana, Burkina Faso, Benin, Togo
65 Nigeria, Cameroon
66 Equatorial Guinea, Republic of the
     Congo, Gabon, Central African Republic
67 Comoros, Democratic Republic of the
     Congo, Zambia
68 Tanzania, Malawi, Mozambique
69 Mauritius, Zimbabwe, Botswana,
     Madagascar
70 Angola, Namibia, Seychelles
71 South Africa, Swaziland, Lesotho

72 SOUTH AMERICA

74 Argentina
75 Paraguay, Uruguay
76 Chile
77 Peru, Bolivia
78 Colombia
79 Ecuador, Venezuela
80 Guyana, Suriname, French Guiana
81 Brazil

82 NORTH AMERICA

84 Mexico
85 Belize, Guatemala
86 Honduras, El Salvador, Costa Rica
87 Nicaragua, Panama
88 Cuba, Jamaica
89 Dominican Republic, Haiti, Bahamas,
     Turks & Caicos Is.
90 Puerto Rico, Antigua & Barbuda,
     St. Kitts & Nevis, Dominica
91 St. Lucia, Barbados,
     St. Vincent & the Grenadines,
     Grenada, Trinidad & Tobago
92 Canada
93 Canadian Provincial & Territorial Flags
94 Alberta
95 British Columbia
96 Manitoba
97 New Brunswick
98 Newfoundland
99 Northwest Territories, Nunavut
100 Nova Scotia, Prince Edward Island
101 Ontario, Québec
102 Southern Ontario
103 Southern Québec
104 Saskatchewan
105 Yukon Territory

POLAR REGIONS

6 Arctic Regions, Greenland
7 Antarctica

8 WORLD INDEX

UNITED STATES

6 U.S. Political
7 U.S. Physical
8 Alabama
9 Alaska
0 Arizona
1 Arkansas
2 California
3 Colorado
4 Connecticut
5 Delaware
6 Florida
7 Georgia
8 Hawaii
9 Idaho
0 Illinois
1 Indiana
2 Iowa
3 Kansas
4 Kentucky
5 Louisiana
6 Maine
7 Maryland
8 Massachusetts
9 Michigan
0 Minnesota
1 Mississippi
2 Missouri
3 Montana
4 Nebraska
5 Nevada
6 New Hampshire
7 New Jersey
8 New Mexico
9 New York
0 North Carolina
1 North Dakota
2 Ohio
3 Oklahoma
4 Oregon
5 Pennsylvania
6 Rhode Island
7 South Carolina
8 South Dakota
9 Tennessee
0 Texas
1 Utah
2 Vermont
3 Virginia
4 Washington
5 West Virginia
6 Wisconsin
7 Wyoming

8 STATE INDEXES

General

- ⊛ National Capital
- ★ Territorial Capital
- • Other City
- International Boundary (subject area)
- International Boundary (non-subject)
- Internal Boundary (state, province, etc.)
- ---- Disputed Boundary
- Perennial River
- Intermittent River
- Canal
- Dam

U.S. States, Canadian Provinces & Territories
(additions and changes to general legend)

- ★ State Capital
- • County Seat
- Built Up Area
- State Boundary
- County Boundary
- National Park
- Other Park, Forest, Grassland
- Indian, Other Reservation
- ■ Point of Interest
- ▲ Mountain Peak
- ·········· Continental Divide
- ········· Time Zone Boundary
- Limited Access Highway
- Other Major Road
- (90) Highway Shield

PROJECTION

The only true representation of the earth, free of distortion, is a globe. Maps are flat, and the process by which the geographic locations (latitude and longitude) are transformed from a three-dimensional sphere to a two-dimensional flat map is called a Projection.

For a detailed explanation of Projections, see *MapScope* in Volume 2 of *Funk & Wagnalls New Encyclopedia.*

TYPES OF SCALE

VISUAL SCALE

Every map has a bar scale, or a Visual Scale, that can be used for measuring. It shows graphically the relationship between map distance and ground distance.

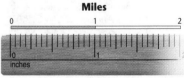

Miles

One inch represents 1 mile

Kilometers

One centimeter represents 10 kilometers

REPRESENTATIVE FRACTION

The scale of a map, expressed as a numerical ratio of map distance to ground distance, is called a Representative Fraction (or RF). It is usually written as 1/50,000 or 1:50,000, meaning that one unit of measurement on the map represents 50,000 of the same units on the ground.

This example is used on pages 20, 21 for India, Bangladesh, and Pakistan.

The Globe is centered on the continent of Asia, as shown on pages 6, 7.

The subject countries are shown in a stronger red/brown color.

LOCATOR

THE WORLD IN THE 21ST CENTURY

The following eight-page section looks at the growing world population and the impact of environmental change as we move into a new century and millennium. Topics covered are:

World Population Trends ....pages S-1,2
Life & Health S-3,4
Climate & Global Warming S-5,6
Deforestation S-7,8

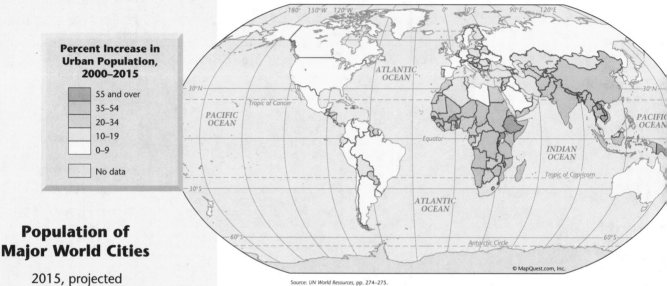

Source: *UN World Resources*, pp. 274–275.

Percent Increase in Urban Population, 2000–2015

- 55 and over
- 35–54
- 20–34
- 10–19
- 0–9
- No data

Urban Population Growth, 2000–2015

The world population will become increasingly urbanized in the early 21st century. It is predicted that the largest increases in urban population will occur in Africa and southern and eastern Asia

Population of Major World Cities

2015, projected

1 Tokyo 28,887,000
2 Mumbai...........26,218,000
3 Lagos...............24,640,000
4 São Paulo 20,320,000
5 Mexico City......19,180,000
6 Shanghai 17,969,000
7 New York..........17,602,000
8 Calcutta............17,305,000
9 Delhi 16,860,000
10 Beijing 15,572,000
11 Los Angeles 14,217,000
12 Buenos Aires 13,856,000
13 Seoul 12,980,000
14 Rio de Janeiro ..11,860,000
15 Osaka 10,609,000

These figures are for "urban agglomerations," which are densely populated urban areas, larger than the cities by themselves.

Source: UN, Dept. for Economic and Social Information and Policy Analysis

© MapQuest.com, Inc.

Population Growth: Urban vs. Rural Areas, 1950–2015

Population (billions)

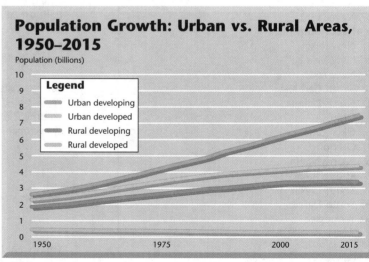

Legend
- Urban developing
- Urban developed
- Rural developing
- Rural developed

Source: *UN World Resources*, p. 146.

Population growth in rural areas will taper off where it has not already. But urban growth will increase, especially in the developing nations.

Developed regions include United States, Canada, Japan, Europe, and Australia and New Zealand.

Developing regions include Africa, Asia (excluding Japan), South America and Central Ame Mexico, and Oceania (excluding Australia and New Zealand). The European successor states the former Soviet Union are classified as developed regions, while the Asian successor states classified as developing regions.

Population Density, 2000

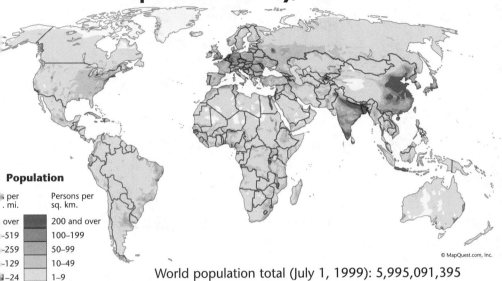

Population

per . mi.	Persons per sq. km.
over	200 and over
–519	100–199
–259	50–99
–129	10–49
–24	1–9
der 1	under 1

© MapQuest.com, Inc.

World population total (July 1, 1999): 5,995,091,395

Source: International Programs Center, U.S. Bureau of the Census

Population Density, Largest Countries

2000
People per square mile

China	330
India	800
United States	70
Indonesia	290
Brazil	50
Russia	20

2050
People per square mile

China	360
India	1,400
United States	100
Indonesia	450
Brazil	70
Russia	20

The world will become more crowded in the 21st century. In mid-1999, China already had the highest population in the world, with an estimated 1.2 billion inhabitants, one-fifth of the total population. India had reached 1 billion, while the United States had the world's third-largest population, with about 273 million, followed by Indonesia, Brazil, and Russia.

Source: Bureau of the Census, U.S. Dept. of Commerce

Anticipated World Population Growth

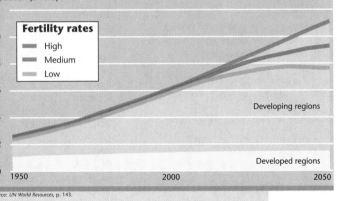

pulation (billions)

Fertility rates
- High
- Medium
- Low

Developing regions

Developed regions

| 1950 | 2000 | 2050 |

rce: UN World Resources, p. 143.

The world population has grown from about 2 billion in 1950 to 6 billion today, and could almost double by 2050. Most of the growth will continue to occur in developing regions, where fertility rates (number of children born per woman of childbearing age) are relatively high.

Where the fertility rate is around 2 children per woman of childbearing age, the population will tend to stabilize. This figure indicates roughly that couples, over a lifetime, are replacing themselves without adding to the population.

Population experts at the United Nations actually give three different projections for future population growth. Under a **high** fertility-rate projection, which assumes rates would stabilize at an average of 2.6 in high-fertility regions and 2.1 in low-fertility regions, the global population would reach 11.2 billion by 2050. Under a **medium** projection, which assumes rates would ultimately stabilize at around replacement levels, the population would rise to 9.4 billion by 2050. Under a **low** fertility-rate projection, which assumes rates would eventually stabilize at lower-than-replacement levels, the world population would still reach about 7.7 billion by 2050.

Population Projections by Continent

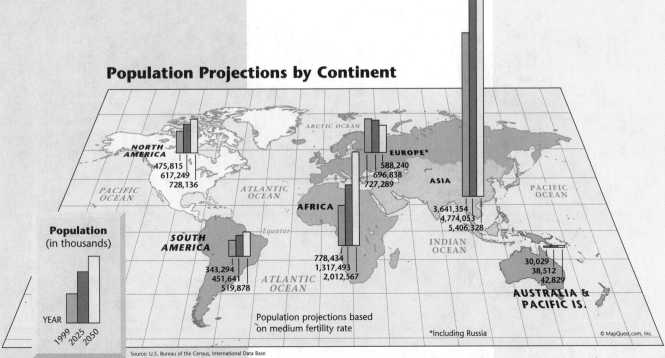

ARCTIC OCEAN

NORTH AMERICA
475,815
617,249
728,136

PACIFIC OCEAN

ATLANTIC OCEAN

EUROPE*
588,240
696,838
727,289

ASIA
3,641,354
4,774,053
5,406,328

PACIFIC OCEAN

AFRICA
778,434
1,317,493
2,012,567

Equator

INDIAN OCEAN

SOUTH AMERICA
343,294
451,641
519,878

ATLANTIC OCEAN

Population (in thousands)

YEAR
1999 2025 2050

30,029
38,512
42,829

AUSTRALIA & PACIFIC IS.

Population projections based on medium fertility rate

*Including Russia

© MapQuest.com, Inc.

Source: U.S. Bureau of the Census, International Data Base

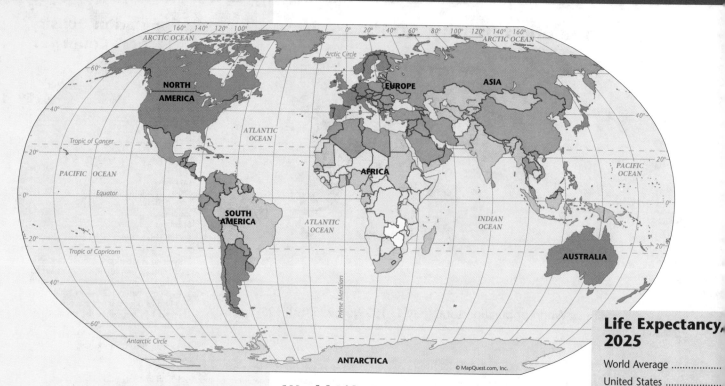

World Life Expectancy, 1999

Life Expectancy
(in years)

- 75–84
- 65–74
- 50–64
- 40–49
- Less than 40

- No data

Life expectancy at birth is a common measure of the number of years a person may expect to live. There are many factors, such as nutrition, sanitation, health and medical services, that contribute to helping people live longer.

As some of the above factors improve in the developing countries, life expectancy there should increase. But most of Sub-Saharan Africa will have less than average life expectancies.

Although it is not indicated here, females almost always have a longer life expectancy than males.

Life Expectancy, 2025

World Average ....

United States ....

Highest
Andorra ....
Austria ....
Australia ....
Canada ....
Cyprus ....
Dominica ....
Israel ....
Japan ....
Kuwait ....
Monaco ....
San Marino ....
Singapore ....
Taiwan ....

Lowest
Malawi ....
Ethiopia ....
Zambia ....
Rwanda ....
Swaziland ....
Botswana ....
Namibia ....
Zimbabwe ....

World Life Expectancy, 2025

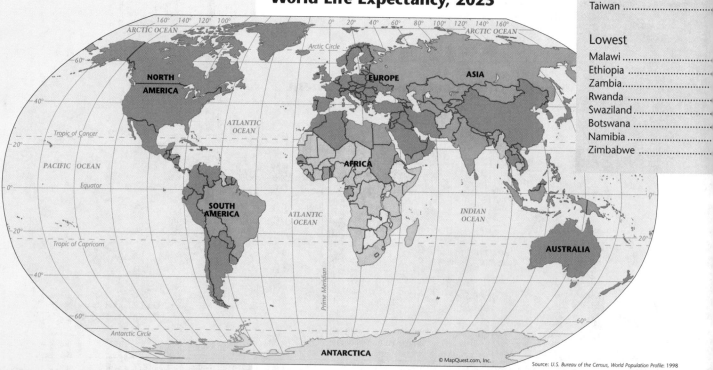

Source: U.S. Bureau of the Census, World Population Profile: 1998

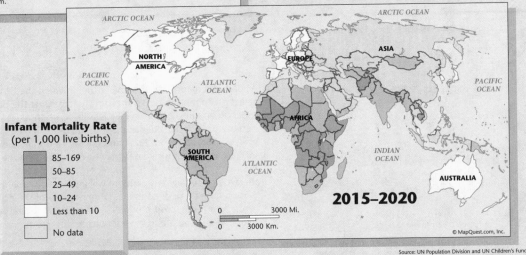

1995–2000

0 — 3000 Mi.
0 — 3000 Km.

MapQuest.com, Inc.

Infant Mortality Averages, 2015–2020

by continent with highest and lowest country

World Average 35

Africa 55
  Sierra Leone 114
  Mauritius 8

Asia 32
  Afghanistan 118
  Japan 4

Australia & Oceania ..15
  Papua
    New Guinea 37
  Australia 5

Europe 8
  Albania 20
  Austria
    & 14 others..........5

North America 22
  Haiti 82
  Canada...................5
  U.S. 5

South America 23
  Guyana.................37
  Chile......................9

Infant Mortality

Infant mortality means the number of deaths before the age of one per 1,000 live births. It is a fairly common way of judging how healthy a country is. Presently there are about 14 countries with infant mortality rates lower than that of the United States.

With improvements in sanitation and health care, it is expected that infant mortality will decline substantially in the 21st century. However, it will continue to be a serious problem especially in Sub-Saharan Africa and other developing regions

Infant Mortality Rate
(per 1,000 live births)

- 85–169
- 50–85
- 25–49
- 10–24
- Less than 10
- No data

2015–2020

0 — 3000 Mi.
0 — 3000 Km.

© MapQuest.com, Inc.

Source: UN Population Division and UN Children's Fund

Food & Nutrition

There has been a general trend towards better nutrition, but Sub-Saharan Africa remains a problem area: increasing numbers of people will be suffering from undernutrition.

On a worldwide basis, the food supply seems adequate. Unfortunately the availability of food and the distribution of people don't always match up.

Undernutrition in Developing Countries, 1969-2010

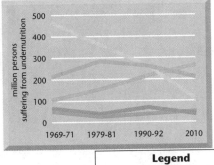

million persons suffering from undernutrition

1969-71 1979-81 1990-92 2010

Legend
- Latin America and the Caribbean
- Near East and North Africa
- Sub-Saharan Africa
- East and Southeast Asia
- South Asia

Fertility

This rate is the number of births related to the number of women of childbearing age. Currently the rate for developed nations is about 1.6, but it is about 2.9 in developing nations.

Africa shows the slowest reduction in the fertility rate. With improvements in infant mortality and the implementation of family planning programs, the rate should stabilize.

Average Daily per Capita Calorie Supply, 1992–1994

by continent with highest and lowest country

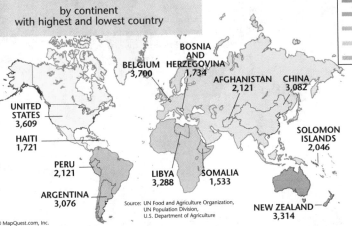

BOSNIA AND HERZEGOVINA 1,734
BELGIUM 3,700
AFGHANISTAN 2,121
CHINA 3,082
UNITED STATES 3,609
HAITI 1,721
PERU 2,121
LIBYA 3,288
SOMALIA 1,533
SOLOMON ISLANDS 2,046
ARGENTINA 3,076
NEW ZEALAND 3,314

Source: UN Food and Agriculture Organization, UN Population Division, U.S. Department of Agriculture

© MapQuest.com, Inc.

Trends in Fertility Rates

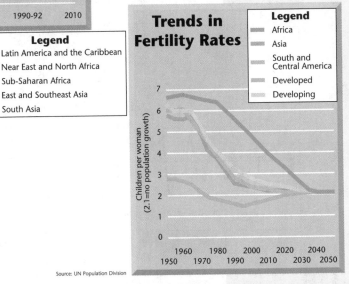

Legend
- Africa
- Asia
- South and Central America
- Developed
- Developing

Children per woman (2.1=no population growth)

1950 1960 1970 1980 1990 2000 2010 2020 2030 2040 2050

Source: UN Population Division

Global Warming

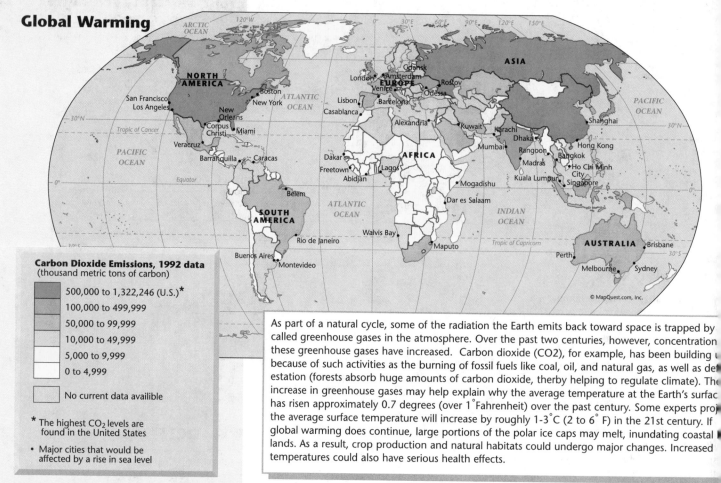

Carbon Dioxide Emissions, 1992 data
(thousand metric tons of carbon)

- 500,000 to 1,322,246 (U.S.)*
- 100,000 to 499,999
- 50,000 to 99,999
- 10,000 to 49,999
- 5,000 to 9,999
- 0 to 4,999

No current data availible

* The highest CO₂ levels are found in the United States

• Major cities that would be affected by a rise in sea level

Source: Estimates or Global, Regional, and National Annual CO2 Emissions from Fossil-Fuel Burning Hydraulic Cement Production, and Gas Flaring: 1950–1992, Oak Ridge National Laboratory, 1995

As part of a natural cycle, some of the radiation the Earth emits back toward space is trapped by called greenhouse gases in the atmosphere. Over the past two centuries, however, concentration these greenhouse gases have increased. Carbon dioxide (CO2), for example, has been building because of such activities as the burning of fossil fuels like coal, oil, and natural gas, as well as de estation (forests absorb huge amounts of carbon dioxide, therby helping to regulate climate). The increase in greenhouse gases may help explain why the average temperature at the Earth's surfac has risen approximately 0.7 degrees (over 1˚Fahrenheit) over the past century. Some experts pro the average surface temperature will increase by roughly 1-3˚C (2 to 6˚F) in the 21st century. If global warming does continue, large portions of the polar ice caps may melt, inundating coastal lands. As a result, crop production and natural habitats could undergo major changes. Increased temperatures could also have serious health effects.

Projections of Rising Global Temperature

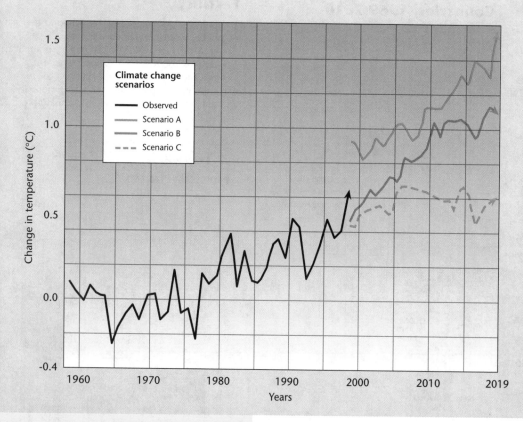

Scientists differ over the magnitude of the mate changes an increase in greenhouse ga may cause. The graph at left shows how avera global surface temperatures would be affec under three different scenarios up to the ye 2019. Scenario B, which a group of NASA scie tists believes to be the most likely, assumes moderate increase in greenhouse gases. Scenario A, they grow at a fast rate, wh Scenario C assumes no increase in greenhou gases. (A temperature change of 1˚C is equi lent to a change of 1.8˚F.)

Sources: NASA Goddard Institute for Space Studies.

Changing Surface Temperatures, 1960–1998

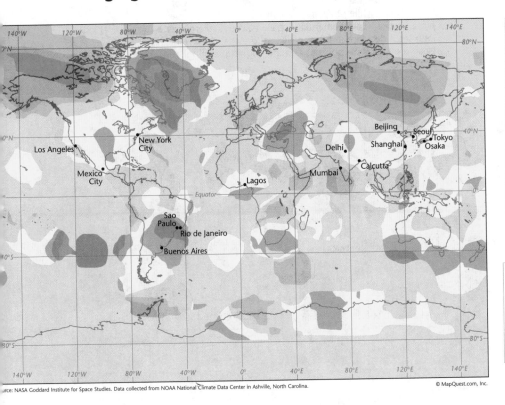

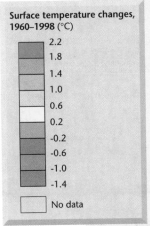

Surface temperature changes, 1960–1998 (°C)

2.2
1.8
1.4
1.0
0.6
0.2
-0.2
-0.6
-1.0
-1.4

No data

The changes in land surface temperatures shown on the map at left are derived from several thousand meteorological stations and satellite measurements. (A change of 1°C is equivalent to 1.8°F.)

Source: NASA Goddard Institute for Space Studies. Data collected from NOAA National Climate Data Center in Ashville, North Carolina.

© MapQuest.com, Inc.

Rising Weather-Related Deaths

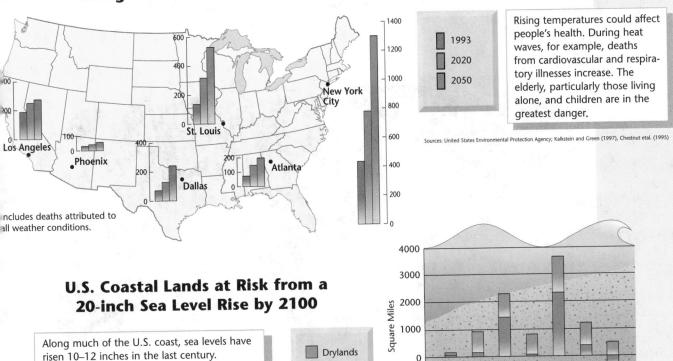

1993
2020
2050

New York City

St. Louis

Los Angeles

Phoenix

Dallas

Atlanta

Includes deaths attributed to all weather conditions.

Rising temperatures could affect people's health. During heat waves, for example, deaths from cardiovascular and respiratory illnesses increase. The elderly, particularly those living alone, and children are in the greatest danger.

Sources: United States Environmental Protection Agency; Kalkstein and Green (1997), Chestnut etal. (1995)

U.S. Coastal Lands at Risk from a 20-inch Sea Level Rise by 2100

Along much of the U.S. coast, sea levels have risen 10–12 inches in the last century.

A projected global sea level rise of about 20 inches by 2100 could:
   –Inundate 5,000 square miles of dryland
   –Drown 15–60% of coastal wetlands

Drylands
Wetlands

Source: United State Environmental Protection Agency

Square Miles

Northeast
Mid-Atlantic
South Atlantic
S & W Florida
Louisiana
Rest of Gulf Coast
West

World Forest Cover

Forests help regulate climate by storing huge amounts of carbon dioxide, while providing habitats for countless animal and plant species. Environmentalists have voiced concern over a long-term decrease in forest cover, as forest lands have been cleared for such purposes as farming, logging, mining, and urban expansion.

Forest Cover

- Forest cover 8,000 years ago that has been lost
- Remaining forest cover (much of it fragmented)

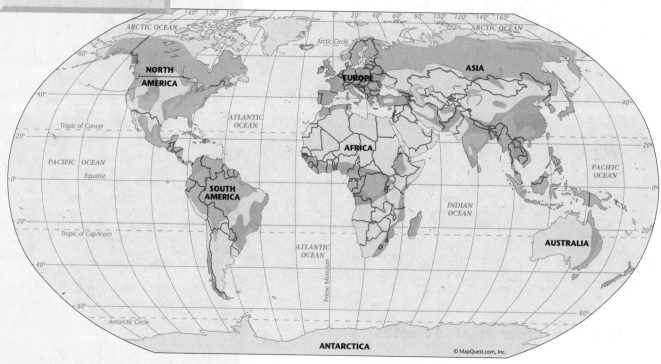

© MapQuest.com, Inc.

Source: *Forest Frontiers Initiative*, World Resource Institute, 1998

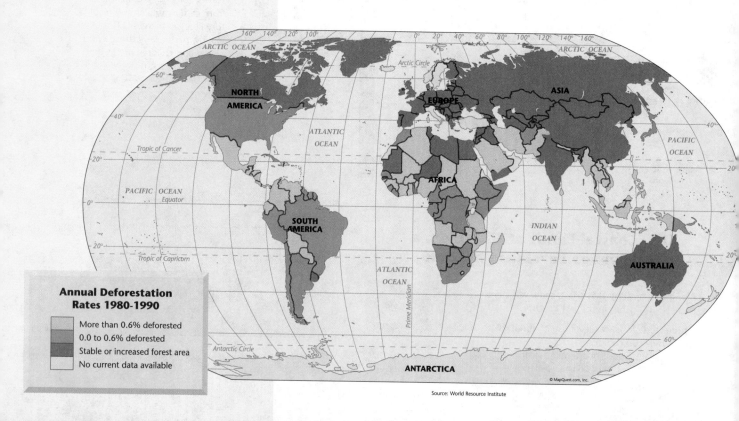

Annual Deforestation Rates 1980-1990

- More than 0.6% deforested
- 0.0 to 0.6% deforested
- Stable or increased forest area
- No current data available

© MapQuest.com, Inc.

Source: World Resource Institute

Tropical Rain Forests

rain forests, found around the Earth with-
egrees of the equator, contain more than
the world's plant and animal species,
being home to many indigenous peoples.
e vital to the balance of nature. In the past
s alone, about one-fifth of the acreage has
eared for logging and other purposes.
in forests, including the major forests pin-
, remain under serious threat.

Tai National Park and surrounding forests (Côte d'Ivoire)
Threat: Logging, Agricultural clearing
Risks: Rich biodiversity

Sundarbans (Bangladesh/India)
Threat: Logging
Risks: The world's largest mangrove forest.
       Habitat for the world's largest
       population of Bengal tigers.
       Economy for 300,000 local families

Ratanari Province (Cambodia)
Threat: Illegal logging
Risks: Habitats for several minority peoples.
       Endangered species of animals.

Western and Gulf Provinces (Papua New Guinea)
Threat: Logging, Pipeline development
Risks: Exceptional area for richness of
       diverse and rare animal species.
       Habitats for several indigenous
       peoples/cultures.

sts of Darien Gap
ombia/Panama)
at: Logging, Highway construction
: Habitats for three indigenous
  peoples/cultures
  Rich biodiversity

Bolivar State (Venezuela)
Threat: Logging, Mining
Risks: Habitats for several indigenous
       peoples/cultures
       Rich biodiversity

The Atlantic Rain Forest (Coastal Brazil)
Threat: Logging, Agricultural clearing
Risks: Biodiversity–70% of the plants and
       20% of the primate species are
       found nowhere else in the world

Cross River and Korup National Park (Cameroon/Nigeria)
Threat: Logging by European and Asian companies
Risks: Rich in plant species-potential wealth of new
       drugs and industrial products.
       Possible cure to deadly diseases.

Eastern Congo Forests (Dem. Rep. of the Congo)
Threat: Agricultural clearing
Risks: Greatest biological diversity of any
       forest on the continent of Africa.
       Many of Africa's remaining Pygmy
       peoples.

© MapQuest.com, Inc.

Source: *Forest Frontiers Initiative*, World Resource Institute, 1998

ercentage of Frontier Forest
nder Moderate or High Threat of Destruction
hrough 2030)

Source: *Forest Frontiers Initiative*, World Resource Institute, 1998

WORLD 39%

AFRICA 77%

NORTH AMERICA 26%

CENTRAL AMERICA 87%

SOUTH AMERICA 54%

EUROPE 100%

ASIA 60%

RUSSIA 19%

OCEANIA 76%

Frontier Forests

According to the World Resources Institute, only about one-fifth of Earth's forest cover of 8,000 years ago survives unfragmented, in the large unspoiled tracts it calls frontier forests. These forests are big enough to provide stable habitats for a rich diversity of plant and animal species. Most surviving forests are in the far north or the tropics, and are under threat.

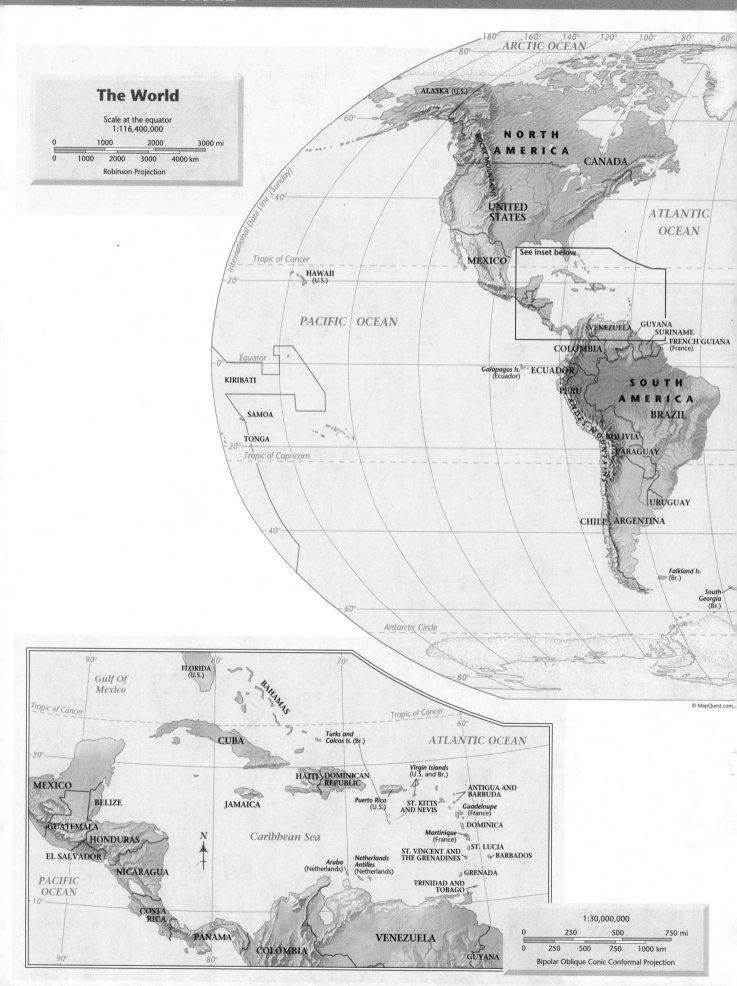

The World

Scale at the equator
1:116,400,000

0   1000   2000   3000 mi

0   1000   2000   3000   4000 km

Robinson Projection

180°   160°   140°   120°   100°   80°   60°

ARCTIC OCEAN

80°

ALASKA (U.S.)

60°

NORTH AMERICA

CANADA

40°

ROCKY MOUNTAINS

UNITED STATES

ATLANTIC OCEAN

Tropic of Cancer

20°

MEXICO

HAWAII (U.S.)

See inset below

International Date Line (Sunday)

PACIFIC OCEAN

VENEZUELA   GUYANA
SURINAME
FRENCH GUIANA (France)

COLOMBIA

Equator

0°

Galápagos Is. (Ecuador)

ECUADOR

KIRIBATI

PERU

SOUTH AMERICA

BRAZIL

ANDES MOUNTAINS

SAMOA

BOLIVIA

PARAGUAY

TONGA

20°

Tropic of Capricorn

URUGUAY

CHILE   ARGENTINA

40°

Falkland Is. (Br.)

South Georgia (Br.)

60°

Antarctic Circle

80°

© MapQuest.com

Inset map

90°   80°   70°

FLORIDA (U.S.)

Gulf Of Mexico

BAHAMAS

Tropic of Cancer

ATLANTIC OCEAN

CUBA

Turks and Caicos Is. (Br.)

60°

20°

Virgin Islands (U.S. and Br.)

HAITI   DOMINICAN REPUBLIC

ANTIGUA AND BARBUDA

MEXICO

Puerto Rico (U.S.)

JAMAICA

ST. KITTS AND NEVIS

Guadeloupe (France)

BELIZE

DOMINICA

GUATEMALA

Martinique (France)

ST. LUCIA

HONDURAS

Caribbean Sea

ST. VINCENT AND THE GRENADINES

BARBADOS

EL SALVADOR

N

NICARAGUA

Aruba (Netherlands)

Netherlands Antilles (Netherlands)

GRENADA

PACIFIC OCEAN

10°

TRINIDAD AND TOBAGO

COSTA RICA

PANAMA

VENEZUELA

COLOMBIA

GUYANA

90°   80°

1:30,000,000

0   250   500   750 mi

0   250   500   750   1000 km

Bipolar Oblique Conic Conformal Projection

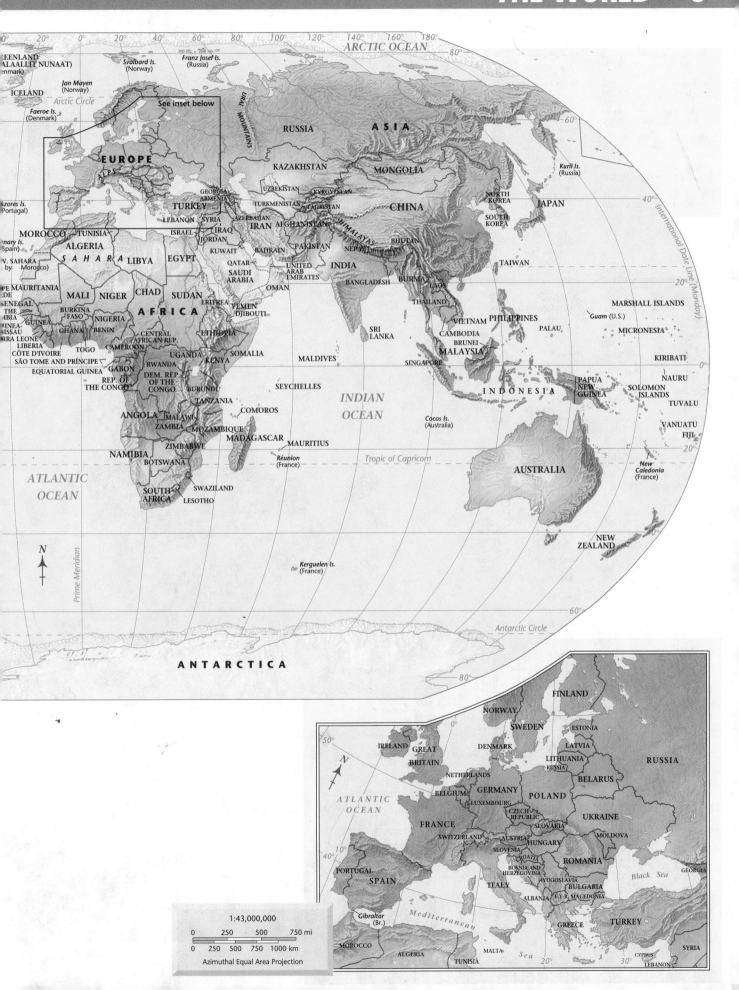

ARCTIC OCEAN

GREENLAND
(KALAALLIT NUNAAT)
(Denmark)

ICELAND

Arctic Circle

Svalbard Is.
(Norway)

Jan Mayen
(Norway)

Franz Josef Is.
(Russia)

Faeroe Is.
(Denmark)

Azores Is.
(Portugal)

EUROPE

ALPS

See inset below

URAL MOUNTAINS

RUSSIA

ASIA

KAZAKHSTAN

MONGOLIA

Kuril Is.
(Russia)

UZBEKISTAN
KYRGYZSTAN
TURKMENISTAN
TAJIKISTAN

GEORGIA
ARMENIA
TURKEY
AZERBAIJAN

NORTH
KOREA

JAPAN

SOUTH
KOREA

CHINA

HIMALAYAS

LEBANON   SYRIA
ISRAEL
JORDAN
IRAQ
IRAN   AFGHANISTAN

BHUTAN

40°

MOROCCO   TUNISIA

KUWAIT
BAHRAIN
PAKISTAN
NEPAL

TAIWAN

Canary Is.
(Spain)

ALGERIA

S A H A R A   LIBYA

EGYPT

QATAR
SAUDI
ARABIA

UNITED
ARAB
EMIRATES

INDIA

BANGLADESH

BURMA
LAOS

20°

W. SAHARA
(by Morocco)

OMAN

THAILAND

MARSHALL ISLANDS

MAURITANIA

MALI   NIGER   CHAD   SUDAN

ERITREA

A F R I C A

SENEGAL
THE
GAMBIA

BURKINA
FASO

NIGERIA

YEMEN
DJIBOUTI

ETHIOPIA

Guam (U.S.)

MICRONESIA

GUINEA
GUINEA-
BISSAU
SIERRA LEONE
LIBERIA
CÔTE D'IVOIRE
GHANA
BENIN
TOGO

CAMEROON

CENTRAL
AFRICAN REP.

UGANDA
KENYA

SOMALIA

SRI
LANKA

MALDIVES

VIETNAM   PHILIPPINES

CAMBODIA
BRUNEI
MALAYSIA

PALAU

KIRIBATI

SÃO TOME AND PRÍNCIPE
EQUATORIAL GUINEA

GABON
REP. OF
THE CONGO

RWANDA
DEM. REP.
OF THE
CONGO
BURUNDI

SINGAPORE

I N D O N E S I A

PAPUA
NEW
GUINEA

NAURU

SOLOMON
ISLANDS

SEYCHELLES

0°

TANZANIA

INDIAN
OCEAN

TUVALU

ANGOLA
MALAWI
ZAMBIA
MOZAMBIQUE

COMOROS

VANUATU

FIJI

ZIMBABWE
MADAGASCAR
MAURITIUS

New
Caledonia
(France)

NAMIBIA
BOTSWANA

Réunion
(France)

Tropic of Capricorn

Cocos Is.
(Australia)

20°

ATLANTIC
OCEAN

SOUTH
AFRICA
SWAZILAND
LESOTHO

AUSTRALIA

N

NEW
ZEALAND

Prime Meridian

Kerguelen Is.
(France)

Antarctic Circle

A N T A R C T I C A

80°

1:43,000,000

0   250   500   750 mi

0   250 500 750 1000 km

Azimuthal Equal Area Projection

FINLAND

NORWAY

SWEDEN

ESTONIA

IRELAND
GREAT
BRITAIN

DENMARK

LATVIA

LITHUANIA

RUSSIA

RUSSIA

NETHERLANDS

BELARUS

ATLANTIC
OCEAN

BELGIUM

GERMANY

POLAND

LUXEMBOURG

N

FRANCE

CZECH
REPUBLIC
SLOVAKIA

UKRAINE

SWITZERLAND

AUSTRIA
HUNGARY

MOLDOVA

SLOVENIA
CROATIA

ROMANIA

PORTUGAL

SPAIN

BOSNIA AND
HERZEGOVINA

YUGOSLAVIA

Black Sea

GEORGIA

ITALY

BULGARIA

ALBANIA   F.Y.R. MACEDONIA

Gibraltar
(Br.)

Mediterranean

GREECE

TURKEY

MOROCCO

Sea

ALGERIA

TUNISIA

MALTA

CYPRUS
LEBANON

SYRIA

MAJOR CITIES

Afghanistan	(metro)
Kabul	2,029,000
Bahrain	
Manama	151,000
Bangladesh	(metro)
Dhaka	8,545,000
Bhutan	
Thimphu	8,900
Brunei	
Band. Seri Begawan	51,000
Burma (Myanmar)	(metro)
Rangoon	3,873,000
Cambodia	
Phnom Penh	800,000
China	
Shanghai	7,500,000
Hong Kong	6,502,000
Beijing	5,700,000
Tianjin	4,500,000
Shenyang	3,600,000
Wuhan	3,200,000
Guangzhou	2,900,000
Chongqing	2,700,000
Harbin	2,500,000
Chengdu	2,500,000
Zibo	2,200,000
Xi'an	2,200,000
Nanjing	2,091,000
Cyprus	
Nicosia	193,000
India	(metro)
Mumbai (Bombay)	12,572,000
Calcutta	10,916,000
Delhi	8,375,000
Madras	5,361,000
Hyderabad	4,280,000
Bangalore	4,087,000
Indonesia	
Jakarta	9,113,000
Surabaya	2,664,000
Bandung	2,356,000
Medan	1,844,000
Iran	
Tehran	6,750,000
Mashhad	1,964,000
Iraq	(metro)
Baghdad	4,336,000
Israel	
Jerusalem	585,000
Japan	
Tokyo	7,968,000
Yokohama	3,320,000
Osaka	2,600,000
Nagoya	2,151,000
Sapporo	1,774,000
Kyoto	1,464,000
Kobe	1,420,000
Fukuoka	1,296,000
Kawasaki	1,209,000
Hiroshima	1,115,000
Jordan	(metro)
Amman	1,183,000
Kazakhstan	
Almaty	1,064,000

North Korea	
P'yŏngyang	2,741,000
South Korea	
Seoul	10,231,000
Pusan	3,814,000
Taegu	2,449,000
Kuwait	
Kuwait	29,000
Kyrgyzstan	
Bishkek	589,000
Laos	
Vientiane	377,000
Lebanon	(metro)
Beirut	1,826,000
Malaysia	(metro)
Kuala Lumpur	1,236,000
Maldives	
Male	55,000
Mongolia	
Ulan Bator	536,000
Nepal	
Kathmandu	419,000
Oman	
Masqat	85,000
Pakistan	(metro)
Karachi	5,181,000
Lahore	2,953,000
Faisalabad	1,104,000
Islamabad	204,000
Philippines	
Manila	1,655,000
Qatar	
Doha	236,000
Russia (Asian)	
Novosibirsk	1,368,000
Yekaterinburg	1,277,000
Omsk	1,161,000
Chelyabinsk	1,084,000
Krasnoyarsk	870,000
Saudi Arabia	(metro)
Riyadh	2,619,000
Jiddah	1,492,000
Singapore	
Singapore	3,737,000
Sri Lanka	
Colombo	615,000
Syria	
Damascus	1,549,000
Halab (Aleppo)	1,542,000
Taiwan	
Taipei	1,770,000
Tajikistan	
Dushanbe	529,000
Thailand	(metro)
Bangkok	6,547,000
Turkey (Asian)	
Ankara	2,938,000
İzmir	2,130,000
Turkmenistan	
Ashgabat	407,000
United Arab Emirates	
Abu Dhabi (metro)	799,000
Uzbekistan	(metro)
Tashkent	2,282,000
Vietnam	(metro)
Ho Chi Minh City	3,521,000
Hanoi	1,236,000
Yemen	(metro)
Sana	927,000

International comparability of city population data is limited by various data inconsistencies.

© MapQuest.com, Inc.

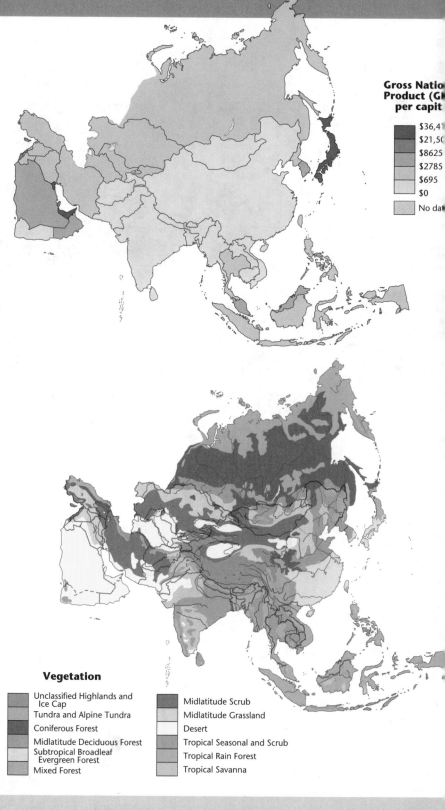

Gross National Product (GNP) per capita

- $36,41...
- $21,50...
- $8625
- $2785
- $695
- $0
- No data

Vegetation

- Unclassified Highlands and Ice Cap
- Tundra and Alpine Tundra
- Coniferous Forest
- Midlatitude Deciduous Forest
- Subtropical Broadleaf Evergreen Forest
- Mixed Forest
- Midlatitude Scrub
- Midlatitude Grassland
- Desert
- Tropical Seasonal and Scrub
- Tropical Rain Forest
- Tropical Savanna

Asia: Population, by nation (in millions)*

CHINA	INDIA	INDON.	PAKIS.	BANGL.	JAPAN	PHILIP.	All other Asian countries
1254.2	1000.8	216.1	138.1	127.1	126.2	79.4	699.5*

*Excluding Russia

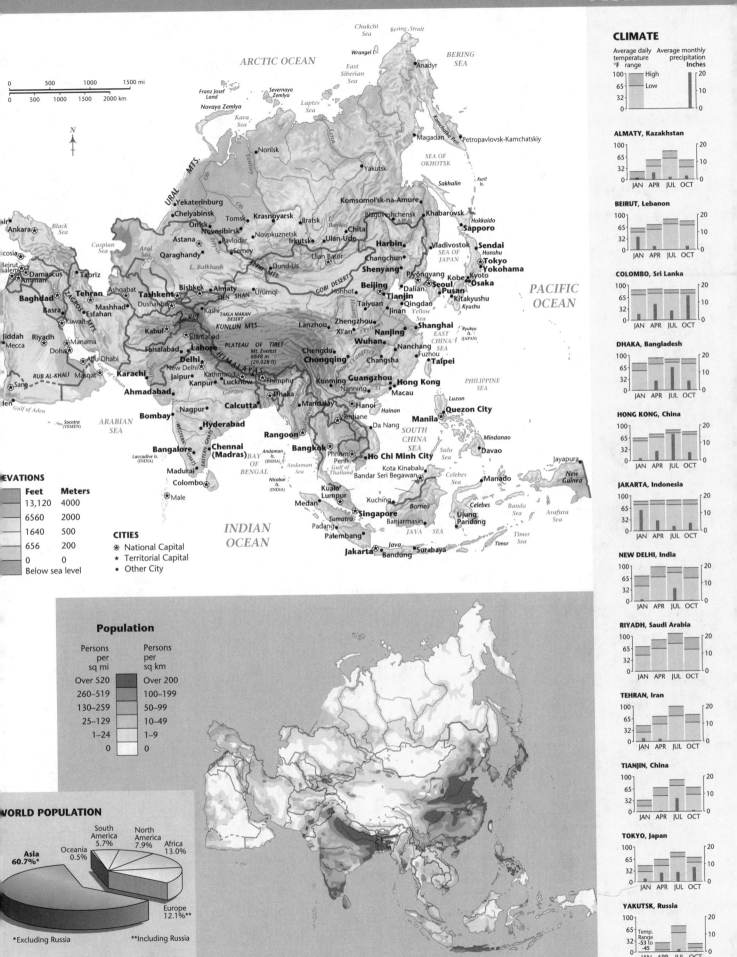

ARCTIC OCEAN

BERING SEA

Chukchi Sea

Bering Strait

Wrangel I.

East Siberian Sea

Franz Josef Land

Severnaya Zemlya

Novaya Zemlya

Laptev Sea

Kara Sea

Anadyr

Magadan   Petropavlovsk-Kamchatskiy

Kamchatka Pen.

SEA OF OKHOTSK

Norilsk

Yakutsk

Sakhalin

Kuril Is.

Hokkaido

Ob

Yenisey

Lena

Amur

Yekaterinburg

Chelyabinsk

Omsk   Tomsk   Krasnoyarsk   Bratsk

Novosibirsk   Novokuznetsk   Chita   Blagoveshchensk   Khabarovsk

Astana   Pavlodar   Irkutsk   Ulan-Ude   Sapporo

Qaraghandy   Semey   Ulan Bator   Harbin   Vladivostok   Sendai
Honshu
Changchun   SEA OF JAPAN   Tokyo
Shenyang   Pyongyang   Yokohama
Hohhot   Beijing   Seoul   Kobe   Kyoto
GOBI DESERT   Dalian   Pusan   Osaka
Taiyuan   Tianjin   Qingdao   Kitakyushu
TIEN SHAN   Jinan   Yellow   Kyushu
Bishkek   Almaty   Ürümqi   Zhengzhou   Sea   Shanghai   Ryukyu
TAKLA MAKAN   Lanzhou   Xi'an   Nanjing   EAST   Is.
DESERT   Wuhan   Nanchang   CHINA   (JAPAN)
KUNLUN MTS.   Chengdu   Changsha   Fuzhou   SEA
PLATEAU OF TIBET   Chongqing   Taipei
Mt. Everest   Kunming   Guangzhou   Hong Kong
8848 m   Nanning   Macau
(29,028 ft)   Mandalay   Hanoi   PHILIPPINE
HIMALAYAS   Vientiane   Da Nang   Luzon   SEA
Hainan   Manila   Quezon City
Rangoon   SOUTH   Mindanao
CHINA   Davao
Bangkok   SEA
Phnom   Ho Chi Minh City   Sulu
Penh   Sea
Kota Kinabalu   Celebes
Bandar Seri Begawan   Sea   Manado
Kuala   Kuching   Banda
Lumpur   Borneo   Ujung   Sea
Medan   Pandang   Arafura
Sumatra   Banjarmasin   Sea
Padang   JAVA SEA   Timor
Palembang   Timor   Sea
Java   New
Jakarta   Bandung   Surabaya   Guinea

Jayapura

PACIFIC OCEAN

URAL MTS.

ALTAI MTS.

L. Baykal

Dund-Us

Caspian Sea

Aral Sea

L. Balkhash

HINDU KUSH

Kashi

ZAGROS MTS.

Black Sea

Ankara

Nicosia

Beirut
Jerusalem   Damascus

Amman   Tabriz

Baghdad   Tehran   Mashhad

Basra   Esfahan   Ashgabat   Tashkent   Dushanbe

Kuwait   Dund   Bishkek

Jiddah   Riyadh   Manama

Mecca   Doha   Abu Dhabi

Sanaa   Masqat

Gulf of Aden

Socotra (YEMEN)

Aden

ARABIAN SEA

RUB AL-KHALI

Gulf of Oman

Kabul   Islamabad

Faisalabad   Lahore

Karachi   Delhi   Jaipur   New Delhi   Kathmandu   Thimphu

Ahmadabad   Kanpur   Lucknow   Dhaka

Ganges

Bombay   Nagpur   Calcutta

Hyderabad   Mandalay

Bangalore   Chennai (Madras)

Madurai   BAY OF BENGAL

Colombo   Andaman Is. (INDIA)

Laccadive Is. (INDIA)   Nicobar Is. (INDIA)

Male

INDIAN OCEAN

Singapore

WESTERN GHATS   EASTERN GHATS

Komsomol'sk-na-Amure

Krasnoyarsk

Huang (Yellow)

Chang (Yangtze)

Gulf of Thailand

Andaman Sea

Celebes

0   500   1000   1500 mi
0   500   1000   1500   2000 km

N

ELEVATIONS

Feet	Meters
13,120	4000
6560	2000
1640	500
656	200
0	0
Below sea level	

CITIES

⊕ National Capital
★ Territorial Capital
• Other City

Population

Persons per sq mi	Persons per sq km
Over 520	Over 200
260–519	100–199
130–259	50–99
25–129	10–49
1–24	1–9
0	0

WORLD POPULATION

Asia 60.7%*
Oceania 0.5%
South America 5.7%
North America 7.9%
Africa 13.0%
Europe 12.1%**

*Excluding Russia   **Including Russia

CLIMATE

Average daily temperature °F range

Average monthly precipitation Inches

High
Low

ALMATY, Kazakhstan
BEIRUT, Lebanon
COLOMBO, Sri Lanka
DHAKA, Bangladesh
HONG KONG, China
JAKARTA, Indonesia
NEW DELHI, India
RIYADH, Saudi Arabia
TEHRAN, Iran
TIANJIN, China
TOKYO, Japan
YAKUTSK, Russia

Temp. Range -53 to -45

JAN APR JUL OCT

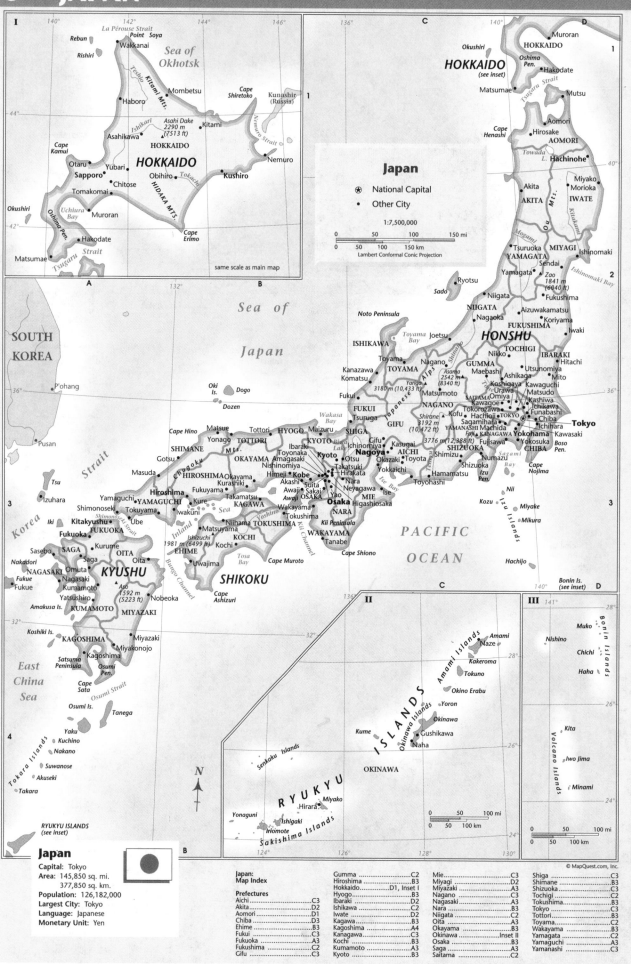

Japan

⊛ National Capital
• Other City

1:7,500,000

0   50   100   150 mi
0 50 100 150 km

Lambert Conformal Conic Projection

Japan

Capital: Tokyo
Area: 145,850 sq. mi.
          377,850 sq. km.
Population: 126,182,000
Largest City: Tokyo
Language: Japanese
Monetary Unit: Yen

Japan:
Map Index

Prefectures

Aichi	C3
Akita	D2
Aomori	D1
Chiba	D3
Ehime	B3
Fukui	C3
Fukuoka	A3
Fukushima	C2
Gifu	C3
Gumma	C2
Hiroshima	B3
Hokkaido	D1, Inset I
Hyogo	B3
Ibaraki	D2
Ishikawa	C2
Iwate	D2
Kagawa	B3
Kagoshima	A4
Kanagawa	C3
Kochi	B3
Kumamoto	A3
Kyoto	C3
Mie	C3
Miyagi	D2
Miyazaki	A3
Nagano	C2
Nagasaki	A3
Nara	C3
Niigata	C2
Oita	A3
Okayama	B3
Okinawa	Inset II
Osaka	C3
Saga	A3
Saitama	C2
Shiga	C3
Shimane	B3
Shizuoka	C3
Tochigi	C2
Tokushima	B3
Tokyo	C3
Tottori	B3
Toyama	C2
Wakayama	B3
Yamagata	C2
Yamaguchi	A3
Yamanashi	C3

Cities and Towns

Aizuwakamatsu	
Akashi	
Akita	
Amagasaki	
Aomori	
Asahikawa	
Ashikaga	
Awaji	
Chiba	
Chitose	
Fujisawa	
Fukue	
Fukui	
Fukuoka	
Fukushima	
Fukuyama	
Funabashi	
Gifu	
Gotsu	
Gushikawa	Ins
Haboro	Ins
Hachinohe	
Hachioji	
Hakodate	D1
Hamamatsu	
Higashiosaka	
Himeji	
Hirakata	
Hirara	Ins
Hirosake	
Hiroshima	
Hitachi	
Ibaraki	
Ichihara	
Ichikawa	
Ichinomiya	
Ise	
Ishinomaki	
Iwaki	
Iwakuni	
Izuhara	
Joetsu	
Kagoshima	
Kanazawa	
Kashiwa	
Kasugai	
Kawagoe	
Kawaguchi	
Kawasaki	
Kitakyushu	
Kitami	
Kobe	
Kochi	
Kofu	
Komatsu	
Koriyama	
Koshigaya	
Kumamoto	
Kurashiki	
Kure	
Kurume	
Kushiro	Ins
Kyoto	
Machida	
Maebashi	
Maizuru	
Masuda	
Matsudo	
Matsue	D1
Matsumoto	
Matsuyama	
Mito	
Miyako	
Miyakonojo	
Miyazaki	
Mombetsu	Ins
Morioka	
Muroran	D1, Inset
Mutsu	
Nagano	
Nagaoka	
Nagasaki	
Nagoya	
Naha	Inset
Nara	
Naze	Inset
Nemuro	Inset
Neyagawa	
Niigata	
Niihama	
Nikko	
Nishinomiya	
Nobeoka	
Numazu	
Obihiro	Inset
Oita	
Okayama	
Okazaki	
Omiya	
Omuta	
Osaka	
Otaru	Inset
Otsu	
Ryotsu	
Saga	
Sagamihara	
Sakai	
Sapporo	Inset
Sasebo	
Sendai	
Shimizu	
Shimonoseki	
Shizuoka	
Suita	
Takamatsu	
Takatsuki	
Tanabe	
Tokorozawa	
Tokushima	
Tokuyama	
Tokyo, capital	
Tomakomai	Inset
Tottori	
Toyama	
Toyohashi	
Toyonaka	
Toyota	
Tsuruga	
Tsuruoka	
Ube	
Urawa	
Utsunomiya	
Uwajima	
Wakayama	
Wakkanai	Inset
Yamagata	
Yamaguchi	
Yao	
Yatsushiro	

© MapQuest.com, Inc.

North Korea and South Korea
⊛ National Capital
• Other City
1:6,625,000
0   50   100 mi
0   50   100 km
Lambert Conformal Conic Projection

© MapQuest.com, Inc.

Cheju Strait
CHEJU   Cheju
Halla-san
1950 m
(6398 ft)
Cheju
same scale as main map

North Korea:
Map Index

Provinces
Chagang B2
Kaesŏng B3
Kangwŏn B3
Namp'o A3
North Hamgyŏng C1
North Hwanghae B3
North P'yŏngan A2
P'yŏngyang A3
South Hamgyŏng B3
South Hwanghae A3
South P'yŏngan A3
Yanggang B2

Cities and Towns
Anju A3
Changjin B2
Changyŏn A3
Ch'ŏngjin C2
Chŏngju A3
Haeju A3
Hamhŭng B3
Hoeryŏng C1
Hŭich'ŏn B2
Hŭngnam B3
Hyesan C2
Ich'ŏn B3
Kaesŏng B4
Kanggye B2
Kilchu C2
Kimch'aek C2
Kosŏng C3
Kowŏn B3
Kusŏng A3
Manp'o B2
Musan C1
Najin D1
Namp'o A3
Ongjin A4
Onsŏng C1
P'anmunjŏm B4
Pukch'ŏng C2
P'ungsan C2
P'yŏnggang B3
P'yŏngsŏng A3
P'yŏngyang, capital ..A3
Sariwŏn A3
Sinp'o B3
Sinŭiju A2
Songnim A3
Tanch'ŏn C2
Wŏnsan B3
Yangdŏk B3

Other Features
Chaeryŏng, river A3
Changjin, river B2
Ch'ŏngch'ŏn, river A3
Hamgyŏng, mts. C2
Imjin, river B3
Kanghwa, bay A4
Korea, bay A3
Musu-dan, point C2
Nangnim-sanmaek, mts. ..B3
Paektu-san, mt. C2
Sŏjosŏn, bay A3
Sup'ung, reservoir A2
Taedong, river B3
Tongjosŏn, bay B3
Tumen, river C1
Yalu, river B2

South Korea:
Map Index

Provinces
Cheju ....Inset
Inch'ŏn B4
Kangwŏn B4
Kwangju B5
Kyŏnggi B4
North Chŏlla B5
North Ch'ungch'ŏng ..B4
North Kyŏngsang C4
Pusan C5
Seoul B4
South Chŏlla B5
South Ch'ungch'ŏng ..B4
South Kyŏngsang C5
Taegu C5
Taejŏn B4

Cities and Towns
Andong C4
Anyang B4
Chech'ŏn C4
Cheju ....Inset
Chinhae C5
Chinju C5
Chonju B5
Ch'ŏnan B4
Ch'ŏngju B4
Ch'unch'ŏn B4
Ch'ungju B4
Inch'ŏn B5
Iri B5
Kangnŭng C4
Kimch'ŏn C4
Kunsan B5
Kwangju B5
Kyŏngju C5
Masan C5
Mokp'o B5
Munsan B4
Nonsan B4
P'ohang C4
Pusan C5
Samch'ŏk C4
Seoul, capital B4
Sokch'o C3
Sŏngnam B4
Sunch'ŏn B5
Suwŏn B4
Taegu C5
Taejŏn B4
Ulchin C4
Ulsan C5
Wando B5
Wŏnju B4
Yŏngju C4
Yŏsu B5

Other Features
Cheju, island ....Inset
Cheju, strait ....Inset
Halla-san, mt. ....Inset
Han, river B4
Hŭksan Chedo, islands ..A5
Kanghwa, bay A4
Koje-do, island C5
Korea, strait C5
Kum, river B4
Naktong, river C5
Soan-kundo, islands ..B5
Sobaek, mts. B5
Taebaek-Sanmaek, mts. ..C3
Tŏkchŏk-kundo, islands ..A4
Ullŭng-do, island D4
Western, channel C5

North Korea
Capital: P'yŏngyang
Area: 47,399 sq. mi.
    122,795 sq. km.
Population: 21,386,000
Largest City: P'yŏngyang
Language: Korean
Monetary Unit: Won

South Korea
Capital: Seoul
Area: 38,330 sq. mi.
    99,301 sq. km.
Population: 46,885,000
Largest City: Seoul
Language: Korean
Monetary Unit: Won

Taiwan
⊛ National Capital
• Other City
1:10,292,000
0   30   60 mi
0   30   60 km
Lambert Conformal Conic Projection

© MapQuest.com, Inc.

Taiwan
Capital: Taipei
Area: 13,969 sq. mi.
    36,189 sq. km.
Population: 22,113,000
Largest City: Taipei
Language: Mandarin Chinese
Monetary Unit: New Taiwan dollar

Taiwan:
Map Index

Cities and Towns
Changhua B1
Chiai B2
Chilung B1
Chunan B1
Chungho B1
Chungli B1
Fangliao B2
Fengshan B2
Fengyüan B1
Hench'un B2
Hsinchu B1
Hsinchuang B1
Hsintien B1
Hsinying B2
Hualien B2
Ilan B1
Kangshan B2
Kaohsiung B2
Makung A2
Miaoli B1
Nant'ou B1
Panch'iao B1
P'ingtung B2

Shanchung B1
T'aichung B1
T'ainan B2
Taipei, capital B1
T'aitung B2
Tanshui B1
T'aoyüan B1
Touliu B2
Yungho B1

Other Features
Choshui, river B2
Chungyang, range B2
East China, sea B1
Kaop'ing, river B2
Lan, island B2
Lü, island B2
Luzon, strait A2
P'enghu (Pescadores),
  islands A2
Pescadores, channel ..A2
Philippine, sea B2
South China, sea A2
Taiwan, strait A1
Tanshui, river B1
Tsengwen, river B2
Yü Shan, mt. B2

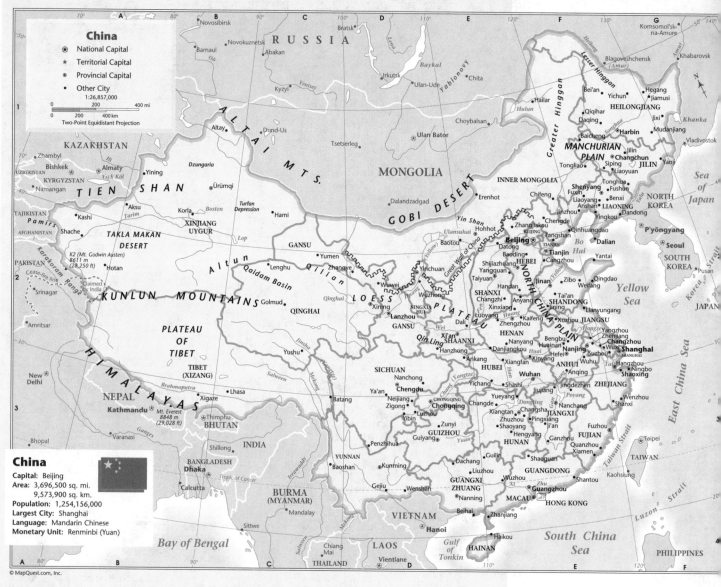

China

- ⊛ National Capital
- ★ Territorial Capital
- ◉ Provincial Capital
- • Other City

1:26,857,000

Two-Point Equidistant Projection

China

Capital: Beijing
Area: 3,696,500 sq. mi.
 9,573,900 sq. km.
Population: 1,254,156,000
Largest City: Shanghai
Language: Mandarin Chinese
Monetary Unit: Renminbi (Yuan)

Hong Kong S.A.R.

- • City

1:1,800,000

Transverse Mercator Projection

© MapQuest.com, Inc.

China:
Map Index

Internal Divisions
Provinces
Anhui E2
Fujian E3
Gansu C1, D2
Guangdong E3
Guizhou D3
Hainan D4
Hebei E2
Heilongjiang F1
Henan E2
Hubei E2
Hunan E3
Jiangsu E2
Jiangxi E3
Jilin F1
Liaoning F1
Qinghai C2
Shaanxi D2
Shandong E2
Shanxi E2
Sichuan D2
Yunnan C3
Zhejiang E3

Autonomous Regions
Guangxi Zhuang D3
Inner Mongolia E1
Ningxia Hui D2
Tibet (Xizang) B2
Xinjiang Uygur B1

Independent Municipalities
Beijing E1
Chongqing D3
Shanghai F2
Tianjin E2

Special Administrative
Regions (S.A.R.)
Hong Kong ....E3, Inset
Macau E3

Cities and Towns
Aberdeen ....Inset
Aksu B1
Altay B1
Ankang D2
Anqing E2
Anshan F1

Anyang E2
Baicheng F1
Baoding E2
Baoshan C3
Baotou E1
Batang C3
Beihai D3
Beijing, capital E2
Bengbu E2
Benxi F1
Cangzhou E2
Changchun F1
Changde E3
Changsha E3
Changzhi E2
Changzhou F2
Chek Keng ....Inset
Chengde E1
Chengdu D2
Chifeng E1
Chung Hau ....Inset
Dachang D3
Dali C3
Dalian F2
Dandong F1
Danjiangkou E2
Daqing F1
Datong E1
Erenhot E1
Fushun F1
Fuxin F1
Fuzhou E3
Ganzhou E3
Gejiu D3
Golmud C2
Guangzhou E3
Guilin D3
Guiyang D3
Haikou E4
Hailar E1
Hami C1
Handan E2
Hangzhou F2
Hanzhong D2
Harbin F1
Hefei E2
Hegang G1
Hengyang E3
Hohhot E1
Hotan A2

Huainan E2
Jiamusi G1
Ji'an E3
Jilin F1
Jinan E2
Jingdezhen E2
Jining E2
Jinzhou F1
Jiujiang E2
Jixi G1
Kaifeng E2
Kashi A2
Korla B1
Kowloon ....Inset
Kunming D3
Lanzhou D2
Lenghu C2
Lhasa C3
Lianyungang E2
Liaoyang F1
Liaoyuan F1
Liuzhou D3
Lo Wu ....Inset
Luoyang E2
Luzhou D2
Mudanjiang F1
Nanchang E3
Nanchong D2
Nanjing E2
Nanning D3
Nanyang E2
Neijiang D3
New Kowloon ....Inset
Ningbo F3
Penzhihua D3
Pingxiang E3
Qingdao F2
Qinhuangdao E2
Qiqihar F1
Quanzhou E3
Sai Kung ....Inset
Shache A2
Handan E2
Shantou E3
Shanxi E2
Shaoguan E3
Shaoxing F2
Shaoyang E3
Shashi E2
Sha Tin ....Inset
Shek Pik ....Inset
Shenyang F1

Shijiazhuang E2
Siping F1
Suzhou F2
Tai'an E2
Taiyuan E2
Tangshan E2
Tianjin E2
Tonghua F1
Tongliao E1
Tsuen Wan ....Inset
Tuen Mun ....Inset
Ürümqi B1
Weifang E2
Wenshan D3
Wenzhou F3
Wuhan E2
Wuhu E2
Wuwei D2
Wuxi F2
Wuzhong D2
Wuzhou E3
Xiamen E3
Xi'an D2
Xiangfan E2
Xiangtan E3
Xigaze B3
Xining D2
Xinxiang E2
Xinyang E2
Xuzhou E2
Ya'an D2
Yangquan E2
Yangzhou E2
Yanji F1
Yantai F2
Yibin D3
Yichang E2
Yichun F1
Yinchuan D2
Yingkou F1
Yining B1
Yueyang E3
Yumen C2
Yushu C2
Zhangjiakou E1
Zhanjiang D3
Zhangye D2
Zhengzhou E2
Zhenjiang E3
Zibo E2

Zigong D3
Zunyi D3

Other Features
Altai, range B1
Altun, range B2
Bayan Har, range C2
Bo Hai, gulf E2
Bosten, lake B1
Brahmaputra, river B3
Chang (Yangtze), river .D2, E2
Deep, bay ....Inset
Dongting, lake E3
Dzungaria, desert basin ..B1
East China, sea F3
Fen, river E2
Gan, river E3
Gobi, desert D1
Greater Hinggan, range ..F1
Great Wall of China D2
Han, river D2
Heilong (Amur), river F1
Himalayas, mts. B3
Hong Kong, island .....Inset
Hongze, lake E2
Huai, river E2
Huang (Yellow), river .D2, E2
Hulun, lake E1
Indus, river A2
Jinsha (Yangtze), river C2
Khanka, lake G1
Kunlun, mts. B2
K2 (Godwin Austen), mt. ..A2
Lantau, island ....Inset
Lesser Hinggan, range F1
Liao, river F1
Loess, plateau D2
Lop, lake C1
Manchurian, plain F1
Mekong, river C3
Nan Ling, mts. E3
New Territories, island .Inset
North China, plain E2
Pamirs, region A2
Poyang, lake E3
Qaidam, basin C2
Qilian, range D2
Qinghai, lake C2
Qin Ling, mts. D2
Salween, river C3
Songhua, river F1
South China, sea ....E4, Inset

Stonecutters (S.I.), island ..Inset
Tai, lake F2
Taiwan, strait F3
Takla Makan, desert A2
Tanggula, range C2
Tarim, river B1
Tibet, plateau C2
Tien Shan, range A1
Tonkin, gulf D4
Turfan, depression C1
Ulansuhai, lake E1
Wei, river E3
Xi, river E3
Yalu, river F1
Yangtze, river C2, D2
Yellow, sea F2
Yin Shan, mts. E1
Yuan, river D3
Zhu, river E3

Vietnam:
Map Index

Cities and Towns
Bac Lieu A5
Bien Hoa B4
Buon Me Thuot B4
Ca Mau A5
Cam Ranh B4
Can Tho A4
Cao Bang B1
Chau Doc A4
Da Lat B4
Da Nang B3
Dien Bien Phu A2
Dong Hoi B3
Ha Giang A1
Haiphong B2
Hanoi, capital A2
Hoa Binh A2
Ho Chi Minh City B4
Hon Gai B2
Hue B3
Khe Sanh B3
Kontum B3
Lang Son B2
Lao Cai A1
Long Xuyen A4
My Tho B4
Nam Dinh B2
Nha Trang B4
Phan Rang B4
Phan Thiet B4
Pleiku B3
Quang Ngai B3
Quang Tri B3
Qui Nhon B4
Rach Gia A4
Soc Trang A5
Son La A2
Tay Ninh B4
Thai Nguyen A2

Thanh Hoa A2
Tuy Hoa B4
Viet Tri A2
Vinh A2
Vung Tau- Con Dao B4
Yen Bai A2

Other Features
Annam, mts. A2
Ba, river B3
Black (Da), river A2
Ca, river A2
Central, highlands B4
Con Son, islands B5
Cu Lao Thu, island B4
Dao Phu Quoc, island A4
Dong Nai, river B4
Fan Si Pan, mt. A1
Gam, river A1
Lo, river A1
Ma, river A2
Mekong, delta B5
Mekong, river A4
Mui Bai Bung, point A5
Ngoc Linh, mt. B3
Red (Hong), river A2
Tonkin, gulf B2

Vietnam

Capital: Hanoi
Area: 127,246 sq. mi.
      329,653 sq. km.
Population: 77,311,000
Largest City: Ho Chi Minh City
Language: Vietnamese
Monetary Unit: Dong

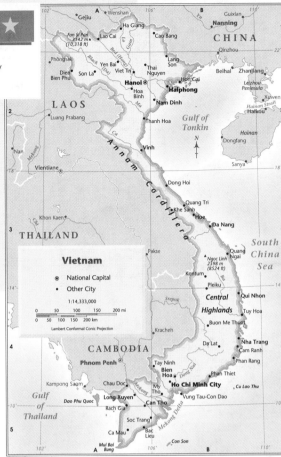

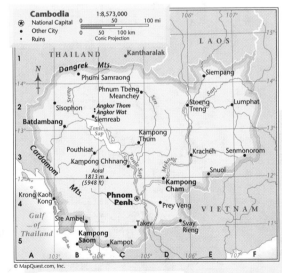

© MapQuest.com, Inc.

Laos

Capital: Vientiane
Area: 91,429 sq. mi.
      236,085 sq. km.
Population: 5,407,000
Largest City: Vientiane
Language: Lao
Monetary Unit: New kip

Laos:
Map Index

Cities and Towns
Attapu D4
Ban Houayxay A1
Champasak C4
Louang Namtha A1
Luang Prabang B2
Muang Khammouan C3
Muang Không C4
Muang Khôngxédôn C4
Muang Paklay A2
Muang Pakxan B2
Muang Vangviang B2
Muang Xaignabouri A2
Muang Xay A1
Muang Xépôn D3
Muang Xon B1
Pakse C4
Phôngsali B1
Saravan D4
Savannakhet C3
Vientiane, capital B3
Xam Nua C1
Xiangkhoang B2

Other Features
Annam, range C3
Banghiang, river C3
Bolovens, plateau D4
Kong, river D4
Luang Prabang, range A3
Mekong, river A1, C3
Nam Ngum, reservoir B2
Ou, river B1
Phou Bia, mt. B2
Xiangkhoang, plateau B2

Mongolia

Capital: Ulan Bator
Area: 604,800 sq. mi.
      1,566,839 sq. km.
Population: 2,617,000
Largest City: Ulan Bator
Language: Mongolian
Monetary Unit: Tughrik

Mongolia:
Map Index

Cities and Towns
Altay B2
Arvayheer C2
Baruun-Urt D2
Bayanhongor C2
Bulgan C2
Buyant-Uhaa D3
Choybalsan D2
Dalandzadgad C3
Darhan C2
Dund-Us B2

Erdenet C2
Mandalgovĭ C2
Mörön C2
Ölgiy A2
Öndörhaan D2
Sühbaatar C2
Tamsagbulag D2
Tsetserleg C2
Ulaangom B2
Ulaan-Uul C2
Ulan Bator, capital C2
Uliastay B2

Other Features
Altai, mts. B2
Bööntsagaan, lake B2
Dörgön, lake B2
Dzavhan, river B2
Gobi, desert C3
Hangayn, mts. B2
Har Us, lake B2
Hovd, river B2
Hövsgöl, lake C1
Hyargas, lake B2
Ih Bogd Uul, mt. C3
Kerulen, river D2
Mongolian, plateau C2
Onon, river C2
Orhon, river C2
Selenge Mörön, river C2
Tavan Bogd Uul, mt. A2
Tesiyn, river C2
Tuul, river C2
Uvs, lake B1

© MapQuest.com, Inc.

Cambodia

Capital: Phnom Penh
Area: 70,238 sq. mi.
      181,964 sq. km.
Population: 11,627,000
Largest City: Phnom Penh
Language: Khmer
Monetary Unit: New riel

Cambodia:
Map Index

Cities and Towns
Batdambang B2
Kampong Cham D4
Kampong Chhnang C3
Kampong Saom B5
Kampong Thum C3
Kampot C5
Kracheh E3
Krong Kaoh Kong A4
Lumphat F2
Phnom Penh, capital C4
Phnum Tbeng Meanchey ...C2
Phumi Samraong B1
Pouthisat B3

Prey Veng D4
Senmonorom F3
Siempang E1
Siemreab B2
Sisophon B2
Snuol E3
Sre Ambel B4
Stoeng Treng D2
Svay Rieng D4
Takev C5

Other Features
Angkor Thom, ruins B2
Angkor Wat, ruins B2
Aoral, mt. C3
Cardamom, mts. A3
Dangrek, mts. B1
Mekong, river D3
San, river E2
Sen, river C2
Sreng, river B2
Thailand, gulf A4
Tonle Sap, lake B2, C3
Tonle Sap, river B2

Thailand

Capital: Bangkok
Area: 198,115 sq. mi.
513,251 sq. km.
Population: 60,609,000
Largest City: Bangkok
Language: Thai
Monetary Unit: Baht

Thailand:
Map Index

Cities and Towns

Aranyaprathet	C3
Bangkok, *capital*	B3
Ban Phai	C2
Buriram	C3
Chaiyaphum	C3
Chiang Mai	B2
Chiang Rai	B2
Chon Buri	B3
Chumphon	B4
Hat Yai	B5
Hua Hin	B3
Khon Kaen	C2
Lampang	B2
Lamphun	B2
Loei	B2
Lop Buri	B3
Nakhon Phanom	C2
Nakhon Ratchasima	C3
Nakhon Sawan	B3
Nakhon Si Thammarat	B4
Nam Tok	B3
Nan	B2
Narathiwat	B5
Nong Khai	C2
Nonthaburi	B3
Pattani	B5
Phatthalung	B5
Phayao	B2
Phetchabun	B2
Phetchaburi	B3
Phichit	B2
Phitsanulok	B2
Phrae	B2
Phra Nakhon Si Ayutthaya	B3
Phuket	B5
Prachuap Khiri Khan	B4
Ranong	B4
Ratchaburi	B3
Rayong	B3
Roi Et	C2
Sakon Nakhon	C2
Sara Buri	B3
Sattahip	B3
Sisaket	C3
Songkhla	B5
Sukhothai	B2
Surat Thani	B4
Surin	C3
Tak	B2
Takua Pa	B4
Trang	B5
Trat	C3
Ubon Ratchathani	C3
Udon Thani	C2
Uttaradit	B2
Yala	B5

Other Features

Bilauktaung, *range*	B3
Chao Phraya, *river*	B3
Chi, *river*	C2
Dangrek, *mts.*	C3
Dawna, *range*	B2
Inthanon, *mt.*	B2
Khorat, *plateau*	C2
Ko Chang, *island*	C3
Ko Kut, *island*	C3
Ko Phangan, *island*	B4
Ko Samui, *island*	B4
Ko Tarutao, *island*	B5
Kra, *isthmus*	B4
Laem, *mt.*	B3
Lam Pao, *reservoir*	C2
Luang, *mt.*	B2
Mae Klong, *river*	B3
Malacca, *strait*	B5
Malay, *peninsula*	B5
Mekong, *river*	C2
Mun, *river*	B2
Nan, *river*	B2
Pa Sak, *river*	B3
Phetchabun, *range*	B3
Ping, *river*	B2
Salween, *river*	A2
Sirinthorn, *reservoir*	C3
Srinagarind, *reservoir*	B3
Tanen, *range*	B2
Thailand, *gulf*	B4
Thale Luang, *lagoon*	B5
Yom, *river*	B2

Burma (Myanmar)

Capital: Rangoon
Area: 261,228 sq. mi.
676,756 sq. km.
Population: 48,081,000
Largest City: Rangoon
Language: Burmese
Monetary Unit: Kyat

Burma:
Map Index

States and Divisions

Chin, *state*	B2
Irrawaddy, *division*	B3
Kachin, *state*	C1
Karen, *state*	C3
Kayah, *state*	C2
Magwe, *division*	B2
Mandalay, *division*	B2
Mon, *division*	C3
Pegu, *division*	B3
Rakhine, *state*	B2
Rangoon, *division*	C3
Sagaing, *division*	B2
Shan, *state*	C2
Tenasserim, *division*	C3

Cities and Towns

Bassein	B3
Bhamo	C1
Haka	B2
Henzada	B3
Kawthaung	C4
Keng Tung	C2
Kyaukpyu	B2
Lashio	C2
Loi-kaw	C2
Mandalay	B2
Maymyo	B2
Meiktila	B2
Mergui	C4
Monywa	B2
Moulmein	C3
Myingyan	B2
Myitkyina	C1
Pa-an	C3
Pegu	C3
Prome	B2
Putao	C1
Rangoon, *capital*	C3
Sagaing	B2
Shwebo	B2
Sittwe	B2
Tamu	B1
Taunggyi	C2
Tavoy	C3
Ye	C3

Other Features

Andaman, *sea*	B3
Arakan Yoma, *mts.*	B2
Bengal, *bay*	B3
Bilauktaung, *range*	C3
Cheduba, *island*	B2
Chin, *hills*	B2
Chindwin, *river*	B1
Coco, *islands*	B3
Hkakabo Razi, *mt.*	C1
Irrawaddy, *river*	B2
Martaban, *gulf*	C3
Mekong, *river*	C2
Mergui, *archipelago*	C4
Mouths of the Irrawaddy, *delta*	B3
Preparis, *island*	B3
Ramree, *island*	B2
Salween, *river*	C2
Shan, *plateau*	C2
Sittang, *river*	C2
Tavoy, *point*	C3
Thailand, *gulf*	C4

Philippines

Capital: Manila
Area: 115,860 sq. mi.
300,155 sq. km.
Population: 79,346,000
Largest City: Manila
Languages: Pilipino, English
Monetary Unit: Philippine peso

Philippines:
Map Index

Regions

Bicol	B3
Cagayan Valley	B2
Central Luzon	A3
Central Mindanao	C5
Central Visayas	B4
*Cordillera Autonomous Region	B2
Eastern Visayas	C4
Ilocos	B2
*Moslem Mindanao Autonomous Region	B5
National Capital Region	B3
Northern Mindanao	C4
Southern Mindanao	C5
Southern Tagalog	B3
Western Mindanao	B5
Western Visayas	B4

Cities and Towns

Angeles	B3
Bacolod	B4
Baguio	B2
Basilan	B5
Batangas	B3
Bislig	C4
Butuan	C4
Cabanatuan	B3
Cadiz	B4
Cagayan de Oro	C4
Calapan	B3
Calbayog	C3
Cebu	B4
Cotabato	C5
Dagupan	B2
Davao	C5
Dipolog	B4
Dumaguete	B4
General Santos	C5
Iligan	C4
Iloilo	B4
Jolo	B5
Laoag	B2
Laoang	C3
Legazpi	B3
Lipa	B3
Lucena	B3
Mamburao	B3
Mandaue	B4
Manila, *capital*	B3
Masbate	B3
Naga	B3
Olongapo	B3
Ormoc	C4
Pagadian	B5
Puerto Princesa	A4
Quezon City	B3
Roxas	B4
San Carlos	B4
San Fernando	B3
San Pablo	B3
Silay	B4
Surigao	C4
Tacloban	C4
Tuguegarao	B2
Vigan	B2
Zamboanga	B5

Other Features

Agusan, *river*	C4
Apo, *volcano*	C5
Babuyan, *channel*	B2
Babuyan, *islands*	B1
Balabac, *island*	A5
Balabac, *strait*	A5
Bashi, *channel*	B1
Basilan, *island*	B5
Bataan, *peninsula*	B3
Batan, *islands*	B1
Bohol, *island*	C4
Bohol, *sea*	C4
Cagayan, *islands*	B4
Cagayan, *river*	B2
Cagayan Sulu, *island*	A5
Calamian, *islands*	A3
Caramoan, *peninsula*	B3
Catanduanes, *island*	C3
Cebu, *island*	B4
Celebes, *sea*	B5
Cordillera Central, *mts.*	B2
Corregidor, *island*	B3
Cuyo, *islands*	B4
Davao, *gulf*	C5
Dinagat, *island*	C4
Diuata, *mts.*	C4
Jolo, *island*	B5
Laguna de Bay, *lake*	B3
Lamon, *bay*	B3
Leyte, *island*	C4
Lingayen, *gulf*	B2
Luzon, *island*	B3
Luzon, *strait*	B2
Manila, *bay*	B3
Marinduque, *island*	B3
Masbate, *island*	B3
Mayon, *volcano*	B3
Mindanao, *island*	C5
Mindoro, *island*	B3
Mindoro, *strait*	B3
Moro, *gulf*	B5
Negros, *island*	B4
Palawan, *island*	A4
Panay, *gulf*	B4
Panay, *island*	B4
Philippine, *sea*	C3
Pulangi, *river*	C5
Samar, *island*	C3
Samar, *sea*	B3
Siargao, *island*	C4
Sibuyan, *island*	B3
Sibuyan, *sea*	B3
Sierra Madre, *mts.*	B2
South China, *sea*	A3
Sulu, *archipelago*	A5
Sulu, *sea*	A4
Tablas, *island*	B3
Tawi Tawi, *island*	A5
Visayan, *islands*	B4
Visayan, *sea*	B4
Zambales, *mts.*	B3
Zamboanga, *peninsula*	B5
*Not on map	

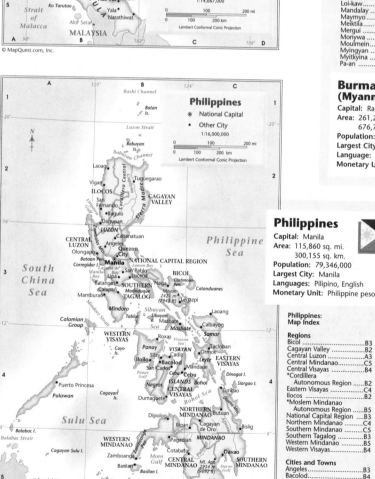

Indonesia: Map Index

Cities and Towns

Amahai	D2
Ambon	D2
Balikpapan	C2
Banda Aceh	A1
Bandar Lampung	B2
Bandung	B2
Banjarmasin	C2
Baubau	D2
Bengkulu	B2
Bogor	B2
Cilacap	B2
Cirebon	C2
Denpasar	C2
Dili	D2
Ende	E2
Fakfak	E2
Gorontalo	D1
Jakarta, *capital*	B2
Jambi	B2
Jayapura	F2
Kediri	C2
Kendari	D2
Kupang	D3
Madiun	C2
Magelang	C2
Malang	C2
Manado	D1
Manokwari	E2
Mataram	C2
Medan	A1
Merauke	F2
Padang	B2
Palangkaraya	C2
Palembang	B2
Palu	C2
Pangkalpinang	B2
Parepare	C2
Pekalongan	C2
Pekanbaru	B1
Pematangsiantar	A1

Pontianak	B2
Raba	C2
Samarinda	C2
Semarang	C2
Sorong	E2
Sukabumi	B2
Surabaya	C2
Surakarta	C2
Tanjungpinang	B1
Tarakan	C1
Tasikmalaya	B2
Tegal	B2
Ternate	D1
Ujung Pandang	C2
Waingapu	D2
Yogyakarta	C2

Other Features

Agung, *mt.*	C2
Alor, *island*	D2
Arafura, *sea*	E2
Aru, *islands*	E2
Babar, *island*	D2
Bali, *island*	C2
Banda, *sea*	D2
Bangka, *island*	B2
Belitung, *island*	B2
Biak, *island*	E2
Borneo, *island*	C1
Buru, *island*	D2
Celebes (Sulawesi), *island*	D2
Celebes, *sea*	D1
Ceram, *island*	D2
Ceram, *sea*	D2
Digul, *river*	E2
Enggano, *island*	B2
Flores, *island*	C2
Flores, *sea*	C2
Greater Sunda, *islands*	B2
Halmahera, *island*	D1
Irian Jaya, *region*	E2
Java, *island*	C2
Java, *sea*	C2
Jaya, *mt.*	E2
Kahayan, *river*	C2
Kai, *islands*	E2
Kalimantan, *region*	C2
Kerinci, *mt.*	B2
Krakatau, *island*	B2
Lesser Sunda, *islands*	C2
Lingga, *island*	B2
Lombok, *island*	C2
Madura, *island*	C2
Makassar, *strait*	C2
Malacca, *strait*	A1
Mentawai, *islands*	A2
Misool, *island*	E2
Moa, *island*	D2
Molucca, *sea*	D2
Moluccas, *islands*	D2
Morotai, *island*	D1
Muna, *island*	D2
Natuna Besar, *island*	B1
New Guinea, *island*	E2
Nias, *island*	A1
Obi, *island*	D2
Peleng, *island*	D2
Savu, *sea*	D2
Semeru, *mt.*	C2
Siberut, *island*	A2
Simeulue, *island*	A1
South China, *sea*	C1
Sudirman, *range*	E2
Sula, *islands*	D2
Sulu, *sea*	D1
Sumatra, *island*	B2
Sumba, *island*	D2
Sumbawa, *island*	C2
Talaud, *islands*	D1
Tanimbar, *islands*	E2
Timor, *island*	D2
Timor, *sea*	D3
Waigeo, *island*	E2
Wetar, *island*	D2
Yapen, *island*	E2

Indonesia

Capital: Jakarta
Area: 741,052 sq. mi.
1,919,824 sq. km.
Population: 216,108,000
Largest City: Jakarta
Language: Bahasa Indonesian
Monetary Unit: New rupiah

Brunei

Capital: Bandar Seri Begawan
Area: 2,226 sq. mi.
5,767 sq. km.
Population: 323,000
Largest City: Bandar Seri Begawan
Language: Malay
Monetary Unit: Brunei dollar

Brunei: Map Index

Cities and Towns

Badas	A2
Bandar Seri Begawan, *capital*	B2
Bangar	C2
Jerudong	B2
Kerangan Nyatan	B3
Kuala Abang	B2
Kuala Belait	A3
Labi	A3
Labu	C2
Lumut	A2
Medit	C2
Muara	C1
Seria	A2
Sukang	B3
Tutong	B2

Other Features

Belait, *river*	B3
Brunei, *bay*	C1
Brunei, *river*	C2
Bukit Pagon, *mt.*	C3
Pandaruan, *river*	C2
South China, *sea*	A2
Temburong, *river*	C2
Tutong, *river*	B2

Singapore: Map Index

Cities and Towns

Bedok	B1
Bukit Panjang	B1
Bukit Timah	B1
Changi	B1
Choa Chu Kang	A1
Jurong	B1
Kranji	B1
Nee Soon	B1
Punggol	B1
Queenstown	B1
Sembawang	B1
Serangoon	B1
Singapore, *capital*	B1
Tampines	B1
Thong Hoe	A1
Toa Payoh	B1
Tuas	A1
Woodlands	B1

Other Features

Ayer Chawan, *island*	A1
Bukum, *island*	B2
Johor, *strait*	B1
Keppel, *harbor*	B2
Pandan, *strait*	A2
Semakau, *island*	B2
Senang, *island*	A2
Sentosa, *island*	B2
Singapore, *island*	B1
Singapore, *strait*	B2
Tekong, *island*	C1
Timah, *hill*	B1
Ubin, *island*	B1

Singapore

Capital: Singapore
Area: 247 sq. mi.
640 sq. km.
Population: 3,532,000
Largest City: Singapore
Languages: Mandarin Chinese, English, Malay, Tamil
Monetary Unit: Singapore dollar

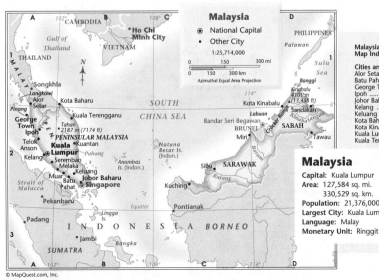

Malaysia

Capital: Kuala Lumpur
Area: 127,584 sq. mi.
330,529 sq. km.
Population: 21,376,000
Largest City: Kuala Lumpur
Language: Malay
Monetary Unit: Ringgit

Malaysia: Map Index

Cities and Towns

Alor Setar	A1
Batu Pahat	B2
George Town	A2
Ipoh	A2
Johor Baharu	B2
Kelang	A2
Keluang	B2
Kota Baharu	B1
Kota Kinabalu	D2
Kuala Lumpur, *capital*	A2
Kuala Terengganu	B2
Kuantan	B2
Kuching	C2
Melaka	B2
Miri	D2
Muar	B2
Sandakan	D2
Seremban	A2
Sibu	C2
Tawau	D2
Telok Anson	A2

Other Features

Banggi, *island*	D1
Baram, *river*	D2
Crocker, *range*	D2
Kinabalu, *mt.*	D1
Kinabatangan, *river*	D2
Labuan, *island*	D2
Langkawi, *island*	A1
Malacca, *strait*	A1
Malay, *peninsula*	A1
Pahang, *river*	B2
Peninsular Malaysia, *region*	B2
Perak, *river*	A2
Pinang, *island*	A2
Rajang, *river*	C2
Sabah, *state*	D2
Sarawak, *state*	C2
Tahan, *mt.*	B2

Australia:
Map Index

States and Territories
Australian Capital Territory......D3
New South Wales.................D3
Northern Territory................C2
Queensland.......................D2
South Australia..................C2
Tasmania..........................D4
Victoria............................D3
Western Australia................B2

Aboriginal Lands
Alawa-Ngandji.....................C1
Balwina...........................B2
Central Australia.................B2
Central Desert...................C2
Daly River.........................B1
Haasts Bluff.......................C2
Lake Mackay.......................B2
Nganyatjara.......................B2
Petermann........................B2
Pitjantjatjara.....................C2
Waani/Garawa....................C1
Yandeyarra.......................A2
Unnamed...........................B2
Unnamed..........................C1
Unnamed..........................D1

Cities and Towns
Adelaide, S.A., capital ..C3, Inset II
Albany, W.A.......................A3
Albury, N.S.W.....................D3
Alice Springs, N.T................C2
Altona, Vic......................Inset V
Armadale, W.A..................Inset I
Armidale, N.S.W..................E3
Asquith, N.S.W.................Inset IV
Auburn, N.S.W.................Inset IV
Balcatta, W.A...................Inset I
Bald Hills, Qld.................Inset III
Ballarat, Vic.....................D3
Bankstown, N.S.W.............Inset IV
Bayswater, W.A................Inset I
Beenleigh, Qld.................Inset III
Belmont, W.A..................Inset I
Bendigo, Vic......................D3
Berwick, Vic....................Inset V
Blacktown, N.S.W.............Inset IV
Botany, N.S.W.................Inset IV

Bourke, N.S.W....................D3
Bowen, Qld........................D2
Box Hill, Vic...................Inset V
Brighton, S.A..................Inset II
Brighton, Qld..................Inset III
Brighton, Vic...................Inset V
Brisbane, Qld.,
  capital.....................E2, Inset III
Broadmeadows, Vic.........Inset V
Broken Hill, N.S.W...............D3
Broome, W.A......................B1
Brown Plains, Qld.............Inset III
Bunbury, W.A.....................A3
Bundaberg, Qld...................E2
Burnside, S.A...................Inset II
Byford, W.A.....................Inset I
Cairns, Qld........................D2
Campbelltown, S.A.............Inset II
Campbelltown, N.S.W.......Inset IV
Canberra, A.C.T.,
  national capital................D3
Cannington, W.A...............Inset I
Canterbury, N.S.W...........Inset IV
Carnarvon, W.A...................A2
Castle Hill, N.S.W.............Inset IV
Caulfield, Vic..................Inset V
Ceduna, S.A.......................C3
Charleville, Qld...................D2
Charters Towers, Qld............D2
Chelsea, Vic....................Inset V
Chermside, Qld................Inset III
City Beach, W.A...............Inset I
Cleveland, Qld.................Inset III
Cloncurry, Qld....................D2
Coburg, Vic.....................Inset V
Coober Pedy, S.A................C2
Coopers Plains, Qld...........Inset III
Cranbourne, Vic..............Inset V
Cronulla, N.S.W...............Inset IV
Dampier, W.A.....................A2
Dandenong, Vic...............Inset V
Darwin, N.T., capital.............C1
Dee Why, N.S.W...............Inset IV
Devonport, Tas....................D4
Doncaster, Vic..................Inset V
Dubbo, N.S.W.....................D3
Elizabeth, S.A..................Inset II
Eltham, Vic.....................Inset V
Emerald, Qld......................D2
Enfield, S.A....................Inset II
Epping, N.S.W..................Inset IV
Esperance, W.A...................B3
Essendon, Vic..................Inset V
Fairfield, N.S.W................Inset IV
Ferntree Gully, Vic...........Inset V
Ferny Grove, Qld.............Inset III

Frankston, Vic..................Inset V
Fremantle, W.A............A3, Inset I
Geelong, Vic......................D3
Geraldton, W.A...................A2
Gladstone, Qld....................E2
Glenelg, S.A....................Inset II
Glen Forrest, W.A.............Inset I
Gold Coast, Qld...................E2
Goodna, Qld....................Inset III
Gosford, N.S.W....................E3
Gosnells, W.A...................Inset I
Grafton, N.S.W....................E3
Grange, S.A.....................Inset II
Greenslopes, Qld.............Inset III
Griffith, N.S.W....................D3
Gympie, Qld.......................E2
Heidelberg, Vic................Inset V
Hobart, Tas., capital.............D4
Holland Park, Qld.............Inset III
Holroyd, N.S.W................Inset IV
Hornsby, N.S.W................Inset IV
Hurstville, N.S.W...............Inset IV
Inala, Qld.......................Inset III
Ipswich, Qld...................Inset III
Kalamunda, W.A..............Inset I
Kalgoorlie, W.A...................B3
Katherine, N.T.....................C1
Keilor, Vic......................Inset V
Kelmscott, W.A................Inset I
Kersbrook, S.A.................Inset II
Kwinana, W.A...................Inset I
Kwinana Beach, W.A..........Inset I
La Perouse, N.S.W............Inset IV
Launceston, Tas...................D4
Leichhardt, N.S.W............Inset IV
Lilydale, Vic...................Inset V
Lismore, N.S.W....................E2
Liverpool, N.S.W..............Inset IV
Lobethal, S.A...................Inset II
Logan, Qld.....................Inset III
Longreach, Qld...................D2
Mackay, Qld.......................D2
Mandurah, W.A...................A3
Manly, Qld.....................Inset III
Manly, N.S.W...................Inset IV
Marion, S.A.....................Inset II
Maryborough, Qld...............E2
Melbourne, Vic.,
  capital.....................D3, Inset V
Melville, W.A...................Inset I
Merredin, W.A....................A3
Midland, W.A...................Inset I
Mildura, Vic.......................D3
Mitcham, S.A...................Inset II
Mona Vale, N.S.W............Inset IV
Moorabbin, Vic................Inset V

Mordialloc, Vic................Inset V
Moree, N.S.W.....................D3
Morningside, Qld.............Inset III
Mosman Park, W.A............Inset I
Mount Barker, S.A............Inset II
Mount Gambier, S.A.............D3
Mount Gravatt, Qld...........Inset III
Mount Isa, Qld....................C2
Mount Nebo, Qld.............Inset III
Mullaloo, W.A..................Inset I
Narrogin, W.A....................A3
Nedlands, W.A.................Inset I
Newcastle, N.S.W................E3
Newman, W.A.....................A2
Newmarket, Qld...............Inset III
Noarlunga, S.A.................Inset II
North Adelaide, S.A...........Inset II
Northcote, Vic.................Inset V
North Sydney, N.S.W........Inset IV
Nunawading, Vic.............Inset V
Oakleigh, Vic..................Inset V
Orange, N.S.W....................D3
Parramatta, N.S.W............Inset IV
Perth, W.A., capital.....A3, Inset I
Pickering Brook, W.A.........Inset I
Port Adelaide, S.A.............Inset II
Port Augusta, S.A................C3
Port Hedland, W.A..............A2
Port Lincoln, S.A.................C3
Port Macquarie, N.S.W..........E3
Port Pirie, S.A....................C3
Prahran, Vic....................Inset V
Preston, Vic....................Inset V
Queenstown, Tas.................D4
Randwick, N.S.W..............Inset IV
Redcliffe, Qld..................Inset III
Redland Bay, Qld.............Inset III
Reynella, S.A...................Inset II
Ringwood, Vic.................Inset V
Rockdale, N.S.W..............Inset IV
Rockhampton, Qld...............E2
Roma, Qld.........................D2
Ryde, N.S.W....................Inset IV
St. Ives, N.S.W................Inset IV
St. Kilda, S.A...................Inset II
St. Kilda, Vic..................Inset V
Salisbury, S.A..................Inset II
Samford, Qld...................Inset III
Sandgate, Qld.................Inset III
Scarborough, W.A.............Inset I
Spearwood, W.A...............Inset I
Springvale, Vic................Inset V
Stirling, S.A....................Inset II
Stirling, S.A....................Inset II
Sunshine, Vic..................Inset V

Sutherland, N.S.W...........Inset IV
Sydney, N.S.W.,
  capital.....................E3, Inset IV
Tamworth, N.S.W................E3
Taree, N.S.W......................E3
Tea Tree Gully, S.A...........Inset II
Tennant Creek, N.T.............C1
Tom Price, W.A....................A2
Toowoomba, Qld.................E2
Townsville, Qld...................D1
Unley, S.A......................Inset II
Victoria Park, W.A.............Inset I
Victoria Point, Qld............Inset III
Wagga Wagga, N.S.W..........D3
Wanneroo, W.A................Inset I
Warrnambool, Vic...............D3
Waverley, Vic..................Inset V
Weipa, Qld........................D1
Whyalla, S.A......................C3
Willoughby, N.S.W............Inset IV
Wollongong, N.S.W.............E3
Woodside, S.A.................Inset II
Woodville, S.A.................Inset II
Woomera, S.A....................C3
Wyndham, W.A...................B1
Wynnum, Qld...................Inset III

Other Features
Arafura, sea.......................C1
Arnhem, cape.....................C1
Arnhem Land, region..........C1
Ashburton, river.................A2
Ashmore and Cartier, islands B1
Australian Alps, mts............D3
Barkly, tableland.................C1
Bass, strait.......................D3
Bate, bay.......................Inset IV
Blue, mts..........................D3
Botany, bay....................Inset IV
Brisbane, river................Inset III
Burdekin, river...................D1
Canning, river...............Inset I
Cape York, peninsula..........D1
Carpentaria, gulf................C1
Coral, sea.........................E1
Daly, river.........................C1
Darling, range....................A3
Darling, river......................D3
Drysdale River Natl. Park.....B1
Eyre, lake.........................C2
Eyre, peninsula..................C3
Fitzroy, river......................B1
Flinders, range...................C3
Flinders, river.....................D1
Frome, lake.......................D2
Gairdner, lake....................C3

Garden, island...................Inset
Gascoyne river...................A2
Gibson, desert...................B2
Gilbert, river.......................D1
Great Artesian, basin...........D2
Great Australian, bight.........B3
Great Barrier, reef...............D1
Great Dividing, range...........D3
Great Sandy, desert............B2
Great Victoria, desert..........B2
Gregory Natl. Park..............C1
Grey, range.......................D2
Groote Eylandt, island........C1
Hamersley, range...............A2
Hobsons, bay..................Inset
Jackson, port...................Inset
Kakadu Natl. Park..............C1
Kangaroo, island................C3
Kimberley, plateau.............B1
King Leopold, range............B1
Kosciusko, mt....................D3
Lakefield Natl. Park............D1
Leeuwin, cape...................A3
Leichhardt, river.................D1
Leveque, cape....................A1
Logan, river.....................Inset
Macdonnell, ranges............C2
Melville, island...................C1
Mitchell, river.....................D1
Moreton, bay...................Inset
Murchison, river.................A2
Murray, river......................C3
Murrumbidgee, river............D3
Musgrave, ranges...............C2
New England, range............E3
North West, cape................A2
Nullarbor, plain..................B3
Port Phillip, bay................Inset
Roper, river........................C1
Rudall River Natl. Park.........B2
St. Vincent, gulf................Inset
Samsonvale, lake.............Inset
Simpson, desert.................C2
Simpson Desert Natl. Park....C2
Spencer, gulf.....................C3
Swan, river......................Inset
Tasman, sea......................E4
Timor, sea.........................B1
Torrens, lake......................C3
Torrens, river...................Inset
Torres, strait......................D1
Uluru (Ayers Rock)..............C2
Victoria, river.....................B1
Witjira Natl. Park.................C2
Yampi, sound.....................A1
York, cape.........................D1

Australia

Capital: Canberra
Area: 2,966,200 sq. mi.
7,684,456 sq. km.
Population: 18,784,000
Largest City: Sydney
Language: English
Monetary Unit: Australian dollar

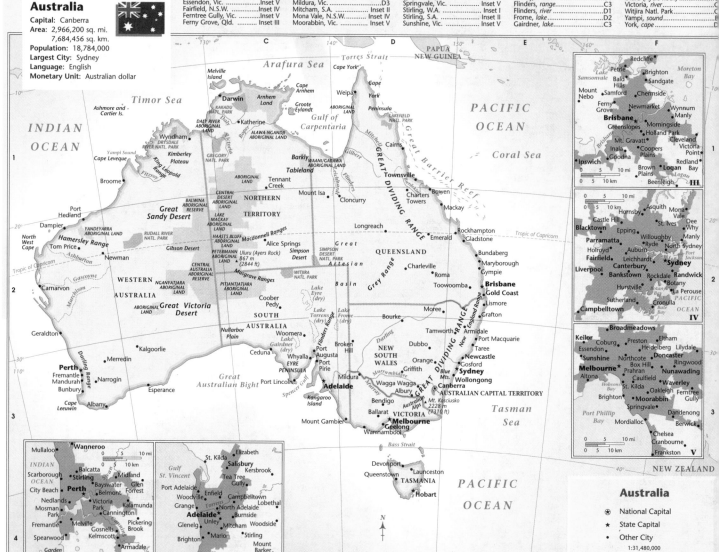

© MapQuest.com, Inc.

Australia

⊛ National Capital
★ State Capital
• Other City

1:31,480,000

Lambert Conformal Conic Projection

**Papua New Guinea:
Map Index**

Cities and Towns
Alotau B3
Arawa B2
Daru A2
Goroka A2
Kavieng B2
Kerema A2
Kimbe B2
Lae A2
Lorengau A2
Madang A2
Morehead A2
Mount Hagen A2
Popondetta A2
Port Moresby, *capital* A2
Rabaul B2
Vanimo A2
Wabag A2
Wau A2
Wewak A1

Other Features
Admiralty, *islands* A2
Bismarck, *archipelago* A2
Bismarck, *range* A2
Bismarck, *sea* A2
Bougainville, *island* B2
Buka, *island* B2
Central, *range* A2
Coral, *sea* B2
D'Entrecasteaux, *islands* B2
Feni, *islands* B2
Fly, *river* A2
Gazelle, *peninsula* B2
Green, *islands* B2
Huon, *peninsula* A2
Karkar, *island* A2
Lihir, *group* B2
Louisiade, *archipelago* B3
Manus, *island* A2
Markham, *river* A2

Milne, *bay* B3
Murray, *lake* A2
Mussau, *island* B2
New Britain, *island* B2
New Guinea, *island* A2
New Hanover, *island* B2
New Ireland, *island* B2
Ninigo, *group* A2
Nuguria, *islands* A2
Owen Stanley, *range* A2
Papua, *gulf* A2
Purari, *river* A2
Ramu, *river* A2
Rossel, *island* B3
St. George's, *channel* B2
Sepik, *river* A2
Solomon, *sea* B2
Tabar, *islands* B2
Tagula, *island* B3
Tanga, *islands* B2
Tauu, *islands* A2
Torres, *strait* A2
Trobriand, *islands* B2
Umboi, *island* A2
Whiteman, *range* A2
Wilhelm, *mt.* A2
Witu, *islands* B2
Woodlark (Muyua), *island* B2

Papua New Guinea

Capital: Port Moresby
Area: 178,704 sq. mi.
  462,964 sq. km.
Population: 4,705,000
Largest City: Port Moresby
Language: English
Monetary Unit: Kina

New Zealand

Capital: Wellington
Area: 104,454 sq. mi.
  270,606 sq. km.
Population: 3,662,000
Largest City: Auckland
Language: English
Monetary Unit: New Zealand dollar

**New Zealand:
Map Index**

Cities and Towns
Alexandra A4
Ashburton B3
Auckland B2
Blenheim B3
Christchurch B3
Collingwood B3
Dunedin B4
East Coast Bays B2
Gisborne C2
Greymouth B3
Hamilton C2
Hastings C2
Hicks Bay C2
Invercargill A4
Kaeo B2
Kaikoura B3
Kaitaia B2
Kawhia B2
Lower Hutt B3
Manukau B2
Milford Sound A3
Napier C2
Nelson B3
New Plymouth B2
Oamaru B4
Palmerston North C3
Queenstown A3
Rotorua C2
Taumaruni C2
Taupo C2
Tauranga C2
Timaru B3
Waimamaku B2
Wanganui B3
Wellington, *capital* B3
Westport B3
Whakatane C2
Whangarei B2

Other Features
Aspiring, *mt.* A3
Banks, *peninsula* B3
Canterbury, *bight* B3
Canterbury, *plains* B3
Clutha, *river* A4
Cook, *mt.* B3
Cook, *strait* B3
Coromandel, *peninsula* C2
East, *cape* C2
Egmont, *cape* B2
Egmont, *mt.* B2
Farewell, *cape* B3
Foveaux, *strait* A4
Great Barrier, *island* C2
Hawea, *lake* A3
Hawke, *bay* C2
Ngauruhoe, *mt.* C2
North, *cape* B1
North, *island* B2
North Taranaki, *bight* B2
Palliser, *cape* C3
Pegasus, *bay* B3
Plenty, *bay* C2
Puysegur, *point* A4
Rangitikei, *river* C2
Raukumara, *range* C2
Ruahine, *range* C2
Ruapehu, *mt.* C2
South, *island* A3
Southern Alps, *mts.* A3
Southland, *plains* A4
South Taranaki, *bight* B2
South West, *cape* A4
Stewart, *island* A4
Tararua, *range* C3
Tasman, *bay* B3
Tasman, *sea* A2
Taupo, *lake* C2
Te Anau, *lake* A4
Tekapo, *lake* B3
Three Kings, *islands* B1
Tongariro, *mt.* C2
Waikato, *river* C2
Wairau, *river* B3
Waitaki, *river* B3
Wanaka, *lake* A3

MAJOR CITIES			
Australia		**Papua New**	
Sydney	3,935,000	**Guinea**	(metro)
Melbourne	3,322,000	Morobe	439,725
Brisbane	1,548,000	Western	398,376
Perth	1,319,000	Highlands	
Adelaide	1,083,000	Southern	390,240
		Highlands	
New Zealand		Eastern	316,802
Auckland	998,000	Highlands	
Wellington	335,000	Madang	288,317
Christchurch	331,000	Port Moresby	271,813
Hamilton	159,000		
Dunedin	112,000		

© MapQuest.com, Inc.

**Micronesia:
Map Index**

Cities and Towns
Colonia A2
Kosrae D2
Palikir, *capital* C2
Weno C2

Other Features
Caroline, *islands* B2
Chuuk, *islands* C2
Eauripik, *atoll* B2
Faraulep, *atoll* B2

Kapingamarangi, *atoll* C2
Kosrae, *island* D2
Mortlock, *islands* C2
Murilo, *atoll* C2
Namoluk, *atoll* C2
Namonuito, *atoll* C2
Ngulu, *atoll* A2
Nukuoro, *atoll* C2
Oroluk, *atoll* C2
Pohnpei, *island* D2
Pulusuk, *island* B2
Ulithi, *atoll* B2
Weno, *island* C2
Yap, *islands* A2

Micronesia

Capital: Palikir
Area: 271 sq. mi.
  702 sq. km.
Population: 132,000
Largest City: Palikir
Language: English
Monetary Unit: U.S. dollar

© MapQuest.com, Inc.

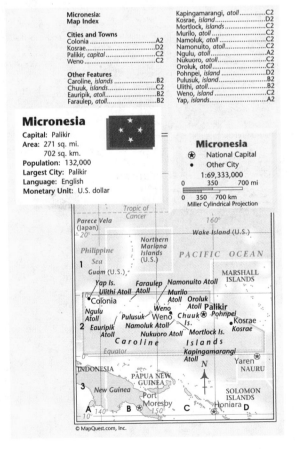

© MapQuest.com, Inc.

Marshall Islands

⊛ National Capital
• Other City

1:25,750,000

0   150   300 mi
0   150   300 km
Mercator Projection

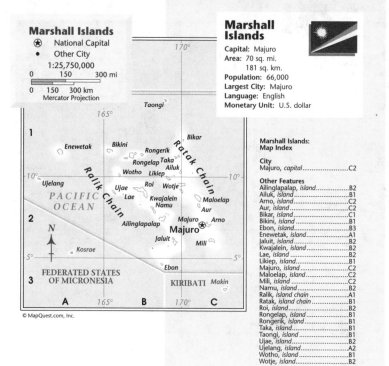

Marshall Islands

Capital: Majuro
Area: 70 sq. mi.
181 sq. km.
Population: 66,000
Largest City: Majuro
Language: English
Monetary Unit: U.S. dollar

Marshall Islands:
Map Index

City
Majuro, capital C2

Other Features
Ailinglapalap, island B2
Ailuk, island B1
Arno, island C2
Aur, island C2
Bikar, island C1
Bikini, island B1
Ebon, island B3
Enewetak, island A1
Jaluit, island B2
Kwajalein, island B2
Lae, island B2
Likiep, island B1
Majuro, island C2
Maloelap, island C2
Mili, island C2
Namu, island B2
Ralik, island chain A1
Ratak, island chain B1
Roi, island B2
Rongelap, island B1
Rongerik, island B1
Taka, island B1
Taongi, island B1
Ujae, island B2
Ujelang, island A2
Wotho, island B1
Wotje, island B2

Nauru

⊛ National Capital
• Other City

1:135,000

0   1   2 mi
0   1   2 km
Lambert Conformal Conic Projection

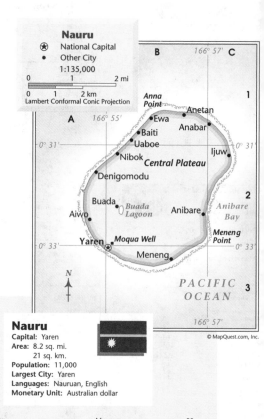

Nauru

Capital: Yaren
Area: 8.2 sq. mi.
21 sq. km.
Population: 11,000
Largest City: Yaren
Languages: Nauruan, English
Monetary Unit: Australian dollar

Nauru:
Map Index

Cities and Towns
Aiwo A2
Anabar C1
Anetan B1
Anibare B2
Baiti B1
Buada B2
Denigomodu A2
Ewa B1
Ijuw C2

Meneng B3
Nibok B2
Uaboe B1
Yaren, capital B3

Other Features
Anibare, bay C2
Anna, point B1
Buada, lagoon B2
Central, plateau B2
Meneng, point C2
Moqua, well B2

Solomon Islands

⊛ National Capital
• Other City

1:24,100,000

0   150   300 mi
0   150   300 km
Mercator Projection

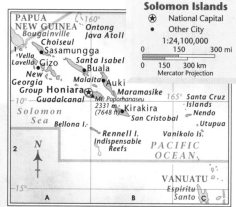

Solomon Islands:
Map Index

Cities and Towns
Auki B1
Buala A1
Gizo A1
Honiara, capital A1
Kirakira B2
Sasamungga A1

Other Features
Bellona, island A2
Choiseul, island A1
Guadalcanal, island A1
Indispensable, reefs B2
Malaita, island B1
Maramasike, island B1
Nendo, island C2
New Georgia Group,
island A1
Ontong Java, island A1
Popomanaseu, mt. B1
Rennell, island B2
San Cristobal, island B2
Santa Cruz, islands C2
Santa Isabel, island A1
Solomon, sea A2
Utupua, island C2
Vanikolo, islands C2
Vella Lavella, island A1

Solomon Islands

Capital: Honiara
Area: 10,954 sq. mi.
28,378 sq. km.
Population: 455,000
Largest City: Honiara
Language: English
Monetary Unit: Dollar

Tuvalu

Capital: Funafuti
Area: 9.4 sq. mi.
24.4 sq. km.
Population: 11,000
Largest City: Funafuti
Languages: Tuvaluan, English
Monetary Unit: Tuvalu dollar,
Australian dollar

Tuvalu:
Map Index

City
Funafuti, capital C3

Other Features
Funafuti, island C3
Nanumanga, island B2
Nanumea, island B1
Niulakita, island C4
Niutao, island B2
Nui, island B2
Nukufetau, island C2
Nukulaelae, island C3
Vaitupu, island C2

Tuvalu

⊛ National Capital
• Other City

1:12,500,000

0   75   150 mi
0   75   150 km
Mercator Projection

© MapQuest.com, Inc.

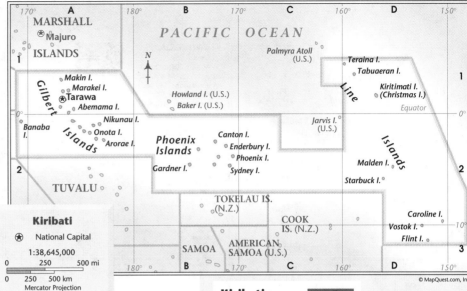

MARSHALL
⊛ Majuro
ISLANDS

PACIFIC OCEAN

Palmyra Atoll (U.S.)

Teraina I.
Tabuaeran I.

Makin I.
Marakei I.
⊛ Tarawa
Abemama I.

Howland I. (U.S.)
Baker I. (U.S.)

Kiritimati I. (Christmas I.)

Equator

Banaba I.
Nikunau I.
Onota I.
Aroraе I.

Jarvis I. (U.S.)

Gilbert Islands

Line Islands

Phoenix Islands

Canton I.
Enderbury I.
Phoenix I.
Sydney I.

Malden I.

Starbuck I.

TUVALU

Gardner I.

Caroline I.

TOKELAU IS. (N.Z.)

COOK IS. (N.Z.)

Vostok I.
Flint I.

SAMOA

AMERICAN SAMOA (U.S.)

© MapQuest.com, Inc.

Kiribati

⊛ National Capital

1:38,645,000

0   250   500 mi
0   250   500 km
Mercator Projection

Kiribati

Capital: Tarawa
Area: 313 sq. mi.
    811 sq. km.
Population: 86,000
Largest City: Tarawa
Languages: I-Kiribati (Gilbertese), English
Monetary Unit: Australian dollar

Kiribati:
Map Index

City
Tarawa, *capital* A1

Other Features
Abemama, *island* A1
Aroraе, *island* A2

Banaba, *island* A2
Canton, *island* B2
Caroline, *island* D2
Enderbury, *island* B2
Flint, *island* D3
Gardner, *island* B2
Gilbert, *islands* A1
Kiritimati (Christmas), *island* ..D1
Line, *islands* D1
Makin, *island* A1
Malden, *island* D2
Marakei, *island* A1
Nikunau, *island* A2
Onota, *island* A2
Phoenix, *island* B2
Phoenix, *islands* B2
Starbuck, *island* D2
Sydney, *island* B2
Tabuaeran, *island* D1
Teraina, *island* D1
Vostok, *island* D3

i:
ap Index

ties and Towns
aloa B3
basa B2
mi B3
utoka A2
mawai A3
abouwalu B2
adi A2
aduri B2
akodu B2
va, *capital* B3
nisea B3

ther Features
nga, *island* B3
gh Water, *sound* B2
cicia, *island* C2
kobia, *island* C1
au, *island* B3
davu, *island* B3
davu, *passage* A3
oa, *island* C2

Koro, *island* B2
Koro, *sea* B2
Lakeba, *island* C3
Lakeba, *passage* C3
Lau, *island group* C2
Laucala, *island* C2
Moala, *island group* B3
Nadi, *bay* A2
Navua, *river* A3
Ono, *island* B3
Ovalau, *island* B2
Qamea, *island* C2
Qelelevu, *island* C2
Rabi, *island* C2
Soso, *bay* B3
Taveuni, *island* C2
Tomanivi, *mt.* B2
Udu, *point* C2
Vanua Balavu, *island* C2
Vanua Levu, *island* B2
Vatu Lele, *island* A3
Vetauua, *island* C1
Viti Levu, *island* A2
Vunaniu, *bay* A3
Washington, *cape* A3
Yasawa, *island group* A2

Fiji

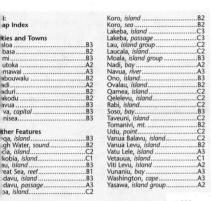

⊛ National Capital
● Other City

1:8,900,000

0   50   100 mi
0   50   100 km
Azimuthal Equal Area Projection

Fiji

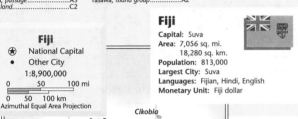

Capital: Suva
Area: 7,056 sq. mi.
    18,280 sq. km.
Population: 813,000
Largest City: Suva
Languages: Fijian, Hindi, English
Monetary Unit: Fiji dollar

Cikobia

Great Sea Reef

Vetauua
Udu Point
Qelelevu

Vanua Levu
Naduri   Labasa
Rabi
Kioa
Laucala
Qamea
Taveuni

Yasawa Group
Bligh Water
Viti Levu
Koro   Nakodu
Vanua Balavu

Lautoka
Nadi Bay
Tomanivi 1323 m (4340 ft)
Ovalau
Lami
Navua   Suva
Gau
Cicia

Koro Sea

Lau Group

Lakeba Passage
Lakeba

Lomawai
Vunaniu Bay
Galoa
Beqa

Vatu Lele
Kadavu Passage
Kadavu   Ono
Vunisea   Soso Bay

Moala Group

Cape Washington

© MapQuest.com, Inc.

Tonga

⊛ National Capital
● Other City

1:11,000,000

0   75   150 mi
0   75   150 km
Mercator Projection

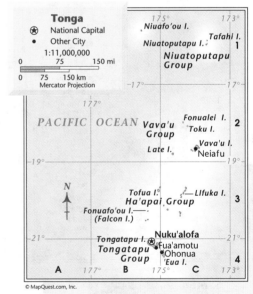

Niuafo'ou I.
Tafahi I.
Niuatoputapu I.
Niuatoputapu Group

PACIFIC OCEAN

Vava'u Group
Fonualei I.
Toku I.
Late I.
Vava'u I.
Neiafu

Tofua I.
Lifuka I.
Ha'apai Group
Fonuafo'ou I. (Falcon I.)

Nuku'alofa
Tongatapu I.
Tongatapu Group
Fua'amotu
Ohonua
'Eua I.

© MapQuest.com, Inc.

Tonga

Capital: Nuku'alofa
Area: 301 sq. mi.
    780 sq. km.
Population: 109,000
Largest City: Nuku'alofa
Languages: Tongan, English
Monetary Unit: Pa'anga

Tonga:
Map Index

Cities and Towns
Fua'amotu B4
Neiafu C2
Nuku'alofa, *capital* B4
Ohonua C4

Other Features
'Eua, *island* C4
Fonuafo'ou (Falcon), *island* ..B3
Fonualei, *island* C2

Ha'apai, *island group* B3
Late, *island* C2
Lifuka, *island* C3
Niuafo'ou, *island* B1
Niuatoputapu, *island* C1
Niuatoputapu, *island group* ..C1
Tafahi, *island* C1
Tofua, *island* B3
Toku, *island* C2
Tongatapu, *island* B4
Tongatapu, *island group* B4
Vava'u, *island* C2
Vava'u, *island group* C2

Palau

⊛ National Capital
● Other City

1:1,900,000

0   5   10 mi
0   5   10 km
Lambert Conformal Conic Projection

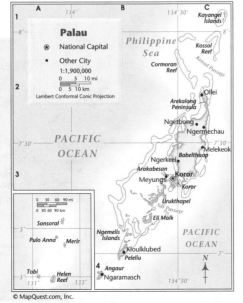

Kayangel Islands

Philippine Sea

Kossol Reef
Cormoran Reef
Kossol Passage

Ollei

Arekalong Peninsula

Ngetbong
Ngermechau

Ngerkeel
Babelthuap
Arakabesan
Meyungs   Koror
Koror

Urukthapel
PACIFIC OCEAN

Eli Malk

Sonsoral

Pulo Anna   Merir

Ngemelis Islands
Kloulklubed
Peleliu

PACIFIC OCEAN

Tobi   Helen Reef

Angaur
Ngaramasch

© MapQuest.com, Inc.

Palau

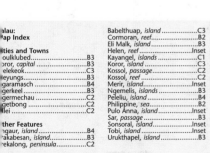

Capital: Koror
Area: 177 sq. mi.
    458 sq. km.
Population: 18,000
Largest City: Koror
Languages: English, Sonsorolese, Angaur, Japanese, Tobi, Palauan
Monetary Unit: U.S. dollar

alau:
ap Index

ities and Towns
oulklubed B3
oror, *capital* B3
elekeok B3
eyungs B3
garamasch B4
germechau C2
getbong C2
lei C2

ther Features
ngaur, *island* B4
akabesan, *island* B3
ekalong, *peninsula* C2

Babelthuap, *island* C3
Cormoran, *reef* B2
Eli Malk, *island* B3
Helen, *reef* ....Inset
Kayangel, *islands* C1
Koror, *island* C3
Kossol, *passage* C2
Kossol, *reef* C2
Merir, *island* ....Inset
Ngemelis, *islands* B3
Peleliu, *island* B4
Philippine, *sea* B2
Pulo Anna, *island* ....Inset
Sar, *passage* B3
Sonsoral, *island* ....Inset
Tobi, *island* ....Inset
Urukthapel, *island* B3

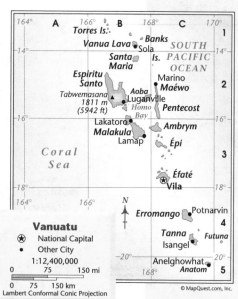

Vanuatu

Capital: Vila
Area: 4,707 sq. mi.
12,194 sq. km.
Population: 189,000
Largest City: Vila
Languages: French, English, Bislama
Monetary Unit: Vatu

Vanuatu:
Map Index

Cities and Towns
Anelghowhat..............C5
Isangel...................C4
Lakatoro.................B3
Lamap....................B3
Luganville................B2
Marino...................C2
Potnarvin................C4
Sola.....................B1
Vila, *capital*...........C3

Other Features
Ambrym, *island*........C3
Anatom, *island*........C5
Aoba, *island*..........B2
Banks, *islands*........B1
Coral, *sea*............C3
Éfaté, *island*.........C3
Épi, *island*...........C3
Erromango, *island*.....C4
Espiritu Santo, *island*..B2
Futuna, *island*........C4
Homo, *bay*.............B2
Maéwo, *island*.........C2
Malakula, *island*......B3
Pentecost, *island*.....C2
Santa Maria, *island*...B2
Tabwemasana, *mt.*......B2
Tanna, *island*.........C4
Torres, *islands*.......B1
Vanua Lava, *island*....B1

Vanuatu
(*) National Capital
• Other City
1:12,400,000
0   75   150 mi
0   75   150 km
Lambert Conformal Conic Projection

© MapQuest.com, Inc.

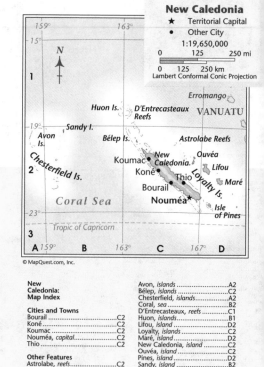

New Caledonia

★ Territorial Capital
• Other City
1:19,650,000
0   125   250 mi
0   125   250 km
Lambert Conformal Conic Projection

New
Caledonia:
Map Index

Cities and Towns
Bourail..................C2
Koné....................C2
Koumac..................C2
Nouméa, *capital*.......C2
Thio....................C2

Other Features
Astrolabe, *reefs*......C2

Avon, *islands*.........A2
Bélep, *islands*........C2
Chesterfield, *islands*..A2
Coral, *sea*............B2
D'Entrecasteaux, *reefs*..C1
Huon, *islands*.........B1
Lifou, *island*.........D2
Loyalty, *islands*......D2
Maré, *island*..........D2
New Caledonia, *island*..C2
Ouvéa, *island*.........D2
Pines, *island*.........D2
Sandy, *island*.........B2

New Caledonia

Capital: Nouméa
Area: 8,548 sq. mi.
21,912 sq. km.
Population: 197,000
Largest City: Nouméa
Language: French
Monetary Unit: CFA Franc

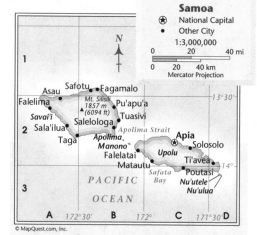

Samoa

(*) National Capital
• Other City
1:3,000,000
0   20   40 mi
0   20   40 km
Mercator Projection

Samoa

Capital: Apia
Area: 1,093 sq. mi.
2,832 sq. km.
Population: 230,000
Largest City: Apia
Languages: Samoan, English
Monetary Unit: Tala

Samoa:
Map Index

Cities and Towns
Apia, *capital*.........C2
Asau....................A2
Fagamalo................B1
Falelatai...............B2
Falelima................A2
Matautu.................C3
Poutasi.................C3
Pu'apu'a................B2
Safotu..................B1
Sala'ilua...............A2
Salelologa..............B2

Solosolo................C2
Taga....................A2
Ti'avea.................D2
Tuasivi.................B2

Other Features
Apolima, *island*.......B2
Apolima, *strait*.......B2
Manono, *island*........B2
Nu'ulua, *island*.......D3
Nu'utele, *island*......D3
Safata, *bay*...........C3
Savai'i, *island*.......A2
Silisili, *mt.*.........B2
Upolu, *island*.........C2

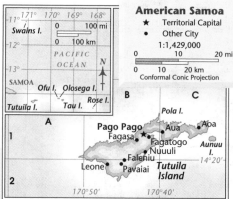

American Samoa

★ Territorial Capital
• Other City
1:1,429,000
0   10   20 mi
0   10   20 km
Conformal Conic Projection

American Samoa:
Map Index

Cities and Towns
Aoa.....................C1
Aua.....................C1
Fagasa..................B1
Fagatogo................B1
Faleniu.................B1
Leone...................B2
Nuuuli..................B1
Pago Pago, *capital*....B1
Pavaiai.................B2

Other Features
Aunuu, *island*.........C1
Ofu, *island*...........A1
Olosega, *island*.......A1
Pola, *island*..........C1
Rose, *island*..........B1
Swains, *island*........A1
Tau, *island*...........A1
Tutuila, *island*.......A1, C2

American Samoa

Capital: Pago Pago
Area: 77 sq. mi.
199 sq. km.
Population: 64,000
Largest City: Pago Pago
Language: Samoan, English
Monetary Unit: U.S. dollar

© MapQuest.com, Inc.

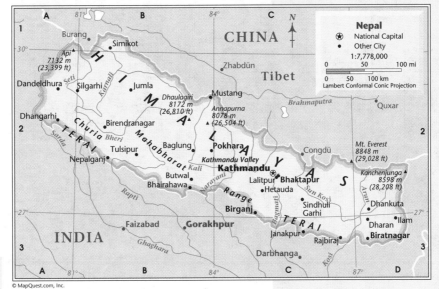

Nepal

- **National Capital**
- **Other City**
- 1:7,778,000
- 0 50 100 mi
- 0 50 100 km
- Lambert Conformal Conic Projection

CHINA
Tibet
INDIA

Nepal:
Map Index

Cities and Towns
Baglung	B2
Bhairahawa	B2
Bhaktapur	C2
Biratnagar	D3
Birendranagar	B2
Birganj	C2
Butwal	B2
Dandeldhura	A2
Dhangarhi	A2
Dhankuta	D2
Dharan	D3
Hetauda	C2
Ilam	D3
Janakpur	C3
Jumla	B2
Kathmandu, *capital*	C2
Lalitpur	C2
Mustang	B2
Nepalganj	B2
Pokhara	B2
Rajbiraj	C3
Silgarhi	B2
Simikot	B1
Sindhuli Garhi	C2
Tulsipur	B2

Other Features
Annapurna, *mt.*	B2
Api, *mt.*	A2
Arun, *river*	D2
Bagmati, *river*	C2
Bheri, *river*	B2
Churia, *mts.*	B2
Dhaulagiri, *mt.*	B2
Everest, *mt.*	C2
Himalayas, *mts.*	B2
Kali, *river*	B2
Kanchenjunga, *mt.*	D2
Karnali, *river*	B2
Kathmandu, *valley*	C2
Mahabharat, *range*	B2
Narayani, *river*	B2
Rapti, *river*	B2
Sarda, *river*	A2
Seti, *river*	A2
Sun Kosi, *river*	C2
Terai, *region*	A2, C3

Maldives

- **Capital:** Male
- **Area:** 115 sq. mi.
  - 298 sq. km.
- **Population:** 300,000
- **Largest City:** Male
- **Language:** Divehi
- **Monetary Unit:** Rufiyaa

Nepal

- **Capital:** Kathmandu
- **Area:** 56,827 sq. mi.
  - 147,220 sq. km.
- **Population:** 24,303,000
- **Largest City:** Kathmandu
- **Language:** Nepali
- **Monetary Unit:** Rupee

INDIAN OCEAN

Maldives

- **National Capital**
- 1:11,579,000
- 0 75 150 mi
- 0 75 150 km
- Lambert Conformal Conic Projection

Maldives:
Map Index

City
Male, *capital*	A2

Other Features
Addu, *atoll*	A5
Ari, *atoll*	A3
Equatorial, *channel*	A5
Fadiffolu, *atoll*	A2
Felidu, *atoll*	A3
Haddummati, *atoll*	A4
Horsburgh, *atoll*	A2
Ihavandiffulu, *atoll*	A1
Kardiva, *channel*	A2
Kolumadulu, *atoll*	A3
Malcolm, *atoll*	A1
Male, *atoll*	A2
Miladummadulu, *atoll*	A1
Mulaku, *atoll*	A3
Nilandu, *atoll*	A3
North Malosmadulu, *atoll*	A2
One and Half Degree, *channel*	A4
South Male, *atoll*	A2
South Malosmadulu, *atoll*	A2
Suvadiva, *atoll*	A4
Tiladummati, *atoll*	A1
Veimandu, *channel*	A3

Sri Lanka:
Map Index

Provinces
Central	B4
Eastern	C4
North Central	B3
Northern	B2
North Western	B4
Sabaragamuwa	B5
Southern	B5
Uva	C5
Western	A4

Cities and Towns
Amparai	C4
Anuradhapura	B3
Batticaloa	C4
Colombo, *capital*	A5
Dehiwala-Mt. Lavinia	A5
Galle	B5

Hambantota	C5
Jaffna	B2
Kalutara	A5
Kandy	B4
Kilinochchi	B2
Kotte	A5
Kurunegala	B4
Mankulam	B2
Mannar	A3
Matale	B4
Matara	B6
Moratuwa	A5
Mullaittivu	B2
Negombo	A4
Nuwara Eliya	B5
Point Pedro	B2
Polonnaruwa	C4
Pottuvil	C5
Puttalam	A3
Ratnapura	B5

Trincomalee	C3
Vavuniya	B3

Other Features
Adam's, *peak*	B4
Adam's Bridge, *shoal*	A3
Aruvi, *river*	B3
Bengal, *bay*	C3
Delft, *island*	A2
Dondra Head, *cape*	B6
Jaffna, *lagoon*	B2
Kalu, *river*	B5
Kelani, *river*	B4
Mahaweli Ganga, *river*	C4
Mannar, *gulf*	A3
Mannar, *island*	A2
Palk, *strait*	A2
Pidurutalagala, *mt.*	B4
Trincomalee, *harbor*	C3
Yan, *river*	B3

Sri Lanka

- **Capital:** Colombo
- **Area:** 25,332 sq. mi.
  - 65,627 sq. km.
- **Population:** 19,145,000
- **Largest City:** Colombo
- **Language:** Sinhalese
- **Monetary Unit:** Rupee

INDIA
Palk Strait
Gulf of Mannar
Bay of Bengal
INDIAN OCEAN

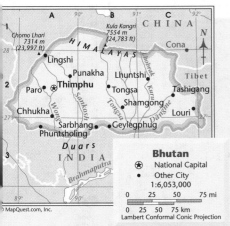

CHINA
Tibet
HIMALAYAS
Duars
INDIA

Bhutan

- **Capital:** Thimphu
- **Area:** 18,147 sq. mi.
  - 47,013 sq. km.
- **Population:** 1,952,000
- **Largest City:** Thimphu
- **Language:** Dzongkha
- **Monetary Unit:** Ngultrum

Bhutan

- **National Capital**
- **Other City**
- 1:6,053,000
- 0 25 50 75 mi
- 0 25 50 75 km
- Lambert Conformal Conic Projection

© MapQuest.com, Inc.

Bhutan:
Map Index

Cities and Towns
Chhukha	A2
Geylegphug	B3
Lhuntshi	C2
Lingshi	A2
Louri	C2
Paro	A2
Phuntsholing	A3
Punakha	B2
Sarbhang	B3
Shamgong	B2
Tashigang	C2

Thimphu, *capital*	A2
Tongsa	B2

Other Features
Chomo Lhari, *mt.*	A1
Dangme, *river*	C2
Duars, *plain*	A3
Himalayas, *mts.*	B1
Kula Kangri, *mt.*	B1
Kuru, *river*	C2
Lhobrak, *river*	B2
Sankosh, *river*	B2
Tongsa, *river*	B2
Wong, *river*	A2

Sri Lanka

- **National Capital**
- **Other City**
- 1:6,400,000
- 0 40 80 mi
- 0 40 80 km
- Mercator Projection

© MapQuest.com, Inc.

India:
Map Index

Internal Divisions
Andaman and Nicobar
  Islands (territory) F6
Andhra Pradesh (state)........C5
Arunachal Pradesh (state)....F3
Assam (state) F3
Bihar (state)................E4
Chandigarh (territory).......C2
Dadra and Nagar
  Haveli (territory)........B4
Daman and Diu (territory)....B4
Delhi (territory)............C3
Goa (state)..................B5
Gujarat (state)..............B4
Haryana (state)..............C3
Himachal Pradesh (state) C2
Jammu and Kashmir (state)....C2
Karnataka (state)............C6

Kerala (state)...............C6
Lakshadweep (territory)......B6
Madhya Pradesh (state).......C4
Maharashtra (state)..........B5
Manipur (state)..............F4
Meghalaya (state)............F3
Mizoram (state)..............F4
Nagaland (state).............F3
Orissa (state)...............D4
Pondicherry (territory)......C6
Punjab (state)...............C2
Rajasthan (state)............B3
Sikkim (state)...............E3
Tamil Nadu (state)...........C6
Tripura (state)..............F4
Uttar Pradesh (state)........C3
West Bengal (state)..........E4

Cities and Towns
Agartala F4
Agra C3

Ahmadabad B4
Aizawl F4
Ajmer B3
Akola C4
Alampur ....Inset II
Aligarh C3
Allahabad D3
Alleppey (Alappuzha)...Inset II
Amdanga ....Inset II
Amravati C4
Amritsar B2
Andheri ....Inset I
Ara D3
Asansol E4
Aurangabad C5
Babu Bheri ....Inset II
Baidyabati ....Inset II
Bally ....Inset II
Bamangachi ....Inset II
Bananga F7
Bandra ....Inset I

Bangalore C6
Bansbaria ....Inset II
Barakpur ....Inset II
Baranagar ....Inset II
Barasat ....Inset II
Bareilly C3
Bargachia ....Inset II
Bauria ....Inset II
Behala ....Inset II
Belapurpada ....Inset I
Belgaum B5
Bellary C5
Bhadrakh E4
Bhadreswar ....Inset II
Bhagalpur E3
Bhamapur D5
Bhandup ....Inset I
Bharatpur C3
Bhatapara D4
Bhatpara ....Inset II
Bhavnagar B4

Bhayandar ....Inset I
Bhimpur ....Inset II
Bhiwandi ....Inset I
Bhopal C4
Bhubaneswar E4
Bhuj A4
Bihar E3
Bijapur C5
Bikaner B3
Bilaspur D4
Bishnupur ....Inset II
Borivli ....Inset II
Buj-Buj ....Inset II
Burdwan E4
Burhanpur C4
Calcutta ....E4, Inset II
Chandannagar ....Inset II
Chandigarh C2
Chandrapur C5
Chembur ....Inset I
Chene ....Inset I

Chennai (Madras)...........D
Cherrapunji ....F
Chirner ....Inset
Cochin (Kochi)...........C
Coimbatore C
Cuddalore C
Cuttack ....D
Daman ....B
Darbhanga ....E
Darjiling ....E
Dehra Dun C
Delhi C
Dhulagarh ....Inset
Dibrugarh ....F
Dispur ....F
Diu ....Inset
Dum-Dum ....Inset
Dumjor ....Inset
Faizabad ....D
Gandhinagar ....B
Ganganagar ....B
Gangtok ....E
Garden Reach ....Inset
Garulia ....Inset
Gauhati ....F
Gaya ....D
Ghatkopar ....Inset
Gorakhpur ....D
Gulbarga C
Guntur C
Gwalior C
Halisahar ....Inset
Haora ....E4, Inset
Hisapur ....Inset
Hubli-Dharwar ....B
Hugli-Chunchura ....Inset
Hyderabad C
Imphal ....F
Indore C
Itanagar ....F
Jabalpur C
Jadabpur ....Inset
Jagdalpur ....D
Jaipur C
Jammu ....B
Jamnagar ....B
Jampur ....Inset
Jamshedpur ....E
Janai ....Inset
Jejur ....Inset
Jhansi C
Jodhpur ....B
Joka ....Inset
Jullundur C
Junagadh ....B
Kakinada ....D
Kalwa ....Inset
Kaman ....Inset
Kamarhati ....Inset
Kanchipuram C
Kanchrapara ....Inset
Kanpur C
Kansaripara ....Inset
Kasinathpur ....Inset
Kathgodam C
Kharagpur ....E
Kohima ....F
Kolhapur ....B
Kolshet ....Inset
Konnagar ....Inset
Kota C
Kozhikode C
Kurla ....Inset
Kurnool C
Lakhpat ....A
Lucknow ....D
Ludhiana C
Madurai C
Malad ....Inset
Malegaon ....B
Mangalore ....B
Mathura C
Meerut C
Moradabad C
Mulund ....Inset
Mumbai (Bombay)......B5, Inset
Mumbra ....Inset
Mysore C
Nagpur C
Nahati ....Inset
Nalikul ....Inset
Nanded C
Nangi ....Inset
Nanole ....Inset
Nasik ....B
Nellore C
New Delhi, capital.......C
Nizamabad C
Ongole C
Panaji ....B
Panihati ....Inset
Patiala C
Patna ....E
Paye ....Inset
Polba ....Inset
Pondicherry C
Port Blair ....F
Pune ....B
Raipur ....D
Rajkot ....B
Ramanbati ....Inset
Ranchi ....E
Raurkela ....E
Rishra ....Inset
Saharanpur Panipat C
Salem C
Sambalpur ....D
Sankrail ....Inset
Sasaram ....D
Sheva ....Inset
Shillong ....F
Sholapur C
Shrirampur ....Inset
Silvassi ....B
Simla C
Singur ....Inset
Sonarpur ....Inset
South Dum-Dum ....Inset
Srinagar ....B
Sugandha ....Inset
Surat ....B
Thane ....Inset
Thanjavur C
Tiruchchirappalli C
Titagarh ....Inset
Trivandrum
  (Thiruvananthapuram)...C7
Trombay ....Inset
Tuticorin ....Inset
Udaipur B4

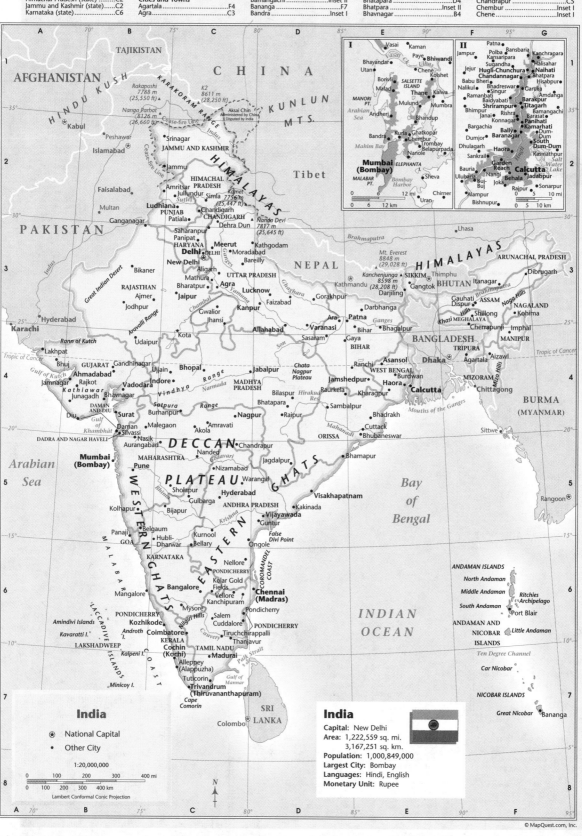

India
Capital: New Delhi
Area: 1,222,559 sq. mi.
  3,167,251 sq. km.
Population: 1,000,849,000
Largest City: Bombay
Languages: Hindi, English
Monetary Unit: Rupee

India
⊛ National Capital
• Other City
1:20,000,000
Lambert Conformal Conic Projection

Bangladesh

⊛ National Capital
• Other City

1:7,491,000

0   50   100 mi
0 50 100 km

Azimuthal Equal Area Projection

© MapQuest.com, Inc.

Bangladesh

Capital: Dhaka
Area: 57,295 sq. mi.
      148,433 sq. km.
Population: 127,118,000
Largest City: Dhaka
Language: Bengali
Monetary Unit: Taka

Bangladesh: Map Index

Cities and Towns

Barisal	D6
Bogra	C4
Brahmanbaria	E5
Chalna	C6
Chandpur	D5
Chittagong	E6
Comilla	E5
Cox's Bazar	E7
Dhaka, capital	D5
Dinajpur	B3
Faridpur	C5
Jaipurhat	B3
Jamalpur	C4
Jessore	C5
Khulna	C6
Kushtia	C5
Mymensingh	D4
Narayanganj	D5
Noakhali	E6
Pabna	C4
Patuakhali	D6
Rajshahi	B4
Rangamati	F6
Rangpur	C3
Saidpur	B3
Sirajganj	C4
Sylhet	E4
Tangail	C4

Other Features

Atrai, river	B4
Barind, region	B4
Bengal, bay	D7
Brahmaputra, river	D3
Chittagong Hills, region	F5
Ganges, river	B4
Jamuna, river	C4
Karnaphuli, reservoir	F6
Karnaphuli, river	E6
Keokradong, mt.	F7
Madhumati, river	C5
Madhupur Tract, region	D4
Meghna, river	D5
Mouths of the Ganges, delta	C7
Old Brahmaputra, river	C4
Padma, river	D5
Sundarbans, region	C7
Surma, river	E3
Tista, river	C2

Pakistan

Capital: Islamabad
Area: 339,697 sq. mi.
      880,044 sq. km.
Population: 138,123,000
Largest City: Karachi
Languages: Urdu, English
Monetary Unit: Pakistani rupee

Pakistan: Map Index

Internal Divisions

Azad Kashmir Province	D2
Baluchistan Province	B4
Federally Administered Tribal Areas	C3
Islamabad Capital Territory	D3
Northern Areas	D2
North-West Frontier Province	D2
Punjab Province	D3
Sind Province	C5

Cities and Towns

Bahawalpur	D4
Bela	C4
Chiniot	D3
Chitral	D2
Dadu	C4
Dera Ghazi Khan	D3
Dera Ismail Khan	D3
Faisalabad	D3
Gilgit	E2
Gujranwala	E3
Gujrat	E3
Gwadar	B5
Hyderabad	C5
Islamabad, capital	D3
Jhang Sadar	D3
Jhelum	D3
Karachi	C5
Kasur	E3
Khuzdar	C4
Lahore	E3
Larkana	C4
Mardan	D2
Mianwali	D3
Mirpur Khas	C5
Multan	D3
Muzaffarabad	D2
Nawabshah	C4
Nok Kundi	B4

Okara	D3
Panjgur	B4
Peshawar	D3
Quetta	C3
Rahimyar Khan	D4
Rawalpindi	D3
Sahiwal	D3
Sargodha	D3
Shikarpur	C4
Sialkot	E3
Sukkur	C4
Surab	C4

Other Features

Arabian, sea	B6
Central Makran, range	B4
Chagai, hills	B4
Chenab, river	D3
Hindu Kush, mts.	D2
Indus, river	C4, E2
Jhelum, river	D3
Karakoram, range	E2
Khojak, pass	C3
Khyber, pass	D2
Kirthar, range	C4
Konar, river	D2
K2 (Godwin Austen), mt.	E2
Makran Coast, range	B5
Mouths of the Indus, delta	B4
Nal, river	B4
Nanga Parbat, mt.	E2
Nara, canal	C4
Nowshak, mt.	D2
Rakaposhi, mt.	E2
Ravi, river	D3
Safed Koh, range	D3
Siahan, range	B4
Sulaiman, range	D3
Sutlej, river	D4
Thar, desert	C4
Tirich Mir, mt.	D2
Toba Kakar, range	C3
Zhob, river	C3

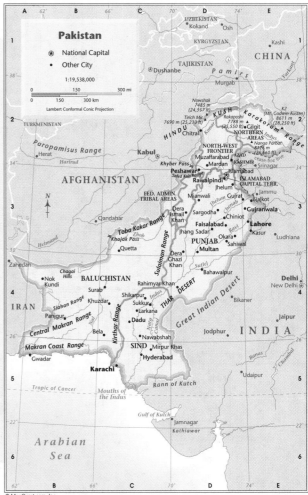

Pakistan

⊛ National Capital
• Other City

1:19,538,000

0   150   300 mi
0 150 300 km

Lambert Conformal Conic Projection

© MapQuest.com, Inc.

India: Map Index

...jjain	C4
...lubaria	Inset II
...ran	Inset I
...tan	Inset I
...adodara	B4
...aranasi	D3
...asai	Inset I
...ellore	C6
...ijayawada	D5
...sakhapatnam	D5
...arangal	C5

Other Features

...mindivi, islands	B6
...ndaman, islands	F6
...ndroth, island	B6
...rabian, sea	A5, Inset I
...ravalli, range	B3
...engal, bay	E5
...hima, river	C5
...rahmaputra, river	F3
...ar Nicobar, island	F7
...auvery, river	C6
...hambal, river	C3
...hata Nagpur, plateau	D4
...omorin, cape	C7
...oromandel, coast	D6
...eccan, plateau	C5
...astern Ghats, mts.	C6
...ephanta, island	Inset I
...alse Divi, point	D5
...anges, river	E3
...haghara, river	D3
...odavari, river	D4
...reat Indian, desert	B3
...reat Nicobar, island	F7
...imalayas, mts.	C2, E3
...irakud, reservoir	D4
...ugli, river	Inset II
...ndus, river	C2
...alpeni, island	B7
...amet, mt.	C2
...anchenjunga, mt.	E3
...arakoram, range	C1
...athiawar, peninsula	B4
...avaratti, island	B6
...hambhat, gulf	B4
...hasi, hills	F3
...olar, gold fields	C5
...rishna, river	C5
...utch, gulf	A4
...accadive, islands	B6
...ttle Andaman, island	F6
...ahanadi, river	D4
...ahim, bay	Inset I
...alabar, coast	B6
...alabar, point	Inset I
...annar, gulf	C7
...anori, point	Inset I
...iddle Andaman, island	F6
...inicoy, island	B7
...izo, hills	F4
...Mouths of the Ganges, delta	E4
...umbai, harbor	Inset I
...aga, hills	F3
...anda Devi, mt.	C2
...armada, river	C4
...icobar, islands	F7
...ilgiri, hills	C6
...orth Andaman, island	F6
...alk, strait	C7
...ann of Kutch, mud flat	B4
...itchies, archipelago	F6
...alsette, island	Inset I
...alt Water, lake	Inset II
...atpura, range	C4
...on, river	D4
...outh Andaman, island	F6
...utlej, river	C2
...en Degree, channel	F7
...lhas, river	Inset I
...asai, creek	Inset I
...indhya, range	C4
...Vestern Ghats, mts.	B5
...amuna, river	C3

Afghanistan: Map Index

Cities and Towns
Asadabad C2
Baghlan B1
Balkh B1
Bamian B2
Baraki Barak B2
Chaghcharan B2
Charikar B1
Farah A2
Feyzabad C1
Gardez B2
Ghazni B2
Herat A2
Jalalabad C2
Kabul, capital B2
Khowst B2
Konduz B1

Kowt-e Ashrow B2
Lashkar Gah A2
Mazar-e Sharif B1
Meymaneh A1
Qalat B2
Qaleh-ye Now B2
Qaleh-ye Panjeh C1
Qandahar B2
Samangan B1
Sar-e Pol B1
Sheberghan B1
Shindand A2
Taloqan B1
Tarin Kowt B2
Zaranj A2
Zareh Sharan B2

Farah, river A2
Fuladi, mt. B2
Gowd-e Zereh, lake A3
Hamun-e Saberi, lake ... A2
Harirud, river A2
Helmand, river A2
Hindu Kush, range B1
Kabul, river B2
Khojak, pass B2
Khyber, pass C2
Konar, river C1
Konduz, river B1
Morghab, river A1
Nowshak, mt. C1
Panj, river A1
Paropamisus, range A2
Registan, region B2
Shibar, pass B2
Vakhan, region C1

Afghanistan
Capital: Kabul
Area: 251,825 sq. mi.
652,396 sq. km.
Population: 25,825,000
Largest City: Kabul
Languages: Pashto, Dari Persian
Monetary Unit: Afghani

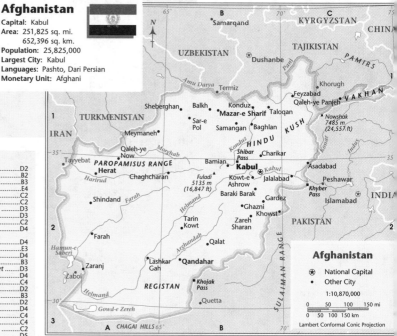

© MapQuest.com, Inc.

Iran
Capital: Tehran
Area: 632,457 sq. mi.
1,638,490 sq. km.
Population: 65,180,000
Largest City: Tehran
Languages: Persian, Turkic, Luri, Kurdish
Monetary Unit: Rial

Iran: Map Index

Cities and Towns
Abadan B3
Ahvaz B3
Arak B3
Ardabil B2
Bakhtaran B2
Bam E4
Bandar Beheshti E4
Bandar-e Abbas D4
Bandar-e Anzali B2
Bandar-e Bushehr C4
Bandar-e Khomeyni B3
Bandar-e Torkeman B2
Birjand D3
Dezful B3

Esfahan C3
Hamadan B3
Ilam B3
Iranshahr E4
Jask D4
Karaj C2
Kashan C3
Kerman D3
Khorramabad B3
Khorramshahr B3
Khvoy A2
Mashhad D2
Neyshabur D2
Orumiyeh (Urmia) A2
Qazvin B2
Qom C3
Rasht B2
Sabzevar D2
Sanandaj B2
Shahr-e Kord C3
Shiraz C4
Sirjan D4
Tabriz A2
Tehran, capital C3
Yasuj C3
Yazd C3
Zabol E3
Zahedan E4
Zanjan B2

Other Features
Aras, river B2

Atrak, river D2
Azerbaijan, region B2
Bakhtiari, region B3
Baluchistan, region E4
Caspian, sea C2
Damavand, mt. C2
Dasht-e Kavir, desert D3
Dasht-e Lut, desert D3
Elburz, mts. C2
Halil, river D4
Hamun-e Jaz Murian, lake .. D4
Hashtadan, region E3
Hormuz, strait D4
Karun, river B3
Kavir-e Namak, desert ... D3
Kerman, region D4
Kharg, island C4
Khorasan, region D2
Khuzestan, region B3
Kopet, mts. D2
Kul, river D4
Larestan, region C4
Mand, river C4
Mazandaran, region C2
Oman, gulf D5
Persian, gulf C4
Qareh, river D4
Qeshm, island D4
Shatt al-Arab, river B3
Urmia, lake B2
Yazd, region C3
Zagros, mts. B3

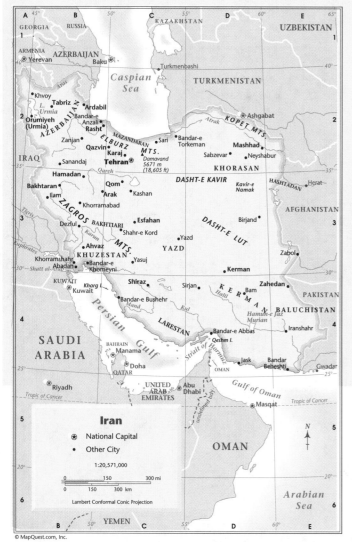

© MapQuest.com, Inc.

Turkmenistan: Map Index

Cities and Towns
Ashgabat, capital C3
Bakhardok C2
Bayramaly D3
Büzmeyin C2
Chardzhou D2
Cheleken A2
Dashhowuz C2
Ensenguly A3
Gazanjyk B2
Gumdag B2
Gushgy D3
Gyzylarbat B2
Kerki D3
Mary C3
Nebitdag B2

Tedzhen C3
Turkmenbashi A2

Other Features
Amu Darya, river D2
Caspian, sea A2
Etrek, river B3
Garabil, plateau D3
Garabogazköl, lake A2
Gushgy, river D3
Kara-Kum, canal D3
Kara-Kum, desert C2
Kopet, mts. B2
Murgab, river D3
Sarygamysh Koli, lake ... B2
Sumbar, river B2
Tedzhen, river C3
Turan, lowland C2

Turkmenistan
Capital: Ashgabat
Area: 188,417 sq. mi.
488,127 sq. km.
Population: 4,366,000
Largest City: Ashgabat
Languages: Turkmen, Russian, Uzbek
Monetary Unit: Manat

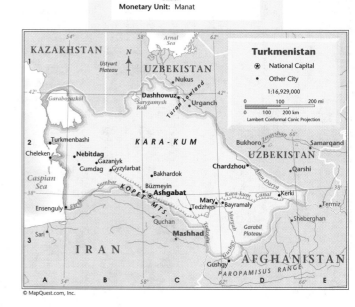

© MapQuest.com, Inc.

Beyneu B2
Ekibastuz D1
Embi B2
Esil C1
Kokshetau C1
Leninsk C2
Lepsi E2
Oral B1
Öskemen
  (Ust-Kamenogorsk) ..E1
Pavlodar D1
Petropavl C1
Qaraghandy (Karaganda) ..D2
Qostanay C1
Qyzylorda C2
Rudnyy C1
Saryshaghan D2
Semey (Semipalatinsk) E1
Shalqar B2
Shymkent (Chimkent) C2
Taldyqorghan D2
Temirtau D1
Zaysan E2
Zhambyl (Dzhambul) D2
Zhezqazghan C2

Other Features
Alakol, lake E2
Aral, sea B2
Balkhash, lake D2
Betpak Dala, plain C2
Caspian, depression B2
Caspian, sea A2
Ili, river D2
Irtysh, river D1
Ishim, river C1
Kazakh Upland region C1
Khan-Tengri, mt. E2
Muyun Kum, desert D2
Syrdarya, river C2
Tengiz, lake C1
Tobol, river C1
Torghay, plateau C1
Ural, river B2
Ustyurt, plateau B2
Zaysan, lake E2

Kazakhstan

Capital: Astana
Area: 1,049,200 sq. mi.
  2,718,135 sq. km.
Population: 16,825,000
Largest City: Almaty
Language: Kazakh
Monetary Unit: Tenge

Kazakhstan: Map Index

Cities and Towns
Astana (Aqmola), capital D1
Almaty (Alma-Ata) D2
Aqtau B2
Aqtobe B1
Aral C2
Arqalyq C1
Atbasar C1
Atyrau B2
Ayagöz E2
Balkhash D2

© MapQuest.com, Inc.

Kazakhstan
⊛ National Capital
• Other City
1:26,667,000
0   125   250 mi
0   125   250 km
Lambert Conformal Conic Projection

Kyrgyzstan: Map Index

Cities and Towns
At-Bashy D2
Balykchy E1
Bishkek, capital D1
Cholpon-Ata E1
Jalal-Abad C2
Jangy-Bazar B2
Karakol F1
Kara-Say F2
Kyzyl-Kyya C2
Naryn C2
Osh C2
Özgön C2
Sary Tash C3
Songköl D2
Sülüktü A3
Talas C1
Tash Kömür C2
Tokmok D1
Toktogul C2

Other Features
Alay, mts. C3
Chatkal, river B2
Chu, river D1
Jengish Chokusu, mt. G1
Kyzyl-Suu, river C3
Naryn, river E2
Tien Shan, mts. E2
Toxkan, river E2
Ysyk-Köl, lake E1

Kyrgyzstan

Capital: Bishkek
Area: 76,642 sq. mi.
  198,554 sq. km.
Population: 4,546,000
Largest City: Bishkek
Language: Kirghiz
Monetary Unit: Som

Uzbekistan

⊛ National Capital
• Other City
1:14,725,000
0   40   80 mi
0   40   80 km
Lambert Conformal Conic Projection

© MapQuest.com, Inc.

Kyrgyzstan
⊛ National Capital
• Other City
1:14,286,000
0   75   150 mi
0   75   150 km
Lambert Conformal Conic Projection

Uzbekistan

Capital: Tashkent
Area: 172,700 sq. mi.
  447,409 sq. km.
Population: 24,102,000
Largest City: Tashkent
Languages: Uzbek, Russian
Monetary Unit: Ruble

Uzbekistan: Map Index

Cities and Towns
Andizhan D2
Bukhara B3
Farghona D2
Gulistan C2
Jizzakh C2
Khujayli A2
Muynoq A2
Namangan D2
Nawoiy C2
Nukus A2
Olmaliq C2
Qarshi C3
Qunghirot A2
Quqon D2
Samarqand C3
Tashkent, capital C2
Termiz C3
Uchquduq B2
Urganch B2
Zarafshon B2

Other Features
Amu Darya, river B2
Aral, sea A2
Chirchiq, river D2
Fergana, valley D2
Kyzylkum, desert B2
Syrdarya, river B2
Turan, lowland A2
Ustyurt, plateau A2
Zeravshan, river B2

Tajikistan

Capital: Dushanbe
Area: 55,300 sq. mi.
  143,264 sq. km.
Population: 6,103,000
Largest City: Dushanbe
Language: Tajik
Monetary Unit: Ruble

Tajikistan: Map Index

Cities and Towns
Dangara A1
Dushanbe, capital A1
Jirgatol B1
Kalai Khum B1
Kansay A1
Khorugh B2
Khudzhand A1
Konibodom B1
Kulob A2
Morghob B1
Navabad A1
Norak A1
Panj A2
Panjakent A2
Qurghonteppa A2
Tursunzoda A1
Uroteppa A1
Zarafobod A1

Other Features
Alay, mts. B1
Bartang, river B1
Communisim, mt. B1
Darya, river A2
Kofarnihon, river A1
Morghob, river B1
Oqsu, river C2
Pamirs, mts. B2
Panj, river A2
Pyandzh, river B1
Qarokul, lake B1
Surkhob, river B1
Syrdarya, river A1, B1
Turkeston, mts. A1
Vahsh, river A1
Zeravshan, mts. A1
Zeravshan, river A1

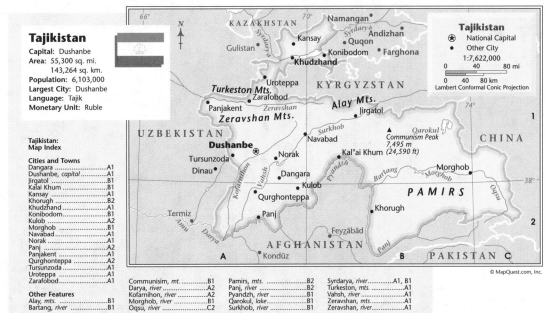

© MapQuest.com, Inc.

Tajikistan
⊛ National Capital
• Other City
1:7,622,000
0   40   80 mi
0   40   80 km
Lambert Conformal Conic Projection

Iraq

**Iraq:
Map Index**

Cities and Towns
Amarah, al-..............C2
Baghdad, capital........B2
Baqubah...............B2
Basra.................C2
Dahuk.................B1
Diwaniyah, ad-........C2
Fallujah, al-..........B2
Hadithah, al-.........B2
Hillah, al-...........B2
Irbil.................B1
Karbala..............B2
Khanaqin............B2
Kirkuk...............B1
Kut, al-.............B2
Mosul...............B1
Najaf, an-...........B2
Nasiriyah, an-.......C2
Qayyarah, al-........B1
Ramadi, ar-.........B2
Rutbah, ar-.........B2

Samarra..............B2
Samawah, as-........C2
Sulaymaniyah, as-....C1
Tall Afar.............B1
Tikrit................B2
Umm Qasr............C2

Other Features
Babylon, ruins.........B2
Diyala, river...........C2

Euphrates, river........C2
Great Zab, river........B1
Haji Ibrahim, mt........B1
Little Zab, river.......B1
Mesopotamia, region....B2
Milh, lake.............B2
Persian, gulf..........C3
Shatt al-Arab, river...C2
Syrian, desert.........B2
Tigris, river..........B1

Capital: Baghdad
Area: 167,975 sq. mi.
435,169 sq. km.
Population: 22,427,000
Largest City: Baghdad
Language: Arabic
Monetary Unit: Dinar

© MapQuest.com, Inc.

Iraq
⊛ National Capital
• Other City
1:12,765,000
0   100   200 mi
0   100   200 km
Lambert Conformal Conic Projection

© MapQuest.com, Inc.

Kuwait

Capital: Kuwait
Area: 6,880 sq. mi.
17,924 sq. km.
Population: 1,991,000
Largest City: Kuwait
Language: Arabic
Monetary Unit: Dinar

Kuwait
⊛ National Capital
• Other City
1:4,667,000
0   25   50 mi
0   25   50 km
Lambert Conformal Conic Projection

**Kuwait:
Map Index**

Cities and Towns
Abdali B1
Ahmadi, al-.............C2
Fuhayhil, al-...........C2
Hawalli.................C2
Jahrah, al-.............B2
Khiran, al-.............C3
Kuwait, capital.........B2
Qasr as-Sabiyah.........C2
Rawdatayn, ar-.........B2
Sulaybikhat, as-........B2
Wafrah, al-............B3

Other Features
Bubiyan, island.........C2
Faylakah, island........C2
Kuwait, bay............B2
Persian, gulf...........C2
Wadi al-Batin, river....A2
Warbah, island.........C1

Saudi Arabia

Capital: Riyadh
Area: 865,000 sq. mi.
2,240,933 sq. km.
Population: 21,505,000
Largest City: Riyadh
Language: Arabic
Monetary Unit: Riyal

**Saudi Arabia:
Map Index**

Cities and Towns
Abha B2
Badanah................B1
Buqayq.................C1
Buraydah...............B1
Dammam, ad-...........C1
Dhahran................C1
Hail...................B1
Harad..................C1
Hillah, al-.............B2
Hufuf, al-.............C1
Jawf, al-..............A1
Jiddah.................A2
Jizan..................B2
Jubayl, al- C1

Khamis Mushayt B2
Kharj, al-.............B1
Mecca.................A2
Medina................A1
Najran................B2
Qalat Bishah...........B2
Qunfudhah, al-.........B2
Rafha.................B1
Ras al-Khafji..........C1
Ras Tanura.............C1
Riyadh, capital........B1
Sulayyil, as-..........B2
Tabuk.................A1
Taif, at-.............B2
Turayf................A1
Unayzah...............B1
Wajh, al-.............A1
Yanbu al-Bahr.........A1

Other Features
Asir, region...........
Dahna, ad-, desert.....
Farasan, islands.......
Hasa, al-, region......
Hijaz, al-, region.....
Jabal Tuwayq, mts......
Nafud, an-, desert.....
Najd, region...........
Persian, gulf..........
Red, sea...............
Rub al-Khali
(Empty Quarter), desert..C
Sabkhat Matti, salt flat..
Sawda, mt..............
Syrian, desert.........
Umm as-Samim, salt flat..
Wadi al-Hamd, river....

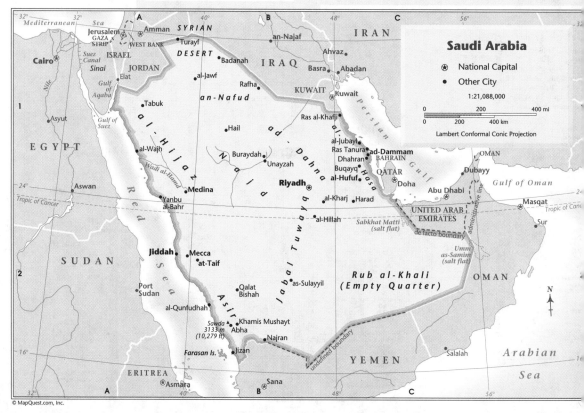

Saudi Arabia
⊛ National Capital
• Other City
1:21,088,000
0   200   400 mi
0   200   400 km
Lambert Conformal Conic Projection

© MapQuest.com, Inc.

Bahrain and Qatar: Map Index

Bahrain
Cities and Towns
Askar B1
Mamtalah, al- B2
Manama, capital. B1
Mina Salman B1

Other Features
Bahrain, gulf A2
Hawar, islands B2
Jiddah, island A1
Muharraq, al-, island....B1
Ras al-Barr, cape B2
Sitrah, island B1
Umm an-Nasan, island......A1

Qatar
Cities and Towns
Doha, capital D3
Dukhan B3
Jumayliyah, al- C2
Khawr, al- D2
Ruways, ar- B3
Umm Bab B3
Umm Said (Musayid) ...D4
Wakrah, al- D3

Other Features
Dawhat as-Salwa, bay ...B3
Ras Laffan, cape D2
Ras Rakan, cape C1
Tuwayyir al-Hamir, hill....C4

Bahrain

Capital: Manama
Area: 268 sq. mi.
694 sq. km.
Population: 629,000
Largest City: Manama
Language: Arabic
Monetary Unit: Dinar

Qatar

Capital: Doha
Area: 4,412 sq. mi.
11,430 sq. km.
Population: 724,000
Largest City: Doha
Language: Arabic
Monetary Unit: Riyal

Bahrain and Qatar
⊛ National Capital
• Other City
1:2,842,000
0   10   20 mi
0   10   20 km
Transverse Mercator Projection

© MapQuest.com, Inc.

United Arab Emirates
⊛ National Capital
• Other City
1:11,579,000
0   50   100   150 mi
0   50   100   150 km
Lambert Conformal Conic Projection

© MapQuest.com, Inc.

United Arab Emirates (U.A.E.)

Capital: Abu Dhabi
Area: 30,000 sq. mi.
77,720 sq. km.
Population: 2,344,000
Largest City: Abu Dhabi
Language: Arabic
Monetary Unit: Dirham

United Arab Emirates: Map Index

Cities and Towns
Abu Dhabi, capital C2
Ajman C2
Aradah B3
Ayn, al- C2
Dubayy C2
Fujayrah, al- D2
Masfut D2
Nashshash, an- C3
Ras al-Khaymah C2

Ruways, ar- B2
Sham, ash- D1
Sharjah C2
Tarif B2
Umm al-Qaywayn.........C2

Other Features
Hormuz, strait D1
Matti, salt flat B3
Oman, gulf D2
Persian, gulf B1
Salamiyah, salt flat C3

Yemen: Map Index

Cities and Towns
Aden B2
Ahwar B2
Amran A1
Ataq B2
Balhaf B2
Bayda, al- B2
Dhamar A2
Ghaydah, al- C1
Habarut C1
Hadiboh C2
Hajjah A1
Hawf C1
Hazm, al- A1
Hudaydah, al- A2
Ibb A2
Lahij A2
Madinat ash-Shab A2
Marib B1
Maydi A1

Mocha (Mukha, al-) A2
Mukalla, al- B2
Qalansiyah C2
Qishn C1
Rida A2
Sadah A1
Sana, capital A1
Sanaw C1
Sayhut C1
Saywun B1
Shabwah B1
Taizz A2
Zabid A2

Other Features
Abd al-Kuri, island C2
Aden, gulf B2
Arabian, sea C2
Bab al-Mandab, strait ...A2
Hadhramaut, district B1
Jabal an-Nabi Shuayb, mt...A1
Jabal Zuqar, island A2
Kamaran, island A1

Perim, island A2
Ras al-Kalb, cape B2
Ras Fartak, cape C1
Red, sea A2
Socotra, island C2
The Brothers, islands C2
Wadi al-Masilah, river B1

Yemen
Capital: Sana
Area: 205,356 sq. mi.
532,010 sq. km.
Population: 16,942,000
Largest City: Sana
Language: Arabic
Monetary Unit: Riyal

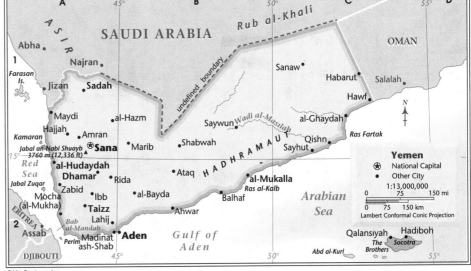

© MapQuest.com, Inc.

Yemen
⊛ National Capital
• Other City
1:13,000,000
0   75   150 mi
0   75   150 km
Lambert Conformal Conic Projection

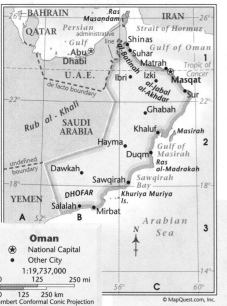

Oman
⊛ National Capital
• Other City
1:19,737,000
0   125   250 mi
0   125   250 km
Lambert Conformal Conic Projection

© MapQuest.com, Inc.

Oman: Map Index

Cities and Towns
Dawkah B2
Duqm C2
Ghabah C2
Hayma C2
Ibri C1
Izki C1
Khaluf C2
Masqat, capital C1

Matrah C1
Mirbat B3
Salalah B3
Sawqirah C2
Shinas C1
Suhar C1
Sur C1

Other Features
Arabian, sea C3
Batinah, al- region C1
Dhofar, region B3

Hormuz, strait C1
Jabal al-Akhdar, al-, mts...C1
Khuriya Muriya, islands...C3
Masirah, gulf C2
Masirah, island C1
Oman, gulf C1
Persian, gulf B1
Ras al-Madrakah, cape ...C2
Ras Musandam, cape C1
Sawqirah, bay C2

Oman

Capital: Masqat
Area: 118,150 sq. mi.
305,829 sq. km.
Population: 2,447,000
Largest City: Masqat
Language: Arabic
Monetary Unit: Rial Omani

Lebanon

Capital: Beirut
Area: 3,950 sq. mi.
　　　10,233 sq. km.
Population: 3,563,000
Largest City: Beirut
Languages: Arabic, French
Monetary Unit: Pound

Lebanon: Map Index

Cities and Towns

Amyun	A1
Baalbek	B1
Babda	A2
Batrun, al-	A1
Beirut, *capital*	A2
Bint Jubayl	A2
Bsharri	B1
Damur, ad-	A2
Duma	A1
Halba	B1
Hirmil, al-	B1
Jazzin	A2
Jubayl	A1
Juniyah	A2
Marj Uyun	A2
Nabatiyah at-Tahta, an-	A2
Qubayyat, al-	B1
Rashayya	A2
Riyaq	B2
Sidon (Sayda)	A2
Sur (Tyre)	A2
Tripoli (Tarabulus)	A1
Zahlah	A2

Other Features

Anti-Lebanon, *mts.*	B1
Awwali, *river*	A2
Bekaa, *valley*	A2
Byblos, *ruins*	A1
Hermon, *mt.*	A2
Ibrahim, *river*	A1
Kebir, *river*	B1
Lebanon, *mts.*	B1
Litani, *river*	A2
Orontes, *river*	B1
Qurnat as-Sawda, *mt.*	B1

Jordan: Map Index

Cities and Towns

Amman, *capital*	A2
Aqabah, al-	A3
Azraq ash-Shishan	B2
Bair	B2
Irbid	A1
Jafr, al-	B2
Jarash	A1
Karak, al-	A2
Maan	A2
Madaba	A2
Mafraq, al-	B1
Mudawwarah, al-	B3
Qatranah, al-	A2
Ramtha, ar-	B1
Ras an-Naqb	A2
Salt, as-	A1
Tafilah, at-	A2
Zarqa, az-	B1

Other Features

Aqaba, *gulf*	A3
Arabah, al-, *river*	A2
Dead Sea, *lake*	A2
Jabal Ramm, *mt.*	A3
Jordan, *river*	A2
Petra, *ruins*	A2
Syrian, *desert*	B1
Tiberias, *lake*	A1
Wadi as-Sirhan, *depression*	B2

Jordan

Capital: Amman
Area: 34,342 sq. mi.
　　　88,969 sq. km.
Population: 4,561,000
Largest City: Amman
Language: Arabic
Monetary Unit: Dinar

Israel

Capital: Jerusalem
Area: 7,992 sq. mi.
　　　20,705 sq. km.
Population: 5,750,000
Largest City: Jerusalem
Languages: Hebrew, Arabic
Monetary Unit: New Shekel

Israel: Map Index

Districts

Central	B1
Haifa	B1
Jerusalem	B2
Northern	B1
Southern	B2
Tel Aviv	B1

Cities and Towns

Acre (Akko)	B1
Ashdod	B2
Ashqelon	B2
Beersheba	B2
Dimona	B2
Elat	B3
Hadera	B1
Haifa	B1
Herzliyya	B1
Holon	B1
Jerusalem, *capital*	
Lod (Lydda)	
Mizpe Ramon	
Nahariyya	
Nazareth	
Netanya	
Petah Tiqwa	
Qiryat Gat	
Qiryat Shemona	
Ramat Gan	
Ramla	
Rehovot	
Tel Aviv-Jaffa	
Tiberias	
Yotvata	
Zefat	

Other Features

Aqaba, *gulf*	
Arabah, al-, *river*	
Besor, *river*	
Dead, *sea*	
Galilee, *region*	
Haifa, *bay*	
Jezreel (Esdraelon), *plain*	
Jordan, *river*	
Judea, *plain*	
Masada, *ruins*	
Meron, *mt.*	
Negev, *region*	
Ramon, *mt.*	
Samarian, *hills*	
Sharon, *plain*	
Tiberias (Galilee), *lake*	
Zevulun, *plain*	

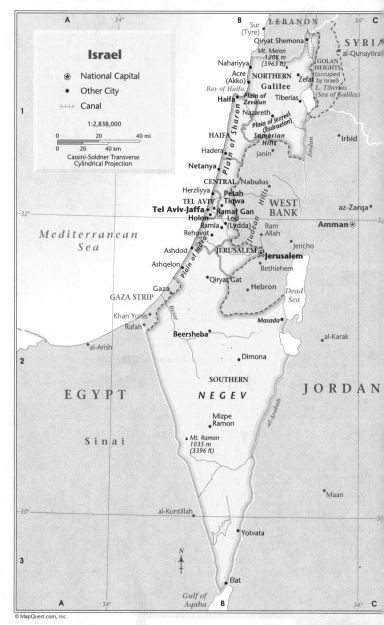

© MapQuest.com, Inc.

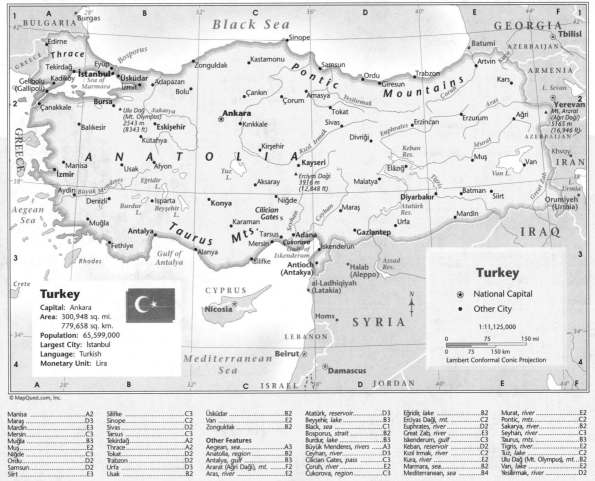

Turkey

Capital: Ankara
Area: 300,948 sq. mi.
779,658 sq. km.
Population: 65,599,000
Largest City: İstanbul
Language: Turkish
Monetary Unit: Lira

Turkey

⊛ National Capital
• Other City

1:11,125,000

0 — 75 — 150 mi
0 — 75 — 150 km
Lambert Conformal Conic Projection

© MapQuest.com, Inc.

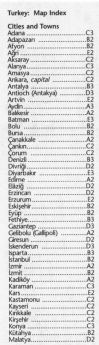

Turkey: Map Index

Cities and Towns

Adana C3
Adapazarı B2
Afyon B2
Ağrı E2
Aksaray C2
Alanya C3
Amasya C2
Ankara, capital C2
Antalya B3
Antioch (Antakya) D3
Artvin E2
Aydın A3
Balıkesir A2
Batman E3
Bolu B2
Bursa B2
Çanakkale A2
Çankırı C2
Çorum C2
Denizli B3
Divriği D2
Diyarbakır E3
Edirne A2
Elâziğ D2
Erzincan D2
Erzurum E2
Eskişehir B2
Eyüp B2
Fethiye B3
Gaziantep D3
Gelibolu (Gallipoli) ..A2
Giresun D2
İskenderun D3
Isparta B3
İstanbul B2
İzmir A2
İzmit B2
Kadıköy A2
Karaman C3
Kars E2
Kastamonu C2
Kayseri C2
Kırıkkale C2
Kırşehir C2
Konya C3
Kütahya B2
Malatya D2
Manisa A2
Maraş D3
Mardin E3
Mersin C3
Muğla B3
Muş E2
Niğde C3
Ordu D2
Samsun C2
Siirt E3
Silifke C3
Sinope C2
Sivas D2
Tarsus C3
Tekirdağ A2
Thrace A2
Tokat D2
Trabzon D2
Urfa D3
Uşak B2
Üsküdar B2
Van E2
Zonguldak B2

Other Features

Aegean, sea A3
Anatolia, region B2
Antalya, gulf B3
Ararat (Ağrı Dağı), mt. .F2
Aras, river E2
Ataturk, reservoir D3
Beyşehir, lake B3
Black, sea C1
Bosporus, strait B3
Burdur, lake B3
Büyük Menderes, rivers .A3
Ceyhan, river D3
Cilician Gates, pass ..C3
Çoruh, river E2
Çukorova, region C3
Eğridir, lake B2
Erciyas Dağı, mt. C2
Euphrates, river D2
Great Zab, river E3
İskenderun, gulf D2
Keban, reservoir D2
Kızıl Irmak, river C2
Kura, river E2
Marmara, sea B2
Mediterranean, sea B4
Murat, river E2
Pontic, mts. C2
Sakarya, river B2
Seyhan, river C3
Taurus, mts. C3
Tigris, river E2
Tuz, lake C2
Ulu Dağ (Mt. Olympus), mt. .B2
Van, lake E2
Yesilirmak, river D2

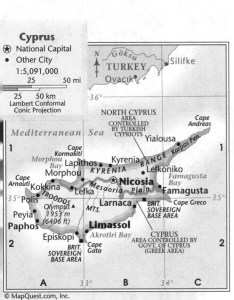

Cyprus

⊛ National Capital
• Other City

1:5,091,000

0 — 25 — 50 mi
0 — 25 — 50 km
Lambert Conformal Conic Projection

© MapQuest.com, Inc.

Cyprus

Capital: Nicosia
Area: 3,572 sq. mi.
9,254 sq. km.
Population: 754,000
Largest City: Nicosia
Languages: Greek, Turkish
Monetary Unit: Pound

Cyprus:
Map Index

Cities and Towns

...kopi A2
...agusta B1
...kina A1
...ithos B1
...assol B2
...oniko B1
...assol B2
...phou A1
...sia, capital B1
...os A2
...ia A1

Yialousa C1

Other Features

Akrotiri, bay B2
Andreas, cape C1
Arnauti, cape A1
British Sovereign
Base Area A2, B2
Famagusta, bay C1
Gata, cape B2
Greco, cape C2
Karpas, peninsula C1
Kormakiti, cape A1
Kyrenia, range B1
Mesaoria, plain B1
Morphou, bay A1
Olympus, mt. A2
Troödos, mts. A2

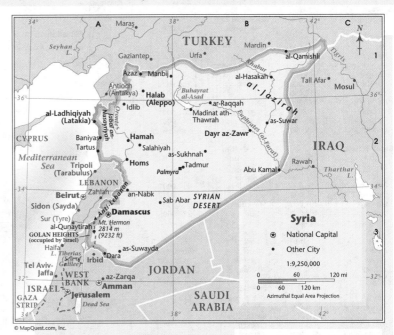

Syria

⊛ National Capital
• Other City

1:9,250,000

0 — 60 — 120 mi
0 — 60 — 120 km
Azimuthal Equal Area Projection

© MapQuest.com, Inc.

Syria

Capital: Damascus
Area: 71,498 sq. mi.
185,228 sq. km.
Population: 17,214,000
Largest City: Damascus
Language: Arabic
Monetary Unit: Pound

Syria:
Map Index

Cities and Towns

Abu Kamal B2
Azaz A1
Baniyas A2
Damascus, capital A3
Dara A3
Dayr az-Zawr B2
Halab (Aleppo) A1
Hamah A2
Hasakah, al- B1
Homs A2
Idlib A2
Ladhiqiyah, al- (Latakia) .A2
Madinat ath-Thawrah ...B2
Manbij A1
Nabk, an- A2
Qamishli, al- B1
Qunaytirah, al- A3
Raqqah, ar- B2
Sab Abar A3
Salahiyah A2
Sukhnah, as- B2
Suwar, as- B2
Suwayda, as- A3
Tadmur B2
Tartus A2

Other Features

Anti-Lebanon, mts. A3
Buhayrat al-Asad, lake .B1
Euphrates (al-Furat), river .B2
Golan Heights, occupied
territory A3
Hermon, mt. A3
Jabal an-Nusayriyah, mts. .A2
Jazirah, al-, region ..B1
Khabur, river B1
Mediterranean, sea A2
Orontes, river A2
Palmyra, ruins B2
Syrian, desert B3
Tigris, river C1

MAJOR CITIES

Albania
Tiranë — 244,000

Andorra
Andorra la Vella — 16,000

Armenia (metro)
Yerevan — 1,278,000

Austria
Vienna — 1,540,000

Azerbaijan (metro)
Baku — 1,848,000

Belarus (metro)
Minsk — 1,708,000

Belgium (metro)
Brussels — 948,000
Antwerp — 456,000

Bosnia and Hercegovina
Sarajevo — 416,000

Bulgaria
Sofia — 1,117,000

Croatia (metro)
Zagreb — 981,000

Czech Republic
Prague — 1,200,000

Denmark
Copenhagen — 632,000

Estonia
Tallinn — 424,000

Finland
Helsinki — 532,000

France
Paris — 2,152,000
Lyon — 1,260,000
Marseille — 1,200,000

Georgia (metro)
Tbilisi — 1,342,000

Germany
Berlin — 3,458,000
Hamburg — 1,708,000
Munich — 1,226,000
Cologne — 964,000
Frankfurt — 647,000
Essen — 612,000
Dortmund — 597,000
Stuttgart — 586,000
Düsseldorf — 571,000
Leipzig — 549,000

Great Britain
London — 7,074,000
Birmingham — 1,021,000
Leeds — 727,000
Glasgow — 616,000
Sheffield — 530,000
Bradford — 483,000
Liverpool — 468,000
Edinburgh — 449,000

Greece (metro)
Athens — 3,073,000

Hungary
Budapest — 1,897,000

Iceland
Reykjavík — 105,000

Ireland
Dublin — 482,000

Italy
Rome — 2,645,000
Milan — 1,304,000
Naples — 1,046,000
Turin — 920,000
Palermo — 688,000
Genoa — 654,000

Latvia
Riga — 821,000

Liechtenstein
Vaduz — 5,000

Lithuania
Vilnius — 580,000

Luxembourg
Luxembourg — 77,000

F.Y.R. Macedonia
Skopje — 430,000

Malta
Valletta — 7,000

Moldova
Chişinău — 656,000

Monaco
Monaco — 27,000

Netherlands
Amsterdam — 717,000
Rotterdam — 591,000

Norway
Oslo — 492,000

Poland
Warsaw — 1,633,000
Łódź — 820,000
Kraków — 745,000
Wrocław — 642,000

Portugal
Lisbon — 582,000

Romania
Bucharest — 2,037,000

Russia (European)
Moscow — 8,368,000
St. Petersburg — 4,232,000
Nizh. Novgorod — 1,376,000
Samara — 1,184,000
Ufa — 1,093,000
Kazan — 1,076,000
Perm — 1,031,000
Rostov-na-Donu — 1,014,000
Volgograd — 999,000

San Marino
San Marino — 3,000

Slovakia
Bratislava — 452,000

Slovenia
Ljubljana — 273,000

Spain
Madrid — 2,867,000
Barcelona — 1,509,000
Valencia — 747,000
Seville — 697,000

Sweden
Stockholm — 718,000

Switzerland
Zürich — 342,000
Bern — 129,000

Turkey (European)
İstanbul — 6,620,000

Ukraine
Kiev — 2,630,000
Kharkiv — 1,555,000
Dnipropetrovsk — 1,147,000
Donetsk — 1,088,000
Odesa — 1,046,000

Yugoslavia (metro)
Belgrade — 1,204,000

International comparability of city population
data is limited by various data inconsistencies.

© MapQuest.com, Inc.

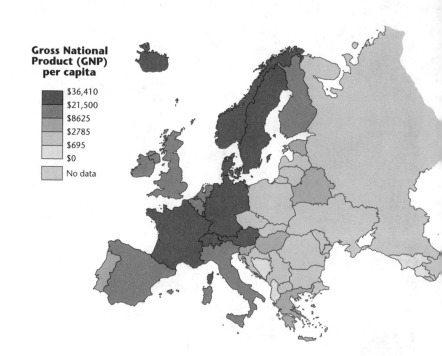

Gross National Product (GNP) per capita

- $36,410
- $21,500
- $8625
- $2785
- $695
- $0
- No data

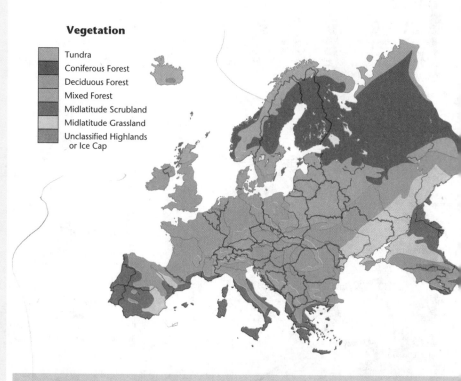

Vegetation

- Tundra
- Coniferous Forest
- Deciduous Forest
- Mixed Forest
- Midlatitude Scrubland
- Midlatitude Grassland
- Unclassified Highlands or Ice Cap

Europe: Population, by nation (in millions)*

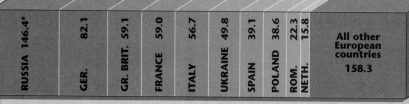

| RUSSIA 146.4* | GER. 82.1 | GR. BRIT. 59.1 | FRANCE 59.0 | ITALY 56.7 | UKRAINE 49.8 | SPAIN 39.1 | POLAND 38.6 | ROM. 22.3 | NETH. 15.8 | All other European countries 158.3 |

*Including Asian Russia as well as the more populous European portion of the country.

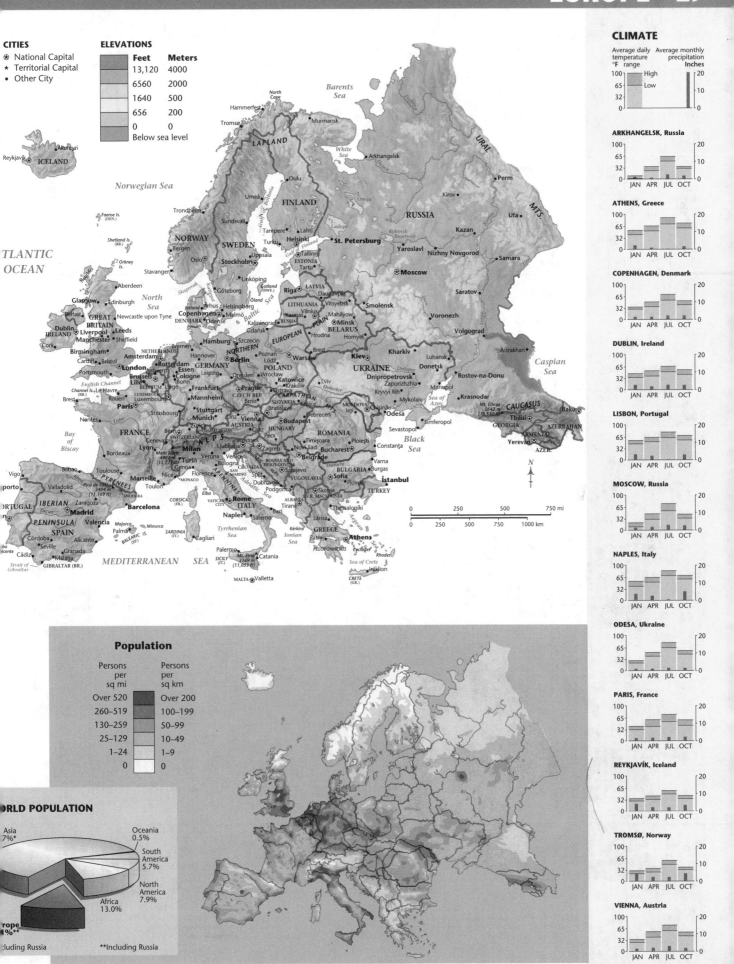

CITIES
⊛ National Capital
★ Territorial Capital
• Other City

ELEVATIONS

Feet	Meters
13,120	4000
6560	2000
1640	500
656	200
0	0
Below sea level	

CLIMATE

Average daily temperature °F range
Average monthly precipitation Inches

High
Low

ARKHANGELSK, Russia
ATHENS, Greece
COPENHAGEN, Denmark
DUBLIN, Ireland
LISBON, Portugal
MOSCOW, Russia
NAPLES, Italy
ODESA, Ukraine
PARIS, France
REYKJAVÍK, Iceland
TROMSØ, Norway
VIENNA, Austria

Population

Persons per sq mi	Persons per sq km
Over 520	Over 200
260–519	100–199
130–259	50–99
25–129	10–49
1–24	1–9
0	0

WORLD POPULATION

Asia 7%*
Oceania 0.5%
South America 5.7%
North America 7.9%
Africa 13.0%
Europe %**

*Including Russia
**Including Russia

Great Britain

National Capital
Other City

1:4,375,000

0 25 50 75 100 mi
0 25 50 75 100 125 150 km

Lambert Conformal Conic Projection

Great Britain
Capital: London
Area: 94,251 sq. mi.
      244,174 sq. km.
Population: 59,133,000
Largest City: London
Language: English
Monetary Unit: Pound

© MapQuest.com, Inc.

Great Britain:
Map Index

CHANNEL ISLANDS
Features
Alderney, island ....In...
Guernsey, island ....In...
Jersey, island ....In...
St. Malo, gulf ....In...
Sark, island ....In...

ENGLAND
Cities and Towns
Aylesbury ....Ins...
Banbury ....
Barnsley ....λ...
Barnstaple ....
Barrow-in-Furness ....
Basildon ....Inse...
Bath ....
Bedford ....
Berwick-upon-Tweed ....
Birkenhead ....
Birmingham ....
Blackburn ....
Blackpool ....
Bolton ....
Boston ....
Bournemouth ....
Bradford ....
Braintree ....Inse...
Brentwood ....Inse...
Brighton ....
Bristol ....
Burnley ....
Bury ....
Bury St. Edmunds............
Buxton ....
Camberley ....Inse...
Cambridge ....
Canterbury ....
Carlisle ....
Chatham ....Inse...
Chelmsford ....D3, Inse...
Cheltenham ....
Chester ....
Chesterfield ....
Chichester ....
Colchester ....
Coventry ....
Cowes ....
Crawley ....Inse...
Crewe ....
Darlington ....
Derby ....
Doncaster ....
Dorchester ....
Dorking ....Inse...
Dover ....
Dudley ....
Dunstable ....Inset
Durham ....
Eastbourne ....
Ely ....
Epsom ....Inset
Ewell ....Inset
Exeter ....
Farnham ....Inse...
Felixstowe ....
Fleetwood.....................
Folkestone ....
Gateshead ....
Gillingham ....
Glastonbury ....
Gloucester ....
Gosport ....
Grantham ....
Gravesend ....Inset
Great Yarmouth ....C...
Grimsby ....
Guildford ....
Halifax ....
Harlow ....Inset
Harrogate ....
Haslemere ....Inse...
Hastings ....
Hereford ....
Hertford ....Inset
High Wycombe ....Inset
Hove ....
Huddersfield ....
Ipswich ....
Kendal ....
Kenilworth ....
Kidderminster ....
King's Lynn ....
Kingston upon Hull ....
Kingston upon Thames...Inset
Lancaster ....
Launceston ....
Leeds ....
Leicester ....D...
Lewes ....D...
Lichfield ....C...
Lincoln ....C...
Liverpool ....
London, capital ......C3, Inset
Lowestoft ....D...
Luton ....
Maidstone ....D...
Manchester ....C...
Margate ....D...
Matlock ....C...
Middlesbrough ....C...
Newcastle-under-Lyme ...C...
Newcastle upon Tyne ....C...
Newmarket ....D...
Newquay ....B...
Northallerton ....C...
Northampton ....C...
North Shields ....C...
Norwich ....D3...
Nottingham ....C...
Oldham ....C...
Oxford ....C...
Penrith ....C...
Penzance ....B4...
Peterborough ....C...
Plymouth ....B4...
Poole ....C4...
Portsmouth ....C...
Preston ....C...
Reading ....C...
Reigate ....Inset III...
Rochdale ....C3...
Rotherham ....C...
St. Albans ....C3, Inset III...

Republic of Ireland

Capital: Dublin
Area: 27,137 sq. mi.
70,303 sq. km.
Population: 3,632,000
Largest City: Dublin
Languages: English, Irish
Monetary Unit: Punt, Euro

Republic of Ireland:
Map Index

Counties
Carlow C2
Cavan C2
Clare B3
Cork B3
Donegal B1
Dublin C2
Galway B2
Kerry B2
Kildare C2
Kilkenny C2
Laois C2
Leitrim B1
Limerick B2
Longford C2
Louth C2
Mayo B2
Meath C2
Monaghan C1
Offaly C2
Roscommon B2
Sligo B1
Tipperary North Riding B2
Tipperary South Riding B2
Waterford C2
Westmeath C2
Wexford C2
Wicklow C2

Cities and Towns
Ardara B1
Arklow C2
Athlone B2
Ballina B1
Bantry B3
Blarney B3
Carlingford C1
Carlow C2
Carrick-on-Shannon B2
Cashel C2
Castlebar B2
Cavan C2
Clara C2
Clifden A2
Clonmel C3
Cóbh B3
Cork B3
Dingle A2
Donegal B1
Drogheda C2
Dublin, capital C2
Dundalk C2
Dungarvan C2
Dún Laoghaire C2
Ennis B2
Enniskillen B2
Galway B2
Kildare C2
Kilkee B2
Kilkenny C2
Killarney B2
Letterkenny C1
Lifford C1
Limerick B2
Longford C2
Mallow B3
Maynooth C2
Monaghan C1
Mullingar C2

Naas C2
Nenagh B2
Port Laoise C2
Roscommon B2
Roscrea C2
Rosslare C2
Shannon B2
Sligo B1
Swords C2
Tipperary B2
Tralee B2
Trim C2
Tuam B2
Tullamore C2
Waterford C2
Westport B2
Wexford C2
Wicklow C2
Youghal C3

Other Features
Achill, island A2
Allen, lake B1
Aran, islands B2
Bantry, bay B3
Barrow, river C2
Benwee Head, cape B1
Blackwater, river B2
Blackwater, river C1
Boggeragh, mts. B2
Boyne, river C2
Caha, mts. B3
Carlingford, lake C1
Carnsore, point C2
Carrantuohill, mt. B3
Celtic, sea B3
Clear, cape B3
Conn, lake B1
Connaught, province B2
Connemara, region B2
Corrib, lake B2
Derg, lake B2
Dingle, bay A2
Donegal, bay B1
Erne, river B1
Errigal, mt. B1
Finn, river C1
Foyle, inlet C1
Galway, bay B2
Grand, canal C2
Irish, sea D2
Killala, bay B1
Knockboy, mt. B3
Lee, river B3
Leinster, province C2
Loop Head, cape B2
Malin Head, cape C1
Mask, lake B2
Maumturk, mts. B2
Mizen Head, cape B3
Moher, cliffs B2
Munster, province B2
Ree, lake B2
Royal, canal C2
Saint George's, channel C3
Shannon, river B2
Suir, river C2
Twelve Pins, mt. B2
Ulster, province C1
Wicklow, mts. C2
Wicklow Head, cape D2

Ireland

⊛ National Capital
• Other City

1:3,960,000

0   30   60 mi
0 30 60 km
Lambert Conformal Conic Projection

© MapQuest.com, Inc.

at Britain: Map Index
...ustell B4
...Helens C3
...ord C3
...sbury C3
...borough C2
...nthorpe C3
...ffield C3
...wsbury C3
...ugh ....Inset III
...hull C3
...hampton C4
...thend-on-Sea D3
...kport C3
...th Shields C2
...ford C3
...venage ....Inset III
...ke-on-Trent C2
...tford-upon-Avon C2
...derland C2
...ndon C3
...nton C3
...ord C3
...kesbury C3
...tford D3
...erton B4
...bridge ....Inset III
...bay B4
...wbridge B4
...o B4
...bridge Wells D3
...kefield C3
...sall C3
...rrington C3
...wick C3
...stminster ....Inset III
...itehaven B2
...gan C3
...chester C3
...ndsor ....Inset III
...verhampton C3
...rcester C3
...vil C4
...k C3

...er Features
...n, river C3
...k Country, region C3
...tol, channel B3
...eviot, hills C3
...swold, hills C3
...mbrian, mts. B2
...tmoor, plateau B4
...e, river B3
...ver, strait D4
...lish, channel C4
...nmoor, plateau B3
...s, region D3
...dden Field, plain C2
...mber, river D3
...n, sea B3
...e, district C2
...th Downs, hills C2
...th, sea D2
...th Foreland, ...
...promontory D3
...se, river C2, D3
...nines, mts. C2
...ell Pike, mt. B2
...y, islands A4
...ern, river C3
...th Downs, hills C3
...head, channel C4
...t, point B4
...s, river C2
...ames, river ....C3, Inset III
...nt, river C2
...eed, river C2
...e, river D3
...h, bay B3
...ght, island C4
...e, river C3
...e, river D3

...E OF MAN
...uglas B2

...RTHERN IRELAND
...es and Towns
...nagh A2
...ymena A2
...ngor B2
...ast A2
...eraine A2
...ywood B2
...ne A2
...donderry A2
...wry A2
...nagh A2
...tadown A2
...angford B2

...her Features
...rim, mts. A2

Bann, river A2
Erne, river A2
Foyle, lake A2
Foyle, river A2
Giant's Causeway, headland A1
Irish, sea B3
Lough Erne, lake A2
Mourne, mts. A2
Neagh, lake A2
North, channel A2
Rathlin, island A1
Slieve Donard, mt. B2
Sperrin, mts. A2
Upper Lough Erne, lake A2

SCOTLAND
Cities and Towns
Aberdeen C1
Aviemore B1
Ayr B2
Campbeltown B2
Clydebank B2
Cupar B2
Dornoch B1
Dumfries B2
Dundee B2
Dunfermline B2
Edinburgh B2
Elgin B1
Fort William B1
Fraserburgh C1
Glasgow B2
Greenock B2
Hamilton B2
Hawick C2
Inverness B1
Kilmarnock B2
Kirkcaldy B2
Kirkwall ....Inset I
Kyle of Lochalsh B1
Lairg B1

Lerwick ....Inset I
Mallaig B1
Montrose C2
Motherwell B2
Newtown St. Boswells C2
Oban B2
Paisley B2
Perth B2
Peterhead C1
Pitlochry B2
Portree A1
St. Andrews B2
Scone B2
Sconser A1
Stirling B2
Stornoway A1
Stranraer B2
Thurso B1
Ullapool B1
Wick B1

Other Features
Arran, island B2
Barra, island A2
Bass Rock, islet C2
Bell Rock (Inchcape), reef C2
Ben Nevis, mt. B2
Bute, island B2
Cheviot, hills C2
Clyde, estuary B2
Clyde, river B2
Coll, island A2
Colonsay, island A2
Dee, river C1
Dornoch, estuary B1
Duncansby, cape B1
Dunsinane, mt. B2
Eigg, island A1
Fair, island ....Inset I
Forth, estuary B2
Forth, river B2

Grampian, mts. B2
Hebrides, sea A1
Hoy, island ....Inset I
Inner Hebrides, islands A2
Islay, island A2
Jura, island B2
Katrine, lake B2
Kinnairds, cape C1
Lammermuir, hills C2
Lewis, island A1
Linnhe, lake A2
Lomond, lake B2
Lorne, estuary A2
Mainland, island ....Inset I
Merrick, mt. B2
Minch, strait A1
Moray, estuary B1
Mull, island A2
Ness, lake B1
North Uist, island A1
Ochil, hills B2
Orkney, islands ....Inset I
Outer Hebrides, islands A1
Rhum, island A1
Sanday, island ....Inset I
Shetland, islands ....Inset I
Sidlaw, hills B2
Skye, island A1
Solway, estuary B2
Southern Uplands, mts. B2
South Ronaldsay, island ....Inset I
South Uist, island A1
Spey, river B1
Stronsay, island ....Inset I
Tay, estuary C2
Tay, lake B2
Tay, river B2
Tiree, island A2
Tweed, river C2
Unst, island ....Inset I
Westray, island ....Inset I

Wrath, cape B1
Yell, island ....Inset I

WALES
Cities and Towns
Aberystwyth B3
Bangor B3
Caerleon C3
Caernarfon B3
Cardiff B3
Carmarthen B3
Conwy B3
Fishguard B3
Holyhead B3
Lampeter B3
Llandrindod Wells B3
Merthyr Tydfil B3
Milford Haven B3
Mold B3
Newport C3
Pembroke B3
Port Talbot B3
Rhondda B3
St. David's B3
Swansea B3
Welshpool B3

Other Features
Anglesey, island B3
Bala, lake B3
Brecon Beacons, mts. B3
Bristol, channel B3
Cambrian, mts. B3
Cardigan, bay B3
Dee, river B3
Lleyn, peninsula B3
Menai, strait B3
Snowdon, mt. B3
Teifi, river B3
Tywi, river B3
Usk, river C3
Wye, river C3

Denmark

Capital: Copenhagen
Area: 16,639 sq. mi.
43,080 sq. km.
Population: 5,357,000
Largest City: Copenhagen
Language: Danish
Monetary Unit: Krone

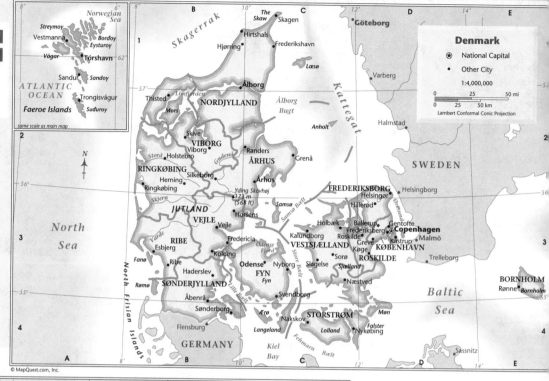

Denmark: Map Index

Counties

Århus	C2
Bornholm	E3
Frederiksborg	D2
Fyn	C3
København	D3
Nordjylland	B2
Ribe	B3
Ringkøbing	B2
Roskilde	D3
Sønderjylland	B3
Storstrøm	C4
Vejle	B3
Vestsjælland	C3
Viborg	B2

Cities and Towns

Åbenrå	B3
Ålborg	B1
Århus	C2
Ballerup	D3
Copenhagen, capital	D3
Esbjerg	B3
Fredericia	B3
Frederiksberg	D3
Frederikshavn	C1
Gentofte	D3
Grenå	C2
Greve	D3
Haderslev	B3
Helsingør	D2
Herning	B2
Hillerød	D3
Hirtshals	B1
Hjørring	B1
Holbæk	C3
Holstebro	B2
Horsens	B3
Kalundborg	C3
Kastrup	D3
Køge	D3
Kolding	B3
Næstved	C3
Nakskov	C4
Nyborg	C3
Nykøbing	C3
Odense	C3
Randers	C2
Ribe	B3
Ringkøbing	B2
Rønne	E3
Roskilde	D3
Sandur	Inset
Silkeborg	B2
Skagen	C1
Skive	B2
Slagelse	C3
Sønderborg	B4
Sorø	C3
Svendborg	C3
Thisted	B2
Tórshavn	Inset
Trongisvágur	Inset
Vejle	B3
Vestmanna	Inset
Viborg	B2

Other Features

Ærø, island	C4
Ålborg, bay	C2
Anholt, island	C2
Baltic, sea	D3
Bordoy, island	Inset
Bornholm, island	E3
Eysturoy, island	Inset
Faeroe, islands	Inset
Falster, island	D4
Fanø, island	B3
Fehmarn, strait	C4
Fyn, island	C3
Gudenå, river	B2
Jutland, peninsula	B3
Kattegat, strait	C1
Læsø, island	C1
Langeland, island	C4
Lille, strait	B3
Limfjorden, channel	B2
Lolland, island	C4
Møn, island	D4
Mors, island	B2
North, sea	A3
North Frisian, islands	B4
Norwegian, sea	Inset
Odense, fjord	C3
Øresund, sound	D3
Rømø, island	B3
Samsø, island	C3
Samsø, strait	C3
Sandoy, island	Inset
Sjælland, island	C3
Skagerrak, strait	B1
Skaw, cape	C1
Skjern, river	B3
Storå, river	B2
Store, strait	C3
Streymoy, island	Inset
Suduroy, island	Inset
Vágar, island	Inset
Varde, river	B3
Yding Skovhøj, hill	B2

Netherlands: Map Index

Provinces

Drenthe	D2
Flevoland	C2
Friesland	C1
Gelderland	D2
Groningen	D1
Limburg	C3
North Brabant	C3
North Holland	B2
Overijssel	D2
South Holland	B2
Utrecht	C2
Zeeland	A3

Cities and Towns

Alkmaar	B2
Almelo	D2
Amersfoort	C2
Amsterdam, capital	B2
Apeldoorn	C2
Arnhem	C3
Assen	D2
Bergen op Zoom	B3
Breda	B3
Delft	B2
Delfzijl	D1
Den Helder	B2
Deventer	D2
Doetinchem	D3
Dordrecht	B3
Edam	C2
Ede	C2
Eindhoven	C3
Emmeloord	C2
Emmen	D2
Enschede	D2
Gouda	B2
Groningen	D1
Haarlem	B2
Heerenveen	C2
Heerlen	C4
Hengelo	D2
Hilversum	C2
Hoogeveen	D2
Hoorn	C2
Leeuwarden	C1
Leiden	B2
Lelystad	C2
Maastricht	C4

Meppel	D2
Middelburg	A3
Nijmegen	C3
Oss	C3
Otterlo	C3
Roermond	D3
Rotterdam	B3
Scheveningen	B2
Schiedam	B3
's Hertogenbosch	C3
Sittard	C4
Sneek	C1
The Hague	B2
Tilburg	C3
Utrecht	C2
Venlo	D3
Vlaardingen	B3
Vlissingen	A3
Weert	C3
Zaanstad	B2
Zwolle	D2

Other Features

Ameland, island	C1
Eems, river	D1
Flevoland, polder	C2
Ijssel, river	D2
Ijsselmeer, sea	C2
Maas, river	C3, D3
Neder Rijn, river	C3
New Waterway, channel	B3
Northeast, polder	C2
North Holland, canal	B2
North Sea, canal	B2
Oosterschelde, channel	A3
Overflakkee, island	A3
Princess Margriet, canal	C1
Schiermonnikoog, island	D1
Schouwen, island	A3
Terschelling, island	B1
Texel, island	B1
Tholen, island	B3
Vaalserberg, mt.	C4
Vlieland, island	B1
Waal, river	C3
Waddenzee, sound	C1
Walcheren, island	A3
Westerschelde, channel	A3
West Frisian, islands	B1
Wilhelmina, canal	B3
Zuid-Willemsvaart, canal	C3

Netherlands

Capital: Amsterdam
Area: 16,033 sq. mi.
41,536 sq. km.
Population: 15,808,000
Largest City: Amsterdam
Language: Dutch
Monetary Unit: Guilder, Euro

© MapQuest.com, Inc.

North Sea

NETHERLANDS
Breda
Middleburg
Eindhoven
Venlo

GERMANY

Knokke
Zeebrugge
Oostende
Brugge
Dunkirk
Oostende-Brugge Canal

Turnhout
KEMPENLAND
Albert Canal
Antwerp
Sint-Niklaas
FLANDERS
ANTWERP
Schelde River
Brugge-Ghent Canal

WEST FLANDERS
Ghent
Mechelen
LIMBURG
Genk
Cologne

Roeselare
EAST FLANDERS
Aalst
BRUSSELS CAPITAL REGION
Schaerbeek
Leuven
Hasselt
Maastricht
Aachen

Ypres
Kortrijk
Anderlecht
Brussels
Ixelles
Uccle
FLEMISH BRABANT
Sint-Truiden
Bonn

Poperinge
Lys
Schelde
Dender
Halle
Wavre
Liège
Limbourg

Mouscron
Senne
WALLOON BRABANT
Verviers

Lille
Tournai
Ath
Gembloux
Meuse
LIÈGE
Spa

Neuffossé Canal
HAINAUT
La Louvière
Namur
Botrange 694 m (2277 ft)

Valenciennes
Mons
Binche
Sambre
Charleroi
WALLONIA
NAMUR
Malmédy
Ourthe

FRANCE
Dinant
ARDENNES
Bastogne

Fumay
Oise
LUXEMBOURG
Neufchâteau
Mosel

Charleville Mézières
Semois
Arlon
LUXEMBOURG
Trier

Luxembourg

Belgium

- ⊛ National Capital
- • Other City
- ⊥⊥⊥ Canal

1:2,381,000

0 — 20 — 40 mi
0 — 20 — 40 km
Lambert Conformal Conic Projection

© MapQuest.com, Inc.

**Belgium:
Map Index**

Internal Divisions

Antwerp (province)............C1
Brussels Cap. Region........C2
East Flanders (province) B2
Flanders (region)............C1
Flemish Brabant (province) C2
Hainaut (province) B2
Liège (province)..............D2
Limburg (province)..........D1
Luxembourg (province) D3
Namur (province)............C2
Walloon Brabant
(province) C2
Wallonia (region)...........C2
West Flanders (province)....B1

Cities and Towns

Aalst C2
Anderlecht....................C2
Antwerp C1
Arlon D3
Ath B2
Bastogne D2
Binche C2
Brugge B1

Brussels, capital............C2
Charleroi.......................C2
Chimay.........................C2
Dinant..........................C2
Gembloux.....................C2
Genk............................D2
Ghent...........................B1
Halle............................C2
Hasselt.........................D2
Ixelles..........................C2
Knokke.........................B1
Kortrijk.........................B2
La Louvière....................C2
Leuven.........................C2
Liège............................D2
Limbourg......................E2
Malmédy.......................D2
Mechelen......................C1
Mons............................B2
Mouscron......................B2
Namur..........................C2
Neufchâteau..................D3
Oostende......................A1
Poperinge......................A2
Roeselare......................B2
Schaerbeek...................C2
Sint-Niklaas...................C1
Sint-Truiden..................D2

Spa..............................D2
Tournai.........................B2
Turnhout.......................C1
Uccle............................C2
Verviers.........................D2
Wavre...........................C2
Ypres............................A2
Zeebrugge.....................B1

Other Features

Albert, canal...................C1
Ardennes, plateau............D2
Botrange, mt...................E2
Brugge-Ghent, canal.........B1
Dender, river..................B2
Kempenland, region..........D1
Leie, river......................B2
Maas, river.....................D2
Meuse, river...................D2
Oostende-Brugge,
canal..........................B1
Ourthe, river...................D2
Rupel, river....................C1
Sambre, river..................C2
Schelde, river..................B2
Semois, river..................D3
Senne, river....................C2

Belgium

Capital: Brussels
Area: 11,787 sq. mi.
30,536 sq. km.
Population: 10,182,000
Largest City: Brussels
Languages: Flemish, French, German
Monetary Unit: Belgian franc, Euro

A   BELGIUM   B
Buurgplaatz 559 m (1835 ft)
Ardennes
Troisvierges
Clervaux
Our
Wiltz
Clerve
Sûre
Vianden
Ettelbruck
Diekirch
Sûre
Echternach
Mersch
Larochette
Redange
Bon Pays
Alzette
Luxembourg
Grevenmacher
GERMANY
Differdange
Remich
Esch-sur-Alzette
Dudelange
FRANCE
Sûre
Mosel

Luxembourg

- ⊛ National Capital
- • Other City

1:1,700,000

0 — 10 — 20 mi
0 — 10 — 20 km
Azimuthal Equal Area Projection

© MapQuest.com, Inc.

**Luxembourg:
Map Index**

Cities and Towns

Clervaux B1
Diekirch.......................B2
Differdange...................A2
Dudelange....................B2
Echternach....................A2
Esch-sur-Alzette A2
Ettelbruck.....................B2
Grevenmacher...............B2
Larochette.....................B2
Luxembourg, capital........B2
Mersch.........................B2
Redange.......................A2
Remich.........................B2
Troisvierges...................B1
Vianden........................B2
Wiltz............................A2

Other Features

Alzette, river..................B2
Ardennes, plateau............A1
Bon Pays, region.............A2
Buurgplaatz, mt...............B1
Clerve, river...................B1
Mosel, river...................B2
Our, river......................B1
Sûre, river......................A2, B2

Liechtenstein

Capital: Vaduz
Area: 62 sq. mi.
161 sq. km.
Population: 32,000
Largest City: Vaduz
Language: German
Monetary Unit: Swiss franc

**Liechtenstein:
Map Index**

Cities and Towns

Balzers B2
Eschen..........................B1
Gamprin........................B1
Malbun.........................B2
Mauren.........................B1
Planken........................B1
Ruggell.........................B1
Schaan.........................B2
Schellenberg..................B1
Triesen.........................B2
Triesenberg...................B2
Vaduz, capital................B2

Other Features

Alps, range A2
Grauspitz, mt..................B2
Rhine, canal...................B1, B2
Rhine, river....................A1, A2
Samina, river..................B2

Ruggell
Schellenberg
Gamprin
Mauren
Eschen
Planken
AUSTRIA
Buchs
Schaan
Vaduz
SWITZERLAND
Triesenberg
Triesen
Malbun
Balzers
Grauspitz 2599 m (8527 ft)

Liechtenstein

- ⊛ National Capital
- • Other City

1:500,000

0 — 2.5 — 5 mi
0 — 2.5 — 5 km
Oblique Mercator Projection

© MapQuest.com, Inc.

Luxembourg

Capital: Luxembourg
Area: 999 sq. mi.
2,588 sq. km.
Population: 429,000
Largest City: Luxembourg
Languages: French, German
Monetary Unit: Luxembourg franc, Euro

France

⊛ National Capital

• Other City

1:5,625,000

0   50   100 mi

0   50   100 km

Lambert Conformal Conic Projection

CORSICA
CORSE

Same scale as main map

© MapQuest.com, Inc.

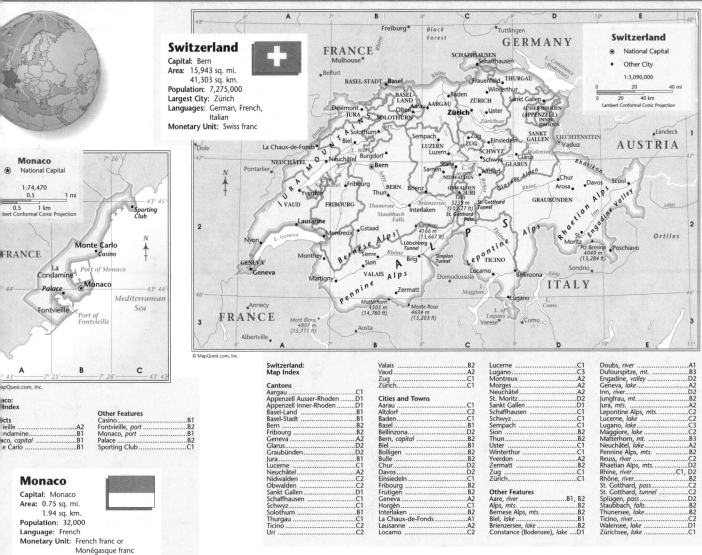

Switzerland

Capital: Bern
Area: 15,943 sq. mi.
41,303 sq. km.
Population: 7,275,000
Largest City: Zürich
Languages: German, French, Italian
Monetary Unit: Swiss franc

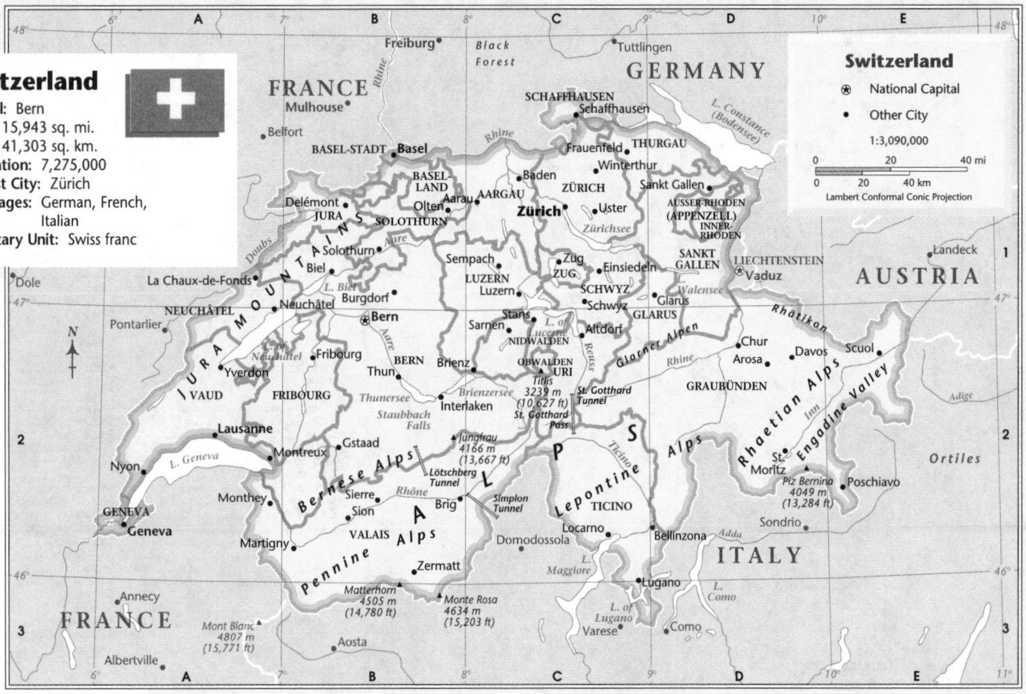
Switzerland
National Capital
Other City
1:3,090,000
0 20 40 mi
0 20 40 km
Lambert Conformal Conic Projection
FRANCE
GERMANY
AUSTRIA
ITALY
LIECHTENSTEIN
Bern
Zürich
Basel
Geneva
Lausanne
Lucerne
Lugano
Schaffhausen
Sankt Gallen
Chur
Vaduz
Mulhouse
Freiburg
Black Forest
Tuttlingen
Belfort
Dole
Pontarlier
Annecy
Albertville
Aosta
Como
Varese
Domodossola
Sondrio
Landeck
JURA MOUNTAINS
ALPS
Bernese Alps
Pennine Alps
Lepontine Alps
Rhaetian Alps
Glarner Alpen
Rhätikon
Engadine Valley
Ortles
L. Geneva
L. Constance (Bodensee)
L. Maggiore
L. of Lugano
Jungfrau 4166 m (13,667 ft)
Matterhorn 4505 m (14,780 ft)
Monte Rosa 4634 m (15,203 ft)
Mont Blanc 4807 m (15,771 ft)
Titlis 3239 m (10,627 ft)
Piz Bernina 4049 m (13,284 ft)
St. Gotthard Tunnel
St. Gotthard Pass
Lötschberg Tunnel
Simplon Tunnel
Staubbach Falls

© MapQuest.com, Inc.

Monaco
National Capital
1:74,470
0.5 1 mi
0.5 1 km
Lambert Conformal Conic Projection
FRANCE
Sporting Club
Monte Carlo
Casino
La Condamine
Port of Monaco
Palace
Monaco
Mediterranean Sea
Fontvieille
Port of Fontvieille
A
B
C
N

apQuest.com, Inc.

aco: Index

cts
ieille ...A2
ndamine ...B1
aco, *capital* ...B1
e Carlo ...B1

Other Features
Casino ...B1
Fontvieille, *port* ...B2
Monaco, *port* ...B1
Palace ...B2
Sporting Club ...C1

Monaco

Capital: Monaco
Area: 0.75 sq. mi.
1.94 sq. km.
Population: 32,000
Language: French
Monetary Unit: French franc or Monégasque franc

Switzerland: Map Index

Cantons
Aargau ...C1
Appenzell Ausser-Rhoden ...D1
Appenzell Inner-Rhoden ...D1
Basel-Land ...B1
Basel-Stadt ...B1
Bern ...B2
Fribourg ...B2
Geneva ...A2
Glarus ...D2
Graubünden ...D2
Jura ...B1
Lucerne ...C1
Neuchâtel ...A2
Nidwalden ...C2
Obwalden ...C2
Sankt Gallen ...D1
Schaffhausen ...C1
Schwyz ...C1
Solothurn ...B1
Thurgau ...C1
Ticino ...C2
Uri ...C2
Valais ...B2
Vaud ...A2
Zug ...C1
Zürich ...C1

Cities and Towns
Aarau ...C1
Altdorf ...C2
Baden ...C1
Basel ...B1
Bellinzona ...D2
Bern, *capital* ...B2
Biel ...B1
Bolligen ...B2
Bulle ...B2
Chur ...D2
Davos ...D2
Einsiedeln ...C1
Fribourg ...B2
Frutigen ...B2
Geneva ...A2
Horgen ...C1
Interlaken ...B2
La Chaux-de-Fonds ...A1
Lausanne ...A2
Locarno ...C2
Lucerne ...C1
Lugano ...C3
Montreux ...A2
Morges ...A2
Neuchâtel ...A2
St. Moritz ...D2
Sankt Gallen ...D1
Schaffhausen ...C1
Schwyz ...C1
Sempach ...C1
Sion ...B2
Thun ...B2
Uster ...C1
Winterthur ...C1
Yverdon ...A2
Zermatt ...B2
Zug ...C1
Zürich ...C1

Other Features
Aare, *river* ...B1, B2
Alps, *mts.* ...B2
Bernese Alps, *mts.* ...B2
Biel, *lake* ...B1
Brienzersee, *lake* ...B2
Constance (Bodensee), *lake* ...D1
Doubs, *river* ...A1
Dufourspitze, *mt.* ...B3
Engadine, *valley* ...D2
Geneva, *lake* ...A2
Inn, *river* ...D2
Jungfrau, *mt.* ...B2
Jura, *mts.* ...A2
Lepontine Alps, *mts.* ...C2
Lucerne, *lake* ...C2
Lugano, *lake* ...C3
Maggiore, *lake* ...C2
Matterhorn, *mt.* ...B3
Neuchâtel, *lake* ...A2
Pennine Alps, *mts.* ...B2
Reuss, *river* ...C2
Rhaetian Alps, *mts.* ...D2
Rhine, *river* ...C1, D2
Rhône, *river* ...B2
St. Gotthard, *pass* ...C2
St. Gotthard, *tunnel* ...C2
Splügen, *pass* ...D2
Staubbach, *falls* ...B2
Thunersee, *lake* ...B2
Ticino, *river* ...C2
Walensee, *lake* ...D1
Zürichsee, *lake* ...C1

ance

ital: Paris
a: 210,026 sq. mi.
544,109 sq. km.
ulation: 58,978,000
gest City: Paris
guage: French
netary Unit: Franc, Euro

France: Map Index

Regions
Alsace ...D2
Aquitaine ...B4
Auvergne ...C4
Basse-Normandie ...B2
Bourgogne ...C3
Bretagne ...B2
Centre ...C3
Champagne-Ardenne ...D2
Corse ...Inset I
Franche-Comté ...D3
Haute-Normandie ...C2
Île-de-France ...C2
Languedoc-Roussillon ...C5
Limousin ...C4
Lorraine ...D2
Midi-Pyrénées ...C5
Nord-Pas-de-Calais ...C1
Pays De La Loire ...B3
Picardie ...C2
Poitou-Charentes ...C3
Provence-Alpes-Côte-d'Azur ...D4
Rhône-Alpes ...D4

Cities and Towns
Abbeville ...C1
Agen ...C4
Aix-en-Provence ...D5
Aix-les-Bains ...D4
Ajaccio ...Inset I
Albi ...C5
Alençon ...C2
Alès ...D4
Amiens ...C2
Angers ...B3
Angoulême ...C4
Annecy ...D4
Arachon ...B4
Argenteuil ...Inset II
Arles ...D5
Arpajon ...Inset II
Arras ...C1
Auch ...C5
Aurillac ...C4
Auxerre ...C3
Avignon ...D5
Ballancourt-sur-Essonne ...Inset II
Bar-le-Duc ...D2
Bastia ...Inset I
Bayeux ...B2
Bayonne ...B5
Beauvais ...C2
Belfort ...D3
Bergerac ...C4
Besançon ...D3
Béziers ...C5
Biarritz ...B5
Blois ...C3
Bondy ...Inset II
Bordeaux ...B4
Boulogne-Billancourt ...Inset II
Boulogne-sur-Mer ...C1
Bourg-en-Bresse ...D3
Bourges ...C3
Brest ...A2
Briançon ...D4
Brive-la-Gallarde ...C4
Caen ...B2
Cahors ...C4
Calais ...C1
Calvi ...Inset I
Cambrai ...C1
Cannes ...D5
Carcassonne ...C5
Carnac ...B3
Châlons-sur-Marne ...D2
Chambéry ...D4
Chamonix-Mont-Blanc ...D4
Chantilly ...C2
Charleville Mézières ...D2
Chartres ...C2
Châteauroux ...C3
Châtellerault ...C3
Chaumont ...D2
Chelles ...Inset II
Cherbourg ...B2
Chevreuse ...Inset II
Choisy-le Roi ...Inset II
Cholet ...B3
Clermont-Ferrand ...C4
Clichy ...Inset II
Cluny ...D3
Cognac ...B4
Colmar ...D2
Compiègne ...C2
Conflans-Sainte-Honorine ...Inset II
Corbeil-Essonnes ...Inset II
Coubert ...Inset II
Créteil ...Inset II
Dammartin-en-Goële ...Inset II
Deauville ...C2
Dieppe ...C2
Digne ...D4
Dijon ...D3
Dôle ...D3
Domont ...Inset II
Douai ...C1
Draguignan ...D5
Dreux ...C2
Dunkirk (Dunkerque) ...C1
Épinal ...D2
Etrechy ...Inset II
Évreux ...C2
Évry ...Inset II
Foix ...C5
Fontainebleau ...C2
Fréjus ...D5
Gap ...D4
Gentilly ...Inset II
Grenoble ...D4
Guéret ...C3
Laon ...C2
La Rochelle ...B3
La-Roche-sur-Yon ...B3
Laval ...B2
Le Creusot ...D3
Le Havre ...C2
Le Mans ...C2
Lens ...C1
Le Puy ...C4
Les Ulis ...Inset II
Levallois-Perret ...Inset II
Lille ...C1
Limoges ...C4
Limours ...Inset II
L'Isle-Adam ...Inset II
Lorient ...B3
Lourdes ...B5
Louvres ...Inset II
Luzarches ...Inset II
Lyon ...D4
Mâcon ...D3
Maisons-Laffitte ...Inset II
Marseille ...D5
Massy ...Inset II
Maurepas ...Inset II
Melun ...Inset II
Mende ...C4
Mennecy ...Inset II
Metz ...D2
Meulan ...Inset II
Montargis ...C2
Montauban ...C4
Montélimar ...D4
Montluçon ...C3
Montpellier ...C5
Montreuil ...Inset II
Mont-Saint-Michel ...B2
Morlaix ...B2
Mulhouse ...D3
Nancy ...D2
Nanterre ...Inset II
Nantes ...B3
Narbonne ...C5
Nevers ...C3
Nice ...D5
Nîmes ...D5
Niort ...B3
Orléans ...C3
Ozoir-la-Ferrière ...Inset II
Palaiseau ...Inset II
Paris, *capital* ...C2, Inset II
Pau ...B5
Périgueux ...C4
Perpignan ...C5
Poissy ...Inset II
Poitiers ...C3
Pontchartrain ...Inset II
Pontoise ...Inset II
Porto-Vecchio ...Inset I
Privas ...D4
Quimper ...A2
Reims ...D2
Rennes ...B2
Roanne ...D3
Rochefort ...B4
Rodez ...C4
Roubaix ...C1
Rouen ...C2
Saint-Brieuc ...B2
Saint-Cloud ...Inset II
Saint-Denis ...Inset II
Saint-Dizier ...D2
Saintes ...B4
Saint-Étienne ...D4
Saint-Germain-en-Laye ...Inset II
Saint-Lô ...B2
Saint-Malo ...B2
Saint-Nazaire ...B3
Saint-Tropez ...D5
Sarcelles ...Inset II
Saumur ...B3
Savigny-sur-Orge ...Inset II
Sedan ...D2
Sevran ...Inset II
Sèvres ...Inset II
Soissons ...C2
Strasbourg ...D2
Tarbes ...C5
Taverny ...Inset II
Toulon ...D5
Toulouse ...C5
Tourcoing ...C1
Tours ...C3
Trouville ...C2
Troyes ...D2
Valence ...D4
Valenciennes ...C1
Vannes ...B3
Verdun ...D2
Versailles ...C2, Inset II
Vesoul ...D3
Vichy ...C3
Vierzon ...C3
Villeneuve-Saint-Georges ...Inset II
Vincennes ...Inset II

Other Features
Adour, *river* ...B5
Aisne, *river* ...D2
Allier, *river* ...C3
Alps, *range* ...D4
Ardennes, *region* ...D1
Argonne, *forest* ...D2
Aube, *river* ...D3
Belfort, *gap* ...D3
Belle, *island* ...B3
Biscay, *bay* ...B4
Blanc, *mt.* ...D4
Cévennes, *mts.* ...C4
Charente, *river* ...B4
Corsica, *island* ...Inset I
Cotentin, *peninsula* ...B2
Dordogne, *river* ...C4
Dover, *strait* ...C1
Durance, *river* ...D5
English, *channel* ...B2
Garonne, *river* ...C4
Geneva, *lake* ...D3
Gironde, *river* ...B4
Hague, *cape* ...B2
Isère, *river* ...D4
Jura, *mts.* ...D3
Landes, *region* ...B5
Lion, *gulf* ...D5
Little St. Bernard, *pass* ...D4
Loire, *river* ...C3
Lot, *river* ...C4
Maritime Alps, *range* ...D4
Marne, *river* ...C2, Inset II
Massif Central, *plateau* ...C4
Meuse, *river* ...D2
Moselle, *river* ...D2
Oise, *river* ...C2, Inset II
Oléron, *island* ...B4
Omaha, *beach* ...B2
Orne, *river* ...B2
Pyrenees, *range* ...C5
Rance, *river* ...B2
Raz, *point* ...A3
Ré, *island* ...B3
Rhine, *river* ...D2
Rhône, *river* ...D4
Saint-Malo, *gulf* ...B2
Sambre, *river* ...C1
Saône, *river* ...D3
Seine, *river* ...C2, Inset II
Somme, *river* ...C2
Utah, *beach* ...B2
Vienne, *river* ...C3
Vignemale, *mt.* ...B5
Vilaine, *river* ...B3
Vosges, *mts.* ...D2
Yeu, *island* ...B3
Yonne, *river* ...C2

Portugal:
Map Index

Districts
Aveiro A2
Beja A4
Braga A2
Bragança B2
Castelo Branco B2
Coimbra A2
Évora B3
Faro A4
Guarda B2
Leiria A3
Lisbon A3
Oporto (Porto) A2
Portalegre B3
Santarém A3
Setúbal A3
Viana do Castelo A2
Vila Real B2
Viseu B2

Cities and Towns
Abrantes A3
Almada A3
Amadora A3
Aveiro A2
Barreiro A3
Beja B3
Braga A2
Bragança B2
Caidasm da Rainha A3
Castelo Branco B3
Chaves B2
Coimbra A2
Covilhã B2
Elvas B3
Estoril A3
Évora B3
Faro B4
Figueira da Foz A2
Grândola A3
Guarda B2
Guimarães A2
Lagos A4
Leiria A3

Leixões A2
Lisbon, capital A3
Mafra A3
Moura B3
Odemira A4
Oeiras A3
Oporto (Porto) A2
Peniche A3
Portalegre B3
Portimão A4
Queluz A3
Santarém A3
Setúbal A3
Sines A4
Valença A1
Viana do Castelo A2
Vila do Conde A2
Vila Nova de Gaia A2
Vila Real B2
Vila Real
   de Santo Antonio B4
Viseu B2

Other Features
Algarve, region A4
Cádiz, gulf B4
Carvoeiro, cape A3
Chança, river B4
Douro, river B2
Espichel, cape A3
Estrela, mt. B2
Estrela, mts. A3
Guadiana, river B3
Lima, river A1
Minho, river A1
Mondego, cape A2
Mondego, river B2
Roca, cape A3
Sado, river A3
São Vicente, cape A4
Seda, river B3
Setúbal, bay A3
Sor, river B3
Sorraia, river A3
Tagus, river A3
Tâmega, river B2
Zêzere, river A3

Portugal

Capital: Lisbon
Area: 35,672 sq. mi.
       92,415 sq. km.
Population: 9,918,000
Largest City: Lisbon
Language: Portuguese
Monetary Unit: Escudo, Euro

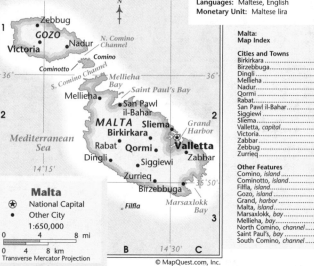

Malta

Capital: Valletta
Area: 122 sq. mi.
       316 sq. km.
Population: 382,000
Largest City: Valletta
Languages: Maltese, English
Monetary Unit: Maltese lira

Malta
- National Capital
- Other City
1:650,000
0   4   8 mi
0   4   8 km
Transverse Mercator Projection

© MapQuest.com, Inc.

Malta:
Map Index

Cities and Towns
Birkirkara ....
Birzebbuga ....
Dingli ....
Mellieha ....
Nadur ....
Qormi ....
Rabat ....
San Pawl il-Bahar ....
Siggiewi ....
Sliema ....
Valletta, capital ....
Victoria ....
Zabbar ....
Zebbug ....
Zurrieq ....

Other Features
Comino, island ....
Cominotto, island ....
Filfla, island ....
Gozo, island ....
Grand, harbor ....
Malta, island ....
Marsaxlokk, bay ....
Mellieha, bay ....
North Comino, channel ....
Saint Paul's, bay ....
South Comino, channel ....

Gibraltar

Area: 2.25 sq. mi.
       5.83 sq. km.
Population: 29,000
Language: English
Monetary Unit: British Pound

Gibraltar:
Map Index

Features
Catalan, bay A2
Detached, mole A2
Eastern, beach A2
Fortress Headquarters A3
Gibraltar, bay A2
Gibraltar, harbor A2
Gibraltar, strait A4
Governor's Residence A2
Great Europa, point A4
Highest point A3
Little, bay A4
Mediterranean, sea A3
North, mole A2
North Front, airfield A1
Rosia, bay A3
Saint Michael's, cave A3
Sandy, bay A3
Signal, hill A2
South, mole A3
The Rock, prom. A2

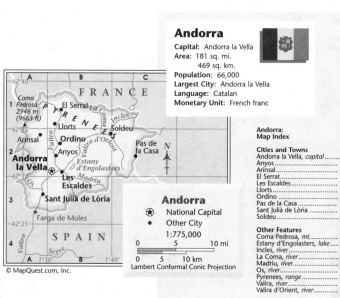

Gibraltar
1:82,200
0   0.5   1 mi
0   0.5   1 km
Miller Cylindrical Projection

© MapQuest.com, Inc.

Andorra

Capital: Andorra la Vella
Area: 181 sq. mi.
       469 sq. km.
Population: 66,000
Largest City: Andorra la Vella
Language: Catalan
Monetary Unit: French franc

Andorra
- National Capital
- Other City
1:775,000
0   5   10 mi
0   5   10 km
Lambert Conformal Conic Projection

© MapQuest.com, Inc.

Andorra:
Map Index

Cities and Towns
Andorra la Vella, capital ......
Anyos ....
Arinsal ....
El Serrat ....
Les Escaldes ....
Llorts ....
Ordino ....
Pas de la Casa ....
Sant Julià de Lòria ....
Soldeu ....

Other Features
Coma Pedrosa, mt. ....
Estany d'Engolasters, lake ....
Incles, river ....
La Coma, river ....
Madriu, river ....
Os, river ....
Pyrenees, range ....
Valira, river ....
Valira d'Orient, river ....

Spain:
Map Index

Regions
Andalusia D4
Aragón F2
Asturias C1
Balearic Islands G3
Basque Country E1
Canary Islands ....Inset I
Cantabria D1
Castile-La Mancha E3
Castile-León D1, E1
Catalonia G2
Estremadura C3
Galicia C1
La Rioja E1
Madrid E2
Murcia F4
Navarra F1
Valencia F2, F3

Cities and Towns
Águilas F4
Albacete F3
Alcalá de Henares ....Inset II
Alcañiz F2
Alcázar de San Juan E3
Alcira F3
Alcobendas ....Inset II
Alcorcón ....E2, Inset II
Alcoy F3
Algeciras D4
Alicante F3
Almadén D3
Almansa F3
Almendralejo C3
Almería E4
Antequera D4
Aranda de Duero E2
Aranjuez E2
Astorga C1
Ávila D2
Avilés D1
Badajoz C3
Badalona H2
Baracaldo E1
Barcelona H2

Baza E4
Béjar D2
Benavente D1
Benidorm F3
Bilbao E1
Burgos E1
Cáceres C3
Cádiz C4
Calatayud F2
Cartagena F4
Castellón de la Plana F3
Ceuta D5
Cieza F3
Ciudad Real E3
Ciudad Rodrigo C2
Córdoba D4
Cornellá de Llogregat G2
Coslada ....Inset II
Cuenca E3
Dos Hermanas D4
Écija D4
El Ferrol B1
Elche F3
Figueras H1
Fuenlabrada ....Inset II
Gerona H1
Getafe ....E2, Inset II
Gijón D1
Granada E4
Guadalajara E2
Guecho E1
Guernica y Luno E1
Hellín F3
Hospitalet H2
Huelva C4
Huesca F1
Ibiza G3
Jaén E3
Jerez de la Frontera C4
La Coruña B1
La Laguna ....Inset I
La Roda E3
Las Palmas ....Inset I
Leganés ....Inset II
León D1
Lérida G2

Linares E3
Logroño E1
Loja D4
Lorca F4
Lucena D4
Lugo C1
Madrid, capital ....E2, Inset II
Mahón J3
Málaga D4
Marbella D4
Mataró H2
Medina del Campo D2
Mérida C3
Mieres D1
Miranda de Ebro E1
Monforte C1
Morón de la Frontera D4
Móstoles ....Inset II
Murcia F4
Orense C1
Oviedo D1
Palencia D1
Palma H3
Pamplona F1
Plasencia C2
Ponferrada C1
Pontevedra B1
Puertollano D3
Reinosa D1
Reus G2
Sabadell H2
Sagunto F3
Salamanca D2
San Baudilio de Llobregat G2
San Fernando C4
San Sebastián F1
Santa Coloma de
   Gramanet H2
Santa Cruz de Tenerife ...Inset I
Santander E1
Santiago de Compostela B1
Segovia D2
Seville D4
Soria E2
Talavera de la Reina D3
Tarragona G2
Tarrasa H2
Telde ....Inset I

Teruel F2
Toledo D3
Tomelloso E3
Torrejón de Ardoz ....Inset II
Torrelavega D1
Torrente F3
Tortosa G2
Úbeda E3
Valdepeñas E3
Valencia F3
Valladolid D2
Vich H2
Vigo B1
Villarreal de los Infantes F3
Vitoria E1
Yecla F3
Zafra C3
Zamora D2
Zaragoza F2

Other Features
Alarcón, reservoir E3
Alboran, sea E4
Alcántara, reservoir C3
Almendra, reservoir C2
Aneto, mt. G1
Balearic, islands G3
Balearic, sea G2
Béticos, mts. D4
Biscay, bay D1
Brava, coast H2
Buendía, reservoir E2
Cabrera, island H3
Cádiz, gulf C4
Canaray, islands ....Inset I
Cantábrica, mts. C1
Cijara, reservoir D3
Duero, river D2
Ebro, river F1
Esla, river D2
Finisterre, cape B1
Formentera, island G3
Fuerteventura, island .....Inset I
Gata, cape E4
Gibraltar, strait D5
Gomera, island ....Inset I
Gran Canaria, island ......Inset I
Gredos, mts. D2

Guadalquivir, river D4
Guadarrama, mts. D2
Guadiana, river C3
Hierro, island ....Inset I
Ibérico, mts. E1
Ibiza, island G3
Jarama, river ....Inset II
Júcar, river F3
Lanzarote, island ....Inset I
La Palma, island ....Inset I
Majorca, island H3
Mediterranean, sea E4
Mequinenza, reservoir F2
Meseta, plateau D3
Miño, river B1
Minorca, island H2
Morena, mts. D3
Mulhacén, mt. E4
Nao, cape G3
Nevada, mts. E4
Orellana, reservoir D3
Ortegal, cape C1
Palos, cape F4
Pyrenees, mts. F1
Ricobayo, reservoir D2
Segura, river E4
Sol, coast D4
Tagus, river D3
Tenerife, island ....Inset I
Toledo, mts. D3
Tormes, river D2
Tortosa, cape G2
Valdecañas, reservoir D3
Valencia, gulf F3
Zújar, reservoir D3

Spain

Capital: Madrid
Area: 194,898 sq. mi.
504,917 sq. km.
Population: 39,168,000
Largest City: Madrid
Language: Spanish
Monetary Unit: Peseta, Euro

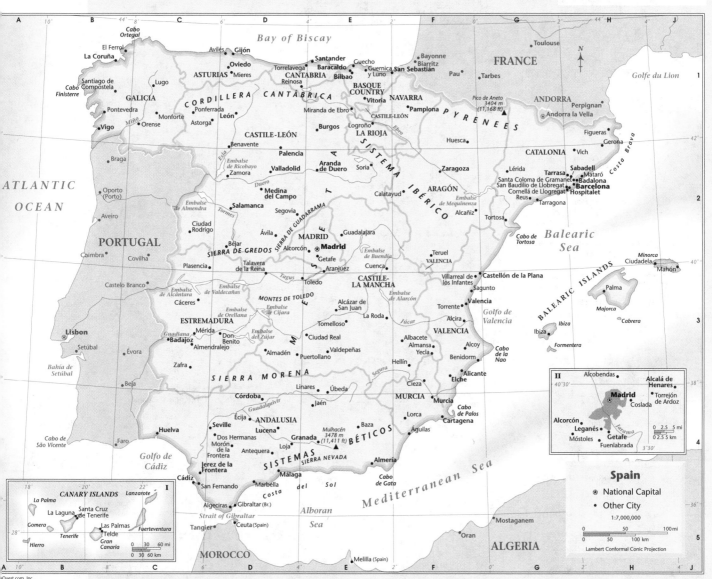

Italy

National Capital
Other City

1:5,614,000

0   50   100   150 mi
0 50 100 150 km
Lambert Conformal Conic Projection

Italy
Capital: Rome
Area: 116,333 sq. mi.
301,381 sq. km.
Population: 56,735,000
Largest City: Rome
Language: Italian
Monetary Unit: Lira, Euro

© MapQuest.com, Inc.

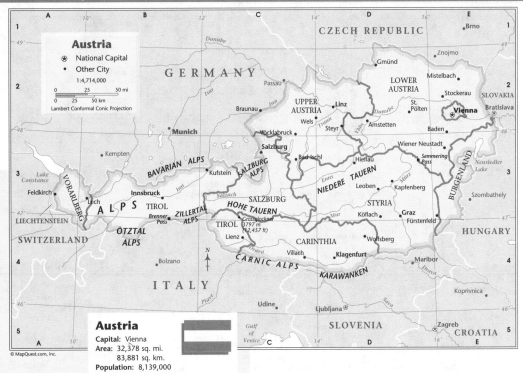

Austria
- ⊛ National Capital
- • Other City

1:4,714,000

0 25 50 mi
0 25 50 km

Lambert Conformal Conic Projection

© MapQuest.com, Inc.

...ria:
...Index

...inces
...enland E3
...inthia C4
...er Austria D2
...urg C3
...a B3, C4
...er Austria C2
...na E2
...rlberg A3

...es and Towns
...etten D2
...n E2
...schl C3
...nau C2
...kirch A3
...enfeld E3
...nd D2
...au D3
...bruck D3
...berg D4
...enfurt D4
...ein D3
...n B3
...en C4
...z C2
...elbach E2
...burg C3

Sankt Pölten D2
Steyr D2
Stockerau E2
Villach C4
Vöcklabruck C2
Wels C2
Wiener Neustadt E3
Wolfsberg D4

Other Features
Alps, range B3
Bavarian Alps, range .B3
Brenner, pass B3
Carnic Alps, range ..C4
Constance, lake A3
Danube, river C2
Drava, river C4
Enns, river D3
Grossglockner, mt. ..C3
Hohe Tauern, mts. ...C3
Inn, river B3, C2
Karawanken, range ...D4
Mur, river D3
Mürz, river D3
Neusiedler, lake E3
Niedere Tauern, range .D3
Ötztal Alps, range ..B4
Salzach, river C3
Salzburg Alps, range .C3
Semmering, pass D3
Traun, river D2
Ybbs, river D2
Zillertal Alps, range .B3

Austria

Capital: Vienna
Area: 32,378 sq. mi.
83,881 sq. km.
Population: 8,139,000
Largest City: Vienna
Language: German
Monetary Unit: Schilling, Euro

Vatican City

Area: 108.7 acres
Population: 811
Languages: Italian, Latin
Monetary Unit: Lira

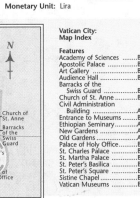

Vatican City

1:24,000

0 .15 .3 mi
0 .15 .3 km
Transverse Mercator Projection

© MapQuest.com, Inc.

Vatican City:
Map Index

Features
Academy of Sciences B1
Apostolic Palace B2
Art Gallery B1
Audience Hall B2
Barracks of the
Swiss Guard B1
Church of St. Anne B1
Civil Administration
Building A2
Entrance to Museums B1
Ethiopian Seminary A2
New Gardens A1
Old Gardens A1
Palace of Holy Office B2
St. Charles Palace B2
St. Martha Palace B2
St. Peter's Basilica B2
St. Peter's Square B2
Sistine Chapel B2
Vatican Museums B1

Index

...ons
...azzi C2
...ia C2
...icata C2
...bria D3
...pania C2
...a-Romagna B1
...-Venezia Giulia C1
...um C2
...uria B1
...bardy B1
...che C2
...se C2
...mont A1
...ia C2
...inia B3
...ia C3
...tino-Alto Adige B1
...any B2
...bria C2
...e d'Aosta A1
...eto B1

...es and Towns
...gento C3
...sandria B1
...ero B2
...a A1
...leia C1
...zo B2
...li Piceno C2
...lino B1
...tta D2
...nza C1
...evento C2
...gna B1
...gna B1
...cia B1
...indisi D2
...iari B3
...anissetta C3
...apobasso C2
...ossa B1
...ua B3
...eonia B3
...erta C2
...el Gandolfo C2
...ania C3
...anzaro D3
...lu C2
...ieti C2
...ggia C1
...avecchia B2
...one B1
...tina d'Ampezzo C1
...enza D2
...mona B1
...one D3
...eo A1
...a C3
...nza B1
...ara B1
...ence B2
...gia B2
...a C1
...inone C2
...ta C3

Genoa B1
Gorizia C1
Grosseto B2
Isernia C2
L'Aquila C2
La Spezia B1
Latina C2
Lecce D2
Livorno B2
Lucca B2
Macerata C2
Manfredonia C2
Mantova B1
Mantua (Mantova) B1
Marsala C3
Matera D2
Merano B1
Messina C3
Milan B1
Modena B1
Monopoli D2
Montepulciano B2
Monza B1
Naples C2
Novara B1
Nuoro B2
Olbia B2
Oristano B3
Otranto D2
Padova B1
Padua (Padova) B1
Palermo C3
Parma B1
Pavia B1
Perugia C2
Pesaro C2
Pescara C2
Pisa B2
Pistoia B2
Placenza B1
Potenza C2
Prato B2
Ragusa C3
Ravenna C1
Reggio di Calabria ..C3
Reggio nell'Emilia ..B1
Rieti C2
Rimini C1
Rome, capital C2
Rovigo B1
Salerno C2
San Gimignano B2
San Remo A2
San Severo C2
Sassari B2
Savona B1
Siena B2
Siracusa C3
Sondrio B1
Sorrento C2
Spoleto C2
Syracuse (Siracusa) .C3
Taranto D2
Teramo C2
Termoli C2
Terni C2
Torre del Greco C2
Trapani C3
Trento B1
Treviso C1
Trieste C1
Turin A1
Udine C1
Venice C1
Ventimiglia A2
Vercelli B1

Verona B1
Vicenza B1
Viterbo C2

Other Features
Adige, river B1
Adriatic, sea C2
Alps, mts. A1, B1
Apennines, range B1
Arno, river B2
Asinara, island B2
Blanc, mt. A1
Bolsena, lake B2
Botte Donato, mt. ...D3
Bracciano, lake C2
Brenner, pass B1
Cagliari, gulf B3
Campagna di Roma, region .C2
Caprara, point C2
Capri, island C2
Carbonara, cape B3
Cervati, mt. C2
Cimone, mt. B1
Como, lake B1
Corno, mt. C2
Dolomites, range B1
Egadi, islands C3
Elba, island B2
Etna, mt. C3
Garda, lake B1
Gennargentu, mts. ...B2
Genoa, gulf B1
Giglio, island B2
Ionian, sea D3
Ischia, island C2
Ligurian, sea B2
Lipari, islands C3
Lombardy, plain B1
Lugano, lake B1
Maggiore, lake B1
Maremma, region B2
Mediterranean, sea ..C3
Messina, strait C3
Montalto, mt. C2
Montecristo, island .B2
Naples, bay C2
Oglio, river B1
Pantelleria, island .C3
Passero, cape C3
Pianosa, island B2
Piave, river C1
Po, river A1, B1
Pontine, islands C2
Pontine, marshes C2
Rosa, mt. A1
Salerno, gulf C2
Sangro, river C2
San Pietro, island ..B3
Santa Maria di Leuca, cape .D3
Sant'Antioco, island .B3
San Vito, cape C2
Sardinia, island B2
Sicily, island C3
Sicily, strait B3
Spartivento, cape ...C3
Stromboli, island ...C3
Taranto, gulf C3
Testa del Gargano, point .D2
Teulada, cape B3
Tiber, river C2
Tirso, river B2
Trasimeno, lake C2
Tyrrhenian, sea B2
Ustica, island C3
Venice, gulf C1
Vesuvius, volcano ...C2

San Marino

Capital: San Marino
Area: 24 sq. mi.
62 sq. km.
Population: 25,000
Largest City: San Marino
Language: Italian
Monetary Unit: Italian lira

San Marino
- ⊛ National Capital
- • Other City

1:280,000

0 2 4 mi
0 2 4 km
Gauss-Krüger Projection

© MapQuest.com, Inc.

San Marino:
Map Index

Cities and Towns
Acquaviva A1
Borgo Maggiore B1
Chiesanuova B2
Domagnano B2
Falciano C1
Montegiardino B2
San Marino, capital .B1
Serravalle B1

Other Features
Ausa, river C1
Marano, river C2
San Marino, river ...A1
Titano, mt. B1

Germany
Capital: Berlin
Area: 137,735 sq. mi.
356,826 sq. km.
Population: 82,087,000
Largest City: Berlin
Language: German
Monetary Unit: Mark, Euro

Germany
⊛ National Capital
● Other City

1:4,066,000

| 0 | 25 | 50 | 75 mi |

| 0 | 25 | 50 | 75 km |

Lambert Conformal Conic Projection

© MapQuest.com, Inc.

Poland

Capital: Warsaw
Area: 120,727 sq. mi.
   312,764 sq. km.
Population: 38,609,000
Largest City: Warsaw
Language: Polish
Monetary Unit: Zloty

Poland:
Map Index

Cities and Towns
Biała Podlaska F2
Białystok F2
Bielsko-Biała D4
Bydgoszcz C2
Bytom D3
Chełm F3
Chojnice C2
Chorzów D3
Ciechanów E2
Częstochowa D3
Darłowo C1
Elbląg D1
Ełk F2

Gdańsk D1
Gdynia D1
Gliwice D3
Głogów C3
Gorzów Wielkopolski B2
Grudziądz D2
Hel D1
Jelenia Góra B3
Katowice D3
Kielce E3
Kołobrzeg B1
Konin D2
Koszalin C1
Kraków D3
Krosnow E4
Kutno D2
Legnica C3

Leszno C3
Łódź D3
Łomża F2
Lublin E3
Nowy Sącz.........................E4
Nysa C3
Olsztyn E2
Opole C3
Ostrołęka E2
Piła C2
Piotrków Trybunalski D3
Płock D2
Poznań C2
Przemyśl F4
Puck D1
Puławy E3
Radom E3
Ruda Śląska D3
Rybnik D3
Rzeszów F3
Sczecinek C2
Siedlce F2
Sieradz D3
Skierniewice D3
Słupsk C1
Sosnowiec D3
Suwałki F1
Świnoujście B2
Szczecin B2
Tarnobrzeg E3
Tarnów E3
Toruń D2
Tychy D3
Ustka C1
Wałbrzych C3
Warsaw, capital E2
Władysławowo D1
Włocławek D2
Wodzisław Śląski D3
Wrocław C3
Zabrze D3
Zakopane D4
Zamość F3
Zielona Góra B3

Other Features
Baltic, sea B1
Beskid, mts. D4
Bug, river E2, F3
Carpathian, mts. E4
Frisches Haff, bay D1
Gdańsk, gulf D1
High Tatra, mts. D4
Mamry, lake E1
Narew, river E2
Neisse, river B3
Noteć, river C2, D2
Oder, river B2, C3
Pilica, river E3
Pomeranian, bay B1
Rysy, mt. E4
San, river F3
Silesia, region C3
Śniardwy, lake E2
Sudeten, mts. B3
Vistula, river D2, E3
Warta, river B2, C2
Wieprz, river F3

Poland

⊛ National Capital
• Other City
⊔⊔⊔ Canal

1:6,687,500

0   50   100 mi
0 50 100 km

Lambert Conformal Conic Projection

© MapQuest.com, Inc.

Germany:
Map Index

States
Baden-Württemberg B4
Bavaria B4
Berlin C2
Brandenburg C2
Bremen B2
Hamburg B2
Lower Saxony B2
Mecklenburg-Western
Pomerania C2
Rhineland-Palatinate A3
Saarland A4
Saxony C3
Saxony-Anhalt B3
Schleswig-Holstein B2
Thuringia B3

Cities and Towns
Aachen A3
Amberg B4
Ansbach B4
Arnsberg B3
Augsburg B4
Baden-Baden B4
Bad Kreuznach A4
Bad Reichenhall C5
Bamberg B4
Bautzen C3
Bayreuth B4
Bergisch Gladbach A3
Berlin, capital C2
Bielefeld B3
Bochum A3
Bonn A3
Bottrop A3
Brandenburg B2
Bremen B2
Bremerhaven B2

Brunswick B2
Büren B3
Chemnitz C3
Coburg B3
Cologne A3
Constance B5
Cottbus C3
Cuxhaven B2
Dachau B4
Darmstadt B4
Dessau C3
Detmold B3
Dortmund A3
Dresden C3
Duisburg A3
Düsseldorf A3
Eberswalde C2
Eisenach B3
Eisenhüttenstadt C2
Eisleben B3
Emden A2
Erfurt B3
Erlangen B4
Essen A3
Esslingen B4
Flensburg B1
Frankfurt am Main B3
Frankfurt an der Oder C2
Freiberg C3
Freiburg A5
Friedrichshafen B5
Fulda B3
Fürth B4
Garmisch-Partenkirchen B5
Gelsenkirchen A3
Gera C3
Giessen B3
Göppingen B4
Görlitz C3
Goslar B3
Gotha B3
Göttingen B3
Greifswald C1
Guben C2
Güstrow C2
Hagen A3
Halberstadt B3

Halle B3
Hamburg B2
Hameln B2
Hamm A3
Hanau B3
Hannover B2
Heidelberg B4
Heidenheim B4
Heilbronn B4
Herne A3
Hildesheim B2
Hindelang B5
Hof B3
Ingolstadt B4
Jena B3
Kaiserslautern A4
Karlsruhe B4
Kassel B3
Kaufbeuren B5
Kempten B5
Kiel B1
Kleve A3
Koblenz A3
Krefeld A3
Kulmbach B3
Landshut B4
Leipzig C3
Leverkusen A3
Lindau B5
Lippstadt B3
Lübeck B2
Luckenwalde C2
Ludwigsburg B4
Ludwigshafen am Rhein B4
Lüneburg B2
Lünen A3
Magdeburg B2
Mainz B4
Mannheim B4
Marburg B3
Marl A3
Meissen C3
Memmingen B5
Moers A3
Mönchengladbach A3
Mühlhausen B3
Mülheim an der Ruhr A3

Munich B4
Münster A3
Naumburg B3
Neubrandenburg C2
Neumünster B1
Neunkirchen A4
Neustrelitz C2
Nienburg B2
Nordenham B2
Nordhausen B3
Nordhorn A2
Northeim B3
Nuremberg B4
Oberammergau B5
Oberhausen A3
Offenbach B3
Oldenburg B2
Osnabrück B2
Paderborn B3
Passau C4
Pforzheim B4
Pirmasens A4
Plauen C3
Potsdam C2
Puttgarden B1
Ratingen A3
Ravensburg B5
Recklinghausen A3
Regensburg C4
Remagen A3
Remscheid A3
Reutlingen B4
Riesa C3
Rosenheim C5
Rostock C1
Saarbrücken A4
Salzgitter B2
Sassnitz C1
Schleswig B1
Schwäbisch Gmünd B4
Schwedt C2
Schweinfurt B3
Schwerin B2
Siegen B3
Singen B5
Solingen A3

Spandau C2
Speyer B4
Stendal B2
Stralsund C1
Straubing C4
Stuttgart B4
Suhl B3
Trier A4
Tübingen B4
Uelzen B2
Ulm B4
Weiden C4
Weimar B3
Wetzlar B3
Wiesbaden B3
Wilhelmshaven B2
Wismar B2
Witten A3
Wittenberg C3
Wittenberge B2
Wolfsburg B2
Worms B4
Wuppertal A3
Würzburg B4
Zittau C3
Zwickau C3

Other Features
Ammersee, lake B4
Baltic, sea C1
Bavarian Alps, mts. B5
Bayerischer Wald, mts. C4
Black, forest A4
Bohemian, forest C4
Chiem, lake C5
Constance, lake B5
Danube, river B4
East Frisian, islands A2
Eifel, plateau A3
Elbe, river B2, C3
Erzgebirge, mts. C3
Fehmarn, island B1
Fichtelberg, mt. C3
Fichtelgebirge, mts. B4
Franconian Jura, mts B4

Frankenwald, mts. B3
Fulda, river B3
Harz, mts. B3
Havel, river C2
Helgoland, island A1
Hünsruck, mts. A4
Inn, river C4
Isar, river C4
Kiel, bay B1
Lahn, river B3
Lech, river B4
Lüneburger Heide, region B2
Main, river B4
Main-Danube, canal B4
Mecklenburg, bay B1
Mittelland, canal B2
Mosel, river A4
Mulde, river C3
Müritz, lake C2
Neckar, river B4
Neisse, river C3
Nord-Ostsee, canal B1
North, sea A1
Northern European, plain B2
North Frisian, islands B1
Oberpfälzer Wald, mts. C4
Odenwald, forest B4
Oder, river C2
Oderhaff, lake C2
Pomeranian, bay C1
Rhine, river A3, A4
Rügen, island C1
Ruhr, river B3
Saale, river B3
Saar, river A4
Salzach, river C4
Schweriner, lake B2
Spessart, mts. B3
Spree, river C3
Starnberg, lake B5
Swabian Jura, mts. B4
Taunus, mts. B3
Thuringian, forest B3
Werra, river B3
Weser, river B2
Zugspitze, mt. B5

Czech Republic:
Map Index

Administrative Regions
Jihočeský B3
Jihomoravský C3
Praha B2
Severočeský A2
Severomoravský C3
Středočeský B3
Východočeský B3
Západočeský A3

Cities and Towns
Břeclav C4
Brno C3
České Budějovice B4
Cheb A2
Děčín B2
Frýdek-Místek D3
Havířov D3
Hradec Králové B2
Jihlava B3
Karlovy Vary A2
Karviná D3
Kladno B2
Klatovy A3
Kolín B2
Liberec B2
Most A2
Olomouc C3
Opava C3
Ostrava D3
Pardubice B2
Plzeň A3
Prague, capital B2
Přerov C3
Prostějov C3
Strakonice A3
Šumperk C3
Svitavy C3
Tábor B3
Trutnov B2
Ústí nad Labem B2
Zlín C3
Znojmo C4

Other Features
Berounka, river A3
Bohemia, region A3
Bohemian, forest A3
Bohemian-Moravian, heights B3
Carpathian, mts. C4
Dyje, river C3
Erzgebirge, mts. A2
Labe, Elbe, river B2
Morava, river C3
Moravia, region C3
Odra, Oder, river C3
Sázava, river B3
Silesia, region B2
Sněžka, mt. B2
Šudeten, mts. B2
Šumava, mts. A3
Vltava, river B3

Czech Republic

Capital: Prague
Area: 30,449 sq. mi.
78,883 sq. km.
Population: 10,281,000
Largest City: Prague
Language: Czech
Monetary Unit: Koruna

Slovakia

Capital: Bratislava
Area: 18,933 sq. mi.
49,049 sq. km.
Population: 5,396,000
Largest City: Bratislava
Language: Slovak
Monetary Unit: New Koruna

Slovakia:
Map Index

Regions
Banskobystrický C2
Bratislavský A2
Košický C2
Nitriansky B2
Prešovský C2
Trenčiansky A2
Trnavský A2
Žilinský B2

Cities and Towns
Banská Bystrica B2
Bardejov C2
Bratislava, capital A2
Humenné C2
Komárno B3
Košice C2
Levice B2
Liptovský Mikuláš B2
Lučenec B2
Martin B2
Michalovce C2
Nitra B2
Nové Zamky B3
Piešťany A2
Poprad B2
Považská Bystrica B2
Prešov C2
Prievidza B2
Ružomberok B2
Spišská Nová Ves C2
Trenčín A2
Trnava A2
Žilina B2
Zvolen B2

Other Features
Biele Karpaty, mts. A2
Carpathian, mts. B2
Danube, river A3
Gerlachovka, mt. B2
Hornád, river C2
Hron, river B2
Ipel', river B2
Laborec, river C2
Male Karpaty, mts. A2
Morava, river A2
Ondava, river C2
Slaná, river C2
Slovenskérudohorie, mts. B2
Tatra, range B2
Váh, river A2

Romania:
Map Index

Cities and Towns
Alba Iulia ....
Alexandria ....
Arad ....
Bacău ....
Baia Mare ....
Bîrlad ....
Bistrița ....
Botoșani ....
Brăila ....
Brașov ....
Bucharest, capital ....
Buzău ....
Călărași ....
Cernavodă ....
Cluj-Napoca ....
Constanța ....
Craiova ....
Dej ....
Deva ....
Dorohoi ....
Drobeta-Turnu Severin ....
Făgăraș ....
Fetești ....
Focșani ....
Galați ....
Giurgiu ....
Hunedoara ....
Iași ....
Lugoj ....
Lupeni ....
Medgidia ....
Mediaș ....
Miercurea Ciuc ....
Oltenița ....
Onești ....
Oradea ....
Petrila ....
Petroșani ....
Piatra Neamț ....
Pitești ....
Ploiești ....
Rădăuți ....
Reghin ....
Reșița ....
Rîmnicu Vîlcea ....
Roman ....
Salonta ....
Satu Mare ....
Sfîntu Gheorghe ....
Sibiu ....
Sighetul Marmației ....

© MapQuest.com, Inc.

Hungary

Capital: Budapest
Area: 35,919 sq. mi.
93,054 sq. km.
Population: 10,186,000
Largest City: Budapest
Language: Hungarian
Monetary Unit: Forint

Romania

Capital: Bucharest
Area: 91,699 sq. mi.
267,174 sq. km.
Population: 22,334,000
Largest City: Bucharest
Language: Romanian
Monetary Unit: Leu

© MapQuest.com, Inc.

Hungary:
Map Index

Counties
Bács-Kiskun B2
Baranya B3
Békés C2
Békéscsaba C2
Borsod-Abaúj-Zemplén C1
Budapest (city) B2
Csongrád C2
Debrecen C2
Dunaújváros B2
Eger C2
Fejér B2
Győr A2
Győr-Moson- Sopron A2
Hajdú-Bihar C2
Heves C2

Hódmezővásárhely C2
Jász-Nagykun-Szolnok C2
Kaposvár A2
Kecskemét B2
Komárom-Esztergom B2
Miskolc C1
Nagykanizsa A2
Nógrád B2
Nyíregyháza C2
Pécs B2
Pest B2
Somogy A2
Sopron A2
Szabolcs- Szatmár-Bereg C1
Szeged C2
Székesfehérvár B2
Szolnok C2
Szombathely A2
Tatabánya B2

Tolna B2
Vas A2
Veszprém A2
Zala ....A
Zalaegerszeg ....A

Cities and Towns
Ajka A2
Baja B2
Békéscsaba C2
Budapest, capital B2
Cegléd B2
Debrecen C2
Dunaújváros B2
Eger C2
Érd B2
Esztergom B2
Gyöngyös B2
Győr A2

Hajdúböszörmény C2
Hódmezővásárhely C2
Jászberény B2
Kaposvár A2
Karcag C2
Kazincbarcika C1
Kecskemét B2
Keszthely A2
Kiskunhalas B2
Komárom B2
Miskolc C1
Mohács B2
Nagykanizsa A2
Nyíregyháza C2
Oroháza C2
Ózd C1
Paks B2
Pápa A2
Pécs B2

Salgótarján B1
Siófok B2
Sopron A2
Szeged C2
Székesfehérvár B2
Szekszárd B2
Szentes C2
Szolnok C2
Szombathely A2
Tatabánya B2
Tokaj C1
Vác B2
Veszprém A2
Zalaegerszeg A2

Other Features
Bakony, mts. A2
Balaton, lake A2
Bükk, mts. C1

Danube, river A2, B2
Drava, river A2
Great Alföld, plain B2
Hernád, river C1
Ipoly, river B1
Kékes, mt. C2
Kiskörei-víztároló, lake C2
Körös, river C2
Little Alföld, plain A2
Maros, river C2
Mátra, mts. B2
Mecsek, mts. B2
Neusiedler (Fertő), lake A2
Rába, river A2
Sió, river B2
Tisza, river C2
Zala, river A2

...ghişoara........................C2
...et D2
...tina C3
...bozia D3
...ceava D3
...cuci D3
...nişoara A3
...goviste C3
...gu Jiu B3
...gu-Mureş C2
...gu Neamţ D2
...gu Ocna D2
...lcea E3
...rda B2
...rnu Măgurele C4
...slui D2
...lău B2

Other Features
...useni, mts. B2
...geş, river C3
...nat, region A3
...caz, reservoir D2
...hor, mts. B2
...strița, river C2
...arpathian, mts. B1
...anube, river B3, D3, E3
...brogea, region E4
...bruja, region D3
...n Gate, reservoir B3
...t, river B3
...oldavia, region C3
...oldoveanu, mt. C3
...ouths of the Danube, delta E3
...ureş, river B2
...lt, river E2
...zelm, lake E3
...et, river D2
...ransylvanian Alps, mts. B3
...alachia, region B3

© MapQuest.com, Inc.

Part of Russia extends onto the continent of Asia.

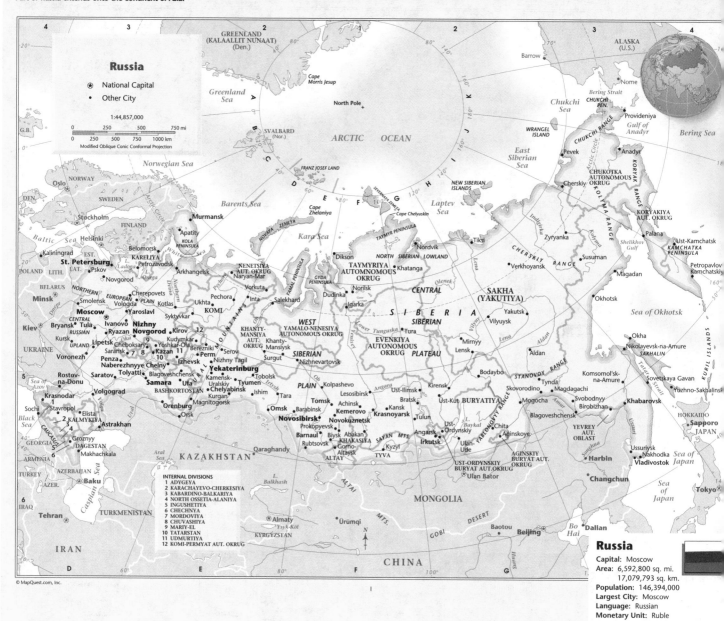

Russia

⊛ National Capital
● Other City

1:44,857,000

0   250   500   750 mi
0   250 500 750 1000 km
Modified Oblique Conic Conformal Projection

INTERNAL DIVISIONS
1 ADYGEYA
2 KARACHAYEVO-CHERKESIYA
3 KABARDINO-BALKARIYA
4 NORTH OSSETIA-ALANIYA
5 INGUSHETIYA
6 CHECHNYA
7 MORDOVIYA
8 CHUVASHIYA
9 MARIY-EL
10 TATARSTAN
11 UDMURTIYA
12 KOMI-PERMYAT AUT. OKRUG

© MapQuest.com, Inc.

Russia

Capital: Moscow
Area: 6,592,800 sq. mi.
        17,079,793 sq. km.
Population: 146,394,000
Largest City: Moscow
Language: Russian
Monetary Unit: Ruble

Russia:
Map Index

Internal Divisions
Adygeya (republic) D5
Aginskiy Buryat (autonomous
  okrug) G4
Altay (republic) F4
Bashkortostan (republic) D4
Buryatiya (republic) G4
Chechnya (republic) D5
Chukotka (autonomous okrug) ...J3
Chuvashiya (republic) D4
Dagestan (republic) D5
Evenkiya (autonomous okrug) F3
Ingushetiya (republic) D5
Kabardino-Balkariya (republic) ...D5
Kalmykiya (republic) D5
Karachayevo-Cherkesiya
  (republic) D5
Kareliya (republic) C3
Khakasiya (republic) F4
Khanty-Mansiya
  (autonomous okrug) E3
Komi (republic) D3
Komi-Permyat
  (autonomous okrug) D3
Koryakiya (autonomous okrug) ...J3
Mariy-El (republic) D4
Mordoviya (republic) D4
Nenetsiya (autonomous okrug) ...D3
North Ossetia Alaniya (republic) .D5
Tatarstan (republic) D4
Taymyriya (autonomous okrug) ...F2
Tyva (republic) F4
Udmurtiya (republic) D4
Ust-Ordynskiy Buryat (autonomous
  okrug) G5
Sakha (Yakutiya) (republic) H3
Yamalo-Nenesiya
  (autonomous okrug) E3
Yevrey (autonomous oblast) H5

Cities and Towns
Abakan F4
Achinsk F4
Aginskoye G4
Aldan H4
Anadyr J3
Angarsk G4
Apatity C3
Arkhangelsk D3
Astrakhan D5
Barabinsk E4
Barnaul F4
Belomorsk C3
Berezniki D4
Birobizhan H5
Biysk F4
Blagoveshchensk D4
Blagoveshchensk H4
Bodaybo G4
Bratsk G4
Bryansk C4
Cheboksary D4
Chelyabinsk E4
Cherepovets C4
Cherskiy J3
Chita G4
Dikson F2
Dudinka F3
Elista D5
Gorno-Altaysk F4
Groznyy D5
Igarka F3
Inta E3
Irkutsk G4
Ishim E4
Ivanovo D4
Izhevsk D4
Kaliningrad C4
Kamensk-Uralskiy E4
Kansk F4
Kemerovo F4
Khabarovsk H5
Khanty-Mansiysk E3

Khatanga G2
Kirensk G4
Kolpashevo F4
Komsomol'sk-na-Amure H4
Kotlas D3
Krasnodar C5
Krasnoyarsk F4
Kudymkar D4
Kurgan E4
Kursk C4
Kyzyl F4
Lensk G3
Lesosibirsk F4
Lipetsk C4
Magadan I4
Magdagachi H4
Magnitogorsk D4
Makhachkala D5
Mirnyy G3
Mogocha G4
Moscow, capital C4
Murmansk C3
Naberezhnyye Chelny D4
Nakhodka H5
Naryan-Mar D3
Nikolayevsk-na-Amure I4
Nizhnevartosk E3
Nizhny Novgorod D4
Nizhny Tagil D4
Nordvik F2
Norilsk F3
Novgorod C4
Novokuznetsk F4
Novosibirsk F4
Okha I4
Okhotsk I4
Omsk E4
Orenburg D4
Orsk D4
Palana J4
Pechora D3
Penza D4
Perm D4
Petropavlovsk-Kamchatskiy I4

Petrozavodsk C3
Pevek J3
Prokopyevsk F4
Providenyia K3
Pskov C4
Rostov-na-Donu C5
Rubtsovsk F4
Ryazan C4
St. Petersburg C4
Salekhard E3
Samara D4
Saransk D4
Saratov D4
Serov E4
Skovorodino H4
Smolensk C4
Sochi C5
Sovetskaya Gavan I5
Stavropol D5
Surgut E3
Susuman I3
Svobodnyy H4
Syktyvkar D3
Tara E4
Tiksi H2
Tobolsk E4
Tolyatti D4
Tomsk F4
Tula C4
Tulun G4
Tura G3
Tynda H4
Tyumen E4
Ufa D4
Ulan-Ude G4
Ussuriysk H5
Ust-Ilimsk G4
Ust-Kamchatsk J4
Ust-Kut G4
Ust-Ordynsk G4
Verkhoyansk H3
Vilyuysk H3
Vladivostok H5

Volgograd D5
Vologda C4
Vorkuta E3
Voronezh C4
Vyatka D4
Yakutsk H3
Yaroslavl C4
Yekaterinburg E4
Yoshkar-Ola D4
Yuzhno-Sakhalinsk I5
Zyryanka I3

Other Features
Aldan, river H4
Amur, river H4
Anadyr, gulf K3
Angara, river F4
Azov, sea C5
Baltic, sea B4
Barents, sea C2
Baykal, lake G4
Bering, sea K4
Bering, strait K3
Black, sea C5
Caspian, sea D6
Caucasus, mts. D5
Central Russian, upland C4
Central Siberian, plateau G3
Central, range I4
Chelyuskin, cape G2
Cherskiy, range H3
Chukchi, peninsula K3
Chukchi, range K2
Chukchi, sea K2
Dnepr, river C4
Dzhugdzhur, range H4
East Siberian, sea J2
Franz Josef Land, islands D1
Gyda, peninsula F2
Indigirka, river I3
Irtysh, river E4
Kamchatka, peninsula J4
Kara, sea E2

Kola, peninsula C3
Kolyma, range J3
Kolyma, river I3
Koryak, range J3
Kuril, islands I5
Ladoga, lake C3
Laptev, sea H2
Lena, river H3
Lower Tunguska, river F3
New Siberian, islands I1
North Siberian, lowland G2
Northern Divina, river D3
Northern European, plain C2
Novaya Zemlya, islands D2
Ob, river E3
Okhotsk, sea I4
Olenek, river G3
Onega, lake C3
Pechora, river D3
Sakhalin, island I4
Sayan, mts. F4
Severnaya Zemlya, islands F1
Shelikhov, gulf I3
Siberia, region H3
Sikhote Alin, range H5
Stanovoy, range H4
Tatar, strait I4
Taymyr, peninsula G2
Ural, mts. D4
Ural, river D4
Ussuri, river H5
Verkhoyansk, range H3
Vilyuy, river H3
Volga, river D5
West Siberian, plain E4
White, sea C3
Wrangel, island I2
Yablonovyy, range G4
Yamal, peninsula E3
Yenisey, river F3
Zhelaniya, cape E2

Armenia

Capital: Yerevan
Area: 11,500 sq. mi.
29,793 sq. km.
Population: 3,409,000
Largest City: Yerevan
Language: Armenian
Monetary Unit: Dram

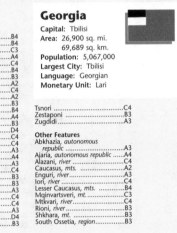

Georgia

- ⊛ National Capital
- • Other City

1:6,547,000

| 0 | 40 | 80 mi |
| 0 | 40 | 80 km |

Lambert Conformal Conic Projection

© MapQuest.com, Inc.

Armenia: Map Index

Cities and Towns

...erdi B1
...at B3
...hat B3
...........................A2
...ashen C2
...............................B2
...atsin B2
...rr C2
...........................D3

Gyumri A2
Hoktemberyan B2
Hrazdan B2
Ijevan C2
Kafan D3
Kirovakan B2
Martuni C2
Meghri D4
Sisian D3
Sotk C2
Stepanavan B2
Tashir B1
Vardenis C2

Vayk C3
Yerevan, *capital* B2

Other Features

Akhuryan, *river* A2
Aragats, *mt.* B2
Aras, *river* B2
Arpa, *river* C3
Debed, *river* B2
Hrazdan, *river* B2
Lesser Caucasus, *mts.* B1
Sevan, *lake* C2
Vorotan, *river* C3

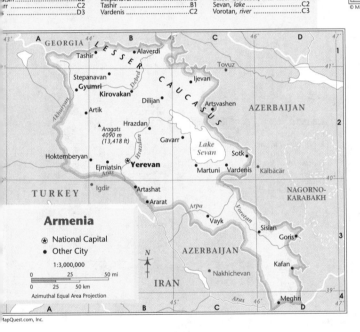

Armenia

- ⊛ National Capital
- • Other City

1:3,000,000

| 0 | 25 | 50 mi |
| 0 | 25 | 50 km |

Azimuthal Equal Area Projection

MapQuest.com, Inc.

Georgia: Map Index

Cities and Towns

Akhalkalaki B4
Akhaltsikhe B4
Akhmeta C3
Batumi A4
Bolnisi C4
Borjomi B4
Chiatura B3
Gagra A2
Gori C4
Gudauta A2
Jvari B3
Khashuri C4
Kobuleti A4
Kutaisi B3
Lagodekhi D4
Marneuli C4
Mtskheta C4
Ochamchire A3
Ozurgeti A4
Poti A3
Rustavi C4
Samtredia B3
Senaki A3
Sukhumi A3
Tbilisi, *capital* C4
Telavi C4
Tqvarcheli A3
Tsiteli-Tsqaro D4
Tskhinvali B3

Tsnori C4
Zestaponi B3
Zugdidi A3

Other Features

Abkhazia, *autonomous*
republic A3
Ajaria, *autonomous republic* A4
Alazani, *river* C4
Caucasus, *mts.* A2
Enguri, *river* A3
Iori, *river* C4
Lesser Caucasus, *mts.* B4
Mqinvartsveri, *mt.* C3
Mtkvari, *river* B3
Rioni, *river* B3
Shkhara, *mt.* B3
South Ossetia, *region* B3

Georgia

Capital: Tbilisi
Area: 26,900 sq. mi.
69,689 sq. km.
Population: 5,067,000
Largest City: Tbilisi
Language: Georgian
Monetary Unit: Lari

Azerbaijan

Capital: Baku
Area: 33,400 sq. mi.
86,528 sq. km.
Population: 7,908,000
Largest City: Baku
Language: Azerbaijani
Monetary Unit: Manat

Azerbaijan

- ⊛ National Capital
- • Other City

1:5,673,000

| 0 | 25 | 50 mi |
| 0 | 25 | 50 km |

Azimuthal Equal Area Projection

Azerbaijan: Map Index

Cities and Towns

Ağcabädi B2
Ağdam B3
Ağstafa A2
Älät C3
Ali Bayramli C3
Astara C3
Baku, *capital* C2
Balakän B2
Bärdä B2
Biläsuvar C3
Gäncä B2
Göyçay B2
Kälbäcär B2
Länkäran C3
Mingäçevir B2
Nakhichevan A3
Quba C2
Şahbuz A3
Şäki B2

Salyan C3
Sumqayit C2
Tovuz A2
Xaçmaz C2
Xankändi B3
Yevlax B2
Zaqatala B2

Other Features

Abşeron, *peninsula* C2
Aras, *river* B3
Bazardüzü Dağı, *mt.* B2
Caucasus, *range* A1
Karabakh, *canal* B2
Kür, *river* A2, C2
Kür-Aras, *lowland* B2
Lesser Caucasus, *range* B2
Mingäçevir, *reservoir* B2
Nagorno-Karabakh,
autonomous region B2
Samur, *river* B2
Talish, *mts.* C3

© MapQuest.com, Inc.

Estonia:
Map Index

Cities and Towns
Haapsalu B2
Kärdla B1
Keila C1
Kohtla-Järve D1
Kunda D1
Kuressaare B2
Mustvee D2
Narva E1
Paldiski C1
Pärnu C2
Rapla C1
Tallinn, *capital* C1
Tapa C1
Tartu D2
Tõrva C2
Türi C2

Valga D3
Viljandi C2
Virtsu B2
Võru D3

Other Features
Baltic, *sea* A1
Finland, *gulf* C1
Hiiumaa, *island* B2
Irbe, *strait* A3
Munamägi, *mt.* D3
Narva, *river* D1
Pärnu, *river* C2
Pedja, *river* D2
Peipus, *lake* D2
Pskov, *lake* D3
Riga, *gulf* B3
Saaremaa, *island* B2
Võrts Järv, *lake* D2

Estonia
Capital: Tallinn
Area: 17,413 sq. mi.
45,111 sq. km.
Population: 1,409,000
Largest City: Tallinn
Language: Estonian
Monetary Unit: Kroon

Estonia
⊛ National Capital
• Other City
1:7,000,000

0   50   100 mi
0 50 100 km
Lambert Conformal Conic Projection
© MapQuest.com, Inc.

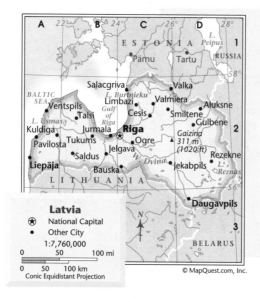

Latvia
Capital: Riga
Area: 24,900 sq. mi.
64,508 sq. km.
Population: 2,354,000
Largest City: Riga
Language: Latvian
Monetary Unit: Lat

Latvia
⊛ National Capital
• Other City
1:7,760,000

0   50   100 mi
0 50 100 km
Conic Equidistant Projection
© MapQuest.com, Inc.

Latvia:
Map Index

Cities and Towns
Aluksne D2
Bauska C2
Cesis C2
Daugavpils D3
Gulbene D2
Jekabpils C2
Jelgava B2
Jurmala B2
Kuldiga A2
Liepāja A2
Limbazi C2
Ogre C2
Pavilosta A2
Rezekne D2
Riga, *capital* C2
Salacgriva C2
Saldus B2
Smiltene C2
Talsi B2
Tukums B2
Valka C2
Valmiera C2
Ventspils A2

Other Features
Baltic, *sea* A2
Burtnieku, *lake* C2
Gaizina, *mt.* C2
Reznas, *lake* D2
Riga, *gulf* B2
Usmas, *lake* B2
Western Dvina, *river* C2

Lithuania
Capital: Vilnius
Area: 25,213 sq. mi.
65,319 sq. km.
Population: 3,585,000
Largest City: Vilnius
Language: Lithuanian
Monetary Unit: Litas

Lithuania
⊛ National Capital
• Other City
1:4,600,000

0   30   60 mi
0 30 60 km
Conic Equidistant Projection

Lithuania:
Map Index

Cities and Towns
Alytus C2
Biržai C1
Druskininkai B2
Jonava C2
Jurbarkas B2
Kaunas B2
Klaipėda A2
Kretinga A2
Kuršėnai B1
Marijampolė B2
Mažeikiai B1
Naujoji Akmenė B1
Palanga A2
Panevėžys B2
Radviliškis B2
Šiauliai B2
Šilalė B2

Šilutė ....A
Tauragė ....B
Telšiai ....B
Ukmergė ....
Utena ....
Vilkaviškis ....
Vilnius, *capital* C

Other Features
Baltic, *sea* ....A
Courland, *lagoon* ....A
Dubysa, *river* ....B
Juozapines, *mt.* ....
Jura, *river* ....A
Merkys, *river* ....
Minija, *river* ....A
Mūša, *river* ....B
Nemunas, *river* ......A2, B
Neris, *river* ....
Nevėžis, *river* ....
Šventoji, *river* ....
Venta, *river* B1

© MapQuest.com, Inc.

Belarus

Map

National Capital (⊛)
Other City (•)

1:8,000,000

0 — 75 — 150 mi
0 — 75 — 150 km

Lambert Conformal Conic Projection

© MapQuest.com, Inc.

Belarus

Capital: Minsk
Area: 80,134 sq. mi.
203,601 sq. km.
Population: 10,402,000
Largest City: Minsk
Languages: Belarussian, Russian
Monetary Unit: Belarus ruble

Belarus:
Map Index

Cities and Towns
Asipovichy...............D3
Babruysk................D3
Baranavichy.............C3
Brest...................A3
Homyel.................E3
Hrodna.................A3
Krychaw................E3
Lida...................B3
Mahilyow...............E3
Maladzyechna...........C2
Mazyr.................D3
Minsk, *capital*.........C3
Orsha.................E2
Pastavy................C2
Pinsk..................C3
Polotsk................D2
Rechytsa...............E3

Salihorsk...............C3
Smilovichi.............D3
Smolevichi.............D2
Vawkavysk.............B3
Vitsyebsk..............E2
Zhlobin...............D3

Other Features
Bug, *river*.............A3
Byarezina, *river*.......D3
Byelaruskaya Hrada, *range*...C3
Dnepr, *river*..........E3
Dnepr-Bug, *canal*......B3
Dzyarzhynskaya Hara, *mt.*....C3
Nyoman, *river*.........B3
Pripyats, *marshes*......C4
Pripyats, *river*........C3
Ptsich, *river*..........D3
Sozh, *river*...........E3
Western Dvina, *river*....D2

Ukraine:
Map Index

Cities and Towns
Balaklava...............C4
Belaya Tserkov.........C2
Berdyansk.............D3
Cherkassy.............C2
Chernigov.............C1
Chernivtsi.............B2
Chornobyl'.............C1
Dneprodzerzhinsk.......D2
Dnipropetrovsk.........D2
Donetsk...............D2
Feodosiya.............D3

Gorlovka...............D2
Ivano-Frankovsk........A2
Izmail.................B3
Kachovka..............C3
Kerch..................D3
Kharkiv................D1
Kherson...............C3
Khmelnytskyy...........B2
Khust.................A2
Kiev, *capital*..........C1
Kirovograd.............C2
Konotop...............C1
Korosten..............B1
Kotovsk................B2
Kovel.................A1

Kramatorsk.............D2
Kremenchug............C2
Kryvyi Rih.............C2
Lisichansk.............D2
Luhansk...............D2
Lutsk..................B1
Lviv...................A2
Makeyevka.............D2
Mariupol..............D3
Melitopol.............D3
Mogilev Podolskiy......B2
Mykolaiv..............C3
Nikopol...............C2
Odesa.................C3
Pervomaysk............C2

Poltava................C2
Priluki.................C1
Rovno.................B1
Sevastopol.............C4
Shostka...............C1
Simferopol............C4
Sumy.................C1
Ternopol..............B2
Uman.................C2
Uzhgorod..............A2
Vinnitsa...............B2
Yalta..................C4
Yevpatoriya............C3
Zaporizhzhia...........D2
Zhitomir..............B1

Other Features
Azov, *sea*............D3
Black, *sea*...........C3
Bug, *river*............A1
Carpathian, *mts.*......A2
Crimean, *mts.*........C4
Crimean, *peninsula*....C3
Desna, *river*.........C1
Dneprodzerzhinsk, *reservoir*...C2
Dnieper, *river*........C1,C3
Dniester, *river*.......B2
Donets, *basin*.........D2
Donets, *river*.........D2
Hoverla, *mt.*.........A2
Kakhovka, *reservoir*....C3

Karkinit, *bay*.........C3
Kerch, *strait*.........D3
Kiev, *reservoir*........C1
Kremenchug, *reservoir*....C2
Pripyat, *river*.........A1
Prut, *river*...........B2
Psel, *river*...........C1
Sluch, *river*..........B1
Southern Bug, *river*....B2
Taganrog, *gulf*........D3
Tisza, *river*..........A2
Volyno-Podol'skaya
Vozvyshennost, *uplands*....B2
Vorskla, *river*........C1

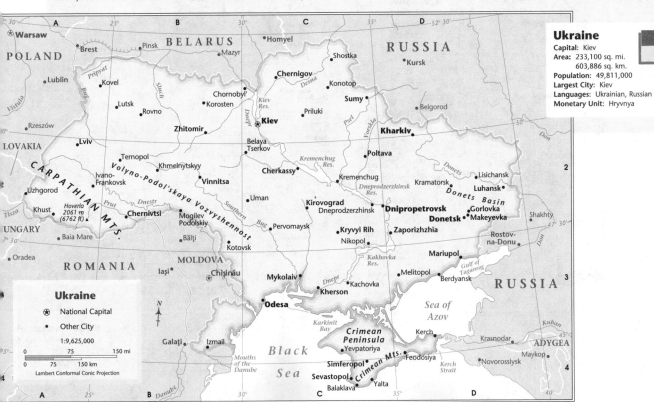

Ukraine

National Capital (⊛)
Other City (•)

1:9,625,000

0 — 75 — 150 mi
0 — 75 — 150 km

Lambert Conformal Conic Projection

MapQuest.com, Inc.

Ukraine

Capital: Kiev
Area: 233,100 sq. mi.
603,886 sq. km.
Population: 49,811,000
Largest City: Kiev
Languages: Ukrainian, Russian
Monetary Unit: Hryvnya

Slovenia

Capital: Ljubljana
Area: 7,821 sq. mi.
20,262 sq. km.
Population: 1,971,000
Largest City: Ljubljana
Languages: Slovenian, Serbo-Croatian
Monetary Unit: Tolar

Slovenia:
Map Index

Cities and Towns

Celje	C2
Idrija	B2
Jesenice	B2
Kočevje	B3
Koper	A3
Kranj	B2
Krško	C3
Ljubljana, *capital*	B2
Maribor	C2
Murska Sobota	D2
Nova Gorica	A3
Novo Mesto	C3
Postojna	B3
Ptuj	C2

Other Features

Adriatic, *sea*	A3
Drava, *river*	C2
Julian Alps, *mts.*	A2
Krka, *river*	B3
Kupa, *river*	B3
Mura, *river*	C2
Sava, *river*	B2
Savinja, *river*	B2
Trieste, *gulf*	A3
Triglav, *mt.*	A2

Slovenia
⊛ National Capital
• Other City
1:5,100,000
0   25   50 mi
0   25   50 km
Lambert Conformal Conic Projection

© MapQuest.com, Inc.

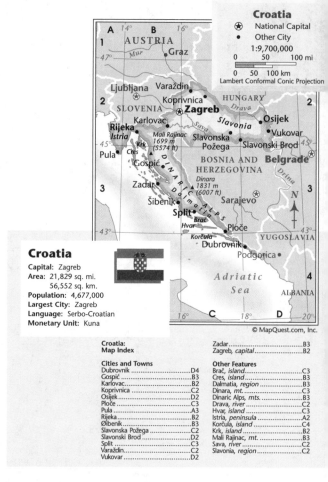

Croatia
⊛ National Capital
• Other City
1:9,700,000
0   50   100 mi
0   50   100 km
Lambert Conformal Conic Projection

© MapQuest.com, Inc.

Croatia

Capital: Zagreb
Area: 21,829 sq. mi.
56,552 sq. km.
Population: 4,677,000
Largest City: Zagreb
Language: Serbo-Croatian
Monetary Unit: Kuna

Croatia:
Map Index

Cities and Towns

Dubrovnik	D4
Gospić	B3
Karlovac	B2
Koprivnica	C2
Osijek	D2
Ploče	C3
Pula	A3
Rijeka	B2
Øibenik	B3
Slavonska Požega	C2
Slavonski Brod	D2
Split	C3
Varaždin	C2
Vukovar	D2
Zadar	B3
Zagreb, *capital*	B2

Other Features

Brač, *island*	C3
Cres, *island*	B3
Dalmatia, *region*	C3
Dinara, *mt.*	C3
Dinaric Alps, *mts.*	B3
Drava, *river*	C2
Hvar, *island*	C3
Istria, *peninsula*	A2
Korčula, *island*	C4
Krk, *island*	B2
Mali Rajinac, *mt.*	B3
Sava, *river*	C2
Slavonia, *region*	C2

Bosnia and Hercegovina:
Map Index

Cities and Towns

Banja Luka	B1
Bihać	A1
Bijeljina	C1
Bosanska Gradiška	B1
Bosanska Krupa	A1
Brčko	B1
Bugojno	B1
Derventa	B1
Doboj	B1
Foča	B2
Gacko	B2
Goražde	B2
Gračanica	B1
Jajce	B1
Livno	B2
Mostar	B2
Pale	B2
Prijedor	A1
Sanski Most	A1
Sarajevo, *capital*	B2
Srebrenica	C1
Teslić	B1
Trebinje	B2
Tuzla	B1
Zavidovići	B1
Zenica	B1
Zvornik	C1

Other Features

Bosna, *river*	B1
Dinara, *mt.*	A2
Dinaric Alps, *mts.*	A1
Drina, *river*	C1
Neretva, *river*	B1
Sava, *river*	B1
Una, *river*	A1
Vrbas, *river*	B1

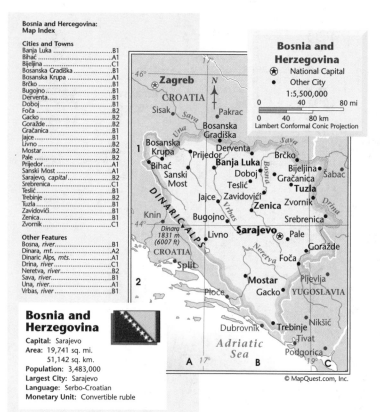

Bosnia and Herzegovina
⊛ National Capital
• Other City
1:5,500,000
0   40   80 mi
0   40   80 km
Lambert Conformal Conic Projection

© MapQuest.com, Inc.

Bosnia and Herzegovina

Capital: Sarajevo
Area: 19,741 sq. mi.
51,142 sq. km.
Population: 3,483,000
Largest City: Sarajevo
Language: Serbo-Croatian
Monetary Unit: Convertible ruble

F.Y.R. Macedonia

Capital: Skopje
Area: 9,928 sq. mi.
25,720 sq. km.
Population: 2,023,000
Largest City: Skopje
Languages: Macedonian, Albanian, Serbo-Croatian, Turkish
Monetary Unit: Denar

F.Y.R. Macedonia:
Map Index

Cities and Towns

Bitola	B2
Blatec	C2
Debar	A2
Gevgelija	C2
Kavadarci	C2
Kičevo	A2
Kočani	C2
Kruševo	B2
Kumanovo	B1
Ohrid	A2
Prilep	B2
Skopje, *capital*	B2
Stip	C2
Struga	A2
Strumica	C2
Tetovo	A1
Titov Veles	B2

Other Features

Belasica, *mts.*	C2
Bregalnica, *river*	C2
Crna, *river*	B2
Crna Gora, *mts.*	B1
Doiran, *lake*	C2
Jakupica, *mts.*	B2
Korab, *mt.*	A2
Kožuf, *mts.*	B2
Nidže, *mts.*	B3
Ogražden, *mts.*	C2
Ohrid, *lake*	A3
Prespa, *lake*	B3
Treska, *river*	B2
Vardar, *river*	C2

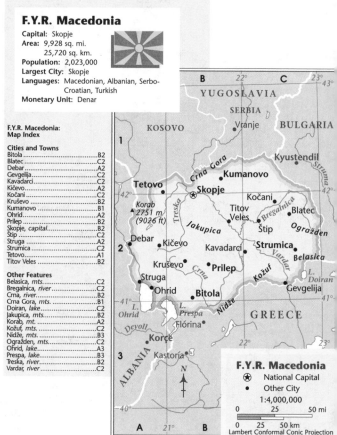

F.Y.R. Macedonia
⊛ National Capital
• Other City
1:4,000,000
0   25   50 mi
0   25   50 km
Lambert Conformal Conic Projection

© MapQuest.com, Inc.

Albania

⊛ National Capital
• Other City

1:3,750,000

0   15   30 mi

0   15   30 km

Lambert Conformal
Conic Projection

Federal Repubic of Yugoslavia

⊛ National Capital
• Other City

1:3,682,000

0   30   60 mi

0   30   60 km

Lambert Conformal Conic Projection

© MapQuest.com, Inc.

Albania:
Map Index

Cities and Towns

Berat	A3
Durrës	A2
Elbasan	B2
Ersekë	B3
Fier	A3
Gjirokastër	B3
Kavajë	A2
Korçë	B3
Krujë	A2
Kukës	B1
Laç	A2
Lushnjë	A3
Peshkopi	B2
Pogradec	B3
Pukë	A1
Sarandë	A4
Shëngjin	A2
Shkodër	A1
Tiranë, capital	A2
Vlorë	A3

Other Features

Adriatic, sea	A2
Buene, river	A2
Devoll, river	B3
Drin, river	A1
Erzen, river	A2
Ionian, sea	A4
Korab, mt.	B2
Mat, river	B2
North Albanian Alps, range	A1
Ohrid, lake	B2
Osum, river	B3
Otranto, strait	A3
Prespa, lake	C3
Scutari, lake	A1
Seman, river	A3
Shkumbin, river	A2
Vijosë, river	A3

Albania

Capital: Tiranë
Area: 11,100 sq. mi.
28,756 sq. km.
Population: 3,365,000
Largest City: Tiranë
Languages: Albanian, Greek
Monetary Unit: Lek

Yugoslavia:
Map Index

Internal Divisions

Kosovo (province)	B3
Montenegro (republic)	A3
Serbia (republic)	B2
Vojvodina (province)	A2

Cities and Towns

Bačka Palanka	A2
Bar	A3
Bečej	A2
Belgrade, capital	C2
Bor	C2
Čačak	B3
Cetinje	A3
Đakovica	B3
Kikinda	B2
Kosovska Mitrovica	B3
Kragujevac	B2
Kraljevo	B3
Kruševac	B3
Leskovac	B3
Nikšić	A3
Niš	B3
Novi Pazar	B3
Novi Sad	A2
Pančevo	B2
Peć	B3
Pirot	C3
Pljevlja	A3
Podgorica	A3

Požarevac	B2
Priboj	A3
Priština	B3
Prizren	B3
Prokuplje	B3
Šabac	A2
Senta	B2
Smederevo	B2
Sombor	A2
Sremska Mitrovica	A2
Subotica	A1
Svetozarevo	B3
Uroševac	B3
Užice	A2
Valjevo	A2
Vranje	B3
Vrbas	A2
Vršac	B2
Zaječar	C3
Zrenjanin	B2

Other Features

Adriatic, sea	A4
Balkan, mts.	C3
Beli Drim, river	B3
Crna Gora, mts.	B3
Danube, river	A2, B2
Đaravica, mt.	B3
Dinaric Alps, mt.	A3
Drina, river	A2
Durmitor, mts.	A3
Fruška Gora, mts.	A2
Ibar, river	B3

Jastrebac, mts.	B3
Južna, river	B3
Kopaonik, mts.	B3
Kotor, gulf	A3
Morava, river	B3
Nišava, river	C3
North Albanian Alps, mts.	B3
Šar Planina, mts.	B3
Sava, river	A2
Scutari, lake	A3
Tara, river	A3
Tisa, river	B2
Velika Morava, river	B2
Veliki, canal	A2
Zapandna Morava, river	B3
Zeta, river	A3
Zlatibor, mts.	A3

Yugoslavia

Capital: Belgrade
Area: 39,449 sq. mi.
102,199 sq. km.
Population: 11,207,000
Largest City: Belgrade
Language: Serbo-Croatian
Monetary Unit: New Yugoslav dinar

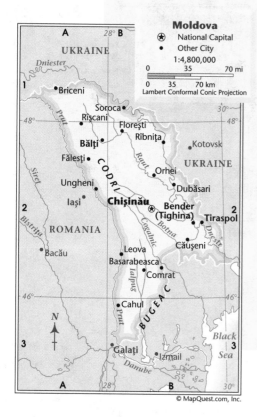

Moldova

★ National Capital
● Other City

1:4,800,000

0 — 35 — 70 mi
0 — 35 — 70 km
Lambert Conformal Conic Projection

© MapQuest.com, Inc.

Moldova

Capital: Chişinău
Area: 13,012 sq. mi.
  33,710 sq. km.
Population: 4,461,000
Largest City: Chişinău
Languages: Moldovan, Russian
Monetary Unit: Moldovan leu

Moldova: Map Index

Cities and Towns

Bălţi A2
Basarabeasca B2
Bender (Tighina) B2
Briceni A1
Cahul B3
Căuşeni B2
Chişinău, capital B2
Comrat B2
Dubăsari B2
Făleşti A2
Floreşti B2
Leova B2
Orhei B2
Rîbniţa B2
Rîşcani A2
Soroca B1
Tiraspol B2
Ungheni A2

Other Features

Botna, river B2
Bugeac, region B3
Codri, region A3
Cogalnic, river B2
Dnestr, river B2
Ialpug, river B2
Prut, river A1, B3
Raut, river B2

Bulgaria: Map Index

Administrative Regions

Burgas E3
Khaskovo D4
Lovech C2
Montana B2
Plovdiv C3
Ruse E2
Sofia City B3
Sofiya B3
Varna F2

Cities and Towns

Asenovgrad C3
Aytos F3
Blagoevgrad B4
Burgas F3
Dimitrovgrad D3
Dobrich F2
Elkhovo E3
Gabrovo D3
Kazanlŭk D3
Khaskovo D4
Kozloduy B2
Kŭrdzhali D4
Kyustendil A3
Lom B2
Lovech C2
Madan C4
Montana B2
Oryakhovo B2
Panagyurishte C3
Pazardzhik C3
Pernik B3
Petrich B4
Pleven C2
Plovdiv C3
Primorsko F3
Razgrad E2
Ruse D2
Samokov B3
Shumen E2
Silistra F1
Sliven E3
Smolyan C4
Sofia, capital B3

Stara Zagora D3
Svilengrad E4
Svishtov D2
Tŭrgovishte E2
Varna F2
Veliko Tŭrnovo D2
Vidin A2
Vratsa B2
Yambol E3

Other Features

Arda, river C4
Balkan, mts. B2
Danube, river B2
Golyama Kamchiya, river E2
Iskŭr, river C2
Kamchiya, river F2
Luda Kamchiya, river E3
Ludogorie, region E2
Maritsa, river D3
Mesta, river B4
Musala, mt. B3
Ogosta, river B2
Osŭm, river C3
Rhodope, mts. C4
Rila, mts. B3
Sredna Gora, mts. C3
Struma, river A3
Stryama, river C3
Thrace, region D4
Thracian, plain C3
Tundzha, river E3
Yantra, river D2

Bulgaria

Capital: Sofia
Area: 42,855 sq. mi.
  111,023 sq. km.
Population: 8,195,000
Largest City: Sofia
Language: Bulgarian
Monetary Unit: Lev

Bulgaria

★ National Capital
● Other City

1:3,210,000

0 — 25 — 50 — 75 mi
0 — 25 — 50 — 75 km
Lambert Conformal Conic Projection

© MapQuest.com, Inc.

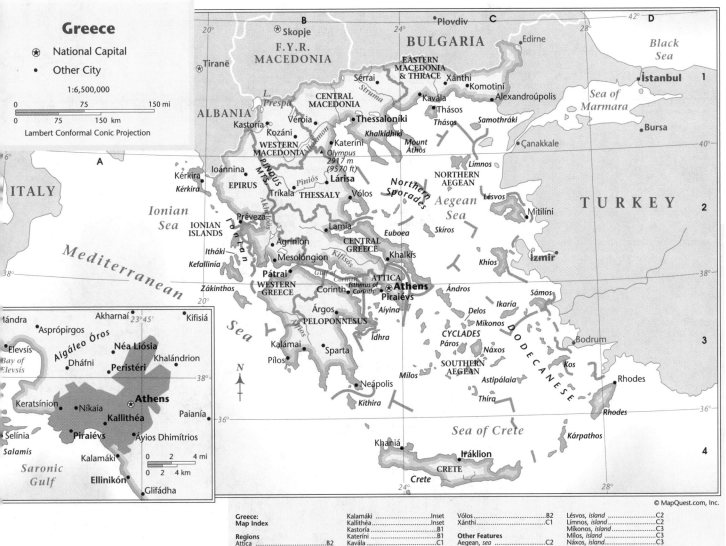

Greece

⊛ National Capital

• Other City

1:6,500,000

0 — 75 — 150 mi
0 — 75 — 150 km
Lambert Conformal Conic Projection

© MapQuest.com, Inc.

Greece:
Map Index

Regions
Attica B2
Central Greece B2
Central Macedonia B1
Crete............................C4
Eastern Macedonia and
   Thrace C1
Epirus B2
Ionian Islands B2
Northern Aegean C2
Peloponnesus B3
Southern Aegean C3
Thessaly......................B2
Western Greece...........B3
Western Macedonia......B1

Cities and Towns
Agrínion B2
Akharnaí ....Inset
Alexandroúpolis C1
Árgos B3
Asprópirgos ....Inset
Athens, *capital* .....B3, Inset
Áyios Dhimítrios ....Inset
Corinth B3
Dháfni ....Inset
Elevsís ....Inset
Ellinikón ....Inset
Glifádha ....Inset
Ioánnina B2
Iráklion C4
Kalámai B3

Kalamáki ....Inset
Kallithéa ....Inset
Kastoría B1
Kateríni B1
Kavála C1
Keratsínion ....Inset
Kérkira A2
Khalándrion ....Inset
Khalkís B2
Khaniá B4
Kifisiá ....Inset
Komotiní C1
Kozáni B1
Lamía B2
Lárisa B2
Mándra ....Inset
Mesolóngion B2
Mitilíni C2
Néa Liósia ....Inset
Neápolis B3
Níkaia ....Inset
Paianía ....Inset
Pátrai B2
Peristéri ....Inset
Pílos B3
Piraiévs ....B3, Inset
Préveza B2
Rhodes D3
Selínia ....Inset
Sérrai B1
Sparta B3
Thásos C1
Thessaloníki B1
Tríkala B2
Véroia B1

Vólos B2
Xánthi C1

Other Features
Aegean, *sea* C2
Aigáleo, *mts.* ....Inset
Aíyina, *island* B3
Akhelóös, *river* B2
Alfíos, *river* B3
Aliákmon, *river* B1
Ándros, *island* C3
Astipálaia, *island* C3
Áthos, *mt.* C1
Corinth, *gulf* B2
Corinth, *isthmus* B3
Crete, *island* C4
Crete, *sea* C4
Cyclades, *islands* C3
Delos, *island* C3
Dodecanese, *islands* ..C3
Elevsís, *bay* ....Inset
Euboea, *island* B2
Idhra, *island* B3
Ikaría, *island* C3
Ionian, *islands* A2
Ionian, *sea.* A2
Itháki, *island* B2
Kárpathos, *island* C4
Kefallínia, *island* B2
Kérkira, *island* A2
Khalkidhikí, *peninsula*....B1
Khíos, *island* C2
Kifissós, *river* B2
Kíthira, *island* B3
Kos, *island* C3

Lésvos, *island* C2
Límnos, *island* C2
Míkonos, *island* C3
Mílos, *island* C3
Náxos, *island* C3
Northern Sporades, *islands*...B2
Olympus, *mt.* B1
Páros, *island* C3
Pindus, *mts.* B2
Piniós, *river* B2
Prespa, *lake* B1
Rhodes, *island* D3
Salamís, *island* ....Inset
Sámos, *island* C3
Samothráki, *island* C1
Saronic, *gulf* ....Inset
Skíros, *island* C2
Struma, *river* B1
Thásos, *island* C1
Thíra, *island* C3
Zákinthos, *island* B3

Greece

Capital: Athens
Area: 50,949 sq. mi.
   131,992 sq. km.
Population: 10,707,000
Largest City: Athens
Language: Greek
Monetary Unit: Drachma

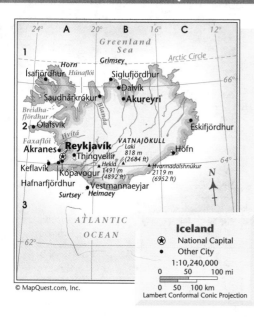

© MapQuest.com, Inc.

Iceland

Capital: Reykjavík
Area: 36,699 sq. mi.
   95,075 sq. km.
Population: 273,000
Largest City: Reykjavík
Language: Icelandic
Monetary Unit: New Icelandic króna

Iceland
⊛ National Capital
• Other City
1:10,240,000
| 0 | 50 | 100 mi |
| 0 | 50 | 100 km |
Lambert Conformal Conic Projection

Iceland:
Map Index

Cities and Towns
Akranes	A2
Akureyri	B2
Dalvík	B2
Eskifjördhur	C2
Hafnarfjördhur	A3
Höfn	C2
Ísafjördhur	A1
Keflavík	A3
Kópavogur	A2
Ólafsvík	A2
Reykjavík, capital	A2
Saudhárkrókur	B2
Siglufjördhur	B1
Thingvellir	A2
Vestmannaeyjar	A3

Other Features
Blanda, river	B2
Breidhafjördhur, fjord	A2
Faxaflói, bay	A2
Greenland, sea	B1
Grímsey, island	B1
Heimaey, island	A3
Hekla, volcano	B3
Horn, cape	A1
Húnaflói, bay	A2
Hvannadalshnúkur, mt.	B3
Hvítá, river	A2
Laki, volcano	B2
Surtsey, island	A3
Vatnajökull, ice cap	B2

Norway

Capital: Oslo
Area: 125,050 sq. mi.
   323,964 sq. km.
Population: 4,439,000
Largest City: Oslo
Language: Norwegian
Monetary Unit: Norwegian krone

Norway:
Map Index

Cities and Towns
Ålesund	B3
Alta	E1
Arendal	B4
Bergen	B3
Bodø	C2
Drammen	C4
Dumbås	B3
Egersund	B4
Florø	A3
Fredrikstad	C4
Gjøvik	C3
Hamar	C3
Hammerfest	E1
Harstad	D2
Haugesund	B4
Kinsarvik	B3
Kirkenes	F2
Kristiansand	B4
Kristiansund	B3
Lakselv	F1
Leikanger	B3
Lillehammer	C3
Mo	C2
Molde	B3
Mosjøen	C2
Moss	C4
Namsos	C3
Narvik	D2
Oslo, capital	C3
Skien	B4
Stavanger	B4
Steinkjer	C3
Tromsø	D2
Trondheim	C3
Vadsø	F1

Other Features
Barents, sea	E1
Boknafjord, fjord	B4
Dovrefjell, mts.	B3
Finnmark, plateau	E2
Glåma, river	C3
Glittertinden, mt.	B3
Hallingdal, valley	B3
Hardangerfjord, fjord	B4
Hardangervidda, plateau	B3
Jotunheimen, mts.	B3
Lofoten, islands	C2
Mjøsa, lake	C3
North, cape	F1
North, sea	A3
Norwegian, sea	A2
Oslofjord, fjord	C4
Skagerrak, strait	B4
Sognafjord, fjord	B3
Tana, river	F1
Trondheimsfjord, fjord	B3
Vesterålen, islands	C2

© MapQuest.com, In.

Finland: Map Index

Internal Divisions

Eastern Finland (province)	C2
Lapland (province)	C1
Oulu (province)	C1
Southern Finland (province)	C2
Western Finland (province)	B2
Central Finland (region)	C2
Central Ostrobothnia (region)	B2
Etelä-Savo (region)	C2
Häme (region)	B2
Itä-Uusimaa (region)	C2
Kainuu (region)	C2
Kymenlaakso (region)	C2
North Karelia (region)	C2
Northern Ostrobothnia (region)	B2
Ostrobothnia (region)	B2
Päijät Häme (region)	C2
Pirkanmaa (region)	B2
Satakunta (region)	B2
Savo (region)	C2
South Karelia (region)	C2
South Ostrobothnia (region)	B2
South-West Finland (region)	B2
Uusimaa (region)	B2

Cities and Towns

Espoo	B2
Hämeenlinna	B2
Hangö	B3
Helsinki, capital	B2
Hyvinkää	B2
Iisalmi	C2
Imatra	C2
Ivalo	C1
Jakobstad	B2
Jämsä	C2
Joensuu	C2
Jyväskylä	C2
Kajaani	C2
Kemi	B1
Kemijärvi	C1
Kokkola	B2
Kolari	B1
Kotka	C2
Kouvola	C2
Kuopio	C2
Lahti	C2
Lappeenranta	C2
Lieksa	D2
Mariehamn (Maarianhamina)	A2
Mikkeli	C2
Muonio	B1
Oulu	C1
Pori	B2
Raahe	B2
Rauma	B2
Rovaniemi	C1
Salo	B2
Savonlinna	C2
Seinäjoki	B2
Tampere	B2
Tornio	B1
Turku	B2
Vaasa	B2
Vantaa	B2
Varkaus	C2
Ylivieska	B2

Other Features

Åland, islands	A2
Baltic, sea	B3
Bothnia, gulf	B2
Finland, gulf	B2
Haltiatunturi, mt.	B1
Iijoki, river	C1
Inari, lake	C1
Kemijoki, river	C1
Kivi, lake	C2
Lapland, region	B1
Lokka, reservoir	C1
Muoniojoki, river	B1
Näsi, lake	B2
Oulu, lake	C2
Oulujoki, river	C1
Ounasjoki, river	B1
Päijänne, lake	C2
Pielinen, lake	C2
Saimaa, lake	C2
Tenojoki, river	C1
Torniojoki, river	C1
Ylikitka, lake	C1

Finland

⊛ National Capital

• Other City

1:10,000,000

0 50 100 150 mi
0 50 100 150 200 km

Lambert Conformal Conic Projection

Finland

Capital: Helsinki
Area: 130,559 sq. mi.
338,236 sq. km.
Population: 5,158,000
Largest City: Helsinki
Languages: Finnish, Swedish
Monetary Unit: Markka, Euro

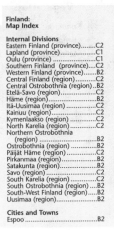

Sweden

⊛ National Capital

• Other City

1:11,333,000

0 50 100 150 mi
0 50 100 150 km

Lambert Conformal Conic Projection

© MapQuest.com, Inc.

Sweden

Capital: Stockholm
Area: 173,732 sq. mi.
450,083 sq. km.
Population: 8,911,000
Largest City: Stockholm
Language: Swedish
Monetary Unit: Krona

Sweden: Map Index

Counties

Älvsborg	B3
Blekinge	C3
Gävleborg	B2
Göteborg och Bohus	B3
Gotland	C3
Halland	B3
Jämtland	B2
Jönköping	B3
Kalmar	C3
Kopparberg	B2
Kristianstad	B3
Kronoberg	B3
Malmöhus	B3
Norrbotten	C1
Örebro	B3
Östergötland	C3
Skaraborg	B3
Södermanland	C3
Stockholm	C3
Uppsala	C2
Värmland	B3
Västerbotten	C2
Västernorrland	C2
Västmanland	C3

Cities and Towns

Borås	B3
Eskilstuna	C3
Falun	B2
Gällivare	D1
Gävle	B3
Göteborg	B3
Halmstad	B3
Haparanda	D1
Härnösand	C2
Helsingborg	B3
Hudiksvall	C2
Jönköping	B3
Kalmar	C3
Karlskrona	C3
Karlstad	B3
Kiruna	D1
Kristianstad	B3
Kristinehamn	B3
Linköping	C3
Luleå	D1
Lund	B3
Malmberget	D1
Malmö	B3
Norrköping	C3
Örebro	C3
Örnsköldsvik	C2
Orrefors	C3
Östersund	B2
Sarjektjakko	D2
Skellefteå	C1
Söderhamn	C2
Stockholm, capital	C3
Sundsvall	C2
Trollhättan	B3
Uddevalla	B3

Umeå	D2
Uppsala	C3
Västerås	C3
Växjö	B3
Visby	C3

Other Features

Ångermanälven, river	C2
Baltic, sea	D2
Bothnia, gulf	D2
Dalälven, river	C2
Faxälven, river	C2
Göta, canal	B3
Gotland, island	C3
Hornavan, lake	C1
Indalsälven, river	B2
Kalixälven, river	C1
Kattegat, strait	B3
Kebnekaise, mt.	C1
Kjölen, mts.	C1
Klarälven, river	B2
Ljusnanälven, river	B2
Luleälven, river	D1
Mälaren, lake	C3
Muonioälven, river	D1
Norra Storfjället, mt.	C1
Öland, island	C3
Öresund, sound	B3
Österdalälven, river	B2
Skagerrak, strait	A3
Skåne, region	B3
Skelleftealven, river	C1
Småland, region	B3
Storavan, lake	C1
Storsjön, lake	B2
Torneälven, river	D1
Uddjaur, lake	C1
Umeälven, river	C2
Vänern, lake	B3
Vättern, lake	B3
Vindelälven, river	C2

MapQuest.com, Inc.

MAJOR CITIES

Algeria
Algiers — 1,483,000
Oran — 590,000
Constantine — 483,000

Angola (metro)
Luanda — 2,081,000

Benin
Cotonou — 402,000
Porto-Novo — 144,000

Botswana
Gaborone — 183,000

Burkina Faso
Ouagadougou — 824,000

Burundi
Bujumbura — 235,440

Cameroon (metro)
Douala — 1,320,000
Yaoundé — 1,119,000

Cape Verde
Praia — 61,000

Central African Republic
Bangui — 474,000

Chad (metro)
N'Djamena — 826,000

Comoros (metro)
Moroni — 30,000

Congo, Democratic Republic of the
Kinshasa — 3,800,000
Lubumbashi — 739,000

Congo, Republic of the
Brazzaville (metro) — 1,004,000

Côte d'Ivoire
Abidjan — 2,793,000
Yamoussoukro — 107,000

Djibouti (metro)
Djibouti — 450,000

Egypt
Cairo — 6,789,000
Alexandria — 3,328,000
Port Said — 470,000
Suez — 418,000

Equatorial Guinea
Malabo — 38,000

Eritrea
Asmara — 358,000

Ethiopia
Addis Ababa — 2,085,000

Gabon
Libreville — 275,000

The Gambia
Banjul — 40,000

Ghana (metro)
Accra — 1,673,000

Guinea (metro)
Conakry — 1,558,000

Guinea-Bissau
Bissau — 138,000

Kenya
Nairobi — 959,000
Mombasa — 401,000

Lesotho
Maseru — 109,000

Liberia (metro)
Monrovia — 962,000

Libya (metro)
Tripoli — 1,682,000

Madagascar (metro)
Antananarivo — 876,000

Malawi
Blantyre — 332,000
Lilongwe — 234,000

Mali
Bamako — 810,000

Mauritania
Nouakchott — 550,000

Mauritius
Port Louis — 146,000

Morocco
Casablanca — 2,943,000
Fez — 564,000
Rabat — 1,220,000

Mozambique (metro)
Maputo — 2,212,000

Namibia
Windhoek — 114,000

Niger
Niamey — 392,000

Nigeria
Lagos — 1,300,000
Ibadan — 1,300,000
Abuja — 250,000

Rwanda
Kigali — 237,000

São Tomé & Príncipe
São Tomé — 43,000

Senegal
Dakar — 1,641,000

Seychelles (metro)
Victoria — 24,000

Sierra Leone
Freetown — 470,000

Somalia
Mogadishu — 997,000

South Africa
Cape Town — 2,350,000
Johannesburg — 1,916,000
Durban — 1,137,000
Pretoria — 1,080,000
Port Elizabeth — 853,000
Bloemfontein — 300,000

Sudan
Omdurman — 1,271,000
Khartoum — 947,000

Swaziland
Mbabane — 38,000

Tanzania (metro)
Dar es-Salaam — 1,747,000

Togo
Lomé — 600,000

Tunisia
Tunis — 674,000

Uganda (metro)
Kampala — 954,000

Western Sahara
el-Aaiún — 90,000

Zambia (metro)
Lusaka — 1,317,000

Zimbabwe (metro)
Harare — 1,410,000

International comparability of city population data is limited by various data inconsistencies.

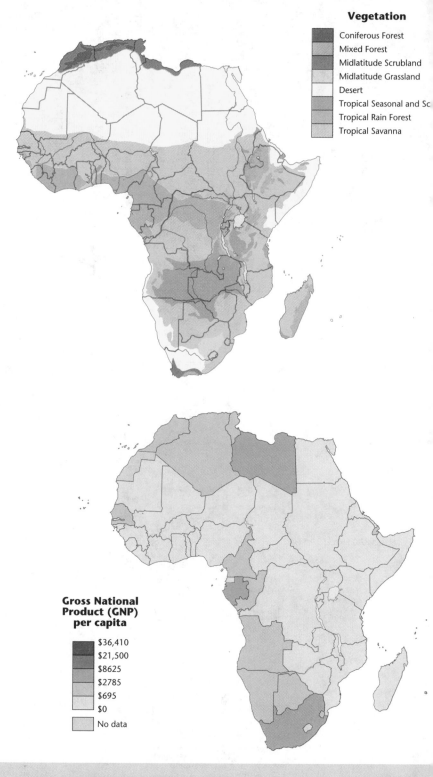

Vegetation

- Coniferous Forest
- Mixed Forest
- Midlatitude Scrubland
- Midlatitude Grassland
- Desert
- Tropical Seasonal and Sc
- Tropical Rain Forest
- Tropical Savanna

Gross National Product (GNP) per capita

- $36,410
- $21,500
- $8625
- $2785
- $695
- $0
- No data

Africa: Population, by nation (in millions)

NIGERIA	EGYPT	ETHIOPIA	CONGO, DEM.REP.	S. AFR.	SUDAN	TANZ.	ALGERIA	MOROC.	KENYA	All other African countries
113.8	67.3	59.7	50.5	43.4	34.5	31.3	31.1	29.7	28.8	288.3

© MapQuest.com, Inc.

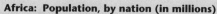

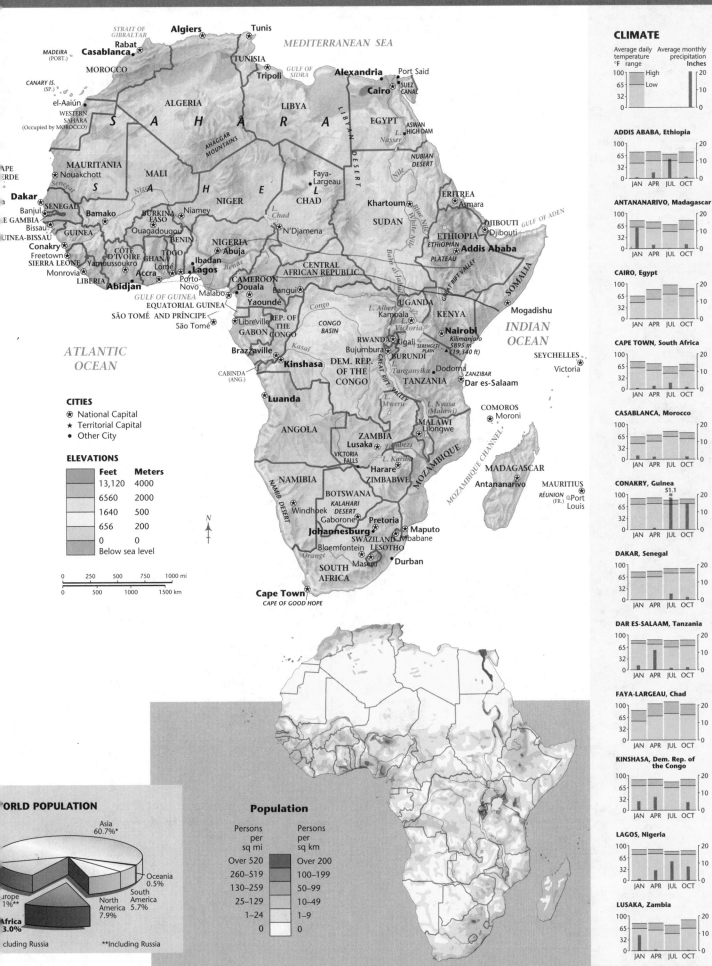

CLIMATE

Average daily temperature °F range — High, Low
Average monthly precipitation Inches

ADDIS ABABA, Ethiopia
ANTANANARIVO, Madagascar
CAIRO, Egypt
CAPE TOWN, South Africa
CASABLANCA, Morocco
CONAKRY, Guinea
DAKAR, Senegal
DAR ES-SALAAM, Tanzania
FAYA-LARGEAU, Chad
KINSHASA, Dem. Rep. of the Congo
LAGOS, Nigeria
LUSAKA, Zambia

CITIES

⊛ National Capital
★ Territorial Capital
• Other City

ELEVATIONS

Feet	Meters
13,120	4000
6560	2000
1640	500
656	200
0	0
Below sea level	

0   250   500   750   1000 mi
0   500   1000   1500 km

N

WORLD POPULATION

Asia 60.7%*
Oceania 0.5%
South America 5.7%
North America 7.9%
Europe 21%**
Africa 13.0%

*Including Russia   **Including Russia

Population

Persons per sq mi	Persons per sq km
Over 520	Over 200
260–519	100–199
130–259	50–99
25–129	10–49
1–24	1–9
0	0

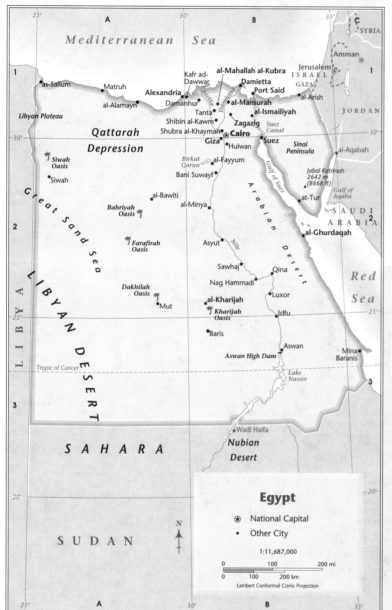

Mediterranean Sea

25° A 30° B 35° C
SYRIA
Amman

as-Sallum
Matruh
al-Alamayn
Libyan Plateau

Qattarah
Depression

Kafr ad-Dawwar
al-Mahallah al-Kubra
Alexandria
Damietta
Damanhur
Port Said
al-Arish
Tanta
al-Mansurah
Shibin al-Kawm
al-Ismailiyah
Shubra al-Khaymah
Zagazig
Cairo
Giza
Hulwan
Suez
Jerusalem
ISRAEL
GAZA
JORDAN
Suez Canal
Sinai Peninsula
al-Aqabah

Birkat Qarun
al-Fayyum
Bani Suwayf

Siwah Oasis
Siwah

Great Sand Sea

Bahriyah Oasis
al-Bawiti
al-Minya

Jabal Katrinah 2642 m (8668 ft)
Gulf of Aqaba
at-Tur
SAUDI ARABIA

al-Ghurdaqah

Farafirah Oasis

Asyut
Qina
Red Sea

Sawhaj
Nag Hammadi

Dakhilah Oasis
Mut
al-Kharijah
Luxor
Kharijah Oasis
Idfu

LIBYA

Baris
Aswan
Mina Baranis

GREAT SAND SEA / LIBYAN DESERT

Tropic of Cancer
Aswan High Dam
Lake Nasser

Wadi Halfa
Nubian Desert

SAHARA

SUDAN

Egypt

- ⊛ National Capital
- • Other City

N

1:11,687,000

0   100   200 mi
0 100 200 km
Lambert Conformal Conic Projection

Egypt

Capital: Cairo
Area: 385,229 sq. mi.
        998,003 sq. km.
Population: 67,273,906
Largest City: Cairo
Language: Arabic
Monetary Unit: Pound

Egypt:
Map Index

Cities and Towns
Alamayn, al-	A1
Alexandria	A1
Arish, al-	B1
Aswan	B3
Asyut	B2
Bani Suwayf	B2
Baris	B3
Bawiti, al-	A2
Cairo, *capital*	B1
Damanhur	B1
Damietta	B1
Fayyum, al-	B2
Ghurdaqah, al-	B2
Giza	B2
Hulwan	B2
Idfu	B3
Ismailiyah, al-	B1
Kafr ad-Dawwar	B1
Kharijah, al-	B2
Luxor	B2
Mahallah al-Kubra, al-	B1
Mansurah, al-	B1
Matruh	A1
Mina Baranis	C3
Minya, al-	B2
Mut	A2
Nag Hammadi	B2
Port Said	B1
Qina	B2
Sallum, as-	A1
Sawhaj	B2
Shibin al-Kawm	B1
Shubra al-Khaymah	B1
Siwah	A2
Suez	B2
Tanta	B1
Tur, at-	B2
Zagazig	B1

Other Features
Aqaba, *gulf*	B2
Arabian, *desert*	B2
Aswan High, *dam*	B3
Bahriyah, *oasis*	A2
Birkat Qarun, *lake*	B2
Dakhilah, *oasis*	A2
Damietta, *river*	B1
Farafirah, *oasis*	A2
Great Sand Sea, *desert*	A2
Jabal Katrinah, *mt.*	B2
Kharijah, *oasis*	B2
Libyan, *desert*	A2
Libyan, *plateau*	A1
Nasser, *lake*	B3
Nile, *river*	B2
Qattarah, *depression*	A2
Red, *sea*	C2
Rosetta, *river*	B1
Sahara, *desert*	A3
Sinai, *peninsula*	B2
Siwah, *oasis*	A2
Suez, *canal*	B1
Suez, *gulf*	B2

© MapQuest.com, Inc.

Libya

Capital: Tripoli
Area: 679,359 sq. mi.
        1,759,997 sq. km.
Population: 4,992,838
Largest City: Tripoli
Language: Arabic
Monetary Unit: Dinar

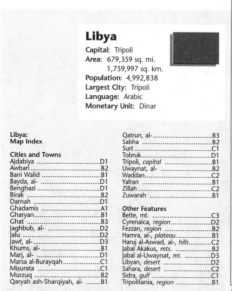

Libya:
Map Index

Cities and Towns
Ajdabiya	D1
Awbari	B2
Bani Walid	B1
Bayda, al-	D1
Benghazi	D1
Birak	B2
Darnah	D1
Ghadamis	A1
Gharyan	B1
Ghat	B3
Jaghbub, al-	D2
Jalu	D2
Jawf, al-	D3
Khums, al-	B1
Marj, al-	D1
Marsa al-Burayqah	C1
Misurata	C1
Murzuq	B2
Qaryah ash-Sharqiyah, al-	B1

Qatrun, al-	B3
Sabha	B2
Surt	C1
Tobruk	D1
Tripoli, *capital*	B1
Uwaynat, al-	B2
Waddan	C2
Yafran	B1
Zillah	C2
Zuwarah	B1

Other Features
Bette, *mt.*	C3
Cyrenaica, *region*	D2
Fezzan, *region*	B2
Hamra, *plateau*	B1
Haruj al-Aswad, al-, *hills*	C2
Jabal Akakus, *mts.*	B2
Jabal al-Uwaynat, *mt.*	D3
Libyan, *desert*	D2
Sahara, *desert*	C2
Sidra, *gulf*	C1
Tripolitania, *region*	B1

Zuwarah
Tripoli
TUNISIA
Gharyan
Yafran
al-Khums
Misurata
Bani Walid
Tripolitania Region
Mediterranean Sea
al-Bayda
al-Marj
Benghazi
Darnah
Tobruk

al-Hamra Plateau
Surt
Gulf of Sidra
Ajdabiya
Ghadamis
al-Qaryah ash-Sharqiyah
Marsa al-Burayqah
al-Jaghbub
Cyrenaica Region

ALGERIA
Waddan
Zillah
Jalu

al-Haruj al-Aswad Hills
Birak
Sabha

Awbari
al-Uwaynat
Murzuq
SAHARA
Fezzan Region
Ghat
Jabal Akakus
al-Qatrun
EGYPT
LIBYAN DESERT
al-Jawf

NIGER
CHAD
Tibesti Massif
Bette 2266 m (7434 ft)
Jabal al-Uwaynat 1907 m (6255 ft)
SUDAN
Tropic of Cancer

Libya

- ⊛ National Capital
- • Other City

1:20,200,000

0   100   200 mi
0 100 200 km
Lambert Conformal Conic Projection

N

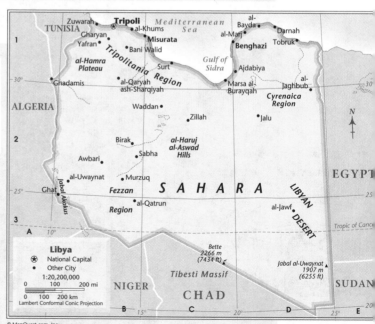

© MapQuest.com, Inc.

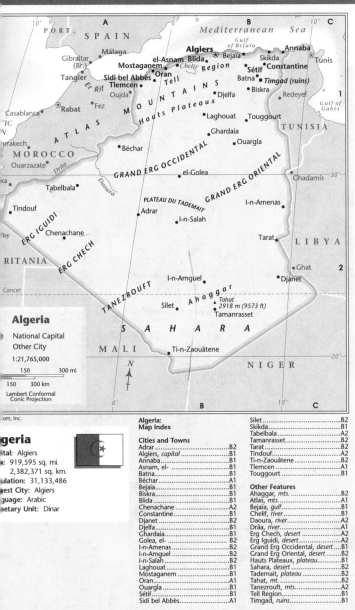

Algeria

⊛ National Capital
• Other City

1:21,765,000

0 — 150 — 300 mi
0 — 150 — 300 km

Lambert Conformal Conic Projection

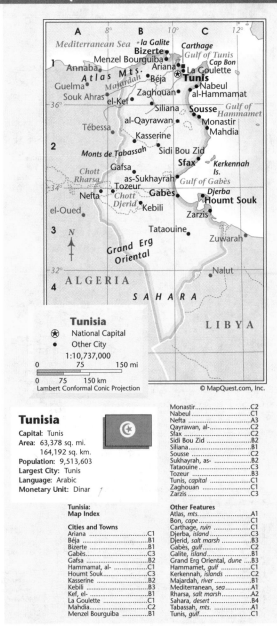

Tunisia

⊛ National Capital
• Other City

1:10,737,000

0 — 75 — 150 mi
0 — 75 — 150 km

Lambert Conformal Conic Projection

© MapQuest.com, Inc.

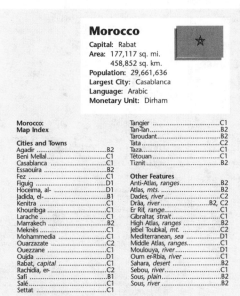

Algeria

Capital: Algiers
Area: 919,595 sq. mi.
2,382,371 sq. km.
Population: 31,133,486
Largest City: Algiers
Language: Arabic
Monetary Unit: Dinar

Algeria:
Map Index

Cities and Towns

Adrar	B2
Algiers, *capital*	B1
Annaba	B1
Batna	B1
Béchar	A1
Bejaïa	B1
Biskra	B1
Blida	B1
Chenachane	A2
Constantine	B1
Djanet	B2
Djelfa	B1
Ghardaia	B1
Golea, el-	B1
I-n-Amenas	B2
I-n-Amguel	B2
I-n-Salah	B2
Laghouat	B1
Mostaganem	B1
Oran	A1
Ouargla	B1
Sétif	B1
Sidi bel Abbès	A1

Silet	B2
Skikda	B1
Tabelbala	A2
Tamanrasset	B2
Tarat	B2
Tindouf	A2
Ti-n-Zaouâtene	B2
Tlemcen	A1
Touggourt	B1

Other Features

Ahaggar, *mts.*	B2
Atlas, *mts.*	A1
Bejaïa, *gulf*	B1
Chelif, *river*	B1
Daoura, *river*	A2
Drâa, *river*	A1
Erg Chech, *desert*	A2
Erg Iguidi, *desert*	A2
Grand Erg Occidental, *desert*	B1
Grand Erg Oriental, *desert*	B1
Hauts Plateaux, *plateau*	B1
Sahara, *desert*	B2
Tademait, *plateau*	B2
Tahat, *mt.*	B2
Tanezrouft, *mts.*	A2
Tell Region	B1
Timgad, *ruins*	B1

Tunisia

Capital: Tunis
Area: 63,378 sq. mi.
164,192 sq. km.
Population: 9,513,603
Largest City: Tunis
Language: Arabic
Monetary Unit: Dinar

Tunisia:
Map Index

Cities and Towns

Ariana	C1
Béja	B1
Bizerte	B1
Gabès	C3
Gafsa	B2
Hammamat, al-	C1
Houmt Souk	C3
Kasserine	B2
Kebili	B3
Kef, el-	B1
La Goulette	C1
Mahdia	C2
Menzel Bourguiba	B1

Monastir	C2
Nabeul	C1
Nefta	A3
Qayrawan, al-	C2
Sfax	C2
Sidi Bou Zid	B2
Siliana	B1
Sousse	C2
Sukhayrah, as-	B2
Tataouine	C3
Tozeur	B3
Tunis, *capital*	C1
Zaghouan	C1
Zarzis	C3

Other Features

Atlas, *mts.*	A1
Bon, *cape*	C1
Carthage, *ruin*	C1
Djerba, *island*	C3
Djerid, *salt marsh*	B3
Gabès, *gulf*	C2
Galite, *island*	B1
Grand Erg Oriental, *dune*	B3
Hammamet, *gulf*	C1
Kerkennah, *islands*	C2
Majardah, *river*	B1
Mediterranean, *sea*	A1
Rharsa, *salt marsh*	A2
Sahara, *desert*	B4
Tabassah, *mts.*	A1
Tunis, *gulf*	C1

Morocco

Capital: Rabat
Area: 177,117 sq. mi.
458,852 sq. km.
Population: 29,661,636
Largest City: Casablanca
Language: Arabic
Monetary Unit: Dirham

Morocco:
Map Index

Cities and Towns

Agadir	B2
Beni Mellal	C1
Casablanca	C1
Essaouira	B2
Fez	C1
Figuig	D1
Hoceima, al-	D1
Jadida, el-	B1
Kenitra	C1
Khouribga	C1
Larache	C1
Marrakech	B2
Meknès	C1
Mohammedia	C1
Ouarzazate	C2
Ouezzane	C1
Oujda	D1
Rabat, *capital*	C1
Rachidia, er-	C2
Safi	B1
Salé	C1
Settat	C1

Tangier	C1
Tan-Tan	B2
Taroudant	B2
Tata	C2
Taza	C1
Tétouan	C1
Tiznit	B2

Other Features

Anti-Atlas, *ranges*	B2
Atlas, *mts.*	B2
Dades, *river*	C2
Drâa, *river*	B2, C2
Er Rif, *range*	C1
Gibraltar, *strait*	C1
High Atlas, *ranges*	B2
Jebel Toubkal, *mt.*	B2
Mediterranean, *sea*	D1
Middle Atlas, *ranges*	C1
Moulouya, *river*	D1
Oum er-Rbia, *river*	B2
Sahara, *desert*	B2
Sebou, *river*	C1
Sous, *plain*	B2
Sous, *river*	B2

Morocco

⊛ National Capital
• Other City

1:13,222,000

0 — 75 — 150 mi
0 — 75 — 150 km

Azimuthal Equal Area Projection

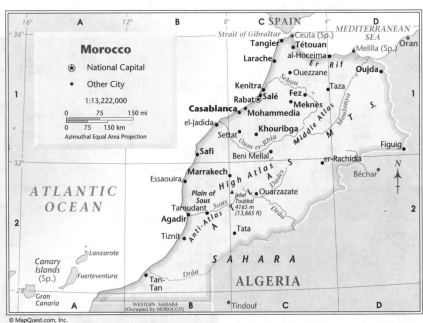

© MapQuest.com, Inc.

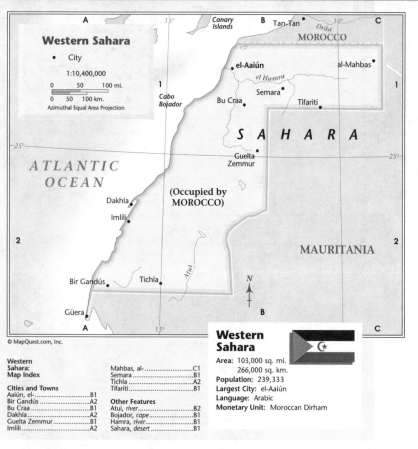

Western Sahara

- City

1:10,400,000

0 50 100 mi.
0 50 100 km.

Azimuthal Equal Area Projection

ATLANTIC OCEAN

(Occupied by MOROCCO)

SAHARA

MOROCCO

MAURITANIA

Tan-Tan
Dráa
el-Aaiún
al-Mahbas
Semara
Tifariti
el Hamra
Bu Craa
Cabo Bojador
Guelta Zemmur
Dakhla
Imlili
Bir Gandús
Tichla
Güera
Atui

© MapQuest.com, Inc.

Western Sahara:
Map Index

Cities and Towns
Aaiún, el- B1
Bir Gandús A2
Bu Craa B1
Dakhla......................A2
Guelta Zemmur B1
Imlili A2

Mahbas, al- C1
Semara B1
Tichla A2
Tifariti B1

Other Features
Atui, river B2
Bojador, cape B1
Hamra, river B1
Sahara, desert B1

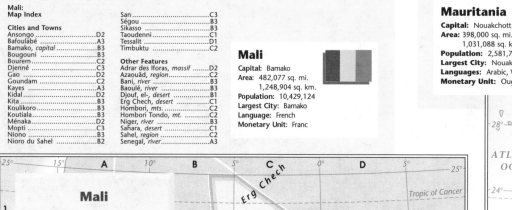

Western Sahara

Area: 103,000 sq. mi.
266,000 sq. km.
Population: 239,333
Largest City: el-Aaiún
Language: Arabic
Monetary Unit: Moroccan Dirham

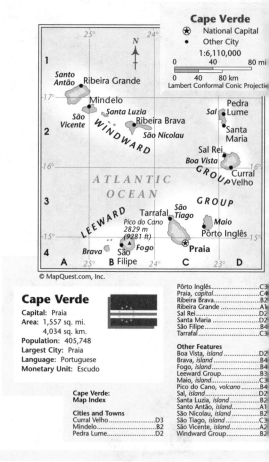

Cape Verde

- ⊛ National Capital
- Other City

1:6,110,000

0 40 80 km
0 40 80 mi

Lambert Conformal Conic Projection

ATLANTIC OCEAN

WINDWARD GROUP
LEEWARD GROUP

Santo Antão
Ribeira Grande
Mindelo
São Vicente
Santa Luzia
Ribeira Brava
São Nicolau
Sal
Pedra Lume
Santa Maria
Sal Rei
Boa Vista
Curral Velho
Tarrafal
São Tiago
Maio
Pôrto Inglês
Pico do Cano 2829 m (9281 ft)
Brava
São Filipe
Fogo
Praia

© MapQuest.com, Inc.

Cape Verde

Capital: Praia
Area: 1,557 sq. mi.
4,034 sq. km.
Population: 405,748
Largest City: Praia
Language: Portuguese
Monetary Unit: Escudo

Cape Verde:
Map Index

Cities and Towns
Curral Velho D3
Mindelo....................B2
Pedra Lume...............D2

Pôrto Inglês..............C3
Praia, capital C4
Ribeira Brava............B2
Ribeira Grande..........A1
Sal Rei......................D2
Santa Maria D2
São Filipe.................B4
Tarrafal C3

Other Features
Boa Vista, island D2
Brava, island B4
Fogo, island B4
Leeward Group..........B3
Maio, island..............D3
Pico do Cano, volcano B4
Sal, island D2
Santa Luzia, island B2
Santo Antão, island ...A1
São Nicolau, island....B2
São Tiago, island C3
São Vicente, island....A2
Windward Group........B2

Mali:
Map Index

Cities and Towns
Ansongo D2
Bafoulabé A3
Bamako, capital B3
Bougouni B3
Bourem.....................C2
Djenné C3
Gao D2
Goundam C2
Kayes A3
Kidal D2
Kita B3
Koulikoro..................B3
Koutiala....................B3
Ménaka D2
Mopti........................C3
Niono B3
Nioro du Sahel B2

San C3
Ségou........................B3
Sikasso B3
Taoudenni C1
Tessalit D1
Timbuktu C2

Other Features
Adrar des Iforas, massif D2
Azaouâd, region C2
Bani, river B3
Baoulé, river B3
Djouf, el-, desert B1
Erg Chech, desert C1
Hombori, mts..............C2
Hombori Tondo, mt......C2
Niger, river B3
Sahara, desert C1
Sahel, region C2
Senegal, river A3

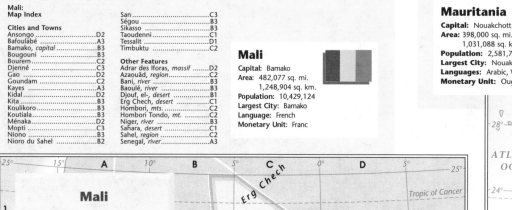

Mali

Capital: Bamako
Area: 482,077 sq. mi.
1,248,904 sq. km.
Population: 10,429,124
Largest City: Bamako
Language: French
Monetary Unit: Franc

Mauritania

Capital: Nouakchott
Area: 398,000 sq. mi.
1,031,088 sq. km.
Population: 2,581,738
Largest City: Nouakchott
Languages: Arabic, Wolof
Monetary Unit: Ouguiya

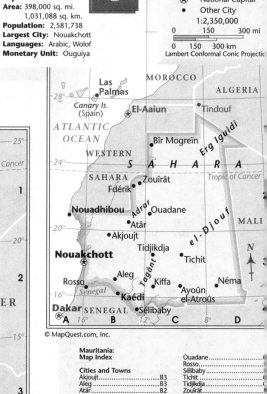

Mauritania

- ⊛ National Capital
- Other City

1:2,350,000

0 150 300 mi
0 150 300 km

Lambert Conformal Conic Projection

MOROCCO
ALGERIA
Las Palmas
Canary Is. (Spain)
El-Aaiun
Tindouf
ATLANTIC OCEAN
WESTERN SAHARA
Bîr Mogreïn
Zouîrât
Fdérik
Nouadhibou
Ouadane
Atâr
Akjoujt
Tropic of Cancer
Erg Iguidi
el-Djouf
MALI
Tidjikdja
Tichit
Nouakchott
Tagânt
Aleg
Kiffa
Rosso
Néma
Senegal
Kaédi
Ayoûn el-Atroûs
Dakar
SENEGAL
Sélibaby

© MapQuest.com, Inc.

Mali

- ⊛ National Capital
- Other City

1:21,265,000

0 200 400 mi
0 200 400 km

Lambert Conformal Conic Projection

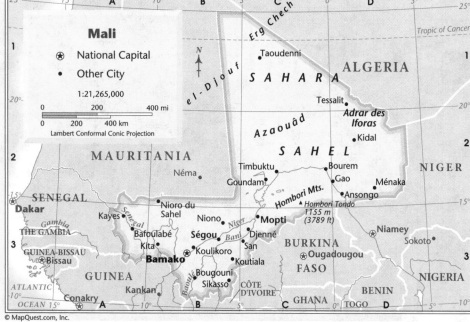

Tropic of Cancer
Erg Chech
el-Djouf
SAHARA
ALGERIA
Taoudenni
Tessalit
Adrar des Iforas
Azaouâd
SAHEL
Kidal
MAURITANIA
Néma
Timbuktu
Bourem
Gao
Goundam
Hombori Mts.
Hombori Tondo 1155 m (3789 ft)
Ménaka
Ansongo
NIGER
Nioro du Sahel
Niono
Niger
Mopti
Djenné
Niamey
Sokoto
SENEGAL
Dakar
Kayes
Gambia
THE GAMBIA
Bafoulabé
Ségou
Bani
Kita
Koulikoro
San
Bamako
Koutiala
BURKINA FASO
GUINEA-BISSAU
Bissau
Bougouní
Sikasso
Ouagadougou
NIGERIA
BENIN
TOGO
GHANA
CÔTE D'IVOIRE
GUINEA
Baoulé
Kankan
ATLANTIC OCEAN
Conakry

© MapQuest.com, Inc.

Mauritania:
Map Index

Cities and Towns
Akjoujt B3
Aleg B3
Atâr B2
Ayoûn el-Atroûs C3
Bîr Mogreïn C1
Fdérik.......................B2
Kaédi........................B3
Kiffa C3
Néma D3
Nouadhibou A2
Nouakchott, capital ...A3

Ouadane....................B2
Rosso........................A3
Sélibaby....................B3
Tichit........................C3
Tidjikdja C3
Zouîrât B2

Other Features
Adrar, region B2
Djouf, el-, desert C2
Erg Iguidi, desert C1
Sahara, desert C1
Senegal, river A3
Tagânt, region C3

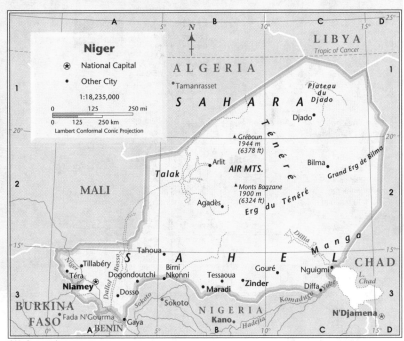

Niger:
Map Index

Cities and Towns
Agadès B2
Arlit B2
Bilma C2
Birni Nkonni B3
Diffa C3
Djado C1
Dogondoutchi A3
Dosso A3
Gaya A3
Gouré C3
Maradi B3
Nguigmi C3
Niamey, *capital* A3
Tahoua A3
Téra A3
Tessaoua B3
Tillabéry A3
Zinder B3

Other Features
Air, *mts.* B2
Bagzane, *mt.* B2
Chad, *lake* C3
Dallol Bosso, *river* A3
Dillia, *river* C2
Djado, *plateau* C1
Erg du Ténéré, *desert* B2
Grand Erg de Bilma,
 desert C2
Gréboun, *mt.* B1
Komadugu Yobe, *river* ...C3
Manga, *region* C2
Niger, *river* A3
Sahara, *desert* A1
Sahel, *region* A3
Talak, *region* B2
Ténéré, *desert* C1

Niger

Capital: Niamey
Area: 497,000 sq. mi.
 1,287,565 sq. km.
Population: 9,962,242
Largest City: Niamey
Language: French
Monetary Unit: CFA franc

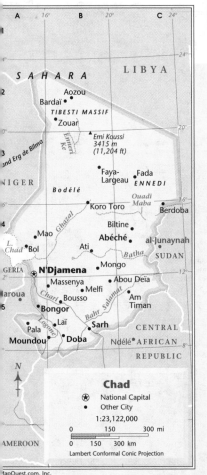

Chad

Capital: N'Djamena
Area: 495,755 sq. mi.
 1,248,339 sq. km.
Population: 7,557,436
Largest City: N'Djamena
Languages: French, Arabic
Monetary Unit: CFA franc

Chad:
Map Index

Cities and Towns
...béché C4
...bou Deïa B5
...m Timan C5
...ozou B2
...ardaï B2
...erdoba C4
...iltine A4
...ol A5
...ongor A5
...ousso A5
...oba A5
...da C3
...aya-Largeau B4
...oro Toro B4
...ao A4
...assenya B5
...iongo B5
...elfi B4
...ongo B5
...oundou B5
...'Djamena, *capital* A4
...arh B5
...ouar B2

Other Features
Bahr Salamat, *river* B5
Batha, *river* C4
Bodélé, *depression* B3
Chad, *lake* A4
Chari, *river* A5
Emi Koussi, *mt.* B3
Ennedi, *plateau* C3
Enneri Ke, *river* B3
Ghazal, *river* B4
Grand Erg de Bilma,
 desert A3
Logone, *river* A5
Ouadi Maba, *river* C4
Sahara, *desert* A2
Tibesti, *massif* B2

Sudan:
Map Index

Cities and Towns
Atbarah C2
Babanusah B3
Damazin, ad- C3
Dunqulah C1
Fashir, al- D1
Halaib D1
Juba C4
Junaynah, al- A2
Kaduqli B3
Kassala D2
Khartoum, *capital* C2
Khartoum North C2
Khashm al-Qirbah C2
Kuraymah C1
Kusti C2
Malakal C3
Nuhud, an- B2
Nyala B2
Omdurman C2
Pibor Post C3
Port Sudan D1
Qadarif, al- C2
Rumbek B3
Sannar C2
Ubayyid, al- C2
Wadi Halfa C1
Wad Madani C2
Waw B3
Yambio B4

Other Features
Akobo, *river* C3
Atbarah, *river* C2
Bahr al-Arab, *river* B3
Bahr al-Ghazal, *river* C3
Bahr al-Jabal, *river* C3
Blue Nile, *river* C2
Kangen, *river* C3
Kinyeti, *mt.* C4
Libyan, *desert* B1
Lol, *river* B3
Nasser, *lake* C1
Nile, *river* C1, C2
Nuba, *mts.* B3
Nubian, *desert* C1
Red, *sea* D1
Red Sea, *hills* D1
Sobat, *river* C3
Sudd, *region* B3
Sue, *river* B3
Wadi al-Malik, *river* B2
Wadi Howar, *river* B2
White Nile, *river* C3

Sudan

Capital: Khartoum
Area: 966,757 sq. mi.
 2,530,459 sq. km.
Population: 34,475,690
Largest City: Khartoum
Language: Arabic
Monetary Unit: Pound

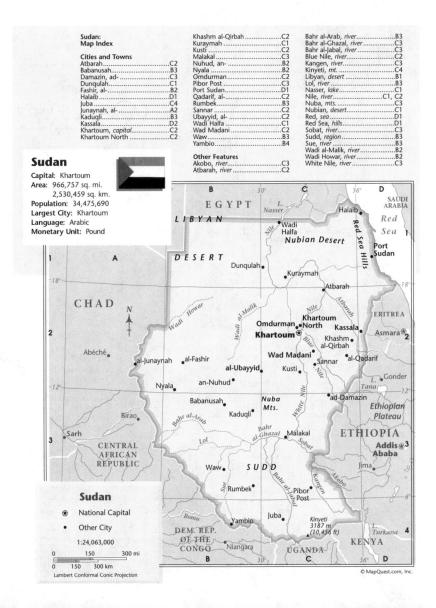

© MapQuest.com, Inc.

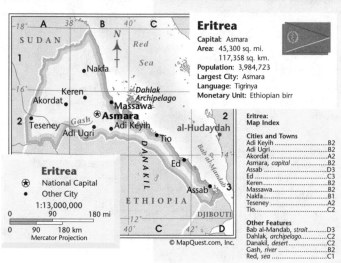

Eritrea

Capital: Asmara
Area: 45,300 sq. mi.
117,358 sq. km.
Population: 3,984,723
Largest City: Asmara
Language: Tigrinya
Monetary Unit: Ethiopian birr

Eritrea

⊛ National Capital
• Other City
1:13,000,000
0   90   180 mi
0   90   180 km
Mercator Projection

Eritrea: Map Index

Cities and Towns
Adi Keyih B2
Adi Ugri B2
Akordat A2
Asmara, capital B2
Assab D3
Ed C3
Keren B2
Massawa B2
Nakfa B1
Teseney A2
Tio C2

Other Features
Bab al-Mandab, strait D3
Dahlak, archipelago C2
Danakil, desert C2
Gash, river B2
Red, sea C1

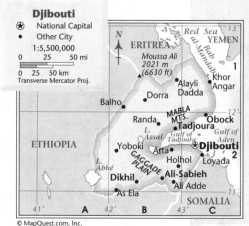

Djibouti

⊛ National Capital
• Other City
1:5,500,000
0   25   50 mi
0   25   50 km
Transverse Mercator Proj.

Djibouti: Map Index

Cities and Towns
Alayli Dadda ....
Ali Adde ....
Ali-Sabieh ....
Arta ....
As Ela ....
Balho ....
Dikhil ....
Djibouti, capital ......
Dorra ....
Holhol ....
Khor Angar ....
Loyada ....
Obock ....
Randa ....
Tadjoura ....
Yoboki ....

Other Features
Abhé, lake ....
Aden, gulf ....
Assal, lake ....
Bab al-Mandab, strait ..
Gaggade, plain ....
Mabla, mts. ....
Moussa Ali, mt. ......
Red, sea ....
Tadjoura, gulf ....

Djibouti

Capital: Djibouti
Area: 8,950 sq. mi.
23,187 sq. km.
Population: 447,439
Largest City: Djibouti
Languages: Cushitic languages
Monetary Unit: Franc

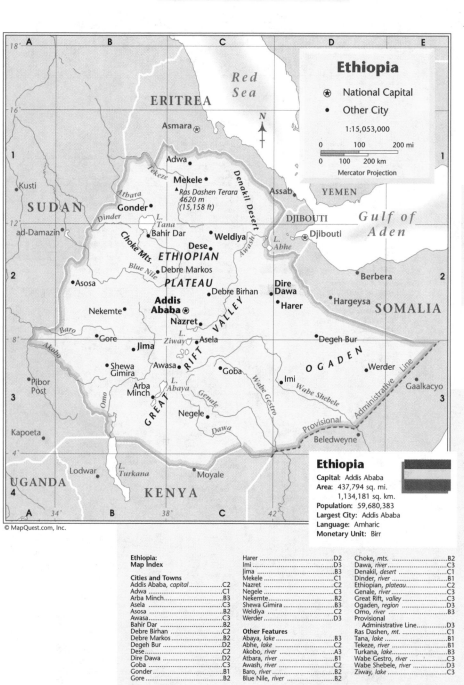

Ethiopia

⊛ National Capital
• Other City
1:15,053,000
0   100   200 mi
0   100   200 km
Mercator Projection

Somalia: Map Index

Cities and Towns
Baraawe A3
Baydhabo A3
Beledweyne B3
Benderbeyla C2
Berbera B1
Boosaaso B1
Burco ....
Ceerigaabo ....
Dhuusamareeb ....
Eyl ....
Gaalkacyo ....
Garoowe ....
Hargeysa ....
Hobyo ....
Jamaame ....
Jawhar ....
Jilib ....
Kismayu ....
Luuq ....
Marka ....
Mogadishu, capital ....
Qardho ....
Xuddur ....

Other Features
Aden, gulf ....
Gees Gwardafuy, cape ..
Juba, river ....
Nugaal, valley ....
Raas Xaafun, cape .....
Surud Ad, mt. ....
Webi Shabeelle, river ..

Somalia

Capital: Mogadishu
Area: 246,300 sq. mi.
638,083 sq. km.
Population: 7,140,643
Largest City: Mogadishu
Language: Somali, Arabic
Monetary Unit: Shilling

Ethiopia

Capital: Addis Ababa
Area: 437,794 sq. mi.
1,134,181 sq. km.
Population: 59,680,383
Largest City: Addis Ababa
Language: Amharic
Monetary Unit: Birr

Ethiopia: Map Index

Cities and Towns
Addis Ababa, capital C2
Adwa C1
Arba Minch B3
Asela C3
Asosa B2
Awasa C3
Bahir Dar B2
Debre Birhan C2
Debre Markos B2
Degeh Bur D2
Dese C2
Dire Dawa D2
Goba C3
Gonder B1
Gore B2

Harer D2
Imi D3
Jima B3
Mekele C1
Nazret C2
Negele C3
Nekemte B2
Shewa Gimira B3
Weldiya C2
Werder D3

Other Features
Abaya, lake B3
Abhe, lake D2
Akobo, river A3
Atbara, river B1
Awash, river C2
Baro, river B3
Blue Nile, river B2
Choke, mts. B2
Dawa, river C3
Denakil, desert C1
Dinder, river B1
Ethiopian, plateau C2
Genale, river C3
Great Rift, valley C3
Ogaden, region D3
Omo, river B3
Provisional
  Administrative Line ...D3
Ras Dashen, mt. C1
Tana, lake B1
Tekeze, river B1
Turkana, lake B3
Wabe Gestro, river D3
Wabe Shebele, river ...D3
Ziway, lake C3

Somalia

⊛ National Capital
• Other City
1:22,100,000
0   150   300 mi
0   150   300 km
Miller Cylindrical Projection

© MapQuest.com, Inc.

Kenya

Capital: Nairobi
Area: 224,961 sq. mi.
582,801 sq. km.
Population: 28,808,658
Largest City: Nairobi
Language: Swahili, English
Monetary Unit: Shilling

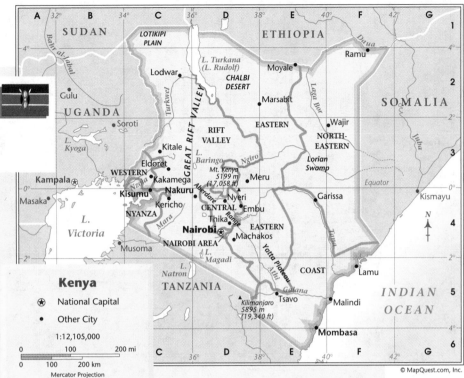

Kenya:
Map Index

Provinces
Central D4
Coast E5
Eastern E3
Nairobi Area D4
North-Eastern F3
Nyanza C4
Rift Valley D3
Western C3

Cities and Towns
Eldoret C3
Embu D4
Garissa E4
Kakamega C3
Kericho C4
Kisumu C4
Kitale C3
Lamu F5
Lodwar C2
Machakos D4
Malindi F5
Marsabit E2
Meru D3
Mombasa E5
Moyale E2

Nairobi, *capital* D4
Nakuru D4
Nyeri D4
Ramu F2
Thika D4
Tsavo E5
Wajir F3

Other Features
Aberdare, *range* D4
Athi, *river* E5
Baringo, *lake* D3
Chalbi, *desert* D2
Daua, *river* F1
Galana, *river* E5
Great Rift, *valley* C3
Kenya, *mt.* D4
Laga Bor, *river* E2
Lorian, *swamp* E3
Lotikipi, *plain* C1
Magadi, *lake* D4
Mara, *river* C4
Ngiro, *river* D3
Nzoia, *river* C3
Tana, *river* F4
Turkana (Rudolf), *lake* D2
Turkwel, *river* C2
Victoria, *lake* B4
Yatta, *plateau* E5

Kenya

⊛ National Capital

• Other City

1:12,105,000

0   100   200 mi
0   100   200 km
Mercator Projection

© MapQuest.com, Inc.

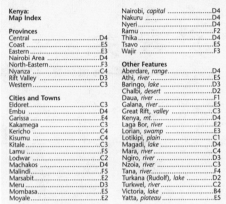

Uganda

Capital: Kampala
Area: 93,070 sq. mi.
241,114 sq. km.
Population: 22,804,973
Largest City: Kampala
Language: English
Monetary Unit: Shilling

Uganda:
Map Index

Cities and Towns
Arua B2
Atiak C2
Entebbe C3
Fort Portal B3
Gulu C2
Jinja C3
Kabale A4
Kampala, *capital* C3
Kitgum C2
Lira C2
Loyoro C2
Masaka B4
Masindi B3
Mbale D3
Mbarara B4
Moroto D2

Mubende B3
Soroti C3
Tororo D3

Other Features
Achwa, *river* C2
Albert, *lake* B3
Albert Nile, *river* B2
Bahr al-Jabal, *river* B2
Edward, *lake* A4
Elgon, *mt.* D3
George, *lake* B4
Kafu, *river* B3
Kagera, *river* B4
Kyoga, *lake* C3
Margherita, *peak* A3
Ruwenzori, *range* B3
Sese, *islands* C4
Victoria, *lake* C4
Victoria Nile, *river* B2,C3

Uganda

⊛ National Capital

• Other City

1:11,600,000

0   75   150 mi
0   75   150 km
Mercator Projection

© MapQuest.com, Inc.

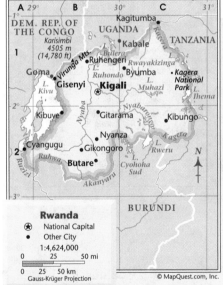

Rwanda

⊛ National Capital

• Other City

1:4,624,000

0   25   50 mi
0   25   50 km
Gauss-Krüger Projection

© MapQuest.com, Inc.

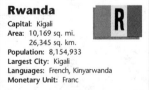

Rwanda

Capital: Kigali
Area: 10,169 sq. mi.
26,345 sq. km.
Population: 8,154,933
Largest City: Kigali
Languages: French, Kinyarwanda
Monetary Unit: Franc

Rwanda:
Map Index

Cities and Towns
Butare B2
Byumba C1
Cyangugu A2
Gikongoro B2
Gisenyi B1
Gitarama B2
Kagitumba C1
Kibungo C2
Kibuye B2
Kigali, *capital* B1
Nyanza B2
Ruhengeri B1

Bulera, *lake* B1
Cyohoha Sud, *lake* C2
Ihema, *lake* C1
Kagera National Park C1
Kagera, *river* C1, C2
Karisimbi, *mt.* B1
Kivu, *lake* B1
Muhazi, *lake* C1
Nyaba, *river* B2
Nyabarongo, *river* C2
Ruhondo, *lake* B1
Ruhwa, *river* B2
Ruzizi, *river* A2
Rwayakizinga, *lake* C1
Rweru, *lake* C2
Virunga, *mts.* B1

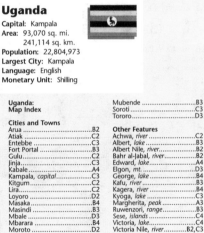

Burundi

⊛ National Capital

• Other City

1:6,548,000

0   50   100 mi
0   50   100 km
Conic Equidistant Projection

© MapQuest.com, Inc.

Burundi

Capital: Bujumbura
Area: 10,740 sq. mi.
27,824 sq. km.
Population: 5,735,937
Largest City: Bujumbura
Languages: French, Kirundi
Monetary Unit: Franc

Burundi:
Map Index

Cities and Towns
Bubanza B2
Bujumbura, *capital* B2
Bururi C2
Cankuzo C2
Gitega B2
Karuzi B2
Makamba B3
Muramvya B2
Muyinga C1
Ngozi B1

Rutana B2
Ruyigi C2

Other Features
Heha, *mt.* B2
Kagera, *river* C1
Malagarasi, *river* C2
Ruvubu, *river* C2
Ruzizi, *river* A1
Tanganyika, *lake* B2

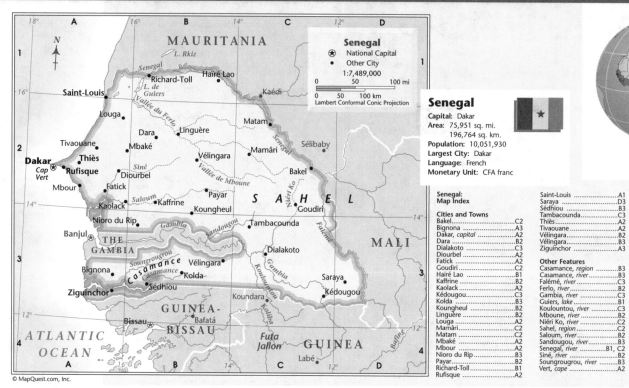

Senegal

Capital: Dakar
Area: 75,951 sq. mi.
196,764 sq. km.
Population: 10,051,930
Largest City: Dakar
Language: French
Monetary Unit: CFA franc

Senegal: Map Index

Cities and Towns

Bakel	C2
Bignona	A3
Dakar, capital	A2
Dara	B2
Dialakoto	C3
Diourbel	A2
Fatick	A2
Goudiri	C2
Hairé Lao	B1
Kaffrine	B2
Kaolack	A2
Kédougou	C3
Kolda	B3
Koungheul	B2
Linguère	B2
Louga	A2
Mamâri	C2
Matam	C2
Mbaké	A2
Mbour	A2
Nioro du Rip	B3
Payar	B2
Richard-Toll	B1
Rufisque	A2
Saint-Louis	A1
Saraya	D3
Sédhiou	B3
Tambacounda	C3
Thiès	A2
Tivaouane	A2
Vélingara	B2
Vélingara	B3
Ziguinchor	A3

Other Features

Casamance, region	B3
Casamance, river	B3
Falémé, river	C3
Ferlo, river	B2
Gambia, river	C3
Guiers, lake	B1
Kouloutou, river	C3
Mboune, river	B2
Niéri Ko, river	C2
Sahel, region	C2
Saloum, river	B2
Sandougou, river	B3
Senegal, river	B1, C2
Siné, river	B2
Soungrougrou, river	B3
Vert, cape	A2

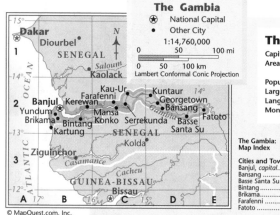

The Gambia

Capital: Banjul
Area: 4,127 sq. mi.
10,692 sq. km.
Population: 1,336,320
Largest City: Banjul
Language: English
Monetary Unit: Dalasi

The Gambia: Map Index

Cities and Towns

Banjul, capital	B2
Bansang	D2
Basse Santa Su	D2
Bintang	B2
Brikama	B2
Farafenni	C2
Fatoto	E2
Georgetown	D2
Kartung	B2
Kau-Ur	C2
Kerewan	B2
Kuntaur	D2
Mansa Konko	C2
Serrekunda	B2
Yundum	B2

Other Feature

Gambia, river	D2

Guinea-Bissau

Capital: Bissau
Area: 13,948 sq. mi.
36,135 sq. km.
Population: 1,234,555
Largest City: Bissau
Language: Portuguese
Monetary Unit: CFA franc

Guinea-Bissau: Map Index

Cities and Towns

Bafatá	C1
Bambadinca	C1
Barro	B1
Bissau, capital	B2
Bissorã	B1
Bolama	B2
Buba	C2
Bubaque	B2
Bula	B1
Cacheu	A1
Cacine	B2
Canchungo	A1
Catió	B2
Farim	B1
Fulacunda	B2
Gabú	C1
Ondame	B2
Pirada	C1
Quebo	C2
Quinhámel	B2
São Domingos	A1

Other Features

Bijagós, islands	A2
Cacheu, river	B1
Corubal, river	D1
Gêba, river	C1

Guinea: Map Index

Cities and Towns

Beyla	D3
Conakry, capital	B3
Coyah	B3
Dabola	C2
Fria	B2
Guéckédou	C3
Kailahun	C3
Kali	C1
Kamsar	A2
Kankan	D2
Kérouané	D3
Kindia	B2
Kissidougou	C3
Kouroussa	D2
Labé	B2
Lélouma	B2
Macenta	D3
Mamou	B2
Niagassola	D1
Nzérékoré	D4
Siguiri	D2
Tougué	C2
Yomou	D4

Other Features

Bafing, river	C2
Futa Jallon, plateau	B1
Gambia, river	B2
Los, islands	A3
Milo, river	D3
Niger, river	C2
Nimba, mts.	D4
Tinkissa, river	C2

Guinea

Capital: Conakry
Area: 94,926 sq. mi.
245,922 sq. km.
Population: 7,538,953
Largest City: Conakry
Language: French
Monetary Unit: Guinea franc

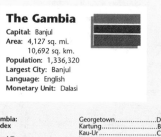

© MapQuest.com, Inc.

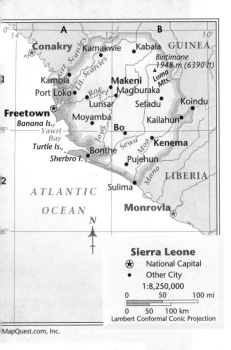

Côte d'Ivoire (Ivory Coast)

⊛ National Capital
• Other City
1:9,789,000

| 0 | 75 | 150 mi |
| 0 | 75 | 150 km |

Lambert Conformal Conic Projection

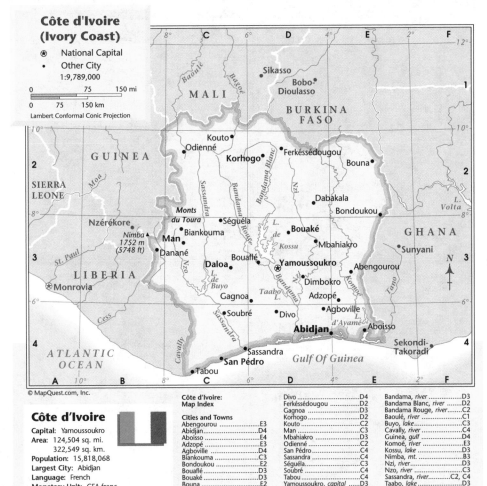

© MapQuest.com, Inc.

Sierra Leone

⊛ National Capital
• Other City
1:8,250,000

| 0 | 50 | 100 mi |
| 0 | 50 | 100 km |

Lambert Conformal Conic Projection

MapQuest.com, Inc.

Sierra Leone

Capital: Freetown
Area: 27,699 sq. mi.
71,759 sq. km.
Population: 5,296,651
Largest City: Freetown
Language: English
Monetary Unit: Leone

**Sierra Leone:
Map Index**

Cities and Towns

...o	B2
...onthe	A2
...eetown, capital	A1
...abala	B1
...ilahun	B1
...amakwie	A1
...mbia	A1
...nema	B2
...oindu	B1
...nsar	A1
...agburaka	B1
...akeni	B1
...oyamba	A1
...rt Loko	A1

Pujehun	B2
Sefadu	B1
Sulima	B2

Other Features

Banana, islands	A1
Bintimane, mt.	B1
Great Scarcies, river	A1
Jong, river	A2
Little Scarcies, river	A1
Loma, mts.	B1
Mano, river	B2
Moa, river	B2
Rokel, river	A1
Sewa, river	B2
Sherbro, island	A2
Turtle, islands	A2
Yawri, bay	A2

Côte d'Ivoire

Capital: Yamoussoukro
Area: 124,504 sq. mi.
322,549 sq. km.
Population: 15,818,068
Largest City: Abidjan
Language: French
Monetary Unit: CFA franc

**Côte d'Ivoire:
Map Index**

Cities and Towns

Abengourou	E3
Abidjan	D4
Aboisso	E4
Adzopé	E3
Agboville	D4
Biankouma	C3
Bondoukou	E2
Bouaflé	D3
Bouaké	D3
Bouna	E2
Dabakala	D2
Daloa	C3
Danané	B3
Dimbokro	D3

Divo	D4
Ferkéssédougou	D2
Gagnoa	D3
Korhogo	D2
Kouto	C2
Man	C3
Mbahiakro	D3
Odienné	C2
San Pédro	C4
Sassandra	C4
Séguéla	C3
Soubré	C4
Tabou	C4
Yamoussoukro, capital	D3

Other Features

Ayamé, lake	E4
Bagoé, river	C1

Bandama, river	D3
Bandama Blanc, river	D2
Bandama Rouge, river	C2
Baoulé, river	C1
Buyo, lake	C3
Cavally, river	C4
Guinea, gulf	D4
Komoé, river	E3
Kossu, lake	D3
Nimba, mt.	B3
Nzi, river	D3
Nzo, river	C3
Sassandra, river	C2, C4
Taabo, lake	D3
Tano, river	E3
Toura, mts.	C2

Liberia

Capital: Monrovia
Area: 38,250 sq. mi.
99,093 sq. km.
Population: 2,923,725
Largest City: Monrovia
Language: English
Monetary Unit: Dollar

**Liberia:
Map Index**

Cities and Towns

Buchanan	A3
Gbarnga	B2
Grand Cess	B3
Greenville	B3
Harbel	A2
Harper	C3
Kakata	A2
Monrovia, capital	A2
Nyaake	C3
Plibo	C3
River Cess	B3
Robertsport	A2
Tapeta	B2
Tubmanburg	B1
Voinjama	B1
Yekepa	B2
Zorzor	B2
Zwedru	B2

Other Features

Bomi, hills	A2
Bong, range	A2
Cavalla, river	C3
Cess, river	B3
Dube, river	C3
Makona, river	A1
Mano, river	A2
Mesurado, cape	A2
Moro, river	A2
Nimba, mts.	B2
Palmas, cape	C3
Putu, range	B3
St. Paul, river	A2
Wutivi, mt.	B1

São Tomé & Príncipe

Capital: São Tomé
Area: 386 sq. mi.
1,000 sq. km.
Population: 154,878
Largest City: São Tomé
Language: Portuguese
Monetary Unit: Dobra

**São Tomé
& Príncipe:
Map Index**

Cities and Towns

...ou	B4
...Neves	B4
...Porto Alegre	B4
...São Tomé, capital	B4
...undi	B1
...Terreiro Velho	C1

Other Features

...Príncipe, island	C1
...São Tomé, island	B4
...São Tomé, mt.	B4

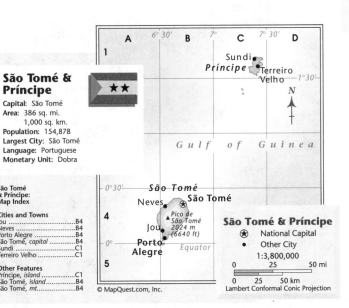

São Tomé & Príncipe

⊛ National Capital
• Other City
1:3,800,000

| 0 | 25 | 50 mi |
| 0 | 25 | 50 km |

Lambert Conformal Conic Projection

© MapQuest.com, Inc.

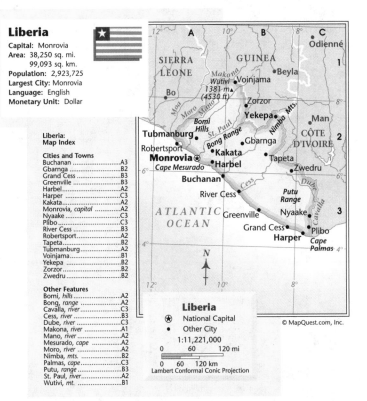

Liberia

⊛ National Capital
• Other City
1:11,221,000

| 0 | 60 | 120 mi |
| 0 | 60 | 120 km |

Lambert Conformal Conic Projection

© MapQuest.com, Inc.

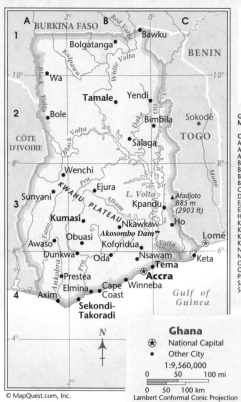

Ghana

Capital: Accra
Area: 92,098 sq. mi.
238,596 sq. km.
Population: 18,887,626
Largest City: Accra
Language: English
Monetary Unit: Cedi

Ghana:
Map Index

Cities and Towns
Accra, *capital* B4
Awaso A3
Axim A4
Bawku B1
Bimbila C2
Bole A2
Bolgatanga B1
Cape Coast B4
Dunkwa B4
Ejura B3
Elmina B4
Ho C3
Keta C4
Koforidua B3
Kpandu C3
Kumasi B3
Nkawkaw B3
Nsawam B4
Obuasi B3
Oda B4
Prestea A4
Salaga B2
Sekondi-Takoradi B4

Sunyani A3
Tamale B2
Tema C4
Wa...................................A1
Wenchi A3
Winneba B4
Yendi B2

Other Features
Afadjoto, *mt.* C3
Afram, *river* B3
Akosombo, *dam* C3
Ankobra, *river* A4
Black Volta, *river* A2
Daka, *river* B2
Guinea, *gulf* C4
Kulpawn, *river* B1
Kwahu, *plateau* B3
Oti, *river* C2
Pra, *river* B3
Pru, *river* B3
Red Volta, *river* B1
Tano, *river* A3
Volta, *lake* C3
Volta, *river* C3
White Volta, *river* B1

Ghana

⊛ National Capital
● Other City

1:9,560,000

0   50   100 mi

0   50   100 km

Lambert Conformal Conic Projection

© MapQuest.com, Inc.

Burkina Faso

⊛ National Capital
● Other City

1:14,785,000

0   100   200 mi

0   100   200 km

Lambert Conformal Conic Projection

© MapQuest.com, Inc.

Burkina Faso

Capital: Ouagadougou
Area: 105,946 sq. mi.
274,472 sq. km.
Population: 11,575,898
Largest City: Ouagadougou
Language: French
Monetary Unit: CFA franc

Burkina Faso:
Map Index

Cities and Towns
Bobo-Dioulasso..................B3
Dédougou.........................C2
Dori..................................D1
Gaoua..............................C3
Koudougou........................C2
Léo..................................C3
Ouagadougou, *capital* D2
Ouahigouya.......................D2
Tenkodogo........................D3

Other Features
Black Volta, *river* B3
Red Volta, *river* D3
Sirba, *river* D3
Téna Kourou, *mt.* B3
White Volta, *river*..............D2

Benin

⊛ National Capital
● Other City

1:14,800,000

0   100   200 mi

0   100   200 km

Lambert Conformal Conic Projection

© MapQuest.com, Inc.

Benin

Capital: Porto-Novo
Area: 43,500 sq. mi.
112,694 sq. km.
Population: 6,305,567
Largest City: Cotonou
Language: French
Monetary Unit: CFA franc

Benin:
Map Index

Cities and Towns
Abomey A4
Bassila A3
Cotonou B4
Djougou A3
Kandi B2
Lokossa A4
Malanville B2
Natitingou A2
Nikki B3
Ouidah B4
Parakou B3
Pobé B4

Porto-Novo, *capital*............B4
Savalou A3
Savé B3
Segbana B2
Tchaourou B3

Other Features
Alibori, *river* B2
Chaîne de l'Atacora, *mts.* ..A2
Couffo, *river* B4
Guinea, *gulf* A4
Mékrou, *river* B2
Mono, *river* A4
Niger, *river* B1
Ouémé, *river* B3
Sota, *river* B2

Togo

Capital: Lomé
Area: 21,925 sq. mi.
56,801 sq. km.
Population: 5,081,413
Largest City: Lomé
Language: French
Monetary Unit: CFA franc

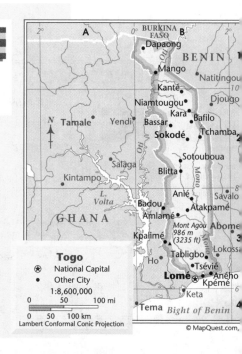

Togo:
Map Index

Cities and Towns
Amlamé B3
Aného B3
Anié B3
Atakpamé B3
Badou B3
Bafilo B2
Bassar B2
Blitta B2
Dapaong B1
Kanté B2
Kara B2
Kpalimé B3
Kpémé B3
Lomé, *capital* B3
Mango B1
Niamtougou B2
Sokodé B2
Sotouboua B2
Tabligbo B3
Tchamba B2
Tsévié B3

Other Features
Agou, *mt.* B3
Benin, *bight* B4
Mono, *river* B2
Oti, *river* B1

Togo

⊛ National Capital
● Other City

1:8,600,000

0   50   100 mi

0   50   100 km

Lambert Conformal Conic Projection

© MapQuest.com, Inc.

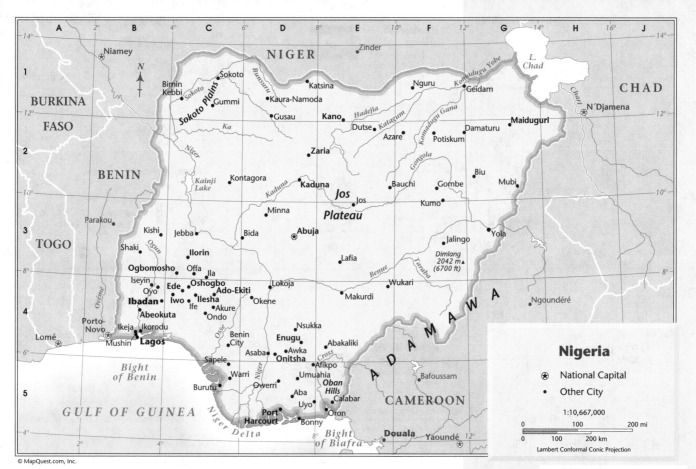

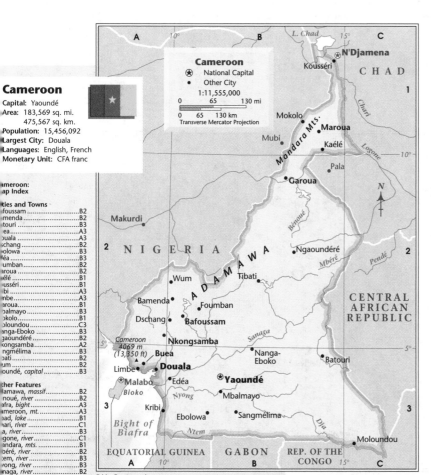

© MapQuest.com, Inc.

Cameroon

Capital: Yaoundé
Area: 183,569 sq. mi.
475,567 sq. km.
Population: 15,456,092
Languages: English, French
Monetary Unit: CFA franc

Cameroon:
Map Index

Cities and Towns

...foussam	B2
...amenda	B2
...atouri	B3
...ea	A3
...ouala	A3
...schang	B2
...olowa	B3
...éa	B2
...umban	B2
...aroua	B1
...élé	B1
...usséri	B1
...bi	A3
...mbe	A3
...aroua	B1
...almayo	B3
...okolo	B1
...oloundou	C3
...anga-Eboko	B3
...gaoundéré	B2
...kongsamba	A2
...oati	B2
...um	B1
...oundé, capital	B3

...ther Features

...damawa, massif	B2
...noué, river	B3
...afra, bight	A3
...ameroon, mt.	A3
...ad, lake	B1
...ari, river	C1
...a, river	B3
...gone, river	C1
...andara, mts.	B1
...béré, river	B3
...em, river	B3
...yong, river	B3
...anaga, river	B2

Nigeria

Capital: Abuja
Area: 356,669 sq. mi.
924,013 sq. km.
Population: 113,828,587
Largest City: Lagos
Language: English
Monetary Unit: Naira

Nigeria:
Map Index

Cities and Towns

Aba	D5
Abakaliki	E4
Abeokuta	B4
Abuja, *capital*	D3
Ado-Ekiti	C4
Afikpo	D5
Akure	C4
Asaba	D4
Awka	D4
Azare	F2
Bauchi	E2
Benin City	C4
Bida	D3
Birnin Kebbi	C1
Biu	G2
Bonny	D5
Burutu	C5
Calabar	E5
Damaturu	F2
Dutse	E2
Ede	C4
Enugu	D4
Geidam	F1
Gombe	F2
Gummi	C1
Gusau	D1
Ibadan	B4
Ife	C4
Ikeja	B4
Ikorodu	B4
Ila	C3
Ilesha	C4
Ilorin	C3
Iseyin	B4
Iwo	C4
Jalingo	F3
Jebba	C3
Jos	E3
Kaduna	D2
Kano	E1
Katsina	D1
Kaura-Namoda	D1
Kishi	B3
Kontagora	C2
Kumo	F2
Lafia	E3
Lagos	B4
Lokoja	D4
Maiduguri	G2

Makurdi	E4
Minna	D3
Mubi	G2
Mushin	B4
Nguru	F1
Nsukka	D4
Offa	C3
Ogbomosho	C3
Okene	D4
Ondo	C4
Onitsha	D4
Oron	E5
Oshogbo	C4
Owerri	D5
Oyo	B4
Port Harcourt	D5
Potiskum	F2
Sapele	C5
Shaki	B3
Sokoto	C1
Umuahia	D5
Uyo	D5
Warri	C5
Wukari	E4
Yola	G3
Zaria	D2

Other Features

Adamawa, *massif*	E5
Benin, *bight*	B5
Benue, *river*	E3
Bunsuru, *river*	D1
Chad, *lake*	G1
Cross, *river*	E4
Dimlang, *mt.*	F3
Gongola, *river*	F2
Guinea, *gulf*	B5
Hadejia, *river*	E1
Jos, *plateau*	E2
Ka, *river*	C2
Kaduna, *river*	D2
Kainji, *lake*	C2
Katagum, *river*	E2
Komadugu Gana, *river*	F2
Komadugu Yobe, *river*	F1
Niger, *delta*	C5
Niger, *river*	C2, D5
Oban, *hills*	E5
Ogun, *river*	B3
Osse, *river*	C4
Sokoto, *plains*	C1
Sokoto, *river*	C1
Taraba, *river*	F3

Equatorial Guinea
⊛ National Capital
• Other City
1:6,250,000
0   40   80 mi
0   40   80 km
Transverse Mercator Projection

© MapQuest.com, Inc.

Equatorial Guinea

Capital: Malabo
Area: 10,831 sq. mi.
28,060 sq. km.
Population: 465,746
Largest City: Malabo
Language: Spanish
Monetary Unit: CFA franc

Equatorial Guinea:
Map Index

Cities and Towns
Aconibe C3
Akurenam C3
Añisoc C3
Bata B3
Calatrava B3
Ebebiyín D2
Evinayong C3
Luba A1
Malabo, *capital* A1
Mbini B3
Mikomeseng C2
Mongomo D3

Niefang C3
Nsok D3
Riaba A1

Other Features
Abia, *river* C3
Biafra, *bight* B1
Bioko, *island* A1
Corisco, *bay* B4
Corisco, *island* B3
Elobey, *islands* B3
Guinea, *gulf* A3
Mbini, *river* C3
Mboro, *river* D4
San Juan, *cape* B3
Santa Isabel, *peak* ...A1

Gabon

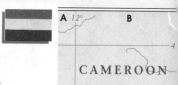

Capital: Libreville
Area: 103,347 sq. mi.
267,738 sq. km.
Population: 1,225,853
Largest City: Libreville
Language: French
Monetary Unit: CFA franc

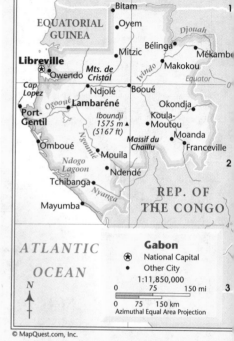

Gabon
⊛ National Capital
• Other City
1:11,850,000
0   75   150 mi
0   75   150 km
Azimuthal Equal Area Projection

© MapQuest.com, Inc.

Gabon:
Map Index

Cities and Towns
Bélinga B1
Bitam A1
Booué A2
Franceville B2
Koula-Moutou B2
Lambaréné A2
Libreville, *capital* ...A1
Makokou B1
Mayumba A2
Mékambo B1
Mitzic A1
Moanda B2
Mouila A2
Ndendé A2
Ndjolé A2

Okondja B2
Omboué A2
Owendo A1
Oyem A1
Port-Gentil A2
Tchibanga A2

Other Features
Chaillu, *mts.* B2
Cristal, *mts.* A1
Djouah, *river* B1
Iboundji, *mt.* A2
Ivindo, *river* B1
Lopez, *cape* A2
Ndogo, *lagoon* A2
Ngounié, *river* A2
Nyanga, *river* A2
Ogooué, *river* A2

Republic of the Congo

⊛ National Capital
• Other City
1:18,000,000
0   100   200 mi
0   100   200 km
Azimuthal Equal Area Projection

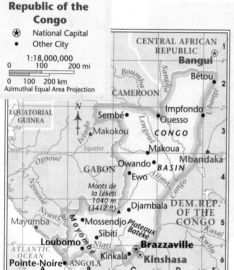

© MapQuest.com, Inc.

Republic of the Congo

Capital: Brazzaville
Area: 132,047 sq. mi.
342,091 sq. km.
Population: 2,716,814
Largest City: Brazzaville
Language: French
Monetary Unit: CFA franc

Republic of the Congo:
Map Index

Cities and Towns
Bétou E2
Brazzaville, *capital* ..C6
Djambala C5
Ewo C4
Impfondo D3
Kinkala C6
Loubomo B6
Makoua C4
Mossendjo B5
Ouesso C3
Owando C4
Pointe-Noire A6

Sembé C3
Sibiti B5

Other Features
Alima, *river* E2
Batéké, *plateau* C5
Congo, *basin* D3
Congo, *river* D4
Ivindo, *river* B3
Lékéti, *mts.* C5
Lengoué, *river* A1
Mayombé, *massif* B5
Niari, *river* B5
Nyanga, *river* A5
Sangha, *river* D2
Ubangi, *river* E2

Central African Republic (C.A.R.)

Capital: Bangui
Area: 240,324 sq. mi.
622,601 sq. km.
Population: 3,444,951
Largest City: Bangui
Language: French
Monetary Unit: CFA franc

Central African Republic:
Map Index

Cities and Towns
Bambari B2
Bangassou B3
Bangui, *capital* A3
Batangafo A2
Berbérati A3
Birao B1
Bossangoa A2
Bouar A2
Bria B2
Kaga Bandoro A2
Mobaye B3
Ndélé B2
Nola A3
Obo C2
Yalinga B2

Other Features
Chari, *river* A2
Chinko, *river* B2
Gribingui, *river* A2
Kadei, *river* A3
Kotto, *river* B2
Lobaye, *river* A2
Mambéré, *river* A2
Massif des Bongos, *range* B2
Mpoko, *river* A2
Ouaka, *river* B2
Ouarra, *river* C2
Ouham, *river* A2
Pendé, *river* A2
Toussoro, *mt.* B2
Ubangi, *river* A3

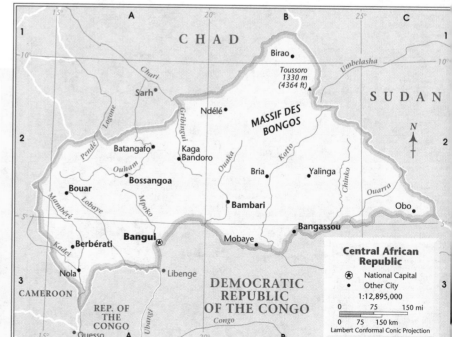

© MapQuest.com, Inc.

Central African Republic
⊛ National Capital
• Other City
1:12,895,000
0   75   150 mi
0   75   150 km
Lambert Conformal Conic Projection

Democratic Republic of the Congo

Capital: Kinshasa
Area: 905,446 sq. mi.
2,345,715 sq. km.
Population: 50,481,305
Largest City: Kinshasa
Language: French
Monetary Unit: Congolese franc

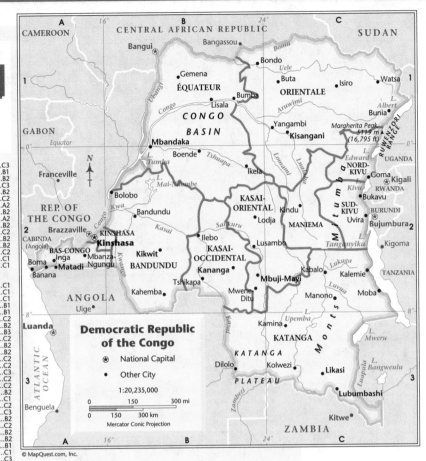

Democratic Republic of the Congo

⊛ National Capital
• Other City

1:20,235,000

0   150   300 mi
0 150 300 km
Mercator Conic Projection

© MapQuest.com, Inc.

Democratic Republic of the Congo:
Map Index

Regions
Bandundu B2
Bas-Congo A2
Équateur B1
Kasai-Occidental B2
Kasai-Oriental B2
Katanga C3
Kinshasa B2
Maniema C2
Nord-Kivu C2
Orientale C1
Sud-Kivu C2

Cities and Towns
Banana A2
Bandundu B2
Boende B2
Bolobo B2
Boma A2
Bondo B1
Bukavu C2
Bumba B1
Bunia C1
Buta C1
Dilolo B3
Gemena B1
Goma C2
Ikela B2
Ilebo B2
Inga A2
Isiro C1
Kabalo C2
Kahemba B2
Kalemie C3
Kamina C3
Kananga B2
Kikwit B2
Kindu C2
Kinshasa, capital A2
Kisangani C1
Kolwezi C3

Likasi C3
Lisala B1
Lodja B2
Lubumbashi C3
Lusambo B2
Manono C2
Matadi A2
Mbandaka B2
Mbanza-Ngungu A2
Mbuji-Mayi B2
Moba C2
Mwene-Ditu B2
Tshikapa B2
Uvira C2
Watsa C1
Yangambi C1

Other Features
Albert, lake C1
Aruwimi, river C1
Bomu, river B1
Congo, river B1
Congo Basin, region B1
Edward, lake C2
Kasai, river B2
Katanga, plateau B3
Kivu, lake C2
Kwa, river B2
Kwango, river B2
Lomami, river C2
Lualaba, river C2
Luapula, river C3
Lukuga, river C2
Luvua, river C2
Mai-Ndombe, lake B2
Margherita, peak C1
Mitumba, mts. C2
Mweru, lake C3
Sankuru, river B2
Tanganyika, lake C2
Tshuapa, river B2
Tumba, lake B2
Ubangi, river B1
Uele, river C1
Upemba, lake C3

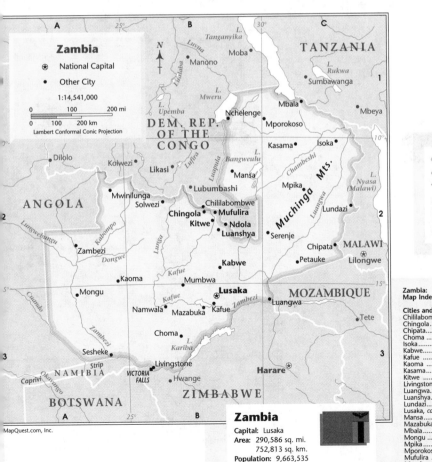

Zambia

⊛ National Capital
• Other City

1:14,541,000

0   100   200 mi
0 100 200 km
Lambert Conformal Conic Projection

MapQuest.com, Inc.

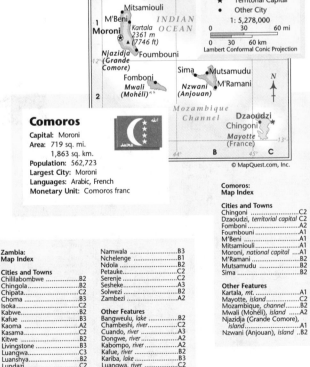

Comoros

⊛ National Capital
★ Territorial Capital
• Other City

1:5,278,000

0   30   60 mi
0 30 60 km
Lambert Conformal Conic Projection

© MapQuest.com, Inc.

Comoros

Capital: Moroni
Area: 719 sq. mi.
1,863 sq. km.
Population: 562,723
Largest City: Moroni
Languages: Arabic, French
Monetary Unit: Comoros franc

Comoros:
Map Index

Cities and Towns
Chingoni C2
Dzaoudzi, territorial capital C2
Fomboni A2
Foumbouni A1
M'Beni A1
Mitsamiouli A1
Moroni, national capital .. A1
M'Ramani B2
Mutsamudu B2
Sima B2

Other Features
Kartala, mt. A1
Mayotte, island C2
Mozambique, channel B2
Mwali (Mohéli), island A2
Njazidja (Grande Comore),
island A1
Nzwani (Anjouan), island .. B2

Zambia

Capital: Lusaka
Area: 290,586 sq. mi.
752,813 sq. km.
Population: 9,663,535
Largest City: Lusaka
Language: English
Monetary Unit: Kwacha

Zambia:
Map Index

Cities and Towns
Chililabombwe B2
Chingola B2
Chipata C2
Choma B3
Isoka C2
Kabwe B2
Kafue B3
Kaoma A2
Kasama C2
Kitwe B2
Livingstone B3
Luangwa C3
Luanshya B2
Lundazi C2
Lusaka, capital B3
Mansa B2
Mazabuka B3
Mbala C1
Mongu A3
Mpika C2
Mporokoso B1
Mufulira B2
Mumbwa B3
Mwinilunga A2

Namwala B3
Nchelenge B1
Ndola B2
Petauke C2
Serenje C2
Sesheke A3
Solwezi B2
Zambezi A2

Other Features
Bangweulu, lake B2
Chambeshi, river C2
Cuando, river A3
Dongwe, river A2
Kabompo, river A2
Kafue, river B2
Kariba, lake B3
Luangwa, river B2
Luapula, river B2
Lunga, river B2
Lungwebungu, river A2
Luvua, river B1
Muchinga, mts. C2
Mweru, lake B1
Tanganyika, lake C1
Victoria, falls B3
Zambezi, river A3, B3

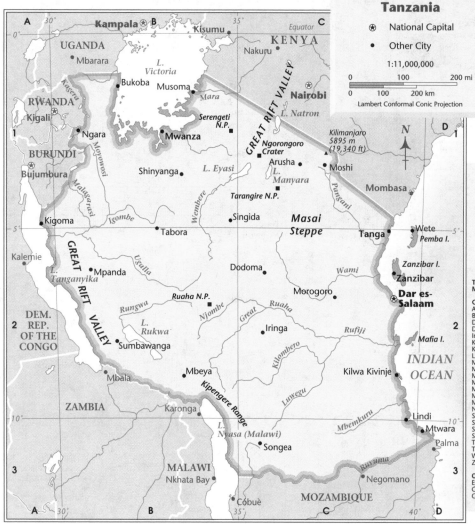

Tanzania

⊛ National Capital

• Other City

1:11,000,000

| 0 | 100 | 200 mi |
| 0 | 100 | 200 km |

Lambert Conformal Conic Projection

Tanzania

Capital: Dar es-Salaam
Area: 364,017 sq. mi.
943,049 sq. km.
Population: 31,270,820
Largest City: Dar es-Salaam
Languages: Swahili, English
Monetary Unit: Shilling

Tanzania:
Map Index

Cities and Towns
Arusha C1
Bukoba B1
Dar es-Salaam, *capital* C2
Dodoma C2
Iringa C2
Kigoma A1
Kilwa Kivinje C2
Lindi C2
Mbeya B2
Morogoro C2
Moshi C1
Mpanda B2
Mtwara D3
Musoma B1
Mwanza B1
Ngara B1
Shinyanga B1
Singida B1
Songea C3
Sumbawanga B2
Tabora B2
Tanga C2
Wete C2
Zanzibar C2

Other Features
Eyasi, *lake* B1
Great Rift, *valley* B2, C1
Great Ruaha, *river* C2

Igombe, *river* B1
Kagera, *river* B1
Kilimanjaro, *mt.* C1
Kilombero, *river* C2
Kipengere, *range* B2
Luwegu, *river* C2
Mafia, *island* C2
Malagarasi, *river* B1
Manyara, *lake* C1
Mara, *river* B1
Masai, *steppe* C1
Mbemkuru, *river* C3
Moyowosi, *river* B1
Natron, *lake* C1
Ngorongoro, *crater* C1
Njombe, *river* B2
Nyasa (Malawi), *lake* B3
Pangani, *river* C1
Pemba, *island* C2
Ruaha Natl. Park B2
Rufiji, *river* C2
Rukwa, *lake* B2
Rungwa, *river* B2
Ruvuma, *river* C3
Serengeti Natl. Park B1
Tanganyika, *lake* A2
Tarangire Natl. Park C1
Ugalla, *river* B2
Victoria, *lake* B1
Wami, *river* B1
Wembere, *river* B1
Zanzibar, *island* C2

© MapQuest.com, Inc.

Malawi

Capital: Lilongwe
Area: 45,747 sq. mi.
118,516 sq. km.
Population: 10,000,416
Largest City: Blantyre
Languages: English, Chichewa
Monetary Unit: Kwacha

Mozambique

Capital: Maputo
Area: 313,661 sq. mi.
812,593 sq. km.
Population: 19,124,335.
Largest City: Maputo
Language: Portuguese
Monetary Unit: Metical

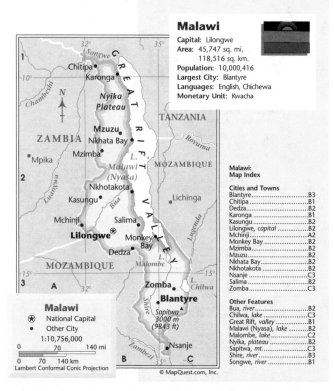

Malawi:
Map Index

Cities and Towns
Blantyre B3
Chitipa B1
Dedza B2
Karonga B1
Kasungu B2
Lilongwe, *capital* B2
Mchinji A2
Monkey Bay B2
Mzimba B2
Mzuzu B2
Nkhata Bay B2
Nkhotakota B2
Nsanje C3
Salima B2
Zomba C3

Other Features
Bua, *river* B2
Chilwa, *lake* C3
Great Rift, *valley* B1
Malawi (Nyasa), *lake* B2
Malombe, *lake* C2
Nyika, *plateau* B1
Sapitwa, *mt.* C3
Shire, *river* B3
Songwe, *river* B1

Mozambique

⊛ National Capital

• Other City

1:25,181,000

| 0 | 150 | 300 mi |
| 0 | 150 | 300 km |

Modified Lambert Conformal Conic Projection

Mozambique:
Map Index

Cities and Towns
Angoche C3
Beira B3
Chimoio B3
Chinde C3
Cuamba C2
Inhambane B5
Lichinga B2
Maputo, *capital* B5
Moçambique D2
Moçímboa da Praia D1
Nacala D2
Nampula D2
Pebane C3
Pemba D2
Quelimane C3
Tete B3
Vilanculos B4
Xai-Xai B5

Other Features
Binga, *mt.* B3
Búzi, *river* B4
Cabora Bassa, *dam* B2
Cabora Bassa, *lake* B2
Changane, *river* B4
Chilwa, *lake* C3
Chire, *river* B3
Lebombo, *mts.* A4
Limpopo, *river* B4
Lugenda, *river* C2
Lúrio, *river* C2
Mozambique, *channel* C3
Namuli, *highlands* C2
Nyasa (Malawi), *lake* B2
Rovuma, *river* C1
Save, *river* B4
Zambezi, *river* B3

© MapQuest.com, Inc.

Malawi

⊛ National Capital

• Other City

1:10,756,000

| 0 | 70 | 140 mi |
| 0 | 70 | 140 km |

Lambert Conformal Conic Projection

© MapQuest.com, Inc.

Mauritius

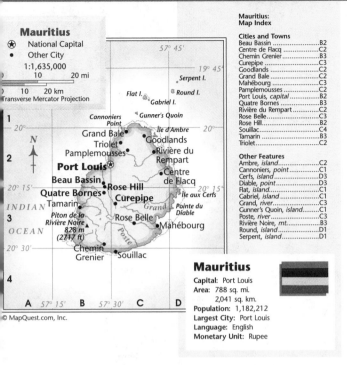

⊛ National Capital
• Other City

1:1,635,000

0 10 20 mi
0 10 20 km
Transverse Mercator Projection

© MapQuest.com, Inc.

Mauritius:
Map Index

Cities and Towns

Beau Bassin	B2
Centre de Flacq	C2
Chemin Grenier	B3
Curepipe	C3
Goodlands	C2
Grand Bale	C2
Mahébourg	C3
Pamplemousses	C2
Port Louis, capital	B2
Quatre Bornes	B3
Rivière du Rempart	C2
Rose Belle	C3
Rose Hill	B2
Souillac	C4
Tamarin	B3
Triolet	C2

Other Features

Ambre, island	C2
Cannoniers, point	C1
Cerfs, island	D3
Diable, point	D3
Flat, island	C1
Gabriel, island	C1
Grand, river	C3
Gunner's Quoin, island	C1
Poste, river	C3
Rivière Noire, mt.	B3
Round, island	D1
Serpent, island	D1

Mauritius

Capital: Port Louis
Area: 788 sq. mi.
2,041 sq. km.
Population: 1,182,212
Largest City: Port Louis
Language: English
Monetary Unit: Rupee

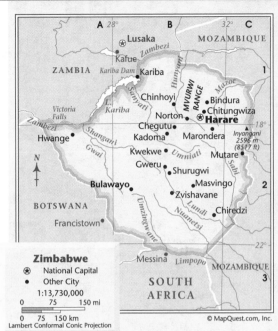

Zimbabwe

⊛ National Capital
• Other City

1:13,730,000

0 75 150 mi
0 75 150 km
Lambert Conformal Conic Projection

© MapQuest.com, Inc.

Zimbabwe

Capital: Harare
Area: 150,872 sq. mi.
390,860 sq. km.
Population: 11,163,160
Largest City: Harare
Language: English
Monetary Unit: Dollar

Zimbabwe:
Map Index

Cities and Towns

Bindura	B1
Bulawayo	B2
Chegutu	B2
Chinhoyi	B1
Chiredzi	B2
Chitungwiza	B1
Gweru	B2
Harare, capital	B1
Hwange	A2
Kadoma	B2
Kariba	B1
Kwekwe	B2
Marondera	B2
Masvingo	B2
Mutare	C2
Norton	B1
Shurugwi	B2
Zvishavane	B2

Other Features

Gwai, river	A2
Hunyani, river	B1
Inyangani, mt.	C2
Kariba, lake	A1
Limpopo, river	B3
Lundi, river	B2
Mazoe, river	B1
Mvurwi, range	B1
Nuanetsi, river	B2
Sabi, river	C2
Sanyati, river	B1
Shangani, river	A2
Umniati, river	B2
Umzingwani, river	B2
Victoria, falls	A1
Zambezi, river	A1, B1

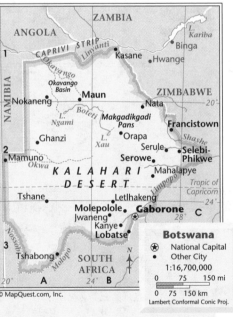

Botswana

⊛ National Capital
• Other City

1:16,700,000

0 75 150 mi
0 75 150 km
Lambert Conformal Conic Proj.

© MapQuest.com, Inc.

Botswana

Capital: Gaborone
Area: 224,607 sq. mi.
581,883 sq. km.
Population: 1,464,167
Largest City: Gaborone
Language: English
Monetary Unit: Pula

Botswana:
Map Index

Cities and Towns

Francistown	B2
Gaborone, capital	B3
Ghanzi	A2
Kanye	B3
Kasane	B1
Letlhakeng	B3
Lobatse	B3
Mahalapye	B2
Mamuno	A2
Maun	A1
Molepolole	B3
Nokaneng	A1
Orapa	B2
Selebi-Phikwe	C2
Serowe	B2

Tshabong	A3
Tshane	A3

Other Features

Boteti, river	A2
Kalahari, desert	A2
Limpopo, river	B2
Linvanti, river	A1
Makgadikgadi, salt pans	B2
Molopo, river	A3
Ngami, lake	A2
Nossob, river	A3
Okavango, basin	A1
Okavango, river	A1
Okwa, river	A2
Shashe, river	C2
Xau, lake	B2

Madagascar

⊛ National Capital
• Other City

1:17,474,000

0 100 200 mi
0 100 200 km
Lambert Conformal Conic Projection

© MapQuest.com, Inc.

Madagascar

Capital: Antananarivo
Area: 226,658 sq. mi.
587,197 sq. km.
Population: 14,873,387
Largest City: Antananarivo
Languages: Malagasy, French
Monetary Unit: Malagasy franc

Madagascar:
Map Index

Cities and Towns

Ambatolampy	B2
Ambatondrazaka	B2
Ambositra	B3
Ampanihy	A3
Andoany	B1
Antalaha	C1
Antananarivo, capital	B2
Antsirabe	B2
Antsiranana	B1
Antsohihy	B1
Farafangana	B3
Fianarantsoa	B3
Ihosy	B3
Mahajanga	A2
Maintirano	A2
Manakara	B3
Marovoay	B2
Morombe	A3
Morondava	A3
Toamasina	B2
Tôlanaro	B3

Toliara	A3
Tsiroanomandidy	B2

Other Features

Alaotra, lake	B2
Ambre, cape	B1
Ankaratra, mts.	B2
Bemaraha, plateau	A2
Betsiboka, river	B2
Kinkony, lake	B2
L'Isalo, mts.	B3
Mahajamba, river	B2
Mangoky, river	A3
Maromokotro, mt.	B1
Menarandra, river	A3
Mozambique, channel	A2
Nosy Be, island	B1
Nosy Sainte Marie, island	B2
Onilahy, river	A3
Saint-André, cape	A2
Sainte-Marie, cape	B4
Sofia, river	B2
Tsaratanana, mts.	B1
Tsiribihina, river	B2

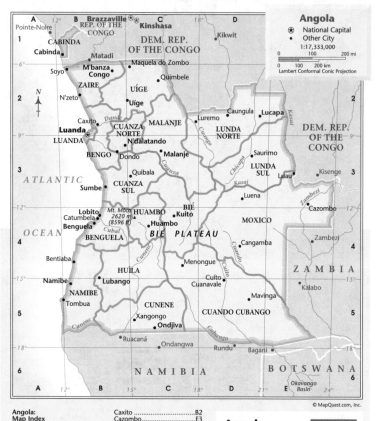

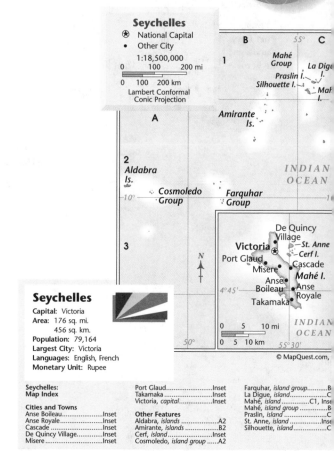

Angola
- ⊛ National Capital
- • Other City

1:17,333,000

0   100   200 mi
0   100   200 km
Lambert Conformal Conic Projection

Seychelles
- ⊛ National Capital
- • Other City

1:18,500,000

0   100   200 mi
0   100   200 km
Lambert Conformal Conic Projection

© MapQuest.com, Inc.

© MapQuest.com, Inc.

Angola:
Map Index

Provinces
Bengo	B3
Benguela	B4
Bié	C4
Cabinda	B1
Cuando Cubango	D5
Cuanza Norte	B2
Cuanza Sul	B3
Cunene	C5
Huambo	C4
Huíla	B4
Luanda	B3
Lunda Norte	D2
Lunda Sul	D3
Malanje	C2
Moxico	D4
Namibe	B5
Uíge	C2
Zaire	B2

Cities and Towns
Benguela	B4
Bentiaba	B4
Cabinda	B1
Cangamba	D4
Catumbela	B4
Caungula	D2
Caxito	B2
Cazombo	E3
Cuíto Cuanavale	D5
Dondo	B3
Huambo	C4
Kuito	C4
Lobito	B4
Luau	E3
Luanda, capital	B2
Lubango	B5
Lucapa	D2
Luena	D3
Luremo	C2
Malanje	C3
Maquela do Zombo	C2
Mavinga	D5
M'banza Congo	B2
Menongue	B5
Namibe	B5
N'dalatando	B2
N'zeto	B2
Ondjiva	C5
Quibala	C3
Quimbele	C2
Saurimo	D3
Soyo	B3
Sumbe	B3
Tombua	B5
Uíge	C2
Xangongo	C5

Other Features
Bié, plateau	C4
Chicapa, river	D3
Cuando, river	D4
Cuango, river	D2
Cuanza, river	C3
Cubal, river	B4
Cubango, river	D5
Cuíto, river	D4
Cunene, river	B5, C4
Dande, river	B2
Kasai, river	D3
Móco, mt.	C4
Zambezi, river	E3

Angola
Capital: Luanda
Area: 481,354 sq. mi.
    1,247,031 sq. km.
Population: 11,177,537
Largest City: Luanda
Language: Portuguese
Monetary Unit: Kwanza

Seychelles
Capital: Victoria
Area: 176 sq. mi.
    456 sq. km.
Population: 79,164
Largest City: Victoria
Languages: English, French
Monetary Unit: Rupee

Seychelles:
Map Index

Cities and Towns
Anse Boileau	Inset
Anse Royale	Inset
Cascade	Inset
De Quincy Village	Inset
Misere	Inset
Port Glaud	Inset
Takamaka	Inset
Victoria, capital	Inset

Other Features
Aldabra, islands	A2
Amirante, islands	B2
Cerf, island	Inset
Cosmoledo, island group	A2
Farquhar, island group	B3
La Digue, island	C
Mahé, island	C1, Inset
Mahé, island group	B
Praslin, island	C
St. Anne, island	Inset
Silhouette, island	C

Namibia
Capital: Windhoek
Area: 318,146 sq. mi.
    824,212 sq. km.
Population: 1,648,270
Largest City: Windhoek
Language: English, Afrikaans
Monetary Unit: Rand

Namibia:
Map Index

Cities and Towns
Bethanien	C4
Gobabis	C2
Grootfontein	C1
Karasburg	C4
Karibib	B2
Katima Mulilo	E1
Keetmanshoop	C4
Khorixas	B2
Lüderitz	B4
Maltahöhe	B3
Mariental	C3
Okahandja	B2
Okakarara	C2
Omaruru	B2
Ondangwa	B1
Opuwo	A1
Oranjemund	B4
Oshakati	B1
Otavi	C1
Otjiwarongo	B2
Outjo	B2
Rehoboth	C3
Rundu	C1

Other Features
Swakopmund	B2
Tsumeb	C1
Tsumkwe	D1
Walvis Bay	B2
Windhoek, capital	C2
Auob, river	C3
Brandberg, mt.	B2
Caprivi, strip	D1
Eiseb, river	D2
Etosha, pan	B1
Fish, river	C4
Kalahari, desert	C3
Kaoko Veld, mts.	A1
Kaukau Veld, region	C1
Kunene, river	A1
Linyanti, river	E1
Namib, desert	A1, B3
Nossob, river	C3
Okavango, river	C1
Omatako, river	C1
Orange, river	C4
Ruacana, falls	B1
Skeleton, coast	A1
Ugab, river	B2
Zambezi, river	E1

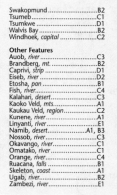

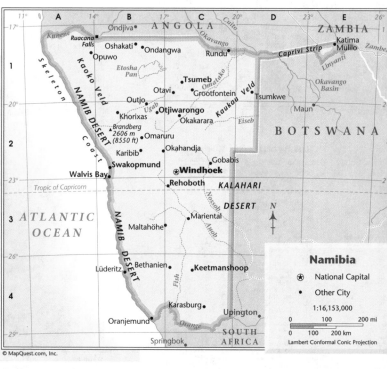

Namibia
- ⊛ National Capital
- • Other City

1:16,153,000

0   100   200 mi
0   100   200 km
Lambert Conformal Conic Projection

© MapQuest.com, Inc.

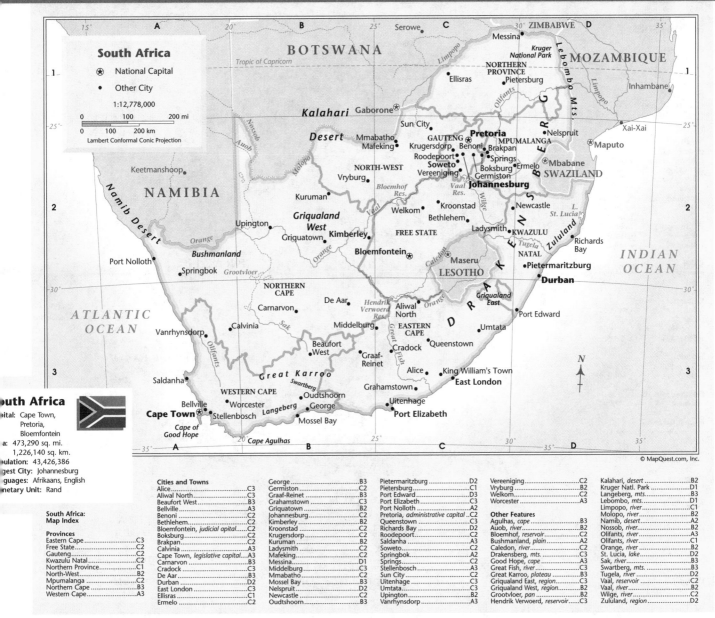

South Africa

⊛ National Capital
• Other City

1:12,778,000

0   100   200 mi
0   100   200 km
Lambert Conformal Conic Projection

© MapQuest.com, Inc.

South Africa

Capital: Cape Town,
         Pretoria,
         Bloemfontein
Area: 473,290 sq. mi.
      1,226,140 sq. km.
Population: 43,426,386
Largest City: Johannesburg
Languages: Afrikaans, English
Monetary Unit: Rand

**South Africa:
Map Index**

Provinces

Eastern Cape	C3
Free State	C2
Gauteng	C2
Kwazulu Natal	C2
Northern Province	C1
North-West	B2
Mpumalanga	C2
Northern Cape	B3
Western Cape	A3

Cities and Towns

Alice	C3
Aliwal North	C3
Beaufort West	B3
Bellville	A3
Benoni	C2
Bethlehem	C2
Bloemfontein, judicial capital	C2
Boksburg	C2
Brakpan	C2
Calvinia	A3
Cape Town, legislative capital	A3
Carnarvon	B3
Cradock	C3
De Aar	B3
Durban	D2
East London	C3
Ellisras	C1
Ermelo	C2

George	B3
Germiston	C2
Graaf-Reinet	B3
Grahamstown	C3
Griquatown	B2
Johannesburg	C2
Kimberley	B2
Kroonstad	C2
Kuruman	B2
Ladysmith	C2
Mafeking	B2
Messina	D1
Middelburg	C3
Mmabatho	C2
Mossel Bay	B3
Nelspruit	D2
Newcastle	C2
Oudtshoorn	B3

Pietermaritzburg	D2
Pietersburg	C1
Port Edward	D3
Port Elizabeth	C3
Port Nolloth	A2
Pretoria, administrative capital	C2
Queenstown	C3
Richards Bay	D2
Roodepoort	C2
Saldanha	A3
Soweto	C2
Springbok	A2
Springs	C2
Stellenbosch	A3
Sun City	C2
Uitenhage	C3
Umtata	C3
Upington	B2
Vanrhynsdorp	A3

Vereeniging	C2
Vryburg	B2
Welkom	C2
Worcester	A3

Other Features

Agulhas, cape	B3
Auob, river	A2
Bloemhof, reservoir	C2
Bushmanland, plain	A2
Caledon, river	C2
Drakensberg, mts.	C3
Good Hope, cape	A3
Great Fish, river	C3
Great Karroo, plateau	B3
Griqualand East, region	C3
Griqualand West, region	B2
Grootvloer, pan	B2
Hendrik Verwoerd, reservoir	C3

Kalahari, desert	B2
Kruger Natl. Park	D1
Langeberg, mts.	B3
Lebombo, mts.	D1
Limpopo, river	C1
Molopo, river	B2
Namib, desert	A2
Nossob, river	B2
Olifants, river	A3
Olifants, river	C1
Orange, river	B2
St. Lucia, lake	D2
Sak, river	B3
Swartberg, mts.	B3
Tugela, river	D2
Vaal, reservoir	C2
Vaal, river	B2
Wilge, river	C2
Zululand, region	D2

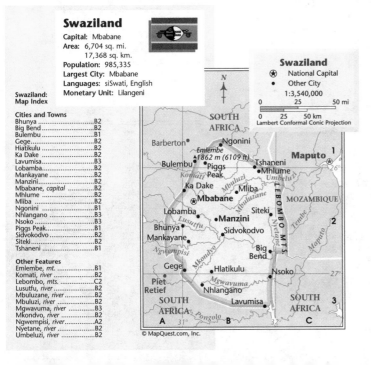

Swaziland

Capital: Mbabane
Area: 6,704 sq. mi.
      17,368 sq. km.
Population: 985,335
Largest City: Mbabane
Languages: siSwati, English
Monetary Unit: Lilangeni

Swaziland

⊛ National Capital
• Other City

1:3,540,000

0   25   50 mi
0   25   50 km
Lambert Conformal Conic Projection

**Swaziland:
Map Index**

Cities and Towns

Bhunya	B2
Big Bend	B2
Bulembu	B1
Gege	B2
Hlatikulu	B2
Ka Dake	B2
Lavumisa	B3
Lobamba	B2
Mankayane	B2
Manzini	B2
Mbabane, capital	B2
Mhlume	B2
Mliba	B2
Ngonini	B1
Nhlangano	B3
Nsoko	B3
Piggs Peak	B1
Sidvokodvo	B2
Siteki	B2
Tshaneni	B1

Other Features

Emlembe, mt.	B1
Komati, river	B2
Lebombo, mts.	C2
Lusutfu, river	B2
Mbuluzane, river	B2
Mbuluzi, river	B2
Mgwavuma, river	B3
Mkondvo, river	B2
Ngwempisi, river	A2
Nyetane, river	B2
Umbeluzi, river	B2

© MapQuest.com, Inc.

Lesotho

Capital: Maseru
Area: 11,716 sq. mi.
      30,352 sq. km.
Population: 2,128,950
Largest City: Maseru
Language: English
Monetary Unit: Loti

**Lesotho:
Map Index**

Cities and Towns

Butha-Buthe	B1
Leribe	B1
Libono	B1
Mafeteng	A2
Maseru, capital	A2
Mohales Hoek	A3
Mokhotlong	C2
Morija	A2
Pitseng	B2
Qachas Nek	B3
Quthing	A3
Roma	A2
Sekake	B2
Teyateyaneng	A2
Thaba-Tseka	B2

Other Features

Caledon, river	A1
Central, range	B2
Drakensberg, mts.	B3
Makhaleng, river	A2
Maloti, mts.	B2
Matsoku, river	B2
Orange, river	A3, B2
Sources, mt.	B1
Thabana Ntlenyana, mt.	C2
Tsedike, river	B3

Lesotho

⊛ National Capital
• Other City

1:5,811,000

0   30   60 mi
0   30   60 km
Lambert Conformal Conic Projection

© MapQuest.com, Inc.

MAJOR CITIES

Argentina
Buenos Aires	2,961,000
Córdoba	1,148,000
Rosario	895,000

Bolivia
La Paz	739,000
Santa Cruz	833,000
El Alto	527,000

Brazil
São Paulo	10,018,000
Rio de Janeiro	5,606,000
Salvador	2,263,000
Belo Horizonte	2,097,000
Fortaleza	1,917,000
Brasília	1,738,000
Curitiba	1,409,000
Recife	1,330,000
Pôrto Alegre	1,296,000
Belém	1,168,000
Manaus	1,138,000

Chile
Santiago	4,641,000
Puente Alto	363,000

Colombia
Bogotá	4,945,000
Cali	1,666,000
Medellín	1,630,000
Barranquilla	994,000

Ecuador
Guayaquil	1,974,000
Quito	1,444,000

Falkland Islands
Stanley	1,200

French Guiana
Cayenne	41,000

Guyana
Georgetown	195,000

Paraguay
Asunción	547,000

Peru
Lima	5,682,000
Arequipa	619,000
Trujillo	509,000

Suriname
Paramaribo	216,000

Uruguay
Montevideo	1,303,000

Venezuela
Caracas	3,673,000
Maracaibo	1,221,000
Barquisimeto	954,000
Valencia	911,000

International comparability of city population data is limited by various data inconsistencies.

CITIES
⊛ National Capital
★ Territorial Capital
• Other City

ELEVATIONS
Feet	Meters
13,120	4000
6560	2000
1640	500
656	200
0	0
Below sea level	

South America: Population, by nation (in millions)

BRAZIL	COLOM.	ARGEN.	PERU	VENEZ.	All other S. Am. countries
171.9	39.3	36.7	26.6	23.2	45.6

© MapQuest.com, Inc.

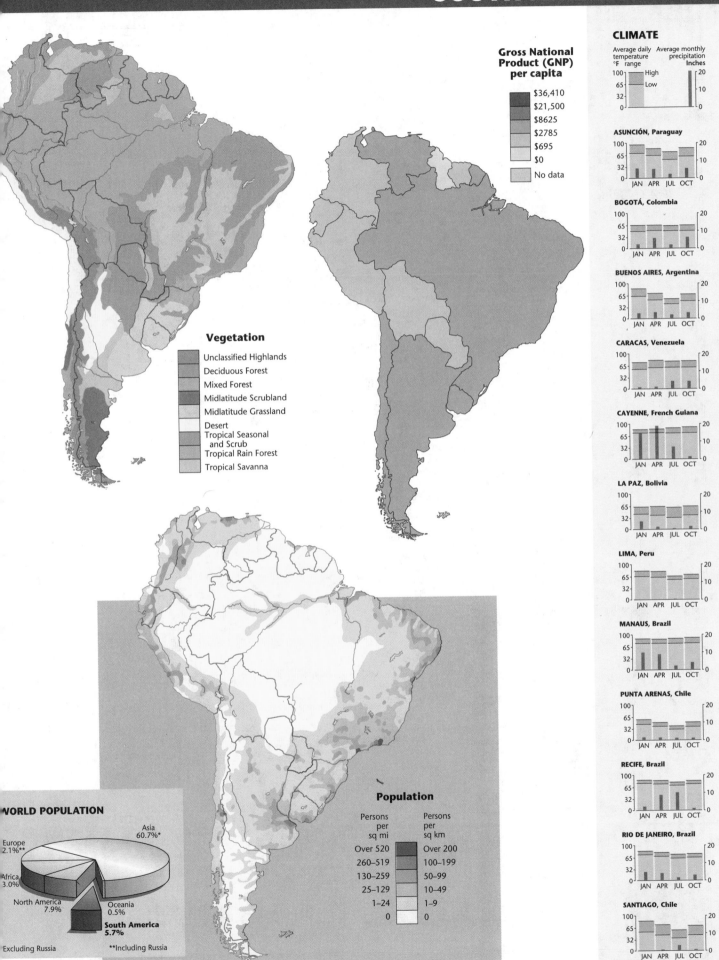

Gross National Product (GNP) per capita

- $36,410
- $21,500
- $8625
- $2785
- $695
- $0
- No data

Vegetation

- Unclassified Highlands
- Deciduous Forest
- Mixed Forest
- Midlatitude Scrubland
- Midlatitude Grassland
- Desert
- Tropical Seasonal and Scrub
- Tropical Rain Forest
- Tropical Savanna

Population

Persons per sq mi	Persons per sq km
Over 520	Over 200
260–519	100–199
130–259	50–99
25–129	10–49
1–24	1–9
0	0

WORLD POPULATION

- Asia 60.7%*
- Europe 2.1%**
- Africa 3.0%
- North America 7.9%
- Oceania 0.5%
- South America 5.7%

*Excluding Russia
**Including Russia

CLIMATE

Average daily temperature °F range
Average monthly precipitation Inches
High
Low

ASUNCIÓN, Paraguay
BOGOTÁ, Colombia
BUENOS AIRES, Argentina
CARACAS, Venezuela
CAYENNE, French Guiana
LA PAZ, Bolivia
LIMA, Peru
MANAUS, Brazil
PUNTA ARENAS, Chile
RECIFE, Brazil
RIO DE JANEIRO, Brazil
SANTIAGO, Chile

PACIFIC OCEAN

ATLANTIC OCEAN

BOLIVIA

PARAGUAY

BRAZIL

URUGUAY

CHILE

Tropic of Capricorn

ATACAMA DESERT

A N D E S

P A T A G O N I A

P A M P A S

G R A N   C H A C O

Chuquicamata
Antofagasta
La Serena
Santiago
Concepción
Puerto Montt
Coihaique
Punta Arenas

JUJUY
San Salvador de Jujuy
Salta
SALTA
Llullaillaco 6723 m (22,057 ft)
Embarcación
FORMOSA
Formosa
Concepción
Asunción
Foz do Iguaçu
Curitiba
Iguaçu Falls
MISIONES
Posadas
Corrientes
CORRIENTES
Santa Maria
Pôrto Alegre
Pelotas
L. dos Patos

San Miguel de Tucumán
TUCUMÁN
CATAMARCA
Ojos del Salado 6880 m (22,572 ft)
Catamarca
La Rioja
LA RIOJA
SANTIAGO DEL ESTERO
Santiago del Estero
CHACO
Presidencia Roque Sáenz Peña
Resistencia
Reconquista
SANTA FE
Curuzú Cuatiá

San Juan
SAN JUAN
Mercedario 6770 m (22,211 ft)
Aconcagua 6960 m (22,834 ft)
Tupungato 6800 m (22,310 ft)
CÓRDOBA
Córdoba
San Francisco
Champaquí 2850 m (9350 ft)
Villa María
Sierras de Córdoba
ENTRE RÍOS
Santa Fe
Paraná
Concordia

Mendoza
Godoy Cruz
San Rafael
MENDOZA
San Luis
Río Cuarto
SAN LUIS
Rosario
San Nicolás

Domuyo 4709 m (15,450 ft)
LA PAMPA
Santa Rosa
DISTRITO FEDERAL
Buenos Aires
Avellaneda
Lanús
Lomas de Zamora
La Plata
Montevideo

BUENOS AIRES
Olavarría
Tandil
Cabo San Antonio
Mar del Plata
Necochea

NEUQUÉN
Neuquén
Bahía Blanca
Bahía Blanca

Concepción

Lanín 3776 m (12,389 ft)
San Carlos de Bariloche
RÍO NEGRO
San Antonio Oeste
Viedma
Punta Rasa
Golfo San Matías
Península Valdés

Chiloé
Esquel
CHUBUT
Rawson
Chubut
Chico

Península Taitao
Comodoro Rivadavia
Golfo San Jorge
Deseado
Cabo Tres Puntas
Puerto Deseado

L. Buenos Aires
SANTA CRUZ
L. San Martín
Fitzroy 3375 m (11,073 ft)
L. Cardiel
L. Viedma
Santa Cruz
Puerto Santa Cruz
Calafate
L. Argentino
Bahía Grande
Río Gallegos
Gallegos
Punta Dungeness
Strait of Magellan

West Falkland I.
East Falkland I.
Stanley
Falkland Islands (Islas Malvinas) (Br.) (claimed by Argentina)

TIERRA DEL FUEGO
Ushuaia
Isla de los Estados
Beagle Channel
Cape Horn

N

Argentina
⊛ National Capital
★ Territorial Capital
● Other City

1:17,760,000

| 0 | 200 | 400 mi |
| 0 | 200 | 400 km |

Modified Chamberlain Trimetric Projection

© MapQuest.com, Inc.

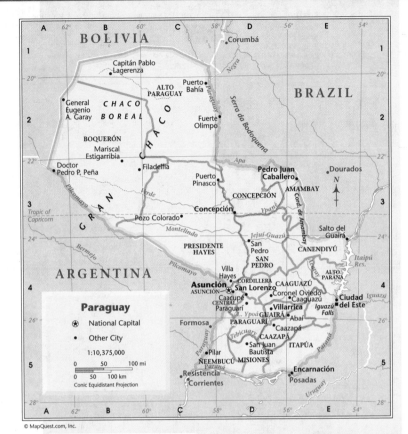

Paraguay

Capital: Asunción
Area: 157,048 sq. mi.
406,752 sq. km.
Population: 5,434,095
Largest City: Asunción
Language: Spanish
Monetary Unit: Guarani

Paraguay:
Map Index

Departments

Alto Paraguay	C2
Alto Paraná	E4
Amambay	E3
Asunción	D4
Boquerón	C2
Caaguazú	D4
Caazapá	D4
Canendiyú	E4
Central	D4
Concepción	D3
Cordillera	D4
Guairá	D4
Itapúa	E5
Misiones	D5
Ñeembucú	C5
Paraguarí	D5
Presidente Hayes	C4
San Pedro	D4

Cities and Towns

Abaí	E4
Asunción, *capital*	D4
Caacupé	D4
Caaguazú	D4
Caazapá	D5
Capitán Pablo Lagerenza	C1
Ciudad del Este	E4
Concepción	D3
Coronel Oviedo	D4
Doctor Pedro P. Peña	A3
Encarnación	E5
Filadelfia	B3
Fuerte Olimpo	D2
General Eugenio A. Garay	A2
Mariscal Estigarribia	B3
Paraguarí	D4
Pedro Juan Caballero	E3
Pilar	C5
Pozo Colorado	C3
Puerto Bahía	C2
Puerto Pinasco	D3
Salto del Guairá	E4
San Juan Bautista	D5
San Lorenzo	D4
San Pedro	D4
Villa Hayes	D4
Villarrica	D4

Other Features

Acaray, *river*	E4
Amambay, *mts.*	E3
Apa, *river*	D3
Chaco Boreal, *region*	B2
Gran Chaco, *region*	B3
Iguazú, *falls*	E4
Itaipú, *reservoir*	E4
Jejuí-Guazú, *river*	D4
Montelindo, *river*	C3
Paraguay, *river*	C2, C5
Paraná, *river*	C5, E5
Pilcomayo, *river*	B3, C4
Tebicuary, *river*	C5
Verde, *river*	C3
Ypané, *river*	D3
Ypoá, *lake*	D4

Argentina

Capital: Buenos Aires
Area: 1,073,518 sq. mi.
2,781,134 sq. km.
Population: 36,737,664
Largest City: Buenos Aires
Language: Spanish
Monetary Unit: Peso

Argentina:
Map Index

Provinces

Buenos Aires	C4
Catamarca	B2
Chaco	C2
Chubut	B5
Córdoba	C3
Corrientes	D2
Distrito Federal	D3
Entre Ríos	D3
Formosa	D1
Jujuy	B1
La Pampa	B4
La Rioja	B2
Mendoza	B3
Misiones	E2
Neuquén	B4
Río Negro	B5
Salta	B2
San Juan	B3
San Luis	B3
Santa Cruz	A6
Santa Fe	C2
Santiago del Estero	C2
Tierra del Fuego	B7
Tucumán	B2

Cities and Towns

Avellaneda	D3
Bahía Blanca	C4
Buenos Aires, *capital*	D3
Calafate	A7
Catamarca	B2
Comodoro Rivadavia	B6
Concordia	D3
Córdoba	C3
Corrientes	D2
Curuzú Cuatiá	D2
Embarcación	C1
Esquel	A5
Formosa	D2
Godoy Cruz	B3
Jesús	D3
La Plata	D4
La Rioja	B2
Lomas de Zamora	D4
Mar del Plata	D4
Mendoza	B3
Necochea	B4
Neuquén	B4
Olavarría	C4
Paraná	C3
Posadas	D2
Presidencia Roque Sáenz Peña	C2
Puerto Deseado	B6
Puerto Santa Cruz	B7
Rawson	B5
Reconquista	D2
Resistencia	D2
Río Cuarto	C3
Río Gallegos	B7
Rosario	C3
Salta	B1
San Antonio Oeste	B5
San Carlos de Bariloche	A5
San Francisco	C3
San Juan	B3
San Luis	B3
San Miguel de Tucumán	B2
San Nicolás	C3
San Rafael	B3
San Salvador de Jujuy	B1
Santa Fe	C3
Santa Rosa	C4
Santiago del Estero	C2
Tandil	D4
Ushuaia	B7
Viedma	C5
Villa María	C3

Other Features

Aconcagua, *mt.*	A3
Andes, *mts.*	A6–B1
Argentino, *lake*	A7
Atuel, *river*	B4
Beagle, *channel*	B7
Bermejo, *river*	C2
Blanca, *bay*	C4
Buenos Aires, *lake*	A6
Cardiel, *lake*	A6
Champaquí, *mt.*	C3
Chico, *river*	B6
Chubut, *river*	A5
Colorado, *river*	B4
Córdoba, *range*	B3
Desaguadero, *river*	B2
Deseado, *river*	B6
Domuyo, *volcano*	A4
Dungeness, *point*	B7
Estados, *island*	C7
Fitzroy, *mt.*	A6
Gallegos, *river*	A7
Gran Chaco, *region*	C1
Grande, *bay*	B7
Iguaçu, *falls*	E2
Iguaçu, *river*	E2
Lanín, *volcano*	A4
Llullaillaco, *volcano*	B1
Magellan, *strait*	B7
Mar Chiquita, *lake*	C3
Mercedario, *mt.*	B3
Negro, *river*	B4
Ojos del Salado, *mt.*	B2
Pampas, *plain*	C4
Paraguay, *river*	D2
Paraná, *river*	D2
Patagonia, *region*	A6
Pilcomayo, *river*	C1
Plata, Río de la, *estuary*	D3
Rasa, *point*	C5
Salado, *river*	B3
Salado, *river*	C2
San Antonio, *cape*	C5
San Jorge, *gulf*	B6
San Martín, *lake*	A6
San Matías, *gulf*	C5
Santa Cruz, *river*	A7
Tres Puntas, *cape*	B6
Tupungato, *mt.*	B3
Uruguay, *river*	D3
Valdés, *peninsula*	C5
Viedma, *lake*	A6

Uruguay

Capital: Montevideo
Area: 68,037 sq. mi.
176,215 sq. km.
Population: 3,308,523
Largest City: Montevideo
Language: Spanish
Monetary Unit: New peso

Uruguay:
Map Index

Cities and Towns

Artigas	B1
Bella Unión	B1
Canelones	C3
Carmelo	A2
Colonia	B3
Durazno	B3
Florida	C3
Fray Bentos	A2
Las Piedras	B3
Melo	C2
Mercedes	A2
Minas	C3
Montevideo, *capital*	B3
Nueva Palmira	A2
Pando	C3
Paso de los Toros	B2
Paysandú	A2
Piedra Sola	B2
Punta del Este	D3
Rivera	C1
Rocha	C3
Salto	B1
San Carlos	D3
San José	B3
Tacuarembó	C1
Treinta y Tres	C2
Trinidad	B2

Other Features

Arapey Grande, *river*	B1
Baygorria, *lake*	B2
Cebollatí, *river*	C2
Cuareim, *river*	B1
Daymán, *river*	B1
Grande, *range*	C2
Haedo, *range*	B2
Merín, *lagoon*	D2
Mirador Nacional, *mt.*	C3
Negra, *lagoon*	D2
Negro, *river*	C2
Paso de Palmar, *lake*	B2
Plata, *river*	B3
Queguay Grande, *river*	B2
Rincón del Bonete, *lake*	B2
Salto Grande, *reservoir*	B1
San José, *river*	B3
San Salvador, *river*	A2
Santa Ana, *range*	C1
Santa Lucía, *river*	B3
Tacuarembó, *river*	C1
Tacuarí, *river*	C2
Uruguay, *river*	A1
Yaguarí, *river*	C1
Yaguarón, *river*	D2
Yi, *river*	B2

© MapQuest.com, Inc.

Chile

Capital: Santiago
Area: 292,135 sq. mi.
756,826 sq. km.
Population: 14,973,843
Largest City: Santiago
Language: Spanish
Monetary Unit: Peso

Chile:
Map Index

Regions
Aisén del General Carlos
  Ibáñez del Campo
Antofagasta C2
Atacama B3
Bío-Bío B6
Coquimbo B4
El Libertador General
  Bernardo O'Higgins B4
La Araucanía B6
Los Lagos B7
Magallanes y Antártica
  Chilena B9
Maule B5, B6
Región Metropolitana ....B4, Inset
Tarapacá C1
Valparaíso ....B4, Inset

Cities and Towns
Aguada de Cachinal C2
Aguas Blancas C2
Algarrobo ....Inset

Los Lagos B7
Ancud B7
Angol B6
Antofagasta B2
Arica B1
Balmaceda B8
Calama C2
Casablanca ....Inset
Castro B7
Cerro Castillo B9
Chaitén B7
Chañaral B3
Chiapa C1

Altamira C3
Ancud B7
Angol B6
Antofagasta B2
Arica B1
Balmaceda B8
Calama C2
Casablanca ....Inset
Castro B7
Cerro Castillo B9
Chaitén B7
Chañaral B3
Chiapa C1

Chile Chico B8
Chillán B6
Chuquicamata C2
Cochrane B8
Coihaique B8
Colina ....Inset
Collaguasi C2
Concepción B6
Conchalí ....Inset
Constitución B5
Copiapó B3
Coquimbo B3
Curicó B4

El Tabo
El Trebolar
Freirina
Gatico
Illapel
Iquique
Lampa
La Serena
La Unión
Lebu
Linares
Los Andes
Los Ángeles
Maipú
Mamiña
Melipilla
Ñuñoa
Osorno
Ovalle
Parral
Pisagua
Porvenir
Potrerillos
Puente Alto
Puerto Aisén
Puerto Cisnes
Puerto Montt
Puerto Natales
Puerto Varas
Puerto Williams
Punta Arenas
Punta Delgada
Putre
Quellón
Quillota
Quilpué
Rancagua
Rungue
San Antonio B4
San Bernardo B4
San Félix
San Fernando
San Pedro de Atacama
Santa Inés
Santiago, capital ....B4, In
Socompa
Talagante
Talca
Talcahuano
Taltal
Temuco
Tilomonte
Tocopilla
Tomé
Unión
Valdivia
Vallenar
Valparaíso ....B4, In
Victoria
Viña del Mar ....B4, In

Other Features
Aconcagua, river
Ancud, gulf
Andes, mts. B8,
Atacama, desert
Bascuñán, cape
Bío-Bío, river
Brunswick, peninsula
Buenos Aires, lake
Campana, island
Chiloé, island
Chonos, archipelago
Cochrane, lake
Concepción, bay
Copiapó, river
Corcovado, gulf
Desolación, island
Domeyko, mts.
Dungeness, point
Duque de York, island
Elqui, river
Fitzroy, mt.
Galera, point
Horn, cape
Hoste, island
Imperial, river
Lanín, volcano
Lengua de Vaca, point
Llanquihue, lake
Llullaillaco, volcano
Loa, river
Madre de Dios, island
Magdalena, island
Magellan, strait
Maipó, river ....B4, In
Maule, river
Navarino, island
Occidental, mts.
Ojos del Salado, mt.
Ollagüe, volcano
Penas, gulf
Rapel, river
Reina Adelaida, archipelago
San Martín, lake
San Valentín, mt.
Santa Inés, island
Taitao, peninsula
Tierra del Fuego, island
Toltén, river
Wellington, island

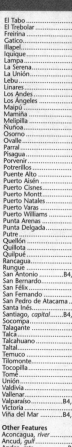

Peru

Capital: Lima
Area: 496,225 sq. mi.
1,285,216 sq. km.
Population: 26,624,582
Largest City: Lima
Languages: Spanish, Quechua
Monetary Unit: Nuevo Sol

Peru:
Map Index

Cities and Towns
Abancay C3
Arequipa C4
Ayacucho C3
Cajamarca B2
Callao B3
Cerro de Pasco B3
Chachapoyas B2
Chiclayo B2
Chimbote B2
Chincha Alta B3
Cuzco C3
Huacho B3
Huancavelica B3
Huancayo B3
Huánuco B2
Huaraz B2
Ica B3
Ilo C4
Iquitos C1
Juliaca C4
La Oroya B3
Lima, *capital* B3
Mollendo C4
Moquegua C4
Moyobamba B2
Nazca C3
Pacasmayo B2
Paita A2
Patavilca B3
Pisco B3
Piura A2
Pucallpa C2
Puerto Maldonado D3
Puno C4
Salaverry B2
San Juan B4
Sicuani C3
Sullana A1
Tacna C4
Talara A1
Tarapoto B2
Tingo María B2
Trujillo B2
Tumbes A1
Yurimaguas B2

Other Features
Amazon, *river* C1
Andes, *mts.* B1, C3
Apurímac, *river* C3
Central, *mts.* B2
Colca, *river* C4
Coropuna, *mt.* C4
Guayaquil, *gulf* A1
Huallaga, *river* B2
Huascarán, *mt.* B2
La Montaña, *region* C2
Machupicchu, *ruins* C3
Madre de Dios, *river* C3
Mantaro, *river* B3
Marañón, *river* B1, B2
Napo, *river* C1
Negra, *point* A2
Occidental, *mts.* B2, C4
Oriental, *mts.* B2, C3
Pastaza, *river* B1
Purús, *river* C3
Putumayo, *river* C1
Santiago, *river* B1
Sechura, *desert* A2
Tambo, *river* C3
Tambo, *river* C4
Tigre, *river* B1
Titicaca, *lake* D4
Ucayali, *river* C2
Urubamba, *river* C3
Vilcabamba, *mts.* C3
Yavarí, *river* C1

Peru map labels

COLOMBIA
ECUADOR
Quito
Guayaquil
Equator
Golfo de Guayaquil
Cuenca
Tumbes
Talara
Sullana
Paita
Piura
Desierto de Sechura
Punta Negra
Chiclayo
Chachapoyas
Cajamarca
Pacasmayo
Trujillo
Salaverry
Chimbote
Patavilca
Huacho
Callao
Lima
Yurimaguas
Moyobamba
Tarapoto
Huaraz
Huascarán 6768 m (22,205 ft)
Tingo María
Huánuco
Cerro de Pasco
La Oroya
Huancayo
Huancavelica
Chincha Alta
Pisco
Ica
Ayacucho
Machupicchu
Cuzco
Abancay
Sicuani
Nazca
Coropuna 6425 m (21,079 ft)
San Juan
Juliaca
Puno
L. Titicaca
La Paz
Arequipa
Mollendo
Moquegua
Ilo
Tacna
Arica
PACIFIC OCEAN
SELVAS
BRAZIL
Cruzeiro do Sul
Pucallpa
Rio Branco
Madre de Dios
Puerto Maldonado
ANDES
Cordillera Occidental
Cordillera Central
Cordillera Oriental
La Montaña
Cordillera de Vilcabamba
Cordillera Oriental
Leticia
Iquitos
Caquetá
Putumayo
Napo
Pastaza
Tigre
Santiago
Marañón
Amazon
Yavarí
Juruá
Itui
Purús
Ucayali
Huallaga
Mantaro
Tambo
Apurímac
Colca
Desaguadero
BOLIVIA
CHILE

Peru
- ⊛ National Capital
- • Other City

1:15,900,000
0 100 200 mi
0 100 200 km
Transverse Mercator Projection

N

© MapQuest.com, Inc.

Bolivia:
Map Index

Departments
Beni A2
Chuquisaca B4
Cochabamba A3
La Paz A3
Oruro A3
Pando A2
Potosí A4
Santa Cruz B3
Tarija B4

Cities and Towns
Aiquile A3
Camiri B4
Cobija A2
Cochabamba A3
Fortín Ravelo A3
Guaqui A3
La Paz, *capital* A3
Llallagua A3
Magdalena B2
Mojos A3
Montero B3
Oruro A3
Potosí A3
Puerto Suárez C2
Riberalta A2
Roboré C3
San Borja A2

San Cristóbal B2
San Ignacio B3
San José de Chiquitos B3
San Matías C2
Santa Ana A3
Santa Cruz B3
Santa Rosa del Palmar B3
Sucre, *capital* A3
Tarija B4
Tarvo B3
Trinidad A2
Tupiza A4
Uyuni A4
Villazón A4
Yacuiba B4

Other Features
Abuná, *river* A2
Altiplano, *plateau* A3
Beni, *river* A2
Chaparé, *river* A3
Cordillera Central, *mts.* A3
Cordillera Occidental, *mts.* A3
Cordillera Oriental, *mts.* A3
Cordillera Real, *mts.* A3
Desaguadero, *river* A3
Grande, *river* B3
Gran Chaco, *region* B4
Guaporé, *river* B2
Ichilo, *river* B3
Illampu, *mt.* A3
Illimani, *mt.* A3

Iténez, *river* B2
Madre de Dios, *river* A2
Mamoré, *river* A2
Ollagüe, *volcano* A4
Paraguá, *river* B2
Paraguay, *river* C4
Pilaya, *river* B4
Pilcomayo, *river* B3
Poopó, *lake* A3
Sajama, *mt.* A3
Salar de Uyuni, *salt flat* A4
San Luis, *lake* B2
San Pablo, *river* B3
Titicaca, *lake* A3
Yata, *river* A2
Yungas, *region* A3

Bolivia

Capital: La Paz, Sucre
Area: 424,164 sq. mi.
1,098,871 sq. km.
Population: 7,982,850
Largest City: La Paz
Languages: Spanish, Quechua, Aymara
Monetary Unit: Boliviano

Bolivia
- ⊛ National Capital
- • Other City

1:15,400,000
0 100 200 mi
0 100 200 km
Transverse Mercator Projection

Bolivia map labels

PERU
BRAZIL
Rio Branco
Iñapari
Cobija
PANDO
Riberalta
Guajará-Mirim
Puerto Maldonado
Madre de Dios
Abuná
Purus
Madeira
Vilhena
Chapada dos Parecis
Mojos
San Borja
Santa Ana
BENI
Trinidad
L. de San Luis
Magdalena
San Cristóbal
Tarvo
Mato Grosso Plateau
LA PAZ
Guaqui
Illampu 6485 m (21,276 ft)
Illimani 6462 m (21,201 ft)
L. Titicaca
La Paz
Cordillera Real
YUNGAS
CORDILLERA OCCIDENTAL
CORDILLERA ORIENTAL
CORDILLERA CENTRAL
Cochabamba
COCHABAMBA
Aiquile
SANTA CRUZ
San Ignacio
Santa Rosa del Palmar
Montero
Santa Cruz
San José de Chiquitos
Roboré
San Matías
Puerto Suárez
Fortín Ravelo
Sajama 6542 m (21,463 ft)
Oruro
ORURO
Llallagua
ALTIPLANO
Poopó
L. Poopó
Sucre
Potosí
POTOSÍ
Camiri
CHUQUISACA
Salar de Uyuni
Uyuni
Ollagüe 5869 m (19,255 ft)
Tupiza
Villazón
TARIJA
Tarija
Yacuiba
PARAGUAY
GRAN CHACO
Mariscal Estigarribia
La Quiaca
Tartagal
Calama
CHILE
ARGENTINA
San Salvador de Jujuy
Concepción
Desaguadero
Beni
Mamoré
Iténez
Guaporé
Paraguay
Itonama
San Pablo
Grande
Pilcomayo
Bermejo

N

© MapQuest.com, Inc.

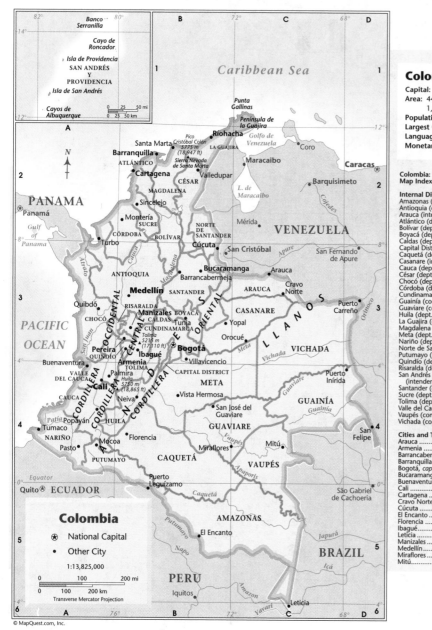

Banco Serranilla
Cayo de Roncador
Isla de Providencia
SAN ANDRÉS Y PROVIDENCIA
Isla de San Andrés
Cayos de Albuquerque
0 25 50 mi
0 25 50 km

Colombia
⊛ National Capital
● Other City
1:13,825,000
0 100 200 mi
0 100 200 km
Transverse Mercator Projection

© MapQuest.com, Inc.

Colombia
Capital: Bogotá
Area: 440,831 sq. mi.
1,142,049 sq. km.
Population: 39,309,422
Largest City: Bogotá
Language: Spanish
Monetary Unit: Peso

Colombia: Map Index

Internal Divisions
Amazonas (commissary)...........B5
Antioquia (dept.)...................B3
Arauca (intendency)...............C3
Atlántico (dept.)....................B2
Bolívar (dept.)......................B2
Boyacá (dept.).....................B3
Caldas (dept.)......................B3
Capital District.....................B4
Caquetá (dept.)....................B4
Casanare (intendency)...........C3
Cauca (dept.).......................A4
César (dept.)........................B2
Chocó (dept.).......................A3
Córdoba (dept.)....................B2
Cundinamarca (dept.)............B3
Guainía (commissary).............C4
Huila (dept.).........................A4
La Guajira (dept.)..................B2
Magdalena (dept.)................B2
Meta (dept.).........................B4
Nariño (dept.).......................A4
Norte de Santander (dept.).....B2
Putumayo (intendency)..........A4
Quindío (dept.).....................B3
Risaralda (dept.)...................B3
San Andrés y Providencia
(intendency)...................Inset
Santander (dept.).................B3
Sucre (dept.).......................B2
Tolima (dept.)......................B4
Valle del Cauca (dept.)..........A4
Vaupés (commissary)............C4
Vichada (commissary)...........C3

Cities and Towns
Arauca.................................C3
Armenia...............................B3
Barrancabermeja...................B3
Barranquilla..........................B2
Bogotá, capital.....................B3
Bucaramanga.......................B3
Buenaventura.......................A4
Cali.....................................A4
Cartagena............................B2
Cravo Norte..........................C3
Cúcuta.................................B3
El Encanto............................B5
Florencia..............................B4
Ibagué................................B3
Leticia.................................C6
Manizales............................B3
Medellín..............................B3
Miraflores.............................B4
Mitú....................................C4

Mocoa................................A4
Montería..............................B2
Neiva..................................B4
Orocué................................C3
Palmira...............................A4
Pasto..................................A4
Pereira................................B3
Popayán..............................A4
Puerto Carreño.....................D3
Puerto Inírida.......................D4
Puerto Leguízamo..................B5
Quibdó................................A3
Ríohacha..............................B2
San Felipe............................D4
San José del Guaviare............B4
Santa Marta..........................B2
Sincelejo..............................B2
Tumaco................................A4
Tunja...................................B3
Turbo..................................A2
Valledupar............................B2
Villavicencio..........................B3
Vista Hermosa.......................B3
Yopal..................................B3

Other Features
Albuquerque, cays...........Inset
Amazon, river......................C5
Andes, range.......................A4
Apaporis, river......................C4
Atrato, river.........................A3
Caquetá, river......................B5
Cauca, river.........................B3
Cordillera Central, range.........A4
Cordillera Occidental,
range...............................A4
Cordillera Oriental, range.......B4
Cristóbal Colón, peak.............B2
Gallinas, point......................C1
Guainía, river.......................C4
Guajira, peninsula..................C1
Guaviare, river......................C4
Huila, mt.............................A4
Llanos, prairie......................C3
Magdalena, river...................B3
Meta, river...........................C3
Orinoco, river........................D3
Patía, river...........................A4
Providencia, island..............Inset
Putumayo, river.....................B5
Roncador, cay...................Inset
San Andrés, island.............Inset
San Juan, river......................A3
Serranilla, bank..................Inset
Sierra Nevada de Santa
Marta, mts........................B2
Tolima, mt............................B3
Vaupés, river........................B4
Vichada, river.......................C3

Venezuela: Map Index

Internal Divisions
Amazonas (territory)..............C3
Anzoátegui (state).................D2
Apure (state)........................C2
Aragua (state)......................C2
Barinas (state)......................C2
Bolívar (state).......................D2
Carabobo (state)...................C2
Cojedes (state).....................C2
Delta Amacuro (territory)........D2
Dependencias Federales.........C1
Distrito Federal.....................C1
Falcón (state).......................B1
Guárico (state)......................C2
Lara (state)..........................B1
Mérida (state).......................B2
Miranda (state).....................C1
Monagas (state)....................D2
Nueva Esparta (state)............D1
Portuguesa (state).................C2
Sucre (state)........................D1
Táchira (state)......................B2
Trujillo (state).......................B2
Yaracuy (state).....................C1
Zulia (state).........................B2

Cities and Towns
Acarigua..............................C2
Anaco.................................D2
Barcelona............................D1
Barinas...............................B2
Barquisimeto........................C1
Baruta.................................C1
Cabimas..............................B1
Calabozo.............................C2
Canaima..............................D2
Caracas, capital....................C1
Carora................................C1
Carúpano.............................D1
Ciudad Bolívar......................D2
Ciudad Guayana....................D2
Coro...................................C1
Cumaná...............................D1
El Tigre...............................D2
Guanare..............................C2
Güiria.................................D1
La Asunción.........................D1
La Guaira Maiquetía...............C1
Los Teques..........................C1
Maiquetía............................C1
Maracaibo............................B1
Maracay..............................C1
Maturín...............................D2
Mérida................................B2

Petare................................C1
Puerto Ayacucho...................C2
Puerto Cabello......................C1
Puerto La Cruz......................D1
Punto Fijo............................B1
San Cristóbal........................B2
San Felipe............................C1
San Fernando de Apure...........C2
San Juan de Los Morros..........C2
Santa Elena de Uairén............D3
Trujillo................................B2
Tucupita..............................D2
Valencia..............................C1
Valera.................................B2

Other Features
Angel, falls..........................D2
Apure, river..........................C2
Arauca, river........................C2
Bolívar, mt...........................B2
Caroní, river.........................D2
Casiquiare, river....................C2
Caura, river..........................C2
Cojedes, river.......................C2
Guri, reservoir......................D2
Guiana, highlands..................D2
La Tortuga, island..................C1
Llanos, plain........................B2

Maracaibo, lake.....................B2
Margarita, island....................D1
Mérida, mts..........................C2
Meta, river...........................C2
Neblina, mt...........................C3
Negro, river..........................B3
Orinoco, river...................C3, D2
Pacaraima, mts......................D3
Paria, gulf............................D1
Parima, mts..........................D3
Roraima, mt..........................D2
Venezuela, gulf......................B1

Venezuela
Capital: Caracas
Area: 352,144 sq. mi.
912,050 sq. km.
Population: 23,203,466
Largest City: Caracas
Language: Spanish
Monetary Unit: Bolívar

Ecuador

Capital: Quito
Area: 105,037 sq. mi.
272,117 sq. km.
Population: 12,562,496
Largest City: Guayaquil
Language: Spanish
Monetary Unit: Sucre

Ecuador: Map Index

Provinces

Azuay	B4
Bolívar	B3
Cañar	B4
Carchi	C2
Chimborazo	B3
Cotopaxi	B3
El Oro	B4
Esmeraldas	B2
Galápagos	Inset
Guayas	A4
Imbabura	B2
Loja	B5
Los Ríos	B3
Manabí	A3
Morona-Santiago	C4
Napo	C3
Pastaza	C3
Pichincha	B2
Sucumbíos	C3
Tungurahua	B3
Zamora-Chinchipe	B5

Cities and Towns

Ambato	B3
Azogues	B4
Babahoyo	B3
Baquerizo Moreno	Inset
Chone	A3
Cuenca	B4
Esmeraldas	B2
Guaranda	B3
Guayaquil	B4
Ibarra	B2
Jipijapa	A3
La Libertad	A4
Latacunga	B3
Loja	B4
Macas	C4
Machala	B4
Manta	A3
Milagro	B4
Nueva Loja	C2
Nuevo Rocafuerte	D3
Otavalo	B2
Portoviejo	A3
Puerto Bolívar	B4
Puyo	C3
Quevedo	B3
Quito, capital	B3
Riobamba	B3
San Lorenzo	B2
Santa Rosa	B4
Santo Domingo de los Colorados	B3
Tena	C3
Tulcán	C2
Zamora	B5

Other Features

Aguarico, river	C3
Andes, mts.	B4
Cayambe, mt.	C3
Chimborazo, mt.	B3
Chira, river	A5
Cordillera Occidental, mts.	B4
Cordillera Oriental, mts.	C4
Cotopaxi, mt.	B3
Curaray, river	C3
Daule, river	B3
Española, island	Inset
Fernandina, island	Inset
Galera, point	A2
Guaillabamba, river	B2
Guayas, gulf	A4
Guayas, river	B4
Isabela, island	Inset
Manta, bay	A3
Marchena, island	Inset
Napo, river	C3
Pastaza, river	C4
Pinta, island	Inset
Plata, island	A3
Puná, island	A4
Putumayo, river	D2
San Cristóbal, island	Inset
San Lorenzo, cape	A3
San Salvador, island	Inset
Santa Cruz, island	Inset
Santa Elena, point	A4
Santa María, island	Inset
Santiago, river	B4
Tigre, river	C3
Vinces, river	B4
Wolf, mt.	Inset
Zamora, river	B4

Ecuador National Capital / Other City
1:8,250,000
0 40 80 mi
0 40 80 km
Transverse Mercator Projection

Venezuela
National Capital / Other City
1:11,110,000
0 100 200 mi
0 100 200 km
Transverse Mercator Projection

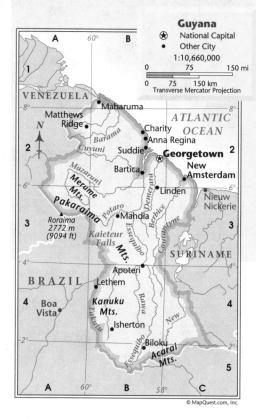

Guyana
- ⊛ National Capital
- • Other City

1:10,660,000

0   75   150 mi
0   75   150 km
Transverse Mercator Projection

© MapQuest.com, Inc.

Guyana
Capital: Georgetown
Area: 83,000 sq. mi.
   214,969 sq. km.
Population: 705,156
Largest City: Georgetown
Language: English
Monetary Unit: Guyana dollar

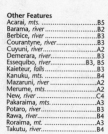

Guyana:
Map Index

Cities and Towns
Anna Regina	B2
Apoteri	B4
Bartica	B3
Biloku	B5
Charity	B2
Georgetown, *capital*	B2
Isherton	B4
Lethem	B4
Linden	B3
Mabaruma	B1
Mahdia	B3
Matthews Ridge	A2
New Amsterdam	C2
Suddie	B2

Other Features
Acarai, *mts.*	B5
Barama, *river*	B2
Berbice, *river*	B3
Courantyne, *river*	B3
Cuyuni, *river*	A2
Demerara, *river*	B3
Essequibo, *river*	B3, B5
Kaieteur, *falls*	B3
Kanuku, *mts.*	B4
Mazaruni, *river*	A2
Merume, *mts.*	A2
New, *river*	C4
Pakaraima, *mts.*	A3
Potaro, *river*	B3
Rawa, *river*	B4
Roraima, *mt.*	A3
Takutu, *river*	B4

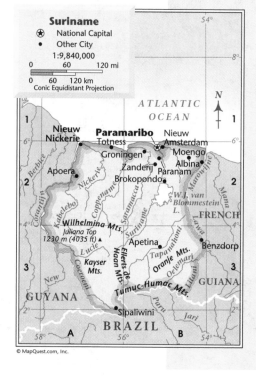

Suriname
- ⊛ National Capital
- • Other City

1:9,840,000

0   60   120 mi
0   60   120 km
Conic Equidistant Projection

© MapQuest.com, Inc.

Suriname
Capital: Paramaribo
Area: 63,037 sq. mi.
   163,265 sq. km.
Population: 431,156
Largest City: Paramaribo
Language: Dutch
Monetary Unit: Suriname guilder

Suriname:
Map Index

Cities and Towns
Albina	B2
Apetina	B3
Apoera	A2
Benzdorp	B3
Brokopondo	B2
Groningen	B2
Moengo	B2
Nieuw Amsterdam	B2
Nieuw Nickerie	A2
Paramaribo, *capital*	B2
Paranam	B2
Sipaliwini	A3
Totness	A2
Zanderij	B2

Other Features
Coereoni, *river*	A3
Coppename, *river*	A2
Corantijn, *river*	A2
Ellerts de Haan, *mts.*	A3
Juliana Top, *mt.*	A3
Kabelebo, *river*	A3
Kayser, *mts.*	A3
Lawa, *river*	B2
Litani, *river*	B3
Lucie, *river*	A3
Marowijne, *river*	B2
Nickerie, *river*	A2
Oelemari, *river*	B3
Oranje, *mts.*	B3
Saramacca, *river*	B2
Suriname, *river*	B3
Tapanahoni, *river*	B3
Tumuc-Humac, *mts.*	B3
Wilhelmina, *mts.*	A2
W.J. van Blommestein, *lake*	B2

French Guiana:
Map Index

Cities and Towns
Apatou	A1
Cacao	B2
Camopi	B2
Cayenne, *capital*	B1
Grand Santi	A1
Iracoubo	B1
Kaw	B1
Kourou	B1
Mana	B1
Maripasoula	A2
Ouanary	C1
Régina	B1
Rémire	B1
Saint-Élie	B1
Saint-Georges	C2
Saint-Laurent du Maroni	A1
Saül	B2

Other Features
Camopi, *river*	B2
Devil's, *island*	B1
Lawa, *river*	A2
Litani, *river*	A2
Mana, *river*	B1
Maroni, *river*	A1
Oyapock, *river*	B2
Salut, *islands*	B1
Tampok, *river*	B2
Tumuc-Humac, *mts.*	A2

French Guiana
Capital: Cayenne
Area: 35,135 sq. mi.
   91,000 sq. km.
Population: 167,982
Largest City: Cayenne
Language: French
Monetary Unit: French franc

French Guiana
- ★ Territorial Capital
- • Other City

1:8,410,000

0   50   100 mi
0   50   100 km
Conic Equidistant Projection

© MapQuest.com, Inc.

Brazil:
Map Index

States and Federal District

Acre..................................A2
Alagoas..............................E2
Amapá...............................C1
Amazonas...........................B2
Bahia.................................D3
Ceará................................E2
Espírito Santo......................D3
Federal District....................D3
Goiás.................................D3
Maranhão...........................D2
Mato Grosso........................C3
Mato Grosso do Sul...............C4
Minas Gerais.......................D3
Pará..................................C2
Paraíba..............................E2
Paraná...............................C4
Pernambuco........................E2
Piauí..................................D2
Rio de Janeiro.........D4, Inset I
Rio Grande do Norte.............E2
Rio Grande do Sul................C4
Rondônia............................B3
Roraima.............................B1
Santa Catarina.....................C4
São Paulo..............C4, Inset II
Sergipe..............................E3
Tocantins............................D3

Cities and Towns

Alagoinhas..........................E3
Altamira.............................C2
Anápolis.............................D3
Aracaju..............................E3
Bacabal..............................D2
Bauru.................................D4
Belém.................................D2
Belford Roxo................Inset I
Belo Horizonte.....................D3
Boa Vista............................B1
Bom Jesus da Lapa...............D3
Brasília, capital...................D3

Cáceres..............................C3
Cachimbo............................C2
Campina Grande...................E2
Campinas............................D4
Campo Grande......................C4
Campos...............................D4
Campos Elísios.............Inset I
Carapicuíba..................Inset II
Corumbá.............................C3
Cotia...........................Inset II
Cruzeiro do Sul....................A2
Cubatão.......................Inset II
Cuiabá................................C3
Curitiba...............................D4
Diadema......................Inset II
Dourados............................C4
Duque de Caxias............Inset I
Feira de Santana...................E3
Floriano..............................D2
Florianópolis........................D4
Fortaleza.............................E2
Foz do Iguaçu......................C4
Goiânia...............................D3
Governador Valadares............D3
Guajara Mirim......................B3
Guarujá.......................Inset II
Guarulhos.....................Inset II
Ilhéus.................................E3
Imbariê........................Inset I
Imperatriz...........................D2
Inhomirim.....................Inset I
Ipiiba..........................Inset I
Itabira................................E3
Itabuna...............................E3
Itajaí..........................Inset I
Itaipu..........................Inset I
Itajaí.................................D4
Itapecerica da Serra.......Inset II
Itapeva.......................Inset II
Itaquaquecetuba...........Inset II
Jaboatão.............................E2
Jacare-Acanga.....................C2
Japeri.........................Inset I
Jir Paraná...........................B3
João Pessoa........................E2
Joinville..............................D4

Juàzeiro.............................D2
Juàzeiro do Norte.................E2
Juiz de Fora.........................D4
Jundiaí...............................C4
Lajes..................................C4
Londrina.............................C4
Macapá...............................C1
Macapá.......................Inset II
Maceió...............................E2
Majé...........................Inset I
Manaus...............................C2
Maraba...............................D2
Mariana..............................D3
Mauá..........................Inset II
Mogi das Cruzes............Inset II
Monjolo.......................Inset I
Montes Claros......................D3
Mozzoro..............................E2
Natal..................................E2
Neves..........................Inset I
Nilópolis......................Inset I
Niterói....................D4, Inset I
Nova Iguaçu.................Inset I
Olinda.................................E2
Osasco........................Inset II
Palmas................................D3
Paranaguá...........................D4
Parnaiba.............................D2
Passo Fundo........................C4
Paulo Afonso.......................E2
Pelotas...............................C5
Petrólina.............................D2
Petrópolis................D4, Inset I
Piracicaba...........................D4
Poá............................Inset II
Pôrto Alegre.........................C5
Pôrto Velho.........................B2
Queimados....................Inset I
Randonopolis.......................C3
Recife.................................E2
Ribeirão Pires................Inset II
Ribeirão Prêto......................D4
Rio Branco..........................B2
Rio de Janeiro.........D4, Inset I
Rio Grande..........................C5
Rio Verde............................C3

Salvador..............................E3
Santa Maria.........................C4
Santana do Livramento...........C5
Santarém............................C2
Santo André..................Inset II
Santos.........................D4, Inset II
São Bernardo do Campo....Inset II
São Caetano do Sul.........Inset II
São Gonçalo..................Inset I
São João de Meriti..........Inset I
São José do Rio Prêto............D4
São Luís..............................D2
São Paulo................D4, Inset II
São Vicente...................Inset II
Sobral.................................D2
Sorocaba.............................D4
Suzano........................Inset II
Taboão da Serra.............Inset II
Tefé...................................B2
Teresina..............................D2
Tubarão...............................D4
Uberaba..............................D3
Uberlândia...........................D3
Vincente de Carvalho.......Inset II
Vitória................................D4
Vitória da Conquista..............D3
Volta Redonda......................D4

Other Features

Acaraí, range......................C1
Açúcar, mt..................Inset I
Amazon, basin.....................B2
Amazon, river......................B2
Araguaia, river....................C3
Aripuaná, river....................C2
Baleia, point........................E3
Bandeira, mt.......................D3
Billings, reservoir..........Inset II
Branco, river.......................B1
Brazilian, highlands..............D3
Caviana, island....................D1
Chapada dos Parecis, range....C3
Corcovado, mt..............Inset I
Corumbau, point..................E3
Furnas, reservoir..................D4

Geral, range.........................C4
Grande, river........................D3
Guandu, river...............Inset I
Guaporé, river.......................B3
Guiana, highlands.................B1
Içá, river..............................B2
Iguaçu, falls.........................C4
Itaipu, reservoir....................C4
Japurá, river.........................B2
Jari, river.............................C1
Javari, river..........................A2
Juruá, river...........................B2
Juruena, river.......................C3
Madeira, river.......................B2
Mantiqueira, range................D4
Mar, range...........................D4
Marajó, island.......................D2
Mato Grosso, plateau............C3
Mexiana, island.....................D1
Neblina, mt..........................B1
Negro, river..........................B2
Órgãos, range...............Inset I
Pantanal, lowland..................C4
Pará, river............................C2
Paraguai, river......................C3
Paraná, river.........................C4
Parima, range.......................B1
Parnaíba, river......................D2
Patos, lagoon.......................C5
Paulo Afonso, falls................E2
Pedra Açú, mt...............Inset I
Purus, river...........................B2
Roncador, range....................C3
São Francisco, river...............D3
Selvas, region.......................B2
Sobradinho, reservoir.............D3
Tapajós, river........................C2
Taquari, river........................C3
Teles Pires, river...................C2
Tietê, river....................Inset II
Tocantins, river.....................D2
Turucuí, reservoir..................C1
Tumucumaque, range............C1
Uruguai, river........................C4
Xingu, river...........................C3

Brazil

Capital: Brasília
Area: 3,286,470 sq. mi.
　　　8,514,171 sq. km.
Population: 171,853,126
Largest City: São Paulo
Language: Portuguese
Monetary Unit: Real

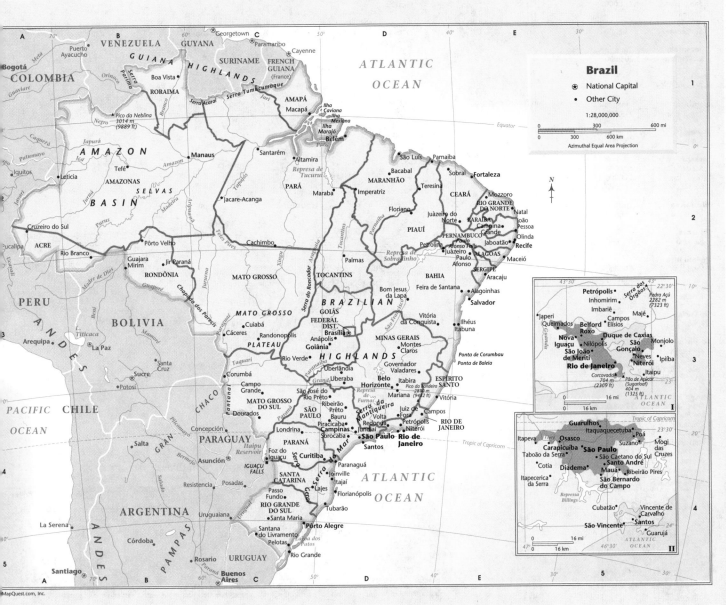

MAJOR CITIES

Antigua & Barbuda
St. Johns 27,000

Bahamas
Nassau 172,000

Barbados
Bridgetown 6,000

Belize
Belize City 45,000
Belmopan 4,000

Canada (metro)
Toronto 4,264,000
Montréal 3,327,000
Vancouver 1,832,000
Ottawa 1,010,000

Costa Rica
San José 324,000

Cuba
Havana 2,185,000

Dominica
Roseau 16,000

Dominican Republic
Santo Domingo 2,135,000

El Salvador (metro)
San Salvador 1,214,000

Grenada
St. George's 30,000

Guatemala (metro)
Guatemala 2,205,000

Haiti
Port-au-Prince 884,000

Honduras (metro)
Tegucigalpa 995,000

Jamaica (metro)
Kingston 587,000

Mexico
Mexico City 8,489,000
Guadalajara 1,633,000
Puebla 1,223,000

Nicaragua (metro)
Managua 1,124,000

Panama
Panamá 465,000

Puerto Rico
San Juan 428,000

St. Kitts & Nevis
Basseterre 15,000

St. Lucia
Castries 45,000

St. Vincent & Grenadines
Kingstown 15,000

Trinidad & Tobago
Port of Spain 43,000

United States
New York 7,381,000
Los Angeles 3,554,000
Chicago 2,722,000
Houston 1,744,000
Philadelphia 1,478,000
San Diego 1,171,000
Phoenix 1,159,000
Washington, D.C. 543,000

International comparability of city population
data is limited by various data inconsistencies.

CITIES
⊛ National Capital
★ Territorial Capital
• Other City

ELEVATIONS

	Feet	Meters
	13,120	4000
	6560	2000
	1640	500
	656	200
	0	0
	Below sea level	

N

	0	250	500	750	1000 mi
	0	500	1000	1500 km	

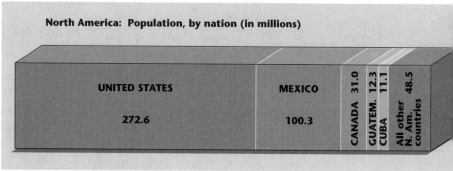

North America: Population, by nation (in millions)

UNITED STATES	MEXICO	CANADA	GUATEM.	CUBA	All other N. Am. countries
272.6	100.3	31.0	12.3	11.1	48.5

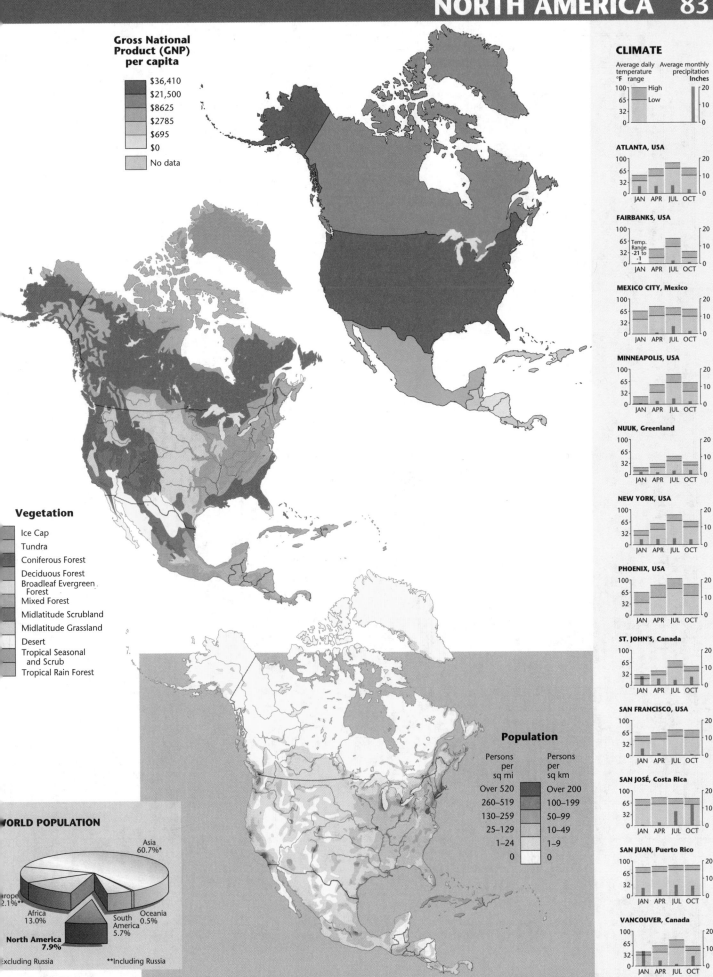

Gross National Product (GNP) per capita

- $36,410
- $21,500
- $8625
- $2785
- $695
- $0
- No data

Vegetation

- Ice Cap
- Tundra
- Coniferous Forest
- Deciduous Forest
- Broadleaf Evergreen Forest
- Mixed Forest
- Midlatitude Scrubland
- Midlatitude Grassland
- Desert
- Tropical Seasonal and Scrub
- Tropical Rain Forest

WORLD POPULATION

- Asia 60.7%*
- Europe 2.1%**
- Africa 13.0%
- South America 5.7%
- Oceania 0.5%
- North America 7.9%

*Excluding Russia **Including Russia

Population

Persons per sq mi	Persons per sq km
Over 520	Over 200
260–519	100–199
130–259	50–99
25–129	10–49
1–24	1–9
0	0

CLIMATE

Average daily temperature °F range — High, Low

Average monthly precipitation Inches

ATLANTA, USA

FAIRBANKS, USA
Temp. Range -21 to -1

MEXICO CITY, Mexico

MINNEAPOLIS, USA

NUUK, Greenland

NEW YORK, USA

PHOENIX, USA

ST. JOHN'S, Canada

SAN FRANCISCO, USA

SAN JOSÉ, Costa Rica

SAN JUAN, Puerto Rico

VANCOUVER, Canada

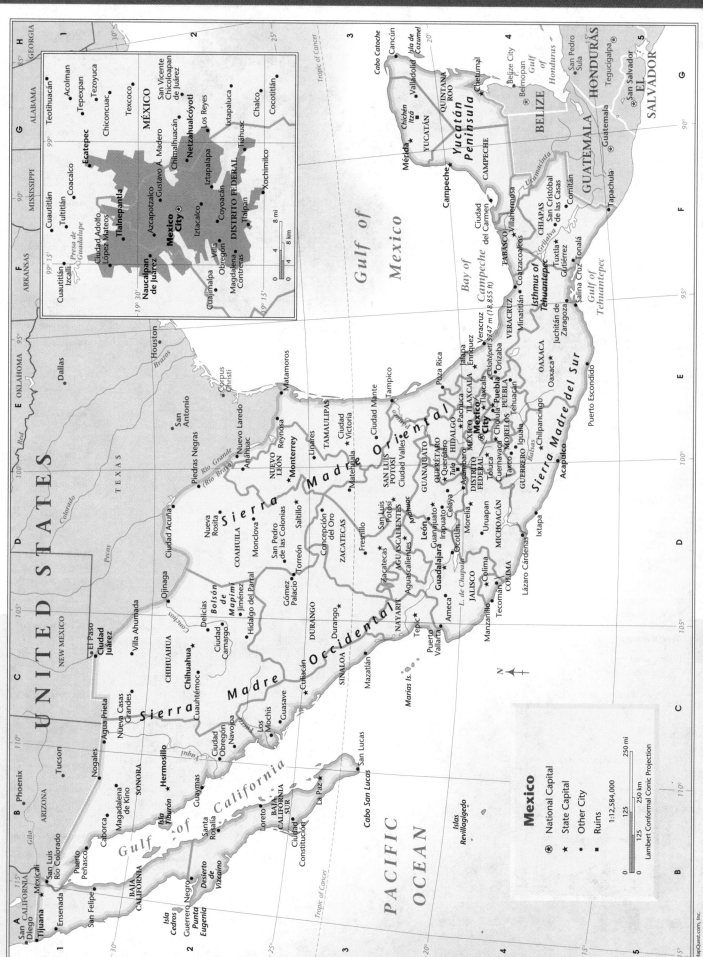

Mexico

Capital: Mexico City
Area: 756,066 sq. mi.
1,958,720 sq. km.
Population: 100,294,036
Largest City: Mexico City
Language: Spanish
Monetary Unit: New peso

Belize

Capital: Belmopan
Area: 8,867 sq. mi.
22,972 sq. km.
Population: 235,789
Largest City: Belize City
Language: English
Monetary Unit: Belize dollar

Belize: Map Index

Cities and Towns

Belize City	B2
Belmopan, capital	B2
Corozal	B1
Dangriga	B2
Hill Bank	B2
Maskall	B2
Neustadt	B1
Orange Walk	A2
Placentia	B3
Progresso	B1
Punta Gorda	B3
San Antonio	B3
San Ignacio	A2

Other Features

Ambergris Cay, island	C2
Belize, river	B2
Glover, reef	C3
Hondo, river	A1
Maya, mts.	B3
New, river	B1
Sarstoon, river	A4
Turneffe, islands	C2
Victoria, peak	B3

Guatemala

Capital: Guatemala City
Area: 42,042 sq. mi.
108,917 sq. km.
Population: 12,335,580
Largest City: Guatemala City
Language: Spanish
Monetary Unit: Quetzal

Guatemala: Map Index

Cities and Towns

Antigua	C5
Champerico	B5
Chinajá	C4
Cobán	C4
Escuintla	C5
Flores	D3
Guatemala City, capital	C5
Huehuetenango	B4
Jutiapa	C5
La Libertad	D3
Mazatenango	B5
Paxbán	C2
Puerto Barrios	E4
Quetzaltenango	B5
Salamá	C4
San José	C5
San Luis	D3
Santo Tomás de Castilla	E4
Tikal	D2
Zacapa	D5

Other Features

Atitlán, lake	B5
Chixoy, river	C4
Honduras, gulf	E3
Izabal, lake	E4
Motagua, river	C4
Pasión, river	C3
Paz, river	C6
Petén-Itzá, lake	D3
San Pedro, river	D2
Sierra Madre, mts.	A5
Sarstún, river	D4
Suchiate, river	A4
Tacaná, volcano	B4
Tajumulco, volcano	C3
Usumacinta, river	C3

© MapQuest.com, Inc.

Mexico: Map Index

States

Aguascalientes	D3
Baja California	A1
Baja California Sur	B2
Campeche	F4
Chiapas	F4
Chihuahua	C2
Coahuila	D2
Colima	D4
Distrito Federal	E4, Inset
Durango	D3
Guanajuato	D3
Guerrero	D4
Hidalgo	E3
Jalisco	D3
México	E4, Inset
Michoacán	D4
Morelos	Inset
Nayarit	C3
Nuevo León	E2
Oaxaca	E4
Puebla	E4
Querétaro	D3
Quintana Roo	G3
San Luis Potosí	D3
Sinaloa	C3
Sonora	B1
Tabasco	F4
Tamaulipas	E3
Tlaxcala	E4
Veracruz	E4
Yucatán	G3
Zacatecas	D3

Cities and Towns

Acámbaro	D4
Acapulco	Inset
Acolman	Inset
Agua Prieta	C1
Aguascalientes, state capital	D3
Ameca	D3
Anáhuac	Inset
Azcapotzalco	Inset
Caborca	B1
Campeche, state capital	F4
Cancún	G3
Celaya	D3
Chalco	Inset
Chetumal, state capital	G4
Chiconcuac	Inset
Chihuahua, state capital	C2
Chilpancingo, state capital	E4
Chimalhuacán	Inset
Cholula	E4
Ciudad Acuña	D2
Ciudad Adolfo López Mateos	Inset
Ciudad Camargo	C2
Ciudad Constitución	B3
Ciudad del Carmen	F4
Ciudad Juárez	C1
Ciudad Madero	E3
Ciudad Obregón	C2
Ciudad Victoria, state capital	E3
Coacalco	Inset
Coatzacoalcos	F4
Cocotitlán	Inset
Colima, state capital	D4
Comitán	F4
Concepción del Oro	D3
Coyoacán	Inset
Cuajimalpa	Inset
Cuauhtémoc	Inset
Cuautitlán	Inset
Cuautitlán Izcalli	Inset
Cuernavaca, state capital	E4
Culiacán, state capital	C3
Delicias	C2
Durango, state capital	D3
Ecatepec	Inset
Ensenada	A1
Fresnillo	D3
Gómez Palacio	D2
Guadalajara, state capital	D3
Guanajuato, state capital	D3
Guasave	C2
Guaymas	B2
Guerrero Negro	B2
Hermosillo, state capital	B2
Hidalgo del Parral	C2
Iguala	E4
Irapuato	D3
Ixtapa	D4
Ixtapaluca	Inset
Iztacalco	Inset
Iztapalapa	Inset
Jalapa Enríquez, state capital	E4
Jiménez	D2
Juchitán de Zaragoza	F4
La Paz, state capital	B3
Lázaro Cárdenas	D4
León	D3
Linares	E3
Loreto	B2
Los Mochis	C2
Los Reyes	Inset
Magdalena de Kino	B1
Magdalena Contreras	Inset
Manzanillo	D4
Matamoros	E2
Matehuala	D3
Mazatlán	C3
Mérida, state capital	G3
Mexicali, state capital	A1
Mexico City, national capital	E4, Inset
Minatitlán	F4
Monclova	D2
Monterrey, state capital	D2
Morelia, state capital	D4
Naucalpan de Juárez	Inset
Navojoa	C2
Netzahualcóyotl	Inset
Nogales	B1
Nueva Casas Grandes	C1
Nuevo Laredo	E2
Oaxaca, state capital	E4
Ocotlán	D3
Ojinaga	D2
Orizaba	E4
Pachuca, state capital	E3
Piedras Negras	D2
Poza Rica	E3
Puebla, state capital	E4
Puerto Escondido	E4
Puerto Peñasco	B1
Puerto Vallarta	C3
Querétaro, state capital	D3
Reynosa	E2
Salina Cruz	E4
Saltillo, state capital	D2
San Cristóbal de las Casas	F4
San Felipe	B1
San Lucas	Inset
San Luis Potosí, state capital	D3
San Luis Río Colorado	B1
San Pedro de las Colonias	D2
Santa Rosalía	B2
San Vicente Chicoloapan	Inset
Tampico	E3
Tapachula	F5
Taxco	E4
Tecomán	D4
Tehuacán	E4
Teotihuacán	Inset
Tepexpan	Inset
Tepic, state capital	D3
Texcoco	Inset
Tijuana	A1
Tláhuac	Inset
Tlalnepantla	Inset
Tlalpan	Inset
Tlaxcala, state capital	E4
Toluca, state capital	E4
Tonalá	D2
Torreón	D2
Tultitlán	Inset
Tuxtla Gutiérrez, state capital	F4
Uruapan	D4
Valladolid	G3
Veracruz	E4
Villa Ahumada	C1
Villahermosa, state capital	F4
Villa Obregón	Inset
Xochimilco	Inset
Zacatecas, state capital	D3

Other Features

Anáhuac, depression	Inset
Balsas, river	D4
Bolsón de Mapimí, depression	D2
California, gulf	C3
Campeche, bay	F4
Catoche, cape	G3
Cedros, island	A2
Chapala, lake	D3
Chichén Itzá, ruins	G3
Citlaltépetl, mt.	E4
Conchos, river	C2
Cozumel, island	G3
Eugenia, point	A2
Fuerte, river	C2
Grijalva, river	F4
Guadalupe, reservoir	Inset
Marías, islands	C3
Mexico, gulf	E2
Revillagigedo, islands	B4
Río Grande (Río Bravo), river	D2
Sierra Madre del Sur, mts.	D4
Sierra Madre Occidental, mts.	C2
Sierra Madre Oriental, mts.	D2
Tehuantepec, gulf	F4
Tehuantepec, isthmus	F4
Tiburón, island	B2
Tula, ruins	D3
Usumacinta, river	F4
Vizcaíno, desert	B2
Yaqui, river	C2
Yucatán, peninsula	G4

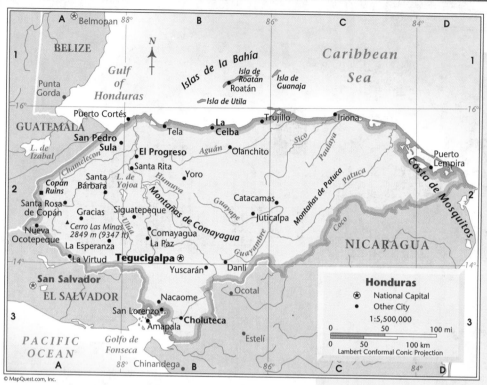

Honduras

Capital: Tegucigalpa
Area: 43,277 sq. mi.
112,117 sq. km.
Population: 5,997,327
Largest City: Tegucigalpa
Language: Spanish
Monetary Unit: Lempira

Honduras:
Map Index

Cities and Towns

Amapala	B3
Catacamas	C2
Choluteca	B3
Comayagua	B2
Danlí	B2
El Progreso	B2
Gracias	A2
Iriona	C2
Juticalpa	B2
La Ceiba	B2
La Esperanza	A2
La Paz	B2
La Virtud	A2
Nacaome	B3
Nueva Ocotepeque	A2
Olanchito	B2
Puerto Cortés	B2
Puerto Lempira	D2
Roatán	B1
San Lorenzo	B3
San Pedro Sula	B2
Santa Bárbara	A2
Santa Rita	B2
Santa Rosa de Copán	A2
Siguatepeque	B2
Tegucigalpa, capital	B2
Tela	B
Trujillo	C
Yoro	B
Yuscarán	B

Other Features

Aguán, river	B
Bahía, islands	C
Caribbean, sea	C
Chamelecon, river	A
Coco, river	A
Comayagua, mts.	B
Copán, ruins	A
Fonseca, gulf	B
Guanaja, island	C
Guayambre, river	B
Guayape, river	B
Honduras, gulf	B
Humuya, river	A
Las Minas, mt.	A
Mosquitos, coast	D
Patuca, mts.	C
Patuca, river	C
Paulaya, river	B
Roatán, island	B
Sico, river	B
Ulúa, river	B
Utila, island	B
Yojoa, lake	B

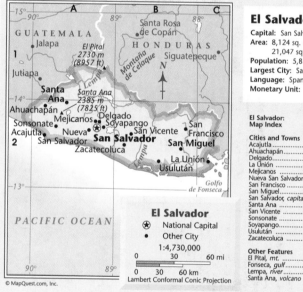

El Salvador

Capital: San Salvador
Area: 8,124 sq. mi.
21,047 sq. km.
Population: 5,839,079
Largest City: San Salvador
Language: Spanish
Monetary Unit: Colón

El Salvador:
Map Index

Cities and Towns

Acajutla	A2
Ahuachapán	A2
Delgado	A2
La Unión	C2
Mejicanos	A2
Nueva San Salvador	A2
San Francisco	B2
San Miguel	B2
San Salvador, capital	A2
Santa Ana	A2
San Vicente	B2
Sonsonate	A2
Soyapango	A2
Usulután	B2
Zacatecoluca	B2

Other Features

El Pital, mt.	A1
Fonseca, gulf	C2
Lempa, river	A1, B2
Santa Ana, volcano	A2

Costa Rica:
Map Index

Cities and Towns

Alajuela	B2
Cartago	C3
Colorado	C3
Golfito	C4
Heredia	B2
La Cruz	A1
Liberia	A2
Limón	C3
Los Chiles	B1
Puerto Jiménez	C4
Puerto Quepos	B3
Puntarenas	B3
San José, capital	B3
Santa Cruz	A2

Other Features

Arenal, lake	B2
Central, range	B2
Chirripó, mt.	C3
Chirripó, river	C4
Coronado, bay	B3
Dulce, gulf	C4
Frío, river	B2
General, river	C3
Grande, river	B3
Guanacaste, range	A2
Irazú, volcano	C3
Nicoya, gulf	B3
Papagayo, gulf	A2
Pirris, river	B3
Reventazón, river	C2
San Carlos, river	B2
San Juan, river	B1
Sarapiquí river	B2
Sixaola, river	C3
Talamanca, range	C3
Tempisque, river	A2

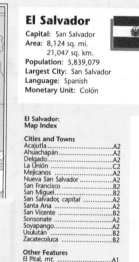

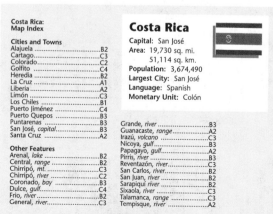

Costa Rica

Capital: San José
Area: 19,730 sq. mi.
51,114 sq. km.
Population: 3,674,490
Largest City: San José
Language: Spanish
Monetary Unit: Colón

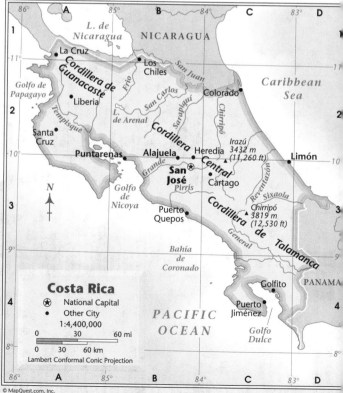

© MapQuest.com, Inc.

Nicaragua

Capital: Managua
Area: 50,880 sq. mi.
131,813 sq. km.
Population: 4,717,132
Largest City: Managua
Language: Spanish
Monetary Unit: Córdoba

Nicaragua:
Map Index

Cities and Towns

Bluefields	C3
Boaco	B2
Bocay	B1
Chinandega	A2
Colonia Nueva Guinea	B3
Corinto	A2
Diriamba	A3
Estelí	B2
Granada	B3
Jinotega	B2
Jinotepe	A3
Juigalpa	B2
La Rosita	B2
León	A2
Managua, *capital*	A2
Masaya	A3
Matagalpa	B2
Nagarote	A2
Ocotal	A2
Prinzapolka	C2
Puerto Cabezas	C1
Puerto Sandino	A2
Rama	B2
Río Blanco	B2
Río Grande	A2
Rivas	B3
San Carlos	B3
San Juan del Norte	C3
San Juan del Sur	B3
Siuna	B2
Somoto	A2
Waspam	C1
Wiwilí	B2

Other Features

Bambana, *river*	B2
Bismuna, *lagoon*	C1
Bluefields, *bay*	C3
Bocay, *river*	B2
Chontaleña, *mts.*	B2
Coco, *river*	A2, C1
Cosigüina, *mt.*	A2
Cosigüina, *point*	A2
Dariense, *mts.*	B2
Escondido, *river*	B2
Fonseca, *gulf*	A2
Gracias a Dios, *cape*	C1
Grande de Matagalpa, *river*	B2
Huapí, *mts.*	B2
Isabelia, *mts.*	B2
Kurinwás, *river*	B2
Maíz, *islands*	C2
Managua, *lake*	A2
Mico, *river*	B2
Miskitos, *cays*	C1
Mogotón, *mt.*	A2
Mosquitos, *coast*	C3
Nicaragua, *lake*	B3
Ometepe, *island*	B3
Perlas, *lagoon*	C2
Perlas, *point*	C2
Prinzapolka, *river*	B2
San Juan, *river*	B3
San Juan del Norte, *bay*	C3
Siquia, *river*	B2
Solentiname, *island*	B3
Tipitapa, *river*	A2
Tuma, *river*	B2
Wawa, *river*	B1
Zapatera, *island*	B3

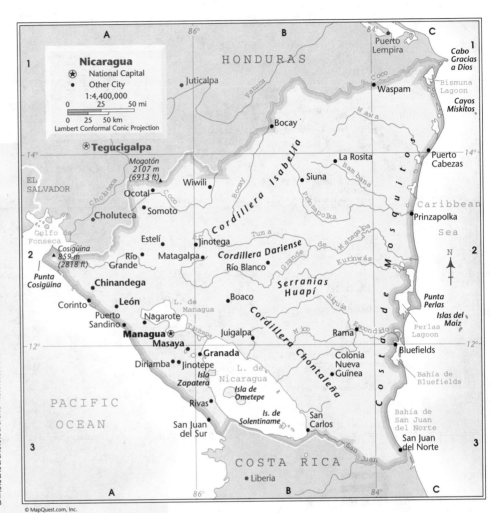

© MapQuest.com, Inc.

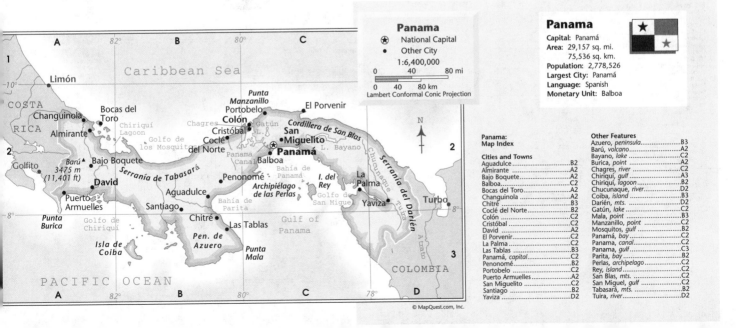

Panama

Capital: Panamá
Area: 29,157 sq. mi.
75,536 sq. km.
Population: 2,778,526
Largest City: Panamá
Language: Spanish
Monetary Unit: Balboa

Panama:
Map Index

Cities and Towns

Aguadulce	B2
Almirante	A2
Bajo Boquete	A2
Balboa	C2
Bocas del Toro	A2
Changuinola	A2
Chitré	B3
Coclé del Norte	B2
Colón	C2
Cristóbal	C2
David	A2
El Porvenir	C2
La Palma	C2
Las Tablas	B3
Panamá, *capital*	C2
Penonomé	B2
Portobelo	C2
Puerto Armuelles	A2
San Miguelito	C2
Santiago	B2
Yaviza	D2

Other Features

Azuero, *peninsula*	B3
Barú, *volcano*	A2
Bayano, *lake*	C2
Burica, *point*	A2
Chagres, *river*	C2
Chiriquí, *gulf*	A3
Chiriquí, *lagoon*	B2
Chucunaque, *river*	D2
Coiba, *island*	B3
Darién, *mts.*	D2
Gatún, *lake*	C2
Mala, *point*	B3
Manzanillo, *point*	C2
Mosquitos, *gulf*	B2
Panamá, *bay*	C2
Panama, *canal*	C2
Parita, *bay*	B2
Perlas, *archipelago*	C2
Rey, *island*	C2
San Blas, *mts.*	C2
San Miguel, *gulf*	C2
Tabasará, *mts.*	B2
Tuira, *river*	D2

© MapQuest.com, Inc.

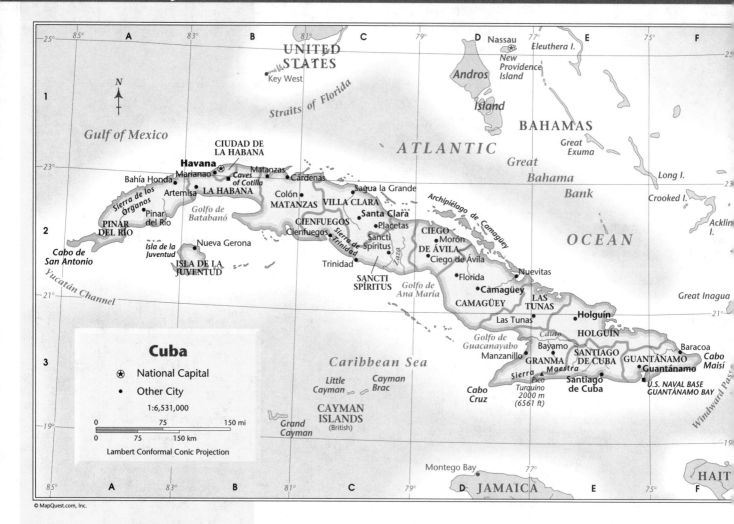

Cuba

- ⊛ National Capital
- • Other City

1:6,531,000

0   75   150 mi
0   75   150 km

Lambert Conformal Conic Projection

© MapQuest.com, Inc.

Cuba

Capital: Havana
Area: 42,804 sq. mi.
    110,890 sq. km.
Population: 11,096,395
Largest City: Havana
Language: Spanish
Monetary Unit: Peso

Cuba:
Map Index

Provinces

Camagüey	D2
Ciego de Ávila	D2
Cienfuegos	C2
Ciudad de La Habana	B1
Granma	E3
Guantánamo	E3
Holguín	E3
Isla de la Juventud (special municipality)	B2
La Habana	B2
Las Tunas	E2
Matanzas	B2
Pinar del Río	A2
Sancti Spíritus	C2
Santiago de Cuba	E3
Villa Clara	C2

Cities and Towns

Artemisa	B2
Bahía Honda	A2
Baracoa	F3
Bayamo	E3
Camagüey	D2
Cárdenas	B1
Ciego de Ávila	D2
Cienfuegos	C2
Colón	C2
Florida	D2
Guantánamo	E3
Havana, capital	B1
Holguín	E3
Las Tunas	E3

Manzanillo	D3
Marianao	B1
Matanzas	B1
Morón	D2
Nueva Gerona	B2
Nuevitas	D2
Pinar del Río	A2
Placetas	C2
Sagua la Grande	C2
Sancti Spíritus	C2
Santa Clara	C2
Santiago de Cuba	E3
Trinidad	C2

Other Features

Ana María, gulf	D2
Batabanó, gulf	B2
Camagüey, archipelago	D2
Cauto, river	E3
Cotilla, caves	B2
Cruz, cape	D3
Florida, straits	B1
Guacanayabo, gulf	D3
Juventud, island	B2
Maestra, mts.	D3
Maísí, cape	F3
Mexico, gulf	A1
Órganos, mts.	A2
San Antonio, cape	A2
Trinidad, mts.	C2
Turquino, mt.	E3
U.S. Naval Base Guantánamo Bay	E3
Windward, passage	F3
Yucatán, channel	A2
Zaza, river	C2

Jamaica

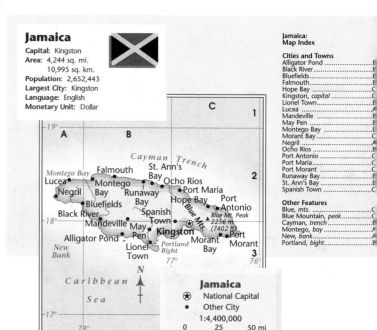

Capital: Kingston
Area: 4,244 sq. mi.
    10,995 sq. km.
Population: 2,652,443
Largest City: Kingston
Language: English
Monetary Unit: Dollar

Jamaica

- ⊛ National Capital
- • Other City

1:4,400,000

0   25   50 mi
0   25   50 km

Lambert Conformal Conic Projection

© MapQuest.com, Inc.

Jamaica:
Map Index

Cities and Towns

Alligator Pond	E
Black River	E
Bluefields	E
Falmouth	E
Hope Bay	C
Kingston, capital	C
Lionel Town	A
Lucea	A
Mandeville	E
May Pen	C
Montego Bay	A
Morant Bay	A
Negril	A
Ocho Rios	C
Port Antonio	C
Port Maria	C
Port Morant	E
Runaway Bay	A
St. Ann's Bay	A
Spanish Town	C

Other Features

Blue, mts.	C
Blue Mountain, peak	C
Cayman, trench	A
Montego, bay	A
New, bank	C
Portland, bight	C

Cotuí..............................B1
Dajabón A1
El Macao D2
El Seibo C2
Hato Mayor C2
Higüey D2
Jimaní A2
La Romana D2
La Vega B1
Luperón B1
Mao A1
Miches C2
Moca A1
Monte Cristi A1
Monte Plata C2
Nagua C1
Neiba A2
Oviedo A3
Pedernales A3
Pedro Santana A1
Puerto Plata B1
Sabana de la Mar C1
Sabaneta A1
Salcedo B1
Samaná C1
San Cristóbal B2
San Francisco de Macorís B1
San José de las Matas ...A1
San Juan A2
San Pedro de Macorís ...C2
Santiago B1
Santo Domingo, capital ..C2
Sousúa B1

Other Features
Bahoruco, mts. A2
Beata, cape A3
Beata, island A3
Calderas, bay B2
Camú, river B1
Central, range B2
Cibao, valley A1
Duarte, mt. B1
Engaño, cape D2
Enriquillo, lake A2
Mona, passage D2
Neiba, mts. A2
Ocoa, bay B2
Oriental, range C2
Ozama, river B2
Samaná, bay C1
Samaná, cape C1
Saona, island D2
Septentrional, range A1
Soco, river C2
Yaque del Norte, river A1
Yaque del Sur, river A2
Yuna, river B2

**Dominican Republic:
Map Index**

Provinces
Azua B2
Bahoruco A2
Barahona A2
Dajabón A1
Distrito Nacional B2
Duarte C1
El Seibo C2
Espaillat B1
Hato Mayor C2
Independencia A2
La Altagracia D2
La Estrelleta A1
La Romana D2
La Vega B2
María Trinidad Sánchez ...B1
Monseñor Nouel B2
Monte Cristi A1
Monte Plata C2
Pedernales A3
Peravia B2
Puerto Plata B1
Salcedo B1
Samaná C1
Sánchez Ramírez B1
San Cristóbal B2
San Juan A2
San Pedro de Macorís C2
Santiago B1
Santiago Rodríguez A1
Valverde B1

Cities and Towns
Azua B2
Baní B2
Barahona A2
Bonao B2
Cabrera C1
Comendador A2

Dominican Republic

Capital: Santo Domingo
Area: 18,704 sq. mi.
48,456 sq. km.
Population: 8,129,734
Largest City: Santo Domingo
Language: Spanish
Monetary Unit: Peso

aiti:
ap Index

Departments
rtibonite C1
entre D1
rand Ande B2
ord C1
ord-Est D1
ord-Ouest B1
uest C2
ud B2
ud-Est C2

Cities and Towns
nse-à-Galets C2
elle-Anse C2
ap-Haïtien C1
ame-Marie A2
nnery C1
onaïves C1
inche C1
acmel C2
rémie A2
éogâne C2
es Cayes B2
iragoâne B2
irebalais C2
ort-au-Prince, capital C2
ort-Salut B2
ort-de-Paix C1
ort-Salut B2
aint-Marc C1

Other Features
Artibonite, river C1
Gonâve, gulf B1
Gonâve, island B2
Gravois, point B3
Pic de la Selle, mt. D2
Port-au-Prince, bay C2
Tortuga, island C1
Vache, island B2
Windward, passage B1

Haiti

Capital: Port-au-Prince
Area: 10,695 sq. mi.
27,614 sq. km.
Population: 6,884,264
Largest City: Port-au-Prince
Languages: French, Creole
Monetary Unit: Gourde

The Bahamas

Capital: Nassau
Area: 5,382 sq. mi.
13,943 sq. km.
Population: 283,705
Largest City: Nassau
Languages: English, Creole
Monetary Unit: Dollar

Turks and Caicos Is.

Capital: Grand Turk
Area: 193 sq. mi.
500 sq. km.
Population: 16,863
Largest City: Grand Turk
Language: English
Monetary Unit: U.S. Dollar

**Bahamas and
Turks & Caicos Islands:
Map Index**

Bahamas

Cities and Towns
Alice Town B2
Arthur's Town B3
Freeport A2
Kemps Bay B3
Marsh Harbour B2
Matthew Town C4
Nassau, capital B2
Nicholls' Town B2
Sandy Point B2

Other Features
Acklins, island C4
Andros, island A3
Cat, island B3
Crooked, island C4
Crooked Island, passage ..C4
Eleuthera, island B2
Exuma, sound B3
Grand Bahama, island A2
Great Abaco, island B2
Great Bahama, bank A3

Great Exuma, island B3
Great Inagua, island C4
Harbour, island C4
Little Inagua, island C4
Long, island C3
Mayaguana, island C4
Mayaguana, passage C4
New Providence, island ...B3
Northeast Providence,
channel B2
Rum, cay C3
Samana, cay C3
San Salvador, island C3
Water, cays A3

Turks & Caicos Islands

Cities and Towns
Cockburn Harbour D4
Grand Turk, capital D4

Other Features
Ambergris, cay D4
Caicos, islands D4
Grand Turk, island D4
Providenciales, island C4
Salt, cay D4
Turks, islands D4

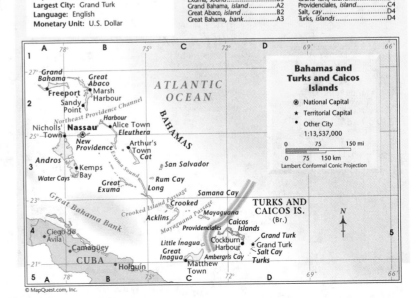

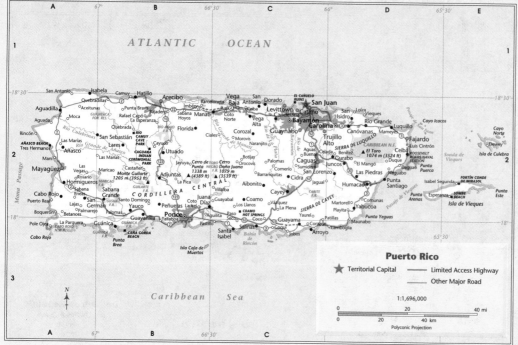

Puerto Rico

Capital: San Juan
Area: 3,492 sq. mi.
9,047 sq. km.
Population: 3,887,652
Largest City: San Juan
Languages: Spanish, English
Monetary Unit: U.S. dollar

Puerto Rico: Map Index

Cities and Towns

Adjuntas	B2
Aguada	A2
Aguadilla	A2
Aguas Buenas	C2
Aguilita	B2
Aibonito	C2
Añasco	A2
Arecibo	B2
Arroyo	C3
Bajadero	B2
Barceloneta	B2
Barranquitas	C2
Bayamón	C2
Cabo Rojo	A2
Caguas	C2
Camuy	B2
Candelaria	C2
Canóvanas	D2
Carolina	D2
Cataño	C2
Cayey	C2
Ceiba	D2
Ceiba	D2
Celada	D2
Ciales	C2
Cidra	C2
Coamo	C2
Coco	C2
Comerío	C2
Coquí	C3
Corazón	C3
Corozal	C2
Coto Laurel	B2
Dorado	C2
Fajardo	D2
Florida	B2
Guánica	B3
Guayama	C2
Guayanilla	B2
Guaynabo	C2
Gurabo	D2
Hatillo	B2
Hormigueros	A2
Humacao	D2
Imbéry	B2
Isabela	A1
Jayuya	B2
Jobos	C3
Juana Díaz	C2
Juncos	D2
Lajas	A2
Lares	B2
Las Piedras	D2
Levittown	C2
Loíza	D2
Luquillo	D2
Manatí	B2
Martorell	D2
Maunabo	D2
Mayagüez	A2
Moca	A2
Naguabo	D2
Pastillo	C3
Patillas	D2
Peñuelas	B2
Ponce	B2
Puerto Real	A2
Punta Santiago	D2

Quebradillas	B2
Río Grande	D2
Sabana Grande	A2
Salinas	C2
San Antonio	A2
San Germán	A2
San Isidro	D2
San Juan, capital	C2
San Lorenzo	D2
San Sebastián	A2
Santa Isabel	C2
Santo Domingo	A2
Trujillo Alto	C2
Utuado	B2
Vega Alta	C2
Vega Baja	C2
Vieques	E2
Villalba	C2
Yabucoa	D2
Yauco	B2

Other Features

Añasco, beach	A2
Arenas, point	D2
Bayamón, river	C2
Brea, point	B2
Cabo Rojo Natl. Wildlife Refuge	A3
Caguana Indian Ceremonial Park	B2
Caja de Muertos, island	C3
Caña Gorda, beach	B3
Caribbean, sea	C3
Caribbean Natl. Forest	D2
Carite Forest Reserve	C2
Coamo Hot Springs	C2
Cordillera Central, mts.	B2
Culebra, island	F1
Culebrinas, river	A2
Doña Juana, mt.	C2
El Cañuelo, ruins	C2
El Toro, mt.	D2
Este, point	F2
Fortín Conde de Mirasol, fort.	E2
Grande de Añasco, river	B2
Grande de Manatí, river	B2
Guajataca Forest Reserve	B2
Guánica Forest Reserve	B3
Guilarte, mt.	B2
Guilarte Forest Reserve	B2
Icacos, key	E1
La Plata, river	C2
Maricao Forest Reserve	B2
Mona, passage	A2
Norte, key	E1
Puerca, point	E1
Punta, mt.	A2
Rincón, bay	A2
Río Abajo Forest Reserve	B2
Río Camuy Cave Park	B2
Rojo, cape	A2
Roosevelt Roads Naval Station	E2
San Juan, passage	E2
Sierra de Cayey, mts.	C2
Sierra de Luquillo, mts.	D2
Sombe, beach	E2
Susua Forest Reserve	B2
Toro Negro Forest Reserve	B2
Vieques, island	E2
Vieques, passage	E2
Vieques, sound	E1
Yeguas, point	C3

Antigua & Barbuda

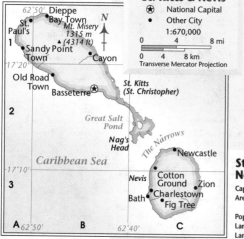

⊛ National Capital
• Other City
1:1,480,000

Antigua and Barbuda

Capital: St. John's
Area: 171 sq. mi.
443 sq. km.
Population: 64,246
Largest City: St. John's
Language: English
Monetary Unit: East Caribbean dollar

Antigua and Barbuda: Map Index

Cities and Towns

Bolands	D5
Cedar Grove	E5
Codrington	E2
Falmouth	E5
Freetown	E5
Old Road	D5
St. John's, capital	D5

Other Features

Antigua, island	D4
Barbuda, island	E3
Boggy, peak	D5
Cobb, cove	E1
Codrington, lagoon	D1
Goat, point	D1
Gravenor, bay	E2
Palmetto, point	D2
Redonda, island	A6
Shirley, cape	E6
Spanish, point	E2
Willoughby, bay	E5

Dominica: Map Index

Cities and Towns

Berekua	B4
Castle Bruce	B2
Colihaut	A2
Glanvillia	A2
La Plaine	B3
Laudat	B3
Marigot	B2
Massacre	B3
Pointe Michel	B3
Pont Cassé	B3
Portsmouth	A2
Rosalie	B3
Roseau, capital	B3
Saint Joseph	A3
Salibia	B2
Salisbury	A2
Soufrière	B4
Vieille Case	B1
Wesley	B1

Other Features

Boiling, lake	B3
Dominica, passage	A1
Grand, bay	B4
Layou, river	B3
Morne Diablotin, mt.	B2
Roseau, river	B3
Toulaman, river	B2

Dominica

Capital: Roseau
Area: 290 sq. mi.
751 sq. km.
Population: 64,881
Largest City: Roseau
Language: English
Monetary Unit: East Caribbean dollar

St. Kitts & Nevis

⊛ National Capital
• Other City
1:670,000

St. Kitts & Nevis: Map Index

Cities and Towns

Basseterre, capital	B2
Bath	C3
Cayon	B1
Charlestown	C3
Cotton Ground	C3
Dieppe Bay Town	B1
Fig Tree	C3
Newcastle	C2
Old Road Town	A1
St. Paul's	A1
Sandy Point Town	A1
Zion	C3

Other Features

Great Salt, pond	C2
Nag's Head, cape	C2
Narrows, strait	C2
Nevis, island	C3
St. Kitts (St. Christopher), island	B2

St. Kitts & Nevis

Capital: Basseterre
Area: 104 sq. mi.
269 sq. km.
Population: 42,838
Largest City: Basseterre
Language: English
Monetary Unit: East Caribbean dollar

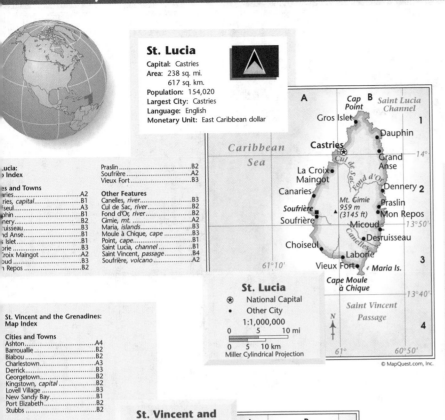

St. Lucia
Capital: Castries
Area: 238 sq. mi.
617 sq. km.
Population: 154,020
Largest City: Castries
Language: English
Monetary Unit: East Caribbean dollar

Lucia:
s Index

es and Towns
aries..............................A2
aries, *capital*..............B1
seul..............................A3
phin..............................B1
ery..............................B2
russeau..........................B3
d Anse..........................B1
Islet..............................B1
orie..............................A3
roix Maingot....................B2
oud..............................B3
Repos..........................B2

Praslin..............................B2
Soufrière..........................A2
Vieux Fort........................B3

Other Features
Canelles, *river*..................B3
Cul de Sac, *river*..............B2
Fond d'Or, *river*................B2
Gimie, *mt.*......................A2
Maria, *islands*..................B3
Moule à Chique, *cape*........B3
Point, *cape*....................B1
Saint Lucia, *channel*..........B1
Saint Vincent, *passage*......B4
Soufrière, *volcano*............A2

St. Lucia
⊛ National Capital
• Other City
1:1,000,000
0   5   10 mi
0   5   10 km
Miller Cylindrical Projection

© MapQuest.com, Inc.

St. Vincent and the Grenadines:
Map Index

Cities and Towns
Ashton..............................A4
Barrouallie........................B2
Biabou..............................B2
Charlestown......................A3
Derrick..............................B3
Georgetown......................B2
Kingstown, *capital*............B2
Lovell Village....................B3
New Sandy Bay..................B1
Port Elizabeth....................B2
Stubbs..............................B2

Other Features
Baleine, *bay*....................B1
Baliceaux, *island*..............B3
Bequia, *island*..................B2
Canouan, *island*..............B3
Grenadines, *islands*..........A3
Mayreau, *island*..............A4
Mt. Wynn, *bay*................B2
Mustique, *island*..............B3
North Mayreau, *channel*....A3
Palm, *island*....................A4
Petit Canouan, *island*........B3
Petit Mustique, *island*........B3
Petit St. Vincent, *island*......A4
St. Vincent, *island*............B2
Savan, *island*..................B3
Soufrière, *mt.*..................B1
Tobago, *cays*..................A4
Union, *island*..................A4
Windward, *islands*............B4

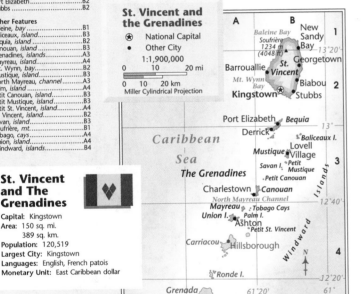

St. Vincent and the Grenadines
⊛ National Capital
• Other City
1:1,900,000
0   10   20 mi
0   10   20 km
Miller Cylindrical Projection

© MapQuest.com, Inc.

St. Vincent and The Grenadines
Capital: Kingstown
Area: 150 sq. mi.
389 sq. km.
Population: 120,519
Largest City: Kingstown
Languages: English, French patois
Monetary Unit: East Caribbean dollar

Barbados
Capital: Bridgetown
Area: 166 sq. mi.
430 sq. km.
Population: 259,191
Largest City: Bridgetown
Language: English
Monetary Unit: Dollar

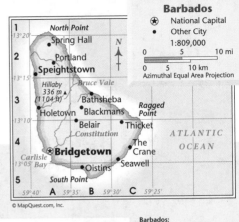

Barbados
⊛ National Capital
• Other City
1:809,000
0   5   10 mi
0   5   10 km
Azimuthal Equal Area Projection

© MapQuest.com, Inc.

Barbados:
Map Index

Cities and Towns
Bathsheba..........................B3
Belair..............................B4
Blackmans..........................B3
Bridgetown, *capital*............A4
Holetown..........................A3
Oistins..............................B5
Portland............................A2
Seawell..............................C4
Speightstown......................A2
Spring Hall........................A2
The Crane..........................C4
Thicket..............................C4

Other Features
Bruce Vale, *river*..............B3
Carlisle, *bay*....................A4
Constitution, *river*............B4
Hillaby, *mt.*....................A3
North, *point*....................A1
Ragged, *point*..................C3
South, *point*....................B5

Trinidad & Tobago
Capital: Port of Spain
Area: 1,980 sq. mi.
5,130 sq. km.
Population: 1,102,096
Largest City: Port of Spain
Language: English
Monetary Unit: Dollar

Charlotteville........................B1
Couva................................A2
Fullarton............................A2
Guayaguayare......................A2
Matelot..............................A2
Moruga..............................A2
Pierreville..........................A2
Plymouth............................B1
Point Fortin........................A2
Port of Spain, *capital*..........A2
Princes Town......................A2
Rio Claro............................A2
St. Augustine......................A2
San Fernando......................A2
San Francique......................A2
Sangre Grande....................A2
Scarborough........................B1
Siparia..............................A2
Toco..................................B2

Trinidad &
Tobago:
Map Index

Cities and Towns
Arima................................A2
Canaan..............................B1
Chaguanas..........................A2

Other Features
El Cerro del Aripo, *mt.*........A2
Paria, *gulf*......................A2
Pitch, *lake*......................A2
Tobago, *island*..................B1
Trinidad, *island*................A2

Trinidad & Tobago
⊛ National Capital
• Other City
1:2,700,000
0   15   30 mi
0   15   30 km
Azimuthal Equal Area Projection

© MapQuest.com, Inc.

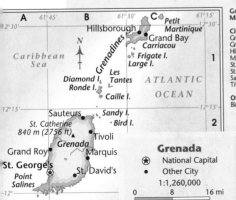

Grenada:
Map Index

Cities and Towns
Grand Bay..........................C1
Grand Roy..........................B2
Hillsborough......................C1
Marquis..............................B2
St. David's..........................B2
St. George's, *capital*..........A2
Sauteurs............................B2
Tivoli................................B2

Other Features
Bird, *island*......................B2

Caille, *island*....................B1
Carriacou, *island*..............C1
Diamond, *island*..............B1
Frigate, *island*..................C1
Grenada, *island*................B2
Grenadines, *island*
group..........................B1, C1
Large, *island*....................C1
Les Tantes, *island*............B1
Petit Martinique, *island*......B1
Ronde, *island*..................B1
St. Catherine, *mt.*............B2
Salines, *point*..................A2
Sandy, *island*..................B2

Grenada
Capital: St. George's
Area: 133 sq. mi.
345 sq. km.
Population: 97,008
Largest City: St. George's
Language: English
Monetary Unit: East Caribbean dollar

Grenada
⊛ National Capital
• Other City
1:1,260,000
0   8   16 mi
0   8   16 km
Transverse Mercator Projection

© MapQuest.com, Inc.

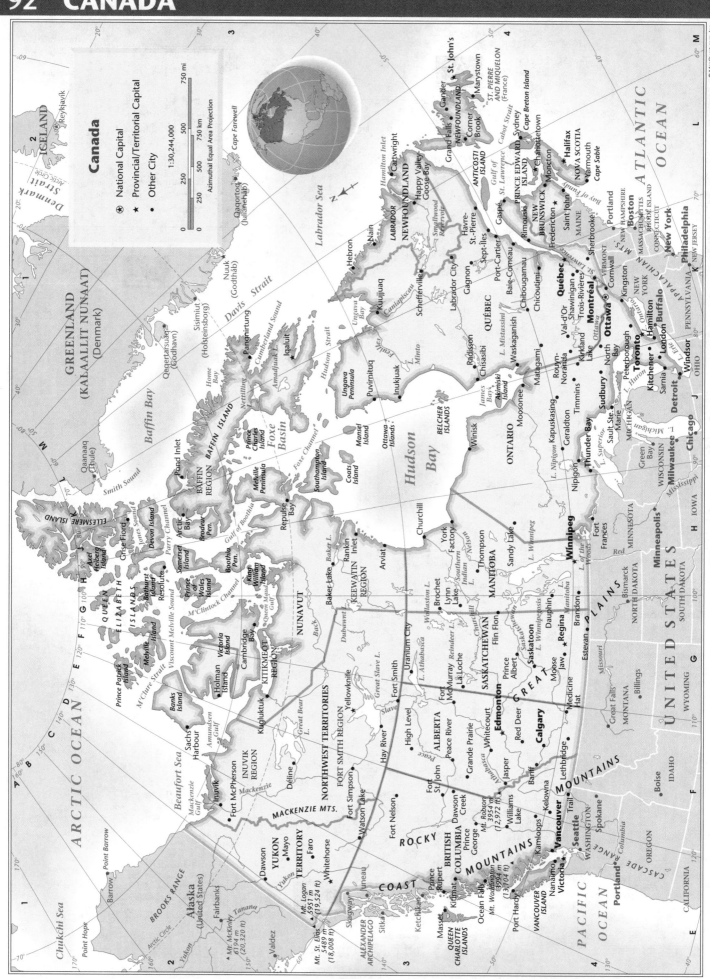

Canada: Map Index

ALBERTA
Cities and Towns
Banff ... F3
Calgary ... F3
Edmonton, capital ... F3
Fort McMurray ... G3
Grande Prairie ... E3
High Level ... F3
Jasper ... E3
Lethbridge ... F4
Medicine Hat ... F4
Peace River ... E3
Red Deer ... F3
Whitecourt ... F3
Other Features
Athabasca, river ... F3
Peace, river ... E3

BRITISH COLUMBIA
Cities and Towns
Dawson Creek ... E3
Fort Nelson ... E2
Fort St. John ... E3
Kamloops ... E4
Kelowna ... F4
Kitimat ... D3
Masset ... D3
Nanaimo ... E4
Ocean Falls ... D3
Port Hardy ... D3
Prince George ... E3
Prince Rupert ... D3
Trail ... F4
Vancouver ... E4
Victoria, capital ... E4
Williams Lake ... E3
Other Features
Coast, mts. ... D3
Fraser, river ... E3
Queen Charlotte, islands ... C3
Robson, mt. ... E3
Rocky, mts. ... G2
Vancouver, island ... E4
Waddington, mt. ... E3

MANITOBA
Cities and Towns
Brandon ... G4
Brochet ... G3
Churchill ... H3
Dauphin ... G3
Flin Flon ... G3
Lynn Lake ... G3
Thompson ... H3
Winnipeg, capital ... G4
York Factory ... H3
Other Features
Hudson, bay ... H3
Manitoba, lake ... G3
Nelson, river ... H3
Saskatchewan, river ... G3
Southern Indian, lake ... G3
Winnipeg, lake ... G3
Winnipegosis, lake ... G3

NEW BRUNSWICK
Cities and Towns
Fredericton, capital ... L4
Moncton ... L4
Saint John ... L4
Other Feature
Fundy, bay ... L4

NEWFOUNDLAND
Cities and Towns
Cartwright ... L3
Corner Brook ... L4
Gander ... L4
Grand Falls ... L4
Happy Valley-Goose Bay ... L3
Hebron ... L3
Labrador City ... L3
Marystown ... L4
Nain ... L3
St. John's, capital ... M4
Other Features
Hamilton, inlet ... M3
Labrador, region ... L3
St. Lawrence, gulf ... L4
Smallwood, reservoir ... L3

NORTHWEST TERRITORIES
Cities and Towns
Déline ... E2
Fort McPherson ... D2
Fort Simpson ... E2
Fort Smith ... F2
Hay River ... F2
Holman Island ... E1
Inuvik ... D2
Sachs Harbour ... E1
Yellowknife, capital ... F2
Other Features
Amundsen, gulf ... E1
Banks, island ... E1
Beaufort, sea ... D1
Great Bear, lake ... E2
Great Slave, lake ... F2
Inuvik, region ... D2
Mackenzie, gulf ... D2
Mackenzie, river ... E2
Mackenzie, mts. ... D2
Melville, island ... F1
M'Clure, strait ... E1
Slave, river ... F2
Victoria, island ... G1
Viscount Melville, sound ... F1

NUNAVUT
Cities and Towns
Arctic Bay ... J1
Baker Lake ... H2
Cambridge Bay ... G2
Grise Fiord ... J1
Iqaluit, capital ... K2
Kugluktuk ... F2
Pangnirtung ... K2
Pond Inlet ... J1
Rankin Inlet ... H2
Repulse Bay ... J2
Resolute ... H1
Other Features
Amadjuak, lake ... K2
Axel Heiberg, island ... H1
Back, river ... G2
Baffin, bay ... L1
Baffin, island ... K2
Baffin, region ... J2
Baker, lake ... H2
Bathurst, island ... G1
Belcher, islands ... J3
Boothia, gulf ... H1
Boothia, peninsula ... H1
Brodeur, peninsula ... J1
Coats, island ... K4
Cumberland, sound ... K4 (L2)
Davis, strait ... M2
Devon, island ... J1
Dubawnt, lake ... G2
Ellesmere, island ... K1
Foxe, basin ... K2
Foxe, channel ... J2
Home, bay ... L2
Hudson, bay ... J3
Hudson, strait ... K2
James, bay ... J3
Jones, sound ... J1
Keewatin, region ... H2
King William, island ... H2
Kitikmeot, region ... F2
Mansel, island ... J2
M'Clintock, channel ... G1
Melville, peninsula ... J2
Nettilling, lake ... K2
Ottawa, islands ... J2
Parry, channel ... J1

Prince Charles, island ... K2
Prince of Wales, island ... H1
Queen Elizabeth, islands ... G2
Queen Maud, gulf ... K1
Smith, sound ... H2
Southampton, island ... J2
Victoria, island ... G1

NOVA SCOTIA
Cities and Towns
Halifax, capital ... L4
Sydney ... M4
Yarmouth ... L4
Other Features
Cabot, strait ... M4
Cape Breton, island ... M4
Fundy, bay ... L4
Sable, cape ... L4

ONTARIO
Cities and Towns
Cornwall ... K4
Fort Frances ... H4
Geraldton ... J4
Hamilton ... J4
Kapuskasing ... J4
Kingston ... K4
Kirkland Lake ... J4
Kitchener ... J4
London ... J4
Moosonee ... J3
Nipigon ... J4
North Bay ... K4
Ottawa, national capital ... K4
Peterborough ... K4
Rouyn-Noranda ... K4
Sandy Lake ... H3
Sarnia ... J4
Sault Ste. Marie ... J4
Sudbury ... J4
Thunder Bay ... J4
Timmins ... J4
Toronto, capital ... K4
Windsor ... J4
Winisk ... J3
Other Features
Akimiski, island ... J3
Albany, river ... H3
Erie, lake ... J4
Hudson, bay ... J3
Huron, lake ... J4
James, bay ... J3
Nipigon, lake ... J4
Ontario, lake ... K4
Ottawa, river ... K4
Superior, lake ... H4
Woods, lake ... H4

PRINCE EDWARD ISLAND
Cities and Towns
Charlottetown, capital ... L4

QUÉBEC
Cities and Towns
Baie-Comeau ... L4
Chibougamau ... K4
Chicoutimi ... K4
Gagnon ... L3
Gaspé ... L4
Havre-St-Pierre ... L3
Inukjuak ... K3
Kuujjuaq ... L3
Matagami ... K4
Montréal ... K4
Port-Cartier ... L4
Puvirnituq ... K2
Québec, capital ... K4
Radisson ... K3
Rimouski ... L4
Rouyn-Noranda ... K4
Schefferville ... L3
Sept-Îles ... L4
Shawinigan ... K4
Sherbrooke ... K4
Trois-Rivières ... K4
Val-d'Or ... K4
Waskaganish ... J3
Other Features
Anticosti, island ... L4
Caniapiscau, river ... L3
Feuilles, river ... K3
Hudson, bay ... J3
Hudson, strait ... K2
James, bay ... J3
Minto, lake ... K3
Mistassini, lake ... K4
Ottawa, river ... K4
St. Lawrence, gulf ... L4
St. Lawrence, river ... K4
Ungava, bay ... L3
Ungava, peninsula ... K2

SASKATCHEWAN
Cities and Towns
Estevan ... G4
La Loche ... G3
Moose Jaw ... G3
Prince Albert ... G3
Regina, capital ... G3
Saskatoon ... G3
Uranium City ... G3
Other Features
Athabasca, lake ... G3
Churchill, river ... G3
Great Plains, plain ... G3
Reindeer, lake ... G3
Saskatchewan, river ... G3
Wollaston, lake ... G3

YUKON TERRITORY
Cities and Towns
Dawson ... D2
Faro ... D2
Mayo ... D2
Watson Lake ... E2
Whitehorse, capital ... D2
Other Features
Beaufort, sea ... D1
Logan, mt. ... C2
St. Elias, mt. ... C2
Yukon, river ... D2

Manitoba
Capital: Winnipeg
Area: 250,947 sq. mi.
650,122 sq. km.
Population: 1,113,898
Largest City: Winnipeg

Nunavut
Capital: Iqaluit
Area: 800,775 sq. mi.
2,074,000 sq. km.
Population: 24,730
Largest City: Iqaluit

Yukon Territory
Capital: Whitehorse
Area: 186,661 sq. mi.
483,578 sq. km.
Population: 30,766
Largest City: Whitehorse

British Columbia
Capital: Victoria
Area: 365,947 sq. mi.
948,049 sq. km.
Population: 3,724,500
Largest City: Vancouver

Nova Scotia
Capital: Halifax
Area: 21,425 sq. mi.
55,505 sq. km.
Population: 909,282
Largest City: Halifax

Saskatchewan
Capital: Regina
Area: 251,866 sq. mi.
652,503 sq. km.
Population: 990,237
Largest City: Saskatoon

Alberta
Capital: Edmonton
Area: 255,287 sq. mi.
661,265 sq. km.
Population: 2,696,826
Largest City: Edmonton

Northwest Territories
Capital: Yellowknife
Area: 520,850 sq. mi.
1,349,000 sq. km.
Population: 39,672
Largest City: Yellowknife

Québec
Capital: Québec
Area: 594,860 sq. mi.
1,541,088 sq. km.
Population: 7,138,795
Largest City: Montréal

Canada
Capital: Ottawa
Area: 3,849,674 sq. mi.
9,973,249 sq. km.
Population: 31,006,347
Largest City: Toronto
Languages: English, French
Monetary Unit: Canadian dollar

Newfoundland
Capital: St. John's
Area: 156,949 sq. mi.
406,604 sq. km.
Population: 551,792
Largest City: St. John's

Prince Edward Island
Capital: Charlottetown
Area: 2,185 sq. mi.
5,661 sq. km.
Population: 134,557
Largest City: Charlottetown

New Brunswick
Capital: Fredericton
Area: 28,355 sq. mi.
73,459 sq. km.
Population: 738,133
Largest City: Saint John

Ontario
Capital: Toronto
Area: 412,581 sq. mi.
1,068,863 sq. km.
Population: 10,753,573
Largest City: Toronto

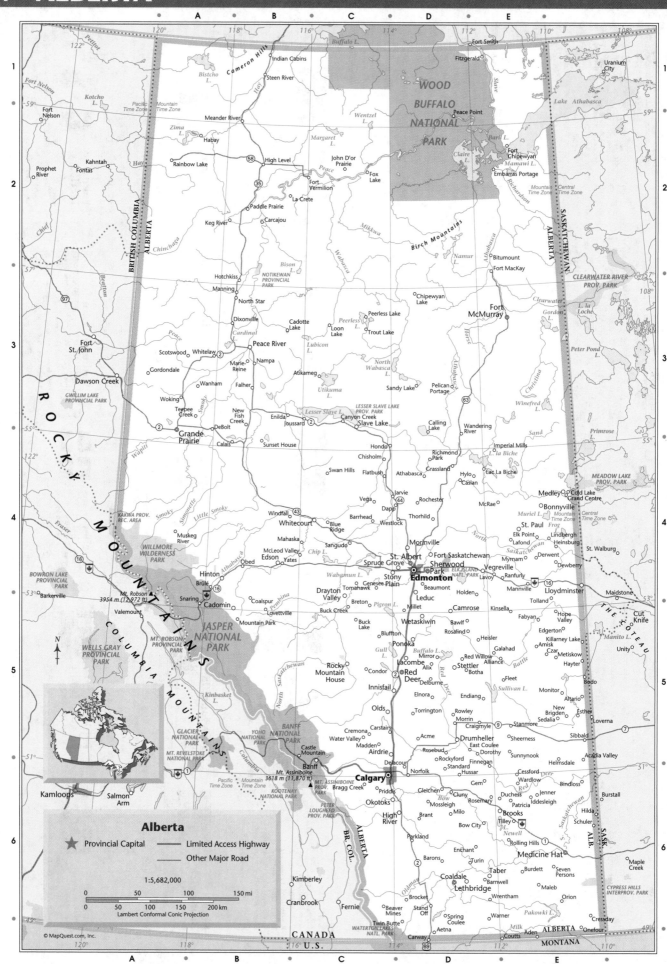

Alberta

★ Provincial Capital ━━ Limited Access Highway
        ━━ Other Major Road

1:5,682,000

0   50   100   150 mi

0   50 100 150 200 km
Lambert Conformal Conic Projection

© MapQuest.com, Inc.

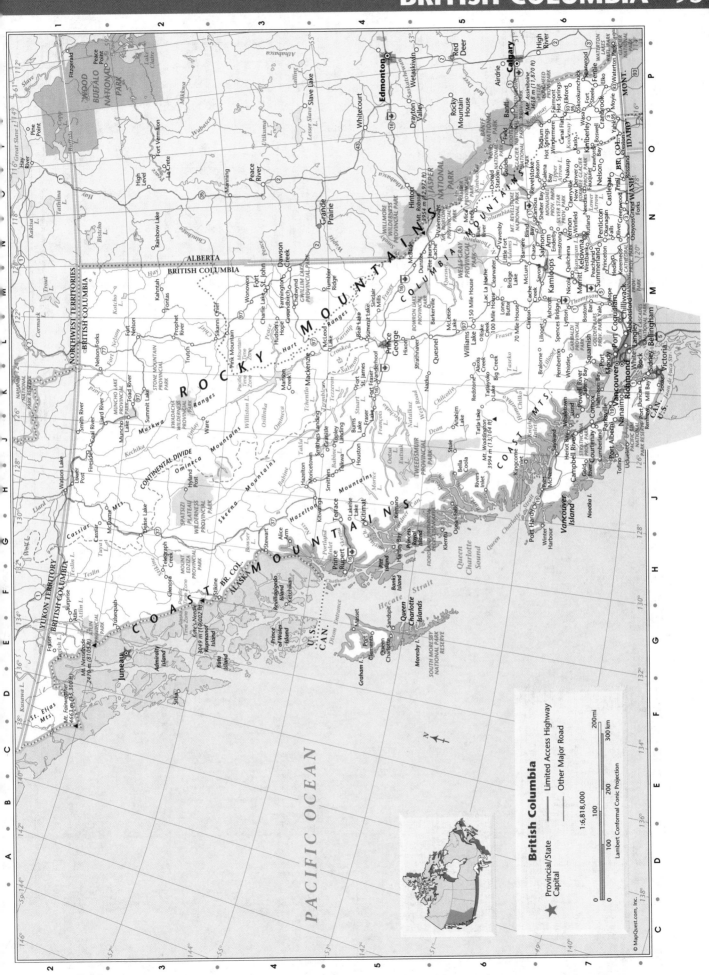

PACIFIC OCEAN

British Columbia

★ Provincial/State Capital

—— Limited Access Highway
—— Other Major Road

1:6,818,000

Lambert Conformal Conic Projection

© MapQuest.com, Inc.

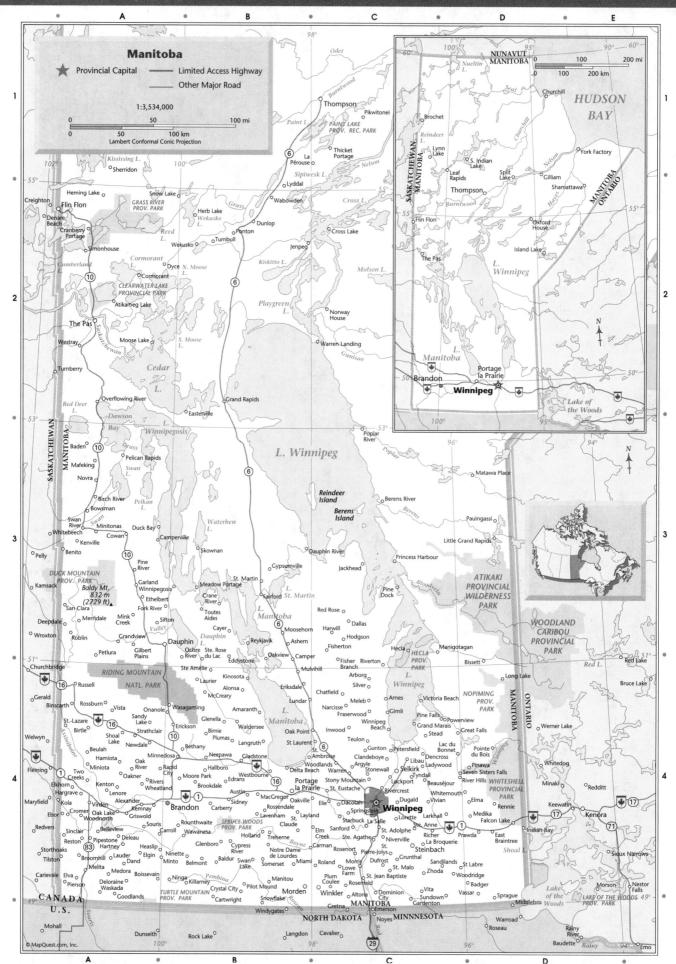

Manitoba

★ Provincial Capital — Limited Access Highway

— Other Major Road

1:3,534,000

0   50   100 mi

0   50   100 km

Lambert Conformal Conic Projection

HUDSON BAY

NUNAVUT
MANITOBA

SASKATCHEWAN
MANITOBA

MANITOBA
ONTARIO

Churchill
Brochet
York Factory
Lynn Lake
S. Indian Lake
Split Lake
Gilliam
Leaf Rapids
Thompson
Shamattawa
Flin Flon
Oxford House
Island Lake
The Pas
L. Winnipeg
Manitoba
Portage la Prairie
Brandon
Winnipeg
Lake of the Woods

SASKATCHEWAN

MANITOBA

ONTARIO

Odei
Burntwood
Thompson
Pikwitonei
Paint L.
PAINT LAKE PROV. REC. PARK
Thicket Portage
La Pérouse
Nelson
Sipiwesk L.
Lyddal
Wabowden
Kississing L.
Sherridon
Snow Lake
Grass
Cross L.
Creighton
Flin Flon
Herb Lake
Wekusko L.
Dunlop
Cross Lake
Denare Beach
GRASS RIVER PROV. PARK
Reed L.
Ponton
Jenpeg
Cranberry Portage
Wekusko
Turnbull
Simonhouse
Cumberland L.
Cormorant L.
Dyce
N. Moose L.
Kiskitto L.
CLEARWATER LAKE PROVINCIAL PARK
Cormorant
Atikameg Lake
Molson L.
Playgreen L.
The Pas
Norway House
Westray
S. Moose L.
Moose Lake
Warren Landing
Gunisao
Turnberry
Cedar L.
Red Deer L.
Overflowing River
Dawson Bay
Easterville
Grand Rapids
Poplar River
Grass
Winnipegosis
Baden
Poplar
L. Winnipeg
Mafeking
Pelican Rapids
Matawa Place
Novra
Swan L.
Birch River
Reindeer Island
Berens River
Bowsman
Pelkan L.
Berens Island
Berens
Swan River
Waterhen L.
Pauingassi
Minitonas
Duck Bay
Whitebeech
Cowan
Camperville
Little Grand Rapids
Kenville
Dauphin River
ATIKAKI PROVINCIAL WILDERNESS PARK
Benito
Skownan
Princess Harbour
Pelly
Gypsumville
Jackhead
WOODLAND CARIBOU PROVINCIAL PARK
DUCK MOUNTAIN PROV. PARK
Pine River
Dauphin
Red L.
Baldy Mt. 832 m (2729 ft)
Garland
Meadow Portage
St. Martin
Pine Dock
Red Lake
Kamsack
Winnipegosis
Crane River
Fairford
St. Martin
Bloodvein
Bruce Lake
San Clara
Ethelbert
Toutes Aides
L. Manitoba
Red Rose
Merridale
Fork River
Cayer
Deepdale
Mink Creek
Sifton
Dauphin
Mooseorn
Harwill
Dallas
Manigotagan
Wroxton
Grandview
Valley
Reykjavik
Hodgson
Hecla
Long Lake
Roblin
Gilbert Plains
Ochre River
Ste. Rose du Lac
Ashern
Fisherton
HECLA PROV. PARK
Bissett
Churchbridge
Petlura
Eddystone
Oakview
Camper
Fisher Branch
Fisher Riverton
Dauphin
L. Manitoba
RIDING MOUNTAIN NATL. PARK
Ste Amélie
Mulvihill
Arborg
L. Winnipeg
Red L.
Gerald
Russell
Laurier
Kinosota
Eriksdale
Chatfield
Silver
Victoria Beach
NOPIMING PROV. PARK
Binscarth
Rossburn
Vista
McCreary
Alonsa
Lundar
Narcisse
Meleb
Arnes
Gimli
Werner Lake
St.-Lazare
Sandy Lake
Onanole
Wasagaming
Amaranth
Fraserwood
Pine Falls
Powerview
Rossburn
Strathclair
Erickson
Glenella
Waldersee
L. Manitoba
Winnipeg Beach
Grand Marais
Great Falls
Whitedog
Birtle
Shoal Lake
Newdale
Bethany
Birnie Plumas
Langruth
Oak Point
Inwood
Teulon
Gunton
Lac du Bonnet
Pointe du Bois
Welwyn
Hamiota
Oak River
Minnedosa
Neepawa
Gladstone
St Laurent
Clandeboye
Libau
Pinawa
Minaki
Fleming
Miniota
Rapid City
Hallboro
Westbourne
St. Ambrose
Woodlands
Argyle
Stonewall
Ladywood
Seven Sisters Falls
Redditt
Two Creeks
Oakner
Moore Park
Edrans
Portage la Prairie
Delta Beach
Warren
Selkirk
Tyndall
River Hills
WHITESHELL PROVINCIAL PARK
Elkhorn
Kenton
Rivers
Brookdale
St. Eustache
Stony Mountain
Beauséjour
Whitemouth
Keewatin
Maryfield
Hargrave
Lenore
Wheatland
Austin
MacGregor
Oakville
Elie
Dacotah
Dugald
Vivian
Elma
Kenora
Kola
Virden
Alexander
Brandon
Sidney
Carberry
Rossendale
Layland
Starbuck
Winnipeg
Lorette
Larkhall
Rennie
Ebor
Cromer
Kemnay
Griswold
Lavenham
St. Claude
Elm Creek
Sanford
La Salle
St. Anne
Richer
Medika
Falcon Lake
71
Redvers
Sinclair
Belleview
Souris
Rounthwaite
Wawanesa
Holland
Ste. Agathe
Niverville
La Broquerie
Prawda
East Braintree
Indian Bay
Storthoaks
Reston
Deleau
Carroll
Cypress River
Glenboro
Treherne
Carman
Rosenort
Pierre-Jolys
Grunthal
Steinbach
Shoal L.
Sioux Narrows
Tilston
Broomhill
Hartney
Elgin
Ninette
Minto
Baldur
Somerset
Notre Dame de Lourdes
Miami
Roland
Lowe Farm
Morris
Dufrost
St. Malo
Sandilands
St Labre
Carievale
Elva
Melita
Medora
Boissevain
Ninga
Killarney
Swan Lake
Manitou
St. Jean Baptiste
Zhoda
Woodridge
Pierson
Waskada
Deloraine
TURTLE MOUNTAIN PROV. PARK
Crystal City
Pilot Mound
Morden
Altona
Dominion City
Vita
Badger
Sprague
Pembina
Plum Coulee
Rosenfeld
Goodlands
Cartwright
Snowflake
Winkler
Gretna
Gardenton
Vassar
Middlebro
Lake of the Woods
LAKE OF THE WOODS PROV. PARK
CANADA
U.S.
MANITOBA
NORTH DAKOTA
Windygates
Emerson
Noyes
MINNESOTA
Warroad
Morson
Nestor Falls
Mohall
Dunseith
Rock Lake
Langdon
Cavalier
Roseau
Rainy River
Emo
©MapQuest.com, Inc.

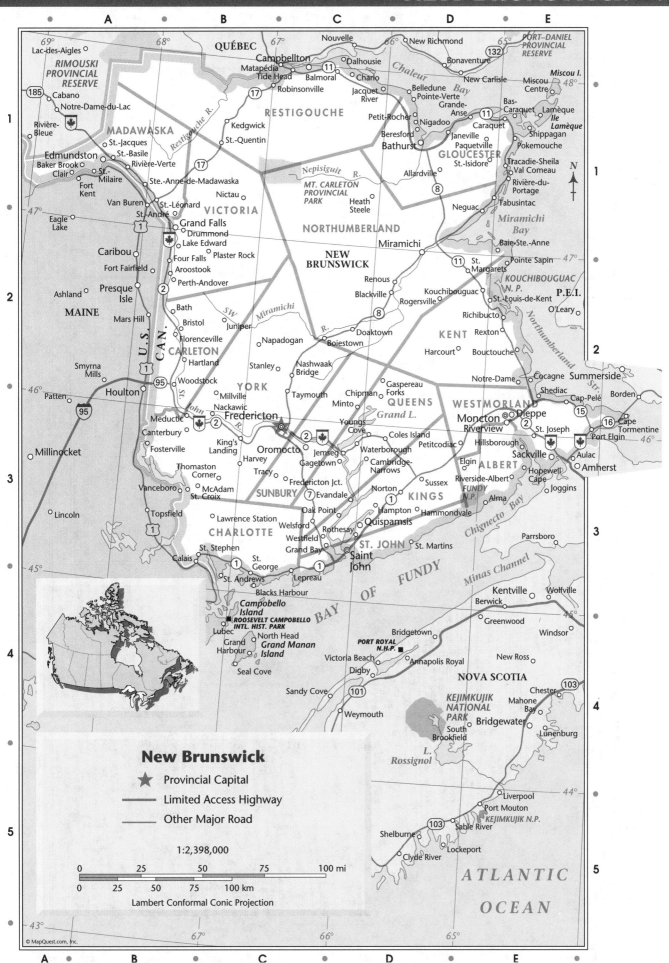

New Brunswick

★ Provincial Capital

— Limited Access Highway

— Other Major Road

1:2,398,000

0   25   50   75   100 mi

0   25   50   75   100 km

Lambert Conformal Conic Projection

© MapQuest.com, Inc.

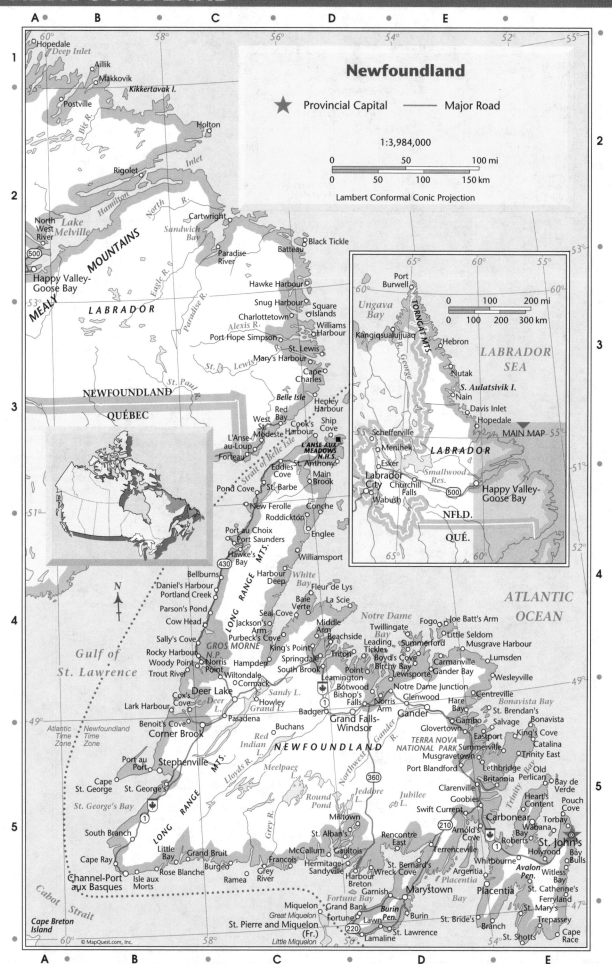

Newfoundland

★ Provincial Capital ———— Major Road

1:3,984,000

0	50	100 mi
0	50 100	150 km

Lambert Conformal Conic Projection

© MapQuest.com, Inc.

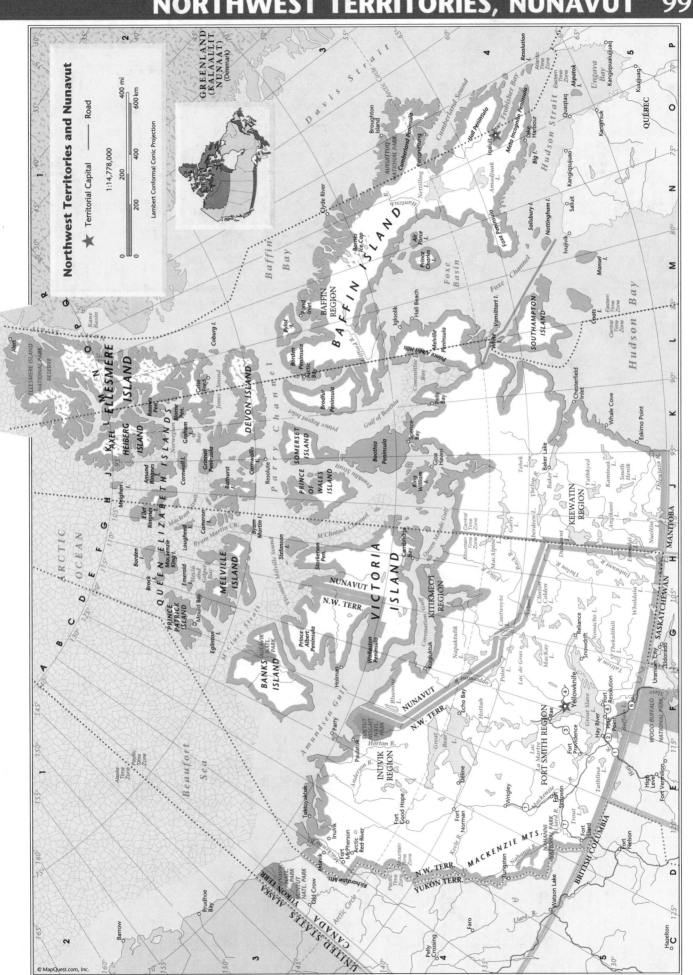

Northwest Territories and Nunavut

1:14,778,000

★ Territorial Capital — Road

400 mi
600 km
200 400
0 200
0

Lambert Conformal Conic Projection

GREENLAND (KALAALLIT NUNAAT) (Denmark)

Davis Strait

Baffin Bay

ARCTIC OCEAN

ELLESMERE ISLAND
ELLESMERE ISLAND NATIONAL PARK RESERVE
Alert
Kane Basin

AXEL HEIBERG ISLAND
Meighen I.
Ellef Ringnes I.
Amund Ringnes I.
QUEEN ELIZABETH ISLANDS
Brock I.
Borden I.
Mackenzie King I.
Emerald I.
Lougheed I.
Cameron I.
Byam Martin I.
Bathurst I.
Cornwall I.
Graham I.
Grinnell Peninsula
Bjorne Pen.
Coburg I.
DEVON ISLAND
Jones Sound
Norwegian Bay
Eureka
Grise Fiord

PRINCE PATRICK ISLAND
Eglinton I.
Mould Bay
M'Clure Strait
MELVILLE ISLAND
Byam Martin Ch.
Viscount Melville Sound
Stefansson I.
Cornwallis I.
Resolute
SOMERSET ISLAND
PRINCE OF WALES ISLAND
Parry Channel
Prince Albert Peninsula

BANKS ISLAND
AULAVIK NATIONAL PARK
Prince Albert Peninsula
Holman
Amundsen Gulf
Sachs Harbour

VICTORIA ISLAND
NUNAVUT
N.W. TERR.
Wollaston Peninsula
Coronation Gulf
Cambridge Bay
Queen Maud Gulf
Bathurst Inlet
M'Clintock Channel
Franklin Strait
Gulf of Boothia
Boothia Peninsula
Spence Bay
Pelly Bay
Gjoa Haven
King William I.
Brodeur Peninsula
Bylot I.
Arctic Bay
Prince Regent Inlet
Borden Peninsula

BAFFIN ISLAND
BAFFIN REGION
Pond Inlet
Clyde River
Barnes Ice Cap
Bylot I.
Cumberland Peninsula
AUYUITTUQ NATIONAL PARK
Broughton Island
Pangnirtung
Cumberland Sound
Hall Beach
Igloolik
Prince Charles I.
Air Force I.
Foxe Basin
Foxe Channel
Nettilling L.
Amadjuak L.
Iqal Peninsula
Iqaluit
Meta Incognita Peninsula
Frobisher Bay
Resolution I.

GREENLAND

Hudson Strait
Quaqtaq
Kangiqsujuaq
Salluit
Ivujivik
Nottingham I.
Salisbury I.
Foxe Peninsula
Mansel I.
Coats I.
Southampton Island
White I.
Vansittart I.
Prince Melville Peninsula
Melville Peninsula
Committee Bay

QUÉBEC
Kangiqsualujjuaq
Kuujjuaq
Ungava Bay
Akpatok I.
Kangirsuk
Aupaluk

Hudson Bay
Chesterfield Inlet
Whale Cove
Eskimo Point
Baker Lake
Rankin Inlet

KEEWATIN REGION
Yathkyed L.
Kaminak L.
South Henik L.
Angikuni L.
Garry L.
Dubawnt L.
Thelon R.
Aberdeen L.

MANITOBA

SASKATCHEWAN
Uranium City
Eldorado
Wholdaia L.
Thekulthili L.
Snowdrift
Nonacho L.
Reliance
Tazin R.

Central Time Zone
Eastern Time Zone

KITIKMEOT REGION
Bluenose L.
Echo Bay
Contwoyto L.
Point L.
MacKay L.
Clinton Colden L.
Aylmer L.
Hottah L.
Lac de Gras

INUVIK REGION
Tuktoyaktuk
Inuvik
Fort McPherson
Arctic Red River
Aklavik
Paulatuk
Horton R.
Anderson R.
Napaktulik L.
Kugluktuk
Coppermine R.
NUNAVUT
N.W. TERR.

FORT SMITH REGION
Great Bear Lake
Déline
Fort Good Hope
Fort Norman
Wrigley
Great Slave Lake
Yellowknife ★
Rae
Hay River
Fort Resolution
Fort Providence
Fort Simpson
La Martre L.
Trout L.
Tathlina L.
Buffalo L.
WOOD BUFFALO NATIONAL PARK
High Level
Fort Vermilion
Fort Nelson
NAHANNI NATIONAL PARK
MACKENZIE MTS.
Tungsten
Keele R.
Mountain R.
Nahanni R.
Liard R.
Fort Liard
Watson Lake

Mackenzie R.

BRITISH COLUMBIA

TUKTUT NOGAIT NATL. PARK
IVVAVIK NATL. PARK
VUNTUT NATL. PARK
Old Crow
Richardson Mts.
ALASKA (UNITED STATES) / CANADA
YUKON TERR.
N.W. TERR.

Pelly Crossing
Faro
Hazelton

Beaufort Sea
Barrow
Prudhoe Bay

Pacific Time Zone
Alaska Time Zone
Mountain Time Zone

Arctic Circle

© MapQuest.com, Inc.

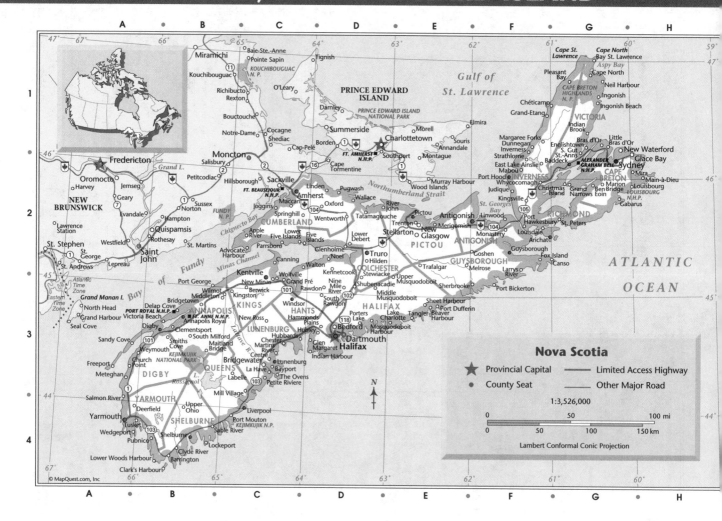

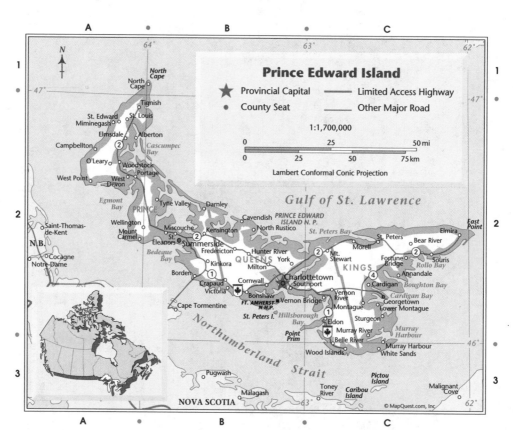

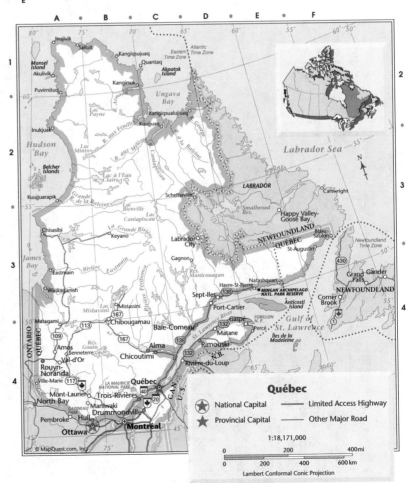

Ontario

⊛ National Capital — Limited Access Highway

★ Provincial/State Capital — Other Major Road

1:15,610,000

0 · 200 · 400 mi

0 · 200 · 400 · 600 km

Lambert Conformal Conic Projection

© MapQuest.com, Inc.

Québec

⊛ National Capital — Limited Access Highway

★ Provincial Capital — Other Major Road

1:18,171,000

0 · 200 · 400 mi

0 · 200 · 400 · 600 km

Lambert Conformal Conic Projection

© MapQuest.com, Inc.

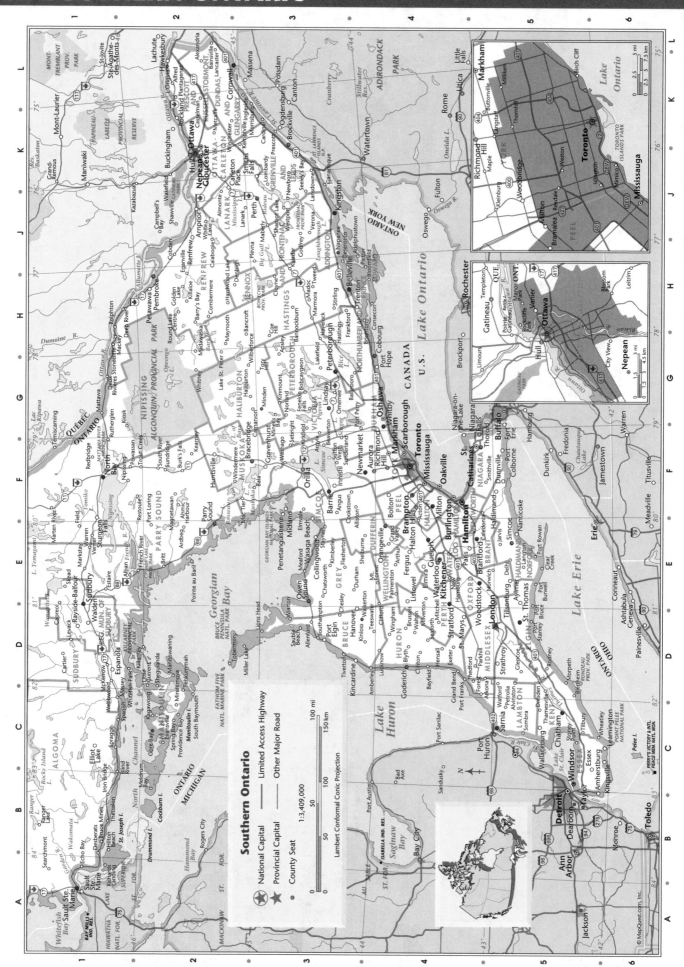

Southern Ontario

★ National Capital — Limited Access Highway
★ Provincial Capital — Other Major Road
• County Seat

1:3,409,000

Lambert Conformal Conic Projection

100 mi
150 km

© MapQuest.com, Inc.

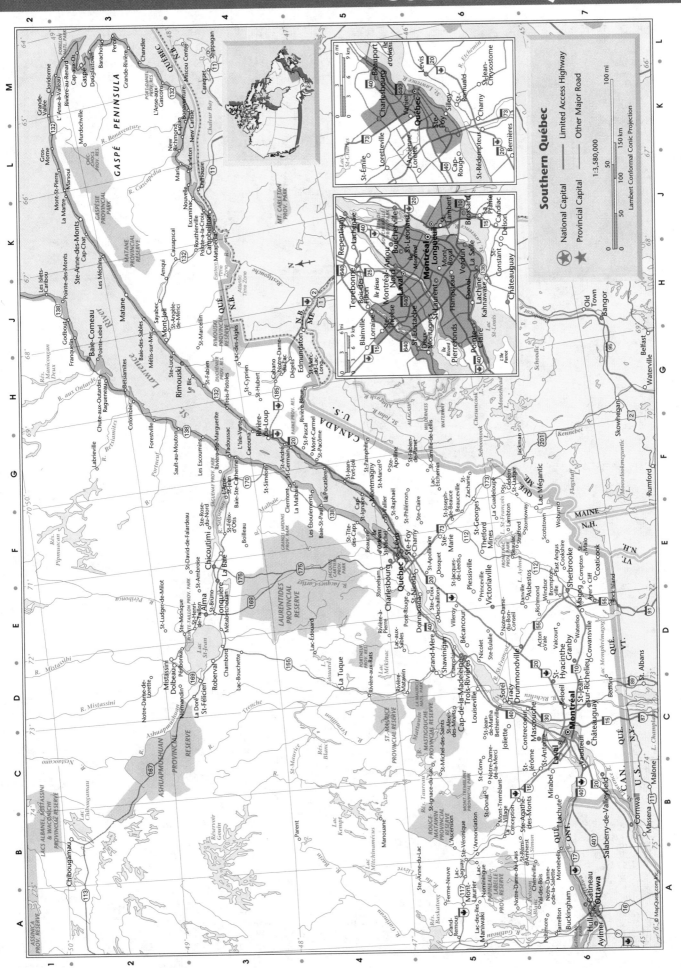

Southern Québec

National Capital
Provincial Capital
Limited Access Highway
Other Major Road

1:3,580,000

Lambert Conformal Conic Projection

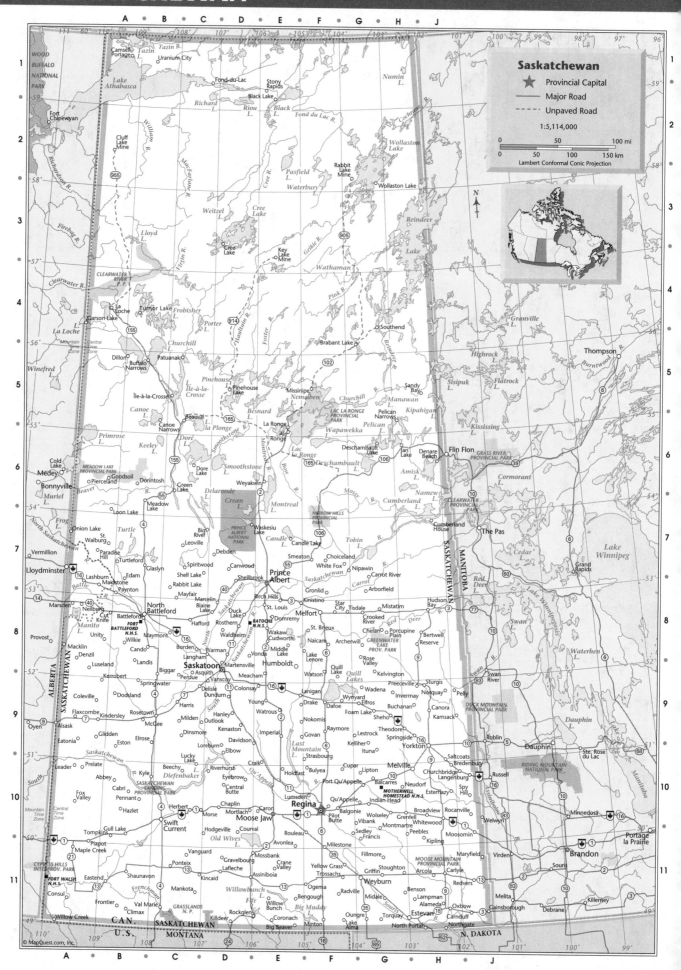

Saskatchewan

★ Provincial Capital
— Major Road
- - - Unpaved Road

1:5,114,000

0   50   100 mi
0   50   100   150 km
Lambert Conformal Conic Projection

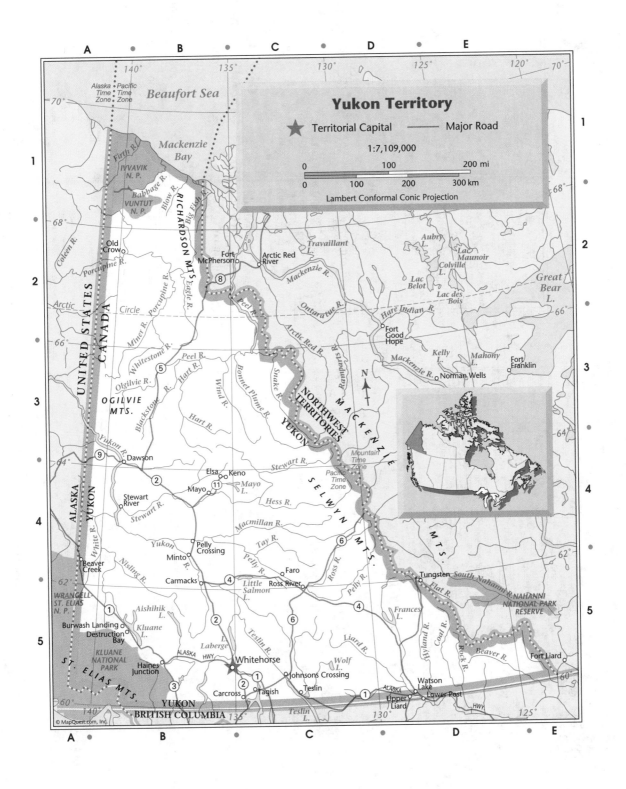

Yukon Territory

★ Territorial Capital — Major Road

1:7,109,000

0   100   200 mi

0   100   200   300 km

Lambert Conformal Conic Projection

Beaufort Sea

Mackenzie Bay

Alaska Time Zone   Pacific Time Zone

IVVAVIK N. P.

Firth R.

Babbage R.

Blow R.

Big Fish R.

VUNTUT N. P.

RICHARDSON MTS.

Eagle R.

Old Crow

Coleen R.

Porcupine R.

Miner R.

Porcupine R.

Arctic Circle

UNITED STATES

CANADA

Whitestone R.

Peel R.

Olgilvie R.

OGILVIE MTS.

Blackstone R.

Hart R.

Wind R.

Hart R.

Bonnet Plume R.

Snake R.

Peel R.

NORTHWEST TERRITORIES

YUKON

Fort McPherson

Arctic Red River

Mackenzie R.

Travaillant

Ontaratue R.

Arctic Red R.

Hare Indian R.

Ramparts R.

MACKENZIE

Aubry L.

Lac Maunoir

Colville

Lac Belot

Lac des Bois

Great Bear L.

Fort Good Hope

Mackenzie R.

Kelly L.

Mahony L.

Norman Wells

Fort Franklin

Yukon R.

Dawson

Stewart River

Stewart R.

Yukon R.

Nisling R.

Beaver Creek

White R.

ALASKA

YUKON

WRANGELL ST. ELIAS N. P.

Burwash Landing

Destruction Bay

Kluane L.

KLUANE NATIONAL PARK

Aishihik L.

ST. ELIAS MTS.

Haines Junction

Elsa

Keno

Mayo

Mayo L.

Hess R.

Macmillan R.

Tay R.

Pelly R.

Stewart R.

SELWYN MTS.

Minto

Pelly Crossing

Carmacks

Little Salmon L.

Ross River

Faro

Ross R.

Pelly R.

Frances L.

Tungsten

Flat R.

South Nahanni R.

NAHANNI NATIONAL PARK RESERVE

MTS.

Mountain Time Zone

Pacific Time Zone

N

Hyland R.

Coal R.

Rock R.

Beaver R.

Fort Liard

Watson Lake

Lower Post

ALASKA HWY

Upper Liard

Liard R.

Wolf L.

Teslin

Johnsons Crossing

Teslin R.

L. Laberge

ALASKA HWY

Whitehorse

Carcross

Tagish

Teslin L.

YUKON

BRITISH COLUMBIA

© MapQuest.com, Inc.

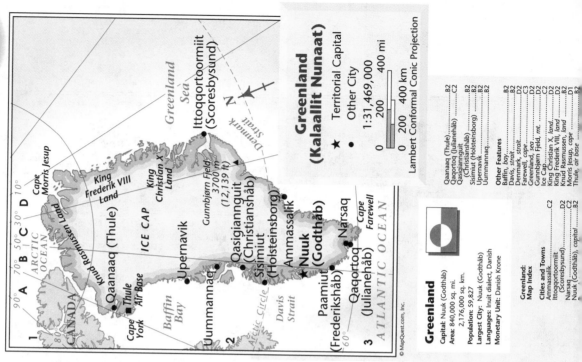

Greenland (Kalaallit Nunaat)

Territorial Capital ★
Other City ●

1:31,469,000

0   200   400 km
0   200   400 mi

Lambert Conformal Conic Projection

© MapQuest.com, Inc.

Greenland

Capital: Nuuk (Godthåb)
Area: 840,000 sq. mi.
2,176,000 sq. km.
Population: 59,827
Largest City: Nuuk (Godthåb)
Languages: Inuit dialect, Danish
Monetary Unit: Danish Krone

Qaanaaq (Thule)	B2
Qaqortoq (Julianehåb)	C2
Qasigiannguit (Christianshåb)	B2
Sisimiut (Holsteinsborg)	B2
Upernavik	B2
Uummannaq	B2

Other Features

Baffin, bay	B2
Davis, strait	B2
Denmark, strait	D3
Farewell, cape	C2
Greenland, sea	D2
Gunnbjörn Field, mt.	D2
Ice Cap	C2
King Christian X, land	D2
King Frederik VIII, land	D2
Knud Rasmussen, land	B2
Morris Jesup, cape	D1
Thule, air base	B2

**Greenland:
Map Index**

Cities and Towns

Ammassalik	C2
Ittoqqortoormiit (Scoresbysund)	D2
Narsaq, cape	C2
Nuuk (Godthåb), capital	B2

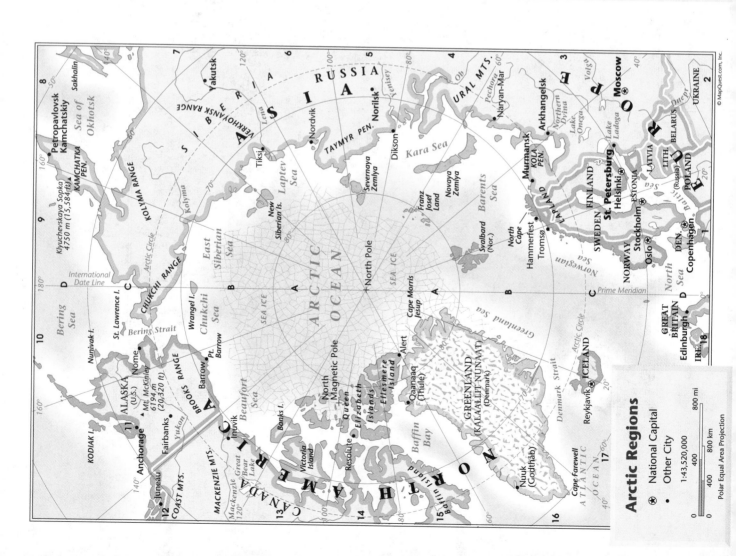

Arctic Regions

National Capital ⊛
Other City ●

1:43,520,000

0   400   800 km
0   400   800 mi

Polar Equal Area Projection

© MapQuest.com, Inc.

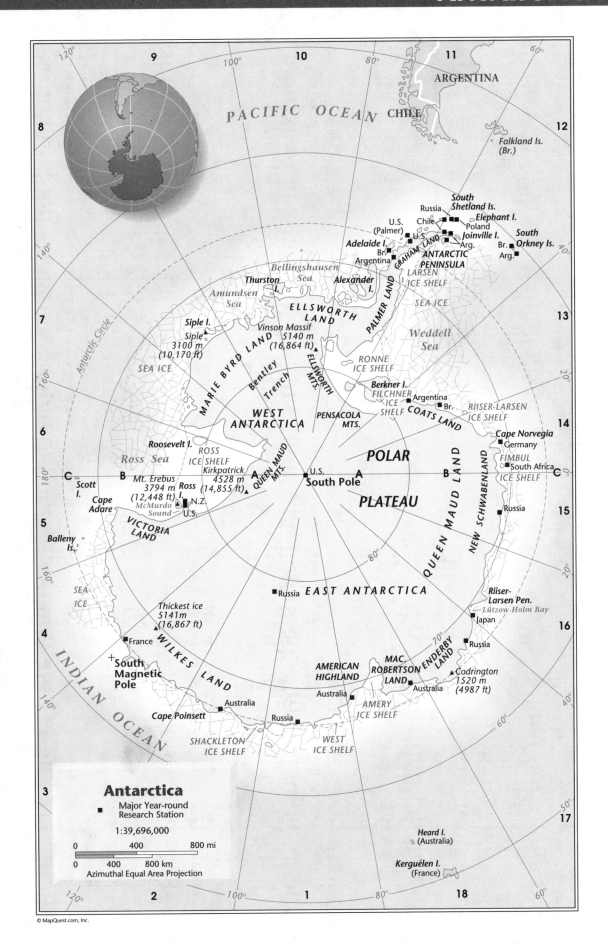

ARGENTINA

PACIFIC OCEAN CHILE

Falkland Is.
(Br.)

Russia
South
Shetland Is.
U.S.
(Palmer)
Chile
Elephant I.
Poland
U.S.
Joinville I.
South
Orkney Is.
Br.
Arg.
Adelaide I.
Br.
Arg.
ANTARCTIC
PENINSULA
Argentina

Bellingshausen
Sea
LARSEN
ICE SHELF
SEA ICE

Thurston
I.
Alexander
I.
ELLSWORTH
LAND
Weddell
Sea

Amundsen
Sea

Siple I.
Siple
3100 m
(10,170 ft)
Vinson Massif
5140 m
(16,864 ft)
RONNE
ICE SHELF

SEA ICE
MARIE BYRD LAND
Bentley
Trench
ELLSWORTH
MTS.
Berkner I.
FILCHNER
ICE
SHELF
Argentina
Br.
RIISER-LARSEN
ICE SHELF
Cape Norvegia
Germany

WEST
ANTARCTICA
PENSACOLA
MTS.
COATS LAND
FIMBUL
South Africa
ICE SHELF

Roosevelt I.
ROSS
ICE SHELF
POLAR
QUEEN MAUD LAND
NEW SCHWABENLAND

Ross Sea
Kirkpatrick
4528 m
(14,855 ft)
QUEEN MAUD
MTS.
U.S.
South Pole
Russia

Scott
I.
Mt. Erebus
3794 m
(12,448 ft)
Ross
I.
N.Z.
U.S.
McMurdo
Sound
PLATEAU

Cape
Adare
VICTORIA
LAND
Riiser-
Larsen Pen.
Lützow-Holm Bay
Japan

Balleny
Is.

SEA
ICE
Russia
EAST ANTARCTICA
Russia

Thickest ice
5141m
(16,867 ft)
Codrington
1520 m
(4987 ft)

France
WILKES LAND
AMERICAN
HIGHLAND
MAC.
ROBERTSON
LAND
ENDERBY
LAND
Australia

South
Magnetic
Pole
Australia

Cape Poinsett
Australia
Russia
AMERY
ICE SHELF

SHACKLETON
ICE SHELF
WEST
ICE SHELF

INDIAN OCEAN

Heard I.
(Australia)

Antarctica
■ Major Year-round
Research Station

1:39,696,000

0   400   800 mi
0   400   800 km
Azimuthal Equal Area Projection

Kerguélen I.
(France)

PALMER LAND
GRAHAM LAND

QUEEN MAUD MTS.

© MapQuest.com, Inc.

A

Aachen A3 40
Aaiún, el- B1 58
Aalst C2 33
Aarau C1 35
Aare, river B1, B2 35
Aba D5 65
Abadan B3 22
Abaí E4 75
Abakaliki E4 65
Abakan D6 44
Abancay C3 77
Abaya, lake B3 60
Abbeville C1 34
Abbey B10 104
Abbotsford L6 95
Abdali B1 24
Abéché C4 59
Abemama, island A1 17
Abengourou E3 63
Åbenrå B3 32
Abeokuta B4 65
Aberdeen Inset 10
Aberdeen C1 30
Aberdeen, lake H4 99
Aberdeen, S. Dak. D1 126
Aberystwyth B3 30
Abha B2 24
Abhe, lake C2 60
Abia, river C3 66
Abidjan D4 63
Abilene, Tex. D2 126
Abkhazia, autonomous republic A3 45
Aboisso E4 63
Abomey A4 64
Abou Deïa B5 59
Abrantes A3 36
Abruzzi C2 38
Abşeron, peninsula C2 45
Abu Dhabi, capital C2 25
Abu Kamal B2 27
Abuja, capital D3 65
Abuná, river A2 77
Acadia Valley E5 94
Acajutla A2 86
Acámbaro D4 84
Acapulco E4 84
Acarai, mts. B5 80
Acaray, river E4 75
Acarigua C2 79
Accra, capital B4 64
Achill, island A2 31
Achinsk D6 44
Achwa, river C2 61
Acklins, island C4 89
Acme D5 94
Acolman Inset 84
Aconcagua, mt. A3 74
Aconcagua, river B4 76
Aconibe C3 66
Acquaviva A1 39
Acre A2 81
Acre (Akko) B1 26
Acton E4 102
Acton Vale D6 103
Açúcar, mt. Inset I 81
Adamawa, massif B2, E5 65
Adams, lake N5 95
Adana C3 27
Adapazarı B2 27
Adare, cape B5 107
Addis Ababa, capital C2 60
Addu, atoll A5 19
Adelaide, island C11 107
Adelaide, S.A., capital C3, Inset II 14
Aden B2 25
Aden E6 94
Aden, gulf B1, C2 60
Adi Keyih B2 60
Adi Ugri B2 60
Adige, river B1 38
Adirondack, mts., N.Y. F1 126
Adjuntus B2 90
Admiralty, islands A2 15
Ado-Ekiti C4 65
Adolphustown H3 102
Adour, river B5 34
Adrar B2 57
Adrar des Iforas, massif D2 58
Adriatic, sea C2 38
Advocate Harbour C2 100
Adwa C1 60
Adygeya, republic E4 44
Adzopé E3 63
Aegean, sea C2 51
Ærø, island C4 32
Aetna D6 94
Afadjoto, mt. C3 64
Afghanistan 22
Afikpo D5 65
Afram, river B3 64
Afyon B2 27
Agadès B2 59
Agadir B2 57
Agartala F4 20
Agboville D4 63
Ağcabädi B2 45
Ağdam B3 45
Agen C4 34
Aginskiy Buryat, autonomous okrug D7 44
Aginskoye D7 44
Agou, mt. B3 64
Agra C3 20
Ağri E2 27
Agrigento C3 38
Agrínion B2 51
Ağstafa A2 45
Agua Prieta C1 84
Aguada A2 90
Aguadilla A2 90
Aguadulce B2 87
Aguán, river B2 86
Aguarico, river C3 79
Aguas Blancas C2 76
Aguas Buenas C2 90
Aguascalientes, state capital D3 84
Águilas F4 37
Aguilita B2 90
Agung, mt. C2 13
Agusan, river C4 12
Ahmadabad B4 20
Ahmadi, al- C2 24
Ahmic Harbour F2 102
Ahuachapán A2 86
Ahvaz B3 22
Ahwar B2 25
Aibonito C2 90
Aigáleo, mts. Inset 51
Ailinglapalap, island B2 16
Aillik B1 98
Ailuk, island B1 16
Aiquile A3 77
Air Force, island O3 99
Air Ronge E5 104
Air, mts. B2 59
Airdrie C5 94
Aishihik, lake B5 105
Aisne, river D2 34
Aiwo A2 16
Aix-en-Provence D5 34
Aix-les-Bains D4 34
Aiyina, island B3 51
Aizawl F4 20
Aizuwakamatsu C2 8
Ajaccio Inset I 34
Ajaria, autonomous republic A4 45
Ajdabiya D1 56
Ajka A2 43
Ajman C2 25
Ajmer B3 20
Akanyaru, river B2 61
Akashi B3 8
Akhalkalaki B4 45
Akhaltsikhe B4 45
Akharnaí Inset 51
Akhdar, river B2 51
Akhmeta C3 45
Akhuryan, river A2 45
Akita D2 8
Akjoujt B3 58
Aklavik A3 99
Akobo, river A3 60
Akola C4 20
Akordat A2 60
Akosombo, dam C3 64
Akpatok, island P4 99
Akranes A2 52
Akron, Ohio E1 126
Aksaray C2 27
Aksu B1 10
Akulivik A1 101
Akure C4 65
Akurenam C3 66
Akureyri B2 52
Akuseki, island A4 8
Alabama E2 126
Alagoas E2 81
Alagoinhas E3 81
Alajuela B2 86
Alakol, lake E2 23
Alamayn, al- A1 56
Alameda H11 104
Alampur Inset II 20
Åland, islands B2 53
Alanya C3 27
Alarcón, reservoir E3 37
Alaska Inset I 126
Alaska, gulf, Alaska Inset I 126
Alaska, range, Alaska Inset I 126
Älät C3 45
Alaverdi B1 45
Alay, mts. B1, C3 23
Alayli Dadda B1 60
Alazani, river C4 45
Alba Iulia B2 43
Albacete F3 37
Alban E1 102
Albania 49
Albany, capital, N.Y. F1 126
Albany, Ga. E2 126
Albany, river C2 101
Albany, W.A. A3 14
Albert Nile, river B2 61
Albert, canal C1 33
Albert, lake B3 61
Alberton A2 100
Albi C5 34
Albina B2 80
Alboran, sea E4 37
Ålborg B1 32
Ålborg, bay C2 32
Albuquerque, cays Inset 78
Albuquerque, N. Mex. C2 126
Albury, N.S.W. D3 14
Alcalá de Henares Inset II 37
Alcañiz F2 37
Alcántara, reservoir C3 37
Alcázar de San Juan E3 37
Alcira F3 37
Alcobendas Inset II 37
Alcorcón E2, Inset II 37
Alcoy F3 37
Aldabra, islands A2 70
Aldan D8 44
Aldan, river D8 44
Alderney, island Inset II 30
Aleg B3 58
Alençon C2 34
Alert Q1 99
Alès D4 34
Alessandria B1 38
Ålesund B3 52
Aleutian islands, Alaska Inset I 126
Alexander A4 96
Alexander, island B11 107
Alexandria A4 15
Alexandria C4 43
Alexandria A1 56
Alexandria L2 102
Alexandria, La. D2 126
Alexandroúpolis C1 51
Alexis Creek L5 95
Alexis, river C3 98
Alfios, river B3 51
Alfred L2 102
Algarrobo Inset 76
Algarve, region A4 36
Algeciras D4 37
Algeria 57
Alghero B2 38
Algiers, capital B1 57
Ali Adde B2 60
Äli Bayramli C3 45
Ali-Sabieh B2 60
Aliákmon, river B1 51
Alibori, river B2 64
Alicante F3 37
Alice C3 71
Alice Arm H3 95
Alice Springs, N.T. C2 14
Alice Town B2 89
Aligarh C3 20
Alima, river D4 66
Aliwal North C3 71
Alix D5 94
Alkmaar B2 32
Allahabad D3 20
Allardville D1 97
Allen, lake B1 31
Allenford D3 102
Allentown, Pa. F1 126
Alleppey (Alappuzah) C7 20
Alliance E5 94
Allier, river C3 34
Alligator Pond B3 88
Alliston F3 102
Allumette, lake H2 102
Alma E3 97
Alma E3 103
Almada A3 36
Almadén D3 37
Almansa F3 37
Almaty (Alma-Ata) D2 23
Almendralejo C3 37
Almelo D2 32
Almendra, reservoir C2 37
Almería E4 37
Almirante A2 87
Almonte J2 102
Alonsa B4 96
Alor Setar A1 13
Alor, island D2 13
Alotau B3 15
Alpena, Mich. E1 126
Alps, mts. 29
Alsace D2 34
Alsask A9 104
Alta E1 52
Altai, mts. B1 10
Altamira C2 81
Altamira C3 76
Altario E5 94
Altay B1 10
Altay B2 11
Altay, republic F4 44
Altdorf C2 35
Altiplano, plateau A3 77
Altona C4 96
Altun, range B2 10
Aluksne D2 46
Alvinston D5 102
Alytus C2 46
Alzette, river B2 33
Am Timan C5 59
Amadjuak, lake O4 99
Amadora A3 36
Amagasaki B3 8
Amahai D2 13
Amakusa, islands A3 8
Amambay, mts. E3 75
Amami, island Inset II 8
Amapá C1 81
Amapala B3 86
Amarah, al- C2 24
Amaranth B4 96
Amarillo, Tex. C2 126
Amasya C2 27
Amazon, basin B2 81
Amazon, river B2 81
Amazonas B2 81
Ambato B3 79
Ambatolampy B2 69
Ambatondrazaka B2 69
Amberg B4 40
Ambergris Cay, island C2 85
Ambergris, cay D4 89
Amberley D3 102
Ambon D2 13
Ambositra B3 69
Ambre, cape B1 69
Ambrym, island C3 18
Amdanga Inset II 20
Ameca D3 84
Ameland, island C1 32
American Samoa 18
Amersfoort C2 32
Amery Ice Shelf, glacier C18 107
Amherst C2 100
Amherstburg B5 102
Amiens C2 34
Amindivi, islands B6 20
Amirante, islands B2 70
Amisk E5 94
Amisk, lake H6 104
Amlamé B3 64
Amman, capital A2 26
Ammassalik C2 106
Ammersee, lake B4 40
Amos A4 101
Ampanihy A3 69
Amparai C4 19
Amqui J3 103
Amran A1 25
Amravati C4 20
Amritsar B2 20
Amsterdam, capital B2 32
Amstetten D2 39
Amu Darya, river B1, D2 23
Amund Ringnes, island J1 99
Amundsen, gulf C2 99
Amundsen, sea B9 107
Amur, river D8 44
Amyun A1 26
Ana María, gulf D2 88
Anabar C1 16
Anaco D2 79
Anadyr C10 44
Anadyr, gulf C11 44
Anahim Lake K5 95
Anáhuac D2 84
Anápolis D3 81
Añasco A2 90
Añasco, beach A2 90
Anatolia, region B2 27
Anatom, island C5 18
Anchorage, Alaska Inset I 126
Ancona C2 38
Ancud B7 76
Ancud, gulf B7 76
Andalusia D4 37
Andaman, islands F6 20
Andaman, sea B3 12
Anderlecht C2 33
Anderson, river C3 99
Andes, mts. 73
Andheri Inset I 20
Andizhan D2 23
Andoany B1 69
Andong C4 9
Andorra 36
Andorra la Vella, capital B2 36
Andreas, cape C1 27
Andros, island A3 89
Ándros, island C3 51
Androth, island B6 20
Anécho B3 64
Anelghowhat C5 18
Anetan B1 16
Aneto, mt. G1 37
Angara, river D6 44
Angarsk D7 44
Angaur B4 17
Angel, falls D2 79
Angeles B3 12
Ångermanälven, river C2 53
Angers B3 34
Angikuni, lake H4 99
Angkor Thom, ruins B2 11
Angkor Wat, ruins B2 11
Anglesey, island B3 30
Angoche C3 68
Angol B6 76
Angola 70
Angoulême C4 34
Angus F3 102
Anholt, island C2 32
Anhui E2 10
Anibare B2 16
Anié B3 64
Añisoc C3 66
Anjou J5 103
Anju A3 9
Ankang D2 10
Ankara, capital C2 27
Ankaratra, mts. B2 69
Ankobra, river A4 64
Ann Arbor, Mich. E1 126
Anna Regina B2 80
Annaba B1 57
Annam, mts. A2 11
Annandale C2 100
Annapolis Royal B3 100
Annapolis, capital, Md. F2 126
Annapurna, mt. B2 19
Annecy D4 34
Anqing E2 10
Ansbach B4 40
Anse Boileau Inset 70
Anse Royale Inset 70
Anse-à-Galets C2 89
Anshan F1 10
Ansongo D2 58
Antalaha C1 69
Antalya B3 27
Antalya, gulf B3 27
Antananarivo, capital B2 69
Antarctic, peninsula C12 107
Antarctica 107
Antequera D4 37
Anti-Atlas, ranges B2 57
Anti-Lebanon, mts. B1 26
Anticosti, island D4 101
Antigonish F2 100
Antigua C5 85
Antigua, island D4 90
Antigua and Barbuda 90
Antioch (Antakya) D3 27
Antofagasta B2 76
Antrim, mts. A2 30
Antsirabe B2 69
Antsiranana B1 69
Antsohihy B1 69
Antwerp C1 33
Anuradhapura B3 19
Anyang E2 10
Anyang B4 9
Anyos B2 36
Aoa C1 18
Aoba, island B2 18
Aomori D1 8
Aoral, mt. C3 11
Aosta A1 38
Aozou B2 59
Apa, river D3 75
Apaporis, river C4 78
Apatity C3 44
Apatou A1 80
Apeldoorn C2 32
Apennines, range B1 38
Apetina B3 80
Api, mt. A2 19
Apia, capital C2 18
Apo, volcano C5 12
Apoera A2 80
Apolima, island B2 18
Apolima, strait B2 18
Apoteri B4 80
Appalachian, mts. E2 126
Apple River C2 100
Apsley G3 102
Apulia C2 38
Apure, river C2 79
Apurímac, river C3 77
Apuseni, mts. B2 43
Aqaba, gulf A3, B3 26
Aqabah, al- A3 26
Aqtau B2 23
Aqtobe B1 23
Aquileia C1 38
Aquitaine B4 34
Ara D3 20
Arabah, al-, river A2, B2 26
Arabian, desert B2 56
Arabian, sea A5, Inset I 20
Aracaju E3 81
Arachon B4 34
Arad A2 43
Aradah B3 25
Arafura, sea E2 13
Aragats, mt. B2 45
Aragón F2 37
Araguaia, river C3 81
Arak B3 22
Arakabesan, island B3 17
Arakan Yoma, mts. B2 12
Aral C2 23
Aral, sea A2, B2 23
Aran, islands B2 31
Aranda de Duero E2 37
Aranjuez E2 37
Aranyaprathet C3 12
Arapey Grande, river B1 75
Ararat B3 45
Ararat (Ağri Daği), mt. F2 27
Aras, river E2 27
Arauca C3 78
Arauca, river C2 79
Aravalli, range B3 20
Arawa B2 15
Arba Minch B3 60
Arborfield G7 104
Arborg C4 96
Archerwill G8 104
Arcola H11 104
Arctic Bay L2 99
Arctic Red River B3 99
Arda, river C4 50
Ardabil B2 22
Ardara B1 31
Ardbeg E2 102
Ardennes, plateau D1 33
Ardennes, region D1 34
Arecibo B2 90
Arekalong, peninsula C2 17
Arenal, lake B2 86
Arenas, point D2 90
Arendal B4 52
Arequipa C4 77
Arezzo B2 38
Argenteuil Inset II 34
Argentia D5 98
Argentina 74
Argentino, lake A7 74
Argeş, river C3 43
Arghandab, river B2 22
Argonne, forest D2 34
Árgos B3 51
Argyle C4 96
Argyle F3 102
Århus C2 32
Ari, atoll A3 19
Ariana C1 57
Arica B1 76
Arichat F2 100
Arima A2 91
Arinsal A2 36
Aripuanã, river C2 81
Arish, al- B1 56
Arizona B2 126
Arkansas D2 126
Arkansas, river D2 126
Arkhangelsk C4 44
Arklow C2 31
Arkona D4 102
Arles D5 34
Arlit B2 59
Arlon D3 33
Armagh A2 30
Armenia 45
Armenia B3 78
Armidale, N.S.W. E3 14
Armstrong N6 95
Armstrong C2 101
Arnaud, river B2 101
Arnes C4 96
Arnhem C3 32
Arnhem Land, region C1 14
Arnhem, cape C1 14
Arno, island C2 16
Arno, river B2 38
Arnold's Cove D5 98
Arnprior J2 102
Arnsberg B3 40
Aroostook B2 97
Arorae, island A2 17
Arpa, river C3 45
Arpajon Inset II 34
Arqalyq C1 23
Arran, island B2 30
Arras C1 34
Arroyo C3 90
Arta B2 60
Artashat B3 45
Artemisa B2 88
Arthur E4 102
Arthur's Town B3 89
Artibonite, river C1 89
Artigas B1 75
Artik A2 45
Artsvashen C2 45
Artvin E2 27
Aru, islands E2 13
Arua B2 61
Aruba, island 82
Arun, river D2 19
Arusha C1 68
Aruvi, river B3 19
Aruwimi, river C1 67
Arvayheer C2 11
As Ela B
Asaba D
Asadabad C
Asahi Dake, mt. Inset
Asahikawa Inset
Asama, mt. C
Asansol E
Asau A
Asbestos E
Ascoli Piceno C
Asela C
Asenovgrad C
Ashburton B
Ashburton, river A
Ashcroft M
Ashdod B
Ashern B
Asheville, N.C. E
Asheweig, river C
Ashgabat, capital C
Ashikaga C
Ashizuri, cape B
Ashmore and Cartier, islands B
Ashqelon B
Ashton A
Ashuapmushuan, river C
Asinara, island B
Asipovichy D
Asir, region B
Askar B1
Asmara, capital B2
Asnam, el- B1
Aso, mt. A3
Asosa B2
Aspiring, mt. A3
Asprópirgos Inset
Asquith C8
Assab D3
Assal, lake B2
Assen D2
Assiniboia D11
Assiniboine, mt. P6
Assiniboine, river A4
Astana (Akmola), capital D1
Astara C3
Asti B1
Astipálaia, island C3
Astorga C1
Astrakhan E4
Astrolabe, reefs C2
Asturias C1
Asunción, capital D4
Aswan B3
Aswan High, dam B3
Asyut B2
At-Bashy D2
Atacama, desert C2
Atakpamé B3
Ataq B2
Atâr B2
Atatürk, reservoir D3
Atbara, river B1
Atbarah C2
Atbarah, river C2
Atbasar C1
Ath B2
Athabasca D4
Athabasca, lake A1
Athabasca, river B4, D3, E2
Athens, capital B3, Inset
Athens, Ga. E2
Athi, river E5
Athlone C2
Áthos, mt. C1
Ati B4
Atiak C2
Atikameg C3
Atikameg Lake A2
Atikokan B3
Atitlán, lake B5
Atlanta, capital, Ga. E2
Atlantic City, N.J. F2
Atlas, mts. A1, B2
Atlin F1
Atlin, lake F1
Atrai, river B4
Atrak, river D2
Atrato, river A3
Attapu D4
Attawapiskat D2
Attawapiskat, river C2
Atuel, river B4
Atyrau B2
Aua C1
Aube, river D3
Auch C5
Auckland B2
Augsburg B4
Augusta, capital, Maine G1
Augusta, Ga. E2
Auki B1
Aulac E3
Aunuu, island C1
Auob, river C3
Aur, island C2
Aurangabad C5
Aurillac C4
Aurora F3
Ausa, river C1
Austin B4
Austin, capital, Tex. D2
Australia
Australian Alps, mts. D3
Australian Capital Territory D3
Austria
Auvergne C4
Auxerre C3
Avalon, peninsula E5
Aveiro A2
Avellaneda D3
Avellino C2
Aviemore B1
Avignon D5
Ávila D2
Avilés D1
Avon, islands A2
Avon, river C3
Avonlea E10
Awaji B3

	Key	Page
island	B3	8
…	C3	60
…, river	C2	60
…	A3	64
…	B2	56
…	D4	65
…river	A2	26
…eiberg, island	K1	99
…	A4	64
…cho	C3	77
…z	E2	23
…	A3	27
…hawan, island	A1	13
…Cliff	D6	103
…ury	Inset III	30
…Dhimítrios	Inset	51
…	E5	102
…	A6	103
…, lake	G4	99
…, lake	E6	103
…	C2	25
…el-Atroûs	C3	58
…	B2	30
…	F3	50
…	C2	58
…	F2	65
…	A1	27
…otzalco	Inset	84
…aijan		45
…aijan, region	B2	22
…	B4	79
…s, islands		5
…	D3	47
…ash-Shishan	B2	26
…	B2	89
…o, peninsula	B3	87
…ver	B3	11
…	B1	26
…ek	C1	60
…l-Mandab, strait	C1	60
…noyo	B3	79
…nusah	B3	59
…island	D2	13
…age, lake	B1	105
…	A2	26
…thuạp, island	C3	17
…e, lake	J4	95
…e, lake	J3	95
…ysk	D3	47
…Bheri	Inset II	20
…yan, channel	B2	12
…yan, islands	B2	12
…on, ruins	B2	24
…ieu	A5	11
…oal	D2	81
…	D2	43
…river	H3	99
…ı Palanka	A2	49
…od	B4	12
…ms	A3	40
…schl	C3	39
…Kreuznach	A4	40
…Reichenhall	C5	40
…	C3	17
…ona	H2	37
…nah	B1	24
…	A2	13
…eck	G1	100
…	C1	35
…	E2	39
…	A3	96
…n-Baden	B4	40
…n-Württemberg	B4	40
…	D4	96
…er	C5	98
…u	B3	64
…	C1	62
…, bay	L1	92
…	M2	99
…, region	N2	99
…g, river	C2	62
…ulabé	A3	18
…ussam	B2	65
…dad, capital	B2	24
…lan	B1	22
…ung	B2	19
…néti, river	C2	19
…io	B2	12
…ane, mt.	B2	59
…mas		89
…walpur	D4	21
…	D3	81
…a Blanca	C4	74
…a Honda	A2	88
…a, islands	B1	86
…Dar	B2	60
…bruco, mts.	A2	89
…al-Arab, river	B2	59
…al-Ghazal, river	C3	59
…al-Jabal, river	C3	59
…Salamat, river	B5	59
…ain		25
…ain, gulf	A2	25
…Mare	B2	43
…	F1	10
…yabati	Inset II	20
…Verte	C4	98
…Comeau	H2	103
…des-Sables	J3	103
…St-Paul	F4	103
…Ste-Anne	E1	97
…Ste-Catherine	G3	103
…io	G3	102
…sville	L2	102
…	B2	26
…	B1	16
…California	A1	84
…California Sur	B2	84
…dero	B2	90
…Boquete	C2	62
…er Brook	A1	97
…er Lake		
…rsfield, Calif.	B2	126

	Key	Page
Bakhardok	C2	22
Bakhtaran	B3	22
Bakhtiari, region	B3	22
Bakony, mts.	A2	43
Baku, capital	C2	45
Bala	F2	102
Bala, lake	B3	30
Balabac, island	A5	12
Balabac, strait	A5	12
Balakän	B2	45
Balaklava	C4	47
Balaton, lake	A2	43
Balboa	C2	87
Balcarres	G10	104
Baldur	B4	96
Baldy, mt.	A3	96
Balearic, islands	G3	37
Balearic, sea	G2	37
Baleia, point	E3	81
Baleine, river	C2	101
Balgonie	F10	104
Balhaf	B2	25
Balho	B1	60
Bali, island	C2	13
Baliceaux, island	B3	91
Balıkesir	A2	27
Balikpapan	C2	13
Balkan, mts.	B2	50
Balkh	B1	22
Balkhash	D2	23
Balkhash, lake	D2	23
Ballancourt-sur-Essonne	Inset II	34
Ballarat, Vic.	D3	14
Balleny, islands	C5	107
Ballerup	D3	32
Ballina	B1	31
Bally	Inset II	20
Ballymena	A2	30
Balmaceda	B8	76
Balmertown	B2	101
Balmoral	C1	97
Balsas, river	E4	84
Baltic, sea		29
Baltimore, Md.	F2	126
Baluchistan, region	E4	22
Balykchy	E1	23
Balzers	B2	33
Bam	D4	22
Bamako, capital	B3	58
Bamangachi	Inset II	20
Bambadinca	C1	62
Bambana, river	B2	87
Bambari	B2	66
Bamberg	B4	40
Bamenda	B2	65
Bamian	B2	22
Ban Houayxay	A1	11
Ban Phai	C2	12
Banaba, island	A2	17
Banana	A2	67
Banana, islands	A1	63
Bananga	F7	20
Banat, region	A3	43
Banbury	C3	30
Bancroft	H2	102
Banda Aceh	A1	13
Bandama Blanc, river	D2	63
Bandama Rouge, river	C2	63
Bandama, river	D3	63
Bandar Beheshti	E4	22
Bandar Lampung	B2	13
Bandar Seri Begawan, capital	B2	13
Bandar-e Abbas	D4	22
Bandar-e Anzali	B2	22
Bandar-e Bushehr	C4	22
Bandar-e Khomeyni	B3	22
Bandar-e Torkeman	C2	22
Bandeira, mt.	Inset I	20
Bandra	Inset I	20
Bandundu	B2	67
Bandung	B2	13
Banff	C5	94
Bangalore	C6	20
Bangar	C2	13
Bangassou	B3	66
Banggi, island	D1	13
Banghiang, river	C3	11
Bangka, island	B2	13
Bangkok, capital	B3	12
Bangladesh		21
Bangor	B2	30
Bangor	B3	30
Bangor, Maine	G1	126
Bangui, capital	A3	66
Bangweulu, lake	B2	67
Bani	B2	89
Bani Suwayf	B2	56
Bani Walid	B1	56
Bani, river	B3	58
Baniyas	A2	27
Banja Luka	B1	48
Banjarmasin	C2	13
Banjul, capital	B2	62
Banks, island	G4	95
Banks, island	D2	99
Banks, island	B1	18
Banks, peninsula	B3	15
Bann, river	H3	102
Bannockburn	H3	102
Bansang	B2	62
Bansbaria	Inset II	20
Banská Bystrica	B2	42
Bantry	B3	31
Bantry, bay	B3	31
Baoding	E2	10
Baoshan	C3	10
Baotou	E1	10
Baoulé, river	B3	58
Baquerizo Moreno	Inset	
Bar	A3	49
Bar-le-Duc	D2	34
Baraawe	A3	60
Barabinsk	D5	44
Baracaldo	E1	37
Barachois	M3	103

	Key	Page
Baracoa	F3	88
Barahona	A2	89
Baraki Barak	B2	22
Barakpur	Inset II	20
Baram, river	D2	13
Barama, river	B2	80
Baranagar	Inset II	20
Baranavichy	C3	47
Barasat	Inset II	20
Barbados		91
Barbuda, island	E3	90
Barcelona	D1	79
Barcelona	H2	37
Barceloneta	B2	90
Bärdä	B2	45
Bardaï	C2	59
Bardejov	C2	42
Bareilly	C3	20
Barents, sea	B3	44
Bargachia	Inset II	20
Bari	D2	38
Baril, lake	E2	94
Barinas	B2	79
Barind, region	B4	21
Baris	B3	56
Barisal	D6	21
Bark, lake	H2	102
Barkerville	M4	95
Barkly, tableland	C1	14
Barletta	D2	38
Barnaul	D6	44
Barnes, ice cap	O3	99
Barnsley	C3	30
Barnstaple	B3	30
Barnwell	D6	94
Baro, river	B2	60
Barons	D6	94
Barquisimeto	C1	79
Barra, river	A2	30
Barrancabermeja	B3	78
Barranquilla	B2	78
Barranquitas	C2	90
Barreiro	A3	36
Barrhead	C4	94
Barrie	F3	102
Barrière	M5	95
Barrington	B4	100
Barro	B1	62
Barrouallie	B2	91
Barrow, Alaska	Inset I	126
Barrow, river	C2	31
Barrow-in-Furness	B2	30
Barry's Bay	H2	102
Bartang, river	B1	23
Bartica	B2	80
Barú, volcano	A2	87
Baruun-Urt	D2	11
Baruta	C1	79
Bas-Caraquet	E1	97
Basarabeasca	B2	50
Basel	B1	35
Bashi, channel	B1	12
Basilan	B5	12
Basilan, island	B5	12
Basildon	Inset III	30
Basilicata	C2	38
Baskatong, reservoir	A5	103
Basque Country	E1	37
Basra	C2	24
Bass Rock, islet	C2	30
Bass, strait	D3	14
Bassar	B2	64
Basse Santa Su	D2	62
Basse-Normandie	B2	34
Bassein	B3	12
Basseterre, capital	B2	90
Bassila	A3	64
Bastia	Inset I	34
Bastogne	D2	33
Bata	B3	66
Bataan, peninsula	B2	12
Batabanó, gulf	B2	88
Batan, islands	B1	12
Batang	B2	10
Batang Duri	C2	13
Batangafo	A2	66
Batangas	B2	12
Batdambang	B2	11
Bate, bay	Inset IV	14
Batéké, plateau	C5	66
Bath	C3	90
Bath	C3	30
Bath	B2	97
Batha, river	C4	59
Bathsheba	B3	91
Bathurst	D1	97
Bathurst, island	J1	99
Batin, Wadi al-, river	A2	24
Batinah, al-, region	C1	25
Batman	E3	27
Batna	B1	57
Baton Rouge, capital, La.	D2	126
Batouri	B3	65
Batroun	A1	26
Batteau	D2	98
Batticaloa	C4	19
Battle, river	A7	104
Battleford	B8	104
Batu Pahat	B2	13
Batumi	A4	45
Baubau	D2	13
Bauchi	E2	65
Bauld, cape	Inset II	98
Bauru	D4	81
Bauska	C3	46
Bautzen	C3	40
Bavaria	B4	40
Bavarian Alps, mts.	B5	40
Bawiti, al-	A2	56
Bawku	B1	64
Bawlf	D5	94
Bay Bulls	E5	98
Bay de Verde	E5	98
Bay Roberts	E5	98
Bay St. Lawrence	G1	100
Bayamo	E3	88
Bayamón	C2	90
Bayamón, river	C2	90
Bayan Har, range	C2	10

	Key	Page
Bayanhongor	C2	11
Bayda, al-	B2	25
Bayda, al-	D1	56
Baydhabo	A3	60
Bayerischer Wald, mts.	C4	40
Bayeux	B2	34
Bayfield	D4	102
Baykal, lake	D7	44
Bayonne	B5	34
Bayport	C3	100
Bayramaly	D3	22
Bayreuth	B4	40
Bays, lake	F2	102
Baza	E4	37
Bazardüzü Daği, mt.	B2	45
Bazin, river	A4	103
Beachside	D4	98
Beagle, channel	B7	74
Bear Lake	C1	94
Bear River	C2	100
Beata, cape	A3	89
Beata, island	A3	89
Beaton	O6	95
Beau Bassin	B2	69
Beauceville	F5	103
Beaufort West	B3	71
Beaufort, sea	B1	105
Beaulac	E6	103
Beaumont	D4	94
Beaumont, Tex.	D2	126
Beauport	L5	103
Beaupré	F4	103
Beauséjour	C4	96
Beauval	C5	104
Beaver Creek	A4	105
Beaver Harbour	E3	100
Beaver Hill, lake	D2	96
Beaver Mines	C6	94
Beaver, river	A6	104
Beaver, river	D5	105
Beaver, river	F3	102
Bécancour	D5	103
Béchar	A1	57
Bedeque, bay	B2	100
Bedford	C3	30
Bedford	D3	100
Bedford	D6	103
Bedok	B1	13
Beechy	C10	104
Beersheba	B2	26
Behala	Inset II	20
Bei'an	F1	10
Beihai	D3	10
Beijing, capital	E2	10
Beira	B3	68
Beirut, capital	A2	26
Béja	B3	36
Béja	B1	57
Bejaïa	B1	57
Bejaïa, gulf	B1	57
Béjar	D2	37
Bekaa, valley	A2	26
Békéscsaba	C2	43
Bela	C4	21
Belair	B4	91
Belapurpada	Inset I	20
Belarus		47
Belaya Tserkov	C2	47
Belasica, mts.	C2	48
Beledweyne	B3	60
Belém	D2	81
Belep, islands	C2	18
Belfast	B2	30
Belford Roxo	Inset I	81
Belfort	D3	34
Belfort, gap	D3	34
Belgaum	B5	20
Belgium		33
Belgrade, capital	B2	49
Beli Drim, river	B3	49
Bélinga	B1	66
Belitung, island	B2	13
Belize		85
Belize City	B2	85
Belize, river	B2	85
Bella Coola	J5	95
Bella Unión	B1	75
Bellary	C5	20
Belle River	C3	100
Belle Isle, strait	C3	98
Belle, island	B3	34
Belle, island	C3	98
Belle-Anse	C2	89
Belledune	D1	97
Belleoram	D4	98
Belleview	A4	96
Belleville	H3	102
Belleville	A3	71
Bellingham	L7	95
Bellingham, Wash.	A1	126
Bellingshausen, sea	B10	107
Bellinzona	D2	35
Bellona, island	A2	16
Belluno	C1	38
Bellville	A3	71
Belmont	B4	96
Belmopan, capital	B2	85
Belo Horizonte	D3	81
Beloeil	C6	103
Belomorsk	C3	44
Bemaraha, plateau	A2	69
Bemidji, Minn.	D1	126
Ben Éoin	G2	100
Ben Nevis, mt.	B2	30
Benavente	D1	37
Bend, Oreg.	A1	126
Bender (Tighina)	B2	50
Benderbeyla	C2	60
Bendigo, Vic.	D3	14
Benevento	C2	38
Bengal, bay	E5	20
Bengbu	E2	10
Benghazi	D1	56
Bengkulu	B2	13
Bengough	E11	104
Benguela	B4	70
Beni Mellal	C1	57

	Key	Page
Beni, river	A2	77
Benidorm	F3	37
Benin		64
Benin City	C4	65
Benin, bight	B5	65
Benito	A3	96
Benoit's Cove	B5	98
Benoni	C2	71
Bénoué, river	B2	65
Benson	G11	104
Bentiaba	B4	70
Benue, river	E3	65
Benxi	F1	10
Benzdorp	B3	80
Beqa, island	B3	17
Bequia, island	B2	91
Berat	A3	49
Berber	B1	60
Berbérati	A3	66
Berbice, river	B3	80
Berdoba	C4	59
Berdyansk	D3	47
Berekua	B4	90
Berens River	C3	96
Berens, island	C3	96
Berens, river	C3	96
Beresford	D1	97
Berezniki	D4	44
Bergamo	B1	38
Bergen	B3	52
Bergen op Zoom	B3	32
Bergerac	C4	34
Bergisch Gladbach	A3	40
Bering, sea	Inset I	126
Bering, strait	C11	44
Berkner, island	B12	107
Berlin, capital	C2	40
Bermejo, river	C2	74
Bermuda, island		82
Bern, capital	B2	35
Bernburg	B3	40
Bernese Alps, mts.	B2	35
Bernières	K6	103
Berounka, river	A3	42
Bertwell	H8	104
Berwick	C2	100
Berwick-upon-Tweed	C2	30
Besançon	D3	34
Beskid, mts.	D4	41
Besnard, lake	D5	104
Besor, river	B2	26
Bessemer	B4	96
Bethanien	C4	70
Bethany	B4	96
Bethel, Alaska	Inset I	126
Bethierville	C5	103
Bethlehem	C2	71
Béticos, mts.	E4	37
Bétou	E2	66
Betsiamites	H3	103
Betsiamites, river	G2	103
Betsiboka, river	B2	69
Bette, mt.	C3	56
Beulah	A4	96
Beyla	D3	62
Beyneu	B2	23
Beyşehir, lake	B3	27
Béziers	C5	34
Bhadrakh	E4	20
Bhadreswar	Inset II	20
Bhagalpur	E3	20
Bhairahawa	B2	19
Bhaktapur	C2	19
Bhamapur	D5	20
Bhamo	B1	12
Bhandup	Inset I	20
Bharatpur	C3	20
Bharatpara	Inset II	20
Bhatpara	Inset II	20
Bhavnagar	B4	20
Bhayandar	Inset I	20
Bheri, river	B2	19
Bhima, river	C5	20
Bhimpur	Inset II	20
Bhiwandi	Inset I	20
Bhopal	C4	20
Bhubaneswar	E4	20
Bhuj	A4	20
Bhunya	B2	71
Bhutan		19
Biabou	B2	91
Biafra, bight	A3	65
Biak, island	E2	13
Biała Podlaska	F2	41
Białystok	F2	41
Biankouma	C3	63
Biarritz	B5	34
Bicaz, reservoir	D2	43
Biche, lake	E4	94
Bida	D3	65
Bié, plateau	C4	70
Biel	B1	35
Biele Karpaty, mts.	A2	42
Bielefeld	B2	40
Bielsko-Biała	D4	41
Bienville, lake	B2	101
Big Beaver	E11	104
Big Bend	B2	71
Big Creek	L5	95
Big Fish, river	B1	105
Big Gull, lake	J3	102
Big Muddy, lake	F11	104
Big River	C7	104
Big Trout Lake	C2	101
Big, river	O4	99
Biggar	C8	104
Bignona	A3	62
Bigstone, river	D1	96
Bihać	A3	48
Bihar	E3	20
Bijagós, islands	A2	62
Bijeljina	C1	48
Bikaner	B3	20
Bikar, island	C1	16
Bikini, island	B1	16

	Key	Page
Bilaspur	D4	20
Biläsuvar	C3	45
Bilauktaung, range	B3, C3	12
Bilbao	E1	37
Billings, Mont.	B1	126
Billings, reservoir	Inset II	81
Bilma	C2	59
Biloku	B5	80
Biloxi, Miss.	E2	126
Biltine	C4	59
Bimbila	C2	64
Binche	C2	33
Bindloss	E6	94
Bindura	B1	69
Binga, mt.	B3	68
Bingen	A4	40
Binscarth	A4	96
Bint Jubayl	A2	26
Bintang	B2	62
Bintimane, mt.	B6	76
Bío-Bío, river	B6	76
Bioko, island	A1	66
Bir Gandús	A2	58
Bir Morgrein	C1	58
Birak	B2	56
Birao	B2	66
Biratnagar	D3	19
Birch Cliff	K5	102
Birch Hills	E7	104
Birch River	A3	96
Birch, mts.	D2	94
Birchy Bay	D4	98
Bird, island	B2	91
Birendranagar	B2	19
Birganj	C2	19
Birjand	D3	22
Birkat Qarun, lake	B2	56
Birkenhead	B3	30
Birkirkara	B2	36
Bîrlad	D2	43
Birmingham	C3	30
Birmingham, Ala.	E2	126
Birni Nkonni	B3	59
Birnie	B4	96
Birnin Kebbi	C1	65
Birobidzhan	E8	44
Birtle	A4	96
Biržai	C1	46
Birzebbuga	C3	36
Biscay, bay	B4	34
Bishkek, capital	D1	23
Bishnupur	Inset II	20
Bishop's Falls	D4	98
Biskra	B1	57
Bislig	C4	12
Bismarck, archipelago	A2	15
Bismarck, capital, N. Dak.	C1	126
Bismarck, range	A2	15
Bismarck, sea	A2	15
Bismuna, lagoon	C1	87
Bison, lake	B2	94
Bissau, capital	B2	62
Bissett	D3	96
Bissorã	B1	62
Bistcho, lake	A1	94
Bistrița	C2	43
Bistrița, river	C2	43
Bitam	A1	66
Bitola	B2	48
Bitumount	E2	94
Biu	G2	65
Biwa, lake	B3	8
Biysk	D6	44
Bizard, island	H5	103
Bizerte	B1	57
Bjorne, peninsula	L1	99
Black (Da), river	A2	11
Black Country, region	C3	30
Black Lake	E1	104
Black River	D2	88
Black Tickle	D2	98
Black Volta, river	A2, B3	64
Black, forest	A4	40
Black, hills, S. Dak.	C1	126
Black, lake	E1	104
Black, sea		29
Blackburn	C3	30
Blackmans	B3	91
Blackpool	C3	30
Blacks Harbour	C3	97
Blackstone, river	B3	105
Blackville	D2	97
Blackwater, river	B2, C1	31
Blagoevgrad	B4	50
Blagoveshchensk	D4	44
Blaine Lake	D8	104
Blainville	H5	103
Blanc, mt.	D4	34
Blanc, reservoir	C4	103
Blanc-Sablon	E3	101
Blanca, bay	C4	74
Blanda, river	B2	52
Blantyre	B3	68
Blarney	B3	31
Blatec	C2	48
Blenheim	B3	15
Blenheim	D5	102
Blida	B1	57
Bligh Water, sound	B2	17
Blind Bay	N6	95
Blind River	C1	102
Blitta	B2	64
Bloemfontein, judicial capital	C2	71
Blois	C3	34
Bloodvein, river	C3	96
Bloomfield	H4	102
Bloomington, Ind.	E2	126
Blossom Park	H6	102
Blow, river	B1	105
Blue Mountain, peak	C2	88
Blue Nile, river	C3	60
Blue Ridge	C4	94
Blue River	N5	95
Blue, mts.	B3	14
Blue, mts.	B2	88
Bluefields	C3	88
Bluefields	C3	87

	Key	Page
Bluenose, *lake*	E3	99
Bluffton	C5	94
Blyth	D4	102
Bo	B2	63
Bo Hai, *gulf*	E2	10
Boa Vista	B1	81
Boa Vista, *island*	D2	58
Boaco	B2	87
Bobcaygeon	G3	102
Bobo-Dioulasso	B3	64
Bocas del Toro	A2	87
Bocay	B1	87
Bocay, *river*	B2	87
Bocholt	A3	40
Bochum	A3	40
Bodaybo	D7	44
Bodo	E5	94
Bodø	C2	52
Boende	B2	67
Boggeragh, *mts.*	B2	31
Boggy, *peak*	D5	90
Bogor	B2	13
Bogotá, *capital*	B3	78
Bogra	C4	21
Bohemia, *region*	A3	42
Bohemian, *forest*	A3	42
Bohemian-Moravian, *heights*	B3	42
Bohol, *island*	C4	12
Bohol, *sea*	C4	12
Boiestown	C2	97
Boilleau	F3	103
Bois-des-Filion	H5	103
Boise, *capital*, Idaho	B1	126
Boissevain	A4	96
Boknafjord, *fjord*	B4	52
Boksburg	C2	71
Bol	A4	59
Bolama	B2	62
Bolands	D5	90
Bole	A2	64
Bolgatanga	B1	64
Bolívar, *mt.*	B2	79
Bolivia		**77**
Bolligen	B2	35
Bolnisi	C4	45
Bolobo	B2	67
Bologna	B1	38
Bolovens, *plateau*	D4	11
Bolsena, *lake*	B2	38
Bolsón de Mapimí, *depression*	D2	84
Bolton	C3	30
Bolton	F4	102
Bolu	B2	27
Bolzano	B1	38
Bom Jesus da Lapa	D3	81
Boma	A2	67
Bombay	B5, Inset I	20
Bombay, *harbor*	Inset I	20
Bomu, *river*	C1	67
Bon Pays, *region*	B2	33
Bon, *cape*	C1	57
Bonaire, *island*		82
Bonao	B2	89
Bonaventure	L3	103
Bonaventure, *river*	L3	103
Bonavista	E5	98
Bonavista, *bay*	E5	98
Bondo	B1	67
Bondoukou	E2	63
Bondy	Inset II	34
Bongor	A5	59
Bonin, *islands*	Inset III	8
Bonn	A3	40
Bonnet Plume, *river*	C3	105
Bonny	D5	65
Bonnyville	E4	94
Bonshaw	B2	100
Bonthe	A2	63
Bööntsagaan, *lake*	B2	11
Boosaaso	B1	60
Boothia, *gulf*	K2	99
Boothia, *peninsula*	K2	99
Booué	A2	66
Bor	C2	49
Borås	B3	53
Bordeaux	B4	34
Borden	B2	100
Borden	C8	104
Borden, *island*	F1	99
Borden, *peninsula*	M2	99
Bordøy, *island*	Inset	32
Borgo Maggiore	B1	39
Borivli	Inset I	20
Borjomi	B4	45
Borneo, *island*	C1	13
Bornholm, *island*	E3	32
Bosanska Gradiška	B1	48
Bosanska Krupa	A1	48
Bosna, *river*	B1	48
Bosnia & Hercegovina		**48**
Boso, *peninsula*	D3	8
Bosporus, *strait*	B2	27
Bossangoa	A2	66
Bosten, *lake*	B1	10
Boston	C3	30
Boston Bar	M6	95
Boston, *capital*, Mass.	F1	126
Boswell	O6	95
Botany, *bay*	Inset IV	14
Boteti, *river*	A2	69
Botha	D5	94
Bothnia, *gulf*	B2, D2	53
Botna, *river*	B2	50
Botoşani	D2	43
Botrange, *mt.*	E2	33
Botswana		**69**
Botte Donato, *mt.*	D3	38
Bottrop	A3	40
Botwood	D4	98
Bouaflé	D3	63
Bouaké	D3	63
Bouar	A2	66
Boucherville	J5	103
Bouctouche	E2	97
Bougainville, *island*	B2	15
Boughton, *bay*	C2	100
Bougouni	B3	58

	Key	Page
Boulder, Colo.	C2	126
Boulogne-Billancourt	Inset II	34
Boulogne-sur-Mer	C1	34
Bouna	E2	63
Bourail	C2	18
Bourem	C2	58
Bourg-en-Bresse	D3	34
Bourges	C3	34
Bourgogne	C3	34
Bourke, N.S.W.	D3	14
Bournemouth	C4	30
Bousso	B5	59
Bow City	D6	94
Bow, *river*	D6	94
Bow, *river*	E6	104
Bowen, Qld.	D2	14
Bowling Green, Ky.	E2	126
Bowser, *lake*	H3	95
Bowsman	A3	96
Boyd's Cove	D4	98
Boyne	C2	31
Boyne, *river*	B4	96
Bozeman, Mont.	B1	126
Brabant Lake	G4	104
Brač, *island*	C3	48
Bracciano, *lake*	C2	38
Bracebridge	F2	102
Bradford	C3	30
Braga	A2	36
Bragança	B2	36
Bragg Creek	C6	94
Brahmanbaria	E5	21
Brahmaputra, *river*	F3	20
Brăila	D3	43
Braintree	Inset III	30
Brakpan	C2	71
Bralorne	L6	95
Bramalea	H5	102
Brampton	F4	102
Branco, *river*	B1	81
Brandberg, *mt.*	B2	70
Brandenburg	C2	40
Brandon	B4, C2	96
Brant	D6	94
Brantford	E4	102
Bras d'Or	G1	100
Brasília, *capital*	D3	81
Braşov	C3	43
Bratislava, *capital*	A2	42
Bratsk	D7	44
Braunau	C2	39
Brava, *coast*	H2	37
Brava, *island*	B4	58
Brazil		**81**
Brazilian, *highlands*	D3	81
Brazzaville, *capital*	C6	66
Brčko	B1	48
Brea, *point*	B3	90
Břeclav	C4	42
Brecon Beacons, *mts.*	B3	30
Breda	B3	32
Bredenbury	H10	104
Bregalnica, *river*	C2	48
Breidhafjördhur, *fjord*	A2	52
Bremen	B2	40
Bremerhaven	B2	40
Brenner, *pass*	B3	39
Brentwood	Inset III	30
Brescia	B1	38
Brest	A3	47
Brest	A2	34
Bretagne	B2	34
Breton	C4	94
Bria	B2	66
Briançon	D4	34
Briceni	A1	50
Bridge Lake	M5	95
Bridgeport, Conn.	F1	126
Bridgetown	B3	100
Bridgetown, *capital*	A4	91
Bridgewater	C3	100
Brienzersee, *lake*	B2	35
Brighton	C4	30
Brighton	H3	102
Brikama	B2	62
Brindisi	D2	38
Brisbane, Qld., *capital*	E2, Inset III	14
Brisbane, *river*	Inset III	14
Bristol	C3	30
Bristol	B2	97
Bristol, *channel*	B3	30
Britannia	E5	98
Britt	E2	102
Brive-la-Gallarde	C4	34
Brno	C3	42
Broadview	H10	104
Brochet	C1	96
Brock, *island*	F1	99
Brocket	D6	94
Brockville	K3	102
Brodfur, *peninsula*	L2	99
Broken Hill, N.S.W.	D3	14
Brokopondo	B2	80
Brolin	C3	30
Bromptonville	E6	103
Brookdale	B4	96
Brooks	E6	94
Brooks range, Alaska	Inset I	126
Broome, W.A.	B1	14
Broomhill	A4	96
Brossard	J6	103
Brownsville, Tex.	D3	126
Bruce Mines	B1	102
Bruce Peninsula N.P.	D2	102
Brugge	B1	33
Brugge-Ghent, *canal*	B1	33
Brûlé	B4	94
Brunei		**13**
Brunei, *bay*	C1	13
Brunei, *river*	B2	13
Brunswick, Ga.	E2	126
Brunswick, *peninsula*	B9	76
Brussels	D4	102
Brussels, *capital*	C2	33
Bryan, Tex.	D2	126
Bryansk	D3	44

	Key	Page
Bsharri	B1	26
Bu Craa	B1	58
Bua, *river*	B2	68
Buada	B2	16
Buala	A1	16
Buba	C2	62
Bubanza	B2	61
Bubaque	B2	62
Bubiyan, *island*	C2	24
Bucaramanga	B3	78
Buchanan	A3	63
Buchanan	H9	104
Buchans	C5	98
Bucharest, *capital*	D3	43
Buck Creek	C4	94
Buck Lake	C4	94
Buckingham	A6	103
Budapest, *capital*	B2	43
Buea	A3	65
Buenaventura	A4	78
Buendía, *reservoir*	E2	37
Buene, *river*	A2	49
Buenos Aires, *capital*	D3	74
Buenos Aires, *lake*	A6	74
Buffalo Narrows	B5	104
Buffalo, *lake*	D5	94
Buffalo, *lake*	E4	99
Buffalo, N.Y.	F1	126
Bug, *river*	E2, F3	41
Bugeac, *region*	B3	50
Bugojno	B1	48
Buhayrat al-Asad, *lake*	B1	27
Buj-Buj	Inset II	20
Bujumbura, *capital*	B2	61
Buka, *island*	B2	15
Bukavu	C2	67
Bukhara	B3	23
Bukit Pagon, *mt.*	C3	13
Bukit Panjang	B1	13
Bukit Timah	B1	13
Bükk, *mts.*	C1	43
Bukoba	B1	68
Bula	B1	62
Bulawayo	B2	69
Bulembu	B1	71
Bulgan	C2	11
Bulgaria		**50**
Bulle	B2	35
Bulyea	F10	104
Bumba	B1	67
Bunbury, W.A.	A3	14
Bundaberg, Qld.	E2	14
Bungo, *channel*	B3	8
Bunia	C1	67
Bunsuru, *river*	D1	65
Buon Me Thuot	B4	11
Buqayq	C1	24
Buraydah	B1	24
Burco	B2	60
Burdekin, *river*	D1	14
Burdett	E6	94
Burdur	B3	27
Burdwan	E4	20
Büren	B3	40
Burgas	F3	50
Burgeo	C5	98
Burgos	E1	37
Burhanpur	C4	20
Burica, *point*	A2	87
Burin	D5	98
Burin, *peninsula*	D5	98
Buriram	C3	12
Burk's Falls	F2	102
Burke, *channel*	J5	95
Burkina Faso		**64**
Burlington	F4	102
Burlington, Vt.	F1	126
Burma (Myanmar)		**12**
Burnley	C3	30
Burns Lake	K4	95
Burntwood	A1	96
Burntwood, *river*	B1, C1, D2	96
Bursa	B2	27
Burtnieku, *lake*	C2	46
Buru, *island*	D2	13
Burundi		**61**
Bururi	B2	61
Burutu	C5	65
Burwash Landing	B5	105
Bury	C3	30
Bury St. Edmunds	D3	30
Buryatiya, *republic*	D7	44
Bushmanland, *plain*	A2	71
Buta	C1	67
Butare	B2	61
Bute, *island*	B2	30
Butha-Buthe	B1	71
Butte, Mont.	B1	126
Buttonville	K5	102
Butuan	C4	12
Butwal	B2	19
Buurgplaatz, *mt.*	B1	33
Buxton	C3	30
Buyant-Uhaa	D3	11
Buyo, *lake*	C3	63
Büyük Menderes, *lake*	A3	27
Buzău	D3	43
Búzi, *river*	B4	68
Büzmeyin	C2	22
Byam Martin, *channel*	G1	99
Byam Martin, *island*	H1	99
Byarezina, *river*	D3	47
Byblos, *ruins*	A1	26
Bydgoszcz	C2	41
Byelaruskaya Hrada, *range*	C3	47
Bylot, *island*	N2	99
Byumba	C1	61

C

	Key	Page
Ca Mau	A5	11
Ca, *river*	A2	11
Caacupé	D4	75
Caaguazú	E4	75
Caaguazú	D5	75
Cabanatuan	B3	12
Cabano	H4	103
Cabimas	B1	79

	Key	Page
Cabinda	B1	70
Cabo Rojo	A2	90
Cabora Bassa, *dam*	B2	68
Cabora Bassa, *lake*	A2	68
Caborca	B1	84
Cabrera	C1	89
Cabrera, *island*	H3	37
Cabri	B10	104
Čačak	B3	49
Cacao	B1	80
Cáceres	C3	81
Cáceres	C3	37
Cache Creek	M6	95
Cacheu	A1	62
Cacheu, *river*	B1	62
Cachimbo	C2	81
Cacine	B2	62
Cacouna	G4	103
Cadiz	B4	12
Cádiz	C4	37
Cádiz, *gulf*	C4	37
Cadomin	B4	94
Cadotte Lake	B2	94
Caen	B2	34
Caerleon	C3	30
Caernarfon	B3	30
Cagayan de Oro	C4	12
Cagayan Sulu, *island*	A5	12
Cagayan, *islands*	B4	12
Cagayan, *river*	B2	12
Cagliari	B3	38
Cagliari, *gulf*	B3	38
Caguas	C2	90
Caha, *mts.*	B3	31
Cahors	C4	34
Cahul	B3	50
Caicos, *islands*	D4	89
Caidasm da Rainha	A3	36
Caille, *island*	B1	91
Cairns, Qld.	D1	14
Cairo, *capital*	B1	56
Cairo, Ill.	E2	126
Caja de Muertos, *island*	B3	90
Cajamarca	B2	77
Calabar	E5	65
Calabogie	J2	102
Calabozo	C2	79
Calabria	D3	38
Calafate	A7	74
Calais	B3	94
Calais	B3	34
Calama	C2	76
Calamian, *islands*	A3	12
Calapan	B3	12
Călăraşi	D3	43
Calatayud	F2	37
Calatrava	B3	66
Calbayog	C3	12
Calcutta	E4, Inset II	20
Caldas, *river*	A1, C2	71
Caledonia	F4	102
Calgary	C5	94
Cali	A4	78
California	B2	126
California, *gulf*	B1	84
Callao	B3	77
Calling Lake	D3	94
Caltanissetta	C3	38
Calvi	Inset I	34
Calvinia	A3	71
Cam Ranh	B4	11
Camagüey	D2	88
Camagüey, *archipelago*	D2	88
Camberley	Inset III	30
Cambodia		**11**
Cambrai	C1	34
Cambrian, *mts.*	B3	30
Cambridge	D3	30
Cambridge Bay	G3	99
Cambridge-Narrows	D3	97
Cameron, *hills*	B1	94
Cameron, *island*	H1	99
Cameroon		**65**
Cameroon, *mt.*	A3	65
Camiri	B4	77
Camopi	B2	80
Camopi, *river*	B2	80
Campana, *island*	A8	76
Campania	C2	38
Campbell River	K6	95
Campbellford	H3	102
Campbellton	A2	100
Campbeltown	B2	30
Campbelltown, N.S.W.	Inset IV	14
Campbelltown, S.A.	Inset II	14
Campeche	F4	84
Campeche, *bay*	F4	84
Campeche, *state capital*	F4	84
Camper	B3	96
Camperville	A3	96
Campina Grande	E2	81
Campinas	D4	81
Campo Grande	C4	81
Campobasso	C2	38
Campobello, *island*	C4	97
Campos	D4	81
Campos Elísios	Inset I	81
Camrose	D4	94
Camsell Portage	A1	104
Camú, *river*	B1	89
Camuy	B2	90
Can Tho	A4	11
Caña Gorda, *beach*	B3	90
Canaan	A4	91
Canada		**92**
Canaima	D3	79
Çanakkale	A2	27
Canal Flats	P6	95
Canary, *islands*	Inset I	37
Canaries	A2	91
Canary, islands		**55**
Canaveral, *cape*, Fla.	E3	126
Canberra, A.C.T., *natl. capital*	D3	14

	Key	Page
Candle Lake	E7	104
Cando	B8	104
Canelles, *river*	B3	91
Canelones	B3	75
Cangamba	D4	70
Cangzhou	E2	10
Caniapiscau, *lake*	C3	101
Caniapiscau, *river*	C2	101
Çankırı	C2	27
Cankuzo	C2	61
Cannes	D5	34
Canning, *river*	Inset I	14
Canoe Narrows	B5	104
Canoe, *lake*	B5	104
Canora	H9	104
Canossa	B1	38
Canouan, *island*	B3	91
Cánovanas	D2	90
Canso	G2	100
Cantabria	D1	37
Cantábrica, *mts.*	C1	37
Canterbury	B3	30
Canterbury	B3	97
Canterbury, *bight*	B3	15
Canterbury, *plains*	B3	15
Canton, *island*	B2	17
Canwood	D7	104
Canyon Creek	C3	94
Cao Bang	B1	11
Cap-aux-Os	M3	103
Cap-Chat	K2	103
Cap-de-la-Madeleine	D5	103
Cap-Haïtien	C1	89
Cap-Pelé	E2	97
Cap-Rouge	K6	103
Cap-St-Ignace	F4	103
Cape Charles	D3	98
Cape Coast	B4	64
Cape Girardeau, Mo.	E2	126
Cape North	G1	100
Cape Race	E5	98
Cape Ray	B5	98
Cape St. George	B5	98
Cape Tormentine	E2	97
Cape Town, *legislative capital*	A3	71
Cape Verde		**58**
Cape York, *peninsula*	D1	14
Capitán Pablo Lagerenza	B1	75
Caplan	L3	103
Caprara, *point*	B2	38
Capreol	D1	102
Capri, *island*	C2	38
Capua	C2	38
Caquetá, *river*	B5	78
Car Nicobar, *island*	F7	20
Caracas, *capital*	C1	79
Caramoan, *peninsula*	B3	12
Carapicuíba	Inset II	81
Caraquet	E1	97
Ceará	E2	81
Cebollatí, *river*	C2	75
Cebu	B4	12
Cebu, *island*	B4	12
Cedar City, Utah	B2	126
Cedar Grove	E5	98
Cedar Rapids, Iowa	D1	126
Cedar, *lake*	B2	94
Cedros, *island*	A2	84
Ceduna, S.A.	C3	14
Ceerigaabo	B1	60
Cefalù	C3	38
Cegléd	B2	43
Ceiba	D2	90
Ceiba	D2	90
Celada	D3	86
Celaya	D3	84
Celebes (Sulawesi), *island*	D2	13
Celebes, *sea*	D1	13
Celje	B3	48
Celtic, *sea*	B3	30
Central African Republic		**D10**
Central Butte	D10	104
Central Makran, *range*	B4	21
Central Siberian, *plateau*	C9	44
Centre	C3	34
Centre	C3	66
Centre de Flacq	C3	69
Centreville	E4	97
Ceram, *island*	D2	13
Ceram, *sea*	D2	13
Cerf, *island*	Inset	69
Cernavodă	D3	43
Cerro Castillo	B9	76
Cerro de Pasco	B3	77
Cervati, *mt.*	C2	38
Cesis	C2	46
České Budějovice	B4	42
Cess, *river*	B3	63
Cessford	E6	94
Cetinje	A3	49
Ceuta	D5	37
Cévennes, *mts.*	C4	34
Ceyhan, *river*	D3	27
Chachapoyas	B2	77
Chaco Boreal, *region*	B2	75
Chad		**59**
Chad, *lake*	A4, A3	59
Chaeryŏng, *river*	A3	9
Chagai, *hills*	B2	21
Chaghcharan	B2	22
Chagres, *river*	C2	87
Chaguanas	A7	91
Chaitén	B7	76
Chaiyaphum	B2	12
Chalco	Inset	84
Chaleur, *bay*	D1	97
Chalna	C6	21
Châlons-sur-Marne	D2	34
Chambal, *river*	C3	20
Chambéry	D4	34
Chambeshi, *river*	B2	67
Chambord	D3	103
Chameleon, *river*	D4	69
Chamonix-Mont-Blanc	D4	34
Champagne Castle, *mt.*	C2	71
Champagne-Ardenne	D2	34
Champaquí, *mt.*	C3	74
Champasak	C4	11

Key Page

...perico B5 85
... plain D5 103
...aral B3 76
...dannagar ....Inset II 20
...digarh C2 20
...dler M3 103
...drapur D5 21
...drapur C5 20
... (Yangtze), river ...D2, E2 10
...gane B4 68
...gchun F1 10
...gde E3 10
...ghua B1 9
... .B1 13
...gjin B2 9
...gjin B2 9
...gsha E3 10
...guinola A2 87
...gyŏn A3 9
...gzhi E2 10
...gzhou F2 10
...nel islands, Calif. ...A2 126
...nel-Port aux Basques B5 98
...tilly C2 34
... Phraya, river B3 12
...ada dos Parecis, range ...C3 81
...ala, lake D3 84
...aré, river A3 77
...leau D3 101
...lin D10 104
...dzhou D2 22
...ente, river B4 34
..., river A5 59
...kar B1 22
...ty B2 80
...eroi C2 33
... .A1 96
...esbourg ......E5, Inset 103
...eston, capital, W. Va. ...E2 126
...eston, S.C. F2 126
...estown C3 90
...estown A3 91
...eville Mézières ...D2 34
...eville, Qld. D2 14
...ie Lake M3 95
... .C1 97
...lotte, N.C. E2 126
...lotte C3 98
...lottetown B2 100
...lotteville B1 91
... .E5, K6 103
...ters Towers, Qld. ...D2 14
...tres C2 34
... .N6 95
...eauguay ...C6, H6 103
...eauroux C3 34
...ellerault C3 34
...field C4 96
...ham ......Inset III 30
...ham C5 102
...ham, sound G4 95
...kal, river B2 23
...sworth E3 102
...tanooga, Tenn. ...E2 126
... Doc A4 11
...mont D2 34
...es B2 36
... .A2 42
...oksary D4 44
...erton C4 9
...hnya, republic ...E4 44
...uba, island B2 12
...utu B2 69
...l ......Inset 9
... island ......Inset 9
..., strait ......Inset 9
... Keng ......Inset 10
...an G8 104
...eken A2 22
...f, river B1 57
...es ......Inset II 34
... .F3 41
...msford ......D3, Inset III 30
...tenham C3 30
...abinsk D5 44
...yuskin, cape B7 44
...nnitz ......Inset I 20
...min Grenier B3 69
...nnitz C3 41
...nab, river D3 21
...hachane ......Inset I 20
...he ......Inset I 20
...néville A6 103
...ngde E1 10
...ngdu D2 10
...nnai (Madras) ...D6 20
...bourg B2 34
...epovets D3 44
...kassy C2 47
...nigov C1 47
...nivtsi B2 47
...rapunji F3 20
...ryville N6 95
...skiy C10 44
...skiy, range C8 44
...sapeake, bay ...F2 126
...sley D3 102
...ster C3 30
...ster C3 100
...sterfield C3 30
...sterfield Inlet K4 99
...sterfield, islands ...A2 14
...sticamp G1 100
...tumal, state capital ...G4 84
...twynd M3 95
...viot, hills C2 30
...vreuse ......Inset II 34
...yenne, capital, Wyo. ...C1 126
...uka A2 19
...apa C2 12
...apa F4 84
...atura B3 45
...au D3 8
...ougamau B2 103

Key Page

Chibougamau, lake B2 103
Chicago, Ill. E1 126
Chicapa, river D3 70
Chichén Itzá, ruins ...G3 84
Chichester C4 30
Chichi, island ......Inset III 8
Chiclayo B2 77
Chico B6 74
Chiconcuac ......Inset 84
Chicoutimi E3 103
Chief, river L2 95
Chiem, lake C5 40
Chiesanuova B2 39
Chieti C2 38
Chifeng E1 10
Chignecto, bay C2 100
Chihuahua, state capital ...C2 84
Chilcotin, river K5 95
Chile 76
Chile Chico B8 76
Chililabombwe B2 67
Chilko, lake K5 95
Chillán B6 76
Chilliwack M6 95
Chiloé, island B7 76
Chilpancingo, state capital ...E4 84
Chilung B1 9
Chilwa, lake B2, C3 68
Chimalhuacán ......Inset 84
Chimay C2 33
Chimborazo, mt. B3 79
Chimbote B2 77
Chimoio B3 68
Chin, hills B2 12
China 10
Chinajá C4 85
Chinandega A2 87
Chincha Alta B3 77
Chinchaga, river A2 94
Chinde C3 68
Chindwin, river B1 12
Chingola B2 67
Chingoni C2 67
Chinhae C5 9
Chinhoyi B1 69
Chiniot D3 21
Chinju C5 9
Chinko, river B2 66
Chioggia C1 38
Chip, lake C4 94
Chipata C2 67
Chipewyan Lake D3 94
Chipman D2 97
Chira, river A5 79
Chirchiq, river C2 23
Chire, river B3 68
Chiredzi B2 69
Chiriquí, gulf A3 87
Chiriquí, lagoon B2 87
Chirner ......Inset I 20
Chirripó, mt. C3 86
Chirripó, river C2 86
Chisasibi A3 101
Chisholm C4 94
Chişinău, capital B2 50
Chita D7 44
Chitipa B1 68
Chitose ......Inset I 8
Chitral D2 21
Chitré B3 87
Chittagong E6 21
Chitungwiza B1 69
Chixoy, river C4 85
Choa Chu Kang A1 13
Choiceland F7 104
Choiseul A3 91
Choiseul, island A1 16
Choisy-le Roi ......Inset II 34
Chojnice C2 41
Choke, mts. B2 60
Cholet B3 34
Cholpon-Ata E1 23
Cholula E4 84
Choluteca B3 86
Choma B3 67
Chomo Lhari, mt. A1 19
Chon Buri B3 12
Chone A3 79
Chŏngjin C2 9
Chŏngju B4 9
Chŏngju A3 9
Chonju B5 9
Chonos, archipelago B7 76
Chontaleña, mts. B2 87
Chornobyl' C1 47
Chorzów D3 41
Choshui, river B2 9
Choybalsan D2 11
Christchurch B3 15
Christina, river E3 94
Christmas Island G2 100
Chu, river D1 23
Chuanan B1 9
Ch'unch'ŏn B4 9
Chungho B1 9
Chungju B4 9
Chungli B1 9
Chungqing, Ind. Mun. ...D3 10
Chungyang, range B2 9
Chuquicamata C2 76
Chur D2 35
Church Point A3 100
Churchbridge A4 96
Churchbridge J10 104
Churchill D1 96
Churchill Falls B3 98
Churchill, lake B4 104

Key Page

Churchill, river D1 96
Churia, mts. B2 19
Chute-aux-Outardes ...H2 103
Chuuk, islands C2 15
Chuvashiya, republic ...D4 44
Ciales C2 90
Cibao, valley A1 89
Cicia, island C2 17
Cidra C2 90
Ciechánow E2 41
Ciego de Ávila D2 88
Cienfuegos C2 88
Cieza F3 37
Cijara, reservoir D3 37
Cikobia, island C1 17
Cilacap B2 13
Cilician Gates, pass ...C3 27
Cimone, mt. B1 38
Cincinnati, Ohio E2 126
Cirebon B2 13
Citlaltépetl, mt. E4 84
City View G6 102
Ciudad Acuña D2 84
Ciudad Bolívar D2 79
Ciudad Camargo C3 84
Ciudad Constitución ...B3 84
Ciudad del Carmen ...F4 84
Ciudad del Este E4 75
Ciudad Guayana D2 79
Ciudad Juárez C1 84
Ciudad Mante E3 84
Ciudad Obregón C2 84
Ciudad Real E3 37
Ciudad Rodrigo C2 37
Ciudad Valles E3 84
Ciudad Victoria,
    state capital ...E3 84
Ciudadela H2 37
Civitavecchia B2 38
Clair A1 97
Claire, lake D2 94
Clandeboye C4 96
Clara C2 31
Clarenville D5 98
Clark's Harbour B4 100
Clarksville, Tenn. E2 126
Clear Creek S5 102
Clear, cape B3 31
Clearwater M5 95
Clearwater, river E3 94
Clementsport B3 100
Clermont F4 103
Clermont-Ferrand C4 34
Clervaux B1 33
Clerve, river B1 33
Cleveland, Ohio E1 126
Clichy ......Inset II 34
Clifden A2 31
Clifford E4 102
Climax B11 104
Clinton B6 95
Clinton D4 102
Clinton Colden, lake ...G4 99
Cloncurry, Qld. D2 14
Clonmel C2 31
Cloridorme M2 103
Clovis, N. Mex. H3 102
Cluff Lake Mine A2 104
Cluj-Napoca B2 43
Cluny D3 34
Cluny D6 94
Clutha, river A4 15
Clyde River B4 100
Clyde River P2 99
Clyde, estuary B2 30
Clyde, river B2 30
Clydebank B2 30
Coacalco ......Inset 84
Coahuila D2 84
Coal River J1 95
Coal, river D5 105
Coaldale D6 94
Coalspur B4 94
Coamo C2 90
Coast, mts. F2, J5 95
Coast, ranges A1, A2 126
Coaticook E6 103
Coats Land, region ...B13 107
Coats, island M4 99
Coatzacoalcos F4 84
Cobán B3 85
Cobden J2 102
Cóbh B3 31
Cobham, river D2 96
Cobija A2 77
Cobourg G4 102
Coburg B3 40
Coburg, island N1 99
Cocagne E2 97
Cochabamba A3 77
Cochin (Kochi) C7 20
Cochrane B8 76
Cochrane D3 101
Cochrane, lake B8 76
Cochrane, river H2 104
Cockburn Harbour ...D4 89
Cockburn, island B2 102
Coclé del Norte B2 87
Coco C2 90
Coco, islands A2 12
Coco, river A2, C1 87
Cocos, islands 5
Cocotitlán ......Inset 84
Cod, cape, Mass. G1 126
Codri, region A3 50
Codrington A3 77
Codrington, mt. C17 107
Cody, Wyo. C1 126
Coe Hill H3 102
Coeroeni, river A3 80
Coeur d'Alene, Idaho ...B1 126
Cogalnic, river B2 50
Cognac B4 34
Coiba, island B3 87
Coihaique B8 76
Coimbatore C6 20
Coimbra A2 36
Cojedes, river C2 79

Key Page

Colca, river C4 77
Colchester D3 30
Cold Lake E4 94
Coleraine A2 30
Coles Island D3 97
Coleville A9 104
Colhaut A2 90
Colima D4 84
Colina ......Inset 76
Coll, island A2 30
Collaguasi C2 76
Collingwood B3 15
Collingwood E3 102
Colmar D2 34
Cologne A3 40
Colombia 78
Colombier H3 103
Colombo, capital A5 19
Colón C2 87
Colón C2 88
Colonia A2 15
Colonia B3 75
Colonia Nueva Guinea ...B3 87
Colonsay E9 104
Colonsay, island A2 30
Colorado C2 86
Colorado C2 126
Colorado, plateau B2 126
Colorado, river B4 74
Colorado, river B4 84
Colorado Springs, Colo. ...C2 126
Columbia, capital, S.C. ...E2 126
Columbia, mts. M4 95
Columbia, plateau B1 126
Columbia, river B1 126
Columbus, capital, Ohio ...E2 126
Columbus, Ga. E2 126
Coma Pedroza, mt. A1 36
Comayagua B2 86
Comayagua, mts. B2 86
Combermere H2 102
Comendador A2 89
Comerío C2 90
Comilla E5 21
Comino, island B1 36
Cominotto, island B1 36
Comitán F4 84
Committee, bay L3 99
Como B1 38
Como, lake B1 38
Comodoro Rivadavia ...B7 76
Comorin, cape C7 20
Comoros 67
Comox K6 95
Compiègne C2 34
Compton E6 103
Comrat B2 50
Con Son, islands B5 11
Conakry, capital B3 62
Concepción B6 76
Concepción B3 75
Concepción del Oro ...D3 84
Conchalí ......Inset 76
Conche D4 98
Conchos, river C2 84
Concord, capital, N.H. ...F1 126
Concordia D3 74
Concordia C5 94
Conche D4 98
Congo, Dem Rep of 67
Congo, Rep of 66
Congo, basin D3 66
Congo, river B3 75
Congo, river B1 67
Conn, lake B1 31
Connecticut F1 126
Connemara, region B2 31
Consecon H4 102
Constance B5 40
Constance (Bodensee), lake ...D1 35
Constanţa E3 43
Constantine B1 57
Constitución B5 76
Consul A11 104
Contrecoeur C6 103
Contwoyto, lake G3 99
Conwy B3 30
Coober Pedy, S.A. C2 14
Cook's Harbour D3 98
Cook, mt. B3 15
Cook, strait B3 15
Cookshire E6 103
Cookstown F3 102
Coos Bay, Oreg. A1 126
Copán, ruins A2 86
Copenhagen, capital ...D3 32
Copiapó B2 76
Copiapó, river B2 76
Coppename, river A2 80
Coppermine, river F3 99
Coquí C3 90
Coquimbo B2 76
Coral, sea D4 14
Corantijn, river A2 80
Corazón A2 86
Corbeil-Essonnes ......Inset II 34
Corcovado, gulf B7 76
Corcovado, mt. ......Inset I 81
Córdoba D4 37
Córdoba C3 74
Córdoba, range B3 74
Corinth B3 51
Corinth, gulf B2 51
Corinth, isthmus B3 51
Corinto A2 87
Corisco, bay A4 66
Corisco, island A4 66
Cork B3 31
Cormack C4 98
Cormoran, reef B2 17
Cormorant A2 96
Cormorant, lake A2 96
Cornélia de Llobregat ...G2 37
Corner Brook C5 98
Corno, mt. C2 38
Cornwall L2 102
Cornwall B2 100
Cornwall, island K1 99
Cornwallis, island J1 99

Key Page

Coro C1 79
Coromandel, peninsula ...C2 15
Coronach E11 104
Coronado, bay B3 86
Coronation, gulf F3 99
Coronel Oviedo D4 75
Coropuna, mt. C4 77
Corozal B1 85
Corozal C2 90
Corpus Christi, Tex. ...D3 126
Corregidor, island B3 12
Corrib, lake B2 31
Corrientes D2 74
Corse ......Inset I 34
Corsica, island ......Inset I 34
Cortina d'Ampezzo ...C1 38
Cortona B2 38
Çoruh, river E2 27
Çorum C2 27
Corumbá C3 81
Corumbau, point E3 81
Corvallis, Oreg. A1 126
Cosenza D3 38
Coslada ......Inset II 37
Cosmoledo, island group ...A2 70
Costa Rica 86
Cotabato C5 12
Côte d'Ivoire 63
Cotentin, peninsula B2 34
Cotia ......Inset II 81
Coto Laurel B2 90
Cotonou B4 64
Cotopaxi, mt. B3 79
Cotswold, hills C3 30
Cottbus C3 40
Cotton Ground C2 90
Cotuí B1 89
Coubert ......Inset II 34
Couffo, river B4 64
Courantyne, river B3 80
Courland, lagoon A2 46
Courtenay K6 95
Courval D10 104
Coutts E6 94
Couva A2 91
Coventry C3 30
Covilhã B2 36
Cow Head C4 98
Cowan A3 96
Cowansville D6 103
Cowes C4 30
Cox's Bazar E7 21
Cox's Cove B4 98
Coyah B3 62
Coyoacán ......Inset 84
Cozumel, island G3 84
Cradock C3 71
Craigmyle D5 94
Craiova B3 43
Cranberry Portage A2 96
Cranbrook P6 95
Crane River B3 96
Crane Valley E11 104
Crapaud B2 100
Cravo Norte C3 78
Crawford Bay O6 95
Crawley ......Inset III 30
Crean, lake D6 104
Cree Lake D3 104
Cree, river E2 104
Cremona B1 38
Cremona C5 94
Cres, island B3 48
Cressday E6 94
Creston O6 95
Crete, island C4 51
Crete, sea C4 51
Créteil ......Inset II 34
Crewe C3 30
Crimean, mts. C4 47
Crimean, peninsula ...C3 47
Cristal, mts. A1 66
Cristóbal C2 87
Cristóbal Colón, peak ...B2 78
Crna Gora, mts. B3 49
Crna, river B3 49
Croatia 48
Crocker, range D2 13
Cromer A4 96
Crooked River G8 104
Crooked, island C4 89
Crooked, river L4 95
Cross Lake C2 96
Cross, river E4 65
Crotone D3 38
Cruz, cape D3 88
Cruzeiro do Sul A2 81
Crystal City B4 96
Cu Lao Thu, island B4 11
Cuajimalpa ......Inset 84
Cuamba C2 68
Cuando, river D4 70
Cuango, river C3 70
Cuanza, river C3 70
Cuauhtémoc C2 84
Cuautitlán ......Inset 84
Cuautitlán Izcalli ......Inset 84
Cuba 88
Cubal, river B4 70
Cubango, river C3 70
Cubatão ......Inset II 81
Cúcuta B3 78
Cuddalore C6 20
Cudworth E8 104
Cuenca B4 79
Cuenca E2 37
Cuernavaca, state capital ...E4 84
Cuiabá C3 81
Cuíto Cuanavale D5 70
Cuito, river C3 70
Cukorova, region C3 27
Culebra, island E2 90
Culebrinas, river A2 90
Culiacán, state capital ...C3 84
Cumaná D1 79
Cumberland K6 95

Key Page

Cumberland House H7 104
Cumberland, lake H6 104
Cumberland, peninsula ...P3 99
Cumberland, sound P3 99
Cumbrian, mts. B2 30
Cunene, river B5, C4 70
Cuneo A1 38
Cupar C3 30
Cupar F10 104
Curaçao, island 82
Curaray, river C3 79
Curepipe C3 69
Curicó B4 76
Curitiba D4 81
Curral Velho D3 58
Curuzú Cuatiá D2 74
Cut Knife A8 104
Cuttack E4 20
Cuxhaven B2 40
Cuyo, islands B4 12
Cuyuni, river A2 80
Cuzco C3 77
Cyangugu A2 61
Cyclades, islands C3 51
Cypress River B4 96
Cyprus 27
Czar E5 94
Czech Republic 42
Częstochowa D3 41

D

Da Lat B4 11
Da Nang B3 11
Dabakala D2 63
Dabola C2 62
Dachang D3 10
Dachau B4 40
Dacotah C4 96
Dades, river C2 57
Dadu C4 21
Dafoe F9 104
Dagestan, republic E4 44
Dagupan B2 12
Dahlak, archipelago C2 60
Dahna, ad-, desert B1 24
Dahuk B1 24
Dajabón A1 89
Daka, river B2 64
Dakar, capital A2 62
Dakhla A2 58
Đakovica B3 49
Đakovo B3 49
Dalälven, river C2 53
Dalandzadgad C3 11
Dalhousie C1 97
Dalhousie K3 103
Dali D2 10
Dalian F2 10
Dallas C3 96
Dallas, Tex. D2 126
Dallol Bosso, river A3 59
Dalmatia, region B3 48
Daloa C3 63
Dalvík B2 52
Daly, river C1 14
Daman B4 20
Damanhur B1 56
Damar, ad- A3 27
Damascus, capital A3 27
Damaturu F2 65
Damavand, mt. C2 22
Damazin, ad- C3 59
Dame-Marie A2 89
Damietta B1 56
Damietta B1 56
Dammam, ad- C2 24
Dammartin-en-Goële ...Inset II 34
Dampier, W.A. A2 14
Damur, ad- A2 26
Danakil, desert C2 60
Danané B3 63
Dand A4 96
Dande, river B2 70
Dandeldhura A2 19
Dandong F1 10
Dangara A1 23
Dangme, river C2 19
Dangrek, mts. C3 12
Dangriga B2 85
Daniel's Harbour C4 98
Danjiangkou E2 10
Danlí B3 86
Danube, river ......D
Danville D6 103
Danville, Va. F2 126
Dao Phu Quoc, island ...A4 11
Dapaong B1 64
Dapp D4 94
Daqing F1 10
Dar es-Salaam, capital ...C2 68
Dara A3 27
Dara B2 62
Đaravica, mt. B3 49
Darbhanga E3 20
Darhan C2 11
Darién, mts. D2 87
Dariense, mts. B2 87
Darjiling E3 20
Darling, range A3 14
Darling, river D3 14
Darlington C2 30
Darłowo C1 41
Darmstadt B4 40
Darnah D1 56
Darnley B2 100
Dartmoor, plateau B4 30
Dartmouth D3 100
Daru A2 15
Darwin, N.T., capital ...C1 14
Dashhowuz C2 22
Dasht-e Kavir, desert ...D3 22
Dasht-e Lut, desert D3 22
Datong E1 10
Daua, river F1 61
Daugavpils D3 46
Daule, river B3 79
Dauphin A3 96
Dauphin River B3 96
Dauphin, lake B3 96

Place	Key	Page
Davao	C5	12
Davao, gulf	C5	12
Davenport, Iowa	D1	126
David	A2	87
Davidson	D9	104
Davis Inlet	E3	98
Davis, strait	M2	92
Davos	D2	35
Dawa, river	C3	60
Dawhat as-Salwa, bay	B3	25
Dawkah	B2	25
Dawson	B3	105
Dawson Creek	M3	105
Dawson, bay	A2	96
Daymán, river	B1	75
Dayr az-Zawr	B2	27
Dayton, Ohio	E2	126
Daytona Beach, Fla.	E3	126
De Aar	B3	71
De Quincy Village	Inset	70
Dead Sea, lake	A2	26
Dead, sea	B2	26
Dean, channel	J5	95
Dean, river	K5	95
Dease Lake	G2	95
Death, valley, Calif.	B2	126
Deauville	C2	34
Debar	A2	48
Debden	D7	104
Debed, river	B2	45
DeBolt	A3	94
Debre Birhan	C2	60
Debre Markos	B2	60
Debrecen	C2	43
Decatur, Ill.	E2	126
Deccan, plateau	C5	20
Děčín	B2	42
Dédougou	C2	64
Dedza	B2	68
Dee, river	B3, C1	30
Deep River	H1	102
Deep, inlet	B1	98
Deepdale	A3	96
Deer Lake	C4	98
Deerfield	A4	100
Degeh Bur	D2	60
Dégelis	H4	103
Dehiwala-Mt. Lavinia	A5	19
Dehra Dun	C2	20
Dej	B2	43
Del Rio, Tex.	C3	126
Delacour	D5	94
Delap Cove	B3	100
Delaronde, lake	C6	104
Delaware	F2	126
Delburne	D5	94
Deleau	A4	96
Delft	B2	32
Delft, island	A2	19
Delfzijl	D1	32
Delgado	A2	86
Delhi	C3	20
Delhi	E5	102
Delicias	C2	84
Déline	D3	99
Delisle	C9	104
Deloraine	A4	96
Delos, island	C3	51
Delson	J6	103
Delta Beach	B4	96
Demerara, river	B3	80
Den Helder	B2	32
Denakil, desert	C1	60
Denare Beach	H6	104
Denbigh	H2	102
Dencross	C4	96
Dender, river	B2	33
Denigomodu	A2	16
Denmark		32
Denmark, strait	D2	106
Dennery	B2	91
Denpasar	C2	13
D'Entrecasteaux, islands	B2	15
D'Entrecasteaux, reefs	C1	18
Denver, capital, Colo.	C2	126
Denzil	A8	104
Dera Ghazi Khan	D3	21
Dera Ismail Khan	D3	21
Derby	C3	30
Derg, lake	B2	31
Derrick	B3	91
Derventa	B1	48
Derwent	E4	94
Des Moines, capital, Iowa	D1	126
Desaguadero, river	B2	74
Desaguadero, river	A3	77
Desberats	B1	102
Deschaillons	D5	103
Deschambault Lake	G6	104
Dese	C2	60
Deseado, river	B6	74
Deseronto	H3	102
Desna, river	C1	47
Desolación, island	B9	76
Desruisseau	B3	91
Dessau	C3	40
Destruction Bay	B5	105
Detmold	B3	40
Detroit, Mich.	E1	126
Deux Rivieres	G1	102
Deux-Montagnes	H5	103
Deva	B3	43
Deventer	D2	32
Devil's, island	B1	80
Devoll, river	B3	49
Devon, island	L1	99
Devonport, Tas.	D4	14
Dewberry	E4	94
Dezful	B3	22
Dháfni	Inset	51
Dhahran	C1	24
Dhaka, capital	D5	21
Dhamar	A2	25
Dhangarhi	D2	19
Dharan	D3	19
Dhaulagiri, mt.	B2	19
Dhofar, region	B3	25
Dhulagarh	Inset	20
Dhuusamareeb	B2	60
Diadema	Inset II	81
Dialakoto	C3	62
Diamond, island	B1	91
Dibrugarh	F3	20
Diefenbaker, lake	C10	104
Diekirch	B2	33
Dien Bien Phu	A2	11
Dieppe	C2	34
Dieppe	E2	97
Dieppe Bay Town	B1	90
Diffa	C3	59
Differdange	A2	33
Digby	B3	100
Digne	D4	34
Digul, river	E2	13
Dijon	D3	34
Dikhil	B2	60
Dikson	B6	44
Dili	D2	13
Dilijan	B2	45
Dillon	B5	104
Dilolo	B3	67
Dimbokro	D3	63
Dimitrovgrad	D3	50
Dimlang, mt.	F3	65
Dimona	B2	26
Dinagat, island	C4	12
Dinajpur	B3	21
Dinant	C2	33
Dinara, mts.	A2, C3	48
Dinaric Alps, mts.	A1, B3	48
Dinder, river	B1	60
Dingle	A2	31
Dingle, bay	A2	31
Dingli	B2	36
Dinsmore	C9	104
Diourbel	A2	62
Dipolog	B4	12
Dire Dawa	D2	60
Diriamba	A3	87
Dispur	F3	20
Diu	B4	20
Diuata, mts.	C4	12
Divo	D4	63
Diviriği	D2	27
Diwaniyah, ad-	C2	24
Dixon Entrance, channel	F4	95
Dixonville	B3	94
Diyala, river	C2	24
Diyarbakır	E3	27
Dja, river	B3	65
Djado	C1	59
Djambala	C5	66
Djanet	B2	57
Djelfa	B1	57
Djenné	C3	58
Djerba, island	C3	57
Djibouti		60
Djibouti, capital	C2	60
Djouah, river	B2	66
Djouf, el-, desert	B1, C3	58
Djougou	A3	64
Dnepr-Bug, canal	B3	47
Dneprodzerzhinsk	D2	47
Dnieper, river	C1, E3	47
Dniester, river	B2	47
Dnipropetrovsk	D2	47
Doaktown	C2	97
Doba	B5	59
Doboj	B1	48
Dobrich	F2	50
Dobruja, region	E3	43
Doctor Pedro P. Peña	A3	75
Dodecanese, islands	C3	51
Dodge City, Kans.	C2	126
Dodoma	B2	68
Dodsland	B9	104
Doetinchem	D3	32
Dogo, island	B2	8
Dogondoutchi	A3	59
Doha, capital	D3	25
Doiran, lake	C2	48
Dolbeau	D3	103
Dôle	D3	34
Dolomites, range	B1	38
Domagnano	B1	39
Domeyko, mts.	C3	76
Dominica		90
Dominica, passage	A1	90
Dominican Republic		89
Dominion City	C4	96
Domont	Inset II	34
Domremy	E8	104
Domuyo, volcano	A4	74
Don Benito	D3	37
Doña Juana, mt.	C2	90
Donald Station	O5	95
Doncaster	C3	30
Dondo	B3	70
Donegal	B1	31
Donegal, bay	B1	31
Donets, basin	D2	47
Donetsk	D2	47
Dong Hoi	B2	11
Dong Nai, river	B4	11
Dongting, lake	E3	10
Dongwe, river	A2	67
Donnacona	E5	103
Dor, lake	C6	104
Dorado	C2	90
Dorchester	C4	30
Dordogne, river	C4	34
Dordrecht	B3	32
Dore Lake	C6	104
Dörgön, lake	B2	11
Dori	D1	64
Dorintosh	B6	104
Dorking	Inset III	30
Dornoch	B1	30
Dorohoi	D2	43
Dorothy	D5	94
Dorra	B1	60
Dortmund	A3	40
Dorval	H6	103
Dos Hermanas	D4	37
Dosquet	E5	103
Dosso	A3	59
Dothan, Ala.	E2	126
Douai	C1	34
Douala	A3	65
Doubs, river	A1	35
Douglas	B2	30
Douglas, channel	H4	95
Douglastown	M3	103
Dourados	C4	81
Douro, river	B2	36
Dover	D3	30
Dover, capital, Del.	F2	126
Dover, strait	D4	30
Dovrefjell, mts.	B3	52
Dozen, island	B2	8
Drâa, river	A1, B2, C2	57
Draguignan	D5	34
Drake	E9	104
Drakensberg, mts.	B3, C3	71
Drammen	C4	52
Drava, river	A2	43
Drayton Valley	C4	94
Dresden	C5	40
Dresden	C5	102
Dreux	C2	34
Drin, river	A1	49
Drina, river	A2	49
Drobeta-Turnu Severin	B3	43
Drogheda	C2	31
Drumheller	D5	94
Drummond	B2	97
Drummondville	D6	103
Druskininkai	B2	46
Dryden	B3	101
Dschang	B2	65
Duars, plain	A3	19
Duarte, mt.	B1	89
Dubăsari	B2	50
Dubawnt, lake	H4	99
Dubawnt, river	H4	99
Dubayy	C2	25
Dubbo, N.S.W.	D3	14
Dube, river	C3	63
Dublin, capital	C2	31
Dubrovnik	D4	48
Dubuque, Iowa	D1	126
Dubysa, river	B2	46
Duchess	E6	94
Duck Bay	A3	96
Duck Lake	D8	104
Dudelange	B2	33
Dudinka	C6	44
Dudley	C3	30
Duero, river	D2	37
Dufourspitze, mt.	B3	35
Dufrost	C4	96
Dugald	C4	96
Duisburg	A3	40
Dukhan	B3	25
Dulce, gulf	C4	86
Duluth, Minn.	D1	126
Dum-Dum	Inset II	20
Duma	A1	26
Dumaguete	B4	12
Dumbás	B2	52
Dumfries	B2	30
Dumjor	Inset II	20
Dún Laoghaire	C2	31
Dunaújváros	B2	43
Duncan	L7	95
Duncansby, cape	B1	30
Dund-Us	B2	11
Dundalk	C2	31
Dundas	C2	30
Dundurn	D9	104
Dunedin	B4	15
Dunfermline	B2	30
Dungarvan	C2	31
Dunkirk (Dunkerque)	C1	34
Dunkwa	B4	64
Dunlop	B2	96
Dunnegan	F1	100
Dunnville	F5	102
Dunqulah	C1	59
Dunsinane, mt.	B2	30
Dunstable	Inset III	30
Dunster	N4	95
Duqm	C2	25
Duque de Caxias	Inset I	81
Duque de York, island	A9	76
Durance, river	D5	34
Durango, Colo.	C2	126
Durango, state capital	D3	84
Durazno	B2	75
Durban	D2	71
Durham	C2	30
Durham	E3	102
Durham, N.C.	F2	126
Durrës	A2	49
Dushanbe, capital	A1	23
Düsseldorf	A3	40
Dutse	E2	65
Dyce	A2	96
Dyje, river	B4	42
Dzaoudzi, territorial capital	C2	67
Dzhugdzhur, range	D8	44
Dzungaria, desert basin	B1	10
Dzyarzhynskaya Hara, mt.	C3	47

E

Place	Key	Page
Eagle, river	B2	98
Eagle, river	B2	105
Ear Falls	B2	101
East Angus	E6	103
East Antarctica	B1	107
East Braintree	D4	96
East China, sea		7
East Coast Bays	B2	15
East Coulee	D6	94
East Frisian, islands	A2	40
East Lake Ainslie	F1	100
East London	C3	71
East Point	C2	100
East Siberian, sea	B10	44
East York	K5	102
East, cape	C2	15
Eastbourne	D4	30
Eastend	B11	104
Eastern Ghats, mts.	C6	20
Easterville	B2	96
Eastmain	A3	101
Eastmain, river	B3	101
Eastport	E5	98
Eatonia	A9	104
Eau Claire, Wis.	D1	126
Ebebiyín	D2	66
Eberswalde	C2	40
Ebolowa	B3	65
Ebon, island	B3	16
Ebor	A4	96
Ebro, river	F1	37
Ecatepec	Inset	84
Echo Bay	E3	99
Echternach	B2	33
Écija	D4	37
Ecuador		79
Ed	C3	60
Edam	C2	32
Eddies Cove	C3	98
Eddystone	B3	96
Ede	C4	65
Ede	C2	32
Edéa	B3	65
Edgerton	E5	94
Edinburgh	B2	30
Edmonton, capital	D4	94
Edmundston	A1	97
Édouard, lake	D4	103
Edrans	B4	96
Edson	B4	94
Edward, lake	A4	61
Edwards plateau, Tex.	C2	126
Eel, river	Inset	70
Éfaté, island	C3	18
Egadi, islands	C3	38
Eganville	H2	102
Egersund	B4	52
Egerton	B4	65
Eglinton, island	E1	99
Egmont, bay	A2	100
Egmont, cape	B2	15
Egmont, mt.	B2	15
Eğridir, lake	B2	27
Egypt		56
Eifel, plateau	A3	40
Eigg, island	A2	30
Eindhoven	C3	32
Eisenach	B3	40
Eisenhüttenstadt	C2	40
Eisleben	B3	40
Ejmiatsin	B2	45
Ejura	B3	64
Ekibastuz	D1	23
Ekwan, river	D2	101
El Cañuelo, ruins	C2	90
El Cerro del Aripo, mt.	A2	91
El Encanto	B5	78
El Ferrol	B1	37
El Macao	D2	89
El Paso, Tex.	C2	126
El Pital, mt.	A1	86
El Porvenir	C2	87
El Progreso	B2	86
El Salvador		86
El Seibo	C2	89
El Serrat	B1	36
El Tabo	Inset	76
El Tigre	D2	79
El Toro, mt.	B1	36
El Trebolar	Inset	76
Elat	B3	26
Elâzığ	D2	27
Elba, island	B2	38
Elbasan	B2	49
Elbe, river	B2, C3	40
Elbert, mt., Colo.	C2	126
Elblag	D1	41
Elbow	D9	104
Elburz, mts.	C2	22
Elche	F3	37
Eldon	C2	100
Eldoret	C2	61
Elephant, island	C12	107
Elephanta, island	Inset I	20
Eleuthera, island	B2	89
Elevsís	Inset	51
Elfros	G9	104
Elgin	B1	30
Elgin	A4	96
Elgin	D3	97
Elgon, mt.	D3	61
Eli Malk, island	B3	17
Elie	C4	96
Elista	E4	44
Elk	F2	41
Elk Point	E4	94
Elkford	P6	95
Elkhorn	A4	96
Elkhovo	E3	50
Elko	P6	95
Elko, Nev.	B1	126
Ellef Ringnes, island	H1	99
Ellerts de Haan, mts.	A3	80
Ellesmere, island	M1	99
Ellice, river	G1	99
Ellinikón	Inset	51
Elliot Lake	C1	102
Ellisras	C1	71
Ellsworth Land, region	B10	107
Ellsworth, mts.	B10	107
Elm Creek	C4	96
Elma	D4	96
Elmina	B4	64
Elmira	C2	100
Elmira	E4	102
Elmsdale	A2	100
Elmvale	F3	102
Elnora	D5	94
Elqui, river	B3	76
Elrose	B9	104
Elsa	B4	105
Elva	A4	96
Elva	B3	36
Ely, Nev.	B2	126
Ely	D3	30
Emba	B2	23
Embarcación	C1	74
Embarras Portage	E2	94
Embi	B2	23
Emden	A2	40
Emerald, island	F1	99
Emerald, Qld.	D2	14
Emerson	C4	96
Emi Koussi, mt.	B3	59
Emilia-Romagna	B1	38
Emlembe, mt.	B1	71
Emmeloord	C2	32
Emmen	D2	32
Emporia, Kans.	D2	126
Ems, river	A2	40
Encarnación	E5	75
Enchant	D6	94
Ende	D2	13
Enderbury, island	B2	17
Enderby	N6	95
Enderby Land, region	C17	107
Endiang	D5	94
Enewetak, island	A1	16
Engadine, valley	D2	35
Engaño, cape	D2	89
Enggano, island	B2	13
Englee	C4	98
English, channel	C4	30
Englishtown	G1	100
Enguri, river	A3	45
Enid, Okla.	D2	126
Enilda	B3	94
Enna	C3	38
Ennadai, lake	H4	99
Ennery	C1	89
Ennis	B2	31
Ennistymon	B2	31
Enns, river	D3	39
Enns	D3	39
Enriquillo, lake	A2	89
Enschede	D2	32
Ensenada	A1	84
Ensenguly	A3	22
Entebbe	C3	61
Enugu	D4	65
Épi, island	C3	18
Épinal	D2	34
Episkopi	A2	27
Epsom	Inset III	30
Equatorial, channel	A5	19
Equatorial Guinea		66
Er Rif, range	C1	57
Erciyes Daği, mt.	C2	27
Érd	B2	43
Erdenet	C2	11
Erebus, mt.	B5	107
Erenhot	E1	10
Erfurt	B3	40
Erg Chech, desert	C1	58
Erg Iguidi, desert	D1	58
Erickson	B4	96
Erie, lake	E5	102
Erie, Pa.	E1	126
Eriksdale	B4	96
Erimo, cape	Inset I	8
Eritrea		60
Erlangen	B4	40
Ermelo	C2	71
Erne, river	A2	30
Errigal, mt.	B1	31
Erromango, island	C4	18
Ersekë	B3	49
Erzen, river	A2	49
Erzgebirge, mts.	C3	40
Erzincan	D2	27
Erzurum	E2	27
Esbjerg	B3	32
Esch-sur-Alzette	A2	33
Eschen	B1	33
Escondido, river	B2	87
Escuintla	C5	85
Escuminac	K3	103
Esfahan	C2	22
Esil	C1	23
Esker	D3	98
Eskifjördhur	C2	52
Eskilstuna	C3	53
Eskimo Point	K4	99
Eskişehir	B2	27
Esla, river	D2	37
Esmeraldas	C1	79
Espanola	D1	102
Española, island	Inset	79
Esperance, W.A.	B3	14
Espichel, cape	A3	36
Espírito Santo	D3	81
Espiritu Santo, island	B2	18
Espoo	A5	74
Esquel	B6	74
Essaouira	B2	57
Essen	A3	40
Essequibo, river	B3, B5	80
Essex	C5	102
Esslingen	B4	40
Estados, island	C7	74
Estaire	E1	102
Estany d'Engolasters, lake	B2	36
Este, point	E2	90
Estelí	A2	87
Esterhazy	H10	104
Estevan	G11	104
Esther	E5	94
Eston	B9	104
Estonia		46
Estoril	A3	36
Estrela, mts.	B2	36
Esztergom	B2	43
Etchemin, river	L6	103
Ethelbert	A3	96
Ethiopia		60
Ethiopia, plateau	C2	60
Etna, mt.	C3	38
Etobicoke	J5	102
Etosha, pan	B1	70
Etrechy	Inset	
Etrek, river		
Ettelbruck		
'Eua, island	B3	
Euboea, island	A	
Eugene, Oreg.	A	
Eugenia, point		
Euphrates, river		
Eureka, Calif.		
Eutsuk, lake	J	
Evandale		
Evansville	E2	
Evansville, Ind.	E2	
Evenkiya, autonomous okrug	C6	
Everest, mt.	C2	
Everett, Wash.	A1	
Évinayong	B3	
Évora	B3	
Évreux	Inset	
Évry	Inset	
Ewa	Inset	
Ewell	Inset III	
Ewo	B4	
Exeter	B4	
Exeter		
Exmoor, plateau	C3	
Extremadura	C3	
Exuma, sound	B1	
Eyasi, lake	B1	
Eyebrow	D10	
Eyl		
Eyre, lake	C2	
Eyre, peninsula	C2	
Eysturoy, island	Inset	

F

Place	Key	Page
Fabyan	E5	
Fada	C3	
Fadiffolu, atoll	A3	
Faenza	B2	
Faeroe, islands	Inset	
Fagamalo	B1	
Fagaras		
Fagasa	B1	
Fagatogo	B1	
Fair, island	Inset I	
Fairbanks, Alaska	Inset I	
Fairford	B3	
Fairmont Hot Springs		
Fairweather, mt.	D1	
Faisalabad	D3	
Faizabad	D3	
Fajardo	D2	
Fakfak	E2	
Falciano	C1	
Falcon Lake	D4	
Falelatai	B2	
Falelima	A2	
Faleniu	C3	
Fălești	A2	
Falher	B3	
Falkland, islands	C7	
Fallujah, al-	B2	
Falmouth	E5	
Falmouth	B4	
False Divi, point	D5	
Falster, island	B4	
Falun	C2	
Famagusta	B1	
Fan Si Pan, mt.	A1	
Fangliao	B3	
Fang	B2	
Farafangana	C2	
Farafenni	C2	
Farah	A2	
Farah, river	A2	
Faraulep, atoll	B2	
Farewell, cape	B3	
Farewell, cape	D2	
Farghona	D2	
Fargo, N. Dak.	D1	
Faridpur	C5	
Farim	B1	
Farmington	M3	
Farmington, N. Mex.		
Farnham	Inset III	
Faro	C4	
Faro	C4	
Farquhar, island group	A6	
Farrellton	B2	
Fashir, al-	A2	
Fatick	A2	
Fatoto	E2	
Fauquier	N6	
Faxafloi, bay		
Faxälven, river	B3	
Faya-Largeau	B3	
Faylakah, island	D1	
Fayum, al-	B2	
Fayyum, al-	B2	
Fderik	B2	
Fehmarn, island	B1	
Fehmarn, strait	B1	
Feira de Santana	E3	
Feldkirch	A3	
Felidu, atoll	A3	
Felixstowe	D3	
Fen, river	E2	
Fenelon Falls	G3	
Fengshan	B3	
Fengyuan	B2	
Feni, islands	B2	
Fens, region	D3	
Feodosiya	P6	
Fergana, valley	E4	
Fergus	E4	
Ferkéssédougou	D2	
Ferlo, river	A3	
Ferme-Neuve	A5	
Fernandina, island	Inset	
Fernie	P6	
Ferrara	B2	
Ferryland	E5	
Fethiye	B2	
Feuilles, river		
Feyzabad		

Name	Key	Page
...arantsoa	B3	69
...	C3	40
...elgebirge, *mts.*	B4	40
...	O5	95
...	E1	102
...	A3	49
...*lake*		
...ree	C3	90
...eira da Foz	A2	36
...eres	H1	37
...ig	D1	57
...		17
...elfia	B3	75
...ner Ice Shelf, *glacier*	B12	107
...*island*	B3	36
...ore	G11	104
...ul Ice Shelf, *glacier*	B14	107
...terre, *cape*	B1	37
...and		53
...nd, *gulf*	C3	53
...y, *river*	J2	95
...*river*	C1	31
...egan		
...	D5	94
...mark, *plateau*	E2	52
...ide	J1	93
...*river*	A1	105
...	C4	70
...er Branch	C3	96
...erton	C3	96
...guard	B3	30
...gerald	E1	94
...roy	B8	76
...roy, *river*	B1	14
...Islands	C2	100
...staff, Ariz.	B2	126
...*island*	C1	69
...bush	C4	94
...combe	A9	104
...	E5	94
...twood	C3	30
...	A4	96
...ning	B1	40
...sburg		
...herton	E3	102
...	C4	98
...r de Lys		
...oland, *polder*	C2	32
...Flon	A2, C2	96
...ders, *range*	C3	14
...ders, *river*	D1	14
...*island*	D3	17
..., Mich.	E1	126
...den Field, *plain*	C2	30
...ence	B2	38
...ence, S.C.	F2	126
...enceville	B4	78
...encia	D3	85
...es, *island*	D2	13
...es, *sea*	C2	13
...eşti	B2	50
...iano	D2	81
...inópolis	D4	81
...ida	B3	75
...ida	D2	88
...ida	B2	90
...ida	E3	126
...ida Keys, Fla.	E3	126
...ida, *straits*	B1	88
...	A3	52
...	A2	15
...m Lake	G9	104
...	B2	48
...şani	D3	43
...ggia	C2	38
...jo	D4	98
...jo, *island*	B4	58
...	C5	34
...kestone	D3	30
...nboni	A2	67
...	F2	104
...nd-du-Lac	C1	104
...nseca, *gulf*	B3, C2	86
...ntainebleau	M2	95
...	A2	35
...nuafobu (Falcon), *island*	B3	17
...nualei, *island*	C4	17
...rest	D4	102
...restville	G3	103
...River	A3	96
...	C1	38
...rmentera, *island*	G3	37
...rmosa	D2	74
...t Albany	D2	101
...t Chipewyan	C2	94
...t Collins, Colo.	C1	126
...t Erie	G5	102
...t Frances	B3	101
...t Fraser	K4	95
...t Good Hope	C3	99
...t Lauderdale, Fla.	E3	126
...t Liard	D4	94
...t MacKay	E2	94
...t McMurray	E3	94
...t McPherson	B3	94
...t Myers, Fla.	E3	126
...t Nelson	L2	95
...t Nelson, *river*	L1	95
...t Norman	C4	94
...t Portal	B3	61
...t Providence	E4	99
...t Qu'Appelle	G10	104
...t Resolution	F4	99
...t Saskatchewan	D4	94
...t Severn	C1	101
...t Simpson	D4	99
...t Smith, Ark.	D2	126
...t Smith, *region*	E4	99
...t St. James	K4	95
...t St. John	M3	95
...t Steele	P6	95
...t Stockton, Tex.	C2	126
...t Vermilion	C2	94
...t Wayne, Ind.	E1	126
...t William	C1	38
...rtaleza	E2	81
...rteau	C3	98
...rth, *estuary*	C2	30

Name	Key	Page
Forth, *river*	B2	30
Fortín Conde de Mirasol, *fort*	E2	90
Fortín Ravelo	B3	77
Fortune	D5	98
Fortune Bridge	C2	100
Fortune, *bay*	D5	98
Foster, *river*	E4	104
Fosterville	B3	97
Fouman	B2	65
Foumbouni	A1	67
Four Falls	B2	97
Foveaux, *strait*	A4	15
Fox Island	F2	100
Fox Lake	C2	94
Fox Valley	A10	104
Foxe, *basin*	N3	99
Foxe, *channel*	M3	99
Foxe, *peninsula*	N4	99
Foz do Iguaçu	C4	81
France		34
Frances, *lake*	D5	105
Franceville	B2	66
Franche-Comté	D3	34
Francis	G10	104
Francistown	B2	69
Francois	C5	98
Franconian Jura, *mts.*	B4	40
Frankenwald, *mts.*	B3	40
Frankford	H3	102
Frankfort, *capital*, Ky.	E2	126
Frankfurt am Main	B3	40
Frankfurt an der Oder	C2	40
Franklin, *strait*	J2	99
Franquelin	J2	103
Franz Josef Land, *islands*	A4	44
Fraser	E1	95
Fraser Lake	K4	95
Fraser, *river*	L5, M4	95
Fraserburgh	C1	30
Fraserdale	D2	101
Fraserwood	C4	96
Fray Bentos	A2	75
Fredericia	B3	32
Frederick	E4	14
Fredericton	C3	97
Fredericton	B2	100
Fredericton Jct.	C3	97
Frederiksberg	D3	32
Frederikshavn	C1	32
Frederikstad	C4	52
Freeport	A2	89
Freeport	A3	100
Freetown	E5	90
Freetown, *capital*	A1	63
Freiberg	C3	40
Freiburg	A5	40
Freirina	B3	76
Fréjus	D5	34
Fremantle, W.A.	A3, Inset I	14
French Guiana		80
French River	E1	102
Frenchman, *river*	B11	104
Fresnillo	D3	84
Fresno, Calif.	B2	126
Fribourg	B2	35
Friedrichshafen	B5	40
Frigate, *island*	C1	91
Friuli-Venezia Giulia	C1	38
Frobisher, *lake*	C4	104
Frog, *lake*	E4	94
Frome, *lake*	D2	14
Frontier	C2	38
Fruška Gora, *mts.*	A2	49
Frutigen	A2	35
Frýdek-Místek	D3	41
Fua'amotu	B4	17
Fuengirola	Inset II	37
Fuerte Olimpo	D2	75
Fuerte, *river*	C2	84
Fuerteventura, *island*	Inset I	37
Fuhayhil, al-	C2	24
Fujairah, al-	D2	25
Fuji, *mt.*	C3	8
Fujian	E3	10
Fujisawa	C3	8
Fukue	A3	8
Fukue, *island*	A3	8
Fukui	C2	8
Fukuoka	B3	8
Fukushima	D2	8
Fukuyama	B3	8
Fulacunda	B2	62
Fuladi, *mt.*	B2	22
Fulda	B3	40
Fulda, *river*	B3	40
Fullarton	A2	91
Funabashi	D3	8
Funafuti, *capital*	C3	16
Funafuti, *island*	C3	16
Fundy, *bay*	A3	100
Furnas, *reservoir*	D4	81
Fürstenfeld	E3	39
Fürth	B4	40
Fushun	F1	10
Futa Jallon, *plateau*	B1	62
Futuna, *island*	C4	18
Fuxin	F1	10
Fuzhou	E3	10
Fyn, *island*	C3	32

G

Name	Key	Page
Gaalkacyo	B2	60
Gabarus	G2	100
Gabès	C3	57
Gabès, *gulf*	C3	57
Gaborone, *capital*	B3	69
Gabon		66
Gabriel, *island*	C2	81
Gabrovo	D3	50
Gabú	C1	62

Name	Key	Page
Gacko	B2	48
Gaeta	C2	38
Gafsa	B2	57
Gagetown	C3	97
Gagnoa	C3	101
Gagnon	D3	63
Gagra	A2	45
Gainesville, Fla.	E3	126
Gainsborough	J11	104
Gairdner, *lake*	C3	14
Gaizina, *mt.*	C2	46
Galahad	E5	94
Galana, *river*	E5	61
Galápagos, *islands*	Inset	79
Galaţi	E3	43
Galena Bay	O6	95
Galicia	C1	37
Galilee, *region*	B1	26
Galle	B5	19
Gallegos, *river*	A7	74
Gallinas, *point*	C1	78
Gällivare	D1	53
Galoa	B3	17
Galveston, Tex.	D3	126
Galway	B2	31
Galway, *bay*	B2	31
Gambia, The		62
Gambia, *river*	B2, C3, D2	62
Gambo	D5	98
Gamprin	B1	33
Gan, *river*	E3	10
Gananoque	J3	102
Gäncä	B2	45
Gander	D5	98
Gander Bay	D4	98
Gandhinagar	B4	20
Ganganagar	B3	20
Ganges, *river*	E3	20
Gangtok	E3	20
Gansu	C1, D2	10
Ganzhou	E3	10
Gao	D2	58
Gaoua	C3	64
Gap	D4	34
Garabil, *plateau*	D3	22
Garabogazköl, *lake*	A2	22
Garda, *lake*	B1	38
Garden Hill	D2	96
Garden Reach	Inset II	20
Garden, *island*	Inset I	14
Garden, *river*	A1	102
Gardenton	C4	96
Gardez	B2	22
Gardner, *canal*	H4	95
Gardner, *island*	B2	17
Garissa	E4	61
Garland	A3	96
Garmisch-Partenkirchen	B5	40
Garnish	D5	98
Garonne, *river*	C4	34
Garoua	B2	65
Garry, *lake*	H3	99
Garson Lake	A4	104
Garulia	Inset II	20
Gary, Ind.	E1	126
Gascoyne *river*	A2	14
Gash, *river*	B2	60
Gaspé	M3	103
Gaspé, *peninsula*	L3	103
Gaspereau Forks	D2	97
Gatal, *cape*	E4	37
Gateshead	C2	30
Gatico	B2	76
Gatineau	A6	103
Gatineau Park	A6	103
Gatineau, *river*	A4, A5	103
Gatún, *lake*	C2	87
Gau, *island*	B3	17
Gauhati	F3	20
Gaultois	D5	98
Gavarr	C2	45
Gävle	C2	53
Gaya	E4	20
Gaya	A3	59
Gazanjyk	B2	22
Gazelle, *peninsula*	B2	15
Gaziantep	D3	27
Gbarnga	B2	63
Gdańsk	D1	41
Gdańsk, *gulf*	D1	41
Gdynia	D1	41
Gêba, *river*	C1	62
Geelong, Vic.	D3	14
Gege	B2	71
Geidam	F1	65
Geikie, *river*	F3	104
Gejiu	D3	10
Gela	C3	38
Gelibolu (Gallipoli)	A2	27
Gelsenkirchen	A3	40
Gem	D6	94
Gembloux	C2	33
General	B1	67
General Eugenio A. Garay	A2	75
General Santos	C5	12
General, *river*	C3	86
Genesee	C4	94
Geneva	A2	35
Geneva, *lake*	A2	35
Genk	D2	33
Gennargentu, *mts.*	B2	38
Genoa	B1	38
Genoa, *gulf*	B1	38
Gentilly	Inset II	34
Gentofte	D3	32
George	B3	71
George Town	A2	13
George, *lake*	C2	101
Georgetown	D2	62
Georgetown	C2	91
Georgetown	C2	100
Georgetown, *capital*	B2	80
Georgia		45
Georgia	E2	126
Georgian, *bay*	E2	102
Gera	C3	40

Name	Key	Page
Geral, *range*	C4	81
Gerald	A4	96
Geraldton	C3	101
Geraldton, W.A.	A2	14
Gerlachovka, *mt.*	C2	42
Germany		40
Germiston	B2	71
Gerona	H2	37
Getafe	E2, Inset II	37
Gevgelija	B3	19
Geylegphug	B3	19
Ghabah	C2	25
Ghadamis	A1	56
Ghaghara, *river*	D3	20
Ghana		64
Ghanzi	A2	69
Ghardaia	B1	57
Gharyan	B1	56
Ghat	B3	56
Ghatkopar	Inset I	20
Ghaydah, al-	C1	25
Ghazal, *river*	B4	59
Ghazni	B2	22
Ghent	B1	33
Ghurdaqah, al-	B2	56
Giant's Causeway, *headland*	A2	30
Gibraltar		36
Gibraltar, *strait*	D5	37
Gibson, *desert*	B2	14
Giessen	B3	40
Gifford, *river*	M2	99
Gifu	C3	8
Giglio, *island*	C2	38
Gijón	D1	37
Gikongoro	B2	61
Gilbert Plains	A3	96
Gilbert, *islands*	A1	17
Gilbert, *river*	D1	14
Gilgit	E2	21
Gilliam	D1	96
Gillingham	D3	30
Gimie, *mt.*	A2	91
Gimli	C4	96
Giresun	D2	27
Gironde, *river*	B4	34
Gisborne	C2	15
Gisenyi	B1	61
Gitarama	B2	61
Gitega	B2	61
Giurgiu	C4	43
Giza	B2	56
Gizo	A1	16
Gjirokastër	B3	49
Gjoa Haven	J3	99
Gjøvik	C3	52
Glace Bay	H1	100
Gladstone	B4	96
Gladstone, Qld.	E2	14
Glåma, *river*	C3	52
Glanvillia	A2	90
Glasgow	B2	30
Glasgow, Mont.	C1	126
Glaslyn	B7	104
Glastonbury	C3	30
Gleichen	D6	94
Glen Margaret	D3	100
Glenboro	B4	96
Glencoe	D5	102
Glenella	B4	96
Glenholme	D2	100
Glenora	G2	95
Glenwood	D5	98
Glidden	C4	104
Glifádha	Inset	51
Glittertinden, *mt.*	B3	52
Gliwice	D3	41
Głogów	C3	41
Gloucester	C3	30
Gloucester	K2	102
Glover, *reef*	C3	85
Glovertown	D5	98
Gmünd	D2	39
Goba	C3	60
Gobabis	C2	70
Gobi, *desert*	D1	10
Godavari, *river*	C5	20
Godbout	J2	103
Goderich	D4	102
Godfrey	J3	102
Godoy Cruz	B3	74
Gods, *lake*	D2	96
Gogama	D3	101
Goiânia	D3	81
Goiás	D3	81
Golan Heights, *occupied terr.*	A3	27
Gold Coast, Qld.	E2	14
Gold River	J6	95
Golden	O5	95
Golden Lake	H2	102
Golea, el-	B2	57
Golfito	C4	86
Golmud	C2	10
Golyama Kamchiya, *river*	A2	50
Goma	C2	67
Gombe	B2	65
Gomera, *island*	Inset I	37
Gómez Palacio	D2	84
Gonaïves	B1	89
Gonâve, *gulf*	B1	89
Gonâve, *island*	B1	89
Gonder	B1	60
Gongola, *river*	F2	65
Goobies	E5	98
Good Hope, *cape*	A3	71
Goodlands	C2	69
Goodsoil	A6	104
Goose Bay	C2	102
Göppingen	B4	40
Gorakhpur	D3	20
Goražde	B2	48
Gordon, *lake*	E3	94
Gordondale	A3	94
Gore	B2	60
Gore Bay	C2	102
Gori	C4	45
Goris	D3	45
Gorizia	C1	38

Name	Key	Page
Görlitz	C3	40
Gorlovka	D2	47
Gorno-Altay, *republic*	D6	44
Gorno-Altaysk	D6	44
Goroka	A2	15
Gorontalo	D1	13
Gorzów Wielkopolski	B2	41
Gosford, N.S.W.	E3	14
Goshen	F2	100
Goslar	B3	40
Gospić	B3	48
Gosport	C4	30
Göta, *canal*	B3	53
Göteborg och Bohus	B3	53
Gotha	B3	40
Gotland, *island*	C3	53
Gotsu	B3	8
Göttingen	B3	40
Gouda	B2	32
Goudiri	C2	62
Gouin, *reservoir*	B3	103
Goundam	C2	58
Gouré	C3	59
Governador Valadares	D3	81
Gowd-e Zereh, *lake*	A3	22
Göyçay	B2	45
Gozo, *island*	A1	36
Graaf-Reinet	B3	71
Gračanica	B1	48
Gracias	A2	86
Grafton, N.S.W.	E2	14
Graham Land, *region*	C11	107
Graham, *island*	F4	95
Graham, *island*	K1	99
Grahamstown	C3	71
Gran Canaria, *island*	Inset I	37
Gran Chaco, *region*	B3	75
Granada	B3	87
Granada	E4	37
Granby	D6	103
Grand Anse	B3	91
Grand Bahama, *island*	A2	89
Grand Bale	C2	69
Grand Bank	D5	98
Grand Bay	C1	91
Grand Bay	C3	97
Grand Bend	D4	102
Grand Bruit	B5	98
Grand Canyon, Ariz.	B2	126
Grand Centre	E4	94
Grand Cess	B3	63
Grand Erg Occidental, *desert*	B1	57
Grand Erg Oriental, *desert*	B2	57
Grand Falls	B1	97
Grand Falls-Windsor	D5	98
Grand Forks	N6	95
Grand Forks, N. Dak.	D1	126
Grand Island, Nebr.	D1	126
Grand Junction, Colo.	B2	126
Grand Manan, *island*	C4	97
Grand Marais	C4	98
Grand Narrows	G2	100
Grand Pré	C2	100
Grand Rapids	B2	96
Grand Rapids, Mich.	E1	126
Grand Roy	B2	91
Grand Santi	A1	80
Grand Turk, *capital*	D4	89
Grand Turk, *island*	D4	89
Grand Valley	E4	102
Grand, *canal*	C2	31
Grand, *harbor*	Inset	36
Grand, *lake*	D2	97
Grand, *lake*	C4	98
Grand, *river*	C3	69
Grand-Etang	F1	100
Grand-Mère	D5	103
Grand-Remous	A5	103
Grande Baleine, *river*	A2	101
Grande de Añasco, *river*	A2	90
Grande de Manatí, *river*	C2	90
Grande de Matagalpa, *river*	B2	87
Grande Prairie	A3	94
Grande, *bay*	B7	74
Grande, *range*	C2	75
Grande, *river*	B3	77
Grande, *river*	D3	81
Grande, *river*	D1	97
Grande-Anse	C2	100
Grande-Rivière	M3	103
Grande-Vallée	M2	103
Grândola	A3	36
Grandview	A3	96
Granisle	J4	95
Grantham	C3	30
Granville Lake	A1	96
Gras, *lake*	E3	99
Grass, *river*	A3, B2	96
Grassland	D4	94
Grauspitz, *mt.*	B2	33
Gravelbourg	D11	104
Gravenhurst	F3	102
Gravesend	Inset III	30
Gravois, *point*	B3	89
Graz	D3	39
Great Abaco, *island*	B3	89
Great Alföld, *plain*	B2	43
Great Artesian, *basin*	D2	14
Great Australian, *bight*	B3	14
Great Bahama, *bank*	B2	15
Great Barrier, *island*	C2	15
Great Barrier, *reef*	D2	14
Great basin, Nev.	B2	126
Great Bear, *lake*	D3	99
Great Britain		30
Great Dividing, *range*	D1, D2	14
Great Exuma, *island*	B3	89
Great Falls	E3	94
Great Falls, Mont.	B1	126
Great Fish, *river*	C3	71
Great Inagua, *island*	C4	89
Great Indian, *desert*	B3	20
Great Karroo, *plateau*	B3	71
Great Nicobar, *island*	F7	20
Great Rift, *valley*	—	55

Name	Key	Page
Great Ruaha, *river*	C2	68
Great Salt, *lake*, Utah	B1	126
Great Sand Sea, *desert*	A2	56
Great Sandy, *desert*	B2	14
Great Scarcies, *river*	A1	63
Great Sea, *reef*	B1	17
Great Slave, *lake*	F4	99
Great Victoria, *desert*	B2	14
Great Wall of China	D2	10
Great Yarmouth	D3	30
Great Zab, *river*	B1	24
Great, *plains*	C1	126
Greater Hinggan, *range*	F1	10
Greater Sunda, *islands*	B2	13
Gréboun, *mt.*	B1	59
Gredos, *mts.*	D2	37
Greece		51
Greeley, Colo.	C1	126
Greely, *fjord*	L1	99
Green Bay, Wis.	E1	126
Green Lake	C6	104
Green, *islands*	B2	15
Greenland		106
Greenland, *sea*	D2	106
Greenock	B2	30
Greensboro, N.C.	F2	126
Greenville	B3	63
Greenville, S.C.	E2	126
Greenwood	N6	95
Greifswald	C1	40
Grená	C2	32
Grenada		91
Grenada, *island*	B3	91
Grenadines, *islands*	A3, B1, C1	91
Grenfell	H10	104
Grenoble	D4	34
Gretna	C4	96
Greve	D3	32
Grevenmacher	B2	33
Grey River	C5	98
Grey, *range*	D2	14
Greymouth	B3	15
Gribingui, *river*	A2	66
Griffin	G11	104
Griffith, N.S.W.	D3	14
Grijalva, *river*	F4	84
Grimsby	C3	30
Grimsey, *island*	B1	52
Grinnell, *peninsula*	J1	99
Griqualand East, *region*	C3	71
Griqualand West, *region*	B2	71
Griquatown	B2	71
Grise Ford	M1	99
Griswold	A4	96
Groningen	B2	80
Groningen	D1	32
Gronlid	F7	104
Groote Eylandt, *island*	C1	14
Grootfontein	C1	70
Grootvloer, *pan*	B2	71
Gros Islet	B1	91
Gros Morne Natl. Park	C4	98
Gros-Morne	L2	103
Grosseto	B2	38
Grossglockner, *mt.*	C3	39
Groundbirch	M3	95
Groznyy	E4	44
Grudziądz	D2	41
Grunthal	C4	96
Guacanayabo, *gulf*	D3	88
Guadalajara	E2	37
Guadalajara, *state capital*	D3	84
Guadalcanal, *island*	A1	16
Guadalquivir, *river*	D4	37
Guadalupe, *reservoir*	Inset	84
Guadarrama, *mts.*	D2	37
Guadeloupe, *island*		82
Guadiana, *river*	C3	37
Guaíllabamba, *river*	C2	78
Guainía, *river*	C4	78
Guajara Mirim	B3	81
Guajira, *peninsula*	C1	78
Guam		5
Guanacaste, *range*	A2	86
Guanaja, *island*	B2	86
Guanajuato, *state capital*	D3	84
Guanare	C2	79
Guandu, *river*	Inset I	81
Guangdong	E3	10
Guangxi Zhuang	D3	10
Guangzhou	E3	10
Guánica	B3	90
Guantánamo	E3	88
Guaporé, *river*	A3	77
Guaqui	A3	77
Guaranda	B3	78
Guaranda	B2	36
Guarda	B2	36
Guarujá	Inset II	81
Guarulhos	Inset II	81
Guasave	C2	84
Guatemala		85
Guatemala City, *capital*	C5	85
Guaviare, *river*	C4	78
Guayaguayare	A2	91
Guayama	C3	90
Guayambre, *river*	B2	86
Guayanilla	B2	90
Guayape, *river*	B2	86
Guayaquil	B4	79
Guayaquil, *gulf*	A4	79
Guayas, *river*	B4	79
Guaymas	C2	84
Guaynabo	C2	90
Guben	C3	40
Gudaut'a	A2	45
Gudenå, *river*	B2	32
Guécho	E1	37
Guéckédou	C3	62
Guelma	E4	102
Guelph	D4	102
Guelta Zemmur	B1	58
Guéret	C3	34
Guernica Y Luno	E1	37
Guernsey, *island*	Inset II	34
Guerrero	D4	84
Guerrero Negro	B2	84
Guiana, *highlands*	D2	79
Guiers, *lake*	B1	62
Guilarte, *mt.*	B2	90

Key Page

Guildford C3 30
Guilin E3 10
Guimarães A2 36
Guinea 62
Guinea, gulf 55
Guinea-Bissau 62
Güiria D1 79
Guiyang D3 10
Guizhou D3 10
Gujranwala E3 21
Gujrat E3 21
Gulbarga C5 20
Gulbene D2 46
Gulf Coastal, plain D3 126
Gulistan C2 23
Gull Lake B10 104
Gull, lake C5 94
Gulu C2 61
Gumdag B2 22
Gummi C1 65
Gunisao, river C2 96
Gunnbjørn Fjeld, mt. D2 106
Gunton C4 96
Guntur D5 20
Gurabo D2 90
Guri, reservoir D2 79
Gusau D1 65
Gushgy D3 22
Gushgy, river D3 22
Gushikawa ....Inset II 8
Gustavo A. Madero ....Inset 84
Güstrow C2 40
Guyana 80
Guysborough F2 100
Gwadar B5 21
Gwai, river A2 69
Gwalior C3 20
Gweru B2 69
Gyda, peninsula B5 44
Gympie, Qld. E2 14
Gyöngyös B2 43
Győr A2 43
Gypsumville B3 96
Gyumri A2 45
Gyzylarbat B2 22

H

Ha Giang A1 11
Ha'apai, island group B3 17
Haapsalu B2 46
Haarlem B2 32
Habarut C1 25
Habay A2 94
Haboro ....Inset I 8
Hachijo, island C3 8
Hachinohe D1 8
Hachioji C3 8
Haddummati, atoll A4 19
Hadejia, river E1 65
Hadera B1 26
Haderslev B3 32
Hadhramaut, district B1 25
Hadithah, al- B2 24
Haedo, range B2 75
Haeju A3 9
Hafford C8 104
Hafnarfjördhur A3 52
Hagen A3 40
Hague, cape B2 34
Haha, island ....Inset III 8
Haifa B1 26
Haifa, bay B1 26
Haikou E4 10
Hail B1 24
Hailar E1 10
Hainan D4 10
Haines Junction B5 105
Haiphong B2 11
Hairé Lao B1 62
Haiti 89
Hajdúböszörmény C2 43
Haji Ibrahim, mt. B1 24
Hajjah A1 25
Haka A1 11
Hakodate ....D1, Inset I 8
Halab (Aleppo) A1 27
Halaib D1 59
Halba B1 26
Halberstadt B3 40
Haldimand F5 102
Halfmoon Bay L6 95
Haliburton G2 102
Halifax C3 30
Halifax, capital D3 100
Halil, river D4 22
Halisahar ....Inset II 20
Hall Beach M3 99
Hall, peninsula P4 99
Halla-san, mt. ....Inset 9
Hallboro B4 96
Halle C2 33
Halle B3 40
Hallingdal, valley B3 52
Halmahera, island D1 13
Halmstad B3 53
Haltiatunturi, mt B1 53
Halton Hills F4 102
Hamadan B3 22
Hamah A2 27
Hamamatsu C3 8
Hamar C3 52
Hambantota C5 19
Hamburg B2 40
Hämeenlinna B2 53
Hameln B2 40
Hamersley, range A2 14
Hamgyŏng, mts. C2 9
Hamhŭng B2 9
Hami C1 10
Hamilton C2 15
Hamilton B2 30
Hamilton F4 102
Hamilton, inlet D2 98
Hamiota A4 96
Hamm A3 40
Hammamat C1 57
Hammamet, gulf C1 57
Hammerfest E1 53

Hammonds Plains D3 100
Hammondvale D3 97
Hampden C4 98
Hampstead J5 103
Hampton D3 97
Hamun-e Jaz Murian, lake D4 22
Hamun-e Saberi, lake A2 22
Han, river E2 10
Han, river B4 9
Hanau B3 40
Handan E2 10
Hangayn, mts. B2 11
Hangö B3 53
Hangzhou F2 10
Hanley D9 104
Hannibal, Mo. D2 126
Hannover B2 40
Hanoi, capital A2 11
Hanover D3 102
Hantzsch, river O3 99
Hanzhong D2 10
Haora ....E4, Inset II 20
Haparanda D1 53
Happy Valley-Goose Bay A2, E4 98
Har Us, lake B2 11
Harad C1 24
Harare, capital B1 69
Harbel A2 63
Harbin F1 10
Harbour Breton D5 98
Harbour Deep C4 98
Harbour, island B2 89
Harcourt D2 97
Hardangerfjord, fjord B4 52
Hardangervidda, plateau B3 52
Hardwood Lake H2 102
Hare Bay D5 98
Harer D2 60
Hargeysa A2 60
Hargrave A4 96
Harirud, river A2 22
Harlow ....Inset III 30
Härnösand C3 53
Harper C3 63
Harris C9 104
Harrisburg, capital, Pa. F1 126
Harrogate C2 30
Harstad D2 52
Hart, ranges L3 95
Hart, river B3 105
Hartford, capital, Conn. F1 126
Hartland B2 97
Hartley Bay H4 95
Hartney A4 96
Harvey C3 97
Harwill C3 96
Harz, mts. B3 40
Hasa, al-, region C1 24
Hasakah, al- B1 27
Hashtadan, region A3 22
Haslemere ....Inset III 30
Hasselt D2 33
Hastings C2 15
Hastings D4 30
Hastings H3 102
Hat Yai B5 12
Hatillo B2 90
Hato Mayor C2 89
Hatteras cape, N.C. F2 126
Hattiesburg, Miss. E2 126
Haugesund B4 52
Haultain, river D4 104
Haute-Normandie C2 34
Havana, capital B1 88
Havel, river C2 40
Havelock H3 102
Havířov D3 42
Havre, Mont. C1 126
Havre-St-Pierre D3 101
Hawaii ....Inset II 126
Hawaii island, Hawaii ....Inset II 126
Hawalli C2 24
Hawar, islands B2 25
Hawea, lake A3 15
Hawf C1 25
Hawick C2 30
Hawke Harbour D2 98
Hawke's Bay C4 98
Hawke, bay C2 15
Hawkesbury L2 102
Hay River E4 99
Hay, river A2, B1 94
Hayes, river D1, D2 96
Hayma C2 25
Hayter E5 94
Hazelton J3 95
Hazelton, mts. H3 95
Hazlet B10 104
Hazm, al- A1 25
Heart's Content E5 98
Heaslip A4 96
Heath Steele C1 97
Hebei E2 10
Hebrides, sea A1 30
Hebron E3 98
Hecate, strait G4 95
Hecla and Griper, bay F1 99
Hedley M6 95
Heerenveen C2 32
Heerlen C4 32
Hefei E2 10
Hegang G1 10
Heha, mt. B2 61
Heidelberg B4 40
Heidenheim B4 40
Heilbronn B4 40
Heilong (Amur), river F1 10
Heilongjiang F1 10
Heimaey, island A3 52
Heinsburg E4 94
Heisler D5 94
Hekla, volcano B3 52
Helen, reef ....Inset 17
Helena, capital, Mont. B1 126
Heligoland, island A1 40
Hellín F3 37

Helmand, river A2 22
Helmsdale E5 94
Helsingborg B3 53
Helsingør D2 32
Helsinki, capital B2 53
Heming Lake A2 96
Henan E2 10
Henashi, cape C1 8
Hengch'un B2 9
Hengelo D2 32
Hengyang E3 10
Henley Harbour D3 98
Henzada B3 12
Herat A2 22
Herb Lake A2 96
Herbert C10 104
Heredia B2 86
Hereford C3 30
Heriot Bay K6 95
Hermitage-Sandyville D5 98
Hermon, mt. A3 27
Hermosillo, state capital B2 84
Hernád, river C1 43
Herne A3 40
Herning B3 32
Hertford ....Inset III 30
Herzliyya B1 26
Hess, river C4 105
Hesse B3 40
Hetauda C2 19
Hiatikulu B2 71
Hicks Bay C2 15
Hidaka, mts. ....Inset I 8
Hidalgo E3 84
Hidalgo del Parral C2 84
Hieflau D3 39
Hierro, island ....Inset I 37
Higashiosaka B3 8
High Atlas, ranges B2 57
High Level B2 94
High River D6 94
High Tatra, mts. D4 41
High Wycombe ....Inset III 30
Highrock A1 96
Highrock, lake A1 96
Higüey D2 89
Hiiumaa, island B2 46
Hijaz, al-, region A1 24
Hilda E6 94
Hildesheim B2 40
Hill Bank B2 85
Hillaby, mt. A3 91
Hillah, al- B2 24
Hillerød D3 32
Hillsborough C1 91
Hillsborough E3 97
Hillsborough, bay B2 100
Hilo, Hawaii ....Inset II 126
Hilton Beach B1 102
Hilversum C2 32
Himalayas, mts. 7
Himeji B3 8
Hinche C1 89
Hindelang B5 40
Hindu Kush, range B1 22
Hino, cape B3 8
Hinton B4 94
Hirakata B3 8
Hirakud, reservoir D4 20
Hirmil, al- B1 26
Hirosaki D1 8
Hiroshima B3 8
Hirtshals B1 32
Hisabpur ....Inset II 20
Hitachi D2 8
Hixon L4 95
Hjørring B1 32
Hkakabo Razi, mt. C1 12
Hküsan Chedo, islands A5 9
Ho C3 64
Ho Chi Minh City B4 11
Hoa Binh A2 11
Hobart, Tas., capital D4 14
Hobsons, bay ....Inset V 14
Hobyo C2 60
Hoceima, al- D1 57
Hodgeville D10 104
Hodgson C3 96
Hódmezővásárhely C2 43
Hoeryŏng C1 9
Hof B3 40
Höfn C2 52
Hohe Tauern, mts. C3 39
Hohhot E1 10
Hokkaido, island ....D1, Inset I 8
Hoktemberyan B2 45
Holbæk C3 32
Holden D4 94
Holetown A3 91
Holguín E3 88
Holhol B2 60
Holman E2 99
Holon B1 26
Holstebro B2 32
Holton C2 98
Holyhead B3 30
Holyrood E5 98
Holywood B2 30
Homathko, river K5 95
Hombori Tondo, mt. C2 58
Hombori C2 58
Homer, Alaska ....Inset I 126
Homo, bay B2 18
Homs A2 27
Homyel E3 47
Hon Gai B2 11
Hondo C3 94
Hondo, river B1 85
Honduras 86
Honduras, gulf A1 86
Hong Kong, S.A.R. E3 10
Hong Kong, island ....Inset 10
Hongze, lake E2 10
Honiara, capital A1 17

Honolulu, capital, Hawaii ....Inset II 126
Honshu, island C2 8
Hoogeveen D2 32
Hoorn C2 32
Hope M6 95
Hope Bay C2 88
Hope Valley E5 94
Hopedale A1 98
Hopedale E3 98
Hopewell Cape E3 97
Horgèn C1 35
Hormigueros A2 90
Hormuz, strait D4 22
Horn, cape C9 76
Horn, cape A1 52
Hornád, river C2 42
Hornavan, lake C1 53
Hornepayne D3 101
Horsburgh, atoll A2 19
Horse, river D3 94
Horsens B3 32
Horton, river D3 99
Hospitalet H2 37
Hotan A2 10
Hotchkiss B2 94
Hottah, lake E3 99
Houghton, Mich. E1 126
Houmt Souk C3 57
Houston J4 95
Houston, Tex. D3 126
Hovd, river B2 11
Hove C4 30
Hoverla, mt. A2 47
Hövsgöl, lake C1 11
Howley C4 98
Hoy, island ....Inset I 30
Hradec Králové B2 42
Hrazdan B2 45
Hrazdan, river B2 45
Hrodna A3 47
Hron, river B2 42
Hsinchu B1 9
Hsinchuang B1 9
Hsintien B1 9
Hsinying B2 9
Hua Hin B3 12
Huacho B3 77
Huai, river E2 10
Huainan E2 10
Hualien B2 9
Huallaga, river B2 77
Huambo C4 70
Huancavelica B3 77
Huancayo B3 77
Huang (Yellow), river D2, E2 10
Huánuco B2 77
Huapí, mts. B2 87
Huaraz B2 77
Huascarán, mt. B2 77
Hubbards C3 100
Hubei E2 10
Hubli-Dharwar C5 20
Hudaydah, al- A2 25
Huddersfield C3 30
Hudson Bay H8 104
Hudson's Hope M3 95
Hudson, bay J3 92
Hudson, strait O4 99
Hue B3 11
Huehuetenango B4 85
Huelva C4 37
Huesca F1 37
Hufuf, al- C1 24
Hugli, river ....Inset II 20
Hugli-Chunchura ....Inset II 20
Hüichŏn B2 9
Huila, mt. A4 78
Hüksan Chedo, islands A5 9
Hull A6 103
Hulun, lake E1 10
Hulwan B2 56
Humber, river D3 30
Humboldt E8 104
Humenné C2 42
Humuya, river B2 86
Húnaflói, bay A2 52
Hunan E3 10
Hunedoara B3 43
Hungary 43
Hŭngnam B3 9
Hünsruck, mts. A4 40
Hunter River B2 100
Huntington, W. Va. E2 126
Huntsville F2 102
Huntsville, Ala. E2 126
Hunyani, river B1 69
Huon, islands B1 18
Huon, peninsula A2 15
Huron, lake E1 126
Hussar D5 94
Hutchinson, Kans. D2 126
Hvannadalshnúkur, mt. B3 52
Hvar, island C3 48
Hvíta, river A2 52
Hwange A2 69
Hyargas, lake B2 11
Hyderabad C5 20
Hyderabad C5 21
Hyesan C2 9
Hyland Post H2 95
Hyland, river D5 105
Hylo D4 94
Hyvinkää B2 53

I

Ialomiţa, river D3 43
Ialpug, river B2 50
Iaşi D2 43
Ibadan B4 65
Ibagué B3 78
Ibar, river B3 49
Ibaraki B3 8

Ibarra B2 79
Ibb A2 25
Ibérico, mts. F2 37
Ibiza G4 37
Ibiza, island G3 37
Iboundji, mt. A2 66
Ibrahim, river A1 26
Ibri C1 25
Ica B3 77
Içá, river B2 81
Icacos, key D2 90
Ice Cap C2 106
Iceland 52
Ichŏn B3 9
Ichihara D3 8
Ichikawa D3 8
Ichilo, river B3 77
Ichinomiya C3 8
Idaho B1 126
Idaho Falls, Idaho B1 126
Iddesleigh E6 94
Idfu B3 56
Idhra, island B3 51
Idlib A2 27
Idrija B2 48
Ife C4 65
Igarka C6 44
Igloolik M3 99
Igombe, river B1 68
Iguaçu, falls C4 81
Iguaçu, river E2 74
Iguala E4 84
Iguazú, falls E4 75
Ih Bogd Uul, mt. C3 11
Ihavandiffulu, atoll A1 19
Ihosy B3 69
Ilan B1 9
Iijoki, river C1 53
Iisalmi C2 53
Ijevan C2 45
IJssel, river D2 32
IJsselmeer, sea C2 32
Ijuw C2 16
Ikaría, island C3 51
Ikeja B4 65
Ikela B2 67
Iki, island A3 8
Ikorodu B4 65
Ila C3 65
Ilam D3 19
Ilam B3 22
Ilebo B2 67
Ilesha C4 65
Ilford D1 96
Ilhéus E3 81
Ili, river D2 23
Iligan C4 12
Illampu, mt. A3 77
Illapel B4 76
Illimani, mt. A3 77
Illinois E1 126
Ilo C4 77
Iloilo B4 12
Ilorin C3 65
Imatra C2 53
Imbariê ....Inset I 81
Imbéry B2 90
Imi D3 60
Imijin, river B3 9
Imilili A2 58
Imperatriz D2 81
Imperial E9 104
Imperial Mills E4 94
Imperial, river B6 76
Impfondo D3 66
Imphal F4 20
Inari, lake C1 53
Inch'ŏn B3 9
Incles, strait C1 36
Indalsälven, river B2 53
India 20
Indian Bay D4 96
Indian Brook G1 100
Indian Cabins B1 94
Indian Harbour D3 100
Indian Head G10 104
Indiana E1 126
Indianapolis, capital, Ind. E2 126
Indigirka, river C9 44
Indispensable, reefs B2 16
Indonesia 13
Indore C4 20
Indus, river C4, E2 21
Ingleside K3 102
Ingolstadt B4 40
Ingonish G1 100
Ingonish Beach G1 100
Ingushetiya, republic E4 44
Inhambane B5 68
Inhomirim ....Inset I 81
Inland, sea B3 8
Inn, river B3, C2 39
Inner Hebrides, islands A2 30
Inner Mongolia E1 10
Innisfail D5 94
Innisfil F3 102
Innsbruck B3 39
Inta C5 44
Interlaken B2 35
International Falls, Minn. D1 126
Inthanon, mt. B2 12
Inukjuak A2 101
Inuvik C3 99
Inuvik, region C3 99
Invercargill A4 15
Invermay G9 104
Inverness F1 100
Inverness B2 27
Inyangani, mt. C2 69
Ioánnina B2 51
Ionian, islands A2 51
Ionian, sea A2 51
Iowa D1 126
Ipiíba ....Inset II 81

Ipoh A2
Ipoly, river B1
Ipswich D3
Iqaluit, capital, Nunivut P4
Iquique C1
Iquitos C1
Iracoubo C1
Iráklion C4
Iran ....
Iranshahr E4
Irapuato D3
Iraq ....
Irazú, volcano C3
Irbe, strait A3
Irbid B1
Irbil B1
Ireland ....
Iri B5
Irian Jaya, region C2
Iringa C2
Iriomote, island ....Inset II
Iriona C2
Irish, sea B3
Irkutsk D7
Iron Bridge B1
Iron Gate Reservoir B3
Iroquois Falls ....
Irrawaddy, river B2
Irtysh, river D5
Irtysh, river ....
Isabela A1
Isabela, island ....Inset
Isabela, mts. ....
Ísafjördhur A1
Isangel C4
Isar, river C4
Ischia, island C3
Ise C3
Ise, bay C3
Isère, river D4
Isernia C2
Iseyin B4
Isherton B4
Ishigaki, island ....Inset III
Ishikari, river ....Inset I
Ishim D5
Ishim, river C1
Ishinomaki D2
Ishinomaki, bay D2
Ishizuchi, mt. B3
Isiro C1
Iskenderun D3
Iskŭr, river C2
Islamabad, capital D2
Island Lake D2
Island, lake A2
Islay, island A2
Isle aux Morts ....
Islington J6 1
Ismailiyah, al- B1
Isoka C2
Isparta B3
Israel ....
Istanbul B2
Istria, peninsula A2
Italy ....
Izmir B2
Izmit B2
Itabira D3
Itabuna E3
Itaipu ....Inset
Itaipú, reservoir E4
Itajaí D4
Itanagar F3
Itapecerica da Serra ....Inset II
Itapeva ....Inset II
Itaquaquecetuba ....Inset II
Iténez, river B2
Itháki, island B2
Ittoqqortoormiit (Scoresbysund) D2 1
Ivalo C1
Ivano-Frankivsk A2
Ivanovo D3
Ivindo, river B1
Ivujivik A1 1
Iwaki D2
Iwakuni B3
Iwo C4
Iwo Jima, island ....Inset III
Ixelles C2
Ixtapa D4
Ixtapaluca ....Inset
Izabal, lake E4
Izhevsk D4
Izki C1
Izmail B3
Iztacalco ....Inset
Iztapalapa ....Inset
Izu, islands C3
Izu, peninsula C3
Izuhara A3

J

Jabal al-Akhdar, al-, mts. C1
Jabal al-Uwaynat, mt. D3
Jabal an-Nabi Shuayb, mt. A2
Jabal an-Nusayriyah, mts. A2
Jabal Katrinah, mt. B2
Jabal Ramm, mt. A3
Jabal Tuwayq, mts. B2
Jabal Zuqar, island A2
Jabalpur C4
Jaboatão E2
Jacare-Acanga C2
Jackhead C3
Jackson's Arm C4
Jackson, capital, Miss. D2 1
Jackson, port ....Inset IV 1
Jackson, Wyo. B1 1
Jacmel C2
Jacobabad C3
Jacques-Cartier, river E4
Jadabpur ....Inset II
Jadida, el- C1
Jaén E4

Key Page
... B2 19
... B2 26
pur D5 20
ıb, al- D2 56
, al- B2 24
ca **88**
... C3 20
hat B3 21
... B1 48
a, *capital* B2 13
stad B2 53
ca, *mts.* B2 48
bad C2 23
ad C2 22
Enríquez,
te *capital* E4 84
... F3 65
... D4 84
... D2 56
island B2 16
ame A3 60
our C4 21
... B2 13
bay J3 92
u B2 20
agar B4 20
r Inset II 20
... C2 53
edpur E4 20
a, *river* C4 21
ke H6 104
ayen, *island* 5
... Inset II 20
our C3 19
lle D1 97
-Bazar B2 23
... **8**
, *sea* B2 8
ese Alps, *mts.* C3 8
... Inset I 81
á, *river* B2 81
a, *river* Inset II 37
... A1 26
iver C1 81
... D4 94
... E5 102
... D4 22
bac, *mts.* B3 49
erény B2 43
island C2 13
sea C2 13
, *river* A2 81
al- A1 24
al- D3 56
ar B3 60
mt. E2 13
ura F2 13
a B2 90
h, al-, *region* B1 27
... A2 26
... C3 65
Toubkal, *mt.* C2 57
re, *lake* D5 98
son City, *capital*, Mo. D2 126
Guazú, *river* D4 75
... Inset II 20
pils C2 46
a Góra B3 41
va B2 46
eg C3 97
... B3 40
sh Chokusu, *mt.* G1 23
r E6 94
eg B2 96
ie A2 89
de la Frontera C4 37
, *island* Inset II 30
long B2 13
alem, *capital* B2 26
ice B2 48
re C5 21
, *island* J5 103
... A1 96
g Sadar D3 21
si C3 20
m D3 21
m, *river* D3 21
... E3 10
usi G1 10
su E2 10
xi E3 10
ah A2 24
ah, *island* A1 25
va B3 42
... A3 60
... F1 10
... F1 10
... B3 60
ní A2 89
nez D2 84
... E2 10
dezhen E3 10
g E2 10
... C3 61
ega B2 87
tepe A3 87
a (Yangtze), *river* C2 10
ou F1 10
apa A3 79
araná B3 81
tol B1 23
river B3 43
ang E3 10
... G1 10
... B2 24
kh C2 23
Pessoa E2 81
s C3 90
pur B3 20
Batt's Arm D4 98
suu C2 53
su C2 8
gins C2 100
nnesburg C2 71
n D'or Prairie C2 94
nsons Crossing C5 105
or Baharu B2 13
or, *strait* B1 13
ville D4 81

Joinville, *island* C12 107
Joka Inset II 20
Joliet, Ill. E1 126
Joliette C5 103
Jolo B5 12
Jolo, *island* B5 12
Jonava C2 46
Jones, *sound* L1 99
Jonesboro, Ark. D2 126
Jong, *river* A2 63
Jönköping B3 53
Jonquière E3 103
Joplin, Mo. D2 126
Jordan **26**
Jordan, *river* A2 26
Jos E3 65
Jos, *plateau* E2 65
Jotunheimen, *mts.* B3 52
Jou B4 63
Joussard C3 94
Juan de Fuca, *strait* L7 95
Juana Díaz B2 90
Juàzeiro D2 81
Juàzeiro do Norte E2 81
Juba C4 59
Juba, *river* A3 60
Jubayl A1 26
Jubayl, al- C1 24
Jubilee, *lake* D5 98
Júcar, *river* F3 37
Juchitán de Zaragoza F4 84
Judique F2 100
Juigalpa B2 87
Juiz de Fora D4 81
Juliaca C4 77
Julian Alps, *mts.* A2 48
Juliana Top, *mt.* A3 80
Jullundur C2 20
Jumayliyah, al- C2 25
Jumla B2 19
Junagadh B4 20
Junaynah, al- A2 59
Juncos D2 90
Jundiai D4 81
Juneau, *capital*, Alaska Inset I 126
Jungfrau, *mt.* B2 35
Juniper B2 97
Juniyah A2 26
Juozapines, *mt.* C2 46
Jura, *island* B2 30
Jura, *mts.* A2 35
Jura, *river* A2 46
Jurbarkas B2 46
Jurmala B2 46
Jurong A1 13
Juruá, *river* B2 81
Juruena, *river* C3 81
Jutiapa D5 85
Juticalpa B2 86
Jutland, *peninsula* B3 32
Juventud, *island* B2 88
Južna, *river* B3 49
Jvari B3 45
Jwaneng B3 69
Jyväskylä C2 53

K

K2 (Godwin Austen), *mt.* A2 10
Ka Dake B2 71
Ka, *river* C2 65
Kabala B1 63
Kabale A4 61
Kabalo C2 67
Kabardino-Balkariya,
republic E4 44
Kabelebo, *river* A2 80
Kabompo, *river* A2 67
Kabul, *capital* B2 22
Kabul, *river* B2 22
Kabwe B2 67
Kachovka C3 47
Kadavu, *island* B3 17
Kadei, *river* A3 66
Kadoma B2 69
Kaduna D2 65
Kaduna, *river* D2 65
Kaduqli B3 59
Kaédi B3 58
Kaélé B1 65
Kaeo B2 15
Kaesŏng B4 9
Kafan D3 45
Kaffrine B2 62
Kafr ad-Dawwar B1 56
Kafu, *river* B3 61
Kafue B3 67
Kafue, *river* B2 67
Kaga Bandoro A2 66
Kagawong C2 102
Kagera, *river* B4, C1, C2 61
Kagitumba C1 61
Kagoshima A4 8
Kahayan, *river* C2 13
Kahemba B2 67
Kahnawake H6 103
Kahntah M2 95
Kahoolawe *island*,
Hawaii Inset II 126
Kai, *islands* E2 13
Kaieteur, *falls* B3 80
Kaifeng E2 10
Kaikoura B3 15
Kailahun C3 62
Kailahun B1 63
Kainji, *lake* C2 65
Kaiserslautern A4 40
Kaitaia B2 15
Kajaani C2 53
Kakamega C3 61
Kakata A2 63
Kakeroma, *island* Inset II 8
Kakhovka, *reservoir* C3 47
Kakinada D5 20
Kaladar H3 102
Kalahari, *desert* A2 69
Kalámai B3 51
Kalamáki Inset 51
Kälbäcär B2 45

Kalemie C2 67
Kalgoorlie, W.A. B3 14
Kali C1 62
Kali, *river* B2 19
Kalimantan, *region* C2 13
Kaliningrad D3 44
Kalixälven, *river* D1 53
Kallithéa Inset 51
Kalmar C3 53
Kalmykiya, republic E4 44
Kalpeni, *island* B7 20
Kalu, *river* B5 19
Kalundborg C3 32
Kalutara A5 19
Kalwa Inset I 20
Kamakwie A1 63
Kaman Inset I 20
Kamaran, *island* A1 25
Kamarhati Inset II 20
Kambia A1 63
Kamchatka, *peninsula* D10 44
Kamchiya, *river* F2 50
Kamensk-Uralsky D5 44
Kamet, *mt.* C2 20
Kamina C3 67
Kaminak, *lake* J4 99
Kamloops M6 95
Kampala, *capital* C3 61
Kampong Cham D4 11
Kampong Chhnang C3 11
Kampong Saom B5 11
Kampong Thum C3 11
Kampot C5 11
Kamsack J9 104
Kamsar A2 62
Kamui, *cape* Inset I 8
Kananga B2 67
Kanazawa C2 8
Kanchenjunga, *mt.* D2 19
Kanchipuram C6 20
Kanchrapara Inset II 20
Kandi B2 64
Kandy B4 19
Kane, *basin* P1 99
Kangaroo, *island* C3 14
Kangen, *river* C3 59
Kanggye B2 9
Kanghwa, *bay* A4 9
Kangiqsualujjuaq C2 101
Kangiqsujuaq B1 101
Kangirsuk B1 101
Kangnŭng C4 9
Kangshan B2 9
Kankan D2 62
Kano E1 65
Kanpur D3 20
Kansaripara Inset II 20
Kansas D2 126
Kansas City, Kans. D2 126
Kansas City, Mo. D2 126
Kansay A1 23
Kansk D6 44
Kanté B2 64
Kanuku, *mts.* B4 80
Kanye B3 69
Kaohsiung B2 9
Kaoko Veld, *mts.* A1 70
Kaolack A2 62
Kaoma A2 67
Kaop'ing, *river* B2 9
Kapfenberg D3 39
Kapingamarangi, *atoll* C2 15
Kapiskau, *river* D2 101
Kaposvár A2 43
Kapuskasing D3 101
Kara B2 64
Kara, *sea* B5 44
Kara-Kum, *canal* D3 22
Kara-Kum, *desert* C2 22
Kara-Say F2 23
Karabakh, *canal* B2 45
Karachayevo-Cherkesiya,
republic E4 44
Karachi C5 21
Karaj C2 22
Karak, al- A2 26
Karakol F1 23
Karakoram, *range* C1 20
Karaman C3 27
Karasburg C4 70
Karawanken, *range* D4 39
Karbala B2 24
Karcag C2 43
Kardiva, *channel* A2 19
Kärdla B1 46
Kareliya, republic C3 44
Kariba B1 69
Kariba, *lake* A1 69
Karibib B2 70
Karisimbi, *mt.* B1 61
Karkar, *island* A2 15
Karkinit, *bay* C3 47
Karlovac B2 48
Karlovy Vary A2 42
Karlskrona C3 53
Karlsruhe B4 40
Karlstad B3 53
Karnali, *river* B2 19
Karnaphuli, *reservoir* F6 21
Karnaphuli, *river* E6 21
Karonga B1 68
Karpas, *peninsula* C1 27
Kárpathos, *island* C4 51
Kars E2 27
Kartala, *mt.* A1 67
Kartung B2 62
Karun, *river* B3 22
Karuzi C2 61
Karviná D3 42
Kasai, *river* B2 67
Kasama C2 67
Kasane B1 69
Kasba, *lake* H4 99
Kashan C3 22
Kashi A2 10
Kashiwa D3 8
Kasinathpur Inset II 20
Kaslo O6 95
Kassala D2 59

Kassel B3 40
Kasserine B2 57
Kastamonu C2 27
Kastoría B1 51
Kastrup D3 32
Kasugai C3 8
Kasungu B2 68
Kasur E3 21
Katagum, *river* E2 65
Katanga, *plateau* B3 67
Kateríni B1 51
Kate's Needle, *mt.* F2 95
Katherine, N.T. C1 14
Kathgodam C3 20
Kathiawar, *peninsula* B4 20
Kathmandu, *capital* C2 19
Katowice D3 41
Katrine, *lake* B2 30
Katsina D1 65
Kattegat, *strait* C2 32
Kau-Ur C2 62
Kauai *island*, Hawaii Inset II 126
Kaufbeuren B5 40
Kaukau Veld, *region* C2 70
Kaunas B2 46
Kaura-Namoda D1 65
Kavadarci C2 48
Kavajë A2 49
Kavála C1 51
Kavaratti, *island* B6 20
Kavieng B2 15
Kavir-e Namak, *desert* D3 22
Kaw B1 80
Kawagoe C3 8
Kawaguchi C3 8
Kawasaki C3 8
Kawhia B2 15
Kawthaung C4 12
Kayangel, *islands* C1 17
Kayes A3 58
Kayser, *mts.* A3 80
Kayseri C2 27
Kazakh Upland, *region* C2 23
Kazakhstan **23**
Kazan D4 44
Kazanlŭk D3 50
Kazincbarcika C1 43
Kearney F2 102
Kearney, Nebr. D1 126
Keban, *reservoir* D2 27
Kebili B3 57
Kebir, *river* B1 26
Kebnekaise, *mt.* C1 53
Kechika, *river* J2 95
Kecskemét B2 43
Kėdainiai B2 46
Kedgwick B1 97
Kediri C2 13
Kédougou C3 62
Keele, *river* C4 99
Keeley, *lake* B6 104
Keetmanshoop C4 70
Keewatin, *region* J4 99
Kef, el- B1 57
Kefallinía, *island* B2 51
Keflavík A3 52
Keg River B2 94
Keila C1 46
Kékes, *mt.* C2 43
Kelang A2 13
Kelani, *river* B4 19
Kelliher G9 104
Kelowna N6 95
Kelsey C1 96
Keluang B2 13
Kelvington G8 104
Kemano J4 95
Kemerovo D6 44
Kemi B1 53
Kemijärvi C1 53
Kemijoki, *river* C1 53
Kemnay A4 96
Kempenland, *region* D1 33
Kemps Bay B3 89
Kempt, *lake* B4 103
Kempten B5 40
Kemptville K2 102
Kenaston D9 104
Kendal C2 30
Kendari D2 13
Kenema B2 63
Keng Tung C2 12
Kenilworth C3 30
Kenitra C1 57
Kennetcook D2 100
Keno B4 105
Kenora B3 101
Kensington B2 100
Kenton A4 96
Kentucky E2 126
Kentville C2 100
Kenville A3 96
Kenya **61**
Kenya, *mt.* D4 61
Keokradong, *mt.* F7 21
Kerangan Nyatan B3 13
Keratsínion Inset 51
Kerch D3 47
Kerch, *strait* D3 47
Kerema A2 15
Keremeos N6 95
Keren B2 60
Kerewan B2 62
Kerguelen, *islands* 5
Kericho C4 61
Kerinci, *mt.* B2 13
Kerkennah, *islands* C2 57
Kerki D3 22
Kérkira A2 51
Kérkira, *island* A2 51
Kerman D3 22
Kerman, *region* D4 22
Kérouané D3 62
Kerrobert A9 104
Kerulen, *river* D2 11
Keszthely A2 43
Keta C4 64
Ketchikan, Alaska Inset I 126
Key Lake Mine E3 104

Key West, Fla. E3 126
Keyano B3 101
Khabarovsk E8 44
Khabur, *river* B1 27
Khakasiya, republic D6 44
Khalándrion Inset 51
Khalkidhikí, *peninsula* B1 51
Khalkís B2 51
Khaluf C2 25
Khambhât, *gulf* B4 20
Khamis Mushayt B2 24
Khan-Tengri, *mt.* E2 23
Khanaqin C2 24
Khaniá B4 51
Khanka, *lake* G1 10
Khanty-Mansiya,
autonomous okrug C5 44
Khanty-Mansiysk C5 44
Kharagpur E4 20
Kharg, *island* C4 22
Kharijah, al- B2 56
Kharijah, *oasis* B2 56
Kharj, al- B1 24
Kharkiv D1 47
Khartoum North C2 59
Khartoum, *capital* C2 59
Khashm al-Qirbah C2 59
Khashuri B4 45
Khasi, *hills* F3 20
Khaskovo D4 50
Khatanga B7 44
Khawr, al- D2 25
Kherson C3 47
Khíos, *island* C2 51
Khiran, al- C3 24
Khmelnytskyy B2 47
Khojak, *pass* C3 21
Khon Kaen C2 12
Khor Angar C1 60
Khorasan, *region* D2 22
Khorat, *plateau* C3 12
Khorixas B2 70
Khorramabad B3 22
Khorramshahr B3 22
Khorugh B2 23
Khouribga C1 57
Khowst B2 22
Khudzhand A1 23
Khujayli A2 23
Khulna C6 21
Khums, al- B1 56
Khuriya Muriya, *islands* C3 25
Khust A2 47
Khuzdar C4 21
Khuzestan, *region* B3 22
Khvoy A2 22
Khyber, *pass* D2 21
Kibungo C2 61
Kibuye B2 61
Kičevo A2 48
Kidal D2 58
Kidderminster C3 30
Kiel B1 40
Kiel, *bay* B1 40
Kielce E3 41
Kiev, *capital* C1 47
Kiev, *reservoir* C1 47
Kiffa C3 58
Kifisiá Inset 51
Kifissós, *river* B2 51
Kigali, *capital* B1 61
Kigoma A1 68
Kii, *channel* B3 8
Kii, *peninsula* B3 8
Kikinda B2 49
Kikkertavak, *island* B2 98
Kikwit B2 67
Kilchu C2 9
Kildare C2 31
Kilimanjaro, *mt.* C1 68
Kilinochchi B2 19
Kilkee B2 31
Kilkenny C2 31
Killala, *bay* B1 31
Killaloe H2 102
Killarney B2 31
Killarney B4 96
Killarney D1 102
Killarney Lake E5 94
Killdeer D11 104
Killeen, Tex. D2 126
Kilmarnock B2 30
Kilombero, *river* C2 68
Kilwa Kivinje C2 68
Kimbe B2 15
Kimberley B2 71
Kimberley O6 95
Kimberley E3 102
Kimberley, *plateau* B1 14
Kimch'aek C2 9
Kimch'ŏn C4 9
Kinabalu, *mt.* D1 13
Kinabatangan, *river* D2 13
Kinbasket, *lake* B5 94
Kinbasket, *lake* O5 95
Kincaid C11 104
Kincardine D3 102
Kindersley A9 104
Kindia B2 62
Kindu C2 67
King Leopold, *range* B1 14
King William, *island* J3 99
King's Cove E5 98
King's Landing B3 97
King's Lynn D3 30
King's Point C4 98
Kingcome Inlet J6 95
Kingman, Ariz. B2 126
Kingston C3 100
Kingston J3 102
Kingston upon Hull C3 30
Kingston upon Thames Inset III 30
Kingston, *capital* C3 88
Kingstown, *capital* B2 91
Kingsville F2 100
Kingsville C5 102
Kinistino E8 104
Kinkala C6 66
Kinkora B2 100

Kinloss D3 102
Kinmount G3 102
Kinnairds, *cape* C1 30
Kinosota B4 96
Kinsarvik B3 52
Kinsella E5 94
Kinshasa, *capital* A2 67
Kinyeti, *mt.* C4 59
Kioa, *island* C2 17
Kiosk G1 102
Kipengere, *range* B2 68
Kipling H10 104
Kirakira B2 16
Kirensk D7 44
Kiribati **17**
Kırıkkale C2 27
Kiritimati (Christmas),
island D1 17
Kirkcaldy B2 30
Kirkenes F2 52
Kirkfield G3 102
Kirkland Lake D3 101
Kirkpatrick, *mt.* A5 107
Kirkuk B1 24
Kirkwall Inset I 30
Kirov D4 44
Kirovakan B2 45
Kirovograd C2 47
Kirşehir C2 27
Kirthar, *range* C4 21
Kiruna D1 53
Kisangani C1 67
Kishi B3 65
Kiskitto, *lake* B2 96
Kiskörei-víztároló, *lake* C2 43
Kiskunhalas B2 43
Kismayo A4 60
Kissidougou C3 62
Kississing, *lake* A1 96
Kisumu C4 61
Kita B3 58
Kita, *island* Inset III 8
Kitakami, *river* D2 8
Kitakyushu A3 8
Kitale C3 61
Kitami Inset I 8
Kitami, *mts.* Inset I 8
Kitchener E4 102
Kitgum C2 61
Kíthira, *island* B3 51
Kitikmeot, *region* G3 99
Kitimat H4 95
Kitwanga H3 95
Kitwe B2 67
Kivi, *lake* C2 53
Kivu, *lake* B1 61
Kızıl Irmak, *river* C2 27
Kjølen, *mts.* C1 53
Kladno B2 42
Klagenfurt D4 39
Klaipėda A2 46
Klamath Falls, Oreg. A1 126
Klarälven, *river* B2 53
Klatovy A3 42
Kleinburg J5 102
Klemtu H5 95
Kleve A3 40
Kloulklubed B3 17
Kluane, *lake* B5 105
Knee, *lake* D1 96
Knight, *inlet* K6 95
Knockboy, *mt.* B3 31
Knokke B1 33
Knoxville, Tenn. E2 126
Ko Chang, *island* C3 12
Ko Kut, *island* C4 12
Ko Phangan, *island* B4 12
Ko Samui, *island* B4 12
Ko Tarutao, *island* B5 12
Kobe B3 8
Koblenz A3 40
Kobuleti A4 45
Kočani C2 48
Kočevje B3 48
Kochi B3 8
Kodiak, Alaska Inset I 126
Kofarnihon, *river* A2 23
Köflach D3 39
Koforidua B3 64
Kofu C3 8
Køge D3 32
Kohima F3 20
Kohtla-Järve D1 46
Koindu B1 63
Koje-do, *island* C5 9
Kokkina A1 27
Kokkola B2 53
Kokshetau C1 23
Kola A4 96
Kola, *peninsula* C3 44
Kolari B1 53
Kolda B3 62
Kolding B3 32
Kolhapur B5 20
Kolín B2 42
Kołobrzeg B1 41
Kolpashevo D6 44
Kolshet Inset I 20
Kolumadulu, *atoll* A3 19
Kolwezi C3 67
Kolyma, *range* C10 44
Kolyma, *river* C9 44
Komadugu Gana, *river* F2 65
Komadugu Yobe, *river* F1 65
Komárno B3 42
Komárom B2 43
Komati, *river* B2 71
Komatsu C2 8
Komi, republic C4 44
Komi-Permyat,
autonomous okrug D4 44
Komoé, *river* E3 63
Komotiní C1 51
Komsomolsk-na-Amure D8 44
Konar, *river* D2 21
Konduz B1 22
Konduz, *river* B1 22
Koné C2 18
Kong, *river* D4 11

Key Page
Konibodom B1 23
Konin D2 41
Konnagar Inset II 20
Konotop C1 47
Kontagora C2 65
Kontum B3 11
Konya C3 27
Kootenay, *lake* O6 95
Kootenay, *river* P6 95
Kopaonik, *mts.* B3 49
Kópavogur A2 52
Koper A3 48
Kopet, *mts.* B2, D2 22
Koprivnica C2 48
Korab, *mt.* B2 49
Korab, *mt.* A2 48
Korçë B3 49
Korčula, *island* C4 48
Korea, *bay* A3 9
Korea, *strait* C5 9
Korhogo D2 63
Koriyama D2 8
Korla B1 10
Koro Toro B4 59
Koro, *island* B2 17
Koro, *sea* B2 17
Koror, *capital* B3 17
Koror, *island* C3 17
Körös, *river* C2 43
Korosten B1 47
Kortrijk B2 33
Koryak, *range* C10 44
Koryakiya,
autonomous okrug C10 44
Kosŏng C3 9
Kos, *island* C3 51
Kosciusko, *mt.* D3 14
Koshigaya C3 8
Koshiki, *islands* A4 8
Košice C2 42
Kosovo, province B3 49
Kosrae D2 15
Kosrae, *island* D2 15
Kossol, *passage* C2 17
Kossol, *reef* C2 17
Kossu, *lake* D3 63
Koszalin C1 41
Kota C3 20
Kota Baharu B1 13
Kota Kinabalu D2 13
Kotcho, *lake* M1 95
Kotka C2 53
Kotlas C4 44
Kotor, *gulf* A3 49
Kotovsk B2 47
Kotto, *river* B2 66
Kouchibouguac D2 97
Koudougou C2 64
Koula-Moutou B2 66
Koulikoro B3 58
Koulountou, *river* C3 62
Koumac C2 18
Koungheul B2 62
Kourou B1 80
Kouroussa D2 62
Kousséri B1 65
Koutiala B3 58
Kouto C2 63
Kouvola C2 53
Kovel A1 47
Kowŏn B3 9
Kowloon Inset 10
Kowt-e Ashrow B2 22
Kozáni B1 51
Kozhikode C6 20
Kozloduy B2 50
Kozu, *island* C3 8
Kožuf, *mts.* C2 48
Kpalimé B3 64
Kpandu C3 64
Kpémé B3 64
Kra, *isthmus* B4 12
Kracheh E3 11
Kragujevac B2 49
Krakatau, *island* B2 13
Kraków D3 41
Kraljevo B3 49
Kramatorsk D2 47
Kranj B2 48
Kranji B1 13
Krasnodar E3 44
Krasnoyarsk D6 44
Krefeld A3 40
Kremenchug C2 47
Kretinga A2 46
Kribi A3 65
Krishna, *river* C5 20
Kristiansand B4 52
Kristianstad B3 53
Kristiansund B3 52
Kristinehamn B3 53
Krk, *island* B2 48
Krka, *river* B3 48
Krong Kaoh Kong A4 11
Kroonstad C2 71
Krosnow E4 41
Krško C3 48
Krugersdorp C2 71
Krujë A2 49
Kruševac B3 49
Kruševo B2 48
Krychaw E3 47
Kryvyi Rih C2 47
Kuala Abang B2 13
Kuala Belait A2 13
Kuala Lumpur, *capital* A2 13
Kuala Terengganu B2 13
Kuantan B2 13
Kuching C2 13
Kuchino, *island* A4 8
Kudymkar D4 44
Kufstein E3 99
Kugluktuk C3 39
Kuito C4 70
Kukës B1 49
Kul, *river* D4 22
Kula Kangri, *mt.* B1 19
Kuldiga A2 46
Kulmbach B3 40

Key Page
Kulob A2 23
Kulpawn, *river* B1 64
Kum, *river* B4 9
Kumamoto A3 8
Kumanovo B1 48
Kumasi B3 64
Kume, *island* Inset II 8
Kumo F2 65
Kunda D1 46
Kunene, *river* A1 70
Kunlun, *mts.* B2 10
Kunming D3 10
Kunsan B5 9
Kuntaur D2 62
Kuopio C2 53
Kupa, *river* B3 48
Kupang D3 13
Kür, *river* A2, C2 45
Kür-Aras, *lowland* B2 45
Kura, *river* E2 27
Kurashiki B3 8
Kuraymah C1 59
Kŭrdzhali D4 50
Kure B3 8
Kuressaare B2 46
Kurgan D5 44
Kuril, *islands* E9 44
Kurinwás, *river* B2 87
Kurla Inset I 20
Kurnool C5 20
Kuršėnai B1 46
Kursk D3 44
Kuru, *river* C2 19
Kuruman B2 71
Kurume A3 8
Kurunegala B4 19
Kushiro Inset I 8
Kushtia C5 21
Kusŏng A3 9
Kusti C2 59
Kut, al- C2 24
Kütahya B2 27
Kutaisi B3 45
Kutch, *gulf* A4 20
Kutno D2 41
Kuujjuaq C2 101
Kuujjuarapik A2 101
Kuwait 24
Kuwait, *bay* B2 24
Kuwait, *capital* B2 24
Kwa, *river* B2 67
Kwahu, *plateau* B3 64
Kwajalein, *island* B2 16
Kwangju B5 9
Kwango, *river* B2 67
Kwekwe B2 69
Kyaukpyu B2 12
Kyle B10 104
Kyle of Lochalsh B1 30
Kyoga, *lake* C3 61
Kyŏngju C5 9
Kyoto B3 8
Kyrenia B1 27
Kyrgyzstan 23
Kyrenia, *range* B1 27
Kyushu, *island* A3 8
Kyustendil A3 50
Kyzyl D6 44
Kyzyl-Kyya C2 23
Kyzyl-Suu, *river* C3 23
Kyzylkum, *desert* B2 23

L

La Asunción D1 79
La Baie F3 103
La Broquerie C4 96
La Ceiba B2 86
La Chaux-de-Fonds A1 35
La Coma, *river* B1 36
La Conception B5 103
La Condamine B1 35
La Coruña B1 37
La Crete B2 94
La Croix Maingot A2 91
La Crosse, Wis. D1 126
La Cruz A1 86
La Digue, *island* C1 70
La Doré D3 103
La Esperanza A2 86
La Goulette C1 57
La Grande, *river* B3 101
La Guadeloupe F6 103
La Guaira Maiquetía C1 79
La Have C3 100
La Laguna Inset I 37
La Libertad A4 79
La Libertad C3 85
La Loche A4 104
La Louvière C2 33
La Malbaie F4 103
La Martre K2 103
La Martre, *lake* E4 99
La Montaña, *region* C2 77
La Oroya B3 77
La Palma C2 87
La Palma, *island* Inset I 37
La Paz B2 86
La Paz, *capital* A3 77
La Paz, *state capital* B3 84
La Pérouse B1 96
La Pérouse, *strait* Inset I 8
La Plaine B3 90
La Plata D4 74
La Plata, *river* C2 90
La Plonge, *lake* C5 104
La Pocatière F4 103
La Prairie J6 103
La Rioja B2 74
La Rioja E1 37
La Rochelle B3 34
La Roda E3 37
La Romana D2 89
La Ronge E5 104
La Ronge, *lake* E6 104
La Rosita B2 87
La Salle C4 96
La Salle J6 103
La Scie D4 98

Key Page
La Serena B3 76
La Spezia B1 38
La Tortuga, *island* C1 79
La Tuque D4 103
La Unión B7 76
La Unión C2 86
La Vega B1 89
La Virtud A2 86
La-Roche-sur-Yon B3 34
Labasa B2 17
Labé B2 62
Labe (Elbe), *river* B2 42
Labelle C3 100
Laberge, *lake* B5 105
Labi A3 13
Laborec, *river* C2 42
Laborie B3 91
Labrador City D3 98
Labrieville G2 103
Labu C2 13
Labuan, *island* D2 13
Laç A2 49
Lac du Bonnet C4 96
Lac La Biche E4 94
Lac La Hache M5 95
Lac Mégantic F6 103
Lac-aux-Sables D5 103
Lac-Bouchette D3 103
Lac-des-Aigles H4 103
Lac-des-Îles A5 103
Lac-Édouard D4 103
Lac-Etchemin F5 103
Lac-Nominingue A5 103
Lac-Saguay A5 103
Laccadive, *islands* B6 20
Lachenaie J5 103
Lachine H6 103
Lachute B6 103
Lacombe D5 94
Ladhiqiyah, al- (Latakia) A2 27
Ladoga, *lake* C3 44
Ladysmith C2 71
Ladywood C4 96
Lae A2 15
Lae, *island* B2 16
Laem, *mt.* B3 12
Læsø, *island* C1 32
Lafayette, La. D2 126
Lafia E3 65
Lafleche D11 104
Lafond E4 94
Laghouat B1 57
Lagodekhi D4 45
Lagos B4 65
Lagos A4 36
Laguna de Bay, *lake* B3 12
Lahave, *river* C3 100
Lahij A2 25
Lahn, *river* B3 40
Lahore E3 21
Lahti C2 53
Laï B5 59
Lairg B1 30
Lajas A2 90
Lajes C4 81
Lakatoro B3 18
Lake Alma F11 104
Lake Charlotte E3 100
Lake Edward B2 97
Lake Harbour O4 99
Lake Lenore F8 104
Lake St. Peter G2 102
Lake, *district* B2 30
Lakeba, *island* C3 17
Lakeba, *passage* C3 17
Lakefield G3 102
Lakelse Lake H4 95
Lakhpat A4 20
Laki, *volcano* B2 52
Lakselv F1 52
Lalitpur C2 19
Lamaline D5 98
Lamap B3 18
Lambaréné A2 66
Lambton E6 103
Lamèque E1 97
Lamèque, *island* E1 97
Lami B3 17
Lamía B2 51
Lammermuir, *hills* C2 30
Lamon, *bay* B3 12
Lampa Inset 76
Lampang B2 12
Lampeter B3 30
Lampman H11 104
Lamu F5 61
Lan, *island* B2 9
Lanai *island*, Hawaii Inset II 126
Lanark J2 102
Lancaster C2 30
Lancaster L2 102
L'Ancienne-Lorette K5 103
Land's End, *promontory* B4 30
Lander, Wyo. C1 126
Landes, *region* B5 34
Landis B8 104
Landshut C4 40
Lang Son B2 11
Langeburg, *mts.* B3 71
Langeland, *island* C4 32
Langenburg J10 104
Langham D8 104
Langkawi, *island* A1 13
Langley L6 95
Langruth B4 96
Langstaff K5 102
Langton E5 102
Languedoc-Roussillon C5 34
Lanigan E9 104
Lanín, *volcano* A4 74
Länkäran C3 45
L'Annonciation B5 103
Lansdowne J3 102
Lansdowne House C2 101
L'Anse-à-Valleau M2 103
L'Anse-au-Loup C3 98
L'Anse-aux-Gascons M3 103
L'Anse-St-Jean F3 103
Lansing, *capital*, Mich. E1 126

Key Page
Lantau, *island* Inset 10
Lanús D3 74
Lanzarote, *island* Inset I 37
Lanzhou D2 10
Lao Cai A1 11
Laoag B2 12
Laoang C3 12
Laon C2 34
Laos 11
Lapithos B1 27
Lapland, *region* B1 53
Lappeenranta C2 53
Laptev, *sea* B8 44
L'Aquila C2 38
Larache C1 57
Laramie, Wyo. C1 126
Laredo, Tex. D3 126
Lares B2 90
Larestan, *region* C4 22
Large, *island* C1 91
Lárisa B2 51
Lark Harbour B4 98
Larkana C4 21
Larkhall C4 96
Larnaca B2 27
Larne B2 30
Larochette B2 33
Larrys River F2 100
Larsen Ice Shelf, *glacier* C12 107
Las Cruces, N. Mex. C2 126
Las Minas, *mt.* A2 86
Las Palmas Inset I 37
Las Piedras D2 90
Las Piedras B3 75
Las Tablas B3 87
Las Tunas E3 88
Las Vegas, N. Mex. C2 126
Las Vegas, Nev. B2 126
L'Ascension B5 103
Lashburn A7 104
Lashio C2 12
Lashkar Gah A2 22
Last Mountain, *lake* E9 104
Latacunga B3 79
Late, *island* C2 17
Latina C2 38
Latium C2 38
Latvia 46
Lau, *island group* C2 17
Laucala, *island* C2 17
Laudat B3 90
Lauder A4 96
Launceston B4 30
Launceston, Tas. D4 14
Laurie River A1 96
Laurier B4 96
Lausanne A2 35
Lautoka A2 17
Laval B2 34
Laval C6, J5 103
Lavenham B4 96
Lavoy E4 94
Lavumisa B3 71
Lawa, *river* A2, B2 80
Lawn D5 98
Lawrence Station B3 97
Lawton, Okla. D2 126
Layland B4 96
Layou, *river* B3 90
Lázaro Cárdenas D4 84
Le Bic H3 103
Le Creusot D3 34
Le Havre C2 34
Le Mans C2 34
Le Puy C4 34
Leader A10 104
Leading Tickles D4 98
Leaf Rapids D1 96
Leamington C5 102
l'Eau Claire, *lake* B2 101
Lebanon 26
Lebanon, *mts.* B1 26
Lebombo, *mts.* C2, D1 71
Lebu B6 76
Lecce D2 38
Lech B3 39
Lech, *river* B4 40
Leduc D4 94
Lee, *river* B3 31
Leeds C3 30
Leeuwarden C1 32
Leeuwin, *cape* A3 14
Leeward Group B3 58
Lefka A1 27
Lefkoniko B1 27
Leganés Inset II 37
Legazpi B3 12
Legnica C3 41
Leicester C3 30
Leichhardt, *river* D1 14
Leiden B2 32
Leie, *river* B2 33
Leikanger B3 52
Leipzig C3 40
Leiria A3 36
Leitrim H6 102
Leixões A2 36
Lékéti, *mts.* C5 66
Lélouma B2 62
Lelystad C2 32
Lempa, *river* A1, B2 86
Lena, *river* C8 44
Leneinsk C2 23
Lenghu C2 10
Lengoué, *river* C3 66
Lenore A4 96
Lens C1 34
Lensk C7 44
Léo C3 64
Leoben D3 39
Léogâne C2 89
León D3 84
León A2 87
León D1 37
Leone B2 18
Leova B2 50
Leoville C7 104
Lepontine Alps, *mts.* C2 35
Lepreau C3 97

Key Page
Lepsi D2 23
Leribe B1 71
Lérida G2 37
Lerwick Inset I 30
Les Cayes B2 89
Les Éboulements F4 103
Les Escaldes B2 36
Les Escoumins G3 103
Les Islets-Caribou J2 103
Les Méchins K3 103
Les Tantes, *island* B1 91
Les Ulis Inset II 34
Leskovac B3 49
Lesosibirsk D6 44
Lesotho 71
Lesser Caucasus, *mts.* A2, B4 45
Lesser Hinggan, *range* F1 10
Lesser Slave, *lake* C3 94
Lesser Sunda, *islands* C2 13
Lestrock G9 104
Lésvos, *island* C2 51
Leszno C3 41
Lethbridge D6 94
Lethbridge E5 98
Lethem B4 80
Leticia C6 78
Letlhakeng B3 69
Letterkenny C1 31
Leuven C2 33
Levack D1 102
Levallois-Perret Inset II 34
Leveque, *cape* B1 14
Leverkusen A3 40
Levice B2 42
Lévis E5, L6 103
Levittown C2 90
Lewes D4 30
Lewis, *island* A1 30
Lewisporte D4 98
Lewiston, Idaho B1 126
Lewiston, Maine F1 126
Lexington, Ky. E2 126
Leyte, *island* C4 12
Lhasa C3 10
Lhobrak, *river* C2 19
Lhuntshi C2 19
Lianyungang E2 10
Liao, *river* F1 10
Liaoning F1 10
Liaoyang F1 10
Liaoyuan F1 10
Liard River J1 95
Liard, *river* K1 95
Libau C4 96
Liberec B2 42
Liberia 63
Liberia A2 86
Libono B1 71
Libreville, *capital* A1 66
Libya 56
Libyan, *desert* A2, D2 56
Lichfield C3 30
Lichinga B2 68
Lida B3 47
Liechtenstein 33
Liège D2 33
Lieksa D2 53
Lienz C4 39
Liepāja A2 46
Lièvre, *river* A5 103
Lifford C1 31
Lifou, *island* D2 18
Lifuka, *island* C3 17
Liguria B1 38
Ligurian, *sea* B2 38
Lihir, *group* B2 15
Likasi C3 67
Likiep, *island* B1 16
Lille C1 34
Lille, *strait* B3 32
Lillehammer C3 52
Lillooet M6 95
Lillooet, *river* L6 95
Lilongwe, *capital* B2 68
Lima, *capital* B3 77
Lima, *river* A2 36
Limassol B2 27
Limbazi C2 46
Limbe A3 65
Limbourg D2 33
Limerick B2 31
Limfjorden, *channel* B2 32
Límnos, *island* C2 51
Limoges C4 34
Limón C3 86
Limours Inset II 34
Limousin C4 34
Limpopo, *river* C1 71
Linares B5 76
Linares E3 84
Linares E3 37
Lincoln C3 30
Lincoln, *capital*, Nebr. D1 126
Lindau B5 40
Lindbergh E4 94
Linden B3 80
Linden D2 100
Lindi C2 68
Lindsay G3 102
Line, *islands* D1 17
Lingayen, *gulf* B2 12
Lingga, *island* B2 13
Lingshi A2 19
Linguère B2 62
Linköping C3 53
Linnhe, *lake* B2 30
Linvanti, *river* A1 69
Linwood F2 100
Linz D2 39
Lion, *gulf* D5 34
Lionel Town B3 88
Lions Head D3 102
Lipa B3 12
Lipari, *islands* C3 38
Lipetsk D3 44
Lippstadt B3 40
Lipton G10 104
Liptovský Mikuláš B2 42
Lira C2 61

Key
Lisala B1
L'Isalo, *mts.* B3
Lisbon, *capital* A3
Lisichansk D2
L'Isle-Adam Inset II
L'Isle-Verte G3
Lismore, N.S.W. E2
Listowel E4
Litani, *river* A2
Litani, *river* A2, B3
Lithuania
Little Alföld, *plain* A2
Little Andaman, *island* F6
Little Bay B5
Little Bras d'Or G1
Little Current D2
Little Fort M5
Little Grand Rapids D3
Little Inagua, *island* C4
Little Rock, *capital*, Ark. D2
Little Salmon, *lake* C4
Little Scarcies, *river* A1
Little Seldom D4
Little Smoky, *river* A4
Little St. Bernard, *pass* D4
Little Zab, *river* B1
Liuzhou D3
Liverpool C3
Liverpool C3
Liverpool, *bay* B3
Livingstone B3
Livno B2
Livorno B2
Ljubljana, *capital* B2
Ljusnanälven, *river* B2
Llallagua A3
Llandrindod Wells B3
Llanos, *plain* C2
Llanos, *prairie* C3
Llanquihue, *lake* B7
Lleyn, *peninsula* B3
Llorts B1
Lloyd, *lake* B3
Lloydminster E4
Lloydminster A7
Lloyds, *river* C5
Llullaillaco, *volcano* B1
Lo Wu Inset
Lo, *river* A1
Loa, *river* B2
Lobamba B2
Lobatse B3
Lobaye, *river* A2
Lobito B4
Locarno C2
Lockeport B4
Lockport B4
Lod (Lydda) B2
Lodja B2
Lodwar C2
Łódź D3
Loei B2
Loess, *plateau* D2
Lofoten, *islands* C2
Logan, *river* Inset III
Logan, Utah B1
Logone, *river* A5
Logroño E1
Loi-kaw C2
Loire, *river* C3
Loíza D2
Loja B4
Loja D4
Lokka, *reservoir* C1
Lokoja D4
Lokossa A4
Lol, *river* B3
Lolland, *island* C4
Lom B2
Lomami, *river* C2
Lomas de Zamora D4
Lomawai A3
Lombardy B1
Lombardy J3
Lombok, *island* C2
Lomé, *capital* B3
Lomond, *lake* B2
Łomża F2
London D5
London, *capital* C3, Inset III
Londonderry A2
Londrina C4
Lone Butte M5
Long Beach, Calif. B2
Long Island, N.Y. F1
Long Lake D4
Long Range, *mts.* B5, C4
Long Xuyen A4
Long, *island* C3
Longford C2
Longlac C3
Longreach, Qld. D2
Longueuil J5
Longview, Tex. D2
Loon Lake C3
Loon Lake A6
Loop Head, *cape* B2
Lop Buri B3
Lop, *lake* C1
Lorca F4
Loreburn D9
Lorengau A2
Loreto B2
Lorette C4
Loretteville K5
Lorient B3
L'Original L2
Lorne, *estuary* A2
Lorraine D2
Lorraine H5
Los Andes B4
Los Ángeles B6
Los Angeles, Calif. B2
Los Chiles B1
Los Mochis C2
Los Reyes Inset
Los Teques C1
Lot, *river* C4
Louang Namtha A1

Name	Key	Page
…omo	B6	66
…a	A2	62
…h Erne, *lake*	A2	30
…hborough, *lake*	J3	102
…heed, *island*	G1	99
…bourg	H2	100
…dale	F2	100
…eville	D5	103
…iade, *archipelago*	B3	15
…iana	D2	126
…ville, Ky.	E2	126
…des	B5	34
…	C2	19
…res	Inset II	
…ch	C2	50
…r Village	B3	91
…ttville	B4	94
…e Farm	C4	99
…r Arrow, *lake*	N6	95
…r Debert	D2	100
…r Five Islands	C2	100
…r Hutt	B3	15
…r Montague	C2	100
…r Post	H1	95
…r Saxony	B2	40
…r Tunguska, *river*	C6	44
…r Woods Harbour	B4	100
…estoft	D3	30
…da	C2	60
…ro	D2	61
…aba, *river*	C2	67
…da, *capital*	B2	70
…g Prabang	B2	11
…g Prabang, *range*	A3	11
…gwa	C3	67
…gwa	C2	67
…shya	B2	67
…ula, *river*	B2, C3	67
…	E3	70
…	A1	66
…ngo	B5	70
…ock, Tex.	C2	126
…	B2	40
…con, *lake*	C3	94
…	F3	41
…umbashi	C3	67
…pa	D2	70
…	B2	38
…	A2	88
…ena	B3	12
…ena	D4	37
…nec	A2	42
…rn, *lake*	C2	35
…	C1	35
…e, *river*	A3	80
…kenwalde	D3	20
…know	D4	102
…key Lake	C9	104
… Kamchiya, *river*	E3	50
…eritz	B4	70
…	C2	20
…ogorie, *region*	E2	50
…wigsburg	B4	40
…wigshafen am Rhein	B4	40
…	D3	70
…ano	C3	35
…ano, *lake*	C3	35
…anville	B2	18
…enda	C2	68
…	C1	37
…oj	A3	43
…ansk	D2	47
…uga, *river*	C2	67
…yani	E2	10
…eni	B3	43
…erón	B1	89
…uillo	D2	90
…emo	C2	70
…	C2	68
…aka, *capital*	B3	67
…emba	B2	67
…eland	A8	104
…anje	A3	49
…utfu, *river*	B2	71
…ga, *river*	B2	67
…gwebungu, *river*	B2	67
…sar	A1	63
…	E2	10
…embourg		33
…or	B2	56
…arches	Inset II	34
…hou	D3	10
…on, *island*	B3	12
…on, *strait*	B1	47
…	A2	47
…dal	B1	96
…n, *bay*	C4	30
…n Lake	C1	96
…on	D4	34
…ton	M6	95

M

Name	Key	Page
Maastricht	C4	32
Mabaruma	B1	80
Maberly	J3	102
Mabou	F1	100
Mac Tier	F2	102
MacAlpine, *lake*	H3	99
Macapá	C1	81
Macas	B4	79
Macau, S.A.R.	E3	10
Maccan	C2	100
Macdonnell, *ranges*	C2	14
Macedonia, F.Y.R.		48
Maceió	E2	81
Macenta	D3	62
Macerata	C2	38
Macfarlane, *river*	C2	104
Macgregor	B4	96
Machakos	D4	61
Machala	B4	79
Machida	C3	8
Machupicchu, *ruins*	C3	77
MacKay, *lake*	F4	99
Mackay, Qld.	D2	14
Mackenzie	L3	95
Mackenzie King, *island*	F1	99
Mackenzie, *bay*	B1	105
Mackenzie, *mts.*	C3	99
Mackenzie, *river*	B3, D4	99
Mackey	H1	102
Macklin	A8	104
Maclean, *strait*	G1	99
Macmillan, *river*	C4	105
Mâcon	D3	34
Macon, Ga.	E2	126
Madaba	A2	26
Madagascar		69
Madan	C4	50
Madang	A2	15
Madawaska	G2	102
Madden	C5	94
Madeira, *island*		55
Madeira, *river*	B2	81
Madhumati, *river*	C5	21
Madhupur Tract, *region*	D4	21
Madinat ath-Thawrah	B2	27
Madison, *capital*, Wis.	E1	126
Madiun	C2	13
Madoc	H3	102
Madre de Dios, *island*	A9	76
Madre de Dios, *river*	A2, C3	77
Madrid, *capital*	E2, Inset I	37
Madriu, *river*	B3	36
Madura, *island*	C2	13
Madura	C7	20
Maebashi	C2	8
Maella, *mts.*	D3	88
Maéwo, *island*	C2	18
Mafeking	A3	96
Mafeteng	A2	71
Mafia, *island*	C2	61
Mafikeng	C2	71
Mafra	A3	36
Mafraq, al-	B1	26
Magadalena de Kino	B1	84
Magadan	D9	44
Magburaka	B1	63
Magdagachi	D8	44
Magdalena	B2	77
Magdalena Contreras	Inset	84
Magdalena, *island*	B7	76
Magdalena, *river*	B3	78
Magdeburg	B2	40
Magelang	C2	13
Magellan, *strait*	B9	76
Maggiore, *lake*	B1	38
Magnetawan	F2	102
Magnitogorsk	D4	44
Magog	D6	103
Mahabharat, *range*	B2	19
Mahajamba, *river*	B2	69
Mahajanga	B2	69
Mahalapye	B2	69
Mahallah al-Kubra, al-	B1	56
Mahanadi, *river*	D4	20
Mahaska	C4	94
Mahbas, al-	C1	58
Mahdia	B3	80
Mahé, *island*	C1, Inset	70
Mahébourg	C3	69
Mahilyow	E3	47
Mahim, *bay*	Inset I	20
Mahón	J3	37
Mai-Ndombe, *lake*	B2	67
Maidstone	D3	30
Maidstone	A7	104
Maiduguri	G2	65
Main Brook	C3	98
Main, *river*	B4	40
Main-à-Dieu	H1	100
Main-Danube, *canal*	B4	40
Maine	G1	126
Mainland, *island*	Inset I	30
Maintirano	A2	69
Mainz	B4	40
Maio, *island*	C3	58
Maipo, *river*	B4, Inset	76
Maipú	Inset	76
Maisons-Laffitte	Inset II	34
Maitland Bridge	B3	100
Maíz, *islands*	C2	87
Maizuru	C2	8
Majardah, *river*	B1	57
Maji	Inset I	60
Majorca, *island*	H3	37
Majuro, *capital*	C2	16
Majuro	C2	16
Makamba	B3	61
Makassar, *strait*	C2	13
Makeni	B1	63
Makeyevka	D2	47
Makhachkala	E4	44
Makhaleng, *river*	A2	71
Makin, *island*	A1	17
Makokou	B1	66
Makona, *river*	A1	63
Makoua	C4	66
Makran Coast, *range*	B5	21
Makung	A2	9
Makurdi	E4	65
Malabar, *coast*	B6	20
Malabo, *capital*	A1	66
Malacca, *strait*	A1, A2	13
Malad	Inset I	20
Maladzyechna	C2	47
Málaga	D4	37
Malagarasi, *river*	B1	68
Malaita, *island*	B1	16
Malakal	C3	59
Malakula, *island*	B3	18
Malang	C2	13
Malanje	C3	70
Malanville	B2	64
Mälaren, *lake*	C3	53
Malatya	D2	27
Malawi		68
Malay, *peninsula*	A1	13
Malaysia		13
Malbaie, *river*	F4	103
Malbun	B2	33
Malcolm, *atoll*	A1	19
Malden, *island*	D2	17
Maldives		19
Male Karpaty, *mts.*	A2	42
Male, *atoll*	A2	19
Male, *capital*	A2	19
Maleb	E6	94
Malegaon	B4	20
Mali		58
Mali Rajinac, *mt.*	B3	48
Malindi	F5	61
Maliag	B1	30
Mallow	B2	31
Malmberget	D1	53
Malmédy	E2	33
Malmö	B3	53
Maloelap, *island*	C2	16
Malombe, *lake*	C2	68
Maloti, *mts.*	B2	71
Malta		36
Maltahöhe	B3	70
Malton	J5	102
Mamâri	C2	62
Mamawi, *lake*	E2	94
Mambéré, *river*	A2	66
Mamburao	B3	12
Mamiña	C2	76
Mamoré, *river*	A2	77
Mamou	B2	62
Mamry, *lake*	E1	41
Mamtalah, al-	B2	25
Mamuno	A2	69
Man	C3	63
Mana	B1	80
Mana, *river*	B1	80
Manado	D1	13
Managua, *capital*	A2	87
Managua, *lake*	A2	87
Manakara	B3	69
Manama, *capital*	B1	25
Manatí	B2	90
Manaus	C2	81
Manawan, *lake*	G5	104
Manbij	A1	27
Manchester	C3	30
Manchester, N.H.	F1	126
Manchurian, *plain*	F1	10
Mand, *river*	C4	22
Mandalay	C2	12
Mandalgov	C2	11
Mandara, *mts.*	B1	65
Mandaue	B4	12
Mandeville	B2	88
Mándra	Inset	51
Mandurah, W.A.	A3	14
Manfredonia	C2	38
Manga, *region*	C2	59
Mangalore	B6	20
Mango	B1	64
Mangoky, *river*	A3	69
Manicouagan, *reservoir*	C3	101
Manicougan Deux, *reservoir*	H2	103
Manigotagan	C3	96
Manila, *bay*	B3	12
Manila, *capital*	B3	12
Manisa	A2	27
Manito, *lake*	A8	104
Manitoba, *lake*	B3, B4, D2	96
Manitou	B4	96
Manitoulin, *island*	C2	102
Manitouwadge	C3	101
Manitowaning	D2	102
Maniwaki	A5	103
Manizales	B3	78
Mankato, Minn.	D1	126
Mankayane	B2	71
Mankota	C11	104
Mankulam	B2	19
Mannar	A3	19
Mannar, *gulf*	C7	20
Mannar, *island*	C7	20
Mannheim	B4	40
Manning	B3	94
Mannville	E4	94
Mano, *river*	A2, B2	63
Manokwari	E2	13
Manono	B2	67
Manono, *island*	B2	18
Manor Park	H5	102
Manori, *point*	Inset I	20
Manouane	B4	103
Manpb	B2	9
Mansa	B2	67
Mansa Konko	C2	62
Mansel, *island*	M4	99
Manson Creek	K3	95
Mansurah, al-	B1	56
Manta	A3	79
Manta, *bay*	A3	79
Mantiqueira, *range*	D4	81
Manyara, *lake*	C1	61
Manzanillo	D3	88
Manzanillo	D4	84
Manzini	B2	71
Mao	A1	89
Mao	A4	59
Maple		Inset I
Maple Creek	A11	104
Maputo, *capital*	B5	68
Maquela do Zombo	C3	70
Mar Chiquita, *lake*	C3	74
Mar del Plata	D4	74
Mar, *range*	D4	81
Mara, *river*	C4	61
Maraba	D2	81
Maracaibo	B1	79
Maracaibo, *lake*	B2	79
Maracay	C1	79
Maradi	B3	59
Marajó, *island*	D2	81
Marakei, *island*	A1	17
Maramasike, *island*	B1	16
Maranhão	D2	81
Marañón, *river*	B1, B2	77
Maras	D3	27
Marathon	C3	101
Marbella	D4	37
Marburg	B3	40
Marcelin	D8	104
Marche	C2	38
Marchena, *island*	Inset	79
Mardan	D2	21
Mardin	E3	27
Maré, *island*	D2	18
Maremma, *region*	B2	38
Margaree Forks	F1	100
Margaret, *lake*	C2	94
Margarita, *island*	D1	79
Margate	D3	30
Margherita, *peak*	A3	61
Maria	L3	103
Maria, *islands*	B3	91
Mariana	D3	81
Marianao	B1	88
Marías, *islands*	C3	84
Marib	B1	25
Marie Byrd Land, *region*	B8	107
Marie-Reine	B3	94
Mariehamn (Maarianhamina)	A2	53
Mariental	C3	70
Marigot	B2	90
Marijampolé	B2	46
Marinduque, *island*	B3	12
Marino	G2	100
Marion Bridge	G2	100
Maripasoula	A2	80
Mariscal Estigarribia	B3	75
Maritime Alps, *range*	D4	34
Maritsa, *river*	D3	50
Mariupol	D3	47
Mariy El, *republic*	D4	44
Marj Uyun	A2	26
Marj, al-	D1	56
Marka	B3	60
Markham	F4, K5	102
Markham, *river*	A2	15
Markstay	E1	102
Marl	A3	40
Marmara, *sea*	B2	27
Marmora	H3	102
Marne, *river*	C2, Inset II	34
Marneuli	A4	45
Maromokotro, *mt.*	B1	69
Marondera	A2	71
Maroni, *river*	A1	80
Maros	D2	13
Maroua	B1	65
Marovoay	B2	69
Marowijne, *river*	B2	80
Marquette, Mich.	E1	126
Marquis	B2	91
Marrakech	B2	57
Marsa al-Burayqah	C1	56
Marsabit	E2	61
Marsala	C3	38
Marsaxlokk, *bay*	C3	36
Marsden	A8	104
Marseille	D5	34
Marsh Harbour	B2	89
Marsoui	L2	103
Martaban, *gulf*	C3	12
Marten River	F1	102
Martensville	D8	104
Martin	B2	42
Martinique, *island*		82
Martins River	C3	100
Martorell	D2	90
Martuni	C2	45
Mary, *river*	D3	98
Mary's Harbour	D3	98
Maryborough, Qld.	E2	14
Maryfield	A4	96
Maryfield	J11	104
Maryland	F2	126
Marystown	D5	98
Masada, *ruins*	B2	26
Masai, *steppe*	C1	68
Masaka	B4	61
Masan	C5	9
Masaya	A3	87
Masbate	B3	12
Masbate, *island*	B3	12
Mascouche	C6	103
Maseru, *capital*	A2	71
Masfut	D2	25
Mashhad	D2	22
Masindi	B3	61
Masirah, *gulf*	C2	25
Masirah, *island*	C2	25
Mask, *lake*	B2	31
Maskall	B2	85
Masqat, *capital*	C1	25
Massachusetts	F1	126
Massacre	B3	90
Massawa	B2	60
Massenya	B5	59
Masset	F4	95
Massey	C1	102
Massif Central, *plateau*	C4	34
Massif des Bongos, *range*	B2	66
Massy	Inset II	34
Masuda	A3	8
Masvingo	B2	69
Mat, *river*	B2	49
Matadi	A2	67
Matagalpa	B2	87
Matagami	A4	101
Matale	B4	19
Matam	C2	62
Matamoros	E2	84
Matane	J3	103
Matanzas	B1	88
Matapédia	C1	97
Matapédia	K4	103
Matara	B6	19
Mataram	C2	13
Mataró	H2	37
Matautu	C2	18
Matawa Place	D3	96
Matehuala	D3	84
Matelot	A2	91
Matera	D2	38
Mathura	C3	20
Matlock	C3	30
Mato Grosso	C3	81
Mato Grosso do Sul	C4	81
Mato Grosso, *plateau*	C3	81
Mátra, *mts.*	C1	42
Matrah	C1	25
Matruh	A1	56
Matsoku, *river*	B2	71
Matsudo	C3	8
Matsue	B3	8
Matsumae	D1, Inset I	8
Matsumoto	C2	8
Matsuyama	B3	8
Mattawa	G1	102
Mattawin, *river*	C5	103
Matterhorn, *mt.*	B3	35
Matthew Town	C4	89
Matthews Ridge	A2	80
Mauá	Inset II	81
Maui, *island*, Hawaii	Inset II	126
Maule, *river*	B5	76
Maumturk, *mts.*	B2	31
Maun	A1	69
Mauna Loa, *mt.*, Hawaii	Inset II	126
Maunabo	D2	90
Mauren	B1	33
Maurepas	Inset II	34
Mauritania		58
Mauritius		69
Mavinga	D5	70
May Pen	B3	88
Maya, *mts.*	A3	85
Maya	A3	8
Mayaguana, *island*	C4	89
Mayaguana, *passage*	C4	89
Mayagüez	A2	90
Maydi	A1	25
Mayfair	C7	104
Maymont	C8	104
Maymyo	C2	12
Maynooth	C2	31
Maynooth	H2	102
Mayo	B4	105
Mayo, *islands*	C4	105
Mayombé, *massif*	B5	66
Mayon, *volcano*	B3	12
Mayotte, *island*	C2	67
Mayreau, *island*	A4	91
Mayumba	A2	66
Mazabuka	B3	74
Mazandaran, *region*	C2	22
Mazar-e Sharif	B1	22
Mazaruni, *river*	A2	80
Mazatenango	B5	84
Mazatlán	C3	84
Mažeikiai	B1	46
Mazoe, *river*	B1	69
Mazyr	D3	47
Mbabane, *capital*	B2	71
Mbahiakro	D3	63
Mbaké	A2	62
Mbala	C1	67
Mbalmayo	B3	65
Mbandaka	A2	67
Mbanza Congo	B2	70
Mbanza-Ngungu	A3	67
Mbarara	B4	61
Mbemkuru, *river*	C3	61
M'Beni	A1	67
Mbéré, *river*	B2	66
Mbeya	B2	68
Mbini	B2	66
Mbini, *river*	C3	66
Mboro	D4	66
Mboune, *river*	B2	62
Mbour	A2	62
Mbuji-Mayi	B2	67
Mbuluzane, *river*	B2	71
Mbuluzi, *river*	B2	71
McAdam	B3	97
McAllen, Tex.	D3	126
McBride	M4	95
McCallum	C5	98
McCreary	B4	96
McDame	H1	95
McGee	B9	104
McKinley *mt.*, Alaska	Inset I	126
McLeese Lake	L5	95
McLeod Lake	M4	95
McLeod Valley	C4	94
M'Clintock, *channel*	D2	99
M'Clure, *strait*	D2	99
McLure	M5	95
McMurdo, *sound*	B5	107
McRae	E4	94
Mealy, *mts.*	A3	98
Meander River	B1	94
Mecca	A2	24
Mechelen	C1	33
Mecklenburg, *bay*	B1	40
Mecklenburg-Western Pomerania	C2	40
Mecsek, *mts.*	B2	42
Medan	A1	13
Medellín	B3	78
Medford, Oreg.	A1	126
Medgidia	E3	43
Media,s	C2	43
Medicine Hat	E6	94
Medika	D4	96
Medina	A1	24
Medina del Campo	D2	37
Medit	B2	13
Mediterranean, *sea*		29
Medley	E4	94
Medora	A4	96
Meductic	B3	97
Meelpaeg, *lake*	C5	98
Meerut	C3	20
Meghna, *river*	D5	21
Meghri	D4	45
Meighen, *island*	J1	99
Meiktila	B2	12
Meissen	C3	40
Mejicanos	A2	86
Mékambo	B1	66
Mekele	C1	60
Mékinac, *lake*	D4	103
Meknès	C1	57
Mekong, *delta*	B2	11
Mekong, *river*	A1, A4, C4, D3	11
Mékrou, *river*	B2	64
Melaka	B2	13
Melbourne, Fla.	E3	126
Melbourne, Vic., *capital*	D3	14
Meldrum Bay	B2	102
Meleb	C4	96
Melekeok	C3	17
Mélèzes, *river*	B2	101
Melfi	B5	59
Melfort	F8	104
Melilla		Inset
Melipilla		Inset 76
Melita	A4	96
Melitopol	D3	47
Mellieha	B2	36
Mellieha, *bay*	B2	36
Melo	C2	75
Melrose	E2	100
Melun	Inset II	34
Melville	H10	104
Melville, *island*	C1	14
Melville, *island*	F1	99
Melville, *lake*	B2	98
Melville, *peninsula*	M3	99
Memmingen	B5	40
Memphis, Tenn.	D2	126
Memphrémagog, *lake*	D6	103
Menai, *strait*	B3	30
Ménaka	D2	58
Mende	C4	34
Mendoza	B3	74
Meneng	B3	16
Menihek	D3	98
Mennecy	Inset II	34
Menongue	C4	70
Mentawai, *islands*	A2	13
Menzel Bourguiba	B1	57
Meppel	D2	32
Mequinenza, *lake*	F2	37
Merano	B1	38
Merauke	F2	13
Mercedario, *mt*	B3	74
Mercedes	A2	75
Mergui	C3	12
Mergui, *archipelago*	C4	12
Mérida	B2	79
Mérida	C3	37
Mérida, *mts.*	B2	79
Mérida, *state capital*	G3	84
Meridian, Miss.	E2	126
Merigomish	E2	100
Merín, *lagoon*	D2	75
Merir, *island*	Inset	17
Merkys, *river*	C2	46
Meron, *mt.*	B1	26
Merredin, W.A.	A3	14
Merrick, *mt.*	B2	30
Merridale	A3	96
Merritt	M6	95
Mersch	B2	33
Mersey, *river*	C3	30
Mersin	C3	27
Merthyr Tydfil	B3	30
Meru	D3	61
Merume, *mts.*	A2	80
Mesaoria, *plain*	B1	27
Meseta, *plateau*	D3	37
Mesolóngion	B2	51
Mesopotamia, *region*	B2	24
Messina	D1	71
Messina	C3	38
Messina, *strait*	D3	38
Mesta, *river*	B4	50
Meta Incognita, *peninsula*	P4	99
Meta, *river*	C3	78
Métabetchouan	E3	103
Metcalfe	K2	102
Meteghan	A3	100
Métis-sur-Mer	J3	103
Metiskow	E5	94
Metz	D2	34
Meulan	Inset II	34
Meuse, *river*	D2	33
Mexicali, *state capital*	A1	84
Mexico		84
Mexico City, *national capital*	E4, Inset	84
Mexico, *gulf*		82
Meymaneh	A1	22
Meyungs	B3	17
Mgwavuma, *river*	B3	71
Mhlume	B2	71
Miami	B4	96

	Key	Page
Miami, Fla.	E3	126
Mianwali	D3	21
Miaoli	B1	9
Mica Creek	N5	95
Michalovce	C2	42
Miches	C2	89
Michigan	E1	126
Michigan, lake	E1	126
Michoacán	D4	84
Mico, river	B2	87
Micoud	B3	91
Micronesia		15
Midale	G11	104
Middelburg	C3	71
Middelburg	A3	32
Middle Andaman, island	F6	20
Middle Arm	C4	98
Middle Atlas, ranges	C1	57
Middle Lake	E8	104
Middle Musquodoboit	D2	100
Middlebro	D4	96
Middlesbrough	C2	30
Middleton	B3	100
Midi-Pyrénées	C5	34
Midland	F3	102
Midland, Tex.	C2	126
Midlands, region	C3	30
Miercurea Ciuc	C2	43
Mieres	D1	37
Mikkeli	C2	53
Mikkwa, river	C2	94
Mikomeseng	C2	66
Míkonos, island	C3	51
Mikura, island	C3	8
Miladummadulu, atoll	A1	19
Milagro	B4	79
Milan	B1	38
Milden	C9	104
Mildura, Vic.	D3	14
Miles City, Mont.	C1	126
Milestone	F10	104
Milford Haven	B3	30
Milford Sound	A3	15
Milh, lake	B2	24
Mili, island	C2	16
Milk, river	E6	94
Mill Bay	L7	95
Mill Village	C3	100
Miller Lake	D2	102
Millet	D4	94
Milliken	K5	102
Milltown	D5	98
Millville	B2	97
Milne, bay	B3	15
Milo	D6	94
Milo, river	D3	62
Mílos, island	C3	51
Milton	B2	100
Milton	F4	102
Milverton	E4	102
Milwaukee, Wis.	E1	126
Mimico	J6	102
Mimilegash	A2	100
Mina Baranis	C3	56
Mina Salman	B1	25
Minami, island	Inset III	8
Minas	C3	75
Minas Gerais	D3	81
Minas, channel	C2	100
Minatitlán	F4	84
Minch, strait	B1	30
Mindanao, island	C5	12
Mindelo	B2	58
Mindemoya	C2	102
Minden	G3	102
Mindoro, island	B3	12
Mindoro, strait	B3	12
Miner's Bay	G3	102
Miner, river	B3	105
Mingäçevir	B2	45
Mingäçevir, reservoir	B2	45
Minho, river	A1	36
Minicoy, island	B7	20
Minija, river	A2	46
Miniota	A4	96
Minitonas	A3	96
Mink Creek	A3	96
Minna	D3	65
Minneapolis, Minn.	D1	126
Minnedosa	B4	96
Minnesota	D1	126
Miño, river	C1	37
Minorca, island	H2	37
Minot, N. Dak.	C1	126
Minsk, capital	C3	47
Minto	B4	96
Minto	C2	97
Minto	B4	105
Minto, lake	B2	101
Minton	F11	104
Minya, al-	B2	56
Miquelon, island	M4	92
Mira	H1	100
Mirabel	B6	103
Mirador Nacional, mt.	C3	75
Miraflores	B4	78
Miragoâne	B2	89
Miramichi	D1	97
Miramichi, bay	E1	97
Miranda de Ebro	E1	37
Mirbat	B3	25
Miri	D2	13
Mirnyy	C7	44
Mirpur Khas	C5	21
Mirror	D5	94
Miscou, island	E1	97
Miscouche	B2	100
Misere	Inset	70
Misery, mt.	B1	90
Miskolc	C1	43
Misool, island	E2	13
Missinipe	F5	104
Mississauga	F4, J6	102
Mississippi	D2	126
Mississippi, lake	J2	103
Mississippi, river	D1	126
Missoula, Mont.	B1	126
Missouri	D2	126

	Key	Page
Missouri, river	D1	126
Mistassibi, river	D1	103
Mistassini	D3	103
Mistassini, lake	B3	101
Mistassini, river	D2	103
Mistatim	G8	104
Mistelbach	E2	39
Misurata	C1	56
Mitchell	D4	102
Mitchell, mt., N.C.	E2	126
Mitchell, river	D1	14
Mitchinamécus, lake	A4	103
Mitilíni	C2	51
Mito	D2	8
Mitsamiouli	A1	67
Mittelland, canal	B2	40
Mitú	C4	78
Mitumba, mts.	C2	67
Mitzic	A1	66
Miyake, island	C3	8
Miyako	D2	8
Miyako, island	Inset II	8
Miyakonojo	A4	8
Miyazaki	A4	8
Mizen Head, cape	B3	31
Mizo, hills	F4	20
Mizpe Ramon	B2	26
Mjøsa, lake	C3	52
Mkondvo, river	B2	71
Mliba	B2	71
Mmabatho	C2	71
Mo	C2	52
Moa	D2	13
Moa, river	B2	63
Moab, Utah	C2	126
Moala, island group	B3	17
Moanda	B2	66
Moba	C2	67
Mobaye	B2	66
Mobile, Ala.	E2	126
Moca	B1	89
Moca	A2	90
Moçambique	D2	68
Mocha, (Mukha, al-)	A2	25
Mocímboa da Praia	D1	68
Môco, mt.	C4	70
Mocoa	A4	78
Modena	B1	38
Moengo	B2	80
Moers	A3	40
Mogadishu, capital	B3	60
Mogami, river	C2	8
Mogi das Cruzes	Inset II	81
Mogilev Podolskiy	B2	47
Mogocha	D7	44
Mogotón, mt.	A2	87
Mohács	B2	43
Mohales Hoek	A3	71
Mohammedia	C1	57
Moher, cliffs	B2	31
Mojave, desert, Calif.	B2	126
Mojos	A2	77
Mokhotlong	C2	71
Mokolo	B1	65
Mokpo	B5	9
Mold	B3	30
Moldavia, region	D2	43
Molde	B3	52
Moldova		50
Moldoveanu, mt.	C3	43
Molepolole	B3	69
Molise	C2	38
Mollendo	C4	77
Molokai island, Hawaii	Inset II	126
Molopo, river	B2	71
Moloundou	C3	65
Molson, lake	C2	96
Molucca, sea	D2	13
Moluccas, islands	D2	13
Mombasa	E5	61
Mombetsu	Inset I	8
Mon Repos	B2	91
Møn, island	D4	32
Mona, passage	D2	89
Monaco		35
Monaco, capital	B1	35
Monaghan	C1	31
Monastery	F2	100
Monastir	C2	57
Mönchengladbach	A3	40
Monclova	D2	84
Moncton	E2	97
Mondego, cape	A2	36
Mondego, river	B2	36
Monforte	C1	37
Monfort	B4	59
Mongolia		11
Mongolian, plateau	C2	11
Mongomo	D3	66
Mongu	A3	67
Monitor	E5	94
Monjolo	Inset I	81
Monkey Bay	B2	68
Mono, river	A4, B2	64
Monopoli	D2	38
Monrovia, capital	A2	63
Mons	B2	33
Mont-Carmel	G4	103
Mont-Joli	H3	103
Mont-Laurier	A5	103
Mont-Royal	J5	103
Mont-Saint-Michel	B2	34
Mont-St-Pierre	L2	103
Mont-Tremblant-Village	B5	103
Montague	C2	100
Montalto, mt.	C3	38
Montana		38
Montana	B1	126
Montargis	C4	34
Montauban	C4	34
Monte Carlo	B1	35
Monte Cristi	A1	89
Monte Plata	C2	89
Montebello	B6	103
Montecristo, island	B2	38
Montegiardino	B2	38
Montego Bay	B2	88
Montélimar	D4	34
Montelindo, river	C3	75

	Key	Page
Montenegro, republic	A3	49
Montepulciano	B2	38
Monterey, Calif.	A2	126
Montería	B2	78
Montero	B3	77
Monterrey, state capital	D2	84
Montes Claros	D3	81
Montevideo, capital	B3	75
Montgomery, capital, Ala.	E2	126
Montluçon	C3	34
Montmagny	F5	103
Montmartre	G10	104
Montpelier, capital, Vt.	F1	126
Montpellier	C5	34
Montréal	C6, J5	103
Montréal, island	J5	103
Montreal, lake	E6	104
Montreuil	Inset II	34
Montreux	A2	35
Montrose	C2	30
Monywa	B2	12
Monza	B1	38
Moore Park	B4	96
Moose Factory	D2	101
Moose Jaw	E10	104
Moose Lake	A2	96
Moose, river	D2	101
Moosehorn	B3	96
Moosomin	J10	104
Moosonee	D2	101
Mopti	C3	58
Moquegua	C4	77
Moradabad	C3	20
Morant Bay	C3	88
Moratuwa	A5	19
Morava, river	A2, C3	42
Morava, river	B3	49
Moravia, region	C3	42
Moray, estuary	B1	30
Morden	B4	96
Mordoviya, republic	E4	44
Moree, N.S.W.	D2	14
Morehead	A2	15
Morelia, state capital	D4	84
Morell	C2	100
Morelos	E4	84
Morena, mts.	D3	37
Moresby, island	F5	95
Moreton, bay	Inset III	14
Morgan City, La.	D3	126
Morghab, river	A1	22
Morghob	B1	23
Morghob, river	B1	23
Morice, lake	J4	95
Moricetown	J3	95
Morija	A2	71
Morinville	D4	94
Morioka	D2	8
Morlaix	B2	34
Morne Diablotin, mt.	B2	90
Morocco		57
Morogoro	C2	68
Morombe	A3	69
Morón	D2	88
Morón	C2	11
Morón de la Frontera	D4	37
Morondava	A3	69
Moroni, national capital	A1	67
Morotai, island	D1	13
Moroto	D2	61
Morpeth	D5	102
Morphou	A1	27
Morris	D5	94
Morris	C4	96
Morrisburg	K3	102
Mors, island	B2	32
Morse	C10	104
Mortlach	D10	104
Mortlock, islands	C2	15
Moruga	A2	91
Moscow, capital	D3	44
Mosel, river	A4	40
Moselle, river	D2	34
Moshi	C1	68
Mosjøen	C2	52
Mosquitos, coast	C3	87
Moss	C4	52
Mossbank	E11	104
Mossel Bay	B3	71
Mossendjo	B5	66
Mossleigh	D6	94
Mossy, river	F6	104
Most	A2	42
Mostaganem	B1	57
Mostar	B2	48
Móstoles	Inset II	37
Mosul	B1	24
Motagua, river	D4	85
Motherwell	B2	30
Mouila	A2	66
Mould Bay	E1	99
Moule à Chique, cape	B3	91
Moulmein	C3	12
Moulouya, river	D1	57
Moundou	B5	59
Mount Carmel	A2	100
Mt. Forest	E4	102
Mount Gambier, S.A.	D3	14
Mount Hagen	A2	15
Mount Isa, Qld.	C2	14
Mt. Stewart	C2	100
Mountain Park	B5	94
Moura	B3	36
Mourne, mts.	A2	30
Mouscron	B2	33
Moussa Ali, mt.	B1	60
Mouths of the Danube, delta	E3	43
Mouths of the Ganges, delta	C7	21
Mouths of the Indus, delta	C5	21
Moyale	E2	61
Moyamba	A1	63
Moyie	P6	95
Moyobamba	B2	77

	Key	Page
Moyowosi, river	B1	68
Mozambique		68
Mozambique, channel		55
Mozzoro	E2	81
Mpanda	B2	68
Mpika	C2	67
Mpoko, river	A2	66
Mporokoso	C1	67
Mqinvartsveri, mt.	C3	45
M'Ramani	B2	67
Mtkvari, river	C4	45
Mtskheta	C4	45
Mtwara	D3	68
Muang Khammouan	C3	11
Muang Không	C4	11
Muang Khôngxédôn	C4	11
Muang Paklay	A2	11
Muang Pakxan	B2	11
Muang Vangviang	B2	11
Muang Xaignabouri	A2	11
Muang Xay	A1	11
Muang Xépôn	D3	11
Muang Xon	B1	11
Muar	B2	13
Muara	C1	13
Mubende	B3	61
Mubi	G2	65
Muchinga, mts.	C2	67
Mudanjiang	F1	10
Mudawwarah, al-	B3	26
Mufulira	B2	67
Muğla	B3	27
Muharraq, al-, island	B1	25
Mühlhausen	B3	40
Mui Bai Bung, point	A5	11
Mukalla, al-	B2	25
Muko, island	Inset III	8
Mulaku, atoll	A3	19
Mulde, river	C3	40
Mulhacén, mt.	E4	37
Mulhouse	D3	34
Mull, island	A2	30
Mullaittivu	B2	19
Mullingar	C2	31
Multan	D3	21
Mulund	Inset I	20
Mulvihill	B4	96
Mumbai	Inset I	20
Mumbwa	B3	67
Mun, river	C3	12
Muna, island	D2	13
Munamägi, mt.	D3	46
Muncho Lake	K2	95
Munich	B4	40
Munsan	B4	9
Münster	A3	40
Munster, province	B2	31
Muonio	B1	53
Muonioälven, river	D1	53
Muoniojoki, river	B1	53
Mur, river	D3	39
Mura, river	C2	48
Muramvya	B2	61
Murat, river	E2	27
Murchison, river	A2	14
Murcia	F4	37
Murdochville	L3	103
Mureș, river	B2	43
Murgab, river	D3	22
Muriel, lake	E4	94
Murilo, atoll	C2	15
Müritz, lake	C2	40
Murmansk	C3	44
Muroran	D1, Inset I	8
Muroto, cape	B3	8
Murray Harbour	C3	100
Murray River	C2	100
Murray, harbour	C2	100
Murray, lake	A2	15
Murray, river	D3	14
Murrumbidgee, river	D3	14
Murska Sobota	D2	48
Mürz, river	D3	39
Murzuq	B2	56
Muş	E2	27
Mûša, river	B1	46
Musala, mt.	B3	50
Musan	C1	9
Musgrave Harbour	E4	98
Musgrave, ranges	C2	14
Musgravetown	E5	98
Mushin	B4	65
Muskeg River	A4	94
Muskegon, Mich.	E1	126
Muskogee, Okla.	D2	126
Muskoka, lake	F2	102
Muskwa, ranges	J2	95
Musoma	B1	68
Musquodoboit Harbour	D3	100
Mussau, island	A2	15
Mustang	B2	19
Mustique, island	B3	91
Mustvee	D2	46
Musu-dan, point	C2	9
Mut	A2	56
Mutare	C2	69
Mutsamudu	B2	67
Mutsu	D1	8
Muyinga	C1	61
Muyun Kum, desert	D2	23
Muzaffarabad	D2	21
Muynoq	A2	23
Mwali (Mohéli), island	A2	67
Mwanza	B1	68
Mwene-Ditu	B2	67
Mweru, lake	B1, C3	67
Mwinilunga	A2	67
My Tho	B4	11
Myingyan	B2	12
Myitkyina	C1	12
Mykolaiv	C3	47
Mymensingh	D4	21
Myrnam	E4	94
Mysore	C6	20
Mzimba	B2	68
Mzuzu	B2	68

N

	Key	Page
N'dalatando	B3	70
N'Djamena, capital	A4	59
N'zeto	B2	70
Naas	C2	31
Nabatiyah at-Tahta, an-	A2	26
Naberezhnyye Chelny	D4	44
Nabeul	C1	57
Nabk, an-	A2	27
Nabouwalu	B2	17
Nacala	D2	68
Nacaome	B3	86
Nackawic	B3	97
Nadi	A2	17
Nadi, bay	A2	17
Nadur	B1	36
Naduri	B2	17
Næstved	C3	32
Nafud, an-, desert	B1	24
Nag Hammadi	B2	56
Naga	B3	12
Naga, hills	F3	20
Nagano	C2	8
Nagaoka	C2	8
Nagarote	A2	87
Nagasaki	A3	8
Nagorno-Karabakh, autonomous region	B2	45
Nagoya	C3	8
Nagpur	C4	20
Nagua	C1	89
Naguabo	D2	90
Nagykanizsa	A2	43
Naha	Inset II	8
Nahanni, river	C4	99
Nahariyya	B1	26
Naicam	F8	104
Naihati	Inset II	20
Nain	E3	98
Nairobi, capital	D4	61
Najaf, an-	B2	24
Najd, region	B1	24
Najin	D1	9
Najran	B2	24
Nakadori, island	A3	8
Nakano, island	A4	8
Nakfa	B1	60
Nakhichevan	A3	45
Nakhodka	E8	44
Nakhon Phanom	C3	12
Nakhon Ratchasima	C3	12
Nakhon Sawan	B3	12
Nakhon Si Thammarat	B4	12
Nakina	C2	101
Nakodu	B2	17
Nakskov	C4	32
Naktong, river	C5	9
Nakuru	D4	61
Nakusp	O6	95
Nal, river	A3	21
Nalikul	Inset II	20
Nam Dinh	B2	11
Nam Ngum, reservoir	B2	11
Nam Tok	B3	12
Namangan	D2	23
Namew, lake	H6	104
Namib, desert	A1, B3	70
Namibe	A2	70
Namibia		70
Namoluk, atoll	C2	15
Namonuito, atoll	C2	15
Nampô	A3	9
Nampa	B3	94
Nampula	C2	68
Namsos	C2	52
Namu, island	B2	16
Namuli, highlands	C2	68
Namur	C2	33
Namur, lake	B3	94
Namwala	B3	67
Nan	B2	12
Nan Ling, mts.	E3	10
Nan, river	B2	12
Nanaimo	L6	95
Nanchang	E3	10
Nanchong	D2	10
Nancy	D2	34
Nanda Devi, mt.	C2	20
Nanded	C4	20
Nanga Parbat, mt.	E2	21
Nanga-Eboko	B3	65
Nangi	Inset II	20
Nangnim-sanmaek, mts.	B3	9
Nanjing	E2	10
Nanning	D3	10
Nanole	Inset I	20
Nanterre	Inset II	34
Nantes	B3	34
Nanticoke	E5	102
Nanumanga, island	B2	16
Nanumea, island	B2	16
Nanyang	E2	10
Nao, cape	G3	37
Napadogan	C2	97
Napaktulik, lake	F3	99
Napanee	J3	102
Napier	C2	15
Naples	C2	38
Naples, bay	C2	38
Napo, river	C1	77
Nara	B3	8
Nara, canal	C4	21
Narathiwat	B5	12
Narayanganj	D5	21
Narayani, river	B2	19
Narbonne	C5	34
Narcisse	C4	96
Nares, strait	O1	99
Narew, river	E2	41
Narrogin, W.A.	A3	14
Narsaq	C2	106
Narva	E1	46
Narva, river	D1	46
Narvik	D2	52
Naryan-Mar	C4	44

	Key	Page
Naryn	E2	[...]
Naryn, river	E2	[...]
Nashshash, an-	C3	[...]
Nashville, capital, Tenn.	E2	[...]
Nashwaak Bridge	C2	[...]
Näsi, lake	B2	[...]
Nasik	B4	[...]
Nasiriyah, an-	C2	[...]
Nass, river	H3	[...]
Nassau, capital	B3	[...]
Nasser, lake	B3	[...]
Nata	E2	[...]
Natal	E2	[...]
Natalkuz, lake	K4	[...]
Natashquan	D3	[...]
Natitingou	A2	[...]
Natron, lake	C1	[...]
Naturna Besar, island	B1	[...]
Naucalpan de Juárez	Inset	[...]
Nauioji Akmene	B2	[...]
Naumburg	B3	[...]
Nauru		[...]
Navabad	A1	[...]
Navarino, island	C9	[...]
Navarra	F1	[...]
Navojoa	C2	[...]
Navua	A3	[...]
Navua, river	A3	[...]
Nawabshah	C3	[...]
Nawoiy	C2	[...]
Náxos, island	C3	[...]
Nayarit	B1	[...]
Nazareth	B1	[...]
Nazca	C3	[...]
Naze	Inset II	[...]
Nazko	L5	[...]
Nazret	C2	[...]
Nchelenge	B1	[...]
Ndélé	B2	[...]
Ndendé	A2	[...]
Ndjolé	A2	[...]
Ndola	B2	[...]
Néa Liósia	Inset	[...]
Neápolis	B3	[...]
Neath	B3	[...]
Nebitdag	A2	[...]
Neblina, mt.	B1	[...]
Nebraska	D1	[...]
Nechako, river	K4	[...]
Neckar, river	B4	[...]
Necochea	D4	[...]
Neder Rijn, river	B3	[...]
Nee Soon	B1	[...]
Needles	N6	[...]
Neepawa	A3	[...]
Nefta	C2	[...]
Negev, region	B2	[...]
Negombo	A4	[...]
Negra, lagoon	D2	[...]
Negra, point	A2	[...]
Negril	A2	[...]
Negro, river	B2	[...]
Negro, river	C2	[...]
Negro, river	B4	[...]
Negros, island	B4	[...]
Neguac	D1	[...]
Neiafu	B3	[...]
Neiba	A2	[...]
Neiba, mts.	B1	[...]
Neijiang	D2	[...]
Neil Harbour	G1	[...]
Neilburg	A8	[...]
Neisse, river	C3	[...]
Neiva	B4	[...]
Nekemte	C6	[...]
Nellore	B3	[...]
Nelson	O6	[...]
Nelson Forks	L1	[...]
Nelson House	B1	[...]
Nelson, river	C1, D1	[...]
Nelspruit	B2	[...]
Néma	D3	[...]
Nemeiben, lake	E5	[...]
Nemunas, river	A2, C2	[...]
Nemuro	Inset I	[...]
Nemuro, strait	Inset I	[...]
Nenagh	B2	[...]
Nenana	C2	[...]
Nenetsiya, autonomous okrug	C4	[...]
Nepal		[...]
Nepalganj	B2	[...]
Nepean	G6, K2	[...]
Nepisiguit, river	C1	[...]
Neretva, river	B2	[...]
Neris, river	C2	[...]
Ness, lake	B1	[...]
Nesselrode, mt.	E1	[...]
Nestaocano, river	C2	[...]
Netanya	B1	[...]
Netherlands		[...]
Nettilling, lake	O3	[...]
Netzahualcóyotl	Inset	[...]
Neubrandenburg	C2	[...]
Neuchâtel	A2	[...]
Neuchâtel, lake	A2	[...]
Neudorf	G10	[...]
Neufchâteau	D3	[...]
Neumünster	B1	[...]
Neunkirchen	A4	[...]
Neuquén	B4	[...]
Neuruppin	C2	[...]
Neusiedler, lake	A3	[...]
Neuss	A3	[...]
Neustrelitz	C2	[...]
Nevada	E2	[...]
Nevada, mts.	E4	[...]
Nevers	C3	[...]
Neves	B4	[...]
Nevis	Inset I	[...]
Nevėžis, river	B2	[...]
Nevinnomyssk	C3	[...]
New Amsterdam	C2	[...]
New Brigden	E5	[...]
New Britain, island	B2	[...]
New Caledonia, island	C3	[...]
New Carlisle	L4	10[...]

Name	Key	Page
Delhi, *capital*	C3	20
Denver	O6	95
England, *range*	E3	14
Ferolle	C4	98
Fish Creek	B3	94
Georgia Group, *islands*	A1	16
Glasgow	E2	100
Guinea, *island*	A2	15
Hamburg	E4	102
Hampshire	F1	126
Hanover, *island*	B2	15
Haven, Conn.	F1	126
Ireland, *island*	B2	15
Jersey	F1	126
Kowloon	Inset	10
Liskeard	E3	101
Mexico	C2	126
Minas	C2	100
Orleans, La.	D3	126
Plymouth	B2	15
Providence, *island*	B3	89
Richmond	C3	100
Ross	C3	100
Sandy Bay	B1	91
Schwabenland, ...gion	B16	107
Siberian, *islands*	B9	44
South Wales	D3	14
Territories, *island*	Inset	10
Waterford	G1	100
Waterway, *channel*	B3	32
York	F1	126
York, N.Y.	F1	126
Zealand		15
...river	C4	80
...er	B1	85
...boro	J3	102
ark, N.J.	F1	126
castle	C2	90
castle	C2	71
castle upon Tyne	C2	30
castle, N.S.W.	E3	14
castle-under-Lyme	C3	30
dale	A4	96
ell, *lake*	E6	94
rman, W.A.	A2	14
market	D3	30
market	F3	102
port	C3	30
port News, Va.	F2	126
quay	B4	30
town St. Boswells	C2	30
agawa	B3	8
habur	D2	22
mi, *lake*	A2	69
oundéré	B2	65
ramasch	B4	17
rkeel	B3	17
melis, *islands*	B3	17
rmechau	C2	17
tbong	C2	17
o, *river*	D3	61
Linh, *mt.*	B3	11
nini	B1	71
rongoro, *crater*	C1	68
unié, *river*	A2	66
zi	B1	61
igmi	C3	59
lu, *atoll*	A2	15
ru	F1	65
vempisi, *river*	A2	71
Trang	B4	11
ngano	B3	71
ara Falls	F4	102
ara-on-the-Lake	F4	102
assola	D1	62
ney, *capital*	A3	59
ntougou	B2	64
re	B5	66
, *island*	A1	13
bo	B2	16
aragua		87
aragua, *lake*	B3	87
ue	D5	34
olls' Town	A2	89
erie, *river*	A2	80
bar, *islands*	F7	20
la	M6	95
olet	D5	103
osia, *capital*	B1	27
oya, *gulf*	B3	86
e, *mts.*	B3	48
dere Tauern, *range*	D3	39
ang	C3	66
burg	B2	40
ri Ko, *river*	C2	62
uw Amsterdam	B2	80
uw Nickerie	A2	80
adoo	D1	97
de	C3	27
er		59
er, *delta*	C5	65
er	B3	58
eria		65
island	C2	8
ata	A2	8
ama	B3	8
au, *island*, Hawaii	Inset II	126
negen	C3	32
	Inset	51
ki	B3	64
co	B3	8
olyevsk-na-Amure	D9	44
sk	A3	49
unau, *lake*	A3	17
ndu, *atoll*	A3	19
giri, *hills*	C6	20
opolis	Inset I	34
ana, *mt.*	B3	63
nes	D5	34
Mile River	D2	100
es	A4	96

Name	Key	Page
Ninga	B4	96
Ningbo	F3	10
Ningxia Hui	D2	10
Ninigo, *group*	A2	15
Niono	B3	58
Nioro du Rip	B3	62
Nioro du Sahel	B2	58
Niort	B3	34
Nipawin	F7	104
Nipigon	C3	101
Nipigon, *lake*	C3	101
Nipissing	F1	102
Nipissing, *lake*	F1	102
Niš	B3	49
Nisåva, *river*	C3	49
Nishino, *island*	Inset III	8
Nishinomiya	B3	8
Nisling, *river*	B4	105
Niterói	D4, Inset I	81
Nitra	B2	42
Niuafo'ou, *island*	B1	17
Niuatoputapu, *island*	C1	17
Niulakita, *island*	C4	16
Niutao, *island*	B2	16
Niverville	C4	96
Nizamabad	C5	20
Nizhnevartosk	C5	44
Nizhny Novgorod	D4	44
Nizhny Tagil	D4	44
Njazidja (Grande Comore), *island*	A1	67
Njombe, *river*	B3	68
Nkawkaw	B3	64
Nkhata Bay	B2	68
Nkhotakota	B2	68
Nkongsamba	A2	65
Noakhali	E6	21
Nobeoka	A3	8
Noel	D2	100
Nogales	B1	84
Nogales, Ariz.	B2	126
Nojima, *cape*	D3	8
Nok Kundi	B4	21
Nokaneng	A1	69
Nokomis	E9	104
Nola	J4	99
Nome, Alaska	Inset I	126
Nonacho, *lake*	G4	99
Nong Khai	C2	12
Nonsan	B4	9
Nonthaburi	B3	12
Nootka, *island*	J6	95
Norak	A1	23
Nord-Ostsee, *canal*	B1	40
Nord-Pas-de-Calais	C1	34
Nordenham	B2	40
Nordhausen	B3	40
Nordhorn	A2	40
Nordvik	B7	44
Norfolk	D5	94
Norfolk, Va.	F2	126
Norilsk	C6	44
Norland	G3	102
Normandin	D3	103
Norquay	H9	104
Norra Storfjället, *mt.*	C1	53
Norris Arm	D4	98
Norris Point	C4	98
Norrköping	C3	53
Norte, *key*	E2	90
N. Albanian Alps, *mts.*	A1, B3	49
North Andaman, *island*	F6	20
North Battleford	B8	104
North Bay	F1	102
North Cape	B1	100
North Carolina	F2	126
North China, *plain*	E2	10
North Comino, *channel*	B1	36
North Dakota	C1	126
North Downs, *hills*	C3	30
North Frisian, *islands*	B4	32
North Holland	B2	32
North Korea		9
North Magnetic Pole	B13	106
North Malosmadulu, *atoll*	A2	19
N. Moose, *lake*	B2	96
North Ossetiya, *republic*	E4	44
North Platte, Nebr.	C1	126
North Portal	H11	104
North Rhine-Westphalia	A3	40
North Rustico	B2	100
North Saskatchewan, *river*	D8	104
North Sea, *canal*	B2	32
North Shields	C2	30
North Siberian, *lowland*	B6	44
North Star	B3	94
North Taranaki, *bight*	B2	15
N. Thompson, *river*	N5	95
North Uist, *island*	A1	30
North Wabasca, *lake*	D3	94
North West River	A2	98
North West, *cape*	A2	14
North York	K5	102
North, *cape*	F1	52
North, *channel*	A2	30
North, *channel*	B1	102
North, *island*	B2	15
North, *river*	B2	98
North, *sea*		29
Northallerton	C2	30
Northampton	C3	30
Northeast, *polder*	C2	32
Northeim	B3	40
Northern Divina, *river*	C4	44
Northern European, *plain*	B2	40
Northern Sporades, *islands*	B2	49
Northern Territory	C2	14
Northgate	H11	104
Northumberland, *strait*	B3, D2	100
Northwest Gander, *river*	D5	98
Norton	D3	97
Northwest, *cape*	B14	107
Norway		52
Norway House	C2	96
Norwegian, *bay*	K1	99
Norwegian, *sea*	A2	52
Norwich	D3	30
Norwich	E4	102
Nossob, *river*	C3	70

Name	Key	Page
Nosy Be, *island*	B1	69
Nosy Sainte Marie, *island*	B2	69
Noteć, *river*	C2, D2	41
Noto, *peninsula*	C2	8
Notre Dame de Lourdes	B4	96
Notre Dame Junction	D4	98
Notre Dame, *bay*	D4	98
Notre-Dame	E2	97
Notre-Dame-de-la-Merci	B5	103
Notre-Dame-de-la-Salette	A6	103
Notre-Dame-de-Lorette	D2	103
Notre-Dame-du-Bon-Conseil	D5	103
Notre-Dame-du-Lac	H4	103
Notre-Dame-du-Laus	A5	103
Nottingham	C3	30
Nottingham, *island*	N4	99
Nouadhibou	A2	58
Nouakchott, *capital*	A3	58
Nouméa, *capital*	C2	18
Nouvelle	K3	103
Nova Gorica	A3	48
Nova Iguaçu	Inset I	81
Novara	B1	38
Novaya Zemlya, *islands*	B4	44
Nové Zamky	B3	42
Novgorod	D3	44
Novi Pazar	B3	49
Novi Sad	A2	49
Novo Mesto	C3	48
Novokuznetsk	D6	44
Novosibirsk	D6	44
Novra	A3	96
Nowshak, *mt.*	D2	21
Nowy Sącz	E4	41
Nsanje	C3	68
Nsawam	B4	64
Nsok	D3	66
Nsoko	B3	71
Nsukka	D4	65
Ntem, *river*	B3	65
Nu'ulua, *island*	D3	18
Nu'utele, *island*	D3	18
Nuba, *mts.*	C3	59
Nubian, *desert*	C1	59
Nueltin, *lake*	J4	99
Nueva Casas Grandes	C1	84
Nueva Gerona	B2	88
Nueva Loja	C2	79
Nueva Ocotepeque	A2	86
Nueva Palmira	A2	75
Nueva Rosita	D2	84
Nueva San Salvador	A2	86
Nuevitas	D2	88
Nuevo Laredo	E2	84
Nuevo León	D2	84
Nuevo Rocafuerte	D3	79
Nuguria, *islands*	B2	15
Nuhud, an-	B2	59
Nui, *island*	B2	16
Nuku'alofa, *capital*	B4	17
Nukufetau, *island*	C2	16
Nukulaelae, *island*	C3	16
Nukuoro, *atoll*	C2	15
Nukus	A2	23
Nullarbor, *plain*	B3	14
Numazu	C3	8
Ñuñoa	Inset	76
Nuoro	B2	38
Nuremberg	B4	40
Nutak	E3	98
Nuuk (Godthåb), *capital*	B2	106
Nuuuli	B1	18
Nuwara Eliya	C3	19
Nyaake	C3	63
Nyaba, *river*	B2	61
Nyala	B3	59
Nyanga, *river*	A2	66
Nyanza	B2	61
Nyasa (Malawi), *lake*	B2, B3	68
Nyborg	C3	32
Nyeri	D4	61
Nyetane, *river*	B2	71
Nyíka, *plateau*	B2	68
Nyíregyháza	C2	43
Nykøbing	C4	32
Nyoman, *river*	B3	47
Nyong, *river*	B3	65
Nysa	C3	41
Nzérékoré	D4	62
Nzi, *river*	D3	63
Nzo, *river*	C3	63
Nzoia, *river*	C3	61
Nzwani (Anjouan), *island*	B2	67

O

Name	Key	Page
O'Leary	A2	100
Oahu, *island*, Hawaii	Inset II	126
Oak Lake	A4	96
Oak Point	C4	96
Oak Point	C3	97
Oak River	A4	96
Oakland, Calif.	A2	126
Oakner	A4	96
Oakview	B3	96
Oakville	C4	96
Oakville	F4	102
Oamaru	B4	15
Oaxaca, *state capital*	E4	84
Ob, *river*	C5	44
Oban	B2	30
Obed	B4	94
Oberammergau	B5	40
Oberhausen	A3	40
Oberpfälzer Wald, *mts.*	C4	40
Obi, *island*	D2	13
Obihiro	Inset I	8
Obo	C2	66
Obock	C2	60
Obuasi	B3	64
Occidental, *mts.*	B2, C4	77
Ocean Falls	J5	95
Ochamchire	A3	45
Ochil, *hills*	B2	30
Ocho Rios	B3	88
Ochre River	B3	96
Ocoa, *bay*	B2	89
Ocotal	A2	87

Name	Key	Page
Ocotlán	D3	84
Oda	B4	64
Odei, *river*	C1	96
Odemira	A4	36
Odense	C3	32
Odense, *bay*	C3	32
Odenwald, *forest*	B4	40
Oder, *river*	B2, C3	41
Oderhaff, *lake*	C3	47
Odesa	C3	47
Odessa, Tex.	C2	126
Odienné	C2	63
Oeiras	A3	36
Oelemari, *river*	B3	80
Oelsnitz	C3	65
Offa	B3	65
Offenbach	B3	40
Ofu, *island*	A1	18
Ogaden, *region*	D3	60
Ogbomosho	A2	65
Ogden, Utah	B1	126
Ogema	F11	104
Ogilvie, *mts.*	B3	105
Oglio, *river*	C2	38
Ogoki, *river*	C2	101
Ogoué, *river*	A2	66
Ogosta, *river*	B2	50
Ogražden, *mts.*	C2	48
Ogre	C2	46
Ogun, *river*	B3	65
Ohio	E1	126
Ohio, *river*	E2	126
Ohonua	C4	17
Ohrid	A2	48
Ohrid, *lake*	B2	49
Øibenik	B3	48
Oise, *river*	C2, Inset II	34
Oistins	B5	91
Oita	A3	8
Ojinaga	D2	84
Ojos del Salado, *mt.*	B2	74
Oka, *river*	D4	44
Okahandja	B2	70
Okakarara	B2	70
Okanagan Falls	N6	95
Okanagan, *lake*	N6	95
Okara	D3	21
Okavango, *basin*	A1	69
Okavango, *river*	A1	69
Okayama	B3	8
Okazaki	C3	8
Okeechobee, *lake*, Fla.	E3	126
Okene	D4	65
Okha	D9	44
Okhotsk	D9	44
Okhotsk, *sea*	D9	44
Oki, *islands*	B2	8
Okinawa, *island*	Inset II	8
Okino Erabu, *island*	Inset II	8
Oklahoma City, *capital*, Okla.	D2	126
Okondja	B2	66
Okotoks	C6	94
Okushiri, *island*	C1, Inset I	8
Okwa, *river*	A2	69
Ólafsvík	A2	52
Olanchito	B2	86
Öland, *island*	C3	53
Olavarría	C4	74
Olbia	B2	38
Old Brahmaputra, *river*	C4	21
Old Crow	E5	105
Old Perlican	E5	98
Old Road	D5	90
Old Road Town	B2	90
Old Wives, *lake*	D10	104
Oldenburg	B2	40
Oldham	C3	30
Oldman, *river*	D6	94
Olds	C5	94
Olenek, *river*	C4	44
Oléron, *island*	B4	34
Olgivie, *river*	B3	105
Ólgiy	A2	11
Olifants, *river*	A3, C1	71
Olinda	E2	81
Oliver	N6	95
Ollagüe, *volcano*	C2	76
Ollei	C2	17
Olmaliq	C2	23
Olomouc	C3	42
Olongapo	B3	12
Olosega, *island*	A1	18
Olsztyn	E2	41
Olt, *river*	C3	43
Oltenița	D3	43
Olympia, *capital*, Wash.	A1	126
Olympus mt., Wash.	A1	126
Olympus, *mt.*	A2	27
Olympus, *mt.*	B1	51
Omagh	A2	30
Omaha, *beach*	B2	34
Omaha, Nebr.	D1	126
Oman		25
Oman, *gulf*	C1, D2	25
Omaruru	B2	70
Omatako, *river*	C1	70
Omboué	A2	66
Omdurman	C2	59
Omemee	G3	102
Ometepe, *island*	B3	87
Omineca, *mts.*	J2	95
Omineca, *river*	K3	95
Omiya	C3	8
Omo, *river*	B3	60
Omsk	D5	44
Omuta	A3	8
Onalone	B4	96
Ondame	B2	66
Ondangwa	B1	70
Ondava, *river*	C2	42
Ondjiva	C2	66
Ondo	C4	65
Öndörhaan	D2	11
Onega, *river*	C1	53
Oneşti	D2	43
Ongjin	A4	9
Ongole	C5	20

Name	Key	Page
Onilahy, *river*	A3	69
Onion Lake	A7	104
Onitsha	D4	65
Ono, *island*	B3	17
Onon, *river*	D2	11
Onota, *island*	A2	17
Onsŏng	C1	9
Ontario	K4	92
Ontong Java, *island*	A1	16
Oostende	A1	33
Oostende-Brugge, *canal*	B1	33
Oosterschelde, *channel*	A3	32
Ootsa, *lake*	J4	95
Opava	C3	41
Opeongo, *lake*	G2	102
Opole	C3	41
Oporto (Porto)	A2	36
Opuwo	A1	70
Oqsu, *river*	C2	23
Oradea	A2	43
Oral	B1	23
Oran	A1	57
Orange Walk	B1	85
Orange, N.S.W.	D3	14
Orange, *river*	A3, B2	71
Orangeville	E4	102
Oranje, *mts.*	B3	80
Oranjemund	B4	70
Orapa	B2	69
Ordino	B2	36
Ordu	D2	27
Örebro	C3	53
Oregon	A1	126
Orellana, *lake*	D3	37
Orenburg	D4	44
Orense	C1	37
Øresund, *sound*	D3	32
Órganos, *mts.*	A2	88
Orhei	B2	50
Orhon, *river*	C2	11
Oriental, *mts.*	B2, C3	77
Oriental, *range*	C2	89
Orillia	F3	102
Orinoco, *river*	C3, D2	79
Orion	E6	94
Oristano	B3	38
Orizaba	E4	84
Orkney, *islands*	Inset I	30
Orlando, Fla.	E3	126
Orléans	C3	34
Orléans, *island*	F5, L5	103
Ormoc	C4	12
Orme, *river*	B2	34
Örnsköldsvik	C2	53
Orocué	C3	78
Oroluk, *atoll*	C2	15
Oromocto	C3	97
Oron	E5	65
Orontes, *river*	A2	27
Oroshaza	C3	43
Orrefors	C3	53
Orsha	C2	47
Orsk	D4	44
Ortegal, *cape*	C1	37
Orumiyeh (Urmia)	A2	22
Oruro	A3	77
Oryakhovo	B2	50
Os, *river*	A3	36
Osaka	B3	8
Osasco	Inset II	81
Osh	C2	23
Oshakati	B1	70
Oshawa	G4	102
Oshogbo	C4	65
Osijek	D2	48
Oslo, *capital*	C3	52
Oslofjord, *fjord*	C4	52
Osnabrück	B2	40
Osorno	B7	76
Osoyoos	N6	95
Oss	C3	32
Osse, *river*	C4	65
Osterdalälven, *river*	B2	53
Östersund	B2	53
Ostrava	D3	42
Ostrołęka	E2	41
Osumi, *islands*	A4	8
Osumi, *peninsula*	A4	8
Osumi, *strait*	A4	8
Osŭm, *river*	C3	50
Otaru	Inset I	8
Otavalo	B2	79
Otavi	B2	70
Oti, *river*	B1, C2	64
Otjiwarongo	B2	70
Otranto	D2	38
Otranto, *strait*	A3	49
Otsu	B3	8
Ottawa	H5, K2	102
Ottawa, *river*	G1, G5 H5, K2	102
Otterlo	C2	32
Ötztal Alps, *range*	B4	39
Ou, *mts.*	B2	8
Ou, *river*	B1	11
Ouadane	C2	58
Ouagadougou, *capital*	D2	64
Ouahigouya	D2	64
Ouaka, *river*	B2	66
Ouanary	C1	80
Ouarra, *river*	C2	66
Ouarzazate	B2	57
Oudtshoorn	B3	71
Ouémé, *river*	B3	64
Ouesso	D3	66
Ouezzane	C1	57
Ouham, *river*	A2	66
Ouidah	B4	64
Oujda	D1	57
Oulu	C1	53
Oulu, *lake*	C2	53
Oulujoki, *river*	C2	53
Oum er-Rbia, *river*	C1	57

Name	Key	Page
Ounasjoki, *river*	B1	53
Oungre	G11	104
Our, *river*	B1	33
Ourthe, *river*	C2	33
Ouse, *river*	C2, D3	30
Outarde, *river*	H2	103
Outer Hebrides, *islands*	A1	30
Outjo	B2	70
Outlook	C9	104
Ouvéa, *island*	C2	18
Ovalau, *island*	B2	17
Ovalle	B4	76
Overflakkee, *island*	B3	32
Overflowing River	A2	96
Oviedo	A3	89
Oviedo	D1	37
Owando	C4	66
Owen Sound	E3	102
Owen Stanley, *range*	A2	15
Owendo	A1	66
Owensboro, Ky.	E2	126
Owerri	D5	65
Oxbow	H11	104
Oxford	C3	30
Oxford	D2	100
Oxford House	D1, D2	96
Oxford, *lake*	D2	96
Oyapock, *river*	B2	80
Oyem	A1	66
Oyo	B4	65
Ozama, *river*	B2	89
Ozark, *plateau*	D2	126
Özd	C1	43
Özgön	C2	23
Ozoir-la-Ferrière	Inset II	34
Ozurgeti	A4	45

P

Name	Key	Page
Pa-an	C3	12
Paamiut (Frederikshåb)	C2	106
Pabna	C4	21
Pacaraima, *mts.*	D3	79
Pacasmayo	B2	77
Pachuca, *state capital*	E3	84
Padang	B2	13
Paddle Prairie	B2	94
Paderborn	B3	40
Padma, *river*	D5	21
Padua (Padova)	B1	38
Paektu-san, *mt.*	C2	9
Pagadian	B5	12
Pago Pago, *capital*	B1	18
Pahang, *river*	B2	13
Paiania	Inset	51
Päijänne, *lake*	C2	53
Paint, *lake*	B1	96
Paisley	B2	30
Paita	A2	77
Pakaraima, *mts.*	A3	80
Pakistan		21
Pakowki, *lake*	E6	94
Paks	B2	43
Pakse	C4	11
Pala	A5	59
Palaiseau	Inset II	34
Palana	D10	44
Palanga	A2	46
Palangkaraya	C2	13
Palau		17
Palawan, *island*	A4	12
Paldiski	C1	46
Pale	B2	48
Palembang	B2	13
Palencia	D1	37
Palermo	C3	38
Palermo	C2	15
Palikir, *capital*	C7	20
Palk, *strait*	K3	95
Palliser, *cape*	C3	15
Palm, *island*	A4	91
Palma	H3	37
Palmas	D3	81
Palmer Land, *region*	B11	107
Palmerston	E4	102
Palmerston North	C3	15
Palmira	A4	78
Palmyra, *ruins*	B2	27
Palos, *cape*	F4	37
Palu	C2	13
Pamirs, *mts.*	B2	23
Pamirs, *region*	A2	10
Pampas, *plain*	C4	74
Pamplemousses	C2	69
Pamplona	F1	37
Panaguyrishte	C3	50
Panaji	B5	20
Panama		87
Panama, *canal*	C2	87
Panamá, *capital*	C2	87
Panama, *gulf*	C3	87
Panay, *gulf*	B4	12
Panay, *island*	B4	12
Pancevo	B2	49
Panch'iao	B1	9
Pandan, *strait*	A2	13
Pandaruan, *river*	C2	13
Pando	C3	75
Panevėžys	C2	46
Pangani, *river*	C1	68
Pangkalpinang	B2	13
Pangnirtung	O2	99
Panihati	Inset II	20
Panj	A2	23
Panj, *river*	B2	23
Panjakent	A1	23
Panjgur	B4	21
P'anmunjŏm	B4	9
Pantanal, *lowland*	C3	81
Pantelleria, *island*	C3	38
Pánuco, *river*	E3	84
Pápa	A2	43
Papagayo, *gulf*	A2	87
Paphos	A2	27
Papua New Guinea		15
Paquetville	D1	97
Pará	C2	81
Pará, *river*	C2	81
Paradise Hill	A7	104

	Key	Page
Paradise River	C2	98
Paraguá, river	B2	77
Paraguai, river	C3	81
Paraguarí	D4	75
Paraguay		75
Paraguay, river	C2, C5	75
Paraíba	E2	81
Parakou	B3	64
Paramaribo, capital	B2	80
Paraná	C3	74
Paraná	C4	81
Paraná, river	D2	74
Paranaguá	D4	81
Paranam	B2	80
Pardubice	B2	42
Parent	B4	103
Parepare	C2	13
Paria, gulf	D1	79
Parima, range	B1	81
Paris, capital	C2, Inset II	34
Paris	E4	102
Parkhill	D4	102
Parkland	D6	94
Parksville	K6	95
Parma	B1	38
Parnaíba	D2	81
Parnaíba, river	D2	81
Pärnu	C2	46
Pärnu, river	C2	46
Paro	A2	19
Paropamisus, range	A2	22
Páros, island	C3	51
Parral	B6	76
Parrsboro	C2	100
Parry	D2	99
Parry, channel	J2	99
Parry Sound	E2	102
Parsnip, river	L4	95
Parson's Pond	C4	98
Pas de la Casa	C2	36
Pasadena	C5	98
Pasfield, lake	E2	104
Pasión, river	C3	85
Paso de los Toros	B2	75
Paso de Palmar, lake	B2	75
Passau	C4	40
Passero, cape	C3	38
Passo Fundo	C4	81
Pastavy	C2	47
Pastaza, river	B1	77
Pastillo	C3	90
Pasto	A4	78
Patagonia, region	A6	74
Patavilca	B3	77
Paterson, N.J.	F1	126
Patía, river	A4	78
Patiala	C2	20
Patillas	C2	90
Patna	E3	20
Patos, lagoon	C5	81
Pátrai	B2	51
Patricia	E6	94
Pattani	B5	12
Patuakhali	D6	21
Patuanak	C5	104
Patuca, mts.	C2	86
Patuca, river	C2	86
Pau	B5	34
Pauingassi	D3	96
Paulatuk	D3	99
Paulaya, river	C2	86
Paulo Afonso	E2	81
Pavaiai	B2	18
Pavia	B1	38
Pavilosta	A2	46
Pavlodar	D1	23
Pavlovsk-Kamchatskiy	D9	44
Paxbán	C2	85
Payar	C2	62
Paye	Inset I	20
Payne, lake	B2	101
Paynton	B7	104
Pays De La Loire	B3	34
Paysandú	A2	75
Paz, river	C6	85
Pazardzhik	C3	50
Peace Point	D1	94
Peace River	B3	94
Peace, river	A3, C2	94
Peachland	N6	95
Pebane	C3	68
Peč	B3	49
Pechora	C4	44
Pechora, river	C4	44
Pécs	B2	43
Pedernales	A2	89
Pedja, river	C2	46
Pedra Açú, mt.	Inset I	81
Pedra Lume	D2	58
Pedro Juan Caballero	E3	75
Pedro Santana	A1	89
Peebles	H10	104
Peel, river	B3, C2	105
Peeress Lake	C3	94
Pegasus, bay	B3	15
Pegu	C3	12
Peipus, lake	D2	46
Pekalongan	B2	13
Pekanbaru	B1	13
Pelee, island	C6	102
Peleliu, island	B4	17
Peleng, island	D2	13
Pelican Narrows	H5	104
Pelican Portage	D3	94
Pelican Rapids	A3	96
Pelican, lake	G5	104
Pelkan, lake	A3	96
Pelly	J9	104
Pelly Bay	L3	99
Pelly Crossing	B4	105
Pelly, river	C4, C5	105
Pelotas	C5	81
Pematangsiantar	A1	13
Pemba	D2	68
Pemba, island	C2	68
Pemberton	L6	95
Pembina	B4	94
Pembina, river	B4	96
Pembroke	B3	30
Pembroke	H2	102

	Key	Page
Penas, gulf	B8	76
Pendé, river	A2	66
Pendleton, Oreg.	B1	126
Penetanguishene	F3	102
P'enghu (Pescadores), islands	A2	9
Peniche	A3	36
Peninsular Malaysia, region	B2	13
Pennant	B10	104
Pennine Alps, mts.	B2	35
Pennines, mts.	C2	30
Pennsylvania	F1	126
Penonomé	B2	87
Penrith	C2	30
Pensacola, Fla.	E2	126
Pensacola, mts.	A11	107
Penticton	N6	95
Peñuelas	B2	90
Penza	D4	44
Penzance	B4	30
Penzhina	D3	10
Peoria, Ill.	E1	126
Perak, river	A2	13
Percé	M3	103
Perdue	C8	104
Pereira	B3	78
Péribonca, river	B3	101
Péribonka	D3	103
Périgueux	C4	34
Perim, island	A2	25
Peristéri	Inset	51
Perlas, archipelago	C2	87
Perlas, lagoon	C2	87
Perm	D4	44
Pernambuco	E2	81
Pernik	B3	50
Perpignan	C5	34
Perrot, island	G6	103
Persian, gulf	C1, C2, C3	24
Perth	B2	30
Perth	J3	102
Perth, W.A., capital	A3, Inset I	14
Perth-Andover	B2	97
Perugia	C2	38
Pervomaysk	C2	47
Pesaro	C2	38
Pescadores, channel	A2	9
Pescara	C2	38
Peshawar	D3	21
Peshkopi	B2	49
Petah Tiqwa	B1	26
Petare	C1	79
Petauke	C2	67
Petawawa	H2	102
Petén-Itzá, lake	D3	85
Peterborough	C3	30
Peterborough	G3	102
Peterhead	C1	30
Petersfield	C4	96
Petit Canouan, island	B3	91
Petit Martinique, island	C1	91
Petit Mustique, island	B3	91
Petit St. Vincent, island	A4	91
Petit-Rocher	D1	97
Petitcodiac	D3	97
Petite Riviere	C3	100
Petlura	A3	96
Petrich	B4	50
Petrila	B3	43
Petrolia	C5	102
Petrólina	D2	81
Petropavl	C1	23
Petropavlovsk-Kamchatskiy	D9	44
Petrópolis	D4, Inset I	81
Petroșani	B3	43
Petrozavodsk	C3	44
Pevek	C10	44
Peyia	A2	27
Pforzheim	B4	40
Phan Rang	B4	11
Phan Thiet	B4	11
Phatthalung	B5	12
Phayao	B2	12
Phetchabun	B2	12
Phetchabun, range	B2	12
Phetchaburi	B2	12
Phichit	B2	12
Philadelphia, Pa.	F2	126
Philippine, sea	C3	12
Philippine, sea	B2	17
Philippines		12
Phitsanulok	B2	12
Phnom Penh, capital	C4	11
Phnum Tbeng Meanchey	C2	11
Phoenix, capital, Ariz.	B2	126
Phoenix, island	B2	17
Phoenix, islands	B2	17
Phôngsali	B1	11
Phou Bia, mt.	B2	11
Phra Nakhon Si Ayutthaya	B3	12
Phuket	B5	12
Phumi Samraong	B1	11
Phuntsholing	A3	19
Pianosa, island	B2	38
Piapot	A10	104
Piatra Neamţ	D2	43
Piauí	D2	81
Piave, river	C1	38
Pibor Post	B3	59
Pic de la Selle, mt.	D2	89
Picardie	C2	34
Pickle Lake	B2	101
Pico da Cano, volcano	B4	58
Picton	H3	102
Pictou	E2	100
Pidurutalagala, mt.	A4	19
Piedmont	A1	38
Piedra Sola	B2	75
Piedras Negras	B2	84
Pielinen, lake	C2	53
Pierceland	A6	104
Pierre, capital, S. Dak.	C1	126
Pierrefonds	G5	103
Pierreville	A2	91
Piest'any	A2	42

	Key	Page
Pietermaritzburg	D2	71
Pietersburg	C1	71
Pigeon, lake	C4	94
Pigeon, lake	G3	102
Piggs Peak	B1	71
Pikangikum	B2	101
Pikes peak, Colo.	C2	126
Pikwitonei	C1	96
Piła	C2	41
Pilar	C5	75
Pilaya, river	B4	77
Pilcomayo, river	B3, C4	75
Pilica, river	E3	41
Pilot Butte	F10	104
Pilot Mound	B4	96
Pílos	B3	51
Pinang, island	A2	13
Pinar del Río	A2	88
Pinawa	D4	96
Pindus, mts.	B2	51
Pine Bluff, Ark.	D2	126
Pine Dock	C3	96
Pine Falls	C4	96
Pine Point	F4	99
Pine River	A3	96
Pinehouse Lake	D5	104
Pines, island	D2	18
Ping, river	B2	12
Pingxiang	E3	10
Piniós, river	B2	51
Pink Mountain	L2	95
Pink, river	F4	104
Pinsk	C3	47
Pinta, island	Inset	79
Piotrków Trybunalski	D3	41
Pipestone	A4	96
Pipmuacan, reservoir	F2	103
Piracicaba	D4	81
Pirada	C1	62
Piraiévs	B3, Inset	51
Pirmasens	A4	40
Pirot	C3	49
Pirris, river	B3	86
Pisa	B2	38
Pisagua	B1	76
Pisco	B3	77
Pisek	B2	38
Pitești	C3	43
Pitlochry	B2	30
Pitseng	B2	71
Pitt, island	H4	95
Pittsburgh, Pa.	E1	126
Piura	A2	77
Placentia	B3	85
Placentia	D5	98
Placentia, bay	D5	98
Placenza	B1	38
Placetas	C2	88
Planken	B1	33
Plantagenet	K2	102
Plasencia	C2	37
Plaster Rock	B2	97
Plata, Río de la, estuary	D3	74
Plata, river	B3	75
Platte, river, Nebr.	C1	126
Playa Grande	C3	40
Pleasant Bay	G1	100
Pleiku	B4	11
Plenty, bay	C2	15
Plessisville	E5	103
Pleven	C2	50
Plevna	J3	102
Pljevlja	A3	49
Płock	D2	41
Ploiești	D3	43
Plovdiv	C3	50
Plum Coulee	C4	96
Plumas	B4	96
Plymouth	B1	91
Plymouth	B4	30
Plzeň	A3	42
Po, river	A1, B1	38
Poá	Inset II	81
Pobé	B4	64
Pocatello, Idaho	B1	126
Podgorica	A3	49
Pogradec	B3	49
Pohang	C4	9
Pohnpei, island	D2	15
Point Fortin	A2	91
Point Leamington	D4	98
Point Pedro	B2	19
Point Prim	B2	100
Pointe au Baril	E2	102
Pointe du Bois	D4	96
Pointe Michel	B3	90
Pointe Sapin	E2	97
Pointe-a-la-Croix	K3	103
Pointe-Claire	H6	103
Pointe-des-Monts	J2	103
Pointe-Lebel	H2	103
Pointe-Noire	A6	66
Poisson Blanc, reservoir	A6	103
Poissy	Inset II	34
Poitiers	C3	34
Poitou-Charentes	C3	34
Pokemouche	E1	97
Pokhara	B2	19
Polar, plateau	A14	107
Polis	A1	27
Polonnaruwa	C4	19
Polotsk	D2	47
Poltava	D2	47
Poltimore	A6	103
Pomeranian, bay	C1	40
Ponce	B2	90
Pond Cove	C3	98
Pond Inlet	N2	99
Pondicherry	C6	20
Ponferrada	C1	37

	Key	Page
Ponoka	D5	94
Pont Cassé	B3	90
Pont-Rouge	E5	103
Pontchartrain	Inset II	34
Ponteix	C11	104
Pontevedra	B1	37
Pontianak	B2	13
Pontic, mts.	D2	27
Pontic, islands	C2	38
Pontine, marshes	C2	38
Pontoise	Inset II	34
Ponton	B2	96
Poole	C4	30
Poopó, lake	A3	77
Popayán	A4	78
Poperinge	A2	33
Poplar River	C3	96
Popomanaseu, mt.	B1	16
Popondetta	A2	15
Poprad	C2	42
Porcupine Plain	G8	104
Porcupine, river	B2	105
Pori	B2	53
Port Alberni	K6	95
Port Antonio	C2	88
Port au Choix	C4	98
Port au Port	B5	98
Port Augusta, S.A.	C3	14
Port Bickerton	F2	100
Port Blair	F6	20
Port Blandford	D5	98
Port Bruce	E5	102
Port Burwell	D3	98
Port Burwell	E5	102
Port Clements	F4	95
Port Colborne	F5	102
Port Coquitlam	L6	95
Port Dufferin	E3	100
Port Elgin	B2	97
Port Elgin	D3	102
Port Elizabeth	B2	91
Port Elizabeth	C3	71
Port Franks	D4	102
Port George	F2	100
Port Glaud	Inset	70
Port Harcourt	D5	65
Port Hardy	J6	95
Port Hawkesbury	F2	100
Port Hedland, W.A.	A2	14
Port Hood	F1	100
Port Hope	G4	102
Port Hope Simpson	C3	98
Port Laoise	C2	31
Port Lincoln, S.A.	C3	14
Port Loko	A1	63
Port Loring	E2	102
Port Louis, capital	B2	69
Port Macquarie, N.S.W.	E3	14
Port Maria	C2	88
Port McNeill	J6	95
Port Moody	L6	95
Port Morant	C3	88
Port Moresby, capital	A2	15
Port Mouton	C4	100
Port Nolloth	A2	71
Port of Spain, capital	A2	91
Port Perry	G3	102
Port Pirie, S.A.	C3	14
Port Renfrew	K7	95
Port Rowan	E5	102
Port Said	B1	56
Port Saunders	C4	98
Port Stanley	D5	102
Port Sudan	D1	59
Port Talbot	B3	30
Port-au-Prince, bay	C2	89
Port-au-Prince, capital	C2	89
Port-Cartier	C3	101
Port-de-Paix	C1	89
Port-Gentil	A2	66
Port-Salut	B2	89
Portage	A2	30
Portage la Prairie	B4, D2	96
Portalegre	B3	36
Porter, lake	C4	104
Porters Lake	D3	100
Porth Edward	D3	71
Portimão	A4	36
Portland	A2	91
Portland Creek	C4	98
Portland, bight	B3	88
Portland, inlet	G4	95
Portland, Maine	F1	126
Portland, Oreg.	A1	126
Portneuf, river	G3	103
Porto Alegre	B4	63
Pôrto Alegre	C5	81
Pôrto Inglês	C3	58
Pôrto Velho	B2	81
Porto-Novo, capital	B4	64
Porto-Vecchio	Inset I	34
Portobelo	C2	87
Portoviejo	A3	79
Portree	A1	30
Portsmouth	C4	30
Portsmouth	A2	90
Portsmouth, Va.	F2	126
Portugal		36
Porvenir	B9	76
Poșada	D2	74
Posadas	D2	74
Poste, river	C3	69
Postojna	B3	48
Postville	B2	98
Potaro, river	B3	80
Potenza	C2	38
Poti	A3	45
Potiskum	F2	65
Potnarvin	C4	18
Potosí	A3	77
Potrerillos	C3	76
Potsdam	C2	40
Pottuvil	C5	19
Pouch Cove	E5	98
Poutasi	C3	18
Pouthisat	B3	11
Považská Bystrica	B2	42
Powassan	F1	102

	Key	Page
Powell River	K6	95
Powerview	C4	96
Poyang, lake	E3	10
Poza Rica	E3	84
Požarevac	B2	49
Poznań	C2	41
Pozo Colorado	C3	75
Pra, river	B4	64
Prachuap Khiri Khan	B4	12
Prague, capital	B2	42
Praia, capital	C4	58
Praslin	B2	91
Praslin, island	C1	70
Prato	B2	38
Prawda	D4	96
Preeceville	H9	104
Prelate	A10	104
Preparis, island	B3	12
Přerov	C2	42
Prescott	K3	102
Prescott, Ariz.	B2	126
Presidencia Roque Sáenz Peña	C2	74
Prešov	C2	42
Prespa, lake	B3	48
Presque Isle, Maine	G1	126
Prestea	A4	64
Preston	C3	30
Pretoria, administrative capital	C2	71
Préveza	B2	51
Prey Veng	D4	11
Priboj	A3	49
Priddis	C6	94
Prievidza	B2	42
Prijedor	A1	48
Prilep	B2	48
Priluki	C1	47
Primorsko	F3	50
Primrose, lake	A6	104
Prince Albert	E7	104
Prince Albert, hills	L3	99
Prince Albert, peninsula	E2	99
Prince Charles, island	N3	99
Prince George	L4	95
Prince of Wales, island	J2	99
Prince Patrick, island	E1	99
Prince Regent, inlet	K2	99
Prince Rupert	G4	95
Princes Town	A2	91
Princess Harbour	C3	96
Princess Margriet, canal	C1	32
Princess Royal, island	H4	95
Princeton	M6	95
Princeville	E5	103
Príncipe, island	C1	63
Prinzapolka	B2	87
Prinzapolka, river	B2	87
Pripyats, marshes	C4	47
Pripyats, river	C3	47
Priština	B3	49
Privas	D4	34
Prizren	B3	49
Progresso	B1	85
Prokopyevsk	D6	44
Prokuplje	B3	49
Prome	B2	12
Prophet River	L2	95
Prostějov	C2	42
Provence-Alpes-Côte-d'Azur	D4	34
Providence Bay	C2	102
Providence, capital, R.I.	F1	126
Providencia, island	Inset	78
Providenciales, island	C4	89
Provideniya	C11	44
Provo, Utah	B1	126
Pru, river	B3	64
Prut, river	B2	47
Przemyśl	F4	41
Psel, river	C1	47
Pskov	D3	44
Pskov, lake	D3	46
Ptsich, river	D3	47
Ptuj	C2	48
Pu'apu'a	B2	18
Pubnico	B4	100
Pucallpa	C2	77
Puck	D1	41
Puebla, state capital	E4	84
Pueblo, Colo.	C2	126
Puente Alto	Inset	76
Puerca, point	D2	90
Puerto Aisén	B8	76
Puerto Armuelles	A2	87
Puerto Ayacucho	C2	79
Puerto Bahía	C2	75
Puerto Barrios	E4	85
Puerto Bolívar	B4	79
Puerto Cabello	C1	79
Puerto Cabezas	B2	87
Puerto Carreño	D3	78
Puerto Cisnes	B7	76
Puerto Cortés	B2	86
Puerto Deseado	B6	74
Puerto Escondido	E4	84
Puerto Inírida	D3	78
Puerto Jiménez	C4	86
Puerto Leguízamo	B5	78
Puerto Lempira	D2	86
Puerto Maldonado	D3	77
Puerto Montt	B7	76
Puerto Natales	B9	76
Puerto Peñasco	B1	84
Puerto Pinasco	D3	75
Puerto Plata	B1	89
Puerto Princesa	A4	12
Puerto Real	A2	90
Puerto Rico		90
Puerto Quepos	B3	86
Puerto Sandino	A2	87
Puerto Santa Cruz	B7	74
Puerto Suárez	C3	77
Puerto Vallarta	C3	84
Puerto Varas	B7	76
Puerto Williams	C9	76
Puertollano	D3	37
Puglia	C2	38
Pugwash	D2	100
Pujehun	A2	63

	Key
Pukatawagan	A1
Pukch'ŏng	A1
Pukë	A1
Pula	B2
Pulangi, river	C2
Puławy	E3
Pulo Anna, island	Inset
Pulusuk, island	B2
Puná, island	A2
Punakha	A2
Pune	B5
Punggol	B1
P'ungsan	C2
Puno	C4
Punta, mt.	B2
Punta Arenas	B9
Punta del Este	B9
Punta Delgada	B9
Punta Gorda	B3
Punta Santiago	D2
Puntarenas	B3
Punto Fijo	B1
Purari, river	A2
Purbeck's Cove	C5
Purus, river	B2
Pusan	C5
Putao	C1
Putre	A3
Puttalam	A3
Puttgarden	C1
Putumayo, river	B5
Puvirnituq	A1
Puyo	C3
Puysegur, point	A4
Pyandzh, river	B1
P'yŏnggang	A3
P'yŏngsŏng	A3
P'yŏngyang, capital	A3
Pyrenees, range	C5

Q

	Key
Qaanaaq (Thule)	B2
Qachas Nek	B3
Qadarif, al-	C2
Qaidam, basin	C2
Qalat	B2
Qalat Bishah	B2
Qaleh-ye Now	C1
Qaleh-ye Panjeh	C1
Qamea, island	B2
Qamishli, al-	F1
Qandahar	B2
Qaqortoq (Julianehåb)	B3
Qaraghandy (Karaganda)	D2
Qardho	B3
Qareh, river	B3
Qarokul, lake	C3
Qarshi	C3
Qaryah ash-Sharqiyah, al-	B1
Qasigiannguit (Christianshåb)	B2
Qasr as-Sabiyah	B2
Qatar	
Qatranah, al-	A2
Qatrun, al-	B2
Qattarah, depression	A2
Qayrawan, al-	B1
Qayyarah, al-	B1
Qazvin	B2
Qelelevu, island	C2
Qeshm, island	D4
Qilian, range	D2
Qin Ling, mts.	D2
Qina	F2
Qingdao	F2
Qinghai	C2
Qinghai, lake	C2
Qinhuangdao	F2
Qiqihar	F1
Qiryat Gat	B2
Qiryat Shemona	B1
Qishn	C3
Qom	C1
Qormi	B2
Qostanay	C1
Qu'Appelle	G10
Qu'Appelle, river	D10
Quang Ngai	B3
Quantaq	C2
Quanzhou	E3
Quatre Bornes	B3
Quba	B1
Qubayyat, al-	B1
Québec, capital	E5, L6
Quebo	B2
Quebradillas	B2
Queen Charlotte	F4
Queen Charlotte, islands	G5
Queen Charlotte, sound	H5
Queen Charlotte, strait	J6
Queen Elizabeth, islands	H1
Queen Maud Land, region	B16
Queen Maud, mts.	A5
Queen Maude, gulf	H3
Queensland	C2
Queenstown	B1
Queenstown	A3
Queenstown	B1
Queenstown, Tas.	D4
Queguay Grande, river	B2
Queimados	Inset
Quelimane	B7
Quellón	B7
Queluz	A3
Querétaro, state capital	D3
Quesnel	L5
Quesnel, lake	M5
Quetta	B2
Quetzaltenango	A5
Quevedo	B3
Quezon City	B3
Qui Nhon	B3
Quibala	A2
Quibdó	A3
Quilchena	M6
Quill Lake	F8
Quill, lakes	F8

Key Page
ta B4 76
ué Inset 76
pele C2 70
per A2 34
ámel B2 62
ana Roo G4 84
amsis D3 97
, *capital* B3 79
ytirah, al- A3 27
udhah, al- B2 24
hirot A2 23
n D2 23
ionteppa A2 23
at as-Sawda, *mt.* B1 26
ng A3 71
orda C2 23
e B2 53
es, *peninsula* L1 99
C2 13
river A2 43
B2 36
, *capital* C1 57
il B2 15
: Lake C7 104
: Lake Mine G2 104
island C2 17
Gia A4 11
dia, er- C2 57
e, Wis. E1 126
ți C2 43
m Hot Springs O6 95
n E3 41
liškis B2 46
lle F11 104
E4 99
B1 24
A1 96
ed, *point* C3 91
eneau H2 103
sa C3 38
iyar Khan D4 21
ow Lake A2 94
er *mt.*, Wash. A1 126
r D4 20
g, *river* C2 13
aj C3 19
B4 20
r Inset II 20
ahi B4 21
ooshi, *mt.* E2 21
gh, *capital*, N.C. F2 126
island chain A1 16
B2 87
adi, ar- B2 24
anbati Inset II 20
at Gan B1 26
ea C5 98
B2 26
an, *mt.* B2 26
ee, *island* B2 12
ha, ar- B1 26
F2 61
, *river* A2 15
agua B4 76
e, *river* B2 34
ni E4 20
a B2 60
ers C2 32
onopolis C3 81
urly E4 94
amati F6 21
er Lake B1 102
itikei, *river* C2 15
oon, *capital* C3 12
pur C3 21
ng B4 12
, *river* B4 76
d City A4 96
d City, S. Dak. C1 126
C1 46
, *river* B2 19
ah, ar- B2 27
al-Khafji C1 24
al-Khaymah C2 25
n-Naqb A2 26
Dashen, *mt.* C1 60
Musandam, *cape* C1 25
Tanura C1 24
point C5 74
ayya A2 26
B2 22
, *island chain* B1 16
naburi B3 12
in, *island* A2 30
ngen A3 40
apura B5 19
umara, *range* C2 15
na B2 53
kela D4 20
river B2 50
nna C1 38
nsburg B5 40
river D3 21
, *river* B4 80
alpindi D3 21
datayn, ar- B2 24
don D2 100
son B5 74
more F9 104
ng B3 12
de-Balfour D1 102
point A3 34
m, *lake* E3 43
rad E2 50
island B3 34
ling C3 30
n, *island* Inset I 8
ytsa E3 47
e E2 81
linghausen A3 40
nquista D2 74
(Hong), *river* A2 11
Bay C3 98
Deer D5 94
Deer, *lake* A2 96
Deer, *river* D5, E6 94
Red Indian, *lake* C5 98
Red Rose C3 96
Red Sucker, *lake* E2 96
Red Volta, *river* B1, D3 64
Red Willow D5 94
Red, *river* C4 96
Red, *river* D2 126
Red, *sea* A1 24
Redange A2 33
Redbridge F1 102
Redding, Calif. A1 126
Redonda, *island* A6 90
Redstone L5 95
Redvers A4 96
Redvers J11 104
Ree, *lake* B2 31
Reed, *lake* A2 96
Regensburg C4 40
Reggio di Calabria C3 38
Reggio nell'Emilia B1 38
Reghin C2 43
Regina F10 104
Régina B1 80
Registan, *region* A2 22
Rehoboth C3 70
Rehovot B2 26
Reigate Inset III 30
Reims D2 34
Reina Adelaida, *archipelago* B9 76
Reindeer, *island* C3 96
Reindeer, *lake* H3 104
Reindeer, *river* G4 104
Reinosa D1 37
Reliance G4 99
Remagen A3 40
Remich B2 33
Rémire B1 80
Remscheid A3 40
Rencontre East D5 98
Renfrew J2 102
Rennell, *island* B2 16
Rennes B2 34
Rennie D4 96
Reno, Nev. B2 126
Renous D2 97
Repentigny K5 103
Reserve H8 104
Resistencia D2 74
Reşiţa A3 43
Resolute J2 99
Resolution, *island* P4 99
Restigouche, *river* B1 97
Reston A4 96
Restoule F1 102
Réunion, *island* 55
Reus G2 37
Reuss, *river* C2 35
Reutlingen B4 40
Revelstoke N6 95
Reventazón, *river* C3 86
Revillagigedo, *islands* B4 84
Rexdale J5 102
Rexton E2 97
Rey, *island* C2 87
Reykjavík B3 96
Reykjavík, *capital* A2 52
Reynosa E2 84
Rezekne D2 46
Reznas, *lake* D2 46
Rhaetian Alps, *mts.* D2 35
Rharsa, *salt marsh* A2 57
Rhine, *canal* B1, B2 33
Rhine, *river* A3, A4 40
Rhineland-Palatinate A4 40
Rhode Island F1 126
Rhodes D3 51
Rhodes, *island* D3 51
Rhodope, *mts.* C4 50
Rhondda B3 30
Rhône, *river* D4 34
Rhône-Alpes D4 34
Rhum, *island* A1 30
Riaba A1 66
Ribe B3 32
Ribeira Brava A2 58
Ribeira Grande A1 58
Ribeirão Pires Inset II 81
Ribeirão Prêto D4 81
Riberalta A2 77
Rîbnița B2 50
Rice, *lake* G3 102
Richard, *lake* C1 104
Richard-Toll B1 62
Richards Bay D2 71
Richards Landing A1 102
Richardson, *mts.* B1 105
Richardson, *river* E2 94
Richelieu, *river* C6 103
Richer C4 96
Richibucto E2 97
Richmond L6 95
Richmond D6 103
Richmond Hill F4, K5 102
Richmond Park D4 94
Richmond, *capital*, Va. F2 126
Ricobayo, *reservoir* D2 37
Rida A2 25
Rideau, *lake* J3 102
Rideau, *river* H6 102
Riesa C3 40
Rieti C2 38
Riga, *capital* C2 46
Riga, *gulf* B2, B3 46
Rigolet B2 98
Riiser-Larsen Ice Shelf, *glacier* B14 107
Riiser-Larsen, *peninsula* C16 107
Rijeka B2 48
Rila, *mts.* B3 50
Rimini C1 38
Rîmnicu Vîlcea C3 43
Rimouski H3 103
Rincón, *bay* C3 90
Rincón del Bonete, *lake* B2 75
Ringkøbing B2 32
Río Blanco B2 87
Rio Branco B2 81
Río Claro A2 91
Río Cuarto C3 74
Rio de Janeiro D4, Inset I 81
Río Gallegos B7 74
Rio Grande C5 81
Río Grande D2 90
Río Grande A2 87
Rio Grande (Río Bravo), *river* D2 84
Rio Grande do Norte E2 81
Rio Grande do Sul C4 81
Rio Verde C3 81
Riobamba B3 79
Ríohacha B2 78
Rioni, *river* B3 45
Riou, *lake* D1 104
Rîşcani A2 50
Rishiri, *island* Inset I 8
Rishra Inset II 20
Riske Creek L5 95
Ritchies, *archipelago* F6 20
Rivas B3 87
River Cess B3 63
River Hills C4 96
River John D2 100
Rivera C1 75
Rivercrest C4 96
Riverhurst D10 104
Rivers A4 96
Rivers Inlet J5 95
Riverside, Calif. B2 126
Riverside-Albert E3 97
Riverton C3 96
Riverview E2 97
Rivière Bleue G4 103
Rivière du Loup C4 101
Rivière du Rempart C2 69
Rivière Noire, *mt.* B3 69
Rivière-à-Pierre D4 103
Rivière-au-Renard M3 103
Rivière-aux-Rats D4 103
Rivière-du-Loup G4 103
Rivière-du-Portage E1 97
Rivière-Matawin D5 103
Rivière-Ste-Marguerite G3 103
Rivière-Verte A1 97
Riyadh, *capital* B1 24
Riyaq B2 26
Roanne D3 34
Roanoke, Va. F2 126
Roatán B1 86
Roatán, *island* B1 86
Robertsport A2 63
Roberval D3 103
Robinsonville C1 97
Roblin A3 96
Roboré C3 77
Robson, *mt.* N4 95
Roca, *cape* A3 36
Rocanville J10 104
Rocha C3 75
Rochdale C3 30
Rochefort B4 34
Rochester D4 94
Rochester, Minn. D1 126
Rochester, N.Y. F1 126
Rock Island D6 103
Rock, *river* D5 105
Rockcliffe Park H5 102
Rockford, Ill. E1 126
Rockglen E11 104
Rockhampton, Qld. E2 14
Rockland K2 102
Rocky Harbour C4 98
Rocky Island, *lake* B1 102
Rocky Mountain House C5 94
Rocky, *mts.* 82
Rockyford D5 94
Roddickton C4 98
Rodez C4 34
Rodney D5 102
Roermond D3 32
Roeselare B2 33
Rogersville D2 97
Roi, *island* B2 16
Roi Et C2 12
Rojo, *cape* A3 90
Rokel, *river* A1 63
Roland C4 96
Rolling Hills E6 94
Rollo, *bay* C2 100
Rolphton H1 102
Roma A2 71
Roma, Qld. D2 14
Roman D2 43
Romania 43
Rome, *capital* C2 38
Rømø, *island* B3 32
Roncador, *cay* Inset 78
Roncador, *range* C3 81
Ronde, *island* B1 91
Rondônia B3 81
Rongelap, *island* B1 16
Rongerik, *island* B1 16
Rønne E3 32
Ronne Ice Shelf, *glacier* B11 107
Roodeport C2 71
Roosevelt, *island* B6 107
Roosevelt Campobello Intl. Hist. Park C4 97
Roper, *river* C1 14
Roraima B1 81
Roraima, *mt.* A3 80
Rosa, *mt.* A1 38
Rosalie B3 90
Rosalind D5 94
Rosario C3 74
Roscommon B2 31
Roscrea C2 31
Rose Belle C3 69
Rose Blanche B5 98
Rose Hill B2 69
Rose Valley G8 104
Rose, *island* B1 18
Roseau, *capital* B3 90
Roseau, *river* B4 96
Rosebud D5 94
Rosemary D6 94
Rosenfeld C4 96
Rosenheim C5 40
Rosenort C4 96
Rosetown B9 104
Rosetta, *river* B1 56
Roskilde D3 32
Ross Ice Shelf, *glacier* A6 107
Ross River C4 105
Ross, *island* B5 107
Ross, *river* C4 105
Ross, *sea* B6 107
Rossburn A4 96
Rosseau, *lake* F2 102
Rossel, *island* B3 15
Rossendale B4 96
Rossignol, *lake* B3 100
Rossland O6 95
Rosslare C2 31
Rosso B3 58
Rosthern D8 104
Rostock C1 40
Rostov-na-Donu E3 44
Roswell, N. Mex. C2 126
Rotherham C3 30
Rothesay D3 97
Rotorua C2 15
Rotterdam B3 32
Roubaix C1 34
Rouen C2 34
Rouleau F10 104
Round Lake Centre H2 102
Round, *island* D1 69
Round, *pond* C5 98
Rounthwaite B4 96
Routhierville J3 103
Rouyn-Noranda A4 101
Rovaniemi C1 53
Rovigo B1 38
Rovno B1 47
Rovuma, *river* C1 68
Rowley D5 94
Roxas B4 12
Royal, *canal* C2 31
Ruacana, *falls* B1 70
Ruahine, *range* C2 15
Ruapehu, *mt.* C2 15
Rub al-Khali (Empty Quarter), *desert* C2 24
Rubtsovsk D6 44
Ruda Śląska D3 41
Rudnyy C1 23
Rufiji, *river* C2 68
Rufisque A2 62
Rügen, *island* C1 40
Ruggell B1 33
Ruhengeri B1 61
Ruhr, *river* B3 40
Ruhwa, *river* B2 61
Rukwa, *lake* B2 68
Rum, *cay* C3 89
Rumbek B3 59
Runaway Bay B2 88
Rundu C1 70
Rungue Inset 76
Rungwa, *river* B2 68
Rupel, *river* C1 33
Ruse D2 50
Russell A4 96
Russia 44
Rustavi C4 45
Rutana B2 61
Rutbah, ar- B2 24
Rutherglen F1 102
Rutland N6 95
Ruvubu, *river* C2 61
Ruvuma, *river* C3 68
Ruways, ar- B2, C1 25
Ruwenzori, *range* B3 61
Ruyigi C2 61
Ruzizi, *river* A1, A2 61
Ružomberok B2 42
Rwanda 61
Rweru, *lake* C2 61
Ryazan D3 44
Rybnik D3 41
Ryotsu C2 8
Rysy, *mt.* E4 41
Ryukyu, *islands* A4, Inset II 8
Rzeszów F3 41

S

's Hertogenbosch C3 32
Saale, *river* B3 40
Saar, *river* A4 40
Saarbrücken A4 40
Saaremaa, *island* B2 46
Saarland A4 40
Sab Abar A3 27
Šabac A2 49
Sabadell H2 37
Sabana de la Mar C1 89
Sabana Grande B2 90
Sabaneta A1 89
Sabha B2 56
Sable *cape*, Fla. E3 126
Sable River B4 100
Sabzevar D2 22
Sachigo, *river* B2 101
Sackville E3 97
Sacramento, *capital*, Calif. A2 126
Sadah A1 25
Sado, *island* C2 8
Sado, *river* A3 36
Safata, *bay* C3 18
Safed Koh, *range* D3 21
Safi B1 57
Safotu B1 18
Saga A3 8
Sagaing B2 12
Sagami, *bay* C3 8
Sagamihara C3 8
Saginaw, Mich. E1 126
Sagua la Grande C2 88
Saguenay, *river* F3 103
Sagunto F3 37
Sahara, *desert* 55
Saharanpur Panipat C3 20
Şahbuz A3 45
Sahel, *region* 55
Sahiwal D3 21
Sai Kung Inset 10
Saidpur B3 21
Saimaa, *lake* C2 53
St. Adolphe C4 96
St. Alban's D5 98
St. Albans C3, Inset III 30
St. Albert D4 94
St-Alexis-des-Monts C5 103
St-Ambroise E3 103
St. Ambroise B4 96
St.-André B1 97
St-André G4 103
St. Andrews C2 30
St. Andrews B3 97
St-Angèle-de-Mérici J3 103
St. Ann's Bay B2 88
St. Anne, *island* Inset 70
St. Anthony D3 98
St-Antoine C6 103
St-Apollinaire E5 103
St-Augustin E3 101
St. Augustine A2 91
St. Augustine, Fla. E3 126
St. Austell B4 30
St. Barbe C3 98
St.-Basile A1 97
St. Bernard's D5 98
St. Brendan's E5 98
St. Bride's D5 98
Saint-Brieuc B2 34
St. Brieux F8 104
St-Bruno E3 103
St-Camille-de-Lellis F5 103
St. Catharines F4 102
St. Catherine's E5 98
St. Catherine, *mt.* B2 91
St-Charles, *lake* K5 103
St. Clair, *lake* C5 102
St. Clair, *river* C5 102
St. Claude B4 96
Saint-Cloud Inset II 34
St. Cloud, Minn. D1 126
St-Côme C5 103
St-Constant J6 103
St. Croix B3 97
St-Cyprien H4 103
St-David-de-Falardeau E3 103
St. David's B2 91
St. David's B3 30
Saint-Denis Inset II 34
Saint-Dizier D2 34
St-Donat B5 103
St. Edward A2 100
St. Eleanors B2 100
St. Elias, *mts.* A5 105
Saint-Élie B1 80
St-Émile K5 103
Saint-Étienne D4 34
St. Eustache C4 96
St-Eustache H5 103
St-Fabien H3 103
St-Fabien-de-Panet F5 103
St-Félicien D3 103
St-Félix-d'Otis F3 103
St-François, *lake* E6 103
St-François, *river* C5 103
St.-Gédéon F6 103
St. George C3 97
St. George's B5 98
St. George's, *bay* B5 98
St. George's, *capital* A2 91
St. George's, *channel* B2 15
Saint George's, *channel* C3 31
St. George, Utah B2 126
St. Georges, *bay* F2 100
St-Georges F5 103
Saint-Georges C2 80
St-Germain G4 103
Saint-Germain-en-Laye Inset II 34
St. Gotthard, *pass* C2 35
St. Gotthard, *tunnel* C2 35
St. Helens C3 30
St-Henri-de-Taillon E3 103
St-Hubert G4 103
St-Hyacinthe D6 103
St-Ignace-du-Lac C5 103
St.-Isidore D1 97
St.-Jacques A1 97
St-Jacques-de-Leeds E5 103
St-Jean, *lake* D3 103
St. Jean Baptiste C4 96
St-Jean-Chrysostome L6 103
St-Jean-de-Matha C5 103
St-Jean-Port-Joli F4 103
St-Jean-sur-Richelieu C6 103
St-Jérôme B6 103
Saint John C3 97
St. John, *river* C3 97
St. John's E5 98
St. John's, *capital* B2 90
Saint Joseph A3 90
St. Joseph E2 97
St. Joseph, *island* B1 102
St. Joseph, Mo. D2 126
St-Joseph-de-Beauce F5 103
St. Kitts (St. Christopher), *island* B2 90
St. Kitts and Nevis 90
St Labre C4 96
St-Lambert J5 103
St Laurent C4 96
St-Laurent J5 103
Saint-Laurent du Maroni A1 80
St. Lawrence D5 98
St. Lawrence, *cape* G1 100
St. Lawrence, *gulf* L4 92
St. Lawrence, *river* K4 92
St. Lawrence Islands N.P. J3 102
St.-Lazare A4 96
St-Leonard J5 103
St.-Léonard B1 97
St. Lewis D3 98
St. Lewis, *river* C3 98
Saint-Lô B2 34
Saint-Louis A1 62
St. Louis A2 100
St. Louis E8 104
St. Louis, Mo. D2 126
St-Louis, *lake* H6 103
St.-Louis-de-Kent E2 97

St.-Louis-de-Kent E2 97

St. Lucia 91
Saint Lucia, *channel* B1 91
St-Ludger F6 103
St. Ludger-de-Milot E3 103
St. Malo C4 96
St.-Malo E6 103
Saint-Malo B2 34
Saint-Malo, *gulf* B2 34
Saint-Marc C1 89
St-Marc-du-Lac-Long H4 103
St-Marcel F5 103
St-Marcellin H3 103
St. Margarets D2 97
St. Martin B3 96
St. Martin, *lake* B3 96
St. Martins D3 97
St. Mary's E5 98
St. Marys D4 102
St-Maurice, *river* C4 103
St-Michel F5 103
St-Michel-des-Saints C5 103
St.-Milaire A1 97
St. Moritz D2 35
Saint-Nazaire B3 34
St-Nicolas E5 103
St-Pacôme G4 103
St-Pamphile G5 103
St-Pascal G4 103
St. Paul E4 94
St. Paul, *capital*, Minn. D1 126
St. Paul, *river* A2 63
St. Paul, *river* C3 98
St. Paul's A1 90
Saint Paul's, *bay* B2 36
St. Peters G2 100
St. Peters C2 100
St. Peters, *bay* C2 100
St. Peters, *island* B2 100
St. Petersburg D3 44
St. Petersburg, Fla. E3 126
St-Philémon F5 103
St. Pierre, *island* M4 92
St. Pierre-Jolys C4 96
St.-Quentin B1 97
St-Raphaël F5 103
St-Rédempteur K6 103
St-Rémi-d'Amherst B5 103
St-Romuald L6 103
St. Shotts E5 98
St-Siméon G4 103
St. Stephen B3 97
St. Thomas D5 102
St-Tite-des-Caps F4 103
Saint-Tropez D5 34
St-Vallier F5 103
Saint Vincent, *passage* B4 91
St. Vincent, *gulf* Inset II 14
St. Vincent, *island* B2 91
St. Vincent and the Grenadines 91
St. Walburg A7 104
St-Zacharie F5 103
Ste-Agathe-des-Monts B5 103
Ste-Amélie B4 96
Ste-Anne-des-Monts K2 103
Ste-Anne-du-Lac A5 103
Ste-Apolline F5 103
Ste-Claire F5 103
Ste-Croix E5 103
Ste-Eulalie D5 103
Ste-Foy E5, K6 103
Ste-Luce H3 103
Ste-Marie E5 103
Ste-Monique E3 103
Ste-Rose-du-Nord F3 103
Ste-Thérèse H5 103
Ste-Véronique A5 103
Ste. Agathe C4 96
Ste. Anne C4 96
Ste. Rose du Lac B3 96
Ste.-Anne-de-Madawaska A1 97
Saintes B4 34
Sajama, *mt.* A3 77
Sak, *river* B3 71
Sakai B3 8
Sakarya, *river* B2 27
Sakha (Yakutiya), republic C8 44
Sakhalin, *island* I4 44
Şaki B2 45
Sakishima, *islands* Inset II 8
Sakon Nakhon C2 12
Sal Rei D2 58
Sal, *island* D2 58
Sala'ilua A2 18
Salaberry-de-Valleyfield B6 103
Salacgriva C2 46
Salado, *river* B3, C2 74
Salaga B2 64
Salahiyah A2 27
Salalah B3 25
Salamá C4 85
Salamanca D2 37
Salamís, *island* Inset 51
Salar de Uyuni, *salt flat* A4 77
Salaverry B2 77
Salcedo B1 89
Saldanha A3 71
Saldus B2 46
Salé C1 57
Salekhard C5 44
Salelologa B2 18
Salem C6 20
Salem, *capital*, Oreg. A1 126
Salerno C2 38
Salerno, *gulf* C2 38
Salford C3 30
Salgótarján B1 43
Salibia B2 90
Salihorsk C3 47
Salima B2 68
Salina Cruz E4 84
Salina, Kans. D2 126
Salinas C3 90
Salines, *point* A2 91
Salisbury A2 90
Salisbury C3 30
Salisbury, *island* N4 99
Salluit A1 101
Sallum, as- A1 56

Name	Key	Page
Sally's Cove	C4	98
Salmon Arm	N6	95
Salmon River	A3	100
Salmon, Idaho	B1	126
Salmon, river	L4	95
Salo	B2	53
Salonta	A2	43
Saloum, river	B2	62
Salsette, island		20
Salt Lake City, capital, Utah	B1	126
Salt Water, lake		Inset II 20
Salt, as-	A1	26
Salt, cay	D4	89
Salta	B1	74
Saltcoats	H9	104
Saltery Bay	K6	95
Saltillo, state capital	D2	84
Salto	B1	75
Salto del Guairá	E4	75
Salut, islands	B1	80
Salvador	E3	81
Salvage	E5	98
Salween, river	C2	10
Salyan	C3	45
Salzach, river	C3	39
Salzburg	C3	39
Salzburg Alps, range	C3	39
Salzgitter	B2	40
Samaná	C1	89
Samaná, bay	C1	89
Samaná, cape	C1	89
Samana, cay	C3	89
Samangan	B1	22
Samar, island	C4	12
Samar, sea	C3	12
Samara	D4	44
Samarian, hills	B1	26
Samarinda	C2	13
Samarqand	C3	23
Samarra	B2	24
Samawah, as-	C2	24
Sambalpur	D4	20
Sambre, river	C2	33
Samch'ŏk	C4	9
Samina, river	B2	33
Samoa		18
Samokov	B3	50
Sámos, island	C3	51
Samothráki, island	C1	51
Samsø, island	C3	32
Samsø, strait	C3	32
Samsonvale, lake	Inset III	14
Samsun	D2	27
Samtredia	B3	45
Samur, river	B2	45
San	C3	58
San Andrés, island	Inset	78
San Angelo, Tex.	C2	126
San Antonio	B4, Inset	76
San Antonio	A3	85
San Antonio	C2	90
San Antonio Oeste	B5	74
San Antonio, cape	D4	74
San Antonio, cape	A2	88
San Antonio, Tex.	D3	126
San Baudilio de Llobregat	G2	37
San Bernardino, Calif.	B2	126
San Bernardo		Inset 76
San Blas, mts.	C2	87
San Borja	A2	77
San Carlos	B4	12
San Carlos	C3	75
San Carlos	B3	87
San Carlos de Bariloche	A5	74
San Carlos, river	B2	86
San Clara	A3	96
San Cristóbal	B2	77
San Cristóbal	B3	79
San Cristóbal de las Casas	F4	84
San Cristóbal, island	B2	16
San Cristóbal, island	Inset	79
San Diego, Calif.	B2	126
San Felipe	D4	78
San Felipe	B1	84
San Félix	B3	76
San Fernando	C4	37
San Fernando	B4	76
San Fernando	A2	91
San Fernando	B2	12
San Fernando de Apure	C2	79
San Francique	A2	91
San Francisco	C3	74
San Francisco	B2	86
San Francisco de Macorís	B1	89
San Francisco, Calif.	A2	126
San Germán	A2	90
San Gimignano	B2	38
San Ignacio	B3	77
San Ignacio	A2	85
San Isidro	D2	90
San Jorge, gulf	B6	74
San José	B3	75
San José	C6	85
San José de Chiquitos	B3	77
San José de las Matas	A1	89
San José del Guaviare	B4	78
San José, Calif.	A2	126
San José, capital	B3	86
San José, river	B2	75
San Juan	B3	74
San Juan	B4	77
San Juan	A2	89
San Juan, capital	C2	90
San Juan, passage	D2	90
San Juan Bautista	D5	75
San Juan de Los Morros	C2	87
San Juan del Norte	C3	87
San Juan del Norte, bay	C3	87
San Juan del Sur	B3	87
San Juan, river	A3	78
San Juan, river	B3	87
San Lorenzo	D4	75
San Lorenzo	B3	79
San Lorenzo	B3	86
San Lorenzo	D2	90
San Lorenzo, cape	A3	79
San Lucas	C3	84
San Lucas, cape	B3	84

Name	Key	Page
San Luis	B3	74
San Luis	D3	85
San Luis Potosí, state capital	D3	84
San Luis Río Colorado	B1	84
San Luis, lake	B2	77
San Marino, capital		39
San Marino, river	A1	39
San Martín, lake	A6	74
San Matías	C3	77
San Matías, gulf	C5	74
San Miguel	B2	86
San Miguel de Tucumán	B2	74
San Miguelito	C2	87
San Nicolás	C3	74
San Pablo	B3	12
San Pablo	B3	77
San Pawl il-Baħar	B2	36
San Pedro	C4	75
San Pédro	C4	63
San Pedro de Atacama	C2	76
San Pedro de las Colonias	D2	84
San Pedro de Macorís	C2	89
San Pedro Sula	A2	86
San Pedro, river	C2	85
San Pietro, island	B3	38
San Rafael	B3	74
San Remo	A2	38
San Salvador de Jujuy	B1	74
San Salvador, capital	A2	86
San Salvador, island	Inset	79
San Salvador, island	A2	89
San Salvador, river	C3	75
San Sebastián	F1	37
San Sebastián	B2	90
San Severo	B2	38
San Valentín, mt.	B8	76
San Vicente	B2	86
San Vito, cape	C3	38
San, river	E2	11
San, river	F3	41
Sana, capital	A1	25
Sanaga, river	B2	65
Sanandaj	B2	22
Sanaw	C1	25
Sancti Spíritus	C2	88
Sand, river	E3	94
Sandakan	D2	13
Sanday, island	Inset I	30
Sandilands	C4	96
Sandougou, river	B3	62
Sandoy, island	Inset	32
Sandspit	G4	95
Sandur		Inset 32
Sandwich, bay	C2	98
Sandy Bay	H5	104
Sandy Cove	A3	100
Sandy Lake	D3	94
Sandy Lake	A4	96
Sandy Lake	B2	101
Sandy Point	B2	89
Sandy Point Town	A1	90
Sandy, island	B2	18
Sandy, island	B2	91
Sandy, lake	C4	96
Sanford	C4	96
Sangha, river	D2	66
Sangmélima	B3	65
Sangre Grande	A2	91
Sangro, river	C2	38
Sangudo	C4	94
Sankosh, river	B2	19
Sankrail		Inset II 20
Sankt Gallen	D1	35
Sankt Pölten	D2	39
Sankuru, river	B2	67
Sannar	C2	59
Sanski Most	A1	48
Sant Julià de Lòria	A3	36
Sant'Antioco, island	B3	38
Santa Ana	A2	77
Santa Ana	A2	86
Santa Ana, river	B1	75
Santa Ana, volcano	A2	86
Santa Bárbara	A2	86
Santa Barbara, Calif.	B2	126
Santa Catarina	C4	81
Santa Clara	C2	88
Santa Coloma de Gramanet	H2	37
Santa Cruz	B3	77
Santa Cruz de Tenerife	Inset I	37
Santa Cruz, island	Inset	79
Santa Cruz, islands	C2	16
Santa Cruz, river	A7	74
Santa Elena de Uairen	D3	79
Santa Elena, point	A4	79
Santa Fe	C3	74
Santa Fe, N. Mex.	C2	126
Santa Inés		Inset 76
Santa Inés, island	B9	76
Santa Isabel	C3	90
Santa Isabel, peak	A1	66
Santa Isabel, river	B1	75
Santa Luzia, island	B2	58
Santa Maria	D2	58
Santa Maria di Leuca, cape	D3	38
Santa Maria, island	B2	18
Santa María, island	Inset	79
Santa Rita	B2	86
Santa Rosa	C4	74
Santa Rosa de Copán	B4	86
Santa Rosa del Palmar	B2	77
Santa Rosalía	B2	84
Santana do Livramento	C5	81
Santander	E1	37
Santarém	A3	36
Santarém	C2	81
Santiago	B3	87
Santiago de Compostela	B1	37
Santiago de Cuba	E3	88
Santiago del Estero	C2	74
Santiago, capital	B4, Inset	76

Name	Key	Page
Santiago, river	B1	77
Santo André	Inset II	81
Santo Antão, island	A1	58
Santo Domingo	B2	90
Santo Domingo de los Colorados	B3	79
Santo Domingo, capital	C2	89
Santo Tomás de Castilla	E4	86
Santos	D4, Inset II	81
Sanyati, river	B1	69
São Bernardo do Campo	Inset II	81
São Caetano do Sul	Inset II	81
São Domingos	A1	62
São Filipe	B4	58
São Francisco, river	D3	81
São Gonçalo	Inset I	81
São João de Meriti	Inset I	81
São José do Rio Prêto	D4	81
São Luís	D2	81
São Nicolau, island	B2	58
São Paulo	D4, Inset II	81
São Tiago, island	C3	58
São Tomé, capital	B4	63
São Tomé, island	B4	63
São Tomé and Príncipe		63
São Vicente, cape	A4	36
São Vicente, island	A2	58
São Vincente	Inset II	81
Saona, island	D2	89
Sapele	C5	65
Sapitwa, mt.	B2	68
Sapporo	Inset I	8
Sar, passage	B3	17
Sar-e Pol	B1	22
Sara Buri	B3	12
Sarajevo, capital	B2	48
Saramacca, river	B2	80
Sarandë	A4	49
Sarandë	D4	44
Sarapiquí, river	B2	86
Saratov	D4	44
Saravan	D4	11
Sarawak, state	C2	13
Sarbhang	A3	19
Sarcelles	Inset II	34
Sardegna, river	A2	19
Sardinia, island	B2	38
Sargodha	D3	21
Sarh	B5	59
Sari	C2	22
Sariwŏn	A3	9
Sarjektjakko	C1	53
Sark, island	Inset II	30
Sarnia	C5	102
Saronic, gulf	Inset	51
Šar Planina, mts.	B3	49
Sarstún, river	D4	85
Sary Tash	C3	23
Sarygamysh Koli, lake	B2	22
Saryshaghan	D2	23
Sasaram	D4	20
Sasebo	A3	8
Saskatchewan, river	G3	92
Saskatoon	D8	104
Sassandra	A4	63
Sassandra, river	C2, C4	63
Sassari	B2	38
Sassnitz	C1	40
Satu, cape	A4	8
Satpura, range	C4	20
Satu Mare	B2	43
Sattahip	B3	12
Sauble Beach	D3	102
Sauðárkrókur	B2	52
Saül	B2	80
Sault Ste. Marie	A1	102
Sault Ste. Marie, Mich.	E1	126
Sault-au-Mouton	G3	103
Saumur	B3	34
Saurimo	D3	70
Sauteurs	B2	91
Sava, river	B1, B2, C2	48
Savai'i, island	A2	18
Savalou	A3	64
Savan, island	B3	91
Savannah, Ga.	E2	126
Savannakhet	C3	11
Savé	B3	64
Savigny-sur-Orge	Inset II	34
Savigna, river	B2	48
Savona	B1	38
Savonlinna	C2	53
Savu, sea	D2	13
Sawda, mt.	B2	24
Sawhaj	B2	56
Sawqirah	C2	25
Sawqirah, bay	C2	25
Saxony	C3	40
Saxony-Anhalt	B3	40
Sayabec	J3	103
Sayan, mts.	D6	44
Sayhut	C1	25
Sayward	K6	95
Sázava, river	B3	42
Scafell Pike, mt.	B2	30
Scarborough	C2	30
Scarborough	B2	91
Scarborough	F4, L5	102
Schaan	B2	33
Schaerbeek	C2	33
Schaffhausen	C1	35
Schefferville	D3	98
Schefferville	C3	101
Schelde, river	B2	33
Schellenberg	B1	33
Scheveningen	B2	32
Schiedam	B3	32
Schiermonnikoog, island	B1	32
Schleswig	B1	40

Name	Key	Page
Schleswig-Holstein	B2	40
Schouwen, island	A3	32
Schreiber	C3	101
Schuler	E6	94
Schwäbisch Gmünd	B4	40
Schwedt	C2	40
Schweinfurt	B3	40
Schwerin	B2	40
Schweriner, lake	B2	40
Schwyz	C1	35
Scilly, islands	A4	30
Scone	B2	30
Sconser	A1	30
Scotstown	E6	103
Scotswood	A3	94
Scott, island	C5	107
Scottsbluff, Nebr.	C1	126
Scugog, lake	G3	102
Scunthorpe	C3	30
Scutari, lake	A1, A3	49
Seaforth	D4	102
Seal Cove	C4	98
Seal, river	D1	96
Searchmont	A1	102
Seattle, Wash.	A1	126
Seawell	C4	91
Sebou, river	C1	57
Sebright	F3	102
Sechura, desert	A2	77
Seda, river	B3	36
Sedalia	E5	94
Sedan	D2	34
Sédhiou	B3	62
Sedley	F10	104
Seeley's Bay	J3	102
Sefadu	B1	63
Segbana	B2	64
Ségou	B3	58
Segovia	D2	37
Séguéla	C3	63
Segura, river	E3	37
Seinäjoki	B2	53
Seine, river	C2, Inset II	34
Sekake	B2	71
Sekondi-Takoradi	B4	64
Selebi-Phikwe	C2	69
Selenge Mörön, river	C2	11
Sélibaby	B4	58
Selinia		Inset 51
Selkirk	C4	96
Selvas, region	B2	81
Selwyn, mts.	C4	105
Seman, river	A3	49
Semara	B1	58
Semarang	C2	13
Sembawang	B1	13
Sembé	C3	66
Semeru, mt.	C2	13
Semey (Semipalatinsk)	E1	23
Semmering, pass	D3	39
Semois, river	D3	33
Sempach	C1	35
Sen, river	D2	11
Senaki	B3	45
Sendai	D2	8
Senegal		62
Senegal, river	B1, C2	62
Senkaku, islands	Inset II	8
Senmonorom	F3	11
Senne, river	C2	33
Senneterre	A4	101
Senta	B2	49
Seoul, capital	B4	9
Sepik, river	A2	15
Sept-Îles	C3	101
Septentrional, range	A1	89
Serangoon	B1	13
Serbia, republic	B2	49
Seremban	A2	13
Serenje	C2	67
Sergipe	E3	81
Seria	A2	13
Serov	D5	44
Serowe	C2	69
Serpent, island	D1	69
Sérrai	B1	51
Serravalle	B1	39
Serrekunda	C2	62
Serule	B2	69
Sese, islands	C4	61
Sesheke	A3	67
Seti, river	A2	19
Sétif	B1	57
Settat	C1	57
Setúbal	A3	36
Setúbal, bay	A3	36
Sevan, lake	C2	45
Sevastopol	C4	47
Seven Persons	E6	94
Seven Sisters Falls	C4	96
Severn, river	C3	30
Severn, river	B2	101
Severnaya Zemlya, islands	A6	44
Seville	D4	37
Sevran	Inset II	34
Sèvres	Inset II	34
Sewa, river	B2	63
Seward, Alaska	Inset I	126
Seychelles		70
Sfax	C2	57
Sfîntu Gheorghe	B2	43
Sha Tin	Inset	10
Shaanxi	D2	10
Shabwah	B1	25
Shache	A2	10
Shackleton Ice Shelf, glacier	C2	107
Shahr-e Kord	C2	22
Shaki	B3	65
Shalqar	B2	23
Sham, ash-	D1	25
Shamattawa	E2	96
Shamgong	B2	19
Shan, plateau	C2	12
Shanchung	B1	9
Shandong	E2	10
Shangani, river	A2	69
Shanghai	F2	10

Name	Key	Page
Shannon	B2	31
Shannon, river	B2	31
Shantou	E3	10
Shanxi	E2	10
Shanxi	F3	10
Shaoguan	E3	10
Shaoxing	F3	10
Shaoyang	E3	10
Sharbot Lake	J3	102
Sharjah	C2	35
Shashe, river	C2	69
Shashi	E2	10
Shatt al-Arab, river	C2	24
Shaunavon	B11	104
Shawinigan	D5	103
Sheberghan	B1	22
Shediac	E2	97
Sheenboro	B2	102
Sheerness	E5	94
Sheet Harbour	E3	100
Sheffield	C3	30
Sheguianda	D2	102
Sheho	G9	104
Shek Pik	Inset	10
Shelburne	B4	100
Shelburne	E3	102
Shelikhov, gulf	C9	44
Shell Lake	C7	104
Shellbrook	D7	104
Shelter Bay	N6	95
Shëngjin	A2	49
Shenyang	F1	10
Sherbro, island	A2	63
Sherbrooke	E2	100
Sherbrooke	E6	103
Sheridan, Wyo.	C1	126
Sherridon	A1	96
Sherwood Park	D4	94
Shetland, islands	Inset I	30
Sheva	Inset I	20
Shewa Gimira	B3	60
Shibar, pass	B2	22
Shibin al-Kawm	B1	56
Shijiazhuang	E2	10
Shikarpur	C4	21
Shikoku, island	B3	8
Shillong	F3	20
Shimizu	C3	8
Shimonoseki	A3	8
Shimonoseki, strait	A3	8
Shinano, river	C2	8
Shinas	C1	25
Shindand	A2	22
Shinyanga	B1	68
Shiono, cape	B3	8
Ship Cove	D3	98
Shippagan	E1	97
Shirane, mt.	C3	8
Shiraz	C4	22
Shire, river	B3	68
Shiretoko, cape	Inset I	8
Shizuoka	C3	8
Shkhara, mt.	B3	45
Shkodër	A1	49
Shkumbin, river	A2	49
Shoal Lake	A4	96
Sholapur	C5	20
Shostka	C1	47
Shreveport, La.	D2	126
Shrewsbury	C3	30
Shrirampur	Inset II	20
Shubenacadie	D2	100
Shubra al-Khaymah	B1	56
Shumen	E2	50
Shurugwi	C2	69
Shwebo	B2	12
Shymkent (Chimkent)	C2	23
Siahan, range	B4	21
Sialkot	D2	21
Siargao, island	C4	12
Šiauliai	B2	46
Sibbald	E5	94
Siberia, region	C7	44
Siberut, island	A2	13
Sibiti	B5	66
Sibiu	C3	43
Sibu	C2	13
Sibuyan, island	B3	12
Sibuyan, sea	B3	12
Sicamous	N6	95
Sichuan	D2	10
Sicily, island	C3	38
Sicily, strait	B3	38
Sico, river	C2	86
Sicuani	C3	77
Sidi bel Abbès	A1	57
Sidi Bou Zid	B2	57
Sidlaw, hills	B2	30
Sidney	L7	95
Sidney	B4	96
Sidon (Sayda)	A2	26
Sidra, gulf	C1	56
Sidvokodvo	B2	71
Siedlce	F2	41
Siegen	B3	40
Siem Pang	E1	11
Siemreab	B2	11
Siena	B2	38
Sieradz	D3	41
Sierra de Cayey, mts.	C2	90
Sierra de Loquillo, mts.	D2	90
Sierra Leone		63
Sierra Madre, mts.	B2	12
Sierra Madre, mts.	C5	85
Sierra Nevada de Santa Marta, mts.	B2	78
Sierra Nevada, mts., Calif.	A2	126
Sifton	A3	96
Siggiewi	B2	36
Sighetul Marmației	B2	43
Sighișoara	C2	43
Siglufjördhur	B1	52
Siguatepeque	B2	86
Siguiri	D2	62
Siirt	E3	27
Sikanni Chief	L2	95

Name	Key	Page
Silay	B4	
Silesia, region	C3	
Silet	B2	
Silgarhi	B2	
Silhouette, island	C3	
Siliana	B1	
Silifke	C3	
Silisili, mt.	A2	
Silistra	F1	
Silkeborg	B2	
Sillery	K6	
Šilutė	A2	
Silvassa	B4	
Silver	C4	
Silver City, N. Mex.	C2	
Sima	B2	
Simcoe, lake	E4	
Simeulue, island	A1	
Simferopol	C4	
Simikot	B1	
Simon, lake	A6	
Simonette, river	A2	
Simonhouse	A2	
Simpson, desert	B2	
Sinai, peninsula	B2	
Sinaloa	C3	
Sincelejo	B2	
Sinclair	C4	
Sinclair Mills	M4	
Sindhuli Garhi	B2	
Siné, river	B2	
Sines	A4	
Singapore		
Singapore, capital	B1	
Singapore, island	B1	
Singapore, strait	B2	
Singen	B5	
Singida	B1	
Singur	Inset II	
Sinoe	C2	
Sinop	B2	
Sint-Niklaas	C1	
Sint-Truiden	D2	
Sinŭiju	A2	
Sió, river	B2	
Siófok	B2	
Sioux City, Iowa	D1	
Sioux Falls, S. Dak.	D1	
Sioux Lookout	B2	
Sipaliwini	A2	
Siparia	A2	
Siping	C1	
Sipiwesk, lake	C1	
Siple, island	B8	
Siple, mt.	B8	
Siquia, river	B2	
Sirajganj	C4	
Sirba, river	D2	
Siret	D2	
Siret, river	D2	
Sirjan	C3	
Sisaket	C3	
Sisian	C3	
Sisimiut (Holsteinsborg)	B2	
Sisophon	B2	
Siteki	B2	
Sitka, Alaska	Inset I	
Sittang, river	B2	
Sittard	C4	
Sittwe	A2	
Sivas	D2	
Siwah	A2	
Sixaola, river	C3	
Sjælland, island	C3	
Skagen	C1	
Skagerrak, strait	A3	
Skåne, region	B3	
Skaw, cape	C1	
Skead	E1	
Skeena, mts.	H3	
Skeena, river	H4	
Skeleton, coast	A1	
Skellefteå	C2	
Skellefteälven, river	C1	
Skien	B4	
Skierniewice	E3	
Skikda	B1	
Skíros, island	C2	
Skive	B2	
Skjern, river	B3	
Skjern, river	B3	
Skookumchuck	P6	
Skopje, capital	B2	
Skovorodino	D8	
Skowhegan	C2	
Skye, island	A1	
Slagelse	C2	
Slaná, river	C2	
Slave Lake	C3	
Slavonia, region	C2	
Slavonska Požega	C2	
Slavonski Brod	D2	
Slieve Donard, mt.	B2	
Sligo	B1	
Sliven	E3	
Slobozia	D3	
Slough	Inset III	
Slovakia		
Slovenia		
Slovenskérudohorie, mts.	B2	
Sluch', river	C1	
Słupsk	C1	
Småland, region	B3	
Smallwood, reservoir	D3	
Smeaton	D8	
Smederevo	B2	
Smilovichi	D3	
Smiltene	D2	
Smith River	J1	
Smithers	J4	
Smithers Landing	J3	
Smiths Cove	B3	
Smiths Falls	J3	
Smithville	F4	

Key Page

y, river A3, A4 94
ensk D3 44
evichi D2 47
...... C4 50
othstone, lake D6 104
othstone, river D6 104
e, river C3 105
ng B1 126
...... A4 94
...... C1 32
ka, mt. B2 42
dwy, lake E2 41
v Lake A2 96
don, mt. B3 30
drift F4 99
flake B4 96
Harbour D3 98
...... E3 11
kundo, islands B5 9
ek, mts. B5 9
...... C3 59
capital B3 50
...... B2 69
river B3 52
...... C2 34
ön, bay A3 9
...... C3 9
dé B2 64
...... C1 65
to, plains C1 65
to, river C1 65
coast D4 37
...... B1 18
eu B2 36
...... C3 30
ull B2 30
...... A3 40
non Is. 16
mon, sea B2 15
olo C2 18
ezi B2 67
alia 60
be, beach E2 90
or A2 49
bra C5 102
...... B4 96
rset, island K2 99
es, river B2 43
ne, river C2 34
oto A2 87
La A2 11
river D4 37
...... Inset II 20
rpur B4 32
erborg B1 38
rio C3 68
ea F1 10
hua, river F1 10
kkhla B5 12
köl D2 23
nam B4 9
nim A3 9
we, river B1 68
ora B1 84
onate A2 86
oral, island ...... Inset 17
...... L7 95
...... A2 43
river B3 36
...... C5 103
...... E2 37
...... B1 50
caba D4 81
ng C3 61
ti A3 36
...... C2 38
iowiec D3 41
bay B3 17
...... B2 64
...... C2 45
uboua C4 63
oré B4 90
rière A2 91
rière, volcano A2 91
...... C4 69
rgrougrou, river B3 64
ces, mt. B1 71
...... A4 96
s. C2 100
...... G11 104
plain B2 57
river B2 57
úa B1 89
h Africa 71
h Andaman, island F6 20
ulatsivik, island E3 98
h Australia C2 14
h Baymouth C2 102
h Bend, Ind. E1 126
h Branch B5 98
h Brook C4 98
h Carolina E2 126
h China, sea ...... E4, Inset 10
h Comino, channel B2 36
h Dakota C1 126
h Downs, hills C3 30
h Dum-Dum ...... Inset II 20
h Georgia, island G1 100
h Henik, lake J4 99
dian Lake D1 96
h Korea 9
h Magnetic Pole C3 107
h Male, atoll A3 19
h Malosmadulu, atoll A2 19
h Milford B3 100
oose, lake 96
h Orkney, islands C12 107

South Ossetia, region B3 45
South Pole A17 107
South Rawdon D3 100
South River F2 102
South Ronaldsay, island ...... Inset I 30
South Saskatchewan, river D8 104
South Shetland, islands C12 107
South Shields C2 30
South Taranaki, bight B2 15
South Uist, island A1 30
South West, cape A4 15
South, island A3 15
Southampton C4 30
Southampton D3 102
Southampton, island L4 99
Southend G4 104
Southend-on-Sea D3 30
Southern Alps, mts. A3 15
Southern Bug, river B2 47
Southern Uplands, mts. B2 30
Southland, plains A4 15
Southport C3 30
Southport B2 100
Sovetskaya Gavan E9 44
Soweto C2 71
Soya, point ...... Inset I 8
Soyapango A2 86
Soyo B2 70
Sozh, river E3 47
Spa D2 33
Spain 37
Sousse C2 57
Spandau C2 40
Spanish C1 102
Spanish Town C3 88
Sparta B3 51
Spartansburg, S.C. E2 126
Spartivento, cape D3 38
Sparwood P6 95
Speightstown A2 91
Spence Bay K3 99
Spencer, gulf C3 14
Spences Bridge M6 95
Sperrin, mts. A2 30
Spessart, mts. B4 40
Spey, river B1 30
Speyer B4 40
Spiritwood C7 104
Spišská Nová Ves E2 42
Spithead, channel C4 30
Split C3 48
Split Lake D1 96
Splügen, pass D2 35
Spokane, Wash. B1 126
Spoleto C2 38
Spragge C1 102
Sprague D4 96
Spree, river C3 40
Spring Bay C2 102
Spring Coulee D6 94
Spring Hall A2 91
Springbok A2 71
Springdale C4 98
Springfield, capital, Ill. E2 126
Springfield, Mass. F1 126
Springfield, Mo. D2 126
Springhill C2 100
Springs C2 71
Springside H9 104
Springstein C4 96
Springwater B9 104
Spruce Grove D4 94
Spy Hill J10 104
Squamish L6 95
Square Islands D3 98
Sre Ambel B4 11
Srebrenica C1 48
Sredna Gora, mts. C3 50
Sremska Mitrovica A2 49
Sreng, river B2 11
Sri Lanka 19
Srinagar B2 20
Stafford C3 30
Stand Off D6 94
Standard D5 94
Stanley C2 97
Stanmore E5 94
Stanovoy, range D8 44
Star City F8 104
Stara Zagora D3 50
Starbuck C4 96
Starbuck, island D2 17
Starnberg, lake B5 40
Start, point B4 30
Staubbach, falls B2 35
Stavanger B4 52
Stavropol E4 44
Stayner E3 102
Stead C4 96
Steen River B1 94
Stefanson, island G2 99
Steinbach C4 96
Steinkjer C3 52
Stellarton E2 100
Stellenbosch A3 71
Stendal B2 40
Stephenville B5 98
Stettler D4 94
Stevenage ...... Inset III 30
Stevenson, lake C3 96
Stewart H3 95
Stewart River B4 105
Stewart, island A4 15
Stewart, river B4, C3 105
Stewiacke D2 100
Steyr E2 39
Stikine G3 95
Stikine, river G3 95
Stirling B2 30
Stirling H3 102
Štip C2 48
Stockerau E2 39
Stockholm, capital C3 52
Stoeng Treng D2 11
Stoke-on-Trent C3 30
Stonecliffe H1 102
Stoneham E4 103
Stonewall C4 96

Stoney Point C5 102
Stony Mountain C4 96
Stony Plain D4 94
Stony Rapids E1 104
Storå, river B2 32
Storavan, lake C1 53
Store, strait C3 32
Storkerson, peninsula G2 99
Stornoway A1 30
Stornoway E6 103
Storsjön, lake B2 53
Storthoaks A4 96
Stoughton G11 104
Strakonice A3 42
Stralsund C1 40
Strangford B2 30
Stranraer B2 30
Strasbourg D2 34
Strasbourg F9 104
Stratford D4 102
Stratford E6 103
Stratford-upon-Avon C3 30
Strathclair A4 96
Strathlorne F1 100
Strathnaver L4 95
Strathroy D5 102
Straubing C4 40
Streymoy, island ...... Inset 32
Stromboli, island C3 38
Stronsay, island ...... Inset I 30
Struga A2 48
Struma, river A3 50
Strumica C2 48
Stryama, river C3 50
Stuart, lake K4 95
Stubbs B2 91
Stuie J5 95
Sturgeon C2 100
Sturgeon Falls D3 101
Sturgis H9 104
Stuttgart B4 40
Subotica A1 49
Suceava D2 43
Suchiate, river A5 85
Sucre, capital A3 77
Sudan 59
Sudbury E1 102
Sudd, region B3 59
Suddie B2 80
Sudeten, mts. B3 41
Sudirman, range D2 13
Suduroy, island ...... Inset 32
Sue, river B3 59
Suez B2 56
Suez, canal B2 56
Suez, gulf B2 56
Sugandha ...... Inset II 20
Suhar C1 25
Sühbaatar C2 11
Suhl B3 40
Suir, river C2 31
Suita B3 8
Sukabumi B3 13
Sukang B3 13
Sukhna, as- B2 27
Sukhothai B2 12
Sukhumi A3 45
Sukkur C4 21
Sula, islands D2 13
Sulaiman, range C4 21
Sulaybikhat, as- B2 24
Sulaymaniyah, as- C1 24
Sulayyil, as- B2 24
Sulima B2 63
Sullana A1 77
Sullivan, lake E5 94
Sulu, archipelago B5 12
Sulu, sea A4 12
Sülüktü A3 23
Sumatra, island B2 13
Šumava, mts. A3 42
Sumba, island D2 13
Sumbar, river B2 22
Sumbawa, island C2 13
Sumbawanga B2 68
Sumbe B2 70
Summerford D4 98
Summerland N6 95
Summerside B2 100
Summerville E5 98
Summit Lake K2 95
Summit Lake L4 95
Šumperk C3 42
Sumqayit C2 45
Sumy C1 47
Sun City C2 71
Sun Kosi, river C2 19
Sunchon B5 9
Sundarbans, region C7 21
Sunderland C2 30
Sunderland F3 102
Sundi C1 63
Sundown C4 96
Sundridge F2 102
Sundsvall C2 53
Sunnynook E5 94
Sunset House B3 94
Sunyani A3 64
Sup'ung, reservoir A2 9
Superior, lake J4 92
Superior, Wis. D1 126
Sur C1 25
Sur (Tyre) A2 26
Surab C4 21
Surabaya C2 13
Surakarta C2 13
Surat B4 20
Surat Thani B4 12
Sûre, river A2, B2 33
Surgut C4 44
Surigao C4 12
Surin C2 12
Suriname 80
Suriname, river B3 80
Surkhob, river B1 23
Surma, river E3 21
Surprise F1 95
Surt C1 56
Surtsey, island A3 52

Surud Ad, mt. B1 60
Sussex D3 97
Susuman C9 44
Sutlej, river D4 21
Sutton West F3 102
Suva, capital B3 17
Suvadiva, atoll A4 19
Suwałki F1 41
Suwanose, island A4 8
Suwar, as- B2 27
Suwayda, as- A3 27
Suwon B2 9
Suzano ...... Inset II 81
Suzhou F2 10
Svalbard, islands 5
Svay Rieng D4 11
Svendborg C3 32
Šventoji, river C2 46
Švetozarevo B3 49
Svilengrad E4 50
Svishtov D2 50
Svitavy C3 42
Svobodnyy D8 44
Swabian Jura, mts. B4 40
Swains, island A1 18
Swakopmund B2 70
Swan Hills C4 94
Swan Lake B4 96
Swan River A3 96
Swan, lake A3 96
Swan, river A3 96
Swan, river ...... Inset I 14
Swansea B3 30
Swaziland 71
Sweden 53
Swift Current D5 98
Swift Current C10 104
Swindon C3 30
Świnoujście B2 41
Switzerland 35
Swords C2 31
Sydney G1 100
Sydney, island B2 17
Sydney, N.S.W., capital ...... E3, Inset IV 14
Syktyvkar C4 44
Sylhet E4 21
Syracuse (Siracusa) C3 38
Syracuse, N.Y. F1 126
Syrdarya, river A1, C2 23
Syria 27
Syrian, desert B1 26
Szczecin B2 41
Szczytno E2 41
Szeged E3 43
Székesfehérvár B2 43
Szekszárd B2 43
Szentes C2 43
Szolnok C2 43
Szombathely A2 43

T

Taabo, lake D3 63
Tabar, islands B2 15
Tabasará, mts. B2 87
Tabasco F4 84
Tabelbala A2 57
Taber D6 94
Tablas, island B3 12
Tabligbo B3 64
Tábor B3 42
Tabora C4 68
Tabou C4 63
Tabriz A1 24
Tabuaeran, island D1 17
Tabuk A1 24
Tabusintac D1 97
Tabwemasana, mt. B2 18
Tacaná, volcano A4 85
Tacloban C4 12
Tacna C4 77
Tacoma, Wash. A1 126
Tacuarembó C1 75
Tacuarembó C1 75
Tacuarí, river D5 75
Tadjoura B2 60
Tadmur B2 27
Tadoussac G3 103
Taebaek-Sanmaek, mts. C3 9
Taedong, river B3 9
Taegu C5 9
Taejon B4 9
Tafahi, island C1 17
Tafilah, at- A2 26
Taga A2 18
Taganrog, gulf D3 47
Tagish C5 105
Tagish, lake E1 95
Tagula, island B3 15
Tagus, river D3 37
Tahan, mt. B2 13
Tahat, mt. C2 57
Tahoua B3 59
Tai, lake F2 10
T'aichung B1 9
Taif, at- B2 24
T'ainan B1 9
Taipei, capital B1 9
Taitao, peninsula A8 76
T'aitung B2 9
Taiwan 9
Taiwan, strait E3 10
Taiyuan E2 10
Taizz A2 25
Tajikistan 23
Tajumulco, volcano B4 85
Tak B2 12
Taka, island B1 16
Takamaka ...... Inset 69
Takamatsu B3 8
Takara, island A4 8
Takatsuki B3 8
Takev C5 11
Takipy A1 96
Takla Makan, desert B2 10
Takla, lake K3 95
Takua Pa B4 12

Takutu, river B4 80
Talagante 76
Talak, region B2 59
Talamanca, range C3 86
Talara A1 77
Talas C1 23
Talaud, islands D1 13
Talavera de la Reina D3 37
Talca B5 76
Talcahuano B6 76
Taldyqorghan D2 23
Talish, mts. C3 45
Tall Afar B1 24
Tallahassee, capital, Fla. E2 126
Tallinn, capital C1 46
Taloqan B1 22
Talsi B2 46
Taltson, river F4 99
Tamale B2 64
Tamanrasset B2 57
Tamarin B3 69
Tamaulipas E3 84
Tambacounda A3 62
Tambo, river C3, C4 77
Tâmega, river B2 36
Tampa, Fla. E3 126
Tampere B2 53
Tampico E3 84
Tampines B1 13
Tampok, river B2 80
Tamsagbulag D2 11
Tamworth, N.S.W. E3 14
Tan-Tan A2 57
Tana B1 60
Tana, river F4 61
Tana, river F1 52
Tanabe B3 8
Tanchon C2 9
Tandil D4 74
Tanega, island A4 8
Tanen, range B2 12
Tanezrouft, mts. A2 57
Tanga C2 68
Tanga, islands B2 15
Tangail C4 21
Tanganyika, lake A2 68
Tanggula, range C2 10
Tangier C1 57
Tangier E3 100
Tangshan E2 10
Tanimbar, islands E2 13
Tanjungpinang B1 13
Tanna, island C4 18
Tano, river A3 64
Tanshui B1 9
Tanzania 68
Taongi, island B1 16
Taoudenni C1 58
Taoyüan B1 9
Tapa C1 46
Tapachula F5 84
Tapajós, river C2 81
Tapanahoni, river B3 80
Tapeta B3 63
Taquari, river C3 81
Tara D5 44
Tara, river A3 49
Tarakan C1 13
Taranto D2 38
Taranto, gulf D2 38
Tarapoto B2 77
Tararua, range C3 15
Tarawa, capital A1 17
Taree, N.S.W. E3 14
Tarija B4 77
Tarin Kowt B2 22
Tarnobrzeg E3 41
Tarnów E3 41
Taroudant B2 57
Tarragona G2 37
Tarrafal C3 58
Tarrasa G2 37
Tarsus C2 27
Tartu C2 46
Tartus A2 27
Tarvo B3 77
Taseko, lake L5 95
Tash Kömür C2 23
Tashigang C2 19
Tashkent, capital C2 23
Tasikmalaya C2 13
Tasman, bay B3 15
Tasman, sea D4 14
Tasmania D4 14
Tata B2 43
Tatabánya B2 43
Tatamagouche D2 100
Tataouine C3 57
Tatar, strait D9 44
Tatarstan, republic C4 44
Tathlina, lake E4 99
Tatla Lake L5 95
Tatlayoko Lake L5 95
Tatra, range B2 42
Tau, island A1 18
Tau, islands B3 15
Tauern, mts. B3 39
Taumaruni C2 15
Taung B2 71
Taunggyi C2 12
Taunton B3 30
Taunton ...... Inset 30
Taunus, mts. B3 40
Taupo C2 15
Taupo, lake C2 15
Tauragė B2 46
Tauranga C2 15
Taureau, reservoir C5 103
Taurus, mts. B2 27
Tauu, islands B3 15
Tavan Bogd Uul, mt. ...... Inset II 11
Taverny ...... Inset II 34
Tavira B4 37
Tavistock D3 102
Tavoy C3 12
Tavoy, island C3 12

Tavoy, point C3 12
Tawau D2 13
Tawi Tawi, island A5 12
Taxco E4 84
Tay Ninh B4 11
Tay, estuary C2 30
Tay, lake B2 30
Tay, river B2 30
Tay, river C4 105
Taymouth C2 97
Taymyr, peninsula B6 44
Taymyriya, autonomous okrug B6 44
Taza C1 57
Tazin, lake A1 104
Tazin, river B1 104
Tbilisi, capital C4 45
Tchamba B2 64
Tchaourou B3 64
Tchentlo, lake K3 95
Tchibanga A2 66
Te Anau, lake A4 15
Tebicuary, river D5 75
Tecomán D4 84
Tecuci D3 43
Tedzhen C3 22
Tedzhen, river C3 22
Teepee Creek A3 94
Tees, river C2 30
Teeswater D3 102
Tefé B2 81
Tegal B2 13
Tegucigalpa, capital B2 86
Tehek, lake J4 99
Tehkummah D2 102
Tehran, capital C2 22
Tehuacán E4 84
Tehuantepec, gulf E4 84
Tehuantepec, isthmus F4 84
Teifi, river B3 30
Tekapo, lake B3 15
Tekeze, river B1 60
Tekirdağ A2 27
Tekong, island C1 13
Tel Aviv-Jaffa B1 26
Tela B2 86
Telavi C4 45
Telde ...... Inset I 37
Telegraph Creek G2 95
Teles Pires, river C2 81
Telford C3 30
Telkwa J4 95
Telok Anson A2 13
Telšiai B2 46
Tema C4 64
Temagami, lake E1 102
Temburong, river C2 13
Temirtau D1 23
Tempisque, river A2 86
Temuco B6 76
Tena C3 79
Téna Kourou, mt. B3 64
Ténéré, desert C1 59
Tenerife, island ...... Inset I 37
Tengiz, lake C1 23
Tenkodogo D3 64
Tennant Creek, N.T. C1 14
Tennessee E2 126
Tennessee, river E2 126
Tenojoki, river C1 53
Tenryu, river C3 8
Teotihuacán ...... Inset 84
Tepexpan ...... Inset 84
Tepic, state capital D3 84
Téra A3 59
Terai, region A2, C3 19
Teraina, island D1 17
Teramo C2 38
Teresina D2 81
Tereul F2 37
Termiz C3 23
Termoli C2 38
Ternate D1 13
Terni C2 38
Ternopil B2 47
Terrace H4 95
Terre Haute, Ind. E2 126
Terrebonne J5 103
Terreiro Velho C1 63
Terrenceville D5 98
Terschelling, island C1 32
Teseney B3 59
Teshio, river ...... Inset I 8
Tesiyn, river B2 11
Teslić B1 48
Teslin C5 105
Teslin, lake C5 105
Teslin, river C5 105
Tessalit D1 58
Tessaoua B3 59
Testa del Gargano, point D2 38
Tete B3 68
Tête Jaune Cache N5 95
Tétouan C1 57
Tetovo A1 48
Teulada, cape B3 38
Teulon C4 96
Tewkesbury C3 30
Texarkana, Tex. D2 126
Texas D2 126
Texcoco ...... Inset 84
Texel, island B1 32
Teyateyaneng A2 71
Tezcoco ...... Inset 84
Tezzeron, lake K4 95
Thaba-Tseka B2 71
Thabana Ntlenyana, mt. B2 71
Thai Nguyen A2 11
Thailand 12
Thailand, gulf B4, C4 12
Thames, river ...... C3, Inset III 30
Thames, river D5 102
Thamesville C4 102
Thane ...... Inset I 20
Thanh Hoa A2 11
Thanjavur C6 20
Thar, desert C4 21
Thásos C1 51
Thásos, island C1 51

	Key	Page
The Crane	C4	91
The Hague	B2	32
The Ovens	C3	100
The Pas	A2, C2	96
Thedford	D4	102
Thekulthili, lake	G4	99
Thelon, river	H4, J4	99
Theodore	H9	104
Thessalon	B1	102
Thessaloníki	B1	51
Thetford	D3	30
Thetford Mines	E5	103
Thicket	C4	91
Thicket Portage	C1	96
Thiès	A2	62
Thika	D4	61
Thimphu, capital	A2	19
Thingvellir	A2	52
Thio	C2	18
Thíra, island	C3	51
Thisted	B2	32
Thlewiaza, river	J4	99
Tholen, island	B3	32
Thomaston Corner	B3	97
Thompson	C1, D2	96
Thompson, river	M6	95
Thong Hoe	A1	13
Thorhild	D4	94
Thornhill	K5	102
Thorold	F4	102
Thrace, region	D4	50
Thracian, plain	C3	50
Three Kings, islands	B1	15
Thule, air base	B2	106
Thun	B2	35
Thunder Bay	C3	101
Thunersee, lake	B2	35
Thuringia	B3	40
Thuringian, forest	B3	40
Thurso	B1	30
Thurston, island	B9	107
Ti'avea	D2	18
Ti-n-Zaouâtene	B2	57
Tiáhuac	Inset	84
Tianjin	E2	10
Tibati	B2	65
Tiber, river	C2	38
Tiberias	B1	26
Tiberias (Galilee), lake	A1, B1	26
Tibesti, massif	B2	59
Tibet (Xizang)	B2	10
Tibet, plateau	B2	10
Tiburón, island	B2	84
Tichit	C3	58
Tichla	A2	58
Ticino, river	C2	35
Tide Head	C1	97
Tidjikdja	C3	58
Tien Shan, range	A1	10
Tierra del Fuego, island	C9	76
Tietê, river	Inset II	81
Tignish	A2	100
Tigre, river	B1	77
Tigris, river	B1	24
Tijuana	A1	84
Tikal	D2	85
Tikrit	B2	24
Tiksi	B8	44
Tiladummati, atoll	A1	19
Tilburg	C3	32
Tilbury	C5	102
Tillabéry	A3	59
Tilley	E6	94
Tillsonburg	E5	102
Tilomonte	C2	76
Tilston	A4	96
Timaru	B3	15
Timbuktu	C2	58
Timgad, ruins	B1	57
Timişoara	A3	43
Timmins	D3	101
Timor, island	D2	13
Timor, sea	B1	14
Tindouf	A2	57
Tingo María	B2	77
Tinkissa, river	C2	62
Tio	C2	60
Tipitapa, river	A2	87
Tipperary	B2	31
Tiranë, capital	A2	49
Tiraspol	B2	50
Tiree, island	A2	30
Tîrgovişte	C3	43
Tîrgu Jiu	B3	43
Tîrgu-Mureş	C2	43
Tîrgu Neamţ	D2	43
Tîrgu Ocna	D2	43
Tirich Mîr, mt.	D2	21
Tirso, river	B2	38
Tiruchchirappalli	C6	20
Tisa, river	B2	49
Tisdale	F8	104
Tista, river	C2	21
Tisza, river	C2	43
Titagarh	Inset II	20
Titano, mt.	B1	39
Titicaca, lake	A3, D4	77
Titov Veles	B2	48
Titova Mitrovica	B3	49
Tivaouane	A2	62
Tiverton	B4	30
Tiverton	D3	102
Tivoli	B2	91
Tiznit	B2	57
Tlaipan	Inset	84
Tlalnepantla	Inset	84
Tlaxcala, state capital	E4	84
Tlemcen	A1	57
Toa Payoh	B1	13
Toad River	K2	95
Toamasina	B2	69
Toba Kakar, range	C3	21
Tobago, cays	A4	91
Tobago, island	B1	91
Tobermory	D2	102
Tobi, island	Inset	17
Tobin, lake	G7	104
Tobol, river	C1	23
Tobolsk	D5	44

	Key	Page
Tobruk	D1	56
Tocantins	D3	81
Tocantins, river	D2	81
Toco	B2	91
Tocopilla	B2	76
Tofino	K6	95
Tofua, island	B3	17
Togo		64
Tokachi, river	Inset I	8
Tokaj	C1	43
Tokara, islands	A4	8
Tokat	D2	27
Tŏkch'ŏk-kundo, islands	A4	9
Tokmok	D1	23
Tokorozawa	C3	8
Toktogul	C2	23
Toku, island	C2	17
Tokuno, island	Inset II	8
Tokushima	B3	8
Tokuyama	A3	8
Tokyo, capital	C3	8
Tōlanaro	B3	69
Toledo	D3	37
Toledo, mts.	D3	37
Toledo, Ohio	E1	126
Toliara	B3	69
Tolima, mt.	B3	78
Tolland	E4	94
Toltén, river	B6	76
Toluca, state capital	E4	84
Tolyatti	D4	44
Tom Price, W.A.	A2	14
Tomahawk	C4	94
Tomakomai	Inset I	8
Tomanivi, mt.	B2	17
Tombua	B5	70
Tomé	B6	76
Tomelloso	E3	37
Tomiko, lake	F1	102
Tompkins	B10	104
Tomsk	D6	44
Tonalá	F4	84
Tonbridge	Inset III	30
Tone, river	C2	8
Tonga		17
Tongariro, mt.	C2	15
Tongatapu, island	B4	17
Tonghua	F1	10
Tongjŏson, bay	B3	9
Tongliao	F1	10
Tongsa	B2	19
Tongsa, river	B2	19
Tonkin, gulf	B2	11
Tonle Sap, lake	B2, C3	11
Tonle Sap, river	C2	11
Toowoomba, Qld.	E2	14
Topeka, Kans.	D2	126
Topley Landing	J4	95
Torbay	B4	30
Torbay	E5	98
Torghay, plateau	C1	23
Tormes, river	D2	37
Torneälven, river	D1	53
Torngat, mts.	D3	98
Tornio	B1	53
Torniojoki, river	B1	53
Toronto, capital	F4, K5	102
Tororo	D3	61
Torquay	G11	104
Tórshavn	Inset	32
Tortosa	G2	37
Tortosa, cape	G2	37
Tortuga, island	C1	89
Toruń	C2	41
Tõrva	D2	46
Tory Hill	G3	102
Tosa, bay	B3	8
Totness	A2	80
Tottori	B3	8
Touggourt	B1	57
Tougué	C2	62
Toulaman, river	B2	90
Touliu	B2	9
Toulon	D5	34
Toulouse	C5	34
Toungoo	C2	12
Toura, mts.	C2	63
Tourcoing	C1	34
Tournai	A2	33
Tours	C3	34
Toussoro, mt.	B3	66
Toutes Aides	B3	96
Tovuz	A2	45
Towada, lake	D1	8
Townsville, Qld.	D1	14
Toxkan, river	E2	23
Toyama	C2	8
Toyama, bay	C2	8
Toyohashi	C3	8
Toyonaka	B3	8
Toyota	C3	8
Tozeur	B3	57
Tqvarcheli	A3	45
Trabzon	D2	27
Tracadie-Sheila	E1	97
Tracy	C3	97
Tracy	D5	103
Trafalgar	E2	100
Trail	O6	95
Tralee	B2	31
Trang	B5	12
Transantarctic, mts.	B4	107
Transylvanian Alps, mts.	C3	43
Trapani	C3	38
Trasimeno, lake	C2	38
Trat	D7	44
Traun, river	D2	39
Traverse City, Mich.	E1	126
Trebinje	C4	99

	Key	Page
Treherne	B4	96
Treinta y Tres	C2	75
Trembleur, lake	K4	95
Trenche, river	C3	103
Trenčín	B2	42
Trent, river	C3	30
Trento	B1	38
Trenton	E2	100
Trenton	H3	102
Trenton, capital, N.J.	F1	126
Tres Puntas, cape	B6	74
Trepassey	E5	98
Treska, river	B2	48
Treviso	C1	38
Trier	A4	40
Triesen	B2	33
Triesenberg	B2	33
Trieste	C1	38
Trieste, gulf	A3	48
Triglav, mt.	A2	48
Tríkala	B2	51
Trim	C2	31
Trincomalee	C3	19
Trinidad	B2	77
Trinidad	B2	75
Trinidad	B3	78
Trinidad	C1	61
Trinidad, island	A2	91
Trinidad, mts.	C2	88
Trinidad and Tobago		91
Trinity East	E5	98
Trinity, bay	E5	98
Triolet	C2	69
Tripoli (Tarabulus)	A1	26
Tripoli, capital	B1	56
Tripolitania, region	B1	56
Trivandrum (Thiruvananthapuram)	C7	20
Trnava	A2	42
Trobriand, islands	B2	15
Trois-Pistoles	G3	103
Trois-Rivières	D5	103
Troisvierges	B1	33
Trollhättan	B3	53
Trombay	Inset I	20
Tromsø	D2	52
Trondheim	C3	52
Trondheimsfjord, fjord	B3	52
Trongisvágur	Inset	32
Troödos, mts.	A2	27
Trossachs	F11	104
Trout Creek	F1	102
Trout Lake	C3	94
Trout River	B4	98
Trout, lake	D4	99
Trout, lake	B2	101
Trouville	C2	34
Trowbridge	C3	30
Troyes	D2	34
Trujillo	B2	77
Trujillo	B2	79
Trujillo	B2	86
Trujillo Alto	C2	90
Truro	B4	30
Truro	D2	100
Trutch	B4	95
Trutnov	B2	42
Tsaratanana, mts.	B1	69
Tsavo	E5	61
Tsedike, river	B3	71
Tsengwen, river	B2	9
Tsetserleg	C2	11
Tsévié	B3	64
Tshabong	A3	69
Tshane	A3	69
Tshaneni	B1	71
Tshikapa	B4	67
Tshuapa, river	B2	67
Tsiribihina, river	B2	69
Tsiroanomandidy	B2	69
Tsiteli-Tsqaro	D4	45
Tskhinvali	B3	45
Tsnori	C4	45
Tsu, island	A3	8
Tsuen Wan	Inset	10
Tsugaru, strait	D1, Inset I	8
Tsumeb	C1	70
Tsumkwe	D1	70
Tsuruga	C3	8
Tsuruoka	C2	8
Tuas	A1	13
Tuasivi	B2	18
Tubarão	D4	81
Tubmanburg	A2	63
Tucson, Ariz.	B2	126
Tucumcari, N. Mex.	C2	126
Tucupita	D2	79
Tucuruí, reservoir	D2	81
Tuen Mun	Inset	10
Tugela, river	D2	71
Tuguegarao	B2	12
Tuktoyaktuk	B3	99
Tuktut Nogait N.P.	D3	99
Tula	D3	44
Tula, ruins	D3	84
Tulcán	B2	79
Tulcea	E3	43
Tullamore	C2	31
Tulsequah	F2	95
Tulsipur	B2	19
Tultitlán	Inset	84
Tulun	D7	44
Tuma, river	B2	87
Tumaco	A4	78
Tumba, lake	B2	67
Tumbes	A1	77
Tumbler Ridge	M3	95
Tumuc-Humac, mts.	A2, B3	80
Tumucumaque, range	C1	81
Tunduru	C2	68
Tundzha, river	D3	50
Tungsten	C4	99

	Key	Page
Tunis, capital	C1	57
Tunis, gulf	C1	57
Tunisia		57
Tupelo, Miss.	E2	126
Tupiza	A4	77
Tupungato, mt.	B3	74
Tur, at-	B2	56
Tura	C7	44
Turan, lowland	A2	23
Turayf	A1	24
Turbo	A2	78
Turda	B2	43
Turfan, depression	C1	10
Türgovishte	E2	50
Türi	C2	46
Turin	A1	38
Turin	D6	94
Turkana (Rudolf), lake	D2	61
Turkeston, mts.	A1	23
Turkey		27
Turkmenbashi	A2	22
Turkmenistan		22
Turks and Caicos Islands		89
Turks, islands	D4	89
Turku	B2	53
Turkwel, river	C2	61
Turnberry	A2	96
Turnbull	B2	96
Turneffe, islands	C2	85
Turnhout	C1	33
Turnor Lake	B4	104
Turnu Măgurele	C4	43
Turquino, mt.	E3	88
Tursunzoda	A1	23
Turtle, lake	B7	104
Turtleford	B7	104
Tuscaloosa, Ala.	E2	126
Tuscany	B2	38
Tusket	B4	100
Tuticorin	C7	20
Tutong	B2	13
Tutong, river	B2	13
Tutuila, island	Al, C2	18
Tuul, river	C2	11
Tuvalu		16
Tuxtla Gutiérrez, state capital	F4	84
Tuy Hoa	B4	11
Tuya, river	G1	95
Tuz, lake	C2	27
Tuzla	B1	48
Tweed	H3	102
Tweed, river	C2	30
Twillingate	D4	98
Twin Butte	D6	94
Twin Falls, Idaho	B1	126
Two Creeks	A4	96
Tychy	D3	41
Tynda	D8	44
Tyndall	C4	96
Tyne Valley	B2	100
Tyne, river	C2	30
Tyrrhenian, sea	B2	38
Tyumen	D5	44
Tyva, republic	D6	44
Tywi, river	B3	30

U

	Key	Page
Uaboe	B1	16
Ubangi, river	B1	67
Ubayyid, al-	C2	59
Ube	A3	8
Ubeda	E3	37
Úbeda	E3	37
Uberaba	D3	81
Uberlândia	D3	81
Ubin, island	B1	13
Ubon Ratchathani	C3	12
Ucayali, river	C2	77
Uccle	C2	33
Uchiura, bay	Inset I	8
Uchquduq	B2	23
Ucluelet	K7	95
Udaipur	B4	20
Uddevalla	B3	53
Uddjaur, lake	C1	53
Udine	C1	38
Udmurtiya, republic	D4	44
Udon Thani	C2	12
Udu, point	C2	17
Uele, river	C1	67
Uelzen	B2	40
Ufa	D4	44
Uga, river	B2	70
Ugalla, river	B2	68
Uganda		61
Uíge	C2	70
Uitenhage	C3	71
Ujae, island	A2	16
Ujelang, island	A2	16
Ujjain	C4	20
Ujung Pandang	C2	13
Ukhta	C4	44
Ukmergė	C2	46
Ukraine		47
Ulaan-Uul	C2	11
Ulaangom	A1	11
Ulan Bator, capital	C2	11
Ulan-Ude	D7	44
Ulansuhai, lake	D1	10
Ulchin	C4	9
Ulhas, river	Inset I	20
Uliastay	B2	11
Ulithi, atoll	A1	15
Ullapool	B1	30
Ulm	B4	40
Ulsan	C5	9
Ulster, province	C1	31
Ulu Dağ (Mt. Olympus), mt.	B2	27
Ulúa, river	B2	86
Ulubaria	Inset II	20
Uluru (Ayers Rock)	C2	14
Uman	C2	47
Umbeluzi, river	B2	71
Umboi, island	A2	15
Umbria	C2	38

	Key	Page
Umeå	D2	53
Umeälven, river	C2	53
Umm al-Qaywayn	C2	25
Umm Bab	B3	25
Umm Qasr	C2	24
Umm Said (Musayid)	D4	25
Umniati, river	B2	69
Umtata	C3	71
Umuahia	D5	65
Umzingwani, river	B2	69
Una, river	A1	48
Unayzah	B1	24
Ungava, bay	L3	92
Ungheni	A2	50
Unión	C2	76
Union	A4	91
Union, island	A4	91
United Arab Emirates		25
United States		126
Unity	A8	104
Unst, island	Inset I	30
Upemba, lake	C3	67
Upernavik	B2	106
Upington	B2	71
Upolu, island	C2	18
Upper Arrow, lake	O6	95
Upper Liard	D5	105
Upper Lough Erne, lake	A3	30
Upper Musquodoboit	E2	100
Upper Ohio	B4	100
Uppsala	C3	53
Ural, mts.	D4	44
Ural, river	A2	23
Uran	Inset I	20
Uranium City	B1	104
Urawa	C3	8
Urganch	B2	23
Urmia, lake	B2	22
Uroševac	B3	49
Uruapan	D4	84
Urubamba, river	C3	77
Uruguai, river	C4	81
Uruguay		75
Uruguay, river	D3	74
Urukthapel, island	B3	17
Ürümqi	B1	10
Usak	B2	27
Ushuaia	D7	74
Usk, river	C3	30
Üsküdar	B2	27
Usmas, lake	B2	46
Ussuri, river	E8	44
Ussuriysk	E8	44
Ust-Ilimsk	D7	44
Ust-Kamchatsk	D10	44
Ust-Kut	D7	44
Ust-Ordynskiy B uryat, autonomous okrug	D7	44
Ust-Ordynskiy	D7	44
Uster	C1	35
Ústí nad Labem	B2	42
Ustica, island	C3	38
Ustka	B1	41
Ustyurt, plateau	A2, B2	23
Usulután	B2	86
Usumacinta, river	F4	84
Utah	B2	126
Utah, beach	B2	34
Utan	Inset I	20
Utena	C2	46
Utikuma, lake	C3	94
Utila, island	B1	86
Utrecht	C2	32
Utsunomiya	C2	8
Uttaradit	B2	12
Utuado	B2	90
Utupua, island	C2	16
Uummannaq	B2	106
Uvira	C2	67
Uvs, lake	B1	11
Uwajima	B3	8
Uwaynat, al-	B2	56
Uyo	D5	65
Uyuni	A4	77
Uzbekistan		23
Uzhhorod	A2	47
Užice	A3	49

V

	Key	Page
Vaal, reservoir	C2	71
Vaal, river	B2	71
Vaalserberg, mt.	D4	32
Vaasa	B2	53
Vác	B2	43
Vache, island	B2	89
Vadodara	B4	20
Vadsø	F1	52
Vaduz, capital	B2	33
Vágar, island	Inset	32
Váh, river	A2	42
Vahsh, river	A1	23
Vaitupu, island	C2	16
Vakhan, region	C1	22
Val Comeau	D2	97
Val Marie	C11	104
Val-d'Or	A4	101
Val-des-Bois	A6	103
Valcourt	D6	103
Valdecaño	D2	37
Valdepeñas	E3	37
Valdés, peninsula	C5	74
Valdivia	B6	76
Valemount	N5	95
Valença	A1	36
Valence	D4	34
Valencia	F3	37
Valencia	C1	79
Valencia, gulf	G3	37
Valenciennes	C1	34
Valera	B2	79
Valga	C2	46
Valira d'Orient, river	B2	36
Valira, river	A2	36
Valjevo	A2	49
Valka	C2	46
Valladolid	G3	84
Valladolid	D2	37
Valle d'Aosta	A1	38

	Key
Valledupar	B2
Vallenar	B3
Valletta, capital	C3
Valley, river	A3
Valmiera	C2
Valparaíso	B4, Inset
Van	E2
Van, lake	E2
Vancouver	L6
Vancouver, island	J6
Vanderhoof	K4
Vänern, lake	B3
Vanguard	C11
Vanier	H5
Vanier	C2
Vanikolo, islands	C2
Vanimo	A2
Vannes	B3
Vanrhynsdorp	A3
Vanscoy	D8
Vansittart, island	M3
Vantaa	B2
Vanua Balavu, island	C2
Vanua Lava, island	B1
Vanua Levu, island	B2
Vanuatu	
Varanasi	D3
Varaždin	C1
Vardar, river	B3
Varde, river	B3
Vardenis	C2
Varkaus	C2
Varna	D2
Vasai	Inset I
Vasai, creek	Inset I
Vaslui	D2
Vassar	D4
Västerås	C3
Vatican City	
Vatnajökull, ice cap	B2
Vättern, lake	B3
Vatu Lele, island	A3
Vaudreuil	C6
Vaupés, river	B4
Vava'u, island	B2
Vavenby	N5
Vavuniya	C3
Vawkavysk	B3
Växjö	B3
Vayk	C3
Vega	C4
Vega Alta	C2
Vega Baja	C2
Vegreville	D4
Veimandu, channel	A3
Vejle	B3
Velika Morava, river	B2
Veliki, canal	A2
Veliko Tŭrnovo	D2
Vélingara	A2
Vélingara	C3
Vella Lavella, island	A1
Vellore	C6
Veneto	B1
Venezuela	
Venezuela, gulf	B1
Venice	C1
Venice, gulf	C1
Venlo	D3
Venta, river	B1
Ventimiglia	A2
Ventspils	A2
Veracruz	E4
Vercelli	C3
Verde, river	C3
Verdun	J6
Verdun	D5
Vereeniging	C2
Verkhoyansk	C8
Verkhoyansk, range	C8
Vermillion, river	C4
Vermont	C1
Vernal, Utah	C1
Verner	E1
Vernon	N6
Vernon Bridge	C2
Vernon River	C2
Véroia	B1
Verona	J3
Versailles	C2, Inset II
Vert, cape	A2
Verviers	D3
Vesoul	D3
Vesterålen, islands	C2
Vestmanna	Inset
Vestmannaeyjar	A3
Vesuvius, volcano	C2
Veszprém	B2
Vetaua, island	C1
Viana do Castelo	B2
Vianden	B2
Vibank	G10
Viborg	B3
Vicenza	B1
Vich	H2
Vichada, river	C3
Vichy	C3
Victoria	B6
Victoria	A1
Victoria	B2
Victoria	C4
Victoria	B5
Victoria Beach	C4
Victoria Beach	D4
Victoria Land, region	B5
Victoria Nile, river	C2
Victoria, capital	Inset
Victoria, capital	L7
Victoria, falls	B3
Victoria, island	B4, C4
Victoria, lake	C1
Victoria, peak	C1
Victoria, Tex.	D3
Victoriaville	E5
Vidin	A2
Viedma	C5
Vieille Case	B2

Key Page

a, *capital* E2 39
e, *river* C3 34
ane, *capital* B3 11
es D2 90
es, *island* E2 90
es, *passage* D2 90
es, *sound* E2 90
on C3 34
Tri A2 11
am 11
Fort B3 91
B2 12
male, *mt.* B5 34
B1 37
awada D5 20
, *river* A3 49
do Conde A2 36
Nova de Gaia A2 36
Real B2 36
Real de Santo Antonio B4 36
capital C3 18
e, *river* B3 34
culos B4 68
bamba, *mts.* C3 77
di C2 46
viškis B2 46
Ahumada C1 84
Hayes D4 75
María C3 74
Obregón Inset 84
h C4 39
ermosa, *state capital* F4 84
oa C2 90
real de los Infantes F3 37
rica D4 75
vicencio B3 78
ón A4 77
Marie A4 101
euve-Saint-Georges Inset II 34
oy E5 103
s, *capital* C2 46
y, *river* C7 44
ysk C8 44
del Mar B4, Inset 76
ennes Inset II 34
ente de Carvalho Inset II 81
s, *river* B3 79
elälven, *river* C2 53
ya, *range* C4 20
A2 11
tsa B2 47
on Massif, *mt.* B10 107
n A4 96
, *river* C3 104
, *islands* 82
ia F2 126
B2 46
ga, *mts.* B1 61
hapatnam D5 20
an, *islands* B4 12
an, *sea* B4 12
C3 53
unt Melville, *sound* F2 99
B2 36
A4 96
Hermosa B4 78
la, *river* D2, E3 41
C4 96
bo C2 38
evu, *island* A2 17
ia E1 37
ia D4 81
ia da Conquista D3 81
ebsk E2 47
n C4 96
ino, *desert* B2 84
dingen B3 32
vostok E8 44
nd, *island* B1 32
ngen A3 32
A3 49
a, *river* B3 42
labruck C2 39
ama B1 63
odina, *province* A2 49
ano, *islands* Inset III 8
, *river* E4 44
grad E4 44
gda D3 44
B2 51
Redonda D4 81
, *lake* C3 64
, *river* C3 64
a D8 104
uta C5 44
nezh D3 44
tan, *river* C3 45
da, *river* C1 47
Järv, *lake* D2 46
D3 46
es, *mts.* D2 34
ok, *island* D3 17
je B3 49
sa B2 50
s A2 49
s, *river* B1 48
B2 49
urg B2 71
var D2 48
niu, *bay* A3 17
Tau-Con Dao B4 11
sea B3 17

W

A1 64
, *river* C3 32
ag A2 15
amun, *lake* C4 94
ana E5 98
asca, *river* C2 94
e Gestro, *river* C3 60
e Shebele, *river* D3 60
owden B2 96
ush D4 98
o, Tex. D2 126
Madani C2 59
dan C2 56
denzee, *sound* C1 32

Key Page

Waddington, *mt.* K5 95
Wadena G9 104
Wadi al-Malik, *river* B2 59
Wadi as-Sirhan, *depression* B2 26
Wadi Halfa C1 59
Wafrah, al- B3 24
Wagga Wagga, N.S.W. D3 14
Waigeo, *island* E2 13
Waikato, *river* C2 15
Waimamaku B2 15
Waingapu D2 13
Wairau, *river* B3 15
Waitaki, *river* B3 15
Wajh, al- A1 24
Wajir F3 61
Wakasa, *bay* B3 8
Wakaw E8 104
Wakayama B3 8
Wakefield C3 30
Wakkanai Inset I 8
Wakomata, *lake* B1 102
Wakrah, al- D3 25
Walachia, *region* B3 43
Wałbrzych C3 41
Walcheren, *island* A3 32
Walden D1 102
Waldersee B4 96
Waldheim D8 104
Walensee, *lake* D1 35
Walkerton D3 102
Wallace D2 100
Wallaceburg C5 102
Walsall C3 30
Walton C2 100
Walton D4 102
Walvis Bay B2 70
Wami, *river* C2 68
Wanaka, *lake* A3 15
Wanapitei, *lake* E1 102
Wandering River D3 94
Wando B5 9
Wanganui C2 15
Wanham A3 94
Wapawekka, *lake* F5 104
Wapawsik B1 96
Wapiti, *river* A4 94
Warangal C5 20
Warbah, *island* C1 24
Wardlow E6 94
Ware K2 95
Warman D8 104
Warner D6 94
Warren C4 96
Warren E1 102
Warren Landing C2 96
Warri C5 65
Warrington C3 30
Warrnambool, Vic. D3 14
Warsaw, *capital* E2 41
Warta, *river* B2, C2 41
Warwick C3 30
Wasa P6 95
Wasaga Beach F3 102
Wasagaming B4 96
Wash, *bay* D3 30
Washago F3 102
Washington A1 126
Washington, *cape* A3 17
Washington, *capital*, D.C. F2 126
Waskada A4 96
Waskaganish A3 101
Waskesiu Lake D7 104
Waspam C1 87
Water Valley C5 94
Water, *cays* A3 89
Waterborough C3 97
Waterbury, *lake* F2 104
Waterford C2 31
Waterhen, *lake* B3 96
Waterloo E4 102
Waterloo D6 103
Watertown, N.Y. F1 126
Watford Inset III 30
Watford D5 102
Wathaman, *lake* G3 104
Watrous E9 104
Watsa C1 67
Watson F8 104
Watson Lake D5 105
Wau A2 15
Wavre C2 33
Waw B3 59
Wawa D3 101
Wawa, *river* B1 87
Wawanesa B4 96
Weagamow Lake B2 101
Webbwood D1 102
Webequie C2 101
Webi Shabeelle, *river* B3 60
Weddell, *sea* B12 107
Wedgeport A4 100
Weert C3 32
Wei, *river* D2 10
Weiden C4 40
Weifang E2 10
Weimar B3 40
Weipa, Qld. D1 14
Weitzel, *lake* D3 104
Wekusko B2 96
Wekusko, *lake* B2 96
Weldiya C2 60
Welkom C2 71
Wellington A2 100
Wellington, *capital* B3 15
Wellington, *island* A8 76
Wels C2 39
Welsford C3 97
Welshpool B3 30
Welwyn A4 96
Wembere, *river* B1 68
Wenchi A3 64
Weno C2 15
Weno, *island* C2 15
Wenshan D3 10
Wentworth D2 100
Wentzel, *lake* C1 94
Wenzhou F3 10
Werder D3 60
Werra, *river* B3 40

Key Page

Weser, *river* B2 40
Wesley B2 90
Wesleyville E4 98
West Antarctica A8 107
West Devon A2 100
West Frisian, *islands* B1 32
West Ice Shelf, *glacier* C1 107
West Palm Beach, Fla. E3 126
West Point A2 100
West Road, *river* K4 95
West Siberian, *plain* C5 44
West St. Modeste C3 98
West Virginia E2 126
Westbank N6 95
Westbourne B4 96
Western Australia B2 14
Western Dvina, *river* C2 46
Western Ghats, *mts.* B5 20
Western Sahara 58
Western, *channel* C5 9
Westerschelde, *channel* A3 32
Westfield C3 97
Westlock D4 94
Westminster Inset III 30
Weston J5 102
Westport B3 15
Westport B2 31
Westport J3 102
Westray A2 96
Westray, *island* Inset I 30
Wetar, *island* D2 13
Wetaskiwin D5 94
Wete C1 68
Wetzlar B3 40
Wewak A1 15
Wexford C2 31
Weyakwin E6 104
Weyburn G11 104
Weymouth A3 100
Whakatane C2 15
Whale Cove K4 99
Whaletown K6 95
Whangarei B2 15
Wheatland A4 96
Wheatley C5 102
Wheeling, W. Va. E1 126
Whistler L6 95
Whitbourne E5 98
Whitby G4 102
White Fox F7 104
White Lake J2 102
White Nile, *river* C3 59
White Rock L6 95
White Sands C3 100
White Volta, *river* B1, D2 64
White, *bay* C4 98
White, *island* L3 99
White, *river* A4 105
White, *sea* C3 44
Whitecourt C4 94
Whitefish Falls D1 102
Whitefish, *bay* A1 102
Whitehaven B2 30
Whitehorse C5 105
Whitelaw A3 94
Whiteman, *range* A2 15
Whitemouth D4 96
Whitestone, *river* B3 105
Whitewood H10 104
Whitney G2 102
Whitney *mt.*, Calif. B2 126
Wholdaia, *lake* H4 99
Whyalla, S.A. C3 14
Whycocomagh F2 100
Wiarton D3 102
Wichita Falls, Tex. D2 126
Wichita, Kans. D2 126
Wick B1 30
Wicklow C2 31
Wicklow Head, *cape* D2 31
Wicklow, *mts.* C2 31
Wiener Neustadt E3 39
Wieprz, *river* F3 41
Wiesbaden B3 40
Wigan C3 30
Wight, *island* C4 30
Wilberforce G2 102
Wilge, *river* C2 71
Wilhelm, *mt.* A2 15
Wilhelmina, *canal* B3 32
Wilhelmina, *mts.* A2 80
Wilhelmshaven B2 40
Wilkes Land, *region* C3 107
Wilkie B8 104
William, *river* B2 104
Williams Harbour D3 98
Williams Lake L5 95
Williamsport C4 98
Williston, *lake* K3 95
Willow Bunch E11 104
Willow Creek A11 104
Willowbunch, *lake* E11 104
Wilmington, Del. F2 126
Wilmington, N.C. F2 126
Wilmot B3 100
Wiltondale C4 98
Wiltz A2 33
Winchester C3 30
Winchester K2 102
Wind, *river* B3 105
Windermere O6 95
Windermere F2 102
Windfall B4 94
Windhoek, *capital* C2 70
Windsor Inset III 30
Windsor C3 100
Windsor C5 102
Windsor D6 103
Windward Group B2 58
Windward, *islands* B4 91
Windward, *passage* F3 88
Winefred, *lake* E3 94
Winfield N6 95
Wingham D4 102
Winisk C1 101
Winisk, *lake* C2 101
Winisk, *river* C2 101
Winkler C4 96
Winneba B4 64

Key Page

Winnemucca, Nev. B1 126
Winnipeg C4, D2 96
Winnipeg Beach C4 96
Winnipeg, *lake* B3, C4, D2 96
Winnipeg, *river* D4 96
Winnipegosis B3 96
Winnipegosis, *lake* A3 96
Winslow, Ariz. B2 126
Winston-Salem, N.C. E2 126
Winter Harbour H6 95
Winterthur C1 35
Wisconsin D1 126
Wismar B2 40
Witless Bay E5 98
Witten A3 40
Wittenberg C3 40
Wittenberge B2 40
Witu, *island* A2 15
Wiwili B2 87
Władysławowo D1 41
Włocławek D2 41
Woburn F6 103
Wodzisław Śląski D3 41
Woking A3 94
Wolf, *lake* C5 105
Wolfsberg D4 39
Wolfsburg B2 40
Wolfville C2 100
Wollaston Lake G2 104
Wollaston, *lake* H2 104
Wollaston, *peninsula* E3 99
Wollongong, N.S.W. E3 14
Wolseley G10 104
Wolverhampton C3 30
Wong, *river* A2 19
Wŏnju B4 9
Wonowon M3 95
Wŏnsan B3 9
Wood Islands C3 100
Woodbridge J5 102
Woodlands B1 13
Woodlands C4 96
Woodlark (Muyua), *island* B2 15
Woodnorth A4 96
Woodridge C4 96
Woods, *lake* B3 101
Woodstock B2 97
Woodstock A2 100
Woodstock E4 102
Woody Point C4 98
Woomera, S.A. C3 14
Worcester C3 30
Worcester A3 71
Worcester, Mass. F1 126
Worms B4 40
Wotho, *island* B1 16
Wotje, *island* B2 16
Wrangel, *island* B10 44
Wrath, *cape* B1 30
Wreck Cove D5 98
Wrentham D6 94
Wrigley D4 99
Wrocław C3 41
Wuhan E2 10
Wuhu E2 10
Wukari E4 65
Wum B2 65
Wuppertal A3 40
Würzburg B4 40
Wutivi, *mt.* B1 63
Wuwei D2 10
Wuxi F2 10
Wuzhong D2 10
Wuzhou E3 10
Wye, *river* C3 30
Wyndham, W.A. B1 14
Wynyard F9 104
Wyoming C1 126

X

Xaçmaz C2 45
Xai-Xai B5 68
Xam Nua C1 11
Xangongo C5 70
Xankändi B3 45
Xánthi C1 51
Xau, *lake* B2 69
Xi'an D2 10
Xi, *river* E3 10
Xiamen E3 10
Xiangfan E2 10
Xiangkhoang B2 11
Xiangtan E3 10
Xigaze B3 10
Xingu, *river* C3 81
Xining D2 10
Xinjiang Uygur B1 10
Xinxiang E2 10
Xinyang E2 10
Xochimilco Inset 84
Xuddur A3 60
Xuzhou E2 10

Y

Ya'an D2 10
Yablonovyy, *range* D7 44
Yabucoa D2 90
Yacuiba B4 77
Yafran B1 56
Yaguarí, *river* C1 75
Yaguarón, *river* D2 75
Yahk O6 95
Yakima, Wash. A1 126
Yaku, *island* A4 8
Yakutsk C8 44
Yala B5 12
Yale M6 95
Yalinga B2 66
Yalta C4 47
Yalu, *river* B2 9
Yamagata D2 8
Yamaguchi A3 8
Yamal, *peninsula* C5 44
Yamalo-Nenesiya, *autonomous okrug* C5 44
Yambio B4 59
Yambol E3 50

Key Page

Yamoussoukro, *capital* D3 63
Yampi, *sound* B1 14
Yamuna, *river* C3 20
Yan, *river* B3 19
Yanbu al-Bahr A1 24
Yangambi C1 67
Yangdŏk B3 9
Yangquan E2 10
Yangtze, *river* C2, D2 10
Yangzhou E2 10
Yanji F1 10
Yantai F2 10
Yantra, *river* D2 50
Yao B3 8
Yaoundé, *capital* B3 65
Yap, *islands* A2 15
Yapen, *island* E2 13
Yaque del Norte, *river* A1 89
Yaque del Sur, *river* A2 89
Yaqui, *river* C2 84
Yare, *river* D3 30
Yaren, *capital* B3 16
Yariga, *mt.* C2 8
Yarmouth A4 100
Yaroslavl D3 44
Yasawa, *island group* A2 17
Yasuj C3 22
Yata, *river* A2 77
Yates B4 94
Yatsushiro A3 8
Yauco B2 90
Yavarí, *river* C1 77
Yaviza D2 87
Yazd C3 22
Yazd, *region* C3 22
Ybbs, *river* D2 39
Ye C3 12
Yeboah C3 30
Yecla F3 37
Yeguas, *point* D2 90
Yekaterinburg D5 44
Yekepa B2 63
Yell, *island* Inset I 30
Yellow Grass F11 104
Yellow, *sea* F2 10
Yellowknife, *capital* F4 99
Yemen 25
Yen Bai A2 11
Yendi B2 64
Yenisey, *river* C6 44
Yeovil C4 30
Yerevan, *capital* B2 45
Yesilhrmak, *river* D2 27
Yeu, *island* B3 34
Yevlax B2 45
Yevpatoriya C3 47
Yevrey, autonomous oblast E8 44
Yi, *river* C2 75
Yialousa C1 27
Yibin D3 10
Yichang E2 10
Yichun F1 10
Yin Shan, *mts.* D1 10
Yinchuan D2 10
Yingkou F1 10
Yining B1 10
Ylikitka, *lake* C1 53
Ylivieska B2 53
Yoboki B2 60
Yogyakarta C2 13
Yojoa, *lake* B2 86
Yokkaichi C3 8
Yokohama C3 8
Yokosuka C3 8
Yola G3 65
Yom, *river* B2 12
Yomou D4 62
Yonago B3 8
Yonaguni, *island* Inset II 8
Yŏngju C4 9
Yonne, *river* C2 34
Yopal B3 78
York C3 30
York B2 100
York K5 102
York Factory E1 96
York, *cape* D1 14
Yorkton H9 104
Yoro B2 86
Yoron, *island* Inset II 8
Yoshino, *river* B3 8
Yoshkar-Ola D4 44
Yŏsu B5 9
Yotvata B3 26
Youghal C3 31
Young E9 104
Youngs Cove D1 97
Ypané, *river* D3 75
Ypoá, *lake* D4 75
Ypres A2 33
Ysyk-Köl, *lake* E1 23
Yü Shan, *mt.* B2 9
Yuan, *river* D3 10
Yubari Inset I 8
Yucatán, *channel* A2 88
Yucatán, *peninsula* G4 84
Yuen Long Inset 10
Yueyang E3 10
Yugoslavia 49
Yukon, *river* D2 92
Yuma, Ariz. B2 126
Yumen C2 10
Yuna, *river* B2 89
Yundum B2 62
Yungas, *region* A3 77
Yungho B1 9
Yunnan C3 10
Yurimaguas B2 77
Yuscarán B3 86
Yushu C2 10
Yuzhno-Sakhalinsk E9 44
Yverdon A2 35

Z

Zaanstad B2 32
Zabbar C2 36
Zabid A2 25
Zabol E3 22

Key Page

Zabrze D3 41
Zacapa D5 85
Zacatecas, *state capital* D3 84
Zacatecoluca B2 86
Zadar B3 48
Zafra C3 37
Zagazig B1 56
Zaghouan C1 57
Zagreb, *capital* B2 48
Zagros, *mts.* B3 22
Zahedan E4 22
Zahlah A2 26
Zaječar C3 49
Zákinthos, *island* B3 51
Zakopane D4 41
Zala, *river* A2 43
Zalaegerszeg A2 43
Zalău B2 43
Zambales, *mts.* B3 12
Zambezi A2 67
Zambezi, *river* A3, B3 67
Zambia 67
Zamboanga B5 12
Zamboanga, *peninsula* B5 12
Zamora D2 37
Zamora B5 79
Zamora, *river* B4 79
Zamość F3 41
Zanderij B2 80
Zanjan B2 22
Zanzibar C2 68
Zao, *mt.* D2 8
Zapandna Morava, *river* B3 49
Zapatera, *island* B3 87
Zaporizhzhia D2 47
Zaqatala B2 45
Zarafobod A1 23
Zarafshon B2 23
Zaragoza F2 37
Zaranj A2 22
Zareh Sharan B2 22
Zaria D2 65
Zarqa, az- B1 26
Zarzis C3 57
Zavidoviči B1 48
Zaysan E2 23
Zaysan, *lake* E2 23
Zebbug A1 36
Zeebrugge B1 33
Zefat B1 26
Zenica B1 48
Zeravshan, *mts.* A1 23
Zeravshan, *river* A1, B2 23
Zermatt B2 35
Zestaponi B3 45
Zeta, *river* A3 49
Zevulun, *plain* B1 26
Zêzere, *river* A3 36
Zhambyl (Dzhambul) D2 23
Zhangjiakou E1 10
Zhangye D2 10
Zhanjiang E3 10
Zhejiang E3 10
Zhelaniya, *cape* B5 44
Zhengzhou E2 10
Zhenjiang E2 10
Zhezqazghan C2 23
Zhitomir B1 47
Zhlobin D3 47
Zhob, *river* C3 21
Zhoda C4 96
Zhu, *river* E3 10
Zhuzhou E3 10
Zibo E2 10
Zielona Góra B3 41
Zigong D3 10
Ziguinchor A3 62
Žilina B2 42
Zillah C2 56
Zillertal Alps, *range* B3 39
Zima, *lake* A2 94
Zimbabwe 69
Zinder B3 59
Zion C3 90
Zittau C3 40
Ziway, *lake* C3 60
Zlatibor, *mts.* A3 49
Zlín C3 42
Znojmo C4 42
Zomba C3 68
Zonguldak B2 27
Zorzor B2 63
Zouar B2 59
Zouîrât B2 58
Zrenjanin B2 49
Zug C1 35
Zugdidi A3 45
Zugspitze, *mt.* B5 40
Zuid-Willemsvaart, *canal* C3 32
Zújar, *reservoir* D3 37
Zululand, *region* D2 71
Zunyi D3 10
Zürich C1 35
Zürichsee, *lake* C1 35
Zurrieq B2 36
Zuwarah B1 56
Zvishavane B2 69
Zvolen B2 42
Zvornik C1 48
Zwedru B2 63
Zwickau C3 40
Zwolle D2 32
Zyryanka C9 44

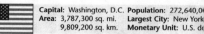

Capital: Washington, D.C. Population: 272,640,0
Area: 3,787,300 sq. mi. Largest City: New York
9,809,200 sq. km. Monetary Unit: U.S. de

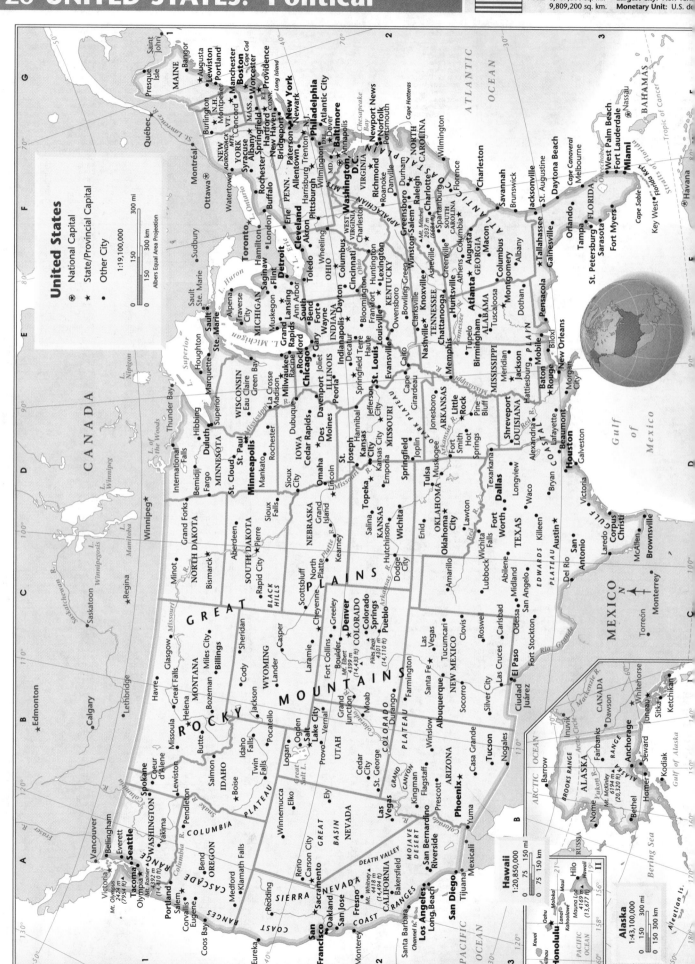

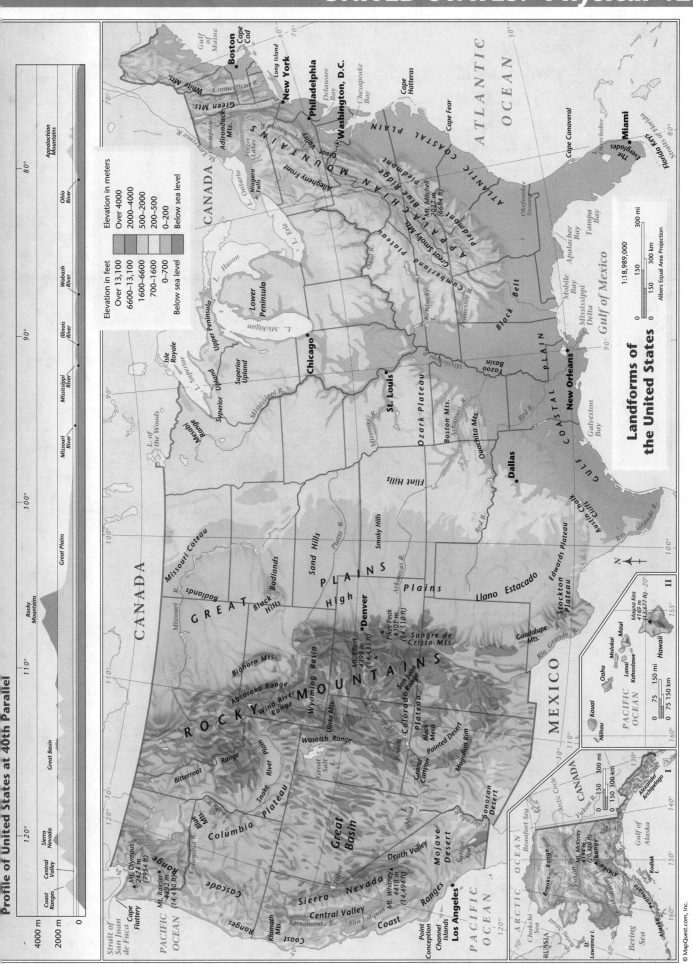

Profile of United States at 40th Parallel

Landforms of the United States

1:18,989,000

Albers Equal Area Projection

© MapQuest.com, Inc.

Capital: Montgomery
Area: 52,400 sq. mi.
135,800 sq. km.
Population: 4,352,000
Largest City: Birmingham

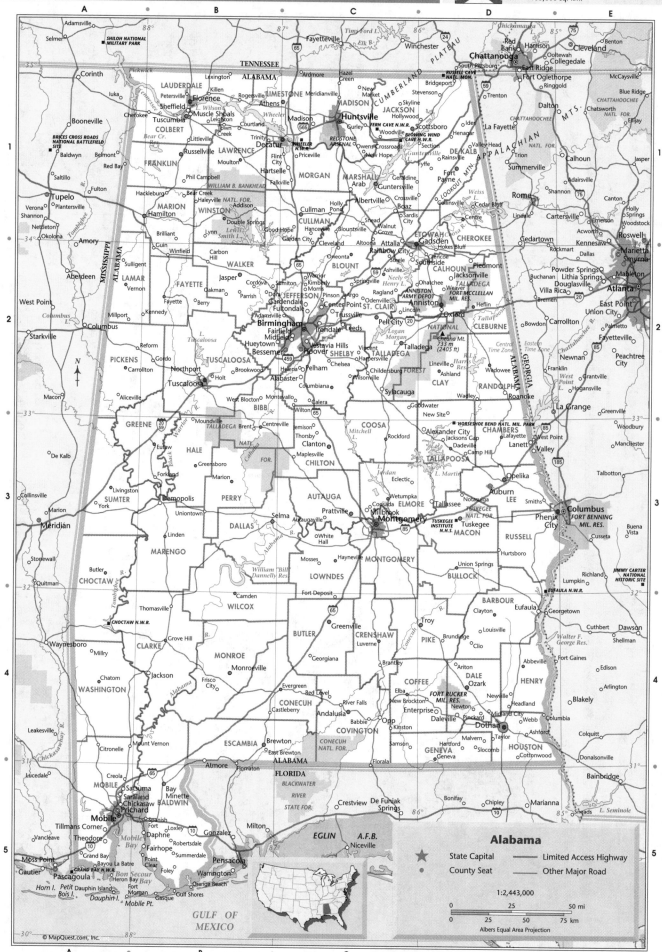

Alabama

★ State Capital
• County Seat
━━ Limited Access Highway
── Other Major Road

1:2,443,000

Albers Equal Area Projection

© MapQuest.com, Inc.

Capital: Juneau
Area: 656,400 sq. mi.
1,700,000 sq. km.
Population: 614,000
Largest City: Anchorage

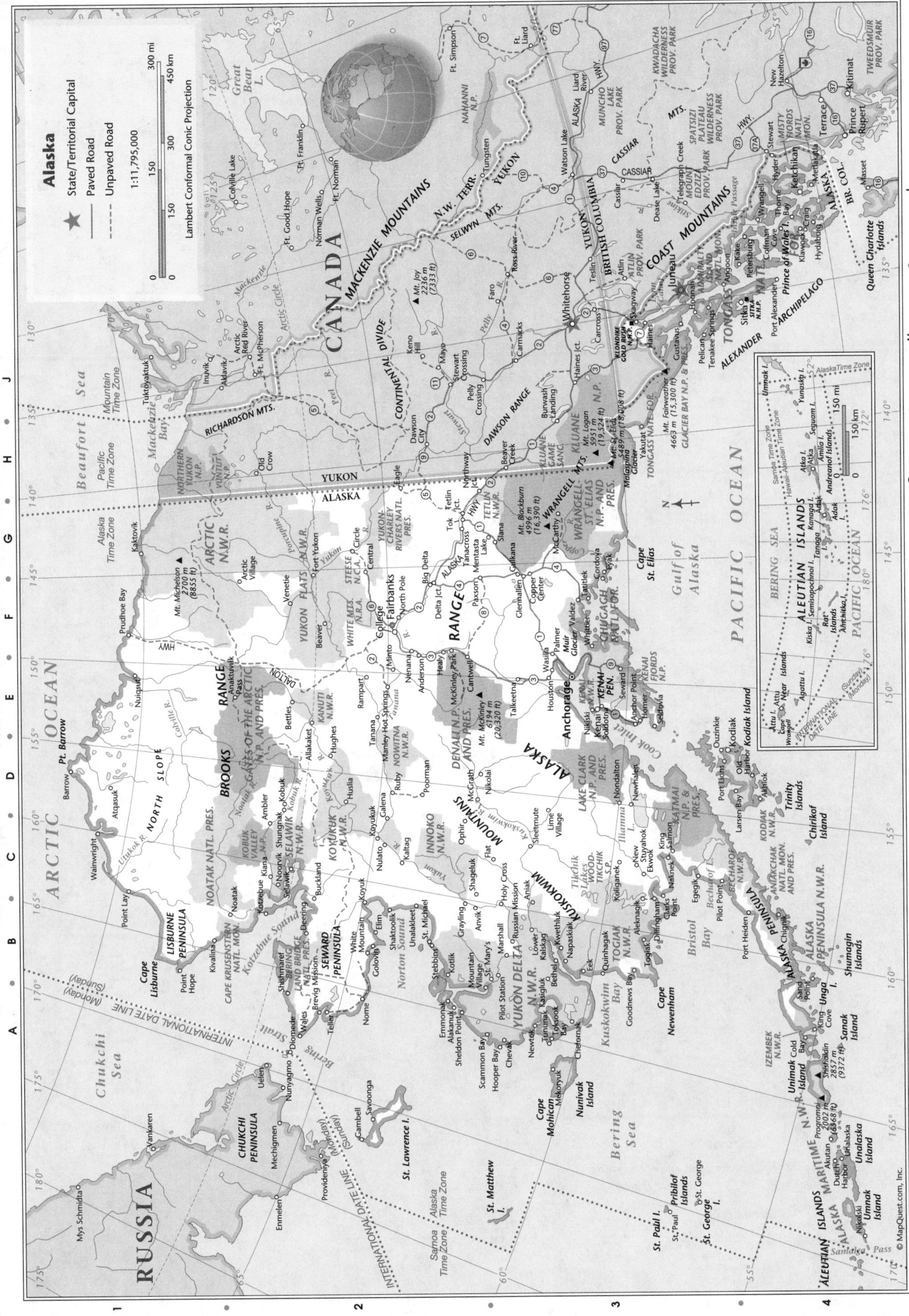

Alaska

★ State/Territorial Capital
——— Paved Road
- - - - Unpaved Road

1:11,795,000

Lambert Conformal Conic Projection

300 mi
150
0

450 km
300
150
0

RUSSIA

CANADA

ARCTIC OCEAN

Beaufort Sea

Chukchi Sea

Bering Sea

Gulf of Alaska

PACIFIC OCEAN

BROOKS RANGE

ALASKA RANGE

MACKENZIE MOUNTAINS

COAST MOUNTAINS

KUSKOKWIM MOUNTAINS

NORTH SLOPE

SEWARD PENINSULA

LISBURNE PENINSULA

CHUKCHI PENINSULA

ALEUTIAN ISLANDS

ALASKA PENINSULA

KENAI PEN.

Anchorage

Fairbanks

Juneau

Whitehorse

Dawson City

Mt. McKinley 6194 m (20,320 ft)

Mt. St. Elias 5489 m (18,008 ft)

Mt. Logan 5951 m (19,524 ft)

INTERNATIONAL DATE LINE

© MapQuest.com, Inc.

Capital: Phoenix
Area: 114,000 sq. mi.
295,300 sq. km.
Population: 4,669,0...
Largest City: Phoenix

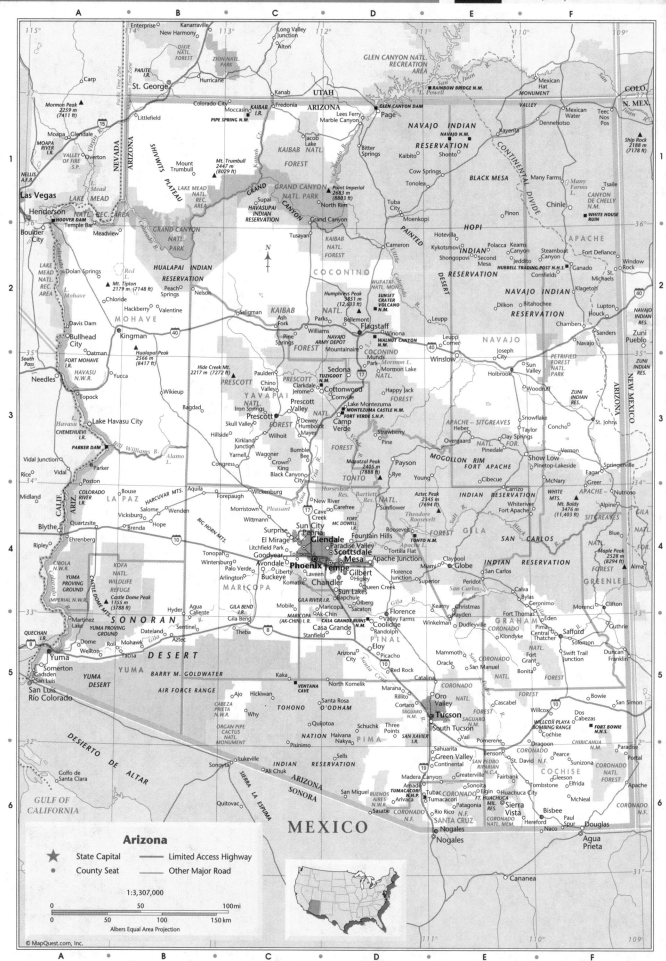

Arizona

★ State Capital
• County Seat
—— Limited Access Highway
—— Other Major Road

1:3,307,000

0   50   100mi
0   50   100   150 km
Albers Equal Area Projection

© MapQuest.com, Inc.

Capital: Little Rock
Area: 53,200 sq. mi.
137,700 sq. km.
Population: 2,538,000
Largest City: Little Rock

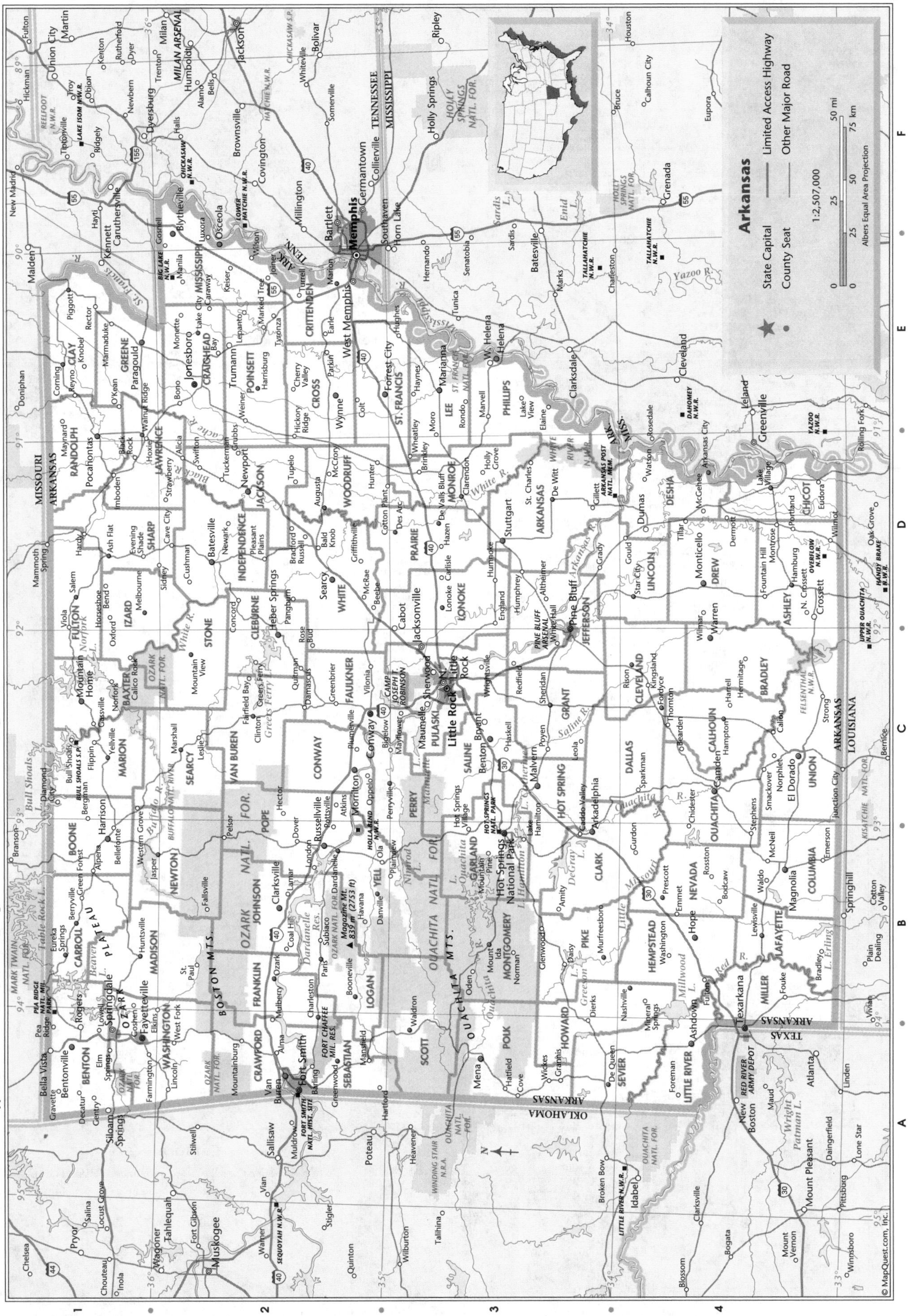

Arkansas
1:2,507,000
Albers Equal Area Projection

Limited Access Highway
Other Major Road

State Capital ★
County Seat ●

50 mi
75 km

MISSOURI

TENNESSEE

MISSISSIPPI

OKLAHOMA

TEXAS

LOUISIANA

ARKANSAS

Little Rock

Memphis

West Memphis

Fort Smith

Fayetteville

Springdale

Rogers

Bentonville

Pine Bluff

Hot Springs

Texarkana

El Dorado

Jonesboro

Paragould

Mountain Home

Harrison

Russellville

Conway

Searcy

Batesville

Magnolia

Camden

Monticello

OZARK MTS.

BOSTON MTS.

OUACHITA MTS.

OZARK NATL. FOR.

OUACHITA NATL. FOR.

Magazine Mt. (2753 ft)
▲ 839 m

MARK TWAIN NATL. FOR.

© MapQuest.com, Inc.

CALIFORNIA REPUBLIC

Capital: Sacramento
Area: 163,700 sq. mi.
424,000 sq. km.
Population: 32,667,
Largest City: Los An

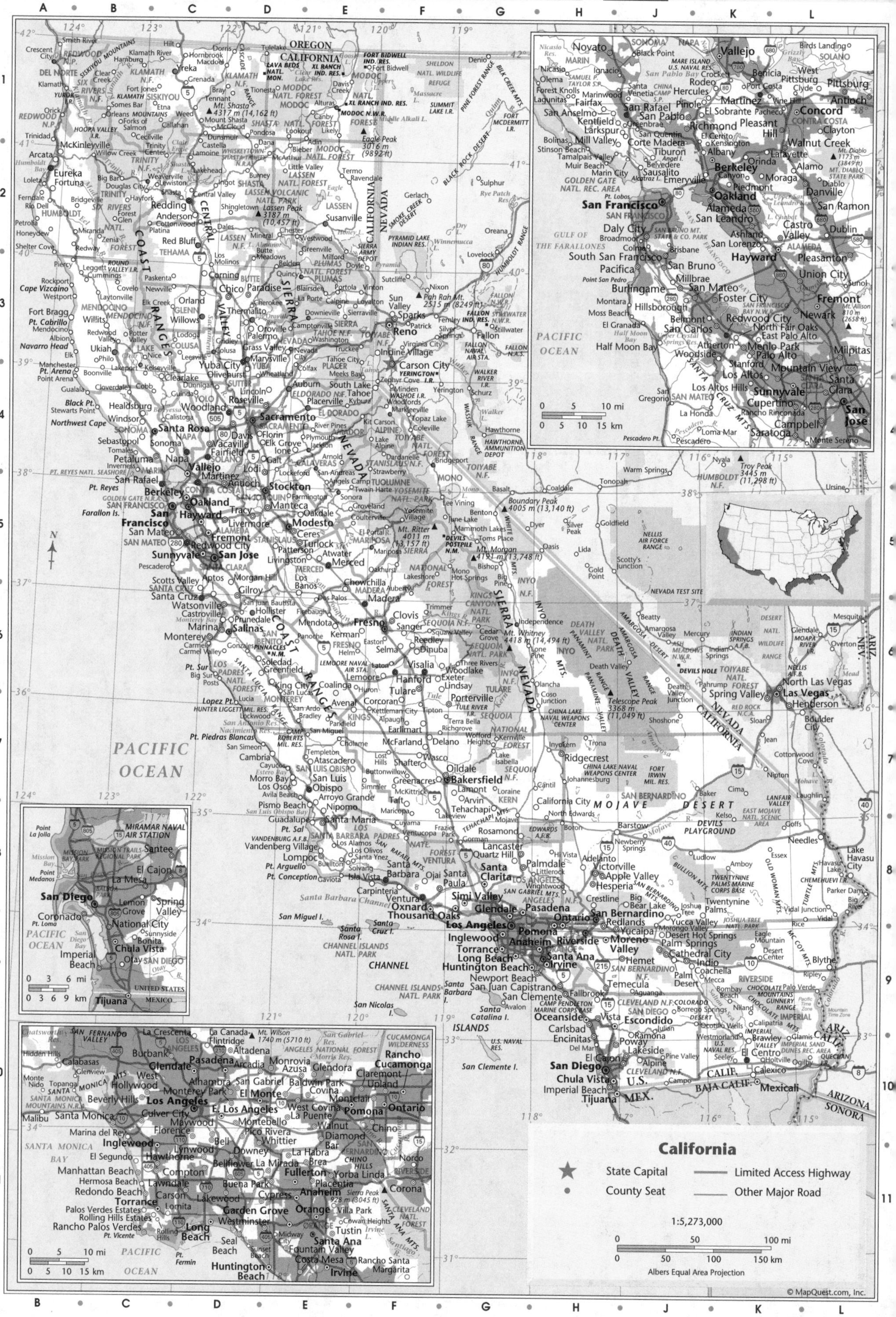

California

★ State Capital   — Limited Access Highway
• County Seat   — Other Major Road

1:5,273,000

0   50   100 mi
0   50   100   150 km

Albers Equal Area Projection

© MapQuest.com, Inc.

OREGON

NEVADA

PACIFIC OCEAN

ARIZONA

MEXICO

PACIFIC OCEAN

Sacramento
San Francisco
Oakland
San Jose
Los Angeles
San Diego
Fresno
Bakersfield
Long Beach
Santa Ana
Anaheim
Riverside
Stockton
Modesto
Berkeley
Vallejo
Concord
Tijuana
Mexicali
Las Vegas

Mt. Whitney 4418 m (14,494 ft)
Death Valley
Mojave Desert
Yosemite National Park
Sierra Nevada
Coast Ranges
Channel Islands National Park

Capital: Denver
Area: 104,100 sq. mi.
269,600 sq. km.
Population: 3,971,000
Largest City: Denver

Colorado

★ State Capital
• County Seat
— Limited Access Highway
— Other Major Road

1:3,137,000

Albers Equal Area Projection

0   25   50 mi
0   25   50   75 km

© MapQuest.com, Inc.

Surrounding states / regions

NEBRASKA
KANSAS
OKLAHOMA
NEW MEXICO
WYOMING
UTAH
ARIZONA

Counties and features

SEDGWICK
PHILLIPS
LOGAN
YUMA
WASHINGTON
MORGAN
WELD
LARIMER
WYOMING COLORADO
NEBRASKA COLORADO
KANSAS COLORADO
COLORADO OKLAHOMA
COLORADO NEW MEXICO
UTAH COLORADO
CHEYENNE
KIT CARSON
LINCOLN
KIOWA
ELBERT
ARAPAHOE
ADAMS
DENVER
JEFFERSON
BOULDER
GILPIN
CLEAR CREEK
GRAND
JACKSON
ROUTT
MOFFAT
RIO BLANCO
GARFIELD
EAGLE
SUMMIT
PARK
DOUGLAS
EL PASO
CROWLEY
KIOWA
BENT
PROWERS
BACA
LAS ANIMAS
OTERO
PUEBLO
FREMONT
TELLER
LAKE
PITKIN
MESA
DELTA
GUNNISON
CHAFFEE
SAGUACHE
CUSTER
HUERFANO
COSTILLA
ALAMOSA
CONEJOS
RIO GRANDE
MINERAL
HINSDALE
OURAY
MONTROSE
SAN MIGUEL
DOLORES
MONTEZUMA
LA PLATA
ARCHULETA
SAN JUAN
SAN JUAN
UNCOMPAHGRE

National forests, parks, grasslands

PAWNEE NATIONAL GRASSLAND
COMANCHE NATIONAL GRASSLAND
ROOSEVELT NATIONAL FOREST
ARAPAHO NATIONAL FOREST
ROCKY MOUNTAIN NATIONAL PARK
ROUTT NATIONAL FOREST
WHITE RIVER NATIONAL FOREST
PIKE NATIONAL FOREST
SAN ISABEL N.F.
GUNNISON NATIONAL FOREST
UNCOMPAHGRE NATIONAL FOREST
GRAND MESA N.F.
RIO GRANDE NATIONAL FOREST
SAN JUAN NATIONAL FOREST
MANTI-LA SAL NATIONAL FOREST
CARSON NATL. FOR.
DINOSAUR NATIONAL MONUMENT
BLACK CANYON OF THE GUNNISON N.M.
CURECANTI N.R.A.
GREAT SAND DUNES N.M.
MESA VERDE NATIONAL PARK
FLORISSANT FOSSIL BEDS N.M.
U.S. AIR FORCE ACADEMY
PUEBLO ORDNANCE DEPOT
FORT CARSON MIL. RES.
BENT'S OLD FORT NATL. HIST. SITE
UINTAH AND OURAY INDIAN RESERVATION
SOUTHERN UTE I.R.
UTE MOUNTAIN INDIAN RESERVATION
NAVAJO INDIAN RESERVATION
BROWNS PARK N.W.R.
MONTE VISTA N.W.R.
ALAMOSA N.W.R.
ARAPAHO N.W.R.
HUTTON LAKE N.W.R.
BAMFORTH N.W.R.
YUCCA HOUSE N.M.
HOVENWEEP N.M.
COLORADO N.M.
AZTEC RUINS N.M.

Mountain ranges

ROCKY MOUNTAINS
FRONT RANGE
LARAMIE MTS.
MEDICINE BOW MTS.
SAWATCH RANGE
SANGRE DE CRISTO MTS.
SAN JUAN MOUNTAINS
CONTINENTAL DIVIDE
ROAN PLATEAU
BOOK CLIFFS
EAST TAVAPUTS PLATEAU
ORANGE CLIFFS
GRAND MESA
BLUE MESA
UNCOMPAHGRE PLATEAU
MANTI-LA SAL
MONUMENT VALLEY

Peaks and elevations

Mt. Elbert 4399 m (14,433 ft)
Mt. Evans 4348 m
Longs Peak 4345 m (14,256 ft)
Grays Peak 4349 m (14,270 ft)
Pikes Peak 4301 m (14,110 ft)
Mt. Massive 4395 m
Blanca Peak 4364 m (14,294 ft)
Crestone Peak 4357 m (14,294 ft)
Uncompahgre Peak 4361 m (14,309 ft)
Mt. Wilson 4342 m (14,246 ft)
Mt. Sneffels 4313 m (14,150 ft)
Mt. Eolus 4293 m (14,084 ft)
Castle Peak 4346 m (14,259 ft)
Mt. Gunnison 3877 m (12,719 ft)
Montezuma Peak 4008 m (13,150 ft)
Bears Ears 2761 m (9058 ft)
Mt. Zirkel 3712 m (12,180 ft)
Bridger Peak 3354 m (11,004 ft)
Mt. Peale 3877 m (12,721 ft)
Black Mesa 1516 m (4973 ft)
Arapaho Peak 4117 m (13,506 ft)
Crested Butte

Cities and towns

Denver
Colorado Springs
Aurora
Lakewood
Pueblo
Arvada
Westminster
Thornton
Boulder
Longmont
Fort Collins
Greeley
Loveland
Englewood
Littleton
Wheat Ridge
Northglenn
Broomfield
Commerce City
Brighton
Lafayette
Louisville
Golden
Evergreen
Central City
Georgetown
Idaho Springs
Empire
Silver Plume
Dillon
Silverthorne
Frisco
Breckenridge
Alma
Fairplay
Leadville
Aspen
Snowmass Village
Glenwood Springs
Carbondale
Basalt
Marble
Gunnison
Crested Butte
Pitkin
Lake City
Creede
Del Norte
Monte Vista
Alamosa
La Jara
Sanford
Manassa
Romeo
Antonito
Conejos
Hooper
Center
Saguache
Moffat
Crestone
San Luis
Blanca
Fort Garland
San Acacio
Walsenburg
La Veta
Aguilar
Trinidad
Raton
Branson
Kim
Pritchett
Campo
Springfield
Walsh
Holly
Granada
Lamar
Las Animas
Hartman
Coolidge
Two Buttes
Wiley
Eads
Haswell
Arlington
Sugar City
Ordway
Olney Springs
Manzanola
Rocky Ford
Swink
La Junta
Fowler
Manzanola
Boone
Pueblo West
Colorado City
Rye
Florence
Canon City
Penrose
Royal Gorge
Silver Cliff
Westcliffe
Salida
Buena Vista
Poncha Springs
Bonanza
Salida
Saguache
Cottonwood
Cascade
Woodland Park
Manitou Springs
Security
Fountain
Monument
Palmer Lake
Larkspur
Castle Rock
Parker
Elizabeth
Kiowa
Elbert
Black Forest
Falcon
Calhan
Ramah
Simla
Matheson
Genoa
Hugo
Limon
Arriba
Flagler
Seibert
Stratton
Vona
Burlington
Bethune
Cheyenne Wells
Kit Carson
Sheridan Lake
Wray
Yuma
Eckley
Otis
Akron
Brush
Fort Morgan
Wiggins
Hillrose
Sterling
Merino
Iliff
Crook
Ovid
Julesburg
Sedgwick
Holyoke
Haxtun
Fleming
Paoli
Amherst
Grant
St. Francis
Ogallala
Sidney
Kimball
Pine Bluffs
Cheyenne
Laramie
Grover
New Raymer
Keota
Nunn
Ault
Pierce
Eaton
Windsor
Kersey
Evans
Platteville
Fort Lupton
Hudson
Keenesburg
Bennett
Byers
Deer Trail
Hugo
Genoa
Greeley
Johnstown
Berthoud
Lyons
Ward
Estes Park
Drake
Granby
Grand Lake
Winter Park
Fraser
Hot Sulphur Springs
Kremmling
Walden
Oak Creek
Yampa
Steamboat Springs
Hayden
Craig
Maybell
Dinosaur
Rangely
Meeker
Silt
Rifle
Parachute
De Beque
Palisade
Clifton
Fruita
Fruitvale
Grand Junction
Collbran
Cedaredge
Orchard City
Paonia
Hotchkiss
Crawford
Delta
Olathe
Montrose
Ridgway
Ouray
Silverton
Ophir
Telluride
Sawpit
Norwood
Naturita
Nucla
Dove Creek
Dolores
Mancos
Cortez
Towaoc
Durango
Bayfield
Ignacio
Pagosa Springs
Chama
Dulce
Navajo
Shiprock
Aztec
Farmington
Bloomfield
Moab
Monticello
Blanding
Vernal
Maeser
Duchesne
Roosevelt
Rangely

Rivers and water features

N. Platte R.
Platte R.
S. Platte R.
Cache la Poudre R.
Big Thompson R.
St. Vrain Cr.
Colorado R.
Gunnison R.
White R.
Yampa R.
Green R.
San Juan R.
Animas R.
Dolores R.
San Miguel R.
Uncompahgre R.
Rio Grande
Conejos R.
Arkansas R.
Purgatoire R.
Apishapa R.
Huerfano R.
Cucharas R.
Big Sandy Cr.
Rush Cr.
Horse Cr.
Republican R.
N. Fork Republican R.
Frenchman Cr.
Beaver Cr.
Bijou Cr.
Kiowa Cr.
Republican R.
Smoky Hill R.
Big Sandy Cr.
Cimarron R.
Two Buttes Cr.
Sand Cr.
Wet Mountain
Laramie R.
Little Snake R.
Yampa R.
Piceance Cr.
Plateau Cr.
Surface Cr.
Cochetopa Cr.
Tomichi Cr.
San Cristobal
Lagoon
Lonetree Res.
Bonny Res.
John Martin Res.
Two Buttes Res.
Grand Lake
Shadow Mountain Lake
Granby Lake
Dillon Res.
Blue Mesa Res.

Time zones

Mountain Time Zone
Central Time Zone

Capital: Hartford
Area: 5,500 sq. mi.
14,400 sq. km.
Population: 3,274,00
Largest City: Bridgep

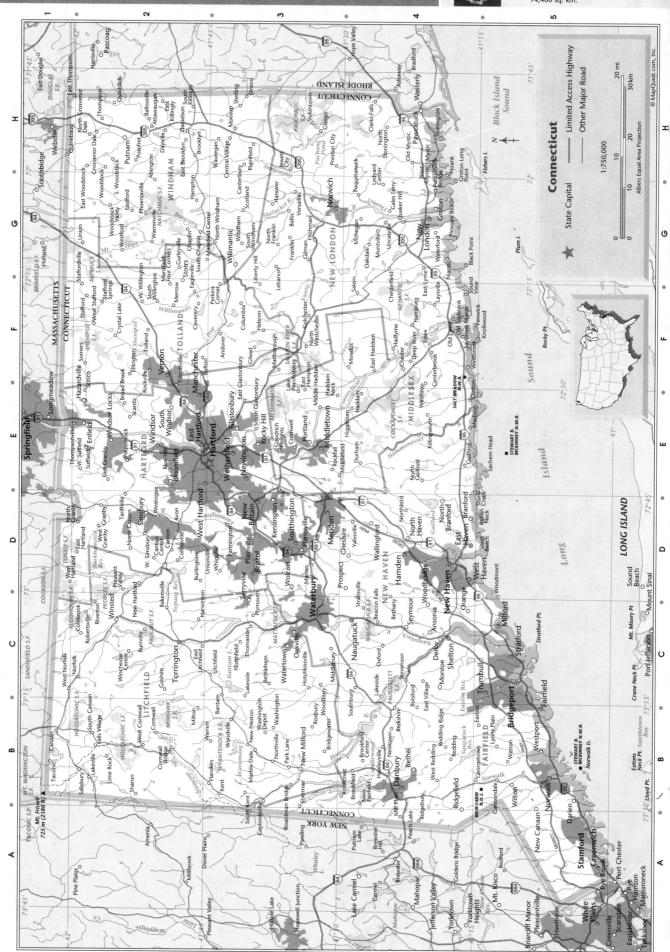

Connecticut

★ State Capital

— Limited Access Highway
— Other Major Road

1:750,000

Albers Equal Area Projection

© MapQuest.com, Inc.

Capital: Dover
Area: 2,500 sq. mi.
6,400 sq. km.
Population: 744,000
Largest City: Wilmington

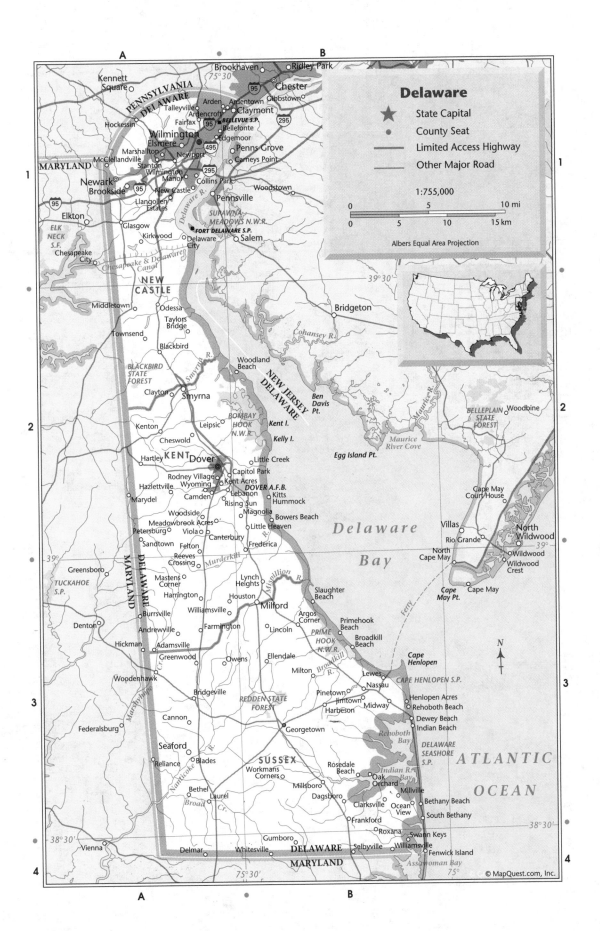

Delaware

★ State Capital
• County Seat
— Limited Access Highway
— Other Major Road

1:755,000

0   5   10 mi
0   5   10   15 km

Albers Equal Area Projection

© MapQuest.com, Inc.

Capital: Tallahassee
Area: 65,800 sq. mi.
170,300 sq. km.
Population: 14,916,0
Largest City: Jackson·

Florida

★ State Capital
• County Seat
— Limited Access Highway
— Other Major Road

1:3,135,000

0   25   50 mi
0   25   50   75 km

Albers Equal Area Projection

© MapQuest.com, Inc.

Capital: Atlanta
Area: 59,400 sq. mi.
153,900 sq. km.

Population: 7,642,000
Largest City: Atlanta

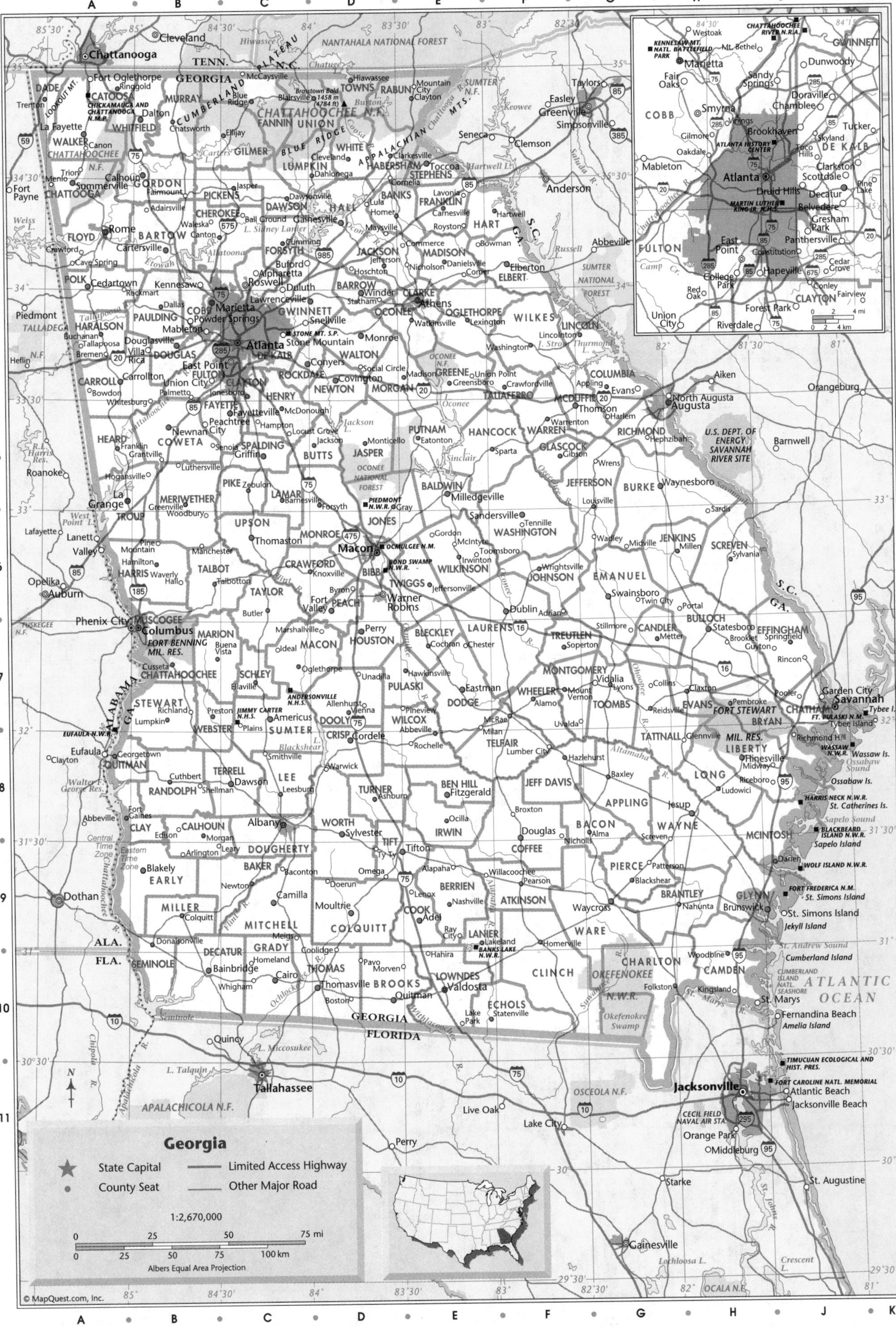

Capital: Honolulu
Area: 10,900 sq. mi.
28,300 sq. km.
Population: 1,193,0
Largest City: Honolu

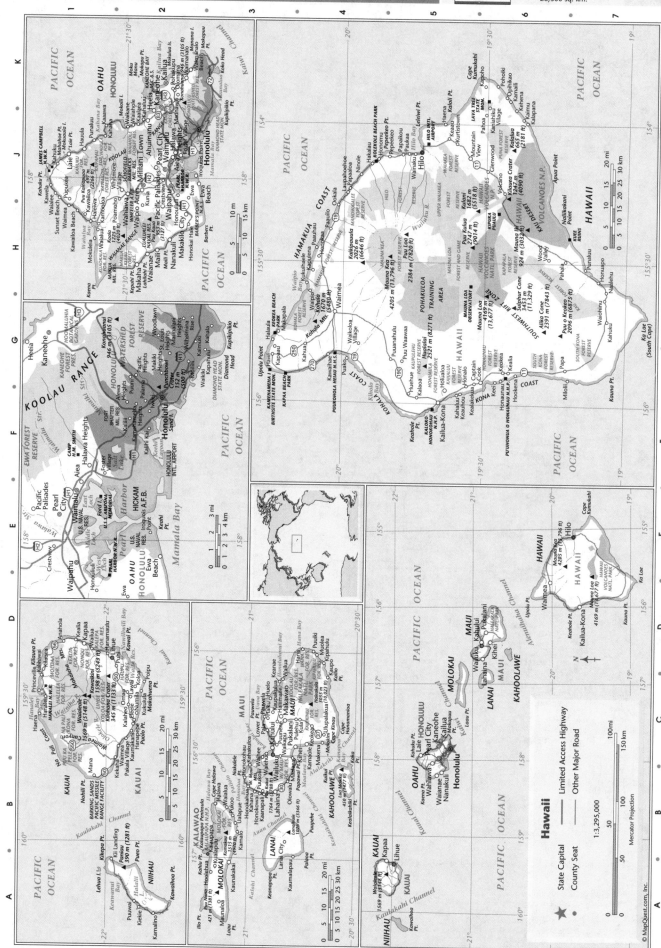

Hawaii

State Capital ★
County Seat ●

Limited Access Highway
Other Major Road

1:3,295,000
Mercator Projection

© MapQuest.com, Inc.

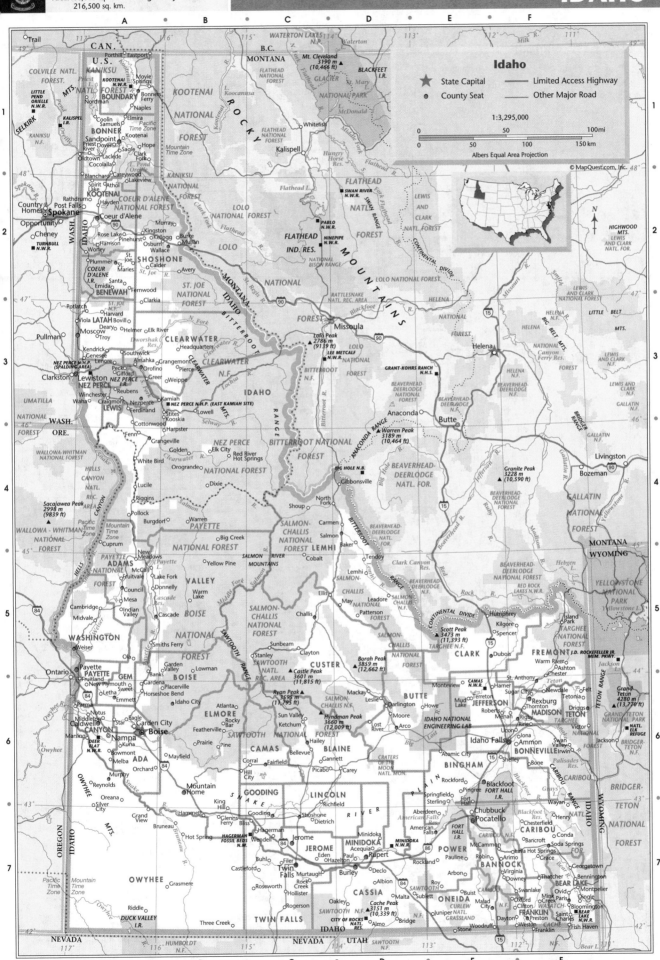

Capital: Boise
Area: 83,600 sq. mi.
216,500 sq. km.
Population: 1,229,000
Largest City: Boise

Idaho

★ State Capital
○ County Seat
━━━ Limited Access Highway
━━━ Other Major Road

1:3,295,000

0   50   100mi
0   50   100   150 km

Albers Equal Area Projection

© MapQuest.com, Inc.

Capital: Springfield
Area: 57,900 sq. mi.
150,000 sq. km.
Population: 12,045,0
Largest City: Chicago

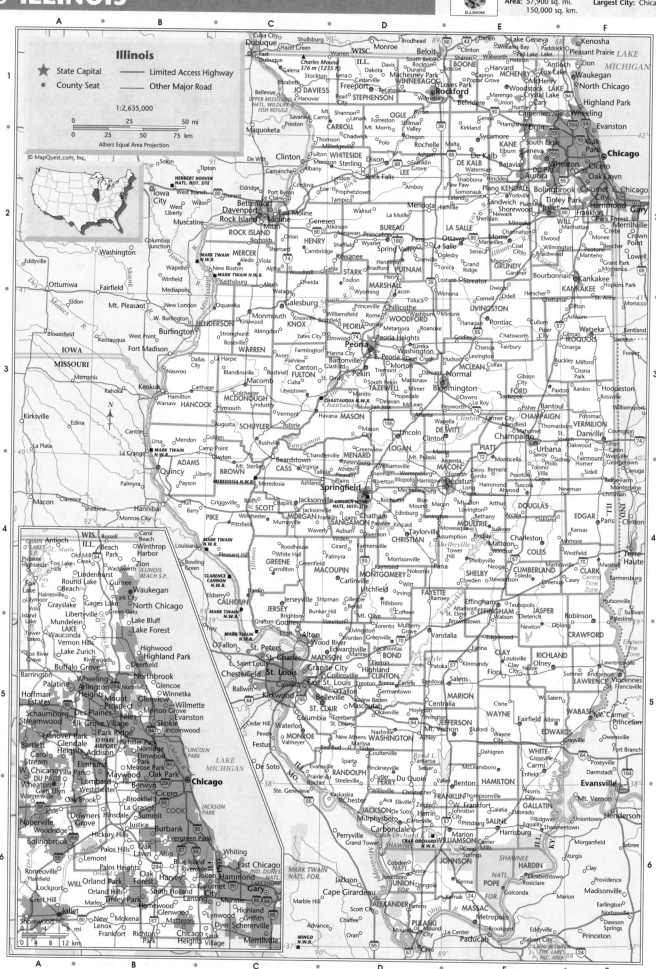

Illinois

★ State Capital — Limited Access Highway
● County Seat — Other Major Road

1:2,635,000

0   25   50 mi
0   25   50   75 km
Albers Equal Area Projection

© MapQuest.com, Inc.

Capital: Indianapolis
Area: 36,400 sq. mi.
94,300 sq. km.
Population: 5,899,000
Largest City: Indianapolis

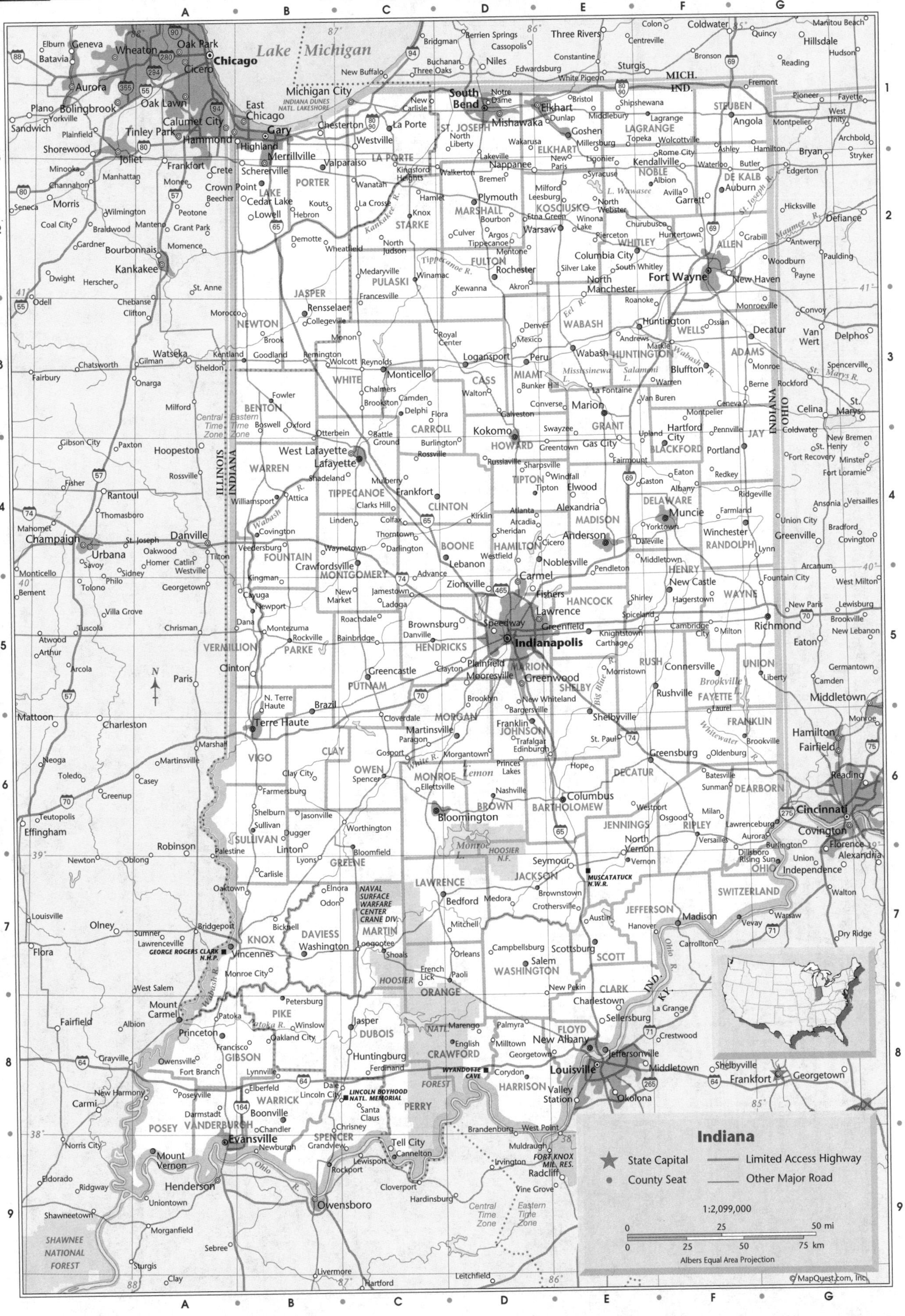

Lake Michigan

MICH.
IND.

ILLINOIS
INDIANA

OHIO
IND.
KY.

Indiana

★ State Capital — Limited Access Highway
● County Seat — Other Major Road

1:2,099,000

0   25   50 mi

0   25   50   75 km

Albers Equal Area Projection

©MapQuest.com, Inc.

SHAWNEE NATIONAL FOREST

HOOSIER N.F.

NAVAL SURFACE WARFARE CENTER CRANE DIV.

MUSCATATUCK N.W.R.

GEORGE ROGERS CLARK N.H.P.

LINCOLN BOYHOOD NATL. MEMORIAL

WYANDOTTE CAVE

FORT KNOX MIL. RES.

Capital: Des Moines
Area: 56,300 sq. mi.
145,800 sq. km.
Population: 2,862,00
Largest City: Des Mo

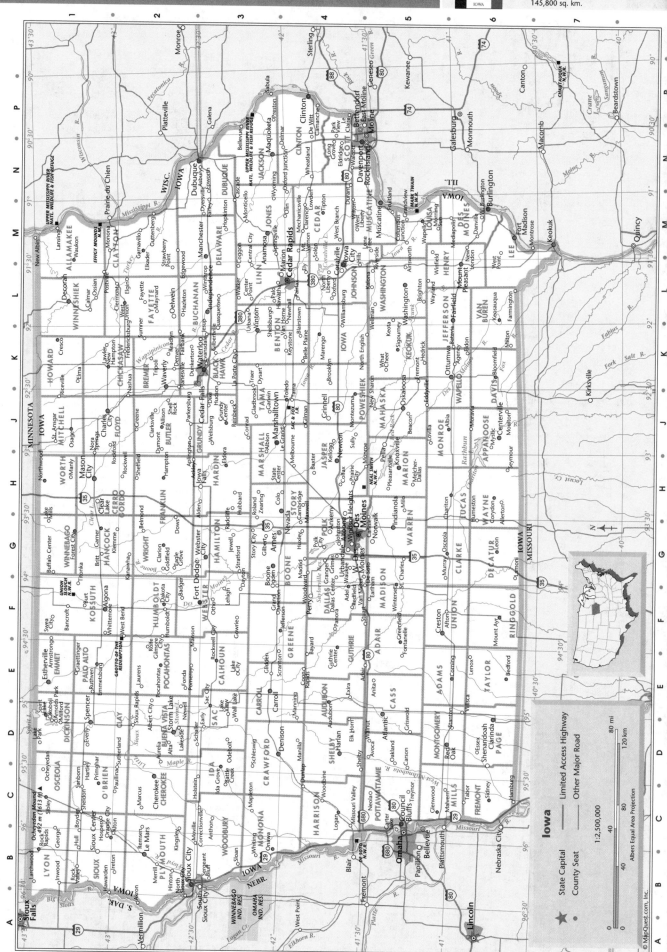

Iowa

State Capital ★
County Seat ●

Limited Access Highway
Other Major Road

1:2,500,000

Albers Equal Area Projection

© MapQuest.com, Inc.

Capital: Topeka
Area: 82,300 sq. mi.
213,100 sq. km.

Population: 2,629,000
Largest City: Wichita

KANSAS

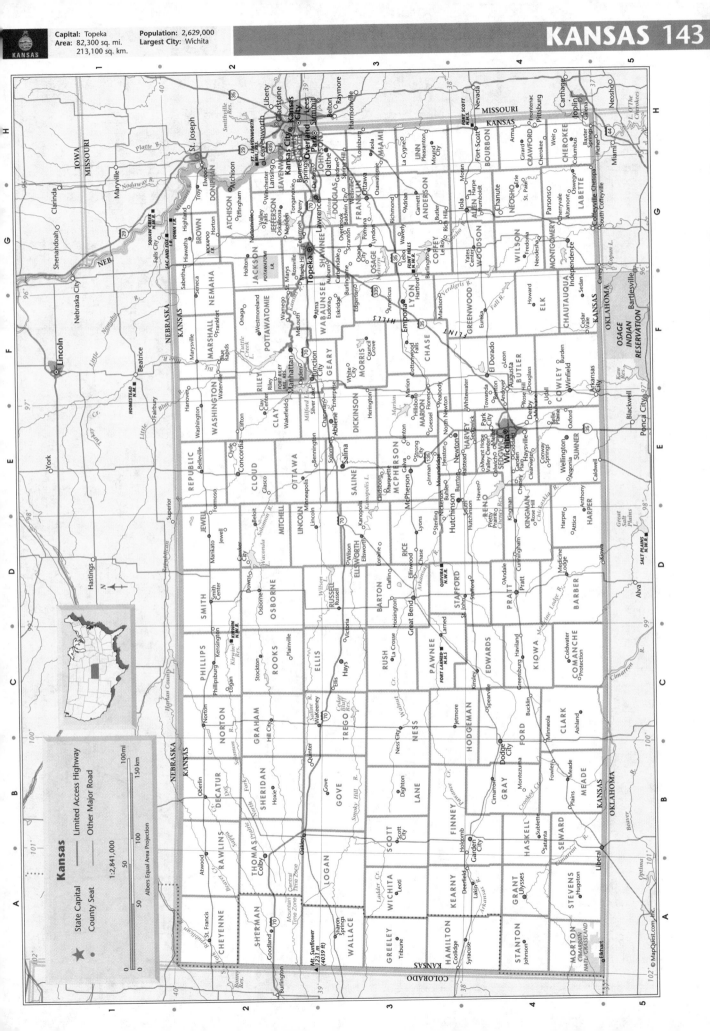

Kansas

Limited Access Highway
Other Major Road

★ State Capital
○ County Seat

★ Topeka

1:2,841,000
Albers Equal Area Projection

0   50   100mi
0   50   100   150 km

© 2002 © MapQuest.com, Inc.

Capital: Frankfort
Area: 40,400 sq. mi.
104,700 sq. km.
Population: 3,936,000
Largest City: Louisville

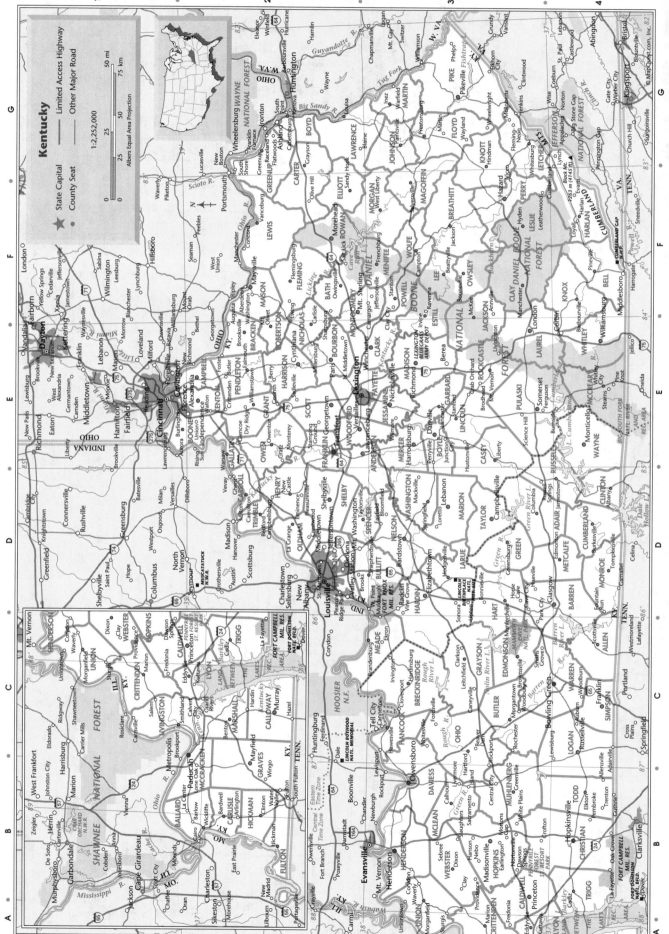

Capital: Baton Rouge
Area: 51,800 sq. mi.
134,300 sq. km.
Population: 4,369,000
Largest City: New Orleans

Louisiana

State Capital ★
Parish Seat •

Limited Access Highway
Other Major Road

1:2,750,000

Albers Equal Area Projection

© MapQuest.com, Inc.

Capital: Augusta
Area: 35,400 sq. mi. 91,700 sq. km.
Population: 1,244,000
Largest City: Portland

A
B
C
D
E
F
1
2
3
4
5
LAURENTIDES PROVINCIAL RESERVE
Baie-St.-Paul
St.-Pascal
Mont-Carmel
La Pocatière
Pohenegamook
Rivière-Bleue
Eastern Time Zone
Atlantic Time Zone
St.-Jacques
Edmundston
St.-Basile
Madawaska
Grand Isle
Lille
Frenchville
Fort Kent
Ste.-Anne-de-Madawaska
St.-Roch-des-Aulnaies
St.-Jean-Port-Joli
St.-Aubert
St. Lawrence River
St.-Ferreol-les-Neiges
St.-Tite-des-Caps
MT. STE.-ANNE PROV. PARK
Ste.-Anne-de-Beaupré
Beaupré
Château-Richer
Île d'Orleans
Cap-St.-Ignace
Montmagny
Ste.-Perpéture
St.-Pamphile
Charlesbourg
Québec
Levis-Lauzon
St.-Romuald
St.-Paul-de-Montminy
Ste.-Claire
St.-Camille-de-Lellis
Lac-Etchemin
St.-Justine
St.-Joseph-de-Beauce
East Broughton
Beauceville
St.-Prosper
St.-Zacharie
Thetford Mines
Ste.-Georges
St.-Methode-de-Frontenac
La Guadeloupe
St.-Martin
L. St.-François
Lambton
St.-Gedeon
FRONTENAC PROV. PARK
Lac Mégantic
L. Mégantic
R. Chaudière
APPALACHIAN
MOUNTAINS
CANADA
U.S.
QUÉBEC
MAINE
St. John R.
Dickey
St. John
St. Francis
Soldier Pond
Sinclair
Van Buren
St.-Léonard
Stockholm
Hamlin
Grand Falls/Grand Sault
Eagle Lake
New Sweden
Winterville
ALLAGASH WILDERNESS WATERWAY
Limestone
Plaster Rock
Caribou
Perham
Washburn
Fort Fairfield
Perth-Andover
Portage
Presque Isle
Mapleton
Clayton Lake
AROOSTOOK
Ashland
Westfield
Masardis
Squa Pan L.
Mars Hill
NEW BRUNSWICK
Southwest Miramichi R.
Munsungan L.
Churchill L.
Aroostook R.
Oxbow
Bridgewater
Grand L. Seboeis
Chamberlain L.
Telos L.
Grand L. Matagamon
Monticello
Littleton
Smyrna Mills
Houlton
Woodstock
Chesuncook L.
Chesuncook
BAXTER STATE PARK
Hodgdon
Linneus
Patten
Nackawic
Mattawamkeag R.
Island Falls
North Amity
Seboomook L.
Pittston Farm
Seboomook
North East Carry
Mt. Katahdin 1606 m (5268 ft)
Sherman Station
Sherman Mills
Haynesville
Orient
Millinocket L.
Pemadumcook L.
Moosehead L.
PISCATAQUIS
Grindstone
Weston
Grand L.
Magaguadavic L.
Moose River
Jackman
Rockwood
Kokadjo
White Cap Mt. 1111 m (3644 ft)
Millinocket
East Millinocket
Reed
Wytopitlock
Danforth
Long Pond
Norcross
Macwahoc
Eaton
McAdam
Oromocto L.
Kingman
Lily Bay
West Seboeis
Moosehead
Lake Parlin
Mattawamkeag
Winn
Brookton
Vanceboro
Eastern Time Zone
Seboeis L.
Penobscot R.
Baskahegan L.
Greenville
PENOBSCOT
Topsfield
Coburn Gore
Kennebec R.
Shirley Mills
SOMERSET
Brownville Junction
Springfield
Lincoln
Lee
Waite
PASSAMAQUODDY INDIAN TOWNSHIP I.R.
Snow Mt. 1204 m (3948 ft)
The Forks
Monson
Sebec L.
Brownville
Seboeis
W. Grand L.
Flagstaff L.
Milo
Princeton
St. Stephen
Eustis
Caratunk
Dover-Foxcroft
Howland
Burlington
Grand Lake Stream
Calais
ST. CROIX ISLAND INTL. HIST. SITE
Stratton
Guilford
Piscataquis R.
Lagrange
Passadumkeag
Woodland
Aziscohos L.
Charleston
South Lagrange
Olamon
Big L.
Alexander
Sugarloaf Mt. 1291 m (4237 ft)
Carrabassett
Bingham
Wellington
Dexter
Hudson
Nicatous L.
MOOSEHORN N.W.R.
Blacks Harbour
Oquossoc
Rangeley
Kingfield
Solon
Exeter Corners
East Corinth
PENOBSCOT I.R.
Milford
Great Pond
Wesley
Perry
PASSAMAQUODDY PLEASANT POINT I.R.
Wilsons Mills
Saddleback Mt. 1255 m (4116 ft)
Salem
Harmony
Corinna
Old Town
Eastport
New Portland
Athens
Hartland
Kenduskeag
Dennysville
Mooselookmeguntic L.
Phillips
Orono
WASHINGTON
MOOSEHORN N.W.R.
Lubec
Richardson Lakes
FRANKLIN
New Vineyard
Madison
Newport
Hermon
Bangor
Amherst
Northfield
Whiting
West Quoddy Head
Umbagog L.
Byron
Weld
Skowhegan
Pittsfield
Carmel
Brewer
HANCOCK
Machias
East Machias
Upton
Mercer
Norridgewock
Hampden
East Holden
Waltham
Deblois
Farmington
Hinckley
Burnham
Clinton
Dixmont
Green Lake
Jonesboro
Cutler
Andover
OXFORD
Mexico
Wilton
Fairfield
Unity
Frankfort
Bucksport
Franklin
Harrington
Columbia Falls
Cross I.
Rumford
Dixfield
Waterville
Brooks
Orland
Cherryfield
Berlin
Newry
Androscoggin R.
Chisholm
Oakland
Albion
Swanville
Ellsworth
Steuben
Milbridge
Jonesport
Winslow
WALDO
Stockton Springs
Trenton
Livermore Falls
China
Belfast
Searsport
Bar Harbor
Winter Harbor
Great Wass I.
Gorham
Bryant Pond
Canton
Belgrade
Gilead
Bethel
KENNEBEC
Liberty
Islesboro Island
Castine
Blue Hill
Somesville
ACADIA NATL. PARK
ACADIA N. P.
WHITE MTN. NATL. FOR.
Livermore
Leeds
South China
Augusta
Searsmont
Buckfield
Winthrop
Lincolnville
Sedgwick
Mt. Desert I.
WHITE MTS.
North Waterford
Paris
Hallowell
Washington
Southwest Harbor
South Paris
Turner
Union
Penobscot Bay
Deer Isle
Bass Harbor
N.H.
MAINE
Norway
Greene
Gardiner
Camden
North Haven
Deer Isle
Stonington
Atlantic
Lovell
Oxford
ANDROSCOGGIN
Jefferson
KNOX
Swans I.
Mechanic Falls
Lewiston
Whitefield
Rockland
Isle au Haut
Long I.
Frenchboro
North Conway
Auburn
Richmond
Waldoboro
Vinalhaven I.
Bridgton
Lisbon
LINCOLN
Thomaston
Owls Head
Isle au Haut ACADIA NATL. PARK
Fryeburg
Casco
Lisbon Falls
SAGADAHOC
Damariscotta
Vinalhaven
Conway
Naples
Bath
Wiscasset
Gray
Brunswick
Port Clyde
SEAL ISLAND N.W.R.
Hiram
Sebago L.
Saco R.
Freeport
Boothbay Harbor
Matinicus I.
Kezar Falls
North Windham
Cornish
Yarmouth
CUMBERLAND
Falmouth
Monhegan I.
Limerick
Westbrook
Portland
Casco Bay
Small Pt.
GULF OF MAINE
Wolfeboro
Hollis Center
South Portland
Cape Elizabeth
Cape Elizabeth
Shapleigh
L. Winnipesaukee
Alfred
Old Orchard Beach
Springvale
YORK
Saco
Saco Bay
Biddeford
Farmington
Sanford
Kennebunk
Kennebunkport
Rochester
North Berwick
Berwick
Somersworth
Dover
Ogunquit
ATLANTIC OCEAN
Durham
Newmarket
Raymond
Epping
York
Kittery
Portsmouth
Exeter
Maine
State/Provincial Capital
County Seat
Limited Access Highway
Other Major Road
1:2,074,000
0 25 50 mi
0 25 50 75 km
Albers Equal Area Projection
© MapQuest.com, Inc.

Capital: Annapolis
Area: 12,400 sq. mi.
32,100 sq. km.
Population: 5,135,000
Largest City: Baltimore

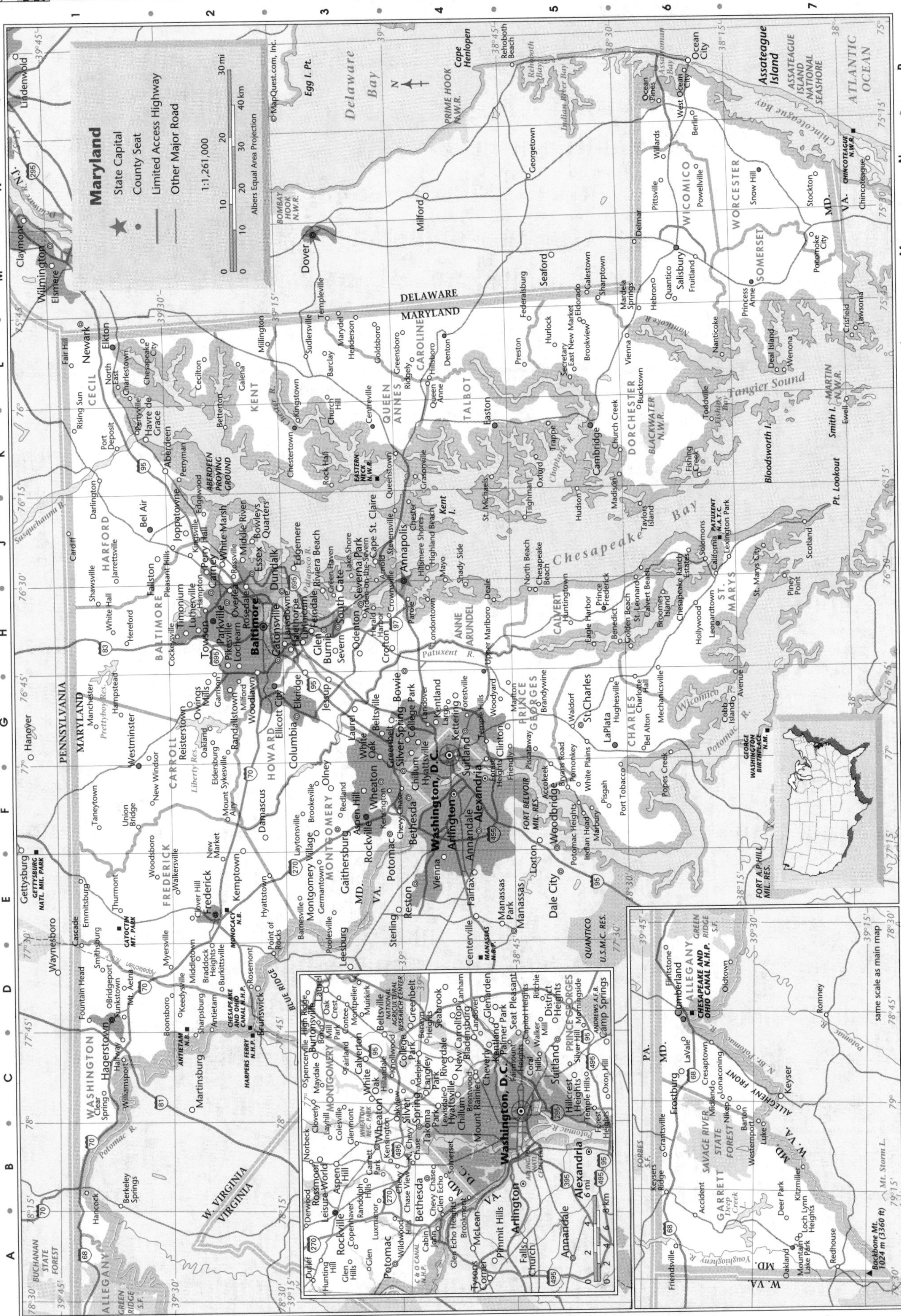

Maryland

★ State Capital
• County Seat
Limited Access Highway
Other Major Road

1:1,261,000
Albers Equal Area Projection

© MapQuest.com, Inc.

30 mi
40 km

ATLANTIC OCEAN

Chesapeake Bay

Delaware Bay

Tangier Sound

PENNSYLVANIA

W. VIRGINIA

VIRGINIA

DELAWARE
MARYLAND

Assateague Island
ASSATEAGUE ISLAND NATIONAL SEASHORE

Baltimore
Washington, D.C.
Annapolis
Frederick
Hagerstown
Cumberland
Salisbury
Ocean City

Counties: ALLEGANY, WASHINGTON, FREDERICK, CARROLL, BALTIMORE, HARFORD, CECIL, KENT, QUEEN ANNES, CAROLINE, TALBOT, DORCHESTER, WICOMICO, SOMERSET, WORCESTER, MONTGOMERY, HOWARD, ANNE ARUNDEL, PRINCE GEORGES, CALVERT, CHARLES, ST. MARYS, GARRETT

same scale as main map

Capital: Boston
Area: 10,600 sq. mi.
27,300 sq. km.
Population: 6,147,000
Largest City: Boston

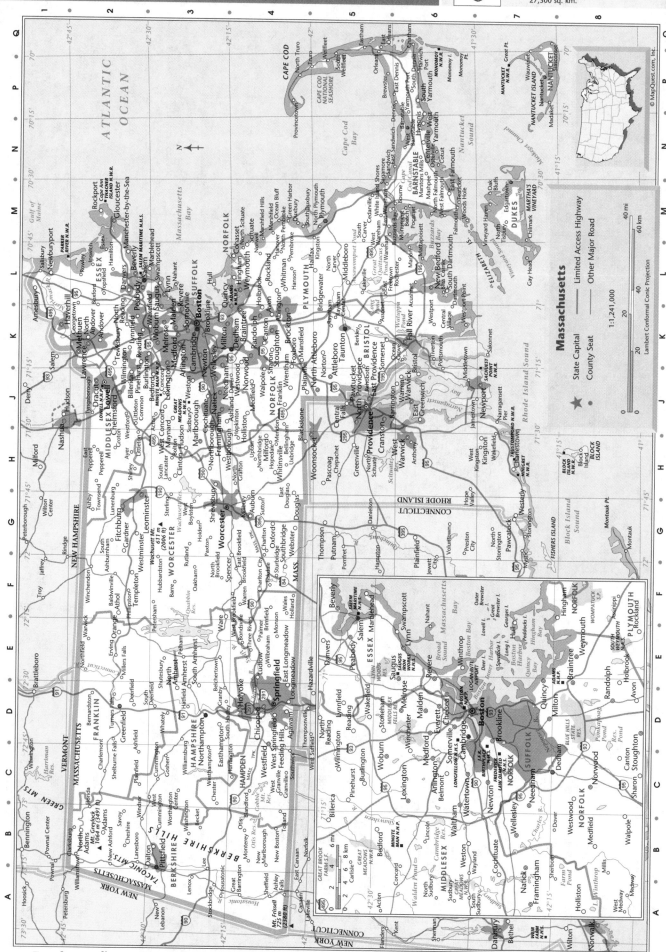

Massachusetts

1:1,241,000

Lambert Conformal Conic Projection

★ State Capital
● County Seat

— Limited Access Highway
— Other Major Road

Capital: Lansing
Area: 96,700 sq. mi.
250,500 sq. km.
Population: 9,817,000
Largest City: Detroit

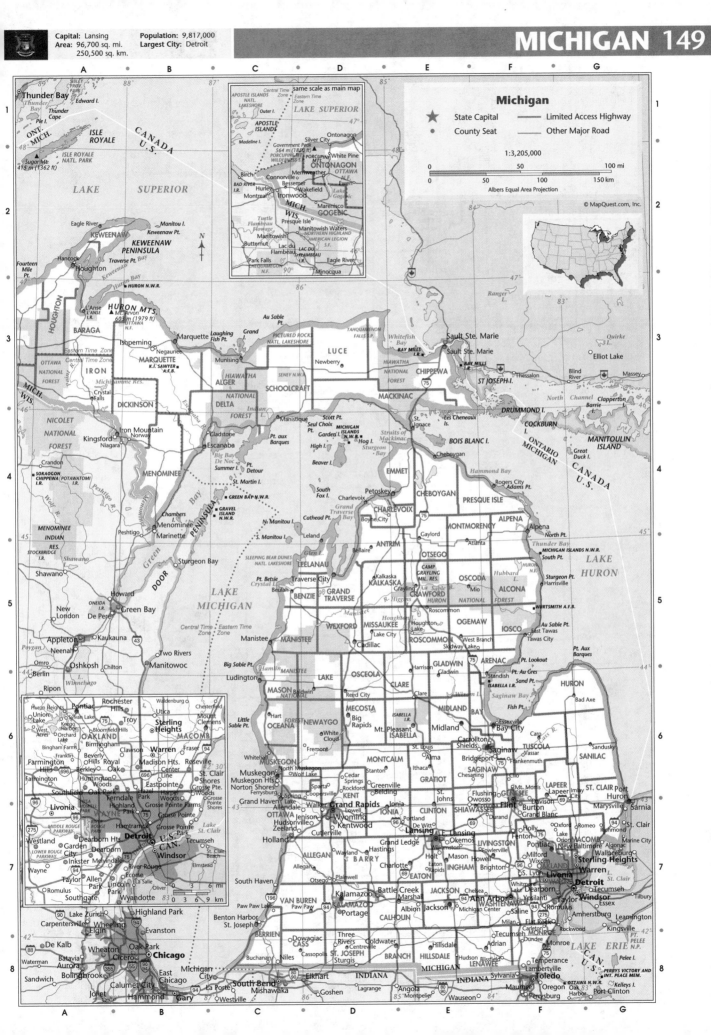

Michigan

★ State Capital   ── Limited Access Highway
• County Seat   ── Other Major Road

1:3,205,000

0   50   100 mi
0   50   100   150 km

Albers Equal Area Projection

© MapQuest.com, Inc.

Capital: St. Paul
Area: 86,900 sq. mi.
225,200 sq. km.
Population: 4,725,000
Largest City: Minneapo

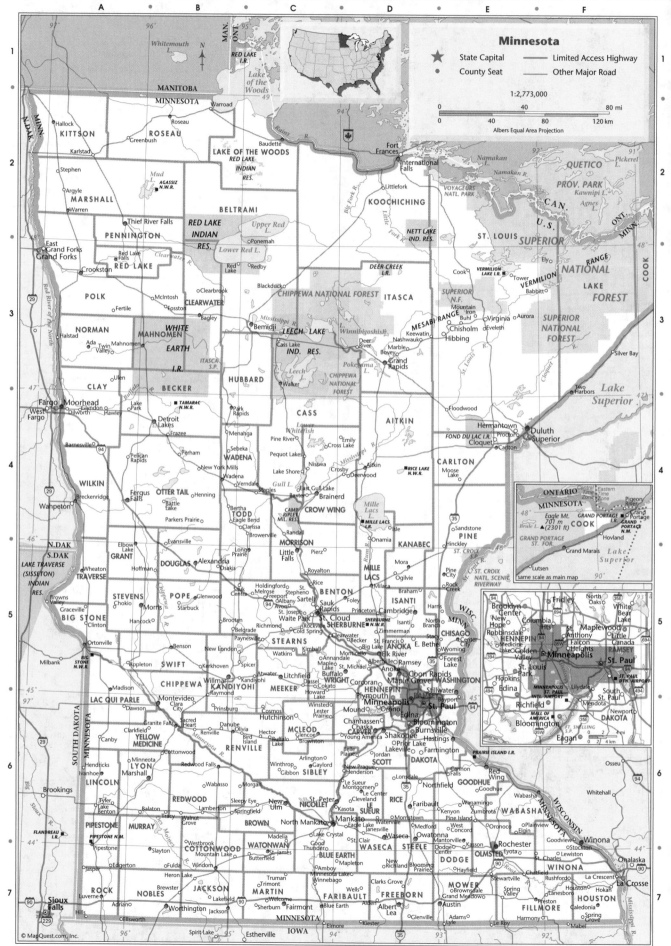

Minnesota

★ State Capital
● County Seat

── Limited Access Highway
── Other Major Road

1:2,773,000

Albers Equal Area Projection

Capital: Jackson
Area: 48,400 sq. mi.
125,400 sq. km.
Population: 2,752,000
Largest City: Jackson

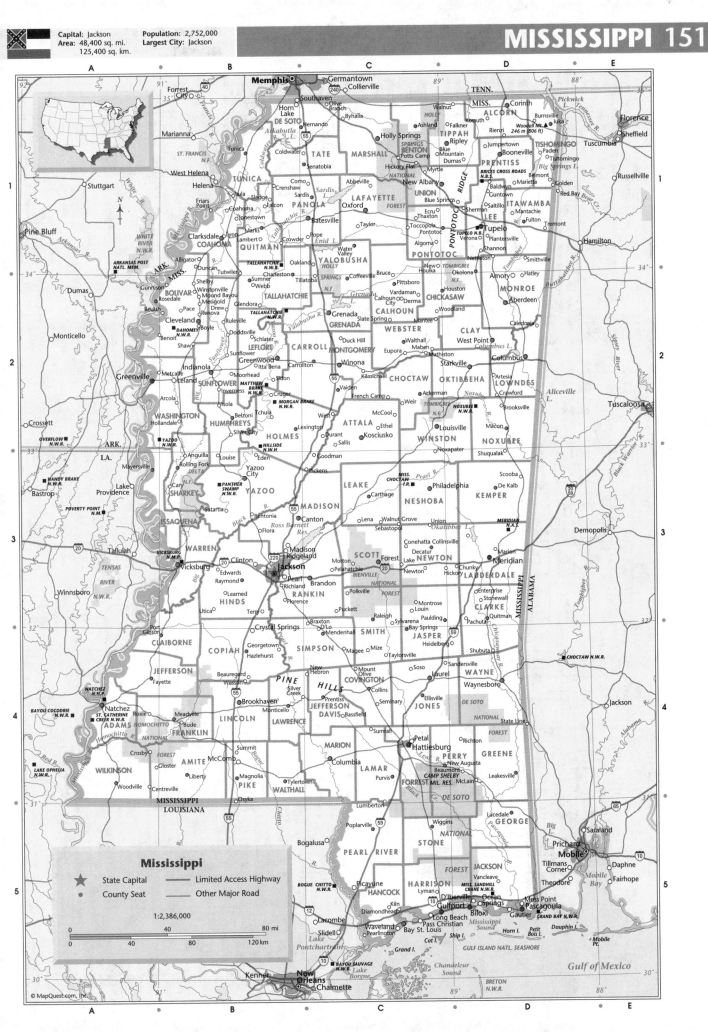

Mississippi

★ State Capital
• County Seat
— Limited Access Highway
— Other Major Road

1:2,386,000

0   40   80 mi

0   40   80   120 km

© MapQuest.com, Inc.

Capital: Jefferson City   **Population:** 5,439,000
Area: 69,700 sq. mi.   **Largest City:** Kansas City
     180,500 sq. km.

Capital: Helena
Area: 147,000 sq. mi.
380,800 sq. km.
Population: 880,000
Largest City: Billings

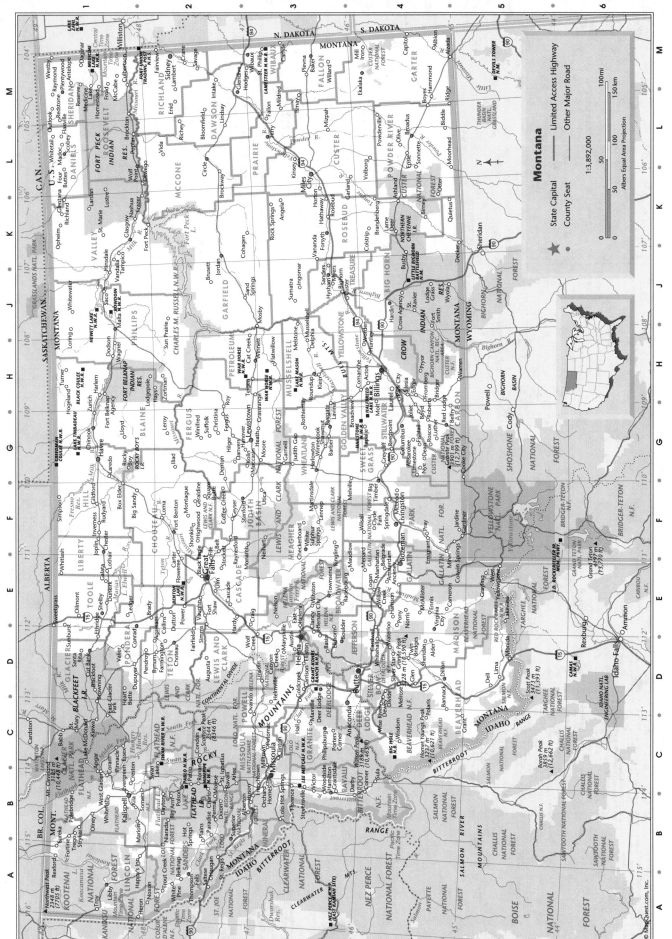

Montana
1:3,892,000

★ State Capital
• County Seat

Limited Access Highway
Other Major Road

Albers Equal Area Projection

Capital: Lincoln
Area: 77,400 sq. mi.
200,300 sq. km.
Population: 1,663,000
Largest City: Omaha

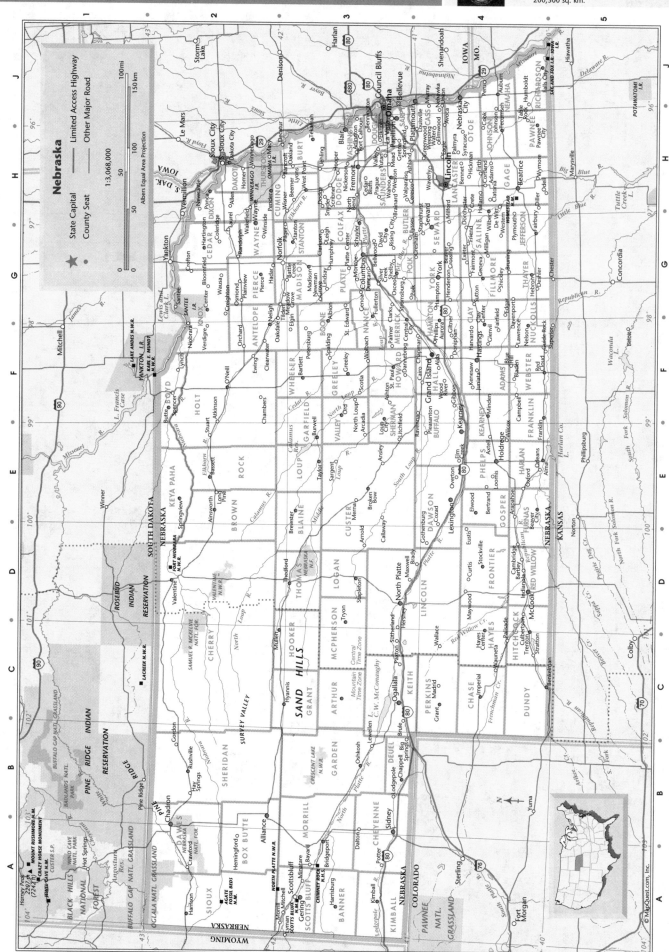

Capital: Carson City **Population:** 1,747,000
Area: 110,600 sq. mi. **Largest City:** Las Vegas
286,400 sq. km.

OREGON | IDAHO
NEVADA

FORT McDERMITT IND. RES.

Denio McDermitt Owyhee
Jackpot

DUCK VALLEY IND. RES.
Owyhee
Mountain City Jarbidge
Matterhorn 3304 m (10,839 ft)
Contact

SHELDON NATL. WILDLIFE REFUGE
Goose L.
FORT BIDWELL IND. RES.
Vya
Massacre L.
Upper L.
Orovada
Paradise Valley
HUMBOLDT NATL. FOR.
Charleston
Pacific Time Zone
Mountain Time Zone

MODOC NATL. FOR.
SUMMIT LAKE IND. RES.
FORT McDERMITT IND. RES.
Jack Creek
North Fork
GREAT SALT LAKE DESERT

Vya
HUMBOLDT
DESERT VALLEY
Tuscarora
ELKO
Montello

WASHOE
Honey L.
Gerlach
Sulphur
Pronto
Golconda
Winnemucca
Valmy
Dunphy
Carlin
Spring Creek
Wells
Deeth
Halleck
Arthur
Lamoille
Cobre
Oasis
Pilot Peak 3263 m (10,704 ft)
West Wendover

SIERRA ARMY DEPOT
Flanigan
Empire
PYRAMID LAKE IND. RES.
Winnemucca L.
Dry L.
Lovelock
Oreana
Mt. Tobin 2979 m (9775 ft)
Battle Mountain
Beowawe
Crescent Valley
Elko
Ruby Dome 3471 m (11,387 ft)
Lee
TE-MOAK IND. RES.
Jiggs
Ruby Valley
Currie
WENDOVER RANGE

PLUMAS NATL. FOR.
Pyramid L.
Sutcliffe
Nixon
PERSHING
Mill City
Imlay
Humboldt
Unionville
LANDER
SHOSHONE RANGE
RUBY MTS.
HUMBOLDT NATL.
Ruby L.
RUBY LAKE N.W.R.
Goshute
Lages
DESERET TEST CENTER

TAHOE N.F.
Lemmon Valley
Sun Valley
Wadsworth
Fernley
Hazen
GREAT BASIN
EUREKA
Newark L.
Cherry Creek
Tippett
GOSHUTE IND. RES.
Ibapah Peak 3684 m (12,087 ft)

Verdi
Reno
STOREY
Steamboat
Sparks
Patrick
CHURCHILL
FALLON N.W.R.
Dixie Valley
Austin
Summit Mt. 3189 m (10,461 ft)
Eureka
WHITE PINE
Steptoe
McGill
HUMBOLDT NATL. FOR.
Mt. Moriah 3678 m (12,067 ft)

Incline Village
Virginia City
Silver Springs
Stillwater
FALLON IND. RES.
STILLWATER N.W.R.
FALLON N.A.S.
Cold Springs
North Toiyabe Peak 3290 m (10,793 ft)
HUMBOLDT NATL.
Ruth
Lane
Ely
Majors Place
Wheeler Peak 3982 m (13,063 ft)
Baker

South Lake Tahoe
Dayton
LYON
Wabuska
Middlegate
FALLON N.A.S.
Ione
YOMBA IND. RES.
Mt. Jefferson 3642 m (11,949 ft)
Duckwater
DUCKWATER IND. RES.
Preston
Lund
Minerva
GREAT BASIN N.P.
SCHELL CREEK RANGE
EGAN RANGE
SNAKE RANGE

Zephyr Cove
Carson City
YERINGTON IND. RES.
Yerington
Schurz
Gabbs
TOIYABE N.F.
Arc Dome 3588 m (11,773 ft)
Round Mountain
Currant
DESERT RANGE EXP. STA.

Minden
Gardnerville
Mason
WALKER RIVER IND. RES.
TOIYABE
SMOKY VALLEY
TOQUIMA RANGE
MONITOR RANGE
HOT CREEK RANGE
GRANT RANGE
HUMBOLDT NATL. FOR.
INDIAN PEAK RANGE

DOUGLAS
WASHOE IND. RES.
Smith
Wellington
Topaz Lake
Mt. Grant 3426 m (11,239 ft)
Babbitt
MINERAL
Luning
Mina
Warm Springs
Nyala
Sunnyside
Atlanta
White R.

ELDORADO N.F.
Walker L.
HAWTHORNE AMMUNITION DEPOT
Hawthorne
Adams–McGill Res.

STANISLAUS NATL. FOR.
TOIYABE N.F.
Basalt
Mt. Montgomery
Coaldale
Tonopah
NYE
Pioche
Caselton
Ursine

YOSEMITE NATL. PARK
Mono L.
Boundary Peak 4005 m (13,140 ft)
ESMERALDA
Silver Peak
Goldfield
Panaca
LINCOLN

Mt. Ritter 4010 m (13,157 ft)
Dyer
White Mt. Peak 4342 m (14,246 ft)
NELLIS AIR FORCE RANGE
Tempiute
Rachel
Hiko
Caliente
DIXIE NATL. FOR.
Mountain Time Zone

DEVILS POSTPILE NATL. MON.
Lida
Gold Point
Scotty's Junction
Ash Springs
Alamo
Elgin
Carp
PAIUTE IND. RES.

SIERRA NATL. FOR.
Mt. Morgan 4190 m (13,748 ft)
INYO NATL. FOR.
NEVADA / CALIFORNIA
PAHRANAGAT N.W.R.
Pacific Time Zone

Madera
KINGS CANYON N.P.
INYO MTS.
DEATH VALLEY
Beatty
NEVADA TEST SITE
NELLIS AIR FORCE RANGE
DESERT NATL.
Mesquite
Burkerville

SIERRA NEVADA
Mt. Whitney 4418 m (14,494 ft)
Amargosa Valley
Mercury
INDIAN SPRINGS A.F.B.
Indian Springs
MOAPA RIVER IND. RES.
Moapa
Glendale
VALLEY OF FIRE S.P.
Overton
ARIZONA

SEQUOIA NATL. PARK
DEATH VALLEY NATIONAL PARK
ASH MEADOWS N.W.R.
DEVILS HOLE (DEATH VALLEY NATL. PARK)
TOIYABE N.F.
NELLIS A.F.B.
Charleston Park
N. Las Vegas
L. Mead

Lindsay
Corcoran
SEQUOIA NATL. FOR.
Kern R.
CHINA LAKE NAVAL WEAPONS CENTER
Pahrump
CLARK
Las Vegas
Spring Valley
Blue Diamond
Paradise
Henderson
Hoover Dam
LAKE MEAD NATL. REC. AREA

Porterville
RED ROCK N.C.A.
Sloan
Boulder City
Red L.

Amargosa R.
Sandy
Goodsprings
BLACK MTS.

Nevada
★ State Capital — Limited Access Highway
● County Seat — Other Major Road

1:3,364,000
0 50 100 mi
0 50 100 150 km
Albers Equal Area Projection
© MapQuest.com, Inc.

FORT IRWIN MIL. RES.
Jean
Nelson
Cottonwood Cove
Searchlight
Cal Nev Ari
L. Mohave

MOJAVE DESERT
MOJAVE NATL. PRESERVE
Bullhead City
Laughlin
Kingman
FORT MOHAVE IND. RES.
Colorado R.

Capital: Concord
Area: 9,400 sq. mi.
24,200 sq. km.
Population: 1,185,000
Largest City: Manchester

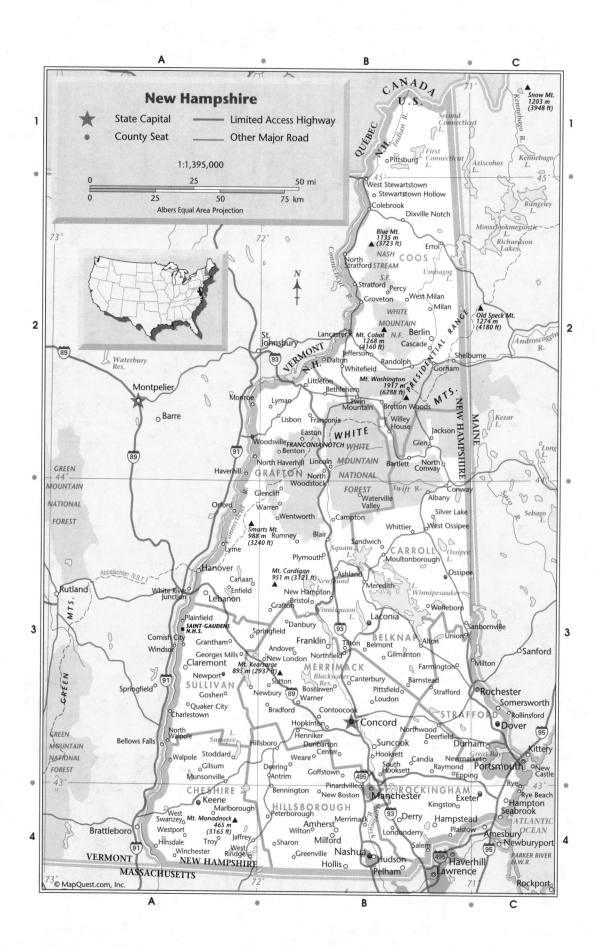

New Hampshire

★ State Capital   ━━━ Limited Access Highway

• County Seat   ━━━ Other Major Road

1:1,395,000

| 0 | 25 | 50 mi |

| 0 | 25 | 50 | 75 km |

Albers Equal Area Projection

Capital: Trenton   Population: 8,115,000
Area: 8,700 sq. mi.   Largest City: Newark
    22,600 sq. km.

NEW JERSEY 157

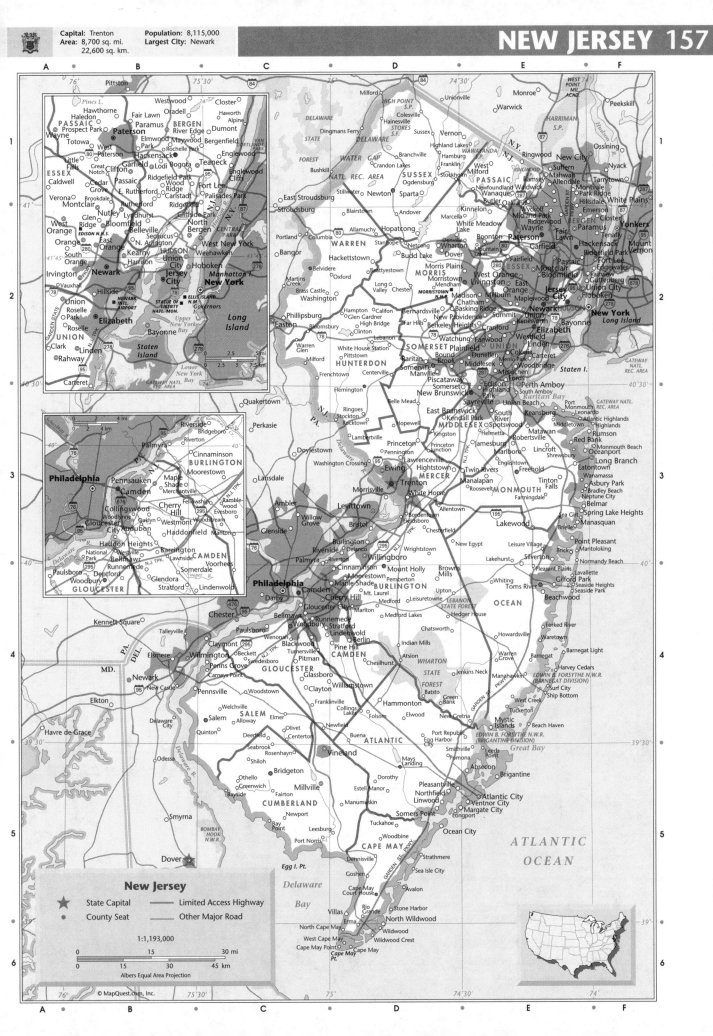

New Jersey

★ State Capital   ━━━ Limited Access Highway

• County Seat   ━━━ Other Major Road

1:1,193,000

0   15   30 mi

0   15   30   45 km

Albers Equal Area Projection

© MapQuest.com, Inc.

Capital: Santa Fe
Area: 121,600 sq. mi.
314,900 sq. km.
Population: 1,737,000
Largest City: Albuquerque

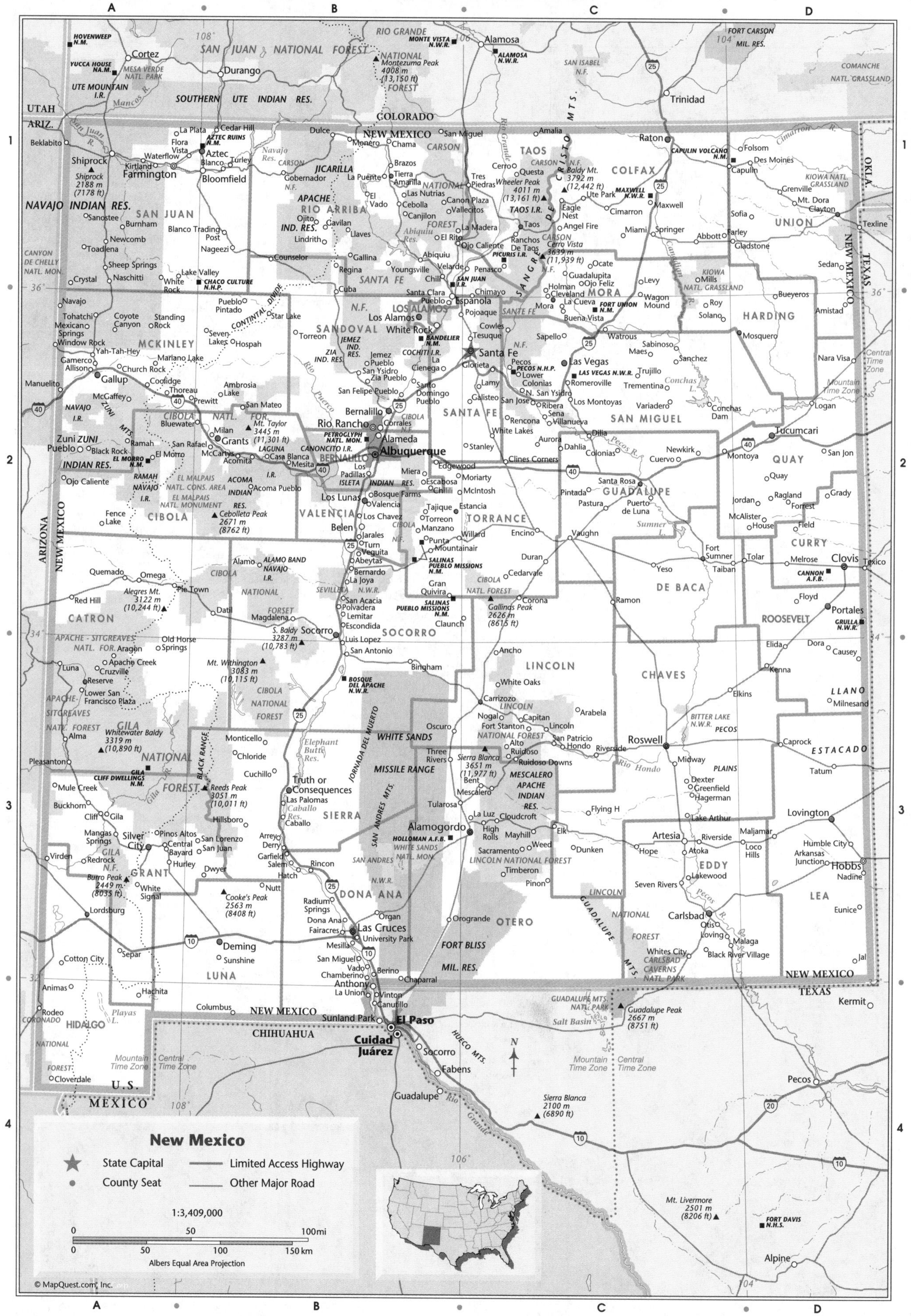

New Mexico

★ State Capital — Limited Access Highway
• County Seat — Other Major Road

1:3,409,000

0   50   100mi
0   50   100   150 km

Albers Equal Area Projection

© MapQuest.com, Inc.

States / Regions: UTAH, ARIZ., COLORADO, OKLA., TEXAS, CHIHUAHUA, U.S., MEXICO, NEW MEXICO

Counties: SAN JUAN, RIO ARRIBA, TAOS, COLFAX, UNION, MCKINLEY, SANDOVAL, LOS ALAMOS, SANTA FE, MORA, HARDING, SAN MIGUEL, QUAY, CIBOLA, VALENCIA, BERNALILLO, TORRANCE, GUADALUPE, CURRY, CATRON, SOCORRO, DE BACA, ROOSEVELT, LINCOLN, CHAVES, SIERRA, OTERO, EDDY, LEA, GRANT, DONA ANA, LUNA, HIDALGO

Selected places:
Farmington, Shiprock, Aztec, Bloomfield, Cortez, Durango, Chama, Raton, Trinidad, Alamosa, Gallup, Grants, Albuquerque, Rio Rancho, Bernalillo, Santa Fe, Las Vegas, Tucumcari, Española, Los Alamos, Taos, Clovis, Portales, Socorro, Truth or Consequences, Silver City, Lordsburg, Deming, Las Cruces, Alamogordo, Roswell, Artesia, Carlsbad, Hobbs, Lovington, El Paso, Ciudad Juárez, Santa Rosa, Fort Sumner, Vaughn, Ruidoso, Cloudcroft

National Forests / Parks / Monuments:
SAN JUAN NATIONAL FOREST, CARSON NATIONAL FOREST, SANTA FE NATIONAL FOREST, CIBOLA NATIONAL FOREST, GILA NATIONAL FOREST, APACHE-SITGREAVES NATIONAL FOREST, LINCOLN NATIONAL FOREST, WHITE SANDS NATIONAL MONUMENT, CARLSBAD CAVERNS NATIONAL PARK, CHACO CULTURE N.H.P., BANDELIER NAT. MON., EL MALPAIS NATL. MONUMENT, PETROGLYPH NATL. MON., SALINAS PUEBLO MISSIONS N.M., CAPULIN VOLCANO N.M.

Indian Reservations:
NAVAJO INDIAN RES., JICARILLA APACHE, ZUNI INDIAN RES., ACOMA INDIAN RES., LAGUNA INDIAN RES., ISLETA INDIAN RES., MESCALERO APACHE INDIAN RES., SOUTHERN UTE INDIAN RES., UTE MOUNTAIN I.R.

Peaks / Elevations:
Wheeler Peak 4011 m (13,161 ft)
Mt. Taylor 3445 m (11,301 ft)
Sierra Blanca 3651 m (11,977 ft)
Whitewater Baldy 3319 m (10,890 ft)
Montezuma Peak 4008 m (13,150 ft)
Baldy Mt. 3792 m (12,442 ft)
Guadalupe Peak 2667 m (8751 ft)
Shiprock 2188 m (7178 ft)

WHITE SANDS MISSILE RANGE, FORT BLISS MIL. RES., HOLLOMAN A.F.B., CANNON A.F.B.

Capital: Albany
Area: 54,700 sq. mi.
141,100 sq. km.

Population: 18,175,000
Largest City: New York

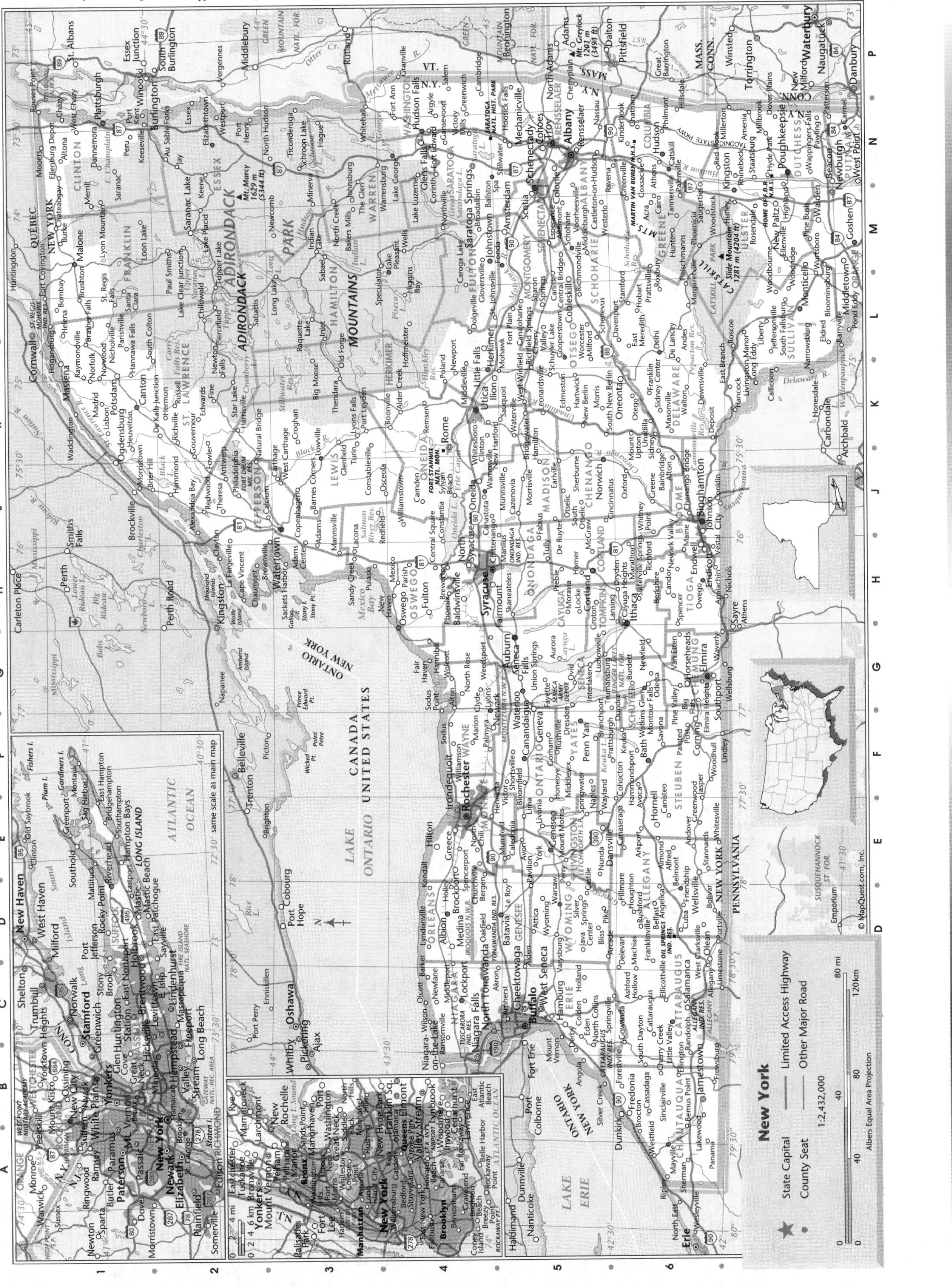

New York
State Capital
County Seat
Limited Access Highway
Other Major Road
1:2,432,000
0 40 80 mi
0 40 80 120 km
Albers Equal Area Projection
© MapQuest.com, Inc.
LAKE ONTARIO
LAKE ERIE
ATLANTIC OCEAN
CANADA
UNITED STATES
PENNSYLVANIA
ADIRONDACK MOUNTAINS
same scale as main map

Capital: Raleigh
Area: 53,800 sq. mi.
139,400 sq. km.
Population: 7,546,000
Largest City: Charlotte

North Carolina

— Limited Access Highway
— Other Major Road

★ State Capital
• County Seat

1:2,600,000

Albers Equal Area Projection

© MapQuest.com, Inc.

ATLANTIC OCEAN

VIRGINIA

SOUTH CAROLINA

NORTH CAROLINA

ONSLOW BAY

LONG BAY

THE GRAND STRAND

Raleigh
Charlotte
Greensboro
Durham
Winston-Salem
High Point
Fayetteville
Wilmington
Asheville
Cary
Gastonia
Chapel Hill
Rocky Mount
Greenville
Wilson
Goldsboro
Kinston
New Bern
Jacksonville
Kannapolis
Concord
Salisbury
Statesville
Hickory
Morganton
Lenoir
Boone
Elizabeth City

(Map of North Carolina showing counties, cities, roads, and geographic features. Inset map of western North Carolina mountains region including Asheville, Mt. Mitchell 2037 m (6684 ft), Great Smoky Mountains, and surrounding areas.)

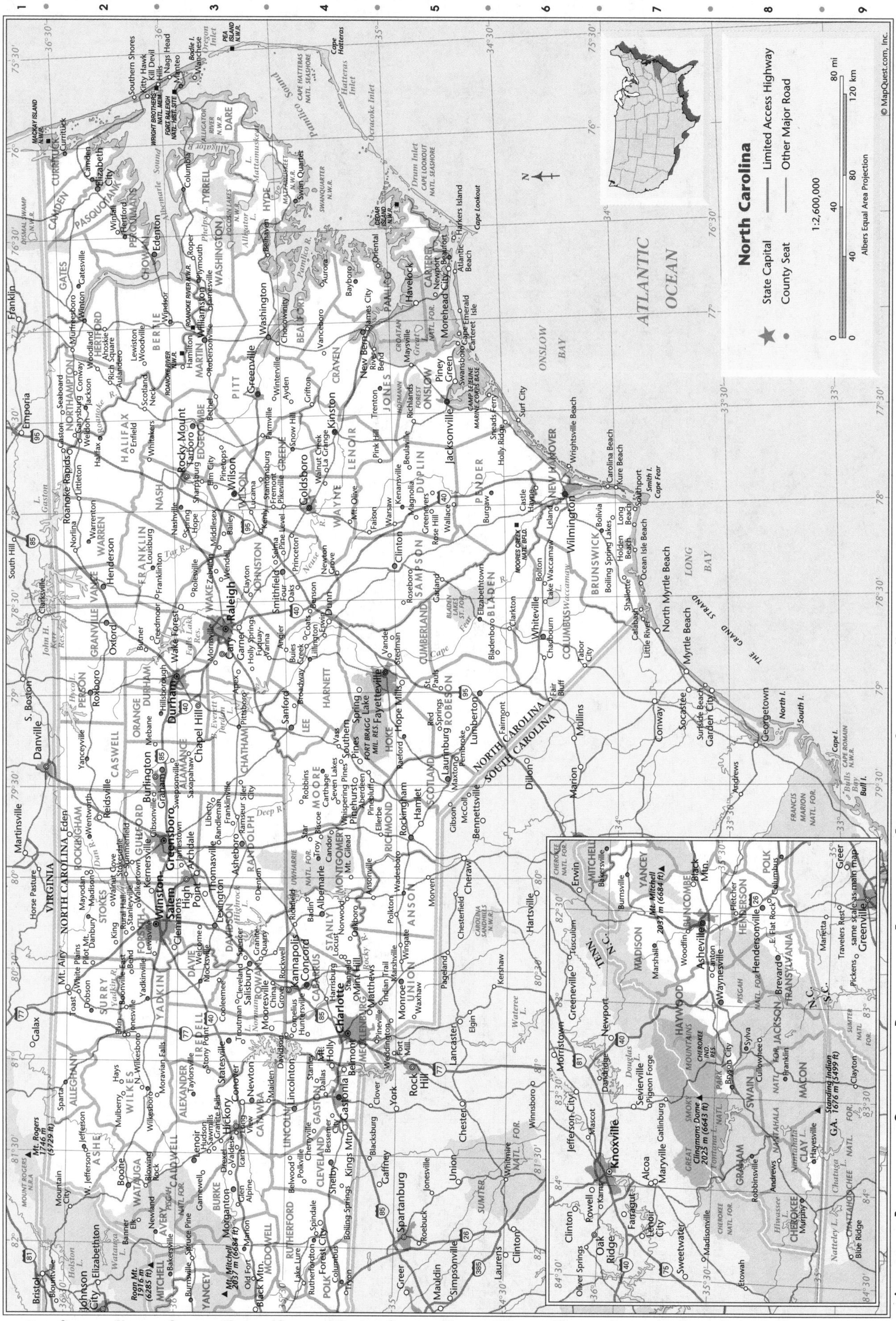

Capital: Bismarck
Area: 70,700 sq. mi.
183,100 sq. km.
Population: 638,000
Largest City: Fargo

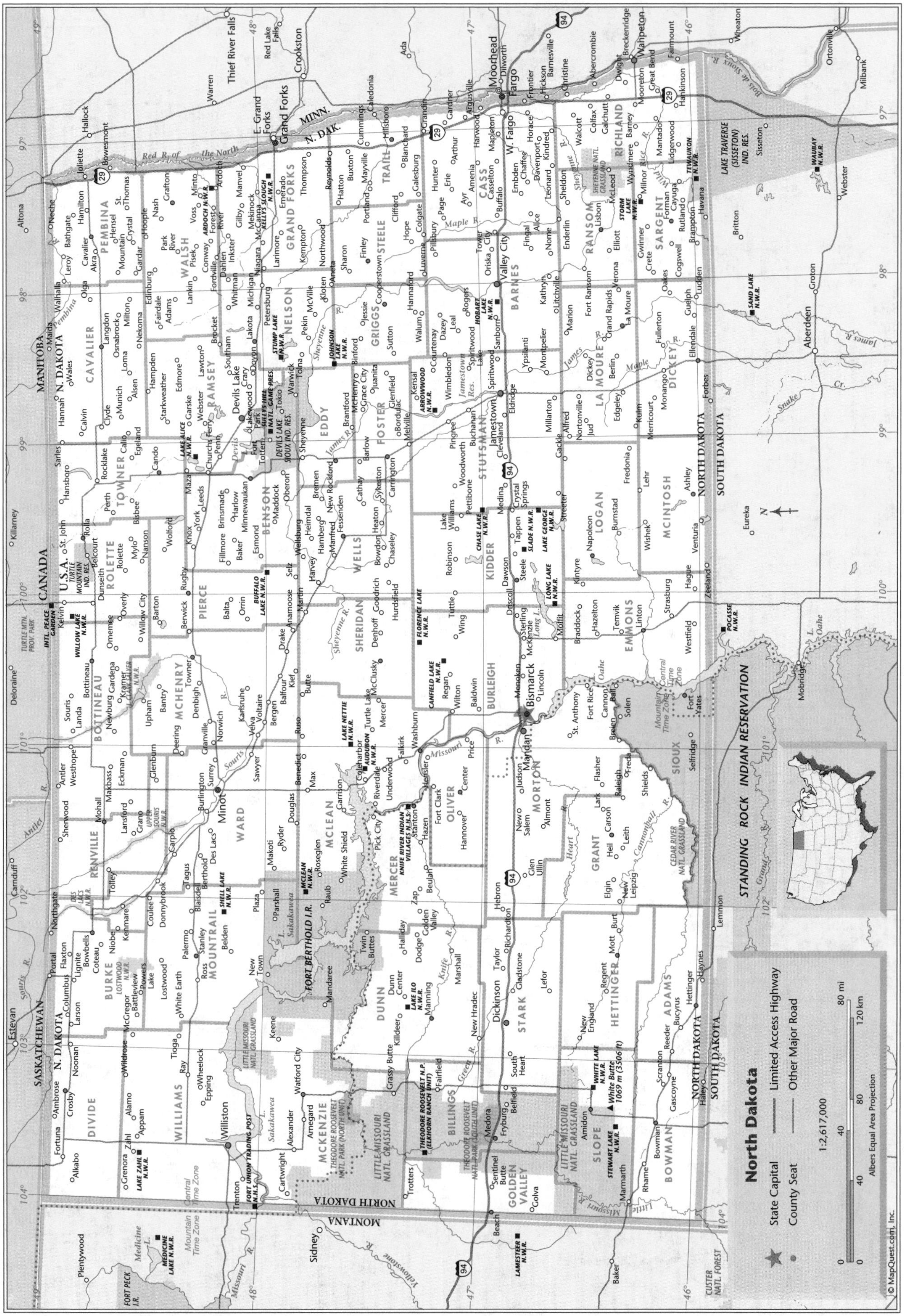

North Dakota

- ★ State Capital
- ● County Seat
- Limited Access Highway
- Other Major Road

1:2,617,000

Albers Equal Area Projection

80 mi
120 km
40 80
40 80

© MapQuest.com, Inc.

Major areas and labels:

MANITOBA • SASKATCHEWAN • CANADA • U.S.A. • MONTANA • SOUTH DAKOTA • MINN. • N. DAK.

Counties: DIVIDE, BURKE, RENVILLE, BOTTINEAU, ROLETTE, TOWNER, CAVALIER, PEMBINA, WALSH, RAMSEY, BENSON, PIERCE, MCHENRY, WARD, MOUNTRAIL, WILLIAMS, MCKENZIE, DUNN, MERCER, OLIVER, MCLEAN, SHERIDAN, WELLS, EDDY, FOSTER, GRIGGS, STEELE, TRAILL, GRAND FORKS, NELSON, STUTSMAN, KIDDER, BURLEIGH, MORTON, GRANT, STARK, BILLINGS, GOLDEN VALLEY, SLOPE, BOWMAN, ADAMS, HETTINGER, SIOUX, EMMONS, LOGAN, LA MOURE, DICKEY, MCINTOSH, SARGENT, RICHLAND, RANSOM, CASS, BARNES

Red R. of the North • Missouri R. • James R. • Sheyenne R. • Knife R. • Little Missouri R. • Souris R. • Cannonball R.

STANDING ROCK INDIAN RESERVATION
FORT BERTHOLD I.R.
DEVILS LAKE SIOUX IND. RES.
TURTLE MOUNTAIN IND. RES.

Bismarck ★ • Mandan • Fargo • Grand Forks • Minot • Jamestown • Williston • Dickinson • Devils Lake • Valley City • Wahpeton

THEODORE ROOSEVELT NAT'L PARK
LITTLE MISSOURI NAT'L GRASSLAND
CEDAR RIVER NAT'L GRASSLAND
SHEYENNE NAT'L GRASSLAND

▲ White Butte 1069 m (3506 ft)

LAKE TRAVERSE (SISSETON) IND. RES.

Capital: Columbus
Area: 44,800 sq. mi.
116,100 sq. km.
Population: 11,209,0
Largest City: Columt

Capital: Oklahoma City **Population:** 3,347,000
Area: 69,900 sq. mi. **Largest City:** Oklahoma City
181,000 sq. km.

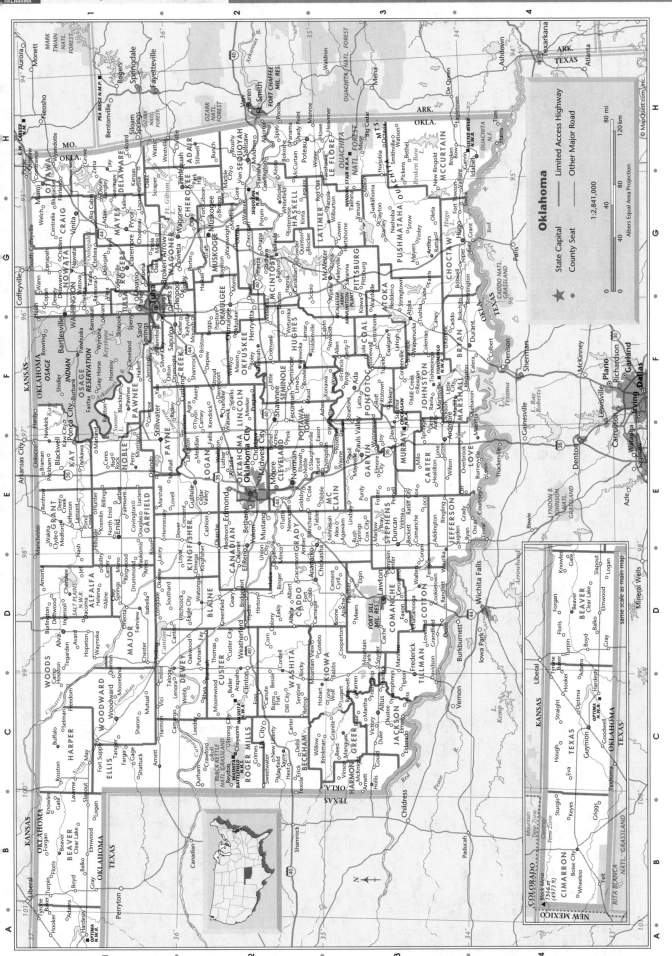

Oklahoma

Limited Access Highway
Other Major Road

★ State Capital
• County Seat

1:2,841,000

© MapQuest.com, Inc.

Capital: Salem
Area: 98,400 sq. mi.
254,800 sq. km.
Population: 3,282,0
Largest City: Portlan

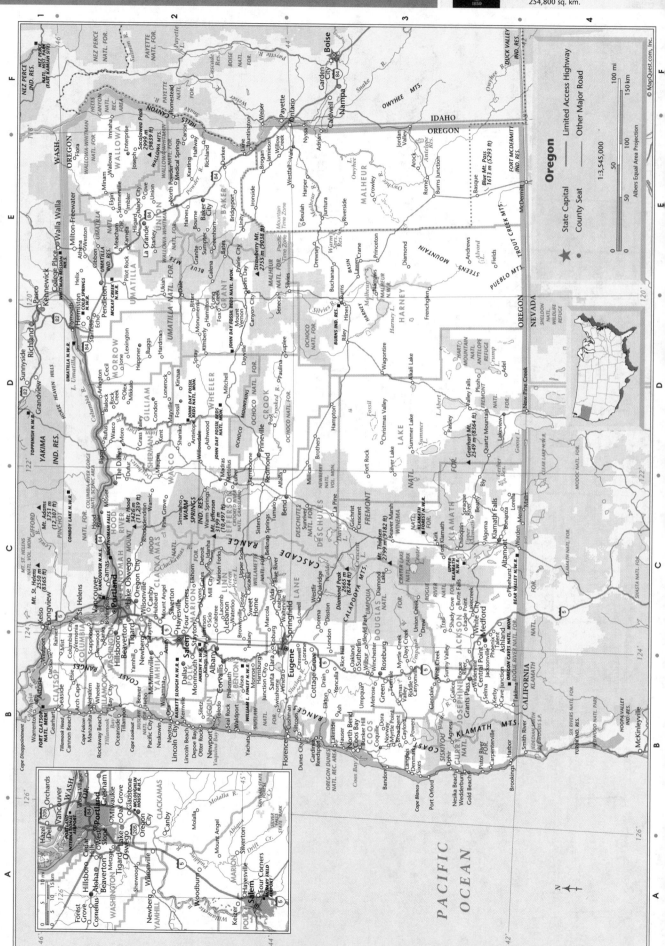

Capital: Harrisburg
Area: 45,300 sq. mi.
117,300 sq. km.
Population: 12,001,000
Largest City: Philadelphia

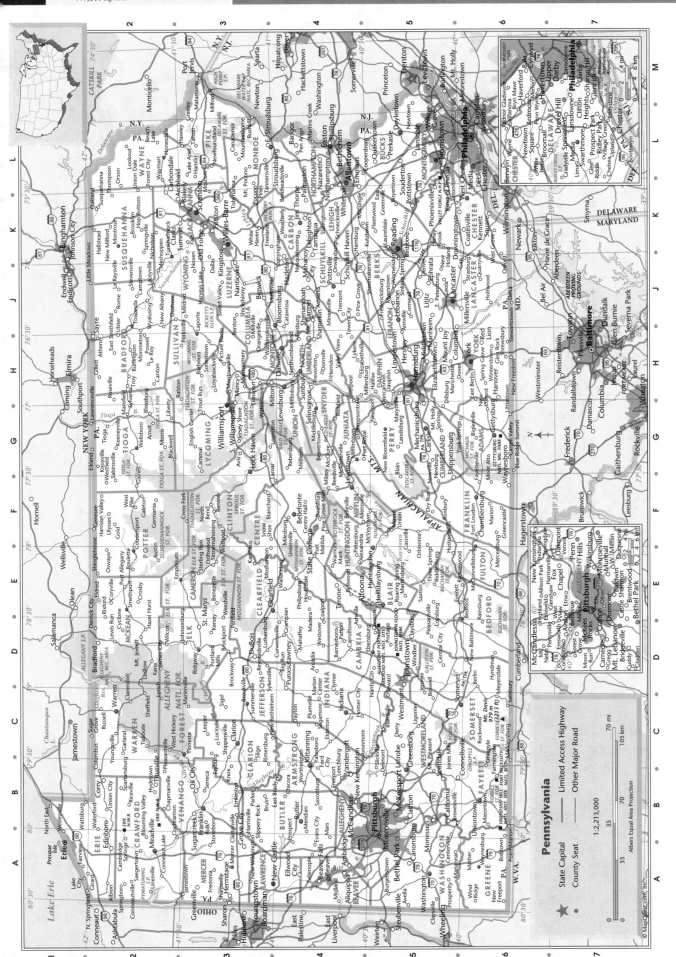

Pennsylvania

State Capital ★
County Seat •

⎯⎯ Limited Access Highway
⎯⎯ Other Major Road

1:2,213,000

0   35   70 mi
0   35   70   105 km

Albers Equal Area Projection

© MapQuest.com, Inc.

Capital: Providence
Area: 1,500 sq. mi.
4,000 sq. km.
Population: 988,000
Largest City: Providence

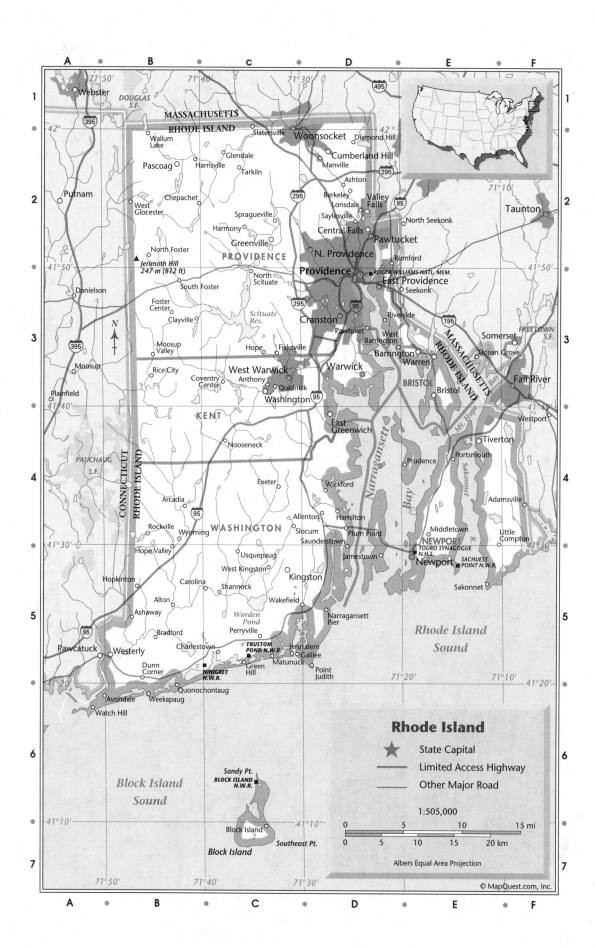

MASSACHUSETTS
RHODE ISLAND

Webster
DOUGLAS S.F.
Wallum Lake
Slatersville
Woonsocket
Diamond Hill
Cumberland Hill
Manville
Glendale
Pascoag
Harrisville
Tarkiln
Ashton
Putnam
Berkeley
Valley Falls
Chepachet
West Glocester
Lonsdale
Saylesville
North Seekonk
Spragueville
Central Falls
Pawtucket
Harmony
Greenville
N. Providence
Rumford
PROVIDENCE
North Foster
Jerimoth Hill
247 m (812 ft)
North Scituate
Providence
ROGER WILLIAMS NATL. MEM.
East Providence
Danielson
South Foster
Seekonk
Foster Center
Scituate Res.
Riverside
Clayville
Cranston
MASSACHUSETTS
Somerset
Ocean Grove
FREETOWN S.F.
Moosup Valley
Hope
Fiskeville
Pawtuxet
West Barrington
RHODE ISLAND
Moosup
Warwick
Barrington
Warren
Fall River
Rice City
West Warwick
BRISTOL
Plainfield
Coventry Center
Anthony
Bristol
Quidnick
Washington
Westport
KENT
East Greenwich
Mt. Hope
PAUCHAUG S.F.
Nooseneck
Narragansett
Tiverton
CONNECTICUT
RHODE ISLAND
Prudence
Portsmouth
Exeter
Wickford
Adamsville
Arcadia
Bay
Rockville
Allenton
Hamilton
Middletown
Little Compton
Wyoming
WASHINGTON
Slocum
Plum Point
NEWPORT
TOURO SYNAGOGUE N.H.S.
Hope Valley
Saunderstown
SACHUEST POINT N.W.R.
Usquepaug
Jamestown
Newport
Hopkinton
West Kingston
Kingston
Sakonnet
Carolina
Shannock
Alton
Wakefield
Ashaway
Worden Pond
Narragansett Pier
Rhode Island Sound
Bradford
Perryville
Pawcatuck
Westerly
Charlestown
TRUSTOM POND N.W.R.
Jerusalem
Galilee
Dunn Corner
NINIGRET N.W.R.
Green Hill
Matunuck
Point Judith
Avondale
Weekapaug
Quonochontaug
Watch Hill

Block Island Sound
Sandy Pt.
BLOCK ISLAND N.W.R.
Block Island
Southeast Pt.
Block Island

Rhode Island

★ State Capital
— Limited Access Highway
— Other Major Road

1:505,000

| 0 | 5 | 10 | 15 mi |
| 0 | 5 | 10 | 15 | 20 km |

Albers Equal Area Projection

© MapQuest.com, Inc.

Capital: Columbia
Area: 32,000 sq. mi.
82,900 sq. km.
Population: 3,836,000
Largest City: Columbia

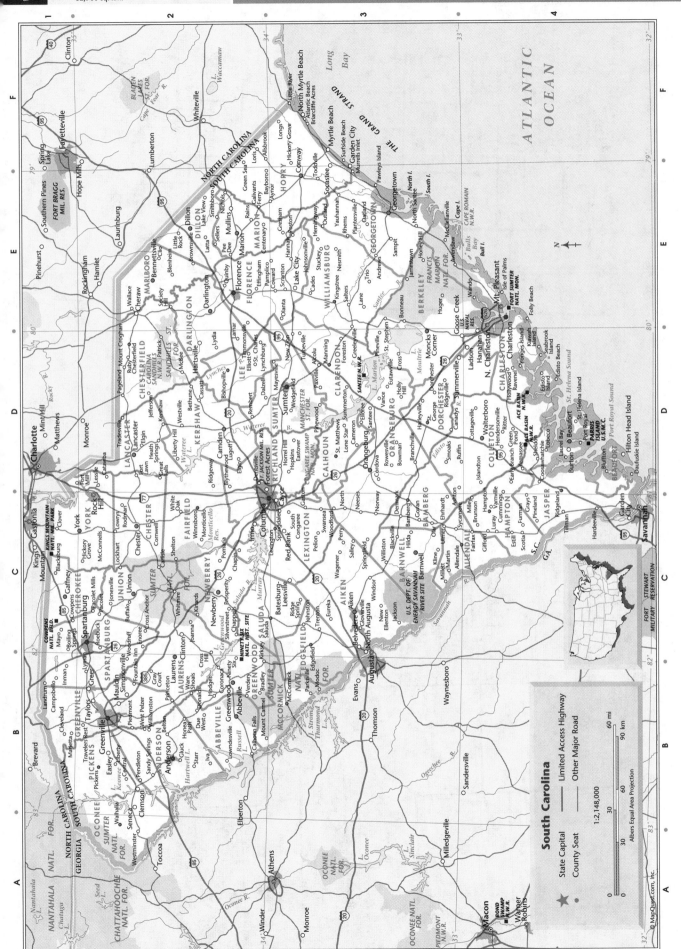

South Carolina

★ State Capital
● County Seat
— Limited Access Highway
— Other Major Road

1:2,148,000

Albers Equal Area Projection

© MapQuest.com, Inc.

ATLANTIC OCEAN

Capital: Pierre
Area: 77,100 sq. mi.
199,700 sq. km.
Population: 738,000
Largest City: Sioux Falls

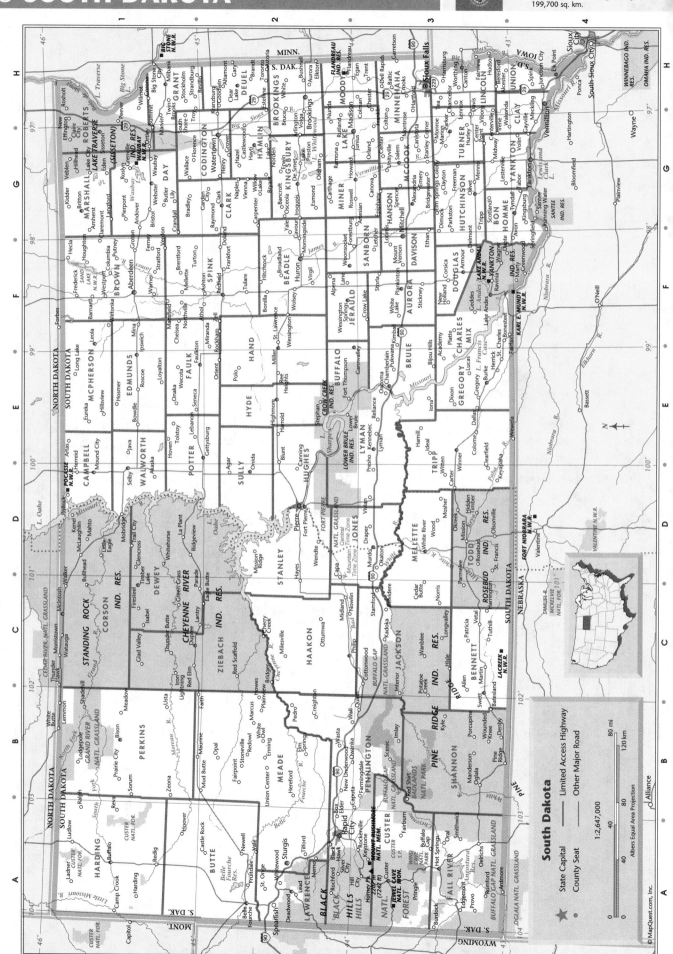

South Dakota

★ State Capital
• County Seat
━━ Limited Access Highway
━━ Other Major Road

1:2,647,000

Albers Equal Area Projection

©MapQuest.com, Inc.

Capital: Nashville
Area: 42,100 sq. mi.
109,200 sq. km.
Population: 5,431,000
Largest City: Memphis

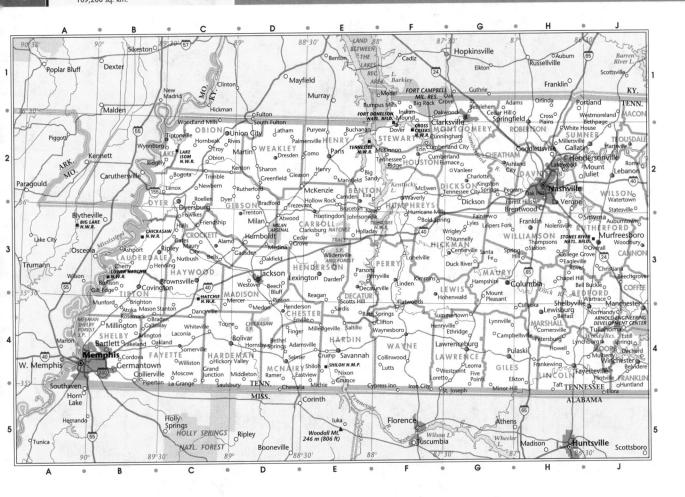

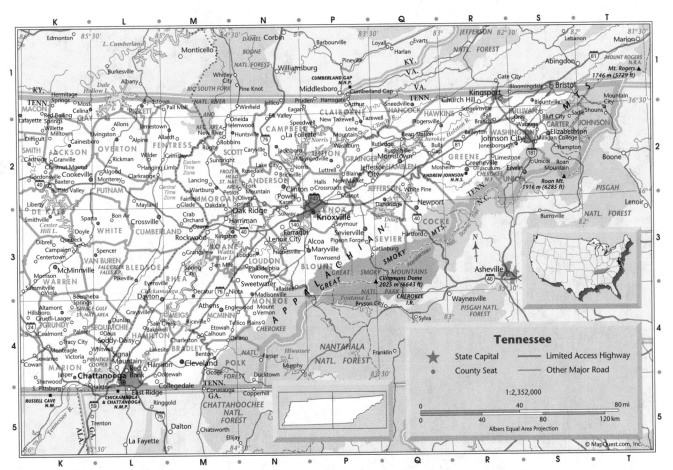

Tennessee

★ State Capital
● County Seat
— Limited Access Highway
— Other Major Road

1:2,352,000

0   40   80 mi

0   40   80   120 km

Albers Equal Area Projection

© MapQuest.com, Inc.

Capital: Austin
Area: 268,600 sq. mi.
695,700 sq. km.
Population: 19,760,0
Largest City: Houston

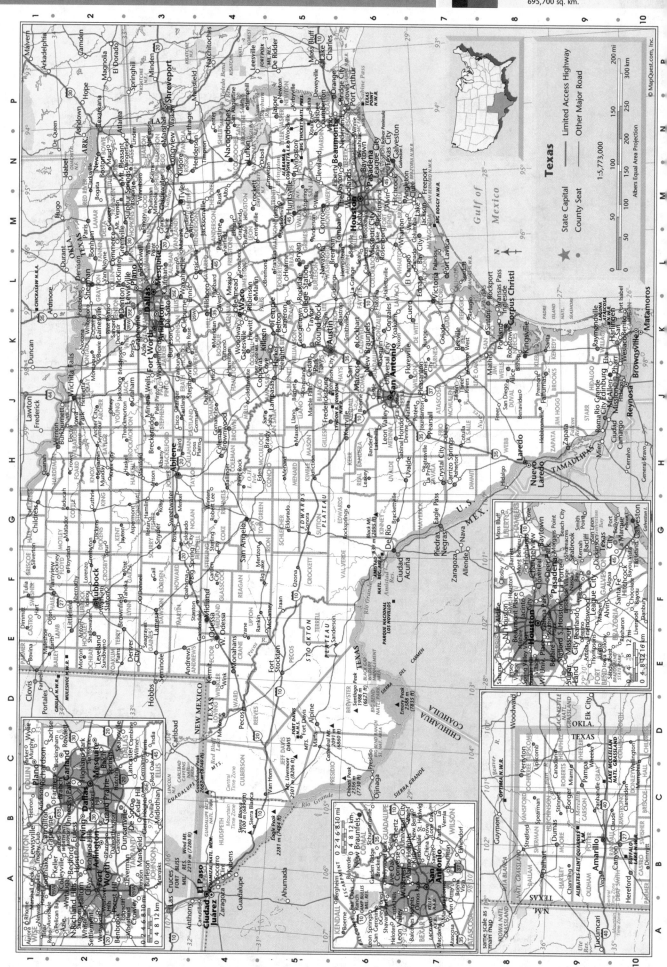

Texas

1:5,773,000

State Capital ★
County Seat •

Limited Access Highway
Other Major Road

Gulf of Mexico

© MapQuest.com, Inc.

Capital: Salt Lake City   **Population:** 2,100,000
Area: 84,900 sq. mi.   **Largest City:** Salt Lake City
219,900 sq. km.

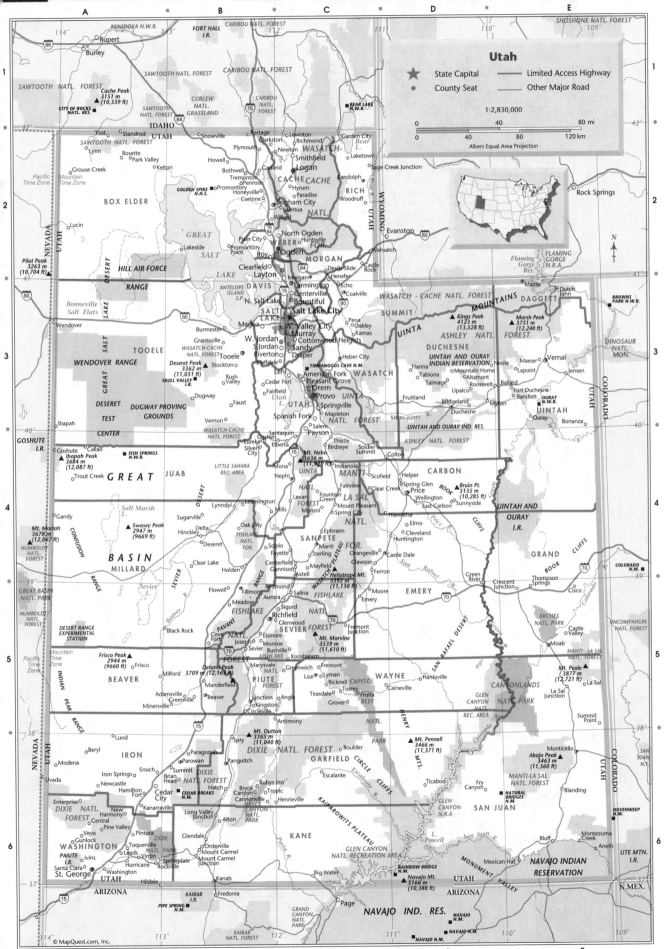

Utah

★ State Capital   ▬ Limited Access Highway
● County Seat   ▬ Other Major Road

1:2,830,000

0   40   80 mi
0   40   80   120 km

Albers Equal Area Projection

Capital: Montpelier
Area: 9,600 sq. mi.
24,900 sq. km.
Population: 591,000
Largest City: Burlington

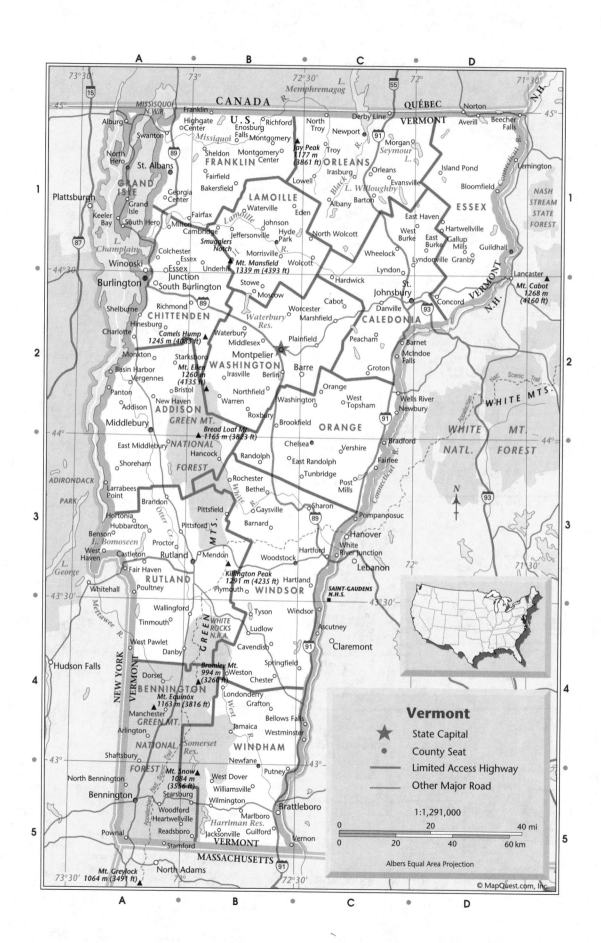

Vermont

★ State Capital
● County Seat
— Limited Access Highway
— Other Major Road

1:1,291,000

0   20   40 mi
0 20 40 60 km

Albers Equal Area Projection

© MapQuest.com, Inc.

Capital: Richmond
Area: 42,800 sq. mi.
110,800 sq. km.
Population: 6,791,000
Largest City: Virginia Beach

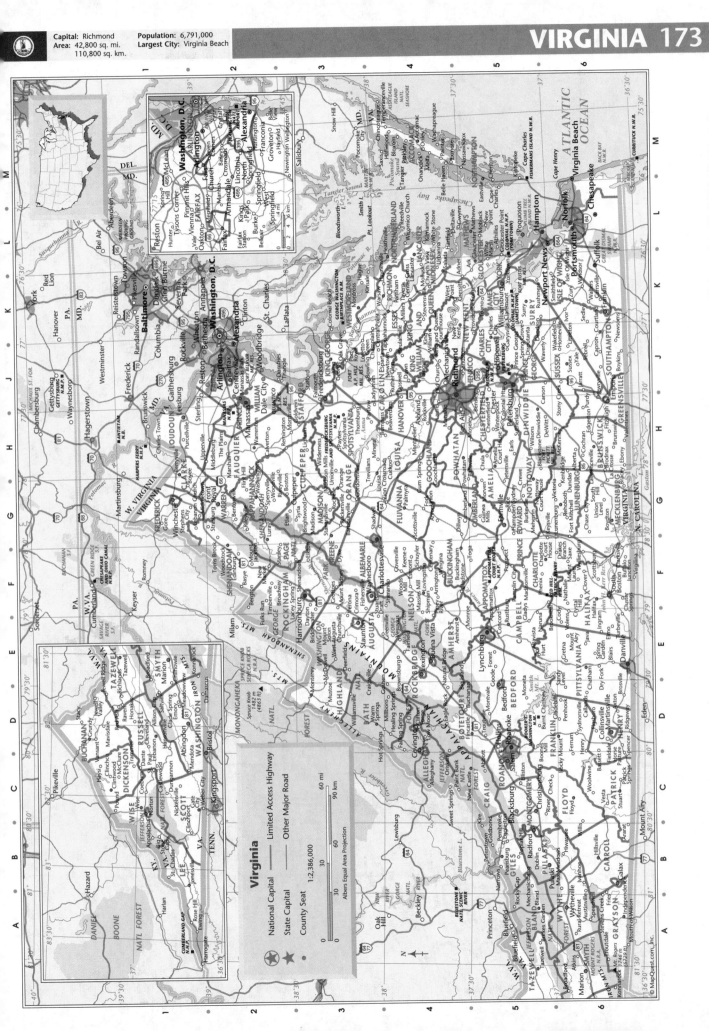

Virginia

Limited Access Highway
Other Major Road

- National Capital
- State Capital
- County Seat

1:2,386,000

Albers Equal Area Projection

0   30   60 mi
0 30 60 90 km

© MapQuest.com, Inc.

Capital: Olympia
Area: 71,300 sq. mi.
184,700 sq. km.
Population: 5,689,0
Largest City: Seattle

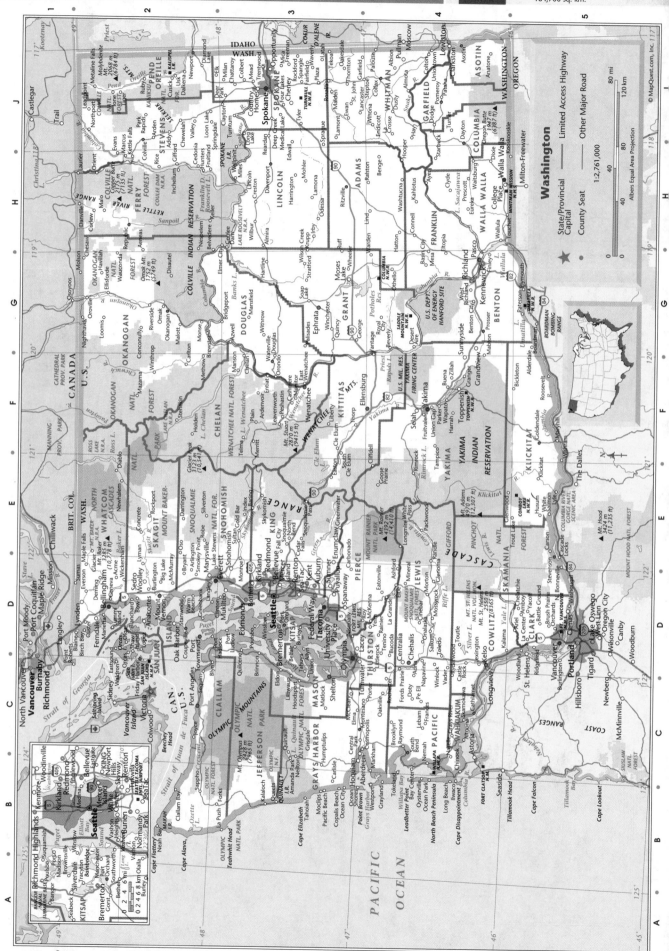

Washington

State/Provincial Capital
County Seat

—— Limited Access Highway
—— Other Major Road

1:2,761,000

Albers Equal Area Projection

©MapQuest.com, Inc. 117

Capital: Charleston
Area: 24,200 sq. mi.
62,800 sq. km.
Population: 1,811,000
Largest City: Charleston

West Virginia

- ★ State Capital
- • County Seat

Limited Access Highway
Other Major Road

1:1,830,000

Albers Equal Area Projection

0 30 60 90 km
0 30 60 mi

BOOKER T. WASHINGTON N.M. ■

Hagerstown
Williamsport
Hedgesville
Shanghai
Martinsburg
BERKELEY
Inwood
Charles Town
JEFFERSON
Harpers Ferry N.H.P.
Shepherdstown
Antietam N.B.
Paw Paw
MORGAN
Berkeley Springs
Hancock
GREEN RIDGE S.F.
BUCHANAN S.F.
Cumberland
Frostburg
Carpendale
Keyser
New Creek
MINERAL
Elk Garden
Mount Storm
Bayard
Henry
GRANT
Petersburg
HARDY
Moorefield
Lost City
Mathias
Baker
Wardensville
HAMPSHIRE
Romney
Springfield
Forks of Capacon
Capon Bridge
Slanesville
Augusta
Rio
Delray
Winchester
Front Royal
Culpeper
VIRGINIA
SHENANDOAH
PARK
Harrisonburg
Waynesboro
Staunton
Buena Vista
Lexington
Covington
WASHINGTON NATL. FOREST
GEORGE
APPALACHIAN
Blacksburg
Radford
Peterstown
Lindside
MONROE
Union
Gap Mills
Waiteville
Alvon
Sweet Springs
Clintonville
GREENBRIER
Frankford
White Sulphur Springs
Lewisburg
Ronceverte
Alderson
Greenville
Renick
Frankford
Trout
Clearco
Richwood
Rupert
Quinwood
Rainelle
Danese
Meadow Bridge
Brooks
Hinton
SUMMERS
Bluestone L.
Athens
Ingleside
Princeton
MERCER
Bluefield
Bramwell
Matoaka
Camp Creek
Oceana
WYOMING
Pineville
Mullens
Herndon
RALEIGH
Beckley
Shady Spring
Bradley
Mt. Hope
Oak Hill
FAYETTE
Fayetteville
Montgomery
Gauley Bridge
Ansted
Lookout
Nallen
NICHOLAS
Summersville
Mount Nebo
Craigsville
Birch River
WEBSTER
Webster Springs
Cowen
Camden on Gauley
POCAHONTAS
Marlinton
Edray
Slaty Fork
Durbin
Frost
Dunmore
Green Bank
Cass
RANDOLPH
Mill Creek
Valley Head
Huttonsville
Bowden
Beverly
Elkins
Norton
Ellamore
Montrose
Parsons
TUCKER
Thomas
Davis
Hambleton
Hendricks
SENECA ROCKS N.R.A.
Circleville
Riverton
Franklin
PENDLETON
Upper Tract
Brandywine
Sugar Grove
Thornwood
MONONGAHELA NATL. FOREST
Elliott Knob (4463 ft)
Spruce Knob (4863 ft)

OHIO
PENNSYLVANIA
MARYLAND

Morgantown
MONONGALIA
Blacksville
Masontown
Reedsville
Newburg
PRESTON
Kingwood
Terra Alta
Rowlesburg
Bruceton Mills
Cuzzart
Albright
Tunnelton
Fellowsville
TAYLOR
Grafton
Flemington
Philippi
BARBOUR
Belington
UPSHUR
Buckhannon
Frenchton
Rock Cave
Hacker Valley
Webster Springs
Diana
Bolair
Erbacon
Cleveland
Alexander
Adrian
French Creek
Wakesville
Ireland
LEWIS
Weston
Jane Lew
Lost Creek
Janelew
West Milford
HARRISON
Clarksburg
Bridgeport
Shinnston
Mannington
MARION
Fairmont
Rivesville
Worthington
Monongah
Wallace
Salem
DODDRIDGE
West Union
New Milton
Pullman
Smithburg
Harrisville
RITCHIE
Pennsboro
Cairo
Petroleum
Macfarlan
Ellenboro
GILMER
Glenville
Tanner
Linn
Troy
Coxs Mills
Cedarville
Stumptown
Normantown
BRAXTON
Gassaway
Sutton
Sutton L.
Flatwoods
Frametown
Strange Creek
Exchange
Rosedale
Orlando
CALHOUN
Grantsville
Arnoldsburg
Annamoriah
Minnora
Big Springs
Looneyville
Newton
Ivydale
CLAY
Clay
Lizemores
Maysel
Procious
Wallback
Nebo
Clendenin
Elkview
KANAWHA
Pond Gap
Smithers
Belva
Gauley Bridge

OHIO
Marietta
Williamstown
Vienna
Parkersburg
WOOD
Belleville
Walker
Rockport
Mineral Wells
Ravenswood
WIRT
Elizabeth
Palestine
Reedy
ROANE
Spencer
Walton
Gandeeville
Newton
JACKSON
Ripley
Cottageville
Sandyville
Evans
Kenna
Gay
Liberty
Fairplain
PUTNAM
Buffalo
Winfield
Poca
Eleanor
Nitro
Scott Depot
Hurricane
St. Albans
South Charleston
CHARLESTON
Marmet
Chesapeake
Cedar Grove
Rand
MASON
Point Pleasant
New Haven
Hartford
Letart
Mason
Glenwood
Leon
Southside

KENTUCKY
Kenova
Ceredo
Huntington
CABELL
Milton
Barboursville
Ona
Culloden
Lesage
Salt Rock
WAYNE
Wayne
Prichard
Fort Gay
Dunlow
Crum
Lavalette
East Lynn
Kiahsville
Genoa
LINCOLN
Hamlin
West Hamlin
Griffithsville
Branchland
Spurlockville
Alkol
Harts
Sod
BOONE
Madison
Danville
Racine
Seth
Whitesville
Van
Bald Knob
Clothier
Sharples
Peytona
Nellis
Barrett
Comfort
LOGAN
Logan
Chapmanville
Man
Amherstdale
Pecks Mill
Holden
MINGO
Williamson
Gilbert
Justice
Kermit
Lenore
Delbarton
Matewan
Naugatuck
Myrtle
Wharncliffe
MCDOWELL
Welch
War
Iaeger
Bradshaw
Keystone
Kimball
Davy
Northfork
Maybeury
Gary
Jolo

NATIONAL FORESTS:
WAYNE NATL. FOREST
JEFFERSON NATL. FOREST
MONONGAHELA NATL. FOREST

Inset (top right — Northern Panhandle)

East Liverpool
Wellsville
Chester
New Cumberland
HANCOCK
Weirton
Steubenville
Follansbee
BROOKE
Wellsburg
Bethany
OHIO
Wheeling
Bellaire
Martins Ferry
Moundsville
MARSHALL
Cameron
Proctor
Littleton
WETZEL
PENNSYLVANIA
P.A.
W. VA.

FREDERICKSBURG AND SPOTSYLVANIA N.M.P.

MONONGAHELA NATL. FOREST
GEORGE WASHINGTON NATL. FOREST
SHENANDOAH MTN.
ALLEGHENY MOUNTAINS

Mt. Davis (3213 ft)
FORBES S.F.
SAVAGE RIVER S.F.
FRIENDSHIP HILL NATL. HIST. SITE
FORT NECESSITY NATL. BFLD.
CHESAPEAKE AND OHIO CANAL N.H.P.

© MapQuest.com, Inc.

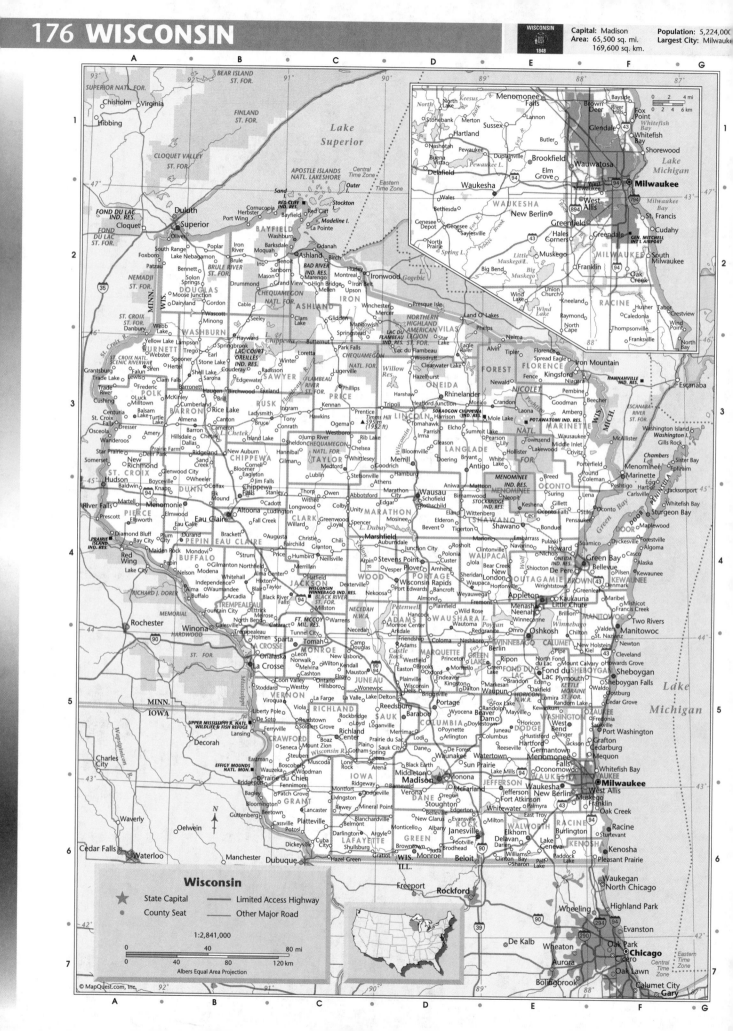

Capital: Cheyenne
Area: 97,800 sq. mi.
253,300 sq. km.
Population: 481,000
Largest City: Cheyenne

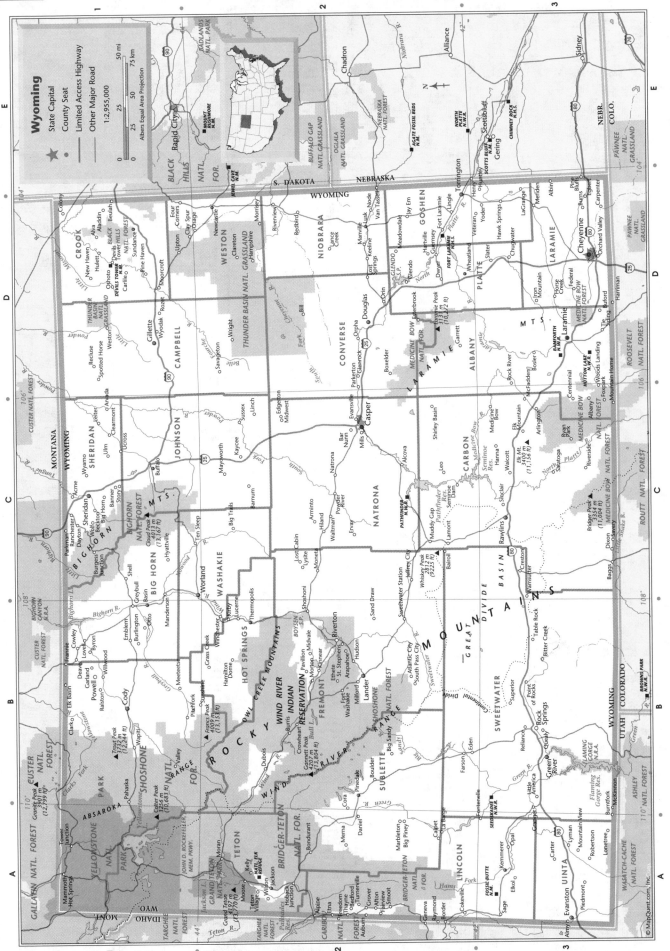

Wyoming

★ State Capital
• County Seat
— Limited Access Highway
— Other Major Road

1:2,955,000

Albers Equal Area Projection

© MapQuest.com, Inc.

178 ALABAMA–CALIFORNIA

Abbreviations
N.H.P. National Historical Park
N.H.S. National Historic Site
N.M. National Monument
N.P. National Park
N.R.A. National Recreation Area

Alabama ... page 128

Cities and Towns
Abbeville D4
Adamsville C2
Alabaster C2
Albertville C1
Alexander City D3
Aliceville A2
Andalusia C4
Anniston D2
Arab C1
Ashford D4
Ashland D2
Ashville C2
Athens C1
Atmore B4
Attalla C1
Auburn D3
Bay Minette B5
Bayou La Batre A5
Bessemer C2
Birmingham C2
Blountsville C1
Boaz C1
Brent B3
Brewton B4
Bridgeport D1
Brundidge D4
Butler A3
Calera C2
Camden B4
Camp Hill D3
Carbon Hill B2
Carrollton A2
Center Point C2
Centre D1
Centreville B3
Chatom A4
Chelsea C2
Cherokee B1
Chickasaw A5
Childersburg C2
Citronelle A4
Clanton C3
Clayton D4
Clio D4
Collinsville D1
Columbiana C2
Cordova B2
Cottonwood D4
Creola A5
Crossville D1
Cullman C1
Dadeville D3
Daleville D4
Daphne B5
Decatur C1
Demopolis B3
Dora B2
Dothan D4
Double Springs B1
East Brewton B4
Elba C4
Enterprise D4
Eufaula D4
Eutaw B3
Evergreen C4
Fairfield C2
Fairhope B5
Falkville C1
Fayette B2
Flomaton B4
Florala C4
Florence B1
Foley B5
Fort Morgan A5
Fort Payne D1
Frisco City B4
Fultondale C2
Gadsden C1
Gardendale C2
Gasque B5
Geneva D4
Georgiana C4
Glencoe D2
Good Hope C1
Goodwater C2
Gordo B2
Grand Bay A5
Greensboro B3
Greenville C4
Grove Hill B4
Guin B2
Gulf Shores B5
Guntersville C1
Haleyville B1
Hamilton B1
Hanceville C1
Hartford D4
Hartselle C1
Hayneville C3
Hazel Green C1
Headland D4
Heflin D2
Helena C2
Henagar D1
Heron Bay A5
Hokes Bluff D2
Holt B2
Hoover C2
Hueytown B2
Huntsville C1
Irondale C2
Jackson B4
Jacksonville D2
Jasper B2
Jemison C3
Lafayette D3
Lanett D3
Leeds C2
Lincoln C2
Linden B3
Lineville D2
Livingston A3
Luverne C4
Madison C1
Marion B3
Meridianville C1
Midfield C2
Midland City D4
Millbrook C3
Mobile A5
Monroeville B4
Montevallo C2
Montgomery, *capital* C3
Moulton B1
Moundville B3
Muscle Shoals B1
New Hope C1
Newton D4
Northport B2
Oneonta C2
Opelika D3
Opp C4
Orange Beach B5
Oxford D2
Ozark D4
Parrish B2
Pelham C2
Pell City C2
Petersville B1
Phenix City D3
Phil Campbell B1
Piedmont D2
Pinson C2
Point Clear B5
Prattville C3
Priceville C1
Prichard A5
Ragland C2
Rainbow City C2
Rainsville D1
Reform A2
Roanoke D2
Robertsdale B5
Rockford C3
Russellville B1
Samson C4
Saraland A5
Sardis City C1
Satsuma A5
Scottsboro C1
Selma B3
Sheffield B1
Slocomb D4
Smiths D3
Southside C2
Spanish Fort B5
Springville C2
Stevenson D1
Sulligent A2
Sumiton B2
Sylacauga C2
Talladega C2
Tallassee D3
Taylor D4
Theodore A5
Thomasville B4
Thorsby C3
Tillmans Corner A5
Town Creek B1
Trinity B1
Troy D4
Trussville C2
Tuscaloosa B2
Tuscumbia B1
Tuskegee D3
Union Springs D3
Uniontown B3
Valley D3
Vernon A2
Vestavia Hills C2
Vincent C2
Warrior C2
Weaver D2
Wedowee D2
West Blocton B2
Wetumpka C3
Winfield B2
York A3

Other Features
Alabama, *river* B4
Appalachian, *mts.* D1
Bear Creek, *reservoir* B1
Black Warrior, *river* B3
Bon Secour, *bay* B5
Cahaba, *river* B3
Cheaha, *mt.* D2
Conecuh, *river* C4
Coosa, *river* D1
Dauphin, *island* A5
Guntersville, *lake* C1
Jordan, *lake* C3
Lewis Smith, *lake* B1
Logan Morgan, *lake* C2
Lookout, *mt.* D1
Martin, *lake* D3
Mitchell, *lake* C3
Mobile, *bay* A5
Neely Henry, *lake* C2
Pickwick, *lake* A1
R.L. Harris, *reservoir* D2
Russell Cave Natl. Monument D1
Tallapoosa, *river* D2
Tennessee, *river* A1
Tombigbee, *river* A4
Tuscaloosa, *lake* B2
Tuskegee Institute Natl. Hist. Site D3
Weiss, *lake* D1
Wheeler, *lake* B1
William "Bill" Dannelly, *reservoir* B3
Wilson, *lake* B1

Alaska ... page 129

Cities and Towns
Adak Inset
Anchorage F2
Barrow D1
Bethel C2
Big Delta F2
College F2
Cordova F2
Craig J3
Delta Jct. F2
Dillingham D3
Fairbanks F2
Haines H3
Homer E3
Juneau, *capital* J3
Kenai E2
Ketchikan J3
Kodiak E3
Kotzebue C1
McKinley Park F2
Metlakatla J3
Nikiski E2
Nome B2
North Pole F2
Palmer F2
Petersburg J3
Prudhoe Bay F1
Seward F2
Sitka H3
Skagway H3
Soldotna E2
Talkeetna E2
Tok G2
Unalaska B4
Valdez F2
Wasilla F2
Whittier F2
Wrangell J3

Other Features
Adak, *island* Inset
Admiralty Island Natl. Monument J3
Agattu, *island* Inset
Alaska, *gulf* F3
Alaska, *peninsula* C3
Alaska, *range* E2
Aleutian, *islands* A4, Inset
Alexander, *archipelago* H3
Amchitka, *island* Inset
Amlia, *island* Inset
Andreanof, *islands* Inset
Aniakchak N.M. and Preserve D3
Atka, *island* Inset
Attu, *island* Inset
Barrow, *point* D1
Beaufort, *sea* H1
Becharof, *lake* D3
Bering, *sea* B3
Bering, *strait* B2
Blackburn, *mt.* G2
Bristol, *bay* C3
Brooks, *range* D1
Cape Krusenstern N.M. C1
Chirikof, *island* D3
Chukchi, *sea* A1
Colville, *river* E1
Cook, *inlet* E3
Copper, *river* G2
Denali Natl. Park and Preserve E2
Fairweather, *mt.* H3
Gates of the Arctic N.P. and Preserve E1
Glacier Bay N.P. and Preserve H3
Iliamna, *lake* D3
Inside Passage, *waterway* J3
Kanaga, *island* Inset
Katmai Natl. Park and Preserve D3
Kenai, *peninsula* E2
Kenai Fjords Natl. Park F3
Kiska, *island* Inset
Klondike Gold Rush N.H.P H3
Kobuk, *river* D1
Kobuk Valley Natl. Park D1
Kodiak, *island* E3
Kotzebue, *sound* C1
Koyukuk, *river* D1
Kuskokwim, *bay* C3
Kuskokwim, *mts.* D2
Kuskokwim, *river* D2
Lake Clark Natl. Park and Preserve E2
Lisburne, *cape* B1
Lisburne, *peninsula* C1
Logan, *mt.* G2
Lynn, *canal* J3
McKinley, *mt.* E2
Malaspina, *glacier* G3
Michelson, *mt.* G1
Mohican, *cape* B2
Muir, *glacier* H3
Near, *islands* Inset
Noatak, *river* D1
Norton, *sound* C2
Nunivak, *island* B3
Porcupine, *river* G1
Pribilof, *islands* B3
Prince of Wales, *island* J3
Progromni, *volcano* C4
Rat, *islands* Inset
St. Elias, *mt.* G2
St. George, *island* B3
St. Lawrence, *island* A2
St. Matthew, *island* A2
St. Paul, *island* A3
Samalga, *pass* B4
Sanak, *island* C4
Seguam, *island* Inset
Semisopochnoi, *island* Inset
Seward, *peninsula* C1
Shishaldin, *volcano* C4
Shumagin, *islands* D4
Sitka N.H.P. H3
Stikine, *river* J3
Tanaga, *island* F3
Tanana, *river* E2
Tikchik, *lakes* D2
Trinity, *islands* E3
Umnak, *island* Inset
Unalaska, *island* B4
Unga, *island* C3
Unimak, *island* C4
Utukok, *river* C1
White Mts. Natl. Rec. Area F1
Wrangell, *mts.* G2
Wrangell-St. Elias N.P. and Preserve G2
Yukon, *river* D2
Yukon-Charley Rivers Natl. Preserve G2
Yunaska, *island* Inset

Arizona ... page 130

Cities and Towns
Ajo C5
Apache Junction D4
Avondale C4
Bagdad B3
Benson E6
Bisbee F6
Bitahochee E2
Buckeye C4
Bullhead City A2
Camp Verde D3
Carefree D4
Casa Grande D5
Catalina E5
Cave Creek D4
Chandler D4
Chinle F1
Chino Valley C3
Cibecue E3
Clarkdale C3
Claypool E4
Clifton F4
Colorado City C1
Coolidge D5
Cornville D3
Cow Springs E1
Crown King C3
Douglas F6
Dudleyville E5
Eagar F3
El Mirage C4
Eloy D5
Flagstaff D2
Florence D4
Fort Defiance F2
Fountain Hills D4
Ganado F2
Geronimo E4
Gila Bend C5
Gilbert D4
Globe E4
Goodyear C4
Grand Canyon C1
Greaterville E6
Green Valley E6
Guthrie F5
Happy Jack D3
Holbrook E3
Huachuca City E6
Kayenta E1
Kearny E4
Kingman A2
Kirkland Junction C3
Lake Havasu City A3
Lake Montezuma D3
Litchfield Park C4
Mammoth E5
Many Farms F1
Marana D5
Mesa D4
Miami E4
Nogales E6
Oracle E5
Oro Valley E5
Page D1
Paradise Valley D4
Parker A3
Payson D3
Peoria C4
Phoenix, *capital* C4
Pima F5
Pinetop-Lakeside F3
Prescott C3
Prescott Valley C3
Quartzsite A4
Queen Creek D4
Randolph D5
Sacaton D4
Safford F5
Sahuarita E6
St. David E6
St. Johns F3
San Carlos E4
Sanders F2
San Manuel E5
Scottsdale D4
Sedona D3
Sells D6
Show Low E3
Sierra Vista E6
Snowflake E3
Somerton A5
South Tucson E5
Springerville F3
Sun City C4
Sun Lakes D4
Superior D4
Surprise C4
Taylor E3
Tempe D4
Thatcher F5
Three Points D5
Tolleson C4
Tombstone E6
Tuba City D1
Tucson E5
Whiteriver F4
Wickenburg C4
Willcox F5
Williams C2
Window Rock F2
Winslow E2
Yuma A5

Other Features
Agua Fria, *river* C4
Alamo, *lake* B3
Apache, *lake* D4
Aztec Peak, *mt.* E4
Baldy, *mt.* F4
Bartlett, *reservoir* D4
Big Horn, *mts.* B4
Bill Williams, *river* A3
Black, *mesa* E1
Black, *river* E4
Canyon De Chelly N.M. F1
Casa Grande Ruins N.M. D5
Castle Dome, *mts.* A4
Castle Dome Peak, *mt.* A4
Chiricahua Natl. Monument F6
Colorado, *river* B2, D1
Coronado Natl. Mem. E6
Gila, *river* B5, D4, F4
Glen Canyon, *dam* D1
Glen Canyon Natl. Rec. Area D1
Grand, *canyon* C1
Grand Canyon Natl. Park B2, C1
Harcuvar, *mts.* B4
Havasu, *lake* A3
Hide Creek, *mt.* C3
Hoover, *dam* A2
Hopi Indian Res. E2
Horseshoe, *reservoir* D4
Hualapai, *mt.* B2
Hubbell Trading Post N.H.S. F2
Humphreys Peak, *mt.* D2
Lake Mead Natl. Rec. Area B1
Little Colorado, *river* D2
Many Farms, *lake* F1
Maple Peak, *mt.* F4
Mazatzal Peak, *mt.* D3
Mohave, *lake* A2
Montezuma Castle N.M. D3
Monument, *valley* F1
Mormon, *lake* D3
Navajo Indian Res. E1, E2
Navajo Natl. Monument E1
Organ Pipe Cactus N.M. C5
Painted, *desert* D2
Parker, *dam* A3
Petrified Forest Natl. Park F3
Pipe Spring Natl. Monument C1
Pleasant, *lake* C4
Point Imperial, *mt.* D1
Powell, *lake* D1
Red, *lake* B2
Saguaro Natl. Monument E5
Salt, *river* E4
San Carlos, *lake* E4
San Pedro, *river* E5
Santa Cruz, *river* D5
Sonoran, *desert* B5
Sunset Crater Volcano N.M. D2
Theodore Roosevelt, *lake* D4
Tipton, *mt.* A2
Tonto Natl. Monument D4
Trumbull, *mt.* B1
Tumacacori Natl Hist. Park D6
Tuzigoot Natl. Monument C3
Ventana, *cave* C5
Verde, *river* D3
Virgin, *river* A1
Walnut Canyon Natl. Monument D2
White, *mts.* F4
White House, *ruin* F1
Wupatki Natl. Monument D2
Yuma, *desert* A5

Arkansas ... page 131

Cities and Towns
Alicia D2
Alma A2
Arkadelphia B3
Arkansas City D4
Ashdown A4
Ash Flat D1
Atkins C2
Augusta D2
Bald Knob D2
Barling A2
Batesville D2
Bay E2
Beebe D2
Bella Vista A1
Benton C3
Bentonville A1
Berryville B1
Blytheville F2
Bodcaw B4
Booneville B2
Brinkley D3
Bryant C3
Bull Shoals C1
Cabot D3
Camden C4
Caraway E2
Carlisle D3
Cave City D2
Charleston A2
Clarendon D3
Clarksville B2
Clinton C2
Conway C2
Corning E1
Crossett D4
Daisy B3
Damascus C2
Danville B2
Dardanelle B2
De Queen A3
Dermott D4
Des Arc D3
De Valls Bluff D3
De Witt D3
Dierks A3
Dumas D4
Earle E2
El Dorado C4
England D3
Eudora D4
Eureka Springs B1
Fairfield Bay C2
Fallsville B2
Farmington A1
Fayetteville A1
Fordyce C4
Foreman A4
Forrest City E2
Fort Smith A2
Fountain Hill D4
Gentry A1
Glenwood B3
Gosnell F2
Gould D4
Gravette A1
Greenbrier C2
Green Forest B1
Greenwood A2
Griffithville D2
Gurdon B4
Hamburg D4
Hampton C4
Harrisburg E2
Harrison B1
Haskell C3
Hatfield A3
Hazen D3
Heber Springs C2
Helena E3
Hope B4
Horseshoe Bend D1
Hot Springs National Park B3
Hot Springs Village B3
Hoxie E1
Hughes E3
Hunter D2
Huntsville B1
Jacksonville C3
Jasper B1
Jonesboro E2
Lake City E2
Lake Hamilton B3
Lake Village D4
Lepanto E2
Lewisville B4
Lincoln A2
Little Rock, *capital* C3
Lonoke D3
Luxora F2
McCrory D2
McGehee D4
McNeil B4
McRae D2
Magnolia B4
Malvern C3
Manila E2
Marianna E3
Marion E2
Marked Tree E2
Marshall C2
Marvell E3
Maumelle C3
Mayflower C3
Melbourne D1
Mena A3
Monticello D4
Morrilton C2
Mountain Home C1
Mountain View
Mount Ida
Mulberry
Murfreesboro
Nashville
Newport
North Crossett
North Little Rock
Oden
Osceola
Ozark
Paragould
Paris
Parkin
Pea Ridge
Pelsor
Perryville
Piggott
Pine Bluff
Pocahontas
Prescott
Rector
Rison
Rogers
Rose Bud
Russell
Russellville
St. Charles
St. Paul
Salem
Searcy
Sheridan
Sherwood
Siloam Springs
Smackover
Springdale
Springhill
Star City
Stuttgart
Texarkana
Tillar
Trumann
Tuckerman
Tupelo
Van Buren
Waldo
Waldron
Walnut Ridge
Warren
Washington
West Fork
West Helena
West Memphis
White Hall
Wynne
Yellville

Other Features
Arkansas, *river*
Arkansas Post Natl. Mem.
Beaver, *lake*
Black, *river*
Boston, *mts.*
Buffalo, *river*
Buffalo Natl. River
Bull Shoals, *lake*
Cache, *river*
Catherine, *lake*
Dardanelle, *reservoir*
DeGray, *lake*
Erling, *lake*
Fort Smith Natl. Hist Site
Greers Ferry, *lake*
Greeson, *lake*
Hamilton, *lake*
Hot Springs Natl. Park
Little Missouri, *river*
Magazine, *mt.*
Maumelle, *lake*
Millwood, *lake*
Mississippi, *river*
Nimrod, *lake*
Norfork, *lake*
Ouachita, *lake*
Ouachita, *mts.*
Ouachita, *river* B3,
Ozark, *plateau*
Pea Ridge Natl. Mil. Park
Red, *river*
St. Francis, *river*
Saline, *river*
Table Rock, *lake*
White, *river* C2,

California ... page 13

Cities and Towns
Adelanto
Alameda
Alamo
Albany
Alhambra
Alpine
Altadena
Alturas
Anaheim E11,
Anderson
Antioch D4,
Apple Valley
Aptos
Arcadia
Arcata
Arnold
Arroyo Grande
Arvin
Ashland
Atascadero
Atherton
Atwater
Auberry
Auburn
Avalon
Avenal
Azusa
Bakersfield
Baldwin Park
Barstow
Bell
Bellflower
Belmont
Belvedere
Benicia
Berkeley C5,
Beverly Hills
Big Bear Lake
Bishop
Black Point
Blythe
Bonita
Boron
Borrego Springs

Key

...wley ...K10
...a ...E11
...igeport ...F4
...bane ...J2
...admoor ...J2
...ellton ...E8
...na Park ...E11
...bank ...C10
...ney ...J3
...a ...D2
...tonwillow ...F7
...abasas ...B10
...exico ...K10
...ifornia City ...H7
...ipatria ...K9
...istoga ...C4
...mbria ...D7
...mpbell ...L4
...nyon ...K2
...rlsbad ...H9
...rmel ...D6
...rmel Valley ...D6
...rpinteria ...F8
...rson ...D11
...stroville ...D6
...thedral City ...J9
...yucos ...E7
...ntral Valley ...C2
...res ...E5
...ester ...D2
...ico ...D3
...ino ...F10
...owchilla ...E5
...ula Vista ...C9, H10
...aremont ...F10
...ayton ...L1
...earlake ...C4
...overdale ...B4
...ovis ...F6
...yde ...L1
...achella ...J9
...alinga ...E6
...obb ...C4
...olfax ...E3
...olusa ...D3
...ompton ...D11
...oncord ...L1
...orcoran ...F6
...orning ...C3
...orona ...F11
...oronado ...B8
...orte Madera ...J1
...osta Mesa ...E11
...ottonwood ...C2
...ovina ...E10
...owan Heights ...E11
...escent City ...A1
...estline ...H8
...ulver City ...C10
...upertino ...L4
...ypress ...D11
...aly City ...J2
...anville ...L2
...avis ...D4
...elano ...F7
...el Mar ...H10
...esert Hot Springs ...J9
...iablo ...L2
...iamond Bar ...E10
...inuba ...F6
...os Palos ...E6
...owney ...D11
...ownieville ...E3
...ublin ...L2
...unsmuir ...C1
...arlimart ...F7
...ast Los Angeles ...D10
...ast Palo Alto ...K3
...l Cajon ...C8, J10
...l Centro ...K10
...l Cerrito ...K1
...l Granada ...J3
...lk Grove ...D4
...l Monte ...D10
...l Segundo ...C11
...l Sobrante ...K1
...merryville ...K2
...ncinitas ...H9
...scondido ...H9
...ureka ...A2
...xeter ...F6
...airfax ...H1
...airfield ...D4
...allbrook ...H9
...erndale ...A2
...irebaugh ...E6
...lorence ...D11
...ort Bragg ...B3
...ortuna ...A2
...oster City ...K3
...ountain Valley ...E11
...razier Park ...G8
...remont ...D5, L3
...resno ...F6
...ullerton ...E11
...alt ...D4
...arden Grove ...E11
...ilroy ...D5
...lendale ...D10, G8
...lendora ...E10
...lenview ...B10
...onzales ...D6
...rass Valley ...D3
...reenacres ...F7
...reenbrae ...J1
...reenfield ...D6
...reenville ...E2
...ridley ...D3
...roveland ...E4
...uadalupe ...E8
...alf Moon Bay ...J3
...anford ...F6
...awthorne ...C11
...ayfork ...B2
...ayward ...C5, L2
...ealdsburg ...C4
...emet ...J9
...ercules ...K1
...ermosa Beach ...C11
...esperia ...H8
...idden Hills ...B10
...illsborough ...J3
...oltville ...K10
...untington Beach ...E11, G9
...uron ...E6
...gnacio ...H1
...mperial Beach ...B9, H10
...ndependence ...G6

Key

Indio ...J9
Inglewood ...C11, G9
Ingot ...C2
Inyokern ...H7
Ione ...E4
Irvine ...E11, H9
Isla Vista ...F8
Jackson ...E4
Joshua Tree ...J8
Julian ...J9
Kelseyville ...C4
Kensington ...K1
Kentfield ...J1
Kerman ...E6
Kernville ...G7
Kettleman City ...F6
King City ...D6
La Canada-Flintridge ...D10
La Crescenta ...D10
Lafayette ...K1
La Habra ...E11
La Honda ...K4
La Isabella ...G7
Lakeport ...C3
Lakeside ...J10
Lakewood ...D11
La Mesa ...C8
La Mirada ...D11
Lamont ...G7
Lancaster ...G8
La Puente ...E10
Larkspur ...J1
Laton ...F6
Lawndale ...C11
Lee Vining ...F5
Lemon Grove ...C8
Lemoore ...F6
Lincoln ...D4
Lindsay ...H8
Littlerock ...D5
Livermore ...E5
Livingston ...E5
Lockeford ...D4
Lodi ...D4
Loma Mar ...K4
Lomita ...C11
Lompoc ...E8
Lone Pine ...G6
Long Beach ...D11, G9
Los Altos ...K3
Los Altos Hills ...K4
Los Angeles ...D10, G8
Los Banos ...C2
Los Molinos ...E7
Los Osos ...E7
Lynwood ...D11
McCloud ...C1
McFarland ...F7
McKinleyville ...A2
Madera ...E6
Malibu ...B10
Mammoth Lakes ...G5
Manhattan Beach ...C11
Manteca ...D5
Marina ...D6
Marina del Rey ...C11
Marin City ...J1
Marinwood ...J1
Mariposa ...F5
Markleeville ...F4
Martinez ...C4, K1
Marysville ...D3
Maywood ...D10
Mecca ...J9
Mendota ...E6
Menlo Park ...K3
Merced ...E5
Midway City ...E11
Millbrae ...J3
Mill Valley ...J1
Milpitas ...L3
Miranda ...B2
Modesto ...E5
Mojave ...G7
Monrovia ...E10
Montara ...J3
Montclair ...F10
Montebello ...D10
Monte Nido ...B10
Monterey ...D6
Monterey Park ...D10
Monte Sereno ...L4
Moraga ...K2
Moreno Valley ...H9
Morgan Hill ...D5
Morongo Valley ...J8
Morro Bay ...E7
Moss Beach ...J3
Mountain View ...K3
Mount Shasta ...C1
Muir Beach ...H1
Napa ...C4
National City ...C9
Needles ...L8
Nevada City ...D3
Newark ...L3
Newberry Springs ...J8
Newport Beach ...H9
Nicasio ...H1
Nice ...C3
Nipomo ...E7
Nipton ...K7
Norco ...F11
North Edwards ...H7
North Fair Oaks ...K3
Novato ...H1
Oakdale ...E5
Oakhurst ...F5
Oakland ...K2, C5
Oceanside ...H9
Oildale ...F7
Ojai ...F8
Olema ...H1
Olivehurst ...D3
Ontario ...F10, H8
Orange ...E11
Orinda ...K1
Orland ...C3
Oroville ...D3
Otay ...C9
Oxnard ...F8
Pacheco ...L1
Pacifica ...J2
Palermo ...D3
Palmdale ...G8
Palm Desert ...J9
Palm Springs ...J9
Palo Alto ...K3
Palos Verdes Estates ...C11
Paradise ...D3
Pasadena ...D10, G8
Patterson ...D5

Key

Petaluma ...C4
Pico Rivera ...D10
Piedmont ...K2
Pine Valley ...J10
Pinole ...K1
Pismo Beach ...E7
Pittsburg ...L1
Placentia ...E11
Placerville ...E4
Pleasant Hill ...L1
Pleasanton ...L2
Pomona ...E10, H8
Port Costa ...K1
Porterville ...G6
Portola ...E3
Poway ...H10
Prunedale ...D6
Quartz Hill ...G8
Quincy ...E3
Ramona ...J9
Rancho Cucamonga ...F10
Rancho Palos Verdes ...C11
Rancho Rinconada ...L4
Rancho Santa Margarita ...F11
Red Bluff ...C2
Redding ...C2
Redlands ...H8
Redondo Beach ...C11
Redwood City ...C5, K3
Reedley ...F6
Richgrove ...F7
Richmond ...J1
Ridgecrest ...H7
Rio Dell ...A2
Riverside ...H9
Rodeo ...K1
Rolling Hills ...C11
Rolling Hills Estates ...C11
Rosamond ...G8
Roseville ...D4
Sacramento, *capital* ...D4
Salinas ...D6
San Andreas ...E4
San Anselmo ...H1
San Bernardino ...H8
San Bruno ...J2
San Carlos ...K3
San Clemente ...H9
San Diego ...B8, H10
San Francisco ...C5, J2
San Gabriel ...D10
Sanger ...F6
San Gregorio ...J4
San Jose ...D5, L4
San Juan Bautista ...D6
San Juan Capistrano ...H9
San Leandro ...K2
San Lorenzo ...K2
San Luis Obispo ...E7
San Mateo ...C5, K3
San Quentin ...J1
San Rafael ...C5, J1
San Ramon ...L2
Santa Ana ...E11, H9
Santa Barbara ...F8
Santa Clara ...L4
Santa Clarita ...G8
Santa Cruz ...C6
Santa Maria ...E8
Santa Monica ...C10
Santa Paula ...F8
Santa Rosa ...C4
Santa Venetia ...J1
Santa Ynez ...E8
Saratoga ...L4
Sausalito ...J2
Scotts Valley ...C5
Seal Beach ...E11
Sebastopol ...C4
Selma ...F6
Shafter ...F7
Shingletown ...D2
Shoshone ...J7
Simi Valley ...G8
Soledad ...D6
Solvang ...E8
Sonoma ...C4
Sonora ...E5
South Lake Tahoe ...F4
South San Francisco ...C8
Spring Valley ...C8
Squaw Valley ...K3
Stanford ...K3
Stinson Beach ...H1
Stockton ...D5
Sunnyvale ...C5, L4
Sunol ...L3
Sunset Beach ...D11
Susanville ...E2
Taft ...F7
Tamalpais Valley ...J1
Tehachapi ...H9
Temecula ...H9
Templeton ...E7
Terra Bella ...F7
Thermalito ...D3
Thousand Oaks ...G8
Tiburon ...J1
Tipton ...F6
Topanga ...B10
Torrance ...C11, G9
Tracy ...D5
Truckee ...E3
Tulare ...F6
Turlock ...E5
Tustin ...E11
Twain Harte ...E4
Twentynine Palms ...J8
Ukiah ...B3
Union City ...L3
Upland ...F10
Vacaville ...D4
Vallejo ...C4, K1
Vandenberg Village ...E8
Ventucopa ...F8
Ventura ...F8
Victorville ...H8
Villa Park ...E11
Vine Hill ...K1
Visalia ...H9
Vista ...H9
Walnut ...E10
Walnut Creek ...L1
Wasco ...F7
Watsonville ...D6
Weaverville ...C2
Weed ...C1
West Covina ...E10
West Hollywood ...C10
Westminster ...E11

Key

Westmorland ...K9
West Pittsburg ...L1
Westwood ...E2
Wheatland ...D3
Whittier ...D10
Willits ...B3
Willow Creek ...B2
Willows ...C3
Windsor ...C4
Wofford Heights ...G7
Woodlake ...F6
Woodland ...D4
Woodside ...K3
Wrightwood ...H8
Yorba Linda ...E11
Yosemite Village ...F5
Yreka ...C1
Yuba City ...D3
Yucaipa ...H8
Yucca Valley ...J8
Zenia ...B2

Other Features

Alameda, *river* ...L3
Alcatraz, *island* ...J2
Allison, *mt.* ...D2
Almanor, *lake* ...D2
Amargosa, *range* ...J6
Amargosa, *river* ...J7
Angel, *island* ...J1
Balboa, *park* ...B8
Berryessa, *lake* ...C4
Boundary, *peak* ...G5
Bullion, *mts.* ...J8
Cascade, *range* ...D1
Central, *valley* ...C2
Chabot, *lake* ...K2
Channel, *islands* ...F9
Channel Islands Natl. Park ...E9, F9
Chatsworth, *reservoir* ...B10
Chino, *river* ...F10
Chocolate, *mts.* ...K9
Clair Engle, *lake* ...C1
Clear, *lake* ...C3
Clear Lake, *reservoir* ...D1
Coast, *ranges* ...C2, D6
Colorado, *desert* ...J9
Colorado, *river* ...L9
Cucamonga, *river* ...F11
Death, *valley* ...H6
Death Valley Natl. Park ...H6
Devils Postpile Natl. Monument ...F5
Diablo, *mt.* ...L1
Eagle, *lake* ...E2
Eagle, *peak* ...E1
Eel, *river* ...B2
Estero, *bay* ...E7
Farallon, *islands* ...B5
Farallones, *gulf* ...H2
Golden Gate Natl. Rec. Area ...C5, J2
Goose, *lake* ...E1
Grizzly, *bay* ...L1
Half Moon, *bay* ...J3
Honey, *lake* ...E2
Humboldt, *bay* ...A2
Imperial, *valley* ...K9
Inyo, *mts.* ...H6
Irvine, *lake* ...F11
Joshua Tree Natl. Park ...K8
Kern, *river* ...G6
Kings, *river* ...F6
Kings Canyon Natl. Park ...G5
Klamath, *mts.* ...B1
Klamath, *river* ...B1
Lanfair, *valley* ...K7
Lassen, *peak* ...D2
Lassen Volcanic Natl. Park ...D2
Lava Beds Natl. Monument ...D1
McCoy, *mts.* ...L9
Mad, *river* ...B2
Merced, *river* ...E5
Middle Alkali, *lake* ...F1
Mission, *bay* ...B8
Mission Bay, *park* ...B8
Mojave, *desert* ...H7
Mojave, *river* ...J8
Mono, *lake* ...G4
Monterey, *bay* ...C6
Morgan, *mt.* ...G5
Morris, *reservoir* ...E10
Napa, *river* ...K1
Nicasio, *reservoir* ...H1
Old Woman, *mts.* ...K8
Oroville, *reservoir* ...D3
Otay, *river* ...C9
Panamint, *range* ...H6
Panamint, *valley* ...H6
Pescadero, *river* ...J4
Pinnacles Natl. Monument ...D6
Point Reyes Natl. Seashore ...B4
Redwood Natl. Park ...A1
Ritter, *mt.* ...F5
Sacramento, *river* ...C3
Salton, *sea* ...K9
San Antonio, *reservoir* ...D7
San Bernardino, *mts.* ...J8
San Clemente, *island* ...G10
San Diego, *bay* ...B9
San Diego, *river* ...B8
San Fernando, *valley* ...B10
San Francisco, *bay* ...J2
San Gabriel, *mts.* ...G8
San Gabriel, *reservoir* ...E10
San Joaquin, *river* ...E5
San Luis Obispo, *bay* ...E8
San Miguel, *island* ...E8
San Nicolas, *island* ...F9
San Pablo, *bay* ...J1
San Rafael, *mts.* ...F8
Santa Ana, *mts.* ...F11
Santa Barbara, *channel* ...F9
Santa Barbara, *island* ...F9
Santa Catalina, *island* ...G9
Santa Cruz, *island* ...F8
Santa Lucia, *range* ...D6
Santa Monica, *bay* ...B11
Santa Monica, *mts.* ...B10
Santa Monica Mts. N.R.A. ...B10
Santa Rosa, *island* ...E8
Santiago, *peak* ...F11
Sequoia Natl. Park ...G6
Sierra, *peak* ...F11
Sierra Nevada, *range* ...D3, G5
Siskiyou, *mts.* ...C1
Tahoe, *lake* ...E3
Tehachapi, *mts.* ...G8
Telescope, *peak* ...H6
Trinity, *river* ...B2

Key

Tule, *river* ...F6
Turtle, *mts.* ...L8
Upper, *lake* ...C3
Upper San Leandro, *reservoir* ...L2
Vizcaino, *cape* ...B3
Whiskeytown-Shasta-Trinity N.R.A. ...D1
White, *mts.* ...G5
Whitney, *mt.* ...G6
Wilson, *mt.* ...D10
Yosemite Natl. Park ...F5

Colorado ....page 133

Cities and Towns

Akron ...G1
Alamosa ...E4
Arvada ...E2
Aspen ...D2
Aurora ...F2
Avon ...D2
Bennett ...F1
Berthoud ...E1
Black Forest ...F2
Boulder ...E1
Breckenridge ...D2
Brighton ...F1
Broomfield ...E1
Brush ...G1
Buena Vista ...D3
Burlington ...H2
Canon City ...E3
Carbondale ...C2
Castle Rock ...F2
Cedaredge ...C3
Center ...D4
Central City ...E2
Cheyenne Wells ...H3
Clifton ...B2
Colorado Springs ...F3
Conejos ...D4
Cortez ...B4
Craig ...C1
Crawford ...C3
Creede ...D4
Cripple Creek ...E3
Dacono ...F1
Del Norte ...D4
Delta ...B3
Denver, *capital* ...F2
Dinosaur ...A1
Dove Creek ...B4
Durango ...C4
Eads ...H3
Eagle ...D2
Eaton ...F1
Englewood ...F2
Estes Park ...E1
Evans ...F1
Evergreen ...E2
Fairplay ...E2
Florence ...E3
Fort Collins ...E1
Fort Lupton ...F1
Fort Morgan ...G1
Fountain ...F3
Frisco ...D2
Fruita ...B2
Fruitvale ...B2
Georgetown ...E2
Glenwood Springs ...C2
Golden ...E2
Grand Junction ...B2
Greeley ...F1
Gunnison ...D3
Gypsum ...D2
Haswell ...G3
Hayden ...C1
Holyoke ...H1
Hot Sulphur Springs ...D1
Hugo ...G2
Idaho Springs ...E2
Johnstown ...F1
Julesburg ...H1
Keota ...F1
Kiowa ...F2
Kit Carson ...H3
Lafayette ...E1
La Junta ...G4
Lake City ...C3
Lakewood ...E2
Lamar ...H3
Las Animas ...G3
Leadville ...D2
Limon ...G2
Littleton ...E2
Longmont ...E1
Louisville ...E1
Loveland ...E1
Manitou Springs ...F3
Meeker ...C1
Milliken ...F1
Monte Vista ...D4
Montrose ...C3
Niwot ...F1
Northglenn ...F2
Olathe ...C3
Orchard City ...C3
Orchard Mesa ...B2
Ordway ...G3
Ouray ...C3
Pagosa Springs ...C4
Palisade ...B2
Palmer Lake ...F2
Paonia ...C3
Parker ...F2
Platteville ...F1
Pritchett ...H4
Pueblo ...F3
Pueblo West ...F3
Rangely ...B1
Rifle ...C2
Rocky Ford ...G3
Saguache ...D3
Salida ...E3
San Luis ...E4
Security ...F3
Silverthorne ...D2
Silverton ...C4
Snowmass Village ...D2
Springfield ...H4
Steamboat Springs ...D1
Sterling ...G1
Telluride ...C4
Thornton ...F2
Trinidad ...F4
Vail ...D2
Vilas ...H4
Walden ...D1
Walsenburg ...F4
Wellington ...E1
Westcliffe ...E3

Key

Westminster ...E2
Wheat Ridge ...F2
Wiley ...H3
Windsor ...F1
Woodland Park ...F3
Wray ...H1
Yuma ...H1

Other Features

Animas, *river* ...C4
Apishapa, *river* ...F4
Arapahoe, *peak* ...E1
Arapaho Natl. Rec. Area ...E1
Arikaree, *river* ...G2
Arkansas, *river* ...F3
Bent's Old Fort Natl. Hist. Site ...G3
Black Canyon of the Gunnison Natl. Monument ...C3
Blanca, *peak* ...E4
Blue Mesa, *reservoir* ...C3
Bonny, *reservoir* ...H2
Castle, *peak* ...D2
Colorado, *plateau* ...A4
Colorado, *river* ...C2
Colorado Natl. Monument ...B2
Crestone, *peak* ...E4
Cucharas, *river* ...F4
Curecanti Natl. Rec. Area ...C3
Dinosaur Natl. Monument ...B1
Dolores, *river* ...B3
Elbert, *mt.* ...D2
Eolus, *mt.* ...C4
Evans, *mt.* ...E2
Florissant Fossil Beds N.M. ...E3
Front, *range* ...E1
Great Sand Dunes N.M. ...E4
Green, *river* ...B1
Gunnison, *mt.* ...C3
Gunnison, *river* ...B3
Hovenweep Natl. Monument ...B4
John Martin, *reservoir* ...G3
Laramie, *mts.* ...E1
Little Snake, *river* ...B1
Longs, *peak* ...E1
Mancos, *river* ...B4
Medicine Bow, *mts.* ...D1
Mesa Verde Natl. Park ...B4
Montezuma, *mt.* ...D4
North Fork Cimarron, *river* ...H4
North Fork Smoky Hill, *river* ...H2
North Platte, *river* ...D1
Park, *range* ...D1
Pikes, *peak* ...E3
Purgatoire, *river* ...G4
Rio Grande, *river* ...E4
Roan, *plateau* ...B2
Rocky, *mts.* ...D1
Rocky Mt. Natl. Park ...E1
Royal Gorge, *canyon* ...E3
Sangre de Cristo, *mts.* ...E3
San Juan, *valley* ...E4
San Luis, *valley* ...E4
Sawatch, *range* ...D2
South Fork Republican, *river* ...G2
South Platte, *river* ...E2, G1
Uncompahgre, *peak* ...C3
U.S. Air Force Academy ...F3
White, *river* ...B1
Wilson, *mt.* ...B4
Yampa, *river* ...C1
Yucca House Natl. Monument ...B4
Zirkel, *mt.* ...D1

Connecticut ....page 134

Cities and Towns

Abington ...G2
Andover ...F3
Ansonia ...C4
Attawaugan ...H2
Avon ...D2
Bakersville ...C2
Ballouville ...H2
Baltic ...G3
Beacon Falls ...C4
Berkshire ...B4
Berlin ...E3
Bethany ...C3
Bethel ...B4
Bethlehem ...C3
Black Point ...F4
Bloomfield ...E2
Blue Hills ...E2
Boardman Bridge ...B3
Bolton ...F2
Botsford ...B4
Branford ...D4
Bridgeport ...C5
Bridgewater ...B3
Bristol ...D3
Broad Brook ...E2
Brookfield ...B4
Brookfield Center ...B4
Brooklyn ...H2
Burlington ...D2
Burrville ...C2
Cannondale ...B5
Canterbury ...H3
Canton ...D2
Canton Center ...D2
Centerbrook ...F4
Central Village ...H3
Chaplin ...G2
Cheshire ...D3
Chester ...F4
Chesterfield ...G4
Clarks Falls ...H4
Clinton ...F4
Colchester ...F3
Colebrook ...D2
Collinsville ...D2
Columbia ...F3
Cornwall ...B2
Cornwall Bridge ...B2
Coventry ...F2
Cromwell ...E3
Danbury ...B4
Danielson ...H2
Darien ...B5
Dayville ...H2
Deep River ...F4
Derby ...C4
Durham ...E3
Eagleville ...F2
East Brooklyn ...H2
Eastford ...G2
East Glastonbury ...E3
East Granby ...E2
East Hampton ...E3

Key

...nville ...H8
...on ...E6
...D5
...nsboro ...E4
...ville ...B5
...ham Park ...J3
...n ...C5
...E10
...ilton ...B6
...pton ...C5
...eville ...J3
...well ...F3
...kinsville ...E7
...ehurst ...F8
...izibah ...G5
...vassee ...D2
...sville ...H8
...B5
...ansville ...D3
...er ...E6
...erville ...E6
...ton ...E6
...D5
...r ...C3
...E3
...rson ...E3
...rsonville ...H8
...sboro ...C4
...nesaw ...B3
...island ...H10
...xville ...D6
...fayette ...A2
...range ...A5
...land ...E9
...nia ...E3
...renceville ...D4
...burg ...E4
...ngton ...C4
...olnton ...C4
...ust Grove ...C5
...sville ...G5
...owici ...H8
...ber City ...B7
...pkin ...B7
...B4, G2
...pleton ...C5
...Donough ...C5
...ntyre ...D6
...con ...F7
...Rae ...E4
...dison ...E4
...nchester ...B6
...B4, H1
...rietta ...G7
...tter ...D7
...shallville ...E5
...dgeville ...H6
...nroe ...D4
...nticello ...D5
...gan ...B8
...ultrie ...D9
...unt Vernon ...F7
...Bethel ...J1
...shville ...E9
...wman ...C9
...wton ...C9
...xdale ...E8
...lla ...C7
...ethorpe ...K3
...rtersville ...B5
...chtree City ...F9
...rson ...H7
...mbroke ...D7
...Y ...J7
...yler ...J7
...der Springs ...B4
...ston ...B7
...man ...E10
...Oak ...H4
...dsville ...G7
...hland ...B7
...mond Hill ...J8
...con ...J7
...ggold ...A2
...erdale ...J4
...chelle ...E8
...kmart ...A3
...me ...A3
...swell ...C3
...lyston ...E3
...dy Springs ...J2
...annah ...J7
...attdale ...K3
...land ...J2
...myrna ...H2
...ellville ...D4
...cial Circle ...D4
...perton ...F7
...arta ...F5
...ingfield ...J7
...Marys ...H10
...Simons Island ...J9
...tenville ...E10
...atesboro ...H7
...tham ...D4
...ne Mountain ...C4
...mmerville ...A3
...rainsboro ...G6
...vania ...H6
...lvester ...D8
...botton ...B6
...nnille ...F6
...omaston ...C6
...omasville ...D10
...omson ...G5
...ton ...E9
...ccoa ...E2
...co Hills ...J2
...enton ...A2
...on ...A2
...cker ...A3
...bee Island ...K8
...adilla ...D7
...ion City ...B4, H4
...ion Point ...E4
...idosta ...E10
...dalia ...G7
...enna ...D7
...la Rica ...B4
...dley ...G6
...rner Robins ...D6
...rrenton ...F5
...ashington ...F4
...atkinsville ...E4
...aycross ...G9
...estoak ...H1
...oodbine ...H10
...rens ...E4
...rightsville ...F6

Key

Zebulon ...C5

Other Features
Alapaha, river ...E9
Allatoona, lake ...B3
Altamaha, river ...G8
Andersonville Natl. Hist. Site ...C7
Appalachian, mts. ...D2
Blackshear, lake ...D8
Blue, ridge ...C2
Brasstown Bald, mt. ...D2
Burton, lake ...D2
Carters, lake ...B2
Chattahoochee, river ...A5, A9, G3
Chattahoochee River N.R.A. ...H1
Chattooga, river ...E2
Chatuge, lake ...D1
Chickamauga and Chattanooga Natl. Military Park ...A2
Coosa, river ...D2
Cumberland, island ...J10
Cumberland Island Natl. Seashore ...J10
Etowah, river ...B3
Flint, river ...C9
Fort Frederica Natl. Monument ...J9
Fort Pulaski Natl. Monument ...K7
Hartwell, lake ...F2
Jackson, lake ...D5
Jekyll, island ...J9
Jimmy Carter Natl. Hist. Site ...C7
J. Strom Thurmond, lake ...G4
Lookout Mt., ridge ...A2
Martin Luther King Jr. N.H.S. ...J3
Ocmulgee Natl. Monument ...D6
Ochlockonee, river ...C10
Ocmulge, river ...E6
Oconee, river ...E5
Oconee, lake ...F6
Ogeechee, river ...F5
Ohoopee, river ...G7
Okefenokee, swamp ...G10
Ossabaw, island ...J8
Russell, lake ...F3
St. Catherines, island ...J8
St. Marys, river ...H10
St. Simons, island ...J9
Sapelo, island ...J9
Savannah, river ...H5
Seminole, lake ...B10
Sidney Lanier, lake ...C3
Sinclair, lake ...E5
Stone Mt. State Park ...C4
Suwannee, river ...F10
Tallapoosa, river ...A4
Tybee, island ...K7
Walter F. George, reservoir ...A8
Wassaw, island ...J9
Weiss, lake ...A3
West Point, lake ...A6
Withlacoochee, river ...E10

Hawaii .....page 138
Cities and Towns
Ahuimanu ...J2
Aiea ...F1, J2
Captain Cook ...G6
Crestview ...E1, J2
Eleele ...C2
Ewa ...D2, J2
Ewa Beach ...E2, J3
Foster Village ...F1, J2
Haena ...C1, J5
Halawa ...B3
Halawa Heights ...F1, J2
Haleiwa ...H1
Hana ...D4
Hanamaulu ...D1
Hanapepe ...C2
Hauula ...J1
Heeia ...G1, K2
Hilo ...E7, J5
Holualoa ...G5
Honalo ...G5
Honokaa ...H4
Honolulu, capital ...C5, F2, J3
Iroquois Point ...E2, J2
Kaanapali ...B3
Kahana ...B3, J1
Kahuku ...J1
Kahului ...C3, D3
Kailua ...C5, K2
Kailua-Kona ...D7, F5
Kalaheo ...C2
Kalaoa ...F5
Kalaupapa ...B3
Kaneohe ...C5, G1, K2
Kapaa ...A5, D1
Kaunakakai ...A3
Keaau ...J5
Kealakekua ...G6
Kealia ...D1, G6
Kekaha ...B2
Kihei ...C4, D3
Kilauea ...C1
Koloa ...C2
Kualapuu ...A3
Kula ...C4
Lahaina ...B3, D6
Laie ...C5, J1
Lanai City ...B3
Lawai ...C2
Lihue ...A5, D2
Maili ...H2
Makaha ...H2
Makakilo City ...H2
Makawao ...C3
Maunawili ...K2
Mililani Town ...J2
Mokuleia ...H1
Mountain View ...B5, H2
Nanakuli ...H2
Pacific Palisades ...E1, J2
Pahala ...H6
Papaikou ...J5
Pearl City ...C5, E1, J2
Pepeekeo ...J5
Pohakupu ...K2
Pukalani ...C3, D6
Pupukea ...J1
Volcano ...J6
Waialua ...B3, H1
Waianae ...B5, H2
Waihee ...C3
Waikiki ...G3
Waikoloa Village ...G4
Wailua ...C3, D1
Wailuku ...C3, D6
Waimalu ...E1, J2
Waimanalo ...K2
Waimanalo Beach ...K2

Key

Waimea ...C2, D6, H1
Waipahu ...E1, J2
Waipio ...H4
Waipio Acres ...J2
Whitmore Village ...J2

Other Features
Alenuihaha, channel ...D6
Alika Cone, mt. ...G6
Diamond Head, point ...G3
Ford, island ...E1
Haleakala, mt. ...C4
Haleakala Natl. Park ...C4, D6
Hamakua, coast ...H4
Hawaii, island ...E6, G5
Hawaii Volcanoes Natl. Park ...E7, H6
Hilo, bay ...J5
Hualalai, mt. ...G5
Kaala, mt. ...H1
Kaena, point ...B5, H1
Kahoolawe, island ...B4, D6
Kahului, bay ...C3
Kaikipauula, mt. ...H4
Kailua, bay ...K2
Kaiwi, channel ...C5, K3
Ka Lae (South Cape), cape ...D7, G7
Kalalua, mt. ...J6
Kalaupapa, peninsula ...B3
Kalaupapa Natl. Hist. Park ...B3
Kaloko-Honokohau Natl. Hist. Park ...F5
Kamakou, mt. ...A3
Kau, desert ...H6
Kauai, channel ...B5, D2
Kauai, island ...A5, B1
Kaukaahi, channel ...C1
Kawaikini, mt. ...C1
Kiholo, bay ...G4
Kilauea, crater ...J6
Kilohana, crater ...C2
Kinau, cape ...C4
Kipuka Puaulu, mt. ...H6
Kohala, coast ...F5
Kohala, mt. ...G4
Kohala, mts. ...G4
Kona, coast ...F6
Konahuanui, mt. ...G2, K2
Koolau Range, mts. ...F1, J1
Kulani, mt. ...H6
Kumukahi, cape ...E7, K5
Lanai, island ...B3, C6
Lehua, island ...A1
Lua Makika, mt. ...C4
Maalaea, bay ...C4
Makaleha, mts. ...C1
Makapuu, point ...C5, K2
Mamala, bay ...E2, J3
Maui, island ...C3, D6
Mauna Iki, mt. ...H6
Mauna Kea, mt. ...E6, H5
Mauna Loa, mt. ...D7, H6
Maunalua, bay ...K3
Mokolii, island ...J2
Mokuauia, island ...J1
Mokulua, island ...K2
Molokai, island ...A3, C5
Molokini, island ...C4
Na Pali, coast ...B1
Niihau, island ...A2, A5
Oahu, island ...B5, D2, K1
Pearl, harbor ...E2
Punchbowl, crater ...G2
Pu'uhonua O Honaunau N.H.P. ...G6
Puu Kainapuaa, mt. ...J1
Puu Kaua, mt. ...H2
Puukohola Heiau Natl. Hist. Site ...G4
Puu Kukui, mt. ...B3
Puu Kulua, mt. ...H5
Puu Loa, mt. ...H5
Puu O Keokeo, mt. ...G6
Sand, island ...F2
Sulphur Cone, mt. ...G6
U.S.S. Arizona Memorial ...E1
Upolu, point ...D6, G3
Waialeale, mt. ...A5, C1
Waianae Range, mts. ...H1
Wailuku, river ...H5
Waimea, canyon ...C2
West Maui, mts. ...B3

Idaho .....page 139
Cities and Towns
Aberdeen ...E7
American Falls ...E7
Ammon ...F6
Arco ...D6
Banks ...A5
Bellevue ...C6
Bennington ...F7
Blackfoot ...E6
Boise, capital ...A6
Bonners Ferry ...A1
Buhl ...C7
Burley ...D7
Caldwell ...A6
Cascade ...A5
Challis ...C5
Chubbuck ...E7
Coeur d'Alene ...A2
Council ...A5
Driggs ...F6
Dubois ...E5
Eagle ...A6
Emmett ...A6
Fairfield ...C6
Filer ...C7
Fish Haven ...F7
Fruitland ...A5
Fruitvale ...A5
Garden City ...A6
Garden Valley ...B5
Glenns Ferry ...C7
Gooding ...C7
Grangeville ...A4
Hailey ...C6
Hayden ...A2
Idaho City ...B6
Idaho Falls ...E6
Jerome ...C7
Kamiah ...A4
Kellogg ...A2
Ketchum ...C6
Kuna ...A6
Laclede ...A1
Lewiston ...A3
McCall ...A5
Malad City ...E7
May ...D5
Middleton ...A6

Key

Montpelier ...F7
Moscow ...A3
Mountain Home ...B6
Murphy ...A6
Nampa ...A6
New Plymouth ...A6
Nezperce ...A3
Orofino ...A3
Osburn ...A2
Paris ...F7
Parma ...A6
Patterson ...D5
Pauline ...E7
Payette ...A5
Pinehurst ...A2
Pocatello ...E7
Post Falls ...A2
Preston ...F7
Priest River ...A1
Rathdrum ...A2
Rexburg ...F6
Rigby ...F6
Rupert ...D7
St. Anthony ...F6
St. Maries ...A2
Salmon ...D5
Sandpoint ...A1
Shelley ...E6
Shoshone ...C7
Soda Springs ...F7
Sugar City ...F6
Sun Valley ...C6
Thatcher ...F7
Twin Falls ...C7
Wallace ...B2
Weiser ...A5
Wendell ...C7

Other Features
American Falls, reservoir ...E7
Bear, lake ...F7
Bear, river ...F7
Big Lost, river ...D6
Bitterroot, range ...B3, D4
Blackfoot, reservoir ...F7
Blackfoot, river ...F6
Bruneau, river ...B7
Cache, mt. ...F6
Caribou, range ...F6
Cascade, reservoir ...A5
Castle, mt. ...C5
Clearwater, mts. ...B3
Clearwater, river ...B4
Craters of the Moon N.M. ...D6
Dworshak, reservoir ...A3
Grays, river ...F6
Hagerman Fossil Beds N.M. ...C7
Hells, canyon ...A5
Hells Canyon Natl. Recreation Area ...A4
Kootenai, river ...A1
Lemhi, river ...D5
Lochsa, river ...B3
Middle Fork Salmon, river ...C5
Nez Perce N.H.P. ...A3, B3
North Fork Clearwater, river ...B3
Owyhee, mt. ...A6
Owyhee, river ...A6
Palisades, reservoir ...F6
Payette, lake ...A5
Payette, river ...A6
Pend Oreille, lake ...A1
Pend Oreille, river ...A1
Priest, river ...A1
Ryan, mt. ...C6
St. Joe, river ...A2
Salmon, river ...B4
Salmon River, mts. ...C5
Sawtooth, range ...B5
Sawtooth Natl. Recreation Area ...C5
Scott, mt. ...C5
Snake, river ...A4
South Fork Selway, river ...B3
Teton, river ...F6
Weiser, river ...A5
Yellowstone Natl. Park ...F5

Illinois .....page 140
Cities and Towns
Abingdon ...C3
Addison ...B5
Albion ...E5
Aledo ...C2
Alsip ...B6
Altamont ...E4
Alton ...C5
Amboy ...D2
Anna ...D6
Antioch ...A4, E1
Arcola ...E4
Arlington Heights ...A5
Arthur ...E4
Ashland ...C4
Athens ...D4
Atlanta ...D3
Atwood ...E4
Auburn ...D4
Aurora ...E2
Barrington ...A5
Barry ...B4
Bartlett ...A5
Bartonville ...D2
Batavia ...E2
Beach Park ...B4
Beardstown ...C3
Beecher ...F2
Belleville ...D5
Belvidere ...E1
Bement ...E4
Benld ...D4
Benton ...E6
Berwyn ...B6
Bethany ...D4
Bloomington ...D3
Blue Island ...B6
Bolingbrook ...A6, E2
Bourbonnais ...F2
Braidwood ...E2
Breese ...D5
Bridgeport ...F5
Brighton ...C5
Brookfield ...B6
Buffalo Grove ...A5
Bunker Hill ...D4
Burbank ...B6
Bushnell ...C3
Byron ...D1
Cahokia ...C5
Cairo ...D6
Calumet City ...C6, F2

Key

Cambridge ...C2
Canton ...C3
Capron ...E1
Carbondale ...D6
Carlinville ...D4
Carlyle ...D5
Carmi ...E5
Carol Stream ...A5
Carpentersville ...E1
Carrier Mills ...E6
Carrollton ...C4
Carterville ...D6
Carthage ...B3
Cary ...E1
Casey ...F4
Catlin ...F3
Centralia ...D5
Cerro Gordo ...E4
Champaign ...E3
Channahon ...E2
Charleston ...E4
Chatham ...D4
Chenoa ...E3
Chester ...D6
Chicago ...B5, F2
Chicago Heights ...B6
Chillicothe ...D3
Christopher ...D6
Cicero ...B6, F2
Clifton ...F2
Clinton ...E3
Coal City ...E2
Colchester ...C3
Collinsville ...C5
Columbia ...C5
Crest Hill ...A6
Crete ...F2
Crystal Lake ...E1
Cuba ...C3
Danville ...F3
Decatur ...E4
Deerfield ...B5
De Kalb ...E2
Delavan ...D3
De Soto ...D6
Des Plaines ...B5
Dixon ...D1
Dolton ...B6
Downers Grove ...B6
Du Quoin ...D6
Dwight ...E2
Earlville ...E2
East Dubuque ...C1
East Moline ...C2
East Peoria ...D3
East St. Louis ...C5
Edwardsville ...C5
Effingham ...E4
Elburn ...E2
Eldorado ...E6
Elgin ...E1
Elizabethtown ...E6
Elk Grove Village ...B5
Elmhurst ...B5
Elmwood ...D2
Elmwood Park ...B5
Erie ...C2
Eureka ...D3
Evanston ...B5, F1
Evergreen Park ...B6
Fairbury ...E3
Fairfield ...E5
Farmer City ...E3
Farmington ...C3
Fisher ...E3
Flora ...E4
Forreston ...D1
Forsyth ...E4
Fox Lake ...A4, E1
Fox Lake Hills ...A4
Fox River Grove ...A5
Frankfort ...B6, F2
Freeburg ...D5
Freeport ...D1
Fulton ...C2
Gages Lake ...B4
Galena ...C1
Galesburg ...C3
Galva ...C2
Geneseo ...C2
Geneva ...E2
Genoa ...E1
Georgetown ...F4
Gibson City ...E3
Gillespie ...D4
Gilman ...F3
Girard ...D4
Glen Ellyn ...A5
Glencoe ...B5
Glendale Heights ...A5
Glenview ...B5
Glenwood ...B6
Godfrey ...C5
Golconda ...E6
Granite City ...C5
Granville ...D2
Grayslake ...A4
Grayville ...E5
Green Oaks ...B4
Greenup ...E4
Greenville ...D5
Gridley ...E3
Gurnee ...A4
Hainesville ...A4
Hamilton ...B3
Hampshire ...E1
Hanover Park ...A5
Hardin ...C4
Harrisburg ...E6
Harristown ...E4
Harvard ...E1
Harvey ...B6
Havana ...C3
Hennepin ...D2
Henry ...D2
Herrin ...D6
Herscher ...E2
Heyworth ...E3
Hickory Hills ...B6
Highland ...D5
Highland Park ...B5, F1
Hillsboro ...D4
Hinckley ...E2
Hinsdale ...B6
Hoffman Estates ...A5
Homer ...F3
Homewood ...B6
Hoopeston ...F3
Huntley ...E1
Island Lake ...A5

Key

Jacksonville ...C4
Jerseyville ...C4
Johnston City ...E6
Joliet ...A6, E2
Jonesboro ...D6
Justice ...B6
Kankakee ...F2
Kaskaskia ...D6
Kewanee ...D2
Kincaid ...D4
Knoxville ...C3
Lacon ...D2
La Grange ...B6
La Harpe ...C3
Lake Bluff ...B5
Lake Forest ...B5
Lake Zurich ...A5
Lanark ...D1
La Salle ...D2
Lansing ...B6
Lawrenceville ...F5
Lemont ...B6
Lena ...D1
Le Roy ...E3
Lewistown ...C3
Lexington ...E3
Libertyville ...B5
Lilymoor ...A4
Lincoln ...D3
Lincolnwood ...B5
Lindenhurst ...A4
Lisle ...B6
Litchfield ...D4
Lockport ...B6
Lombard ...B5
Louisville ...E5
Loves Park ...D1
Lynwood ...C6
McHenry ...E1
Machesney Park ...D1
Mackinaw ...D3
McLeansboro ...E5
Macomb ...C3
Macon ...E4
Mahomet ...E3
Manhattan ...F2
Manito ...D3
Manteno ...E2
Marengo ...E1
Marion ...E6
Marissa ...D5
Marley ...B6
Maroa ...E3
Marseilles ...E2
Marshall ...F4
Mascoutah ...D5
Mason City ...D3
Matteson ...B6
Mattoon ...E4
Maywood ...B5
Melrose Park ...B5
Mendota ...D2
Metamora ...D3
Metropolis ...E6
Milan ...C2
Milford ...F3
Minonk ...D3
Minooka ...E2
Mokena ...B6
Moline ...C2
Momence ...F2
Monmouth ...C3
Monticello ...E3
Morris ...E2
Morrison ...D2
Morton ...D3
Morton Grove ...B5
Mound City ...D6
Mounds ...D6
Mount Carmel ...F5
Mount Carroll ...D1
Mount Morris ...D1
Mount Olive ...D4
Mount Prospect ...B5
Mount Pulaski ...D3
Mount Sterling ...C4
Mount Vernon ...E5
Mount Zion ...E4
Moweaqua ...D4
Mundelein ...A5
Murphysboro ...D6
Naperville ...A6
Nashville ...D5
Neoga ...E4
New Athens ...D5
New Baden ...D5
New Lenox ...B6
Newton ...E5
Niles ...B5
Nokomis ...D4
Normal ...E3
Norridge ...B5
Northbrook ...B5
North Chicago ...B4, F1
Northfield ...B5
Northlake ...B5
Oak Brook ...B6
Oak Forest ...B6
Oak Lawn ...B6, F2
Oak Park ...B5, F2
Oakwood ...F3
Oblong ...F4
O'Fallon ...D5
Oglesby ...D2
Okawville ...D5
Old Mill Creek ...B4
Olney ...E5
Onarga ...F3
Oquawka ...C3
Oregon ...D1
Orion ...C2
Orland Hills ...B6
Orland Park ...B6
Ottawa ...E2
Palatine ...A5
Palestine ...F4
Palos Heights ...B6
Palos Hills ...B6
Pana ...D4
Paris ...F4
Park Forest ...B6
Park Ridge ...B5
Pawnee ...D4
Paxton ...E3
Pecatonica ...D1
Pekin ...D3
Peoria ...D3
Peoria Heights ...D3
Peotone ...F2
Peru ...D2
Petersburg ...D4

Pinckneyville....D5
Pittsfield....C4
Plainfield....A6, E2
Plano....E2
Polo....D2
Pontiac....E3
Princeton....D2
Princeville....D3
Prophetstown....D2
Quincy....B4
Rantoul....E3
Red Bud....D5
Richton Park....B6
Riverdale....D4
Riverton....D4
Riverwoods....B5
Roanoke....D3
Robinson....F4
Rochelle....D2
Rochester....D4
Rock Falls....D2
Rock Island....C2
Rockford....D1
Rockton....D1
Rome....D3
Romeoville....A6
Roodhouse....C4
Roscoe....D1
Rosiclare....E6
Rossville....F3
Round Lake Beach....A4
Rushville....C3
Russell....B4
St. David....D4
St. Elmo....E4
St. Joseph....E3
St. Libory....D5
Salem....E5
Sandoval....D5
Sandwich....E2
Sauk Village....C6
Savanna....C1
Savoy....E3
Schaumburg....A5
Schiller Park....B5
Seneca....E2
Sesser....D5
Shawneetown....E6
Shelbyville....D4
Sheridan....E2
Sherman....D4
Shorewood....A6, E2
Skokie....B5
Somonauk....E2
South Beloit....D1
South Elgin....E2
South Holland....B6
South Jacksonville....C4
Sparta....D5
Spring Valley....D2
Springfield, capital....D4
Staunton....D4
Steeleville....D5
Sterling....D2
Stockland....F3
Stockton....C1
Streamwood....A5
Streator....E2
Sullivan....E4
Summit....B6
Sycamore....E2
Taylorville....D4
Teutopolis....E4
Tilton....F3
Tinley Park....B6, F2
Toledo....E4
Tolono....E4
Toluca....D3
Toulon....D2
Tower Lakes....A5
Tremont....D3
Trenton....D5
Tuscola....E4
Urbana....E3
Vandalia....D5
Vernon Hills....B5
Vienna....E6
Villa Grove....E4
Villa Park....B5
Virden....D4
Virginia....C4
Volo....A4
Wadsworth....B4
Walnut....D2
Wapella....E3
Warren....D1
Warrensburg....D4
Warrenville....A6
Warsaw....B3
Washington....D3
Waterloo....C5
Watseka....F3
Wauconda....A5
Waukegan....B4, F1
Waverly....D4
Westchester....B6
West Chicago....A5
West Frankfort....E6
Westville....F3
Wheaton....A6, E2
Wheeling....B5, F1
White Hall....C4
Wilmette....B5
Wilmington....E2
Winchester....C4
Winnebago....D1
Winnetka....B5
Winthrop Harbor....B4
Woodridge....A6
Wood River....C5
Woodstock....E1
Wyoming....D2
Yorkville....E2
Zeigler....D6
Zion....B4, F1

Other Features
Carlyle, lake....D5
Chautauqua, lake....C3
Chicago, river....B5
Clinton, lake....E3
Crab Orchard, lake....D6
Des Plaines, river....A6, B4
Du Page, river....A6
Fox, lake....A4
Fox, river....A4
Illinois, river....D3
Ind. Dunes Natl. Lakeshore....C6
Kankakee, river....E2
Kaskaskia, river....E4
Lincoln Home Natl. Hist. Site....D4

Marie, lake....A4
Michigan, lake....F1
O'Hare, airport....B5
Ohio, river....D6
Orland, lake....B6
Rend, lake....D5
Rock, river....D2
Sangamon, river....C3
Shelbyville, lake....E4
Spoon, river....C3
Wabash, river....E6

Indiana....page 141

Cities and Towns
Albany....F4
Albion....F2
Alexandria....E4
Anderson....E4
Angola....G1
Arcadia....D4
Argos....D2
Atlanta....D4
Attica....B4
Auburn....F2
Aurora....G6
Austin....E7
Avilla....F2
Bargersville....D5
Batesville....F6
Bedford....D7
Berne....G3
Bicknell....B7
Bloomfield....C6
Bloomington....C6
Bluffton....F3
Boonville....B8
Bourbon....D2
Brazil....B5
Bremen....D2
Brookston....C3
Brookville....F6
Brownsburg....D5
Brownstown....D7
Butler....G2
Cambridge City....F5
Cannelton....C9
Carmel....D5
Chandler....B8
Charlestown....E8
Chesterton....B1
Churubusco....F2
Cicero....D4
Clayton....C5
Clinton....B5
Cloverdale....C5
Columbia City....E2
Columbus....E6
Connersville....F5
Corydon....D8
Covington....B4
Crawfordsville....C4
Crothersville....E7
Crown Point....B2
Culver....D2
Dale....C8
Daleville....E4
Danville....C5
Darmstadt....A8
Decatur....G3
Delphi....C3
Demotte....B2
Dunlap....E1
East Chicago....B1
Eaton....F4
Edinburgh....E6
Elkhart....E1
Ellettsville....C6
Elwood....E4
English....C7
Evansville....A9
Fairmount....E4
Farmland....F4
Ferdinand....C8
Fishers....D5
Flora....C3
Fort Branch....A8
Fort Wayne....F2
Fowler....B3
Frankfort....C4
Franklin....D6
Fremont....G1
French Lick....C7
Galveston....D3
Garrett....F2
Gary....B1
Gas City....E4
Geneva....G3
Georgetown....E8
Goshen....E1
Greencastle....C5
Greenfield....E5
Greensburg....F6
Greentown....E4
Greenwood....D5
Hagerstown....F5
Hammond....A1
Hanover....E7
Hartford City....F3
Hebron....B2
Highland....B1
Hope....E6
Huntertown....F2
Huntingburg....C8
Huntington....F3
Indianapolis, capital....D5
Jasonville....B6
Jasper....C8
Jeffersonville....E8
Kendallville....F2
Kentland....B3
Kingsford Heights....C2
Knox....C2
Kokomo....D3
Kouts....C2
Lafayette....C4
Lagrange....F1
Lakeville....D1
La Porte....C1
Lawrence....D5
Lawrenceburg....G6
Lebanon....D4
Liberty....G5
Ligonier....F2
Lincoln City....B8
Linton....B6
Logansport....D3
Loogootee....C7
Lowell....B2
Madison....F7

Marion....E3
Martinsville....D6
Merrillville....B2
Michigan City....C1
Middlebury....E1
Milan....F6
Milford....E2
Mishawaka....D1
Mitchell....D7
Monon....C3
Monticello....C3
Montpelier....F3
Mooresville....D6
Mount Vernon....A9
Mulberry....C4
Muncie....F4
Nappanee....D2
Nashville....D6
New Albany....E8
Newburgh....B9
New Carlisle....C1
New Castle....F5
New Haven....F2
Newport....B5
New Whiteland....D5
Noblesville....D4
North Judson....C2
North Liberty....D1
North Manchester....E2
North Terre Haute....B5
North Vernon....E6
Notre Dame....D1
Oakland City....B8
Odon....C7
Orleans....D7
Osgood....F6
Ossian....F3
Otterbein....B3
Oxford....B3
Paoli....D7
Pendleton....E4
Peru....C3
Petersburg....B8
Plainfield....D5
Plymouth....D2
Portland....G3
Princeton....A8
Redkey....F4
Rensselaer....B3
Richmond....G5
Rising Sun....G7
Rochester....D2
Rockport....B9
Rockville....B5
Rushville....F5
Salem....D7
Schererville....B2
Scottsburg....E7
Sellersburg....E8
Seymour....E7
Shadeland....C4
Shelbyville....E5
Sheridan....D4
Shoals....C7
South Bend....D1
South Whitley....E2
Speedway....D5
Spencer....C6
Sullivan....B6
Syracuse....E2
Tell City....C9
Terre Haute....B6
Thorntown....C4
Tippecanoe....D2
Tipton....D4
Union City....G4
Upland....E4
Valparaiso....B2
Veedersburg....B4
Vernon....E7
Versailles....F6
Vevay....F7
Vincennes....A7
Wabash....E3
Wakarusa....D1
Walkerton....D2
Warsaw....E2
Washington....B7
Waterloo....F2
Westfield....D4
West Lafayette....C4
Westport....E6
Westville....C1
Williamsport....B4
Winamac....C2
Winchester....G4
Winona Lake....E2
Woodburn....G2
Worthington....C6
Yorktown....F4
Zionsville....D5

Other Features
Big Blue, river....E5
Brookville, lake....F5
Eel, river....E3
George Rogers Clark N.H.P.....A7
Indiana Dunes Natl. Lakeshore....B1
Kankakee, river....C2
Lemon, lake....D6
Lincoln Boyhood Natl. Memorial....C8
Maumee, river....G2
Michigan, lake....B1
Mississinewa, lake....E3
Monroe, lake....D6
Ohio, river....A9
Patoka, lake....B8
St. Joseph, river....G2
Salamonie, river....F3
Tippecanoe, river....C2
Wabash, river....A8
Wawasee, lake....E2
White, river....C6
Whitewater, river....F6

Iowa....page 142

Cities and Towns
Ackley....H2
Adel....F4
Akron....A2
Albia....J5
Algona....E1
Allison....J2
Alta....D2
Altoona....H4
Ames....G3
Anamosa....M3
Ankeny....G4
Asbury....N3

Atlantic....D5
Audubon....E4
Avoca....D5
Batavia....K5
Bayard....E4
Bedford....E6
Belle Plaine....K4
Bellevue....P3
Belmond....G2
Bettendorf....P4
Bloomfield....K6
Boone....G3
Brighton....L5
Britt....G1
Brooklyn....M6
Burlington....M6
Camanche....P4
Carlisle....G5
Carroll....E3
Carter Lake....C5
Cascade....N3
Cedar Falls....K3
Cedar Rapids....L4
Center Point....L3
Centerville....J6
Chariton....H5
Charles City....J1
Cherokee....C2
Clarinda....D6
Clarion....G2
Clarksville....J2
Clear Lake....H1
Clinton....P4
Colfax....H4
Columbus Junction....M5
Coon Rapids....E3
Coralville....L4
Corning....E6
Corydon....H6
Council Bluffs....C5
Cresco....K1
Creston....F5
Dakota City....F2
Dallas Center....G4
Davenport....N4
Decorah....L1
Denison....D4
Denver....K2
Des Moines, capital....G4
De Witt....N4
Dubuque....N2
Durant....N4
Dyersville....M3
Eagle Grove....G2
Eldora....J3
Eldridge....N4
Elgin....L2
Elkader....M2
Emmetsburg....E1
Epworth....N3
Estherville....E1
Evansdale....K3
Fairfield....L6
Farley....M3
Fayette....L2
Forest City....G1
Fort Dodge....F2
Fort Madison....M6
Garner....G1
Gilmore City....F2
Glenwood....C5
Greenfield....F5
Grimes....G4
Grinnell....J4
Grundy Center....J3
Guthrie Center....F4
Guttenberg....M2
Hampton....H2
Harlan....D4
Hartley....D1
Hawarden....B1
Hiawatha....L3
Holstein....C3
Hudson....K3
Hull....B1
Humboldt....F2
Huxley....G4
Ida Grove....D3
Independence....L3
Indianola....G5
Iowa City....L4
Iowa Falls....H2
Jefferson....F4
Jesup....K3
Johnston....G4
Kalona....L5
Keokuk....M7
Keosauqua....L6
Knoxville....H5
Lake City....E3
Lake Mills....G1
Lake View....D3
Lamoni....G6
La Porte City....K3
Laurens....E2
Le Claire....P4
Le Mars....B2
Lenox....E6
Leon....G6
Logan....C4
Lovilia....J5
Madrid....G4
Manchester....M3
Manly....H1
Manning....D4
Manson....E2
Mapleton....C3
Maquoketa....N3
Marengo....K4
Marion....L3
Marshalltown....J3
Mason City....H1
Mediapolis....M5
Melcher-Dallas....H5
Milford....D1
Missouri Valley....C4
Monona....M1
Monroe....H4
Montezuma....J4
Monticello....M3
Mount Ayr....F6
Mount Pleasant....L6
Mount Vernon....M4
Moville....B3
Muscatine....M5
Nashua....J2
Nevada....H3
New Hampton....K1
New London....M6
Newton....H4

Nora Springs....J1
North Liberty....L4
Northwood....H1
Norwalk....G5
Oakland....D5
Oelwein....L2
Ogden....F3
Onawa....B3
Orange City....B1
Osage....J1
Osceola....G5
Oskaloosa....J5
Ottumwa....K5
Park View....N4
Parkersburg....J2
Pella....J5
Perry....F4
Pleasantville....H5
Pocahontas....E2
Polk City....G4
Postville....L1
Prairie City....H4
Primghar....C1
Red Oak....D5
Reinbeck....J3
Remsen....C2
Rock Rapids....B1
Rock Valley....B1
Rockwell City....E3
Sac City....E3
Sanborn....C1
Sergeant Bluff....B3
Sheldon....C1
Shell Rock....J2
Shenandoah....D6
Sibley....C1
Sidney....C6
Sigourney....K5
Sioux Center....B1
Sioux City....B2
Spencer....D1
Spirit Lake....D1
Storm Lake....D2
Story City....G3
Strawberry Point....L2
Stuart....F4
Sumner....K2
Tama....J4
Tipton....M4
Toledo....J4
Traer....K3
Urbandale....G4
Villisca....E6
Vinton....K3
Walcott....N4
Wapello....M5
Washington....L5
Waterloo....K3
Waukee....G4
Waukon....M1
Waverly....K2
Webster City....G2
West Branch....M4
West Burlington....M6
West Des Moines....G4
West Liberty....M4
West Union....L2
Williamsburg....L4
Wilton....M4
Windsor Heights....G4
Winterset....F5
Woodbine....C4

Other Features
Big Sioux, river....A1
Boone, river....G2
Cedar, river....K3
Chariton, river....H6
Clear, lake....H1
Coralville, lake....L4
Des Moines, river....F3
Effigy Mounds Natl. Monument....M1
Floyd, river....B2
Fox, river....K6
Iowa, river....K4
Little Sioux, river....D2
Maple, river....D2
Mississippi, river....M2
Missouri, river....B4
Rathbun, lake....J6
Red Rock, lake....J5
Saylorville, reservoir....G4
Skunk, river....L5
Spirit, lake....D1
Storm, lake....D2
Turkey, river....L2
Wapsipinicon, river....K2
West Nishnabota, river....K2

Kansas....page 143

Cities and Towns
Abilene....E3
Adrian....G3
Alma....F3
Andover....E4
Anthony....D4
Arkansas City....E4
Arma....C4
Ashland....C4
Atchison....G2
Atwood....A2
Augusta....E4
Baldwin City....G3
Baxter Springs....H4
Belle Plaine....E4
Belleville....D2
Beloit....D2
Bonner Springs....H2
Buhler....E3
Burlington....G3
Butler....E3
Caldwell....E4
Caney....G4
Carbondale....G3
Chanute....G4
Chapman....E3
Cheney....D4
Cherryvale....G4
Chetopa....G4
Clay Center....E2
Clearwater....E4
Clifton....E2
Coffeyville....G4
Colby....A2
Coldwater....C4
Columbus....H4
Concordia....E2
Conway Springs....E4

Coolidge
Cottonwood Falls
Council Grove....G5
Derby....G5
De Soto
Dighton
Dodge City
Douglass
El Dorado
Elkhart
Ellinwood
Ellis
Ellsworth
Emporia
Erie
Eudora
Eureka
Fort Scott
Fredonia
Frontenac
Galena
Garden City
Gardner
Garnett
Girard
Goddard
Goodland
Gove
Great Bend
Greensburg
Halstead
Harper
Hays
Haysville
Herington
Hesston
Hiawatha
Hill City
Hillsboro
Holcomb
Holton
Horton
Howard
Hoxie
Hugoton
Humboldt
Hutchinson
Independence
Iola
Iuka
Jetmore
Johnson
Junction City
Kansas City
Kingman
Kinsley
La Crosse
Lakin
Lansing
Larned
Lawrence
Leavenworth
Leoti
Liberal
Lincoln
Lindsborg
Louisburg
Lyndon
Lyons
McPherson
Maize
Manhattan
Mankato
Marion
Marysville
Meade
Medicine Lodge
Minneapolis
Mound City
Moundridge
Mulvane
Neodesha
Ness City
Newton
North Newton
Norton
Oakley
Oberlin
Ogden
Olathe
Osage City
Osawatomie
Osborne
Oskaloosa
Oswego
Ottawa
Overland Park
Paola
Park
Park City
Parsons
Peabody
Phillipsburg
Pittsburg
Plainville
Pratt
Rich Hill
Rose Hill
Rose Hill
Russell
Sabetha
St. Francis
St. John
St. Marys
Salina
Scott City
Sedan
Sedgwick
Seneca
Sharon Springs
Silver Lake
Smith Center
South Hutchinson
Spring Hill
Stafford
Sterling
Stockton
Sublette
Syracuse
Tecumseh
Tonganoxie
Topeka, capital
Towanda
Tribune
Troy
Ulysses
Valley Center

KANSAS–MARYLAND 183

	Key
Falls	G2
eeney	C2
ego	F2
ington	E2
rville	F2
ngton	E4
ville	G3
moreland	F2
ita	E4
ield	F4
Center	G4

er Features

	Key
nsas, *river*	A4, D3
Blue, *river*	F2
r Bluff, *reservoir*	C3
ney, *reservoir*	E4
askia, *river*	D4
arron, *river*	A4
on, *lake*	G3
river	F4
Hills	F4
Larned Natl. Hist. Site	C3
Scott Natl. Hist. Site	H4
apolis, *lake*	E3
sas, *river*	F2
in, *reservoir*	C2
Blue, *river*	E1
ion, *lake*	E3
icine Lodge, *river*	C4
vern, *lake*	G3
ord, *lake*	F2
ouri, *river*	G2
sho, *river*	G3
th Fork Solomon, *river*	B2
ublican, *river*	D1
ne, *river*	C2
ky Hill, *river*	B3
mon, *river*	D2
th Fork Republican, *river*	A2
flower, *mt.*	A2
e Creek, *lake*	F2
igris, *river*	F3
onda, *lake*	D2
on, *lake*	D3

ntucky....................page 144

es and Towns

	Key
rdeen	F2
any	D4
andria	E2
nsville	B4
land	G2
urn	C4
usta	E2
ourville	F4
dstown	D3
dwell	B2
ttyville	F3
ver Dam	C3
ford	D2
ton	C2
ea	E3
y	E2
neville	F3
ling Green	C4
ndenburg	C3
oks	D2
oksville	E2
wnsville	C3
kesville	D4
lington	E1
er	E2
liz	B4, C2
houn	B3
vert City	C2
mpbellsville	D3
mpton	F3
lisle	E2
rollton	D2
rsville	C1
lettsburg	G2
ve City	D3
ntral City	B3
y City	F3
nton	B2
umbia	D3
ncord	F2
bin	E4
inth	E2
vington	E1
estwood	D2
mberland	G4
nthiana	E2
nville	E3
wson Springs	B3, C1
on	B3, C1
Ridge	E2
lington	B3
dyville	A3, C2
monton	D4
on	C3
zabethtown	D3
ton	B4
inence	D2
rfield	D3
mouth	E2
twoods	G2
mingsburg	F2
rence	E2
ster	E2
nkfort, *capital*	E2
nklin	C4
nchburg	F3
lton	B2
orgetown	E2
asgow	D3
atz	E2
ayson	G2
eensburg	D3
eenup	G2
eenville	B3
thrie	B4
rdinsburg	C3
rlan	F4
rrodsburg	E3
rtford	C3
wesville	C3
zard	F3
nderson	B3
ckman	B2
ndman	G3
seville	D3
bson	D3
dgenville	D3
pkinsville	B4
rse Cave	D3
den	F3
dependence	E2

	Key
Inez	G3
Irvine	F3
Jackson	F3
Jamestown	D4
Jeffersontown	D2
Jeffersonville	F3
Jenkins	G3
Junction City	E3
La Fayette	B4, C2
La Grange	D2
Lancaster	E3
Lawrenceburg	E2
Leatherwood	F3
Lebanon	D3
Leitchfield	C3
Lewisport	C3
Lexington	E2
Liberty	E3
Livermore	B3
Livingston	E3
London	E3
Louisa	G2
Louisville	D2
McKee	F3
Mackville	D3
Madisonville	B3
Manchester	F3
Marion	A3, C1
Mayfield	B2
Maysville	F2
Middlesboro	F4
Middletown	D2
Monterey	E2
Monticello	E4
Morehead	F2
Morganfield	B3, C1
Morgantown	C3
Mt. Olivet	E2
Mt. Sterling	F2
Mt. Vernon	E3
Mt. Washington	D2
Muldraugh	C3
Munfordville	D3
Murray	C2
Nebo	B3
New Castle	D2
Nicholasville	E3
Oak Grove	B4
Okolona	D2
Olive Hill	F2
Owensboro	B3
Owenton	E2
Owingsville	F2
Paducah	C2
Paris	E2
Patesville	C3
Phelps	G3
Pikeville	G3
Pine Knot	E4
Pineville	F4
Pleasure Ridge Park	D2
Prestonsburg	G3
Princeton	B3, C2
Providence	B3, C1
Raceland	G2
Radcliff	D3
Richmond	E3
Rochester	C3
Russell Springs	D3
Russellville	C4
St. Matthews	D2
Salyersville	F3
Sandy Hook	F2
Scottsville	C4
Sebree	B3
Shelbyville	D2
Shepherdsville	D2
Slaughters	B3
Smithland	C1
Somerset	E3
South Shore	G2
Springfield	D3
Stanford	E3
Stanton	F3
Sturgis	A3, C1
Taylorsville	D2
Tompkinsville	D4
Valley Station	D2
Vanceburg	F2
Versailles	E2
Vicco	F3
Vine Grove	D3
Walton	E2
Warsaw	E2
West Liberty	F3
Wheelwright	G3
Whitesburg	G3
Whitley City	E4
Wickliffe	B2
Williamsburg	E4
Williamstown	E2
Wilmore	E3
Winchester	E3
Woodbury	C3
Zion	B3

Other Features

	Key
Barkley, *lake*	B4, C2
Barren, *river*	C3
Barren River, *lake*	C4
Big Sandy, *river*	G2
Big South Fork Natl. River and Rec. Area	E4
Buckhorn, *lake*	F3
Cave Run, *lake*	F2
Cumberland, *lake*	E4
Cumberland, *river*	C3
Cumberland Gap Natl. Hist. Park	F4
Dale Hollow, *lake*	D4
Fish Trap, *river*	G3
Green, *river*	B3, D3
Green River, *lake*	D3
Kentucky, *lake*	C2
Kentucky, *river*	D2, E3
Licking, *river*	F2
Lincoln Birthplace Natl. Hist. Site	D3
Mammoth Cave Natl. Park	C3
Nolin River, *lake*	C3
Ohio, *river*	E1
Rough, *river*	C3
Rough River, *lake*	C3
Tennessee, *river*	B2
Tug Fork, *river*	G3

Louisiana ....page 145

Cities and Towns

	Key
Abbeville	E7
Abita Springs	J6
Alexandria	E4
Ama	Inset
Amelia	G7
Amite	J5
Arabi	Inset
Arcadia	D1
Arnaudville	F6
Avondale	Inset
Baker	G5
Baldwin	F7
Ball	E4
Basile	D6
Bastrop	F1
Baton Rouge, *captial*	G6
Bayou Cane	H7
Bayou Vista	G7
Belle Chasse	Inset
Bentley	E3
Bernice	D1
Bertrandville	Inset
Bogalusa	K5
Bossier City	B1
Boyce	D4
Braithwaite	Inset
Breaux Bridge	F6
Bridge City	Inset
Broussard	F6
Bunkie	E5
Buras	K8
Caernarvon	Inset
Cameron	C7
Carencro	E6
Carville	G6
Cecilia	F6
Chalmette	Inset, K7
Charenton	F7
Chauvin	H8
Church Point	E6
Clinton	G5
Colfax	D3
Columbia	E2
Cottonport	E5
Coushatta	C2
Covington	J6
Crowley	E6
Crown Point	Inset
Cullen	C1
Cut Off	J7
Dalcour	Inset
Delcambre	F7
Delhi	G2
Denham Springs	H5
De Quincy	C6
De Ridder	C5
Des Allemands	J7
Destrehan	Inset
Donaldsonville	H6
Edgard	H6
Elton	D6
English Turn	Inset
Erath	E7
Estelle	Inset
Eunice	E6
Farmerville	E1
Ferriday	F3
Franklin	F7
Franklinton	J5
Frenier	Inset
Galliano	J8
Garyville	H6
Glenmora	D5
Golden Meadow	J8
Gonzales	H6
Grambling	D1
Grand Isle	K8
Gray	H7
Greensburg	H5
Greenwood	B2
Gretna	Inset, J7
Gueydan	E6
Hackberry	C6
Hahnville	Inset, J7
Hammond	J5
Harahan	Inset
Harrisonburg	E2
Harvey	Inset
Haughton	C1
Haynesville	C1
Henderson	F6
Homer	C1
Houma	H7
Independence	J5
Inniswold	G6
Iota	D6
Iowa	C6
Jackson	G5
Jeanerette	F7
Jean Lafitte	J7
Jefferson	Inset
Jena	E3
Jennings	D6
Jesuit Bend	Inset
Jonesboro	D2
Jonesville	F3
Kaplan	E6
Kenilworth	Inset
Kenner	Inset, J7
Kentwood	J5
Killona	Inset
Kinder	D6
Krotz Springs	F5
Labadieville	H7
Lacombe	K6
Lafayette	E6
Lafitte	J7
Lake Arthur	D6
Lake Charles	C6
Lake Providence	G1
Laplace	Inset, J6
Larose	J7
Lecompte	E4
Leesville	C4
Livingston	H5
Lockport	H7
Logansport	B3
Luling	Inset
Mamou	E5
Mandeville	J6
Mansfield	B3
Mansura	E4
Many	C3
Marion	E1
Marksville	E4
Marrero	Inset, J7
Melder	D4
Melville	F5
Meraux	Inset
Metairie	Inset, J7
Mimosa Park	Inset
Minden	C1
Monroe	E1
Montegut	H8
Montz	Inset
Morgan City	G7
Moss Bluff	C6
Napoleonville	G7
Natalbany	J5
Natchitoches	C3
Newellton	G2
New Iberia	F6
New Llano	C4
New Orleans	Inset, J7
New Roads	G5
New Sarpy	Inset
Norco	Inset
Oakdale	D5
Oak Grove	G1
Oakville	Inset
Oberlin	D5
Oil City	B1
Olla	E3
Opelousas	E5
Paincourtville	G6
Paradis	Inset
Patterson	G7
Plaquemine	G6
Point a la Hache	K7
Ponchatoula	J6
Port Allen	G5
Port Barre	F5
Port Sulphur	K8
Poydras	Inset
Raceland	H7
Rayne	E6
Rayville	F2
Reserve	H6
Richwood	E2
Ringgold	C2
River Ridge	Inset
Ruston	D1
St. Bernard	Inset
St. Francisville	G5
St. Joseph	G3
St. Martinville	F6
St. Rose	Inset
Scarsdale	Inset
Schriever	H7
Scott	E6
Shreveport	B2
Simmesport	F5
Slidell	K6
Springhill	C1
Stonewall	B2
Sulphur	C6
Sunset	E6
Swartz	F1
Taft	Inset
Tallulah	G2
Terrytown	Inset
Thibodaux	H7
Toca	Inset
Vidalia	G3
Ville Platte	E5
Vinton	B6
Violet	Inset, K7
Vivian	B1
Waggaman	Inset
Walker	H6
Washington	E5
Welsh	D6
Westlake	C6
West Monroe	E1
Westwego	Inset, J7
White Castle	G6
Winnfield	D3
Winnsboro	F2
Zachary	G5
Zwolle	B3

Other Features

	Key
Atchafalaya, *bay*	G8
Atchafalaya, *river*	F5
Barataria, *bay*	K8
Bistineau, *lake*	C2
Black, *river*	F4
Borgne, *lake*	Inset, K6
Breton, *islands*	L8
Caddo, *lake*	A1
Caillou, *bay*	G8
Calcasieu, *lake*	C7
Caney, *lake*	E2
Catahoula, *lake*	E3
Chandeleur, *islands*	M7
Driskill, *mt.*	C2
Grand, *lake*	D7
Jean Lafitte N.H.P. and Preserve	J7
Little, *river*	D2
Marsh, *island*	F7
Mississippi, *river*	G3
Ouachita, *river*	E1
Pearl, *river*	K5
Pontchartrain, *lake*	Inset, J6
Red, *river*	C3
Sabine, *lake*	B7
Sabine, *river*	B5
Terrebonne, *bay*	H8
Timbalier, *bay*	J8
Toledo Bend, *reservoir*	B4
Vermilion, *bay*	F7
West Cote Blanche, *bay*	F7
White, *lake*	E7

Maine ....page 146

Cities and Towns

	Key
Alfred	B5
Amherst	D4
Athens	C4
Auburn	B4
Augusta, *capital*	C4
Bangor	D4
Bar Harbor	D4
Bass Harbor	D4
Bath	C4
Belfast	C4
Berwick	B5
Biddeford	B5
Boothbay Harbor	C4
Brewer	D4
Bridgton	B4
Brunswick	B4
Bucksport	D4
Calais	E3
Camden	C4
Cape Elizabeth	B5
Caribou	D2
Chisholm	B4
Clinton	C4
Conway	A4
Damariscotta	C4
Dexter	C3
Dixfield	B4
Dover-Foxcroft	C3
East Millinocket	D3
Eastport	F4
Ellsworth	D4
Fairfield	C4
Falmouth	B5
Farmington	B4
Fort Fairfield	E2
Fort Kent	D1
Frankfort	D4
Franklin	D4
Freeport	B5
Frenchboro	D4
Frenchville	D1
Fryeburg	B4
Gardiner	C4
Greene	B4
Hallowell	C4
Hampden	D4
Houlton	E2
Howland	D3
Kennebunk	B5
Kittery	B5
Lewiston	B4
Lincoln	D3
Lisbon Falls	B4
Livermore Falls	B4
Machias	E4
Madawaska	D1
Madison	C4
Mars Hill	E2
Mechanic Falls	B4
Mexico	B4
Milbridge	E4
Milford	D4
Millinocket	D3
Milo	D3
Norridgewock	C4
North Amity	E3
North Berwick	B5
North Conway	A4
North East Carry	C3
North Windham	B5
Norway	B4
Oakland	C4
Old Orchard Beach	B5
Old Town	D4
Orono	D4
Oxford	B4
Patten	D3
Portland	B5
Presque Isle	D2
Richmond	C4
Rockland	C4
Rumford	B4
Saco	B5
Sanford	B5
Skowhegan	C4
South Paris	B4
South Portland	B5
Springvale	B5
Thomaston	C4
Van Buren	E1
Waldoboro	C4
Waterville	C4
Westbrook	B5
Westfield	E2
Wilsons Mills	A4
Wilton	B4
Winslow	C4
Winthrop	C4
Wiscasset	C4
Woodland	E3
Yarmouth	B5
York	B5

Other Features

	Key
Acadia Natl. Park	D4
Androscoggin, *river*	B4
Appalachian, *mts.*	A3
Aroostook, *river*	D2
au Haut, *island*	D4
Aziscohos, *lake*	A3
Baskahegan, *lake*	E3
Baxter State Park	D2
Big, *lake*	E3
Casco, *bay*	C4
Chamberlain, *lake*	C2
Chesuncook, *lake*	C2
Churchill, *lake*	C2
Cross, *island*	E4
Deer, *island*	D4
Elizabeth, *cape*	B4
Flagstaff, *lake*	B3
Grand, *lake*	E3
Grand Matagamon, *lake*	D2
Grand Seboeis, *lake*	D2
Great Wass, *island*	E4
Islesboro, *island*	D4
Katahdin, *mt.*	D3
Kennebec, *river*	C3
Long, *island*	D4
Maine, *gulf*	C4
Matinicus, *island*	D4
Mattawamkeag, *river*	D2
Millinocket, *lake*	D3
Monhegan, *island*	C4
Moosehead, *lake*	C3
Mooselookmeguntic, *lake*	B4
Mt. Desert, *island*	D4
Munsungan, *lake*	D2
Nicatous, *lake*	D3
Pemadumcook, *lake*	C3
Penobscot, *bay*	D4
Penobscot, *river*	D3
Piscataquis, *river*	C3
Richardson, *lakes*	B4
Saco, *bay*	B5
Saco, *river*	B5
Saddleback, *mt.*	B4
St. Croix, *river*	E3
St. John, *river*	C2
Sebago, *lake*	B5
Sebec, *lake*	C3
Seboeis, *lake*	D3
Seboomook, *lake*	C3
Snow, *mt.*	B3
Sugarloaf, *mt.*	B3
Swans, *island*	D4
Telos, *lake*	C2
Umbagog, *lake*	A4
Vinalhaven, *island*	D4
West Grand, *lake*	E3
West Quoddy Head, *peninsula*	F4
White Cap, *mt.*	C3

Maryland ....page 147

Cities and Towns

	Key
Aberdeen	K2
Accident	A6
Accokeek	F5
Adelphi	C4
Annapolis, *capital*	J4
Arden-on-the-Severn	H3
Arnold	J3
Aspen Hill	B3, F3
Avenue	G7
Baltimore	H2
Bel Air	J1
Beltsville	C3, G3
Berlin	P6
Berwyn Heights	C4
Bethesda	B4, F4
Bladensburg	C4
Boonsboro	D1
Bowie	G4
Bowleys Quarters	J2
Braddock Heights	D2
Brandywine	G5
Brentwood	C4
Brunswick	D2
Bucktown	K6
Burtonsville	C3
Cabin John	A4
California	J6
Calverton	C3
Cambridge	K5
Cape St. Claire	J3
Camp Springs	C5
Carney	H2
Cascade	D1
Catonsville	H2
Centreville	K3
Chesapeake Beach	H5
Chesapeake Ranch Estates	J6
Chestertown	K3
Cheverly	C4
Chillum	C4, G4
Clinton	G4
Clover Hill	E2
Cloverly	C3
Cockeysville	H2
Colesville	C3
College Park	C4, G4
Columbia	G3
Contee	D3
Copenhaver	A3
Coral Hills	C5
Cresaptown	C6
Crisfield	L7
Crofton	H3
Crownsville	H3
Cumberland	D6
Damascus	F2
Deale	H4
Delmar	M6
Denton	L4
Derwood	A3
District Heights	D5
Dufief	A3
Dundalk	H2
Easton	K4
Edgemere	J3
Edgewood	J2
Eldersburg	G2
Elkridge	G3
Elkton	L1
Ellicott City	G2
Emmitsburg	E1
Essex	J2
Fair Hill	L1
Fallston	J1
Federalsburg	L5
Ferndale	H3
Forest Heights	B5, G4
Forestville	G4
Fountain Head	D1
Frederick	E2
Friendsville	A6
Frostburg	C6
Fruitland	M6
Gaithersburg	F3
Garrison	G2
Germantown	E3
Glen	A3
Glenarden	D4
Glen Burnie	H3
Glen Echo Heights	B4
Glen Hills	A3
Glenmont	B3
Golden Beach	H6
Grantsville	B6
Grasonville	K4
Green Haven	H3
Greenbelt	D4, G3
Greensboro	L4
Hagerstown	D1
Halfway	C1
Hampstead	G1
Hampton	H2
Hancock	B1
Havre de Grace	K1
Herald Harbor	H3
High Ridge	D3
Hillandale	C3
Hillcrest Heights	C5
Hillsmere Shores	J4
Hughesville	G5
Hunting Hill	A3
Hurlock	L5
Hyattstown	E2
Hyattsville	C4, G4
Indian Head	F5
Jarrettsville	J1
Jessup	G3
Joppatowne	J2
Kemptown	E2
Kensington	B3, F3
Kentland	D4, G4
Kettering	G4
Keysers Ridge	B6
Kingstown	K3
Kingsville	J2
Knollwood	C3
Lake Shore	J3
Landover	C4, G4
Langley Park	C4
Lanham	D4
Lansdowne	H3
LaPlata	G5
Largo	G4
Laurel	D3, G3
LaVale	C6
Lawsonia	L7
Layhill	B3
Leonardtown	H6
Lewisdale	C4
Lexington Park	J6
Linthicum	H3
Lochearn	H2
Londontown	H4
Lutherville	H2

	Key
Luxmanor	B3
Manchester	G1
Marlton	G4
Maydale	C3
Middle River	J2
Middletown	D2
Milford	G2
Montgomery Village	F3
Montpelier	D3
Mount Aetna	D1
Mountain Lake Park	A7
Mount Airy	F2
Mount Rainier	C4
Muirkirk	D3
New Carrollton	D4
Norbeck	B3
North Chevy Chase	B4
North East	L1
Oak Crest	D3
Oakland	A7
Oakland	G2
Oakview	C3
Ocean City	P6
Ocean Pines	P6
Odenton	H3
Olney	F3
Overlea	H2
Owings Mills	G2
Oxon Hill	C5
Palmer Park	D4
Parkville	H2
Parole	H4
Perry Hall	J2
Perryman	K2
Perryville	K1
Pikesville	H2
Pleasant Hills	J2
Pocomoke City	M7
Poolesville	E3
Potomac	A3, F3
Potomac Heights	F5
Preston	L5
Prince Frederick	H5
Princess Anne	M7
Randallstown	G2
Randolph Hills	B3
Redhouse	A7
Reisterstown	G2
Rising Sun	K1
Ritchie	D5
Riverdale	C4
Riviera Beach	H3
Rock Hall	K3
Rockville	A3, F3
Rosedale	H2
Rossmoor Leisure World	B3
Rossville	J2
St. Charles	G5
St. Michaels	K4
Salisbury	M6
Seabrook	D4
Seat Pleasant	D5
Severn	H3
Severna Park	H3
Shady Side	H4
Shawsville	H1
Silver Hill	C5
Silver Spring	B4, F4
Snow Hill	N7
South Gate	H3
Spencerville	C3
Stevensville	J3
Suitland	C5, G4
Sykesville	G2
Takoma Park	C4
Taneytown	F1
Temple Hills	C5, G4
Timmont	E1
Timonium	H2
Towson	H2
Upper Marlboro	H4
Waldorf	G5
Walker Mill	D5
Walkersville	E2
Westernport	B7
Westminster	F1
West Ocean City	P6
Wheaton	B3, F3
White Marsh	J2
White Oak	C3, G3
White Plains	G5
Wildwood Hills	A3
Williamsport	C1
Woodlawn	G2
Woodyard	G4

Other Features

	Key
Allegheny Front, mt. ridge	C7
Antietam Natl. Battlefield	D2
Appalachian Natl. Scenic Trail	D2
Assateague Island Natl. Seashore	P7
Assawoman, bay	P6
Backbone, mt.	A7
Chesapeake, bay	J5
Chesapeake and Ohio Canal N.H.P.	A4, D2
Chester, river	K3
Chincoteague, bay	N7
Choptank, river	K5
Deep Creek, lake	A6
Liberty, reservoir	G2
North Branch Potomac, river	C7
Nanticoke, river	L6
Patapsco, river	H3
Patuxent, river	H4
Potomac, river	G6
Susquehanna, river	J1
Wicomico, river	G6
Youghiogheny, river	A6

Massachusetts ....page 148

Cities and Towns

	Key
Abington	L4
Acton	A5, J3
Acushnet	L6
Adams	B2
Amesbury	L1
Amherst	D3
Andover	K2
Arlington	C6, K3
Ashby	J2
Ashfield	C2
Ashland	J3
Assinippi	F8
Assonet	K5
Athol	F2
Attleboro	J5
Auburn	G4
Avon	D8, K4

	Key
Ayer	H2
Baldwinville	F2
Barnstable	N6
Becket	B3
Bedford	B5, J3
Belchertown	E3
Bellingham	J4
Belmont	C6
Berkley	K5
Bernardston	D2
Beverly	F5, L2
Billerica	B5, J2
Blackstone	H4
Blandford	C4
Bliss Corner	L6
Bolton	H3
Bondsville	E4
Boston, capital	D6, K3
Boxford	L2
Braintree	E8, K4
Brewster	P5
Bridgewater	L5
Brimfield	F4
Brockton	K4
Brookfield	F4
Brookline	C7, K3
Burlington	C5, K2
Buzzards Bay	M5
Cambridge	D6, K3
Canton	C8, K4
Carlisle	B5
Cedarville	M5
Centerville	N6
Central Village	K6
Charlton	G4
Charlton City	G4
Chatham	Q6
Chelmsford	J2
Chelsea	D6
Cheshire	B2
Chester	C3
Chicopee	D4
Chilmark	M7
Clarksburg	B2
Clinton	H3
Cochituate	B7, J3
Cohasset	L4
Concord	B6, J3
Cotuit	N6
Dalton	B3
Danvers	E5, L2
Dartmouth	K6
Dedham	C7, K4
Dennis	P6
Douglas	H4
Dover	B8, J4
Dracut	J2
Duxbury	M4
East Brookfield	F4
East Dennis	P6
East Douglas	H4
East Falmouth	M6
East Freetown	L5
Eastham	Q5
Easthampton	D3
East Longmeadow	D4
East Orleans	Q5
East Pepperell	H2
East Wareham	M5
Edgartown	M7
Erving	E2
Essex	L2
Everett	D6
Fall River	K6
Falmouth	M6
Feeding Hills	D4
Fiskdale	F4
Fitchburg	G2
Florida	B2
Foxboro	K4
Framingham	A7, J3
Franklin	J4
Gardner	G2
Gay Head	L7
Georgetown	L2
Gloucester	M2
Granby	D3
Granville	C4
Great Barrington	A4
Greenfield	D2
Green Harbor	M4
Halifax	L5
Hamilton	L2
Hanover	L4
Hanson	L4
Haverhill	K1
Hingham	F8, L4
Holbrook	E8, K4
Holland	F4
Holliston	A8, J4
Holyoke	D4
Hopedale	H4
Hopkinton	H4
Hubbardston	G3
Hudson	H3
Hull	F7, L3
Huntington	C4
Hyannis	N6
Ipswich	L2
Kingston	M5
Lakeville	L5
Lawrence	K2
Lee	B3
Lenox	A3
Leominster	G2
Lexington	C6, K3
Lincoln	B6
Littleton	H2
Littleton Common	J2
Longmeadow	D4
Lowell	J2
Ludlow	E4
Lunenburg	H2
Lynn	E6, L3
Lynnfield	D5, K2
Madaket	P7
Malden	D6, K3
Manchester-by-the-Sea	L2
Mansfield	K4
Marblehead	F5, L3
Marion	L6
Marlborough	H3
Marshfield	M4
Marshfield Hills	M4
Mashpee	N6
Mattapoisett	L6
Maynard	H3
Medfield	B8, J4
Medford	D6, K3
Medway	A8
Melrose	D6, K3

	Key
Mendon	H4
Methuen	K2
Middleboro	L5
Milford	H4
Millis	H4
Milton	D7, K3
Monson	E4
Monterey	B4
Monument Beach	M6
Nahant	E6, L3
Nantucket	P7
Natick	B7, J3
Needham	C7, K3
New Ashford	B2
New Bedford	L6
New Boston	B4
Newburyport	L1
New Marlborough	B4
Newton	C7, K3
North Adams	B2
North Amherst	D3
Northampton	D3
North Andover	K2
North Attleboro	J5
Northborough	H3
Northbridge	H4
North Brookfield	F4
North Carver	L5
North Falmouth	M6
Northfield	E2
North Grafton	H4
North Pembroke	L4
North Plymouth	M5
North Reading	D5, K2
North Scituate	L4
North Sudbury	A6
North Tisbury	M7
Norton	K5
Norwell	L4
Norwood	C8, K4
Oakham	F3
Ocean Bluff	M4
Ocean Grove	K6
Orange	E2
Orleans	Q5
Osterville	N6
Otis	C4
Oxford	G4
Palmer	E4
Paxton	G3
Peabody	E5, L2
Pelham	E3
Pembroke	L4
Pepperell	H2
Petersham	F3
Phillipston	F2
Pinehurst	C5, K2
Pittsfield	B3
Plainville	C2
Plainville	J4
Plymouth	M5
Pocasset	M6
Provincetown	P4
Quincy	E7, K3
Randolph	D8, K4
Raynham	K5
Raynham Center	K5
Reading	D5, K2
Rehoboth	K5
Revere	E6, K3
Rochester	L6
Rockland	E8, L4
Rockport	M2
Rutland	G3
Sagamore	M5
Salem	F5, L2
Salisbury	L1
Sandwich	N5
Saugus	E6, K3
Savoy	B2
Scituate	L4
Sharon	C8, K4
Sheffield	A4
Shelburne Falls	D2
Sherborn	B8
Shirley	H2
Shrewsbury	H3
Shutesbury	E3
Somerset	K5
Somerville	D6, K3
South Amherst	D3
Southbridge	F4
South Carver	M5
South Deerfield	D3
South Dennis	P6
South Duxbury	M4
South Lancaster	H3
South Sudbury	A7
South Wellfleet	P5
South Yarmouth	P6
Spencer	G4
Springfield	D4
Sterling	G3
Stoneham	D5
Stoughton	D8, K4
Sturbridge	F4
Sudbury	A6, J3
Sutton	H4
Swampscott	E6, L3
Taunton	K5
Teaticket	M6
Templeton	G2
Tewksbury	K2
Three Rivers	E4
Tolland	B4
Topsfield	L2
Truro	P5
Turners Falls	D2
Tyngsborough	J2
Upton	H4
Uxbridge	H4
Vineyard Haven	M7
Wakefield	D5, K2
Wales	E4
Walpole	C8, J4
Waltham	C6, K3
Ware	E4
Wareham	M5
Warren	E4
Warwick	E2
Washington	B3
Watertown	C6
Wayland	B7
Webster	G4
Wellesley	B7, J3
West Barnstable	N6
Westborough	H3
West Boylston	G3
West Brookfield	F4
West Concord	J3

	Key
West Cummington	C3
West Falmouth	M6
Westfield	D4
Westford	J2
West Granville	C3
Westhampton	C3
West Medway	A8
Westminster	G2
Weston	B6, J3
Westport	K6
Westport Point	K6
West Springfield	D4
West Wareham	L5
Westwood	C8, K4
West Yarmouth	P6
Weymouth	E8, L4
Whately	D3
White Island Shores	M5
Whitinsville	H4
Whitman	L4
Wilbraham	E4
Williamstown	B2
Wilmington	C5, K2
Winchendon	F2
Winchester	C6
Windsor	B3
Winthrop	E6
Woburn	C5, K3
Worcester	G3
Worthington Center	C3
Wrentham	J4
Yarmouth Port	P6

Other Features

	Key
Adams Natl. Hist. Park	E8, L4
Ann, cape	M2
Berkshire, hills	B4
Boston, bay	E6
Boston Natl. Hist. Park	D6
Boston, harbor	E7
Buzzards, bay	M6
Cape Cod, bay	N5
Cape Cod, canal	M6
Cape Cod Natl. Seashore	P5
Charles, river	C7
Chicopee, river	D4
Cobble Mt., reservoir	C4
Cod, cape	P4
Connecticut, river	E2
Deer, island	E7
Elizabeth, islands	M7
Frederick Law Olmsted N.H.S.	C7
Georges, island	E7
Greylock, mt.	B2
Hingham, bay	A4
Housatonic, river	A4
J.F.K. Birthplace Natl. Hist. Site	D7
Long, island	E7
Longfellow Natl. Hist. Site	D6
Lowell Natl. Hist. Park	J2
Maine, gulf	M1
Martha's Vineyard, island	M7
Massachusetts, bay	F6, M3
Merrimack, river	K1
Minute Man Natl. Hist. Park	B6, J3
Monomoy, island	P5
Muskeget, channel	N7
Nantucket, island	P7
Neponset, river	C7
Otis, reservoir	B4
Peddocks, island	E7
Quabbin, reservoir	F3
Quincy, bay	E7
Salem Maritime N.H.S.	F5, L2
Saugus Iron Works N.H.S.	E6
Shawsheen, river	B6
Spectacle, island	E7
Swift, river	E4
Taconic, mts.	A2
Wachusett, reservoir	G3
Wachusett, river	G3
Walden, pond	B6

Michigan ....page 149

Cities and Towns

	Key
Adrian	E8
Albion	E7
Algonac	G7
Allegan	D7
Allendale	C7
Allen Park	A7
Alma	E6
Alpena	F4
Ann Arbor	F7
Atlanta	E5
Bad Axe	G6
Baldwin	D6
Battle Creek	D7
Bay City	F6
Belding	D6
Bellaire	D5
Belleville	F7
Benton Harbor	C7
Berkley	A6
Bessemer	C2
Beulah	C5
Big Rapids	D6
Birmingham	A6
Blissfield	F8
Bloomfield Hills	A6
Boyne City	D4
Bridgeport	F6
Brighton	F7
Buchanan	C8
Burton	F6
Cadillac	D5
Carleton	F7
Caro	F6
Carrollton	F6
Cassopolis	C8
Cedar Springs	D6
Center Line	B6
Centreville	D8
Charlevoix	D4
Charlotte	E7
Chesaning	E6
Chelsea	E7
Cheboygan	E4
Chesterfield	B6
Christmas	C3
Clare	E6
Clawson	B6
Clio	F6
Coldwater	D8
Connorville	C3
Coopersville	D6
Crystal Falls	A3
Cutlerville	D7
Davison	F6

	Key
Dearborn	A7, F7
Dearborn Hts.	A7
Detroit	B7, F7
De Witt	E7
Dowagiac	C8
Dundee	F8
Durand	F7
Eagle River	A2
East Lansing	E7
Eastpointe	B6
East Tawas	F5
Eaton Rapids	E7
Ecorse	B7
Escanaba	B4
Essexville	F6
Farmington	A6
Farmington Hills	A6
Fenton	F7
Ferndale	B6
Ferrysburg	C6
Flat Rock	F7
Flint	F6
Flushing	F6
Fowlerville	E7
Frankenmuth	F6
Franklin	A6
Fraser	B6
Fremont	D6
Garden City	A7
Gaylord	E4
Gladstone	B4
Gladwin	E6
Grand Blanc	F7
Grand Haven	C6
Grand Ledge	E7
Grand Rapids	D7
Grayling	E5
Greenville	D6
Grosse Pointe	B7
Grosse Pointe Farms	B6
Grosse Pointe Park	B7
Grosse Pointe Shores	B6
Grosse Pointe Woods	B6
Hamtramck	B7
Hancock	A2
Harper Woods	B6
Harrison	E6
Harrisville	F5
Hart	C6
Hastings	D7
Hazel Park	B6
Highland Park	B7
Hillsdale	E8
Holland	C7
Holly	F7
Holt	E7
Houghton	A2
Houghton Lake	E5
Howell	F7
Hudson	E8
Hudsonville	D7
Huntington Woods	A6
Huron Heights	A6
Imlay City	F6
Inkster	A7
Ionia	D7
Iron Mountain	A4
Ironwood	C2
Ishpeming	B3
Ithaca	E6
Jackson	E7
Jenison	D7
Kalamazoo	D7
Kalkaska	D5
Keego Harbor	A6
Kentwood	D7
Kingsford	A4
Lake City	D5
Lake Orion	F7
Lambertville	F8
L'Anse	A3
Lansing, capital	E7
Lapeer	F6
Lincoln Park	A7, F7
Livonia	A7, F7
Lowell	D7
Ludington	C6
Madison Hts.	B6
Manistee	C5
Manistique	C4
Marenisco	D2
Marine City	G7
Marquette	B3
Marshall	E7
Marysville	G7
Mason	E7
Melvindale	A7
Menominee	B4
Merriweather	D2
Michigan Center	E7
Midland	E6
Milan	F7
Milford	F7
Mio	E5
Monroe	F8
Mount Clemens	B6
Mount Morris	F6
Mount Pleasant	E6
Munising	C3
Muskegon	C6
Muskegon Hts.	C6
Negaunee	B3
New Baltimore	G7
Newberry	D3
Niles	C8
North Muskegon	C6
Norton Shores	C6
Norway	B4
Oak Park	A6
Okemos	E7
Ontonagon	D1
Orchard Lake	A6
Otsego	D7
Owosso	E6
Oxford	F7
Paw Paw	C7
Paw Paw Lake	C7
Petoskey	E4
Plainwell	D7
Pontiac	A6, F7
Portage	D7
Port Huron	G7
Portland	E7
Rapid River	C4
Reed City	D6
Richmond	G7
River Rouge	B7
Rockford	D6
Rockwood	A6
Rogers City	F4

	Key
Romeo	F7
Romulus	A7
Roscommon	E5
Royal Oak	B6
Saginaw	F6
St. Clair	G7
St. Clair Shores	B6
St. Ignace	E4
St. Johns	E7
St. Joseph	C7
St. Louis	E6
Saline	F7
Sandusky	G6
Sault Ste. Marie	E3
Shields	F6
Silver City	D1
Skidway Lake	F5
Southfield	A6
Southgate	A7
South Haven	C7
South Lyon	F7
Sparta	D6
Spring Lake	C6
Standish	F5
Stanton	D6
Sterling Heights	B6
Sturgis	D8
Sylvan Lake	A6
Tawas City	F5
Taylor	A7
Tecumseh	F7
Temperance	F8
Three Rivers	D8
Traverse City	D5
Troy	B6
Union Lake	A6
Utica	B6
Vassar	F6
Wakefield	C2
Waldenburg	B6
Walker	D7
Warren	B6
Wayland	D7
Wayne	A7
West Acres	A6
West Branch	E5
Westland	A7
White Cloud	D6
Whitehall	C6
White Pine	D1
Whitmore Lake	F7
Williamston	E7
Wixom	F7
Wolf Lake	C6
Wyandotte	B7
Wyoming	D7
Ypsilanti	F7
Zeeland	C7

Other Features

	Key
Arvon, mt.	A3
Au Sable, river	E5
Beaver, island	D4
Big Bay De Noc, bay	B4
Big Sable, point	C5
Bois Blanc, island	E4
Cass, river	F6
Chambers, island	B4
Detroit, river	B7
Drummond, island	F3
Erie, lake	F8
Escanaba, river	B4
Glen, lake	D4
Gogebic, lake	C2
Government Peak, mt.	D1
Grand, island	C3
Grand Traverse, bay	D4
Green, bay	B4
Hamlin, lake	C5
Hammond, bay	E4
Higgins, lake	E5
High, island	D4
Hog, island	E4
Houghton, lake	E5
Hubbard, lake	F5
Huron, bay	A3
Huron, lake	G5
Huron, mts.	B3
Indian, lake	C4
Isle Royale, island	D2
Isle Royale Natl. Park	D1
Keweenaw, bay	A3
Keweenaw, peninsula	A2
Keweenaw, point	A2
Lookout, point	A7
Manistee, river	D5
Manitou, island	A2
Menominee, river	B4
Michigamme, reservoir	A3
Michigan, lake	C5
North Manitou, island	D4
Paint, river	A3
Pictured Rocks Natl. Lakeshore	C3
Porcupine, mts.	D1
Saginaw, bay	F6
St. Clair, lake	B6
St. Martin, island	B4
Sleeping Bear Dunes Natl. Lakeshore	C5
South Fox, island	D4
South Manitou, island	C5
Straits of Mackinac	E4
Sturgeon, bay	B4
Superior, lake	B2
Thunder, bay	F4
Whitefish, bay	D3
Wixom, lake	E6

Minnesota ....page 1

Cities and Towns

	Key
Ada	
Aitkin	
Albany	
Albert Lea	
Albertville	
Alexandria	
Annandale	
Anoka	
Appleton	
Arlington	
Aurora	
Austin	
Babbitt	
Bagley	
Barnesville	
Baudette	
Baxter	
Bayport	

MINNESOTA–MONTANA 185

Key
Plaine D6
dji C3
on B5
ake D5
sland C6
ning Prairie D7
nington D6
Earth C7
erd C4
enridge A4
klyn Center E5
o D5
sville D6
donia F7
bridge D5
y A6
on Falls E6
on E4
er City E5
hassen D6
ka D6
ield E7
iolm E3
City B6
s Grove D7
water C5
uet E4
to C5
Spring C5
mbia Hts F5
Rapids D5
oran D5
kston A3
oy D4
son A6
oit Lakes B4
orth A4
ge Center E6
th E4
n F6
Lake D6
Bethel D5
Grand Forks A3
a D6
v Lake B5
iver D5
F3
sville B4
th E3
a E7
mont C7
n Heights F5
ault D6
ington D6
us Falls A4
/ D5
st Lake E5
on B3
ey F5
ord C6
coe C6
wood B5
en Valley E5
dview F6
d Forks A3
d Marais F5
d Portage F4
d Rapids D3
ite Falls B6
ck A2
ings E6
ley A4
ield E7
nantown E4
ing E3
ah F7
kins E5
and F4
ard Lake C5
chinson C6
national Falls D2
hoe A6
son B7
sville D6
an D6
on E6
yon E6
rescent F7
Crystal C6
field B7
ville D6
enter D6
ueur D6
iston F7
nfield C5
Canada F5
Falls C5
g Prairie C5
sdale D6
en E5
erne A7
ntosh B3
delia C6
dison A6
nomen B3
kato D6
torville E6
le Grove D5
le Lake D6
pleton D7
plewood E5
shall B6
rose C5
dota F6
ca D5
neapolis E6
neota B6
ntevideo B6
ntgomery E6
nticello D5
orhead A4
a D5
rris B5
und D6
untain Iron E3
untain Lake C7
v Hope E5
vport F6
v Prague D6
v Ulm C6
wa C4
th Branch E5
thfield E6
th Mankato C6
th Oaks F5
ia E6
no D6
noco E6
onville A5
kis B5
atonna D6

Key
Park Rapids B4
Paynesville C5
Pelican Rapids A4
Perham B4
Pigeon River F4
Pine City E5
Pine Island E6
Pipestone A7
Plainview E6
Plymouth D5
Preston E7
Princeton D5
Prinsburg B6
Prior Lake D6
Proctor E4
Ramsey D5
Red Lake Falls A3
Red Wing E6
Redwood Falls B6
Renville B6
Richfield F6
Robbinsdale E5
Rochester E6
Roseau B2
Rushford F7
St. Anthony F5
St. Charles E7
St. Cloud C5
St. Francis D5
St. James C7
St. Joseph C5
St. Louis Park E5
St. Michael D5
St. Paul, *capital* D6
St. Peter D6
Sandstone E4
Sartell C5
Sauk Centre C5
Sauk Rapids C5
Shakopee D6
Silver Bay F3
Slayton B7
Sleepy Eye C6
South St. Paul F5
Spring Valley E7
Springfield C6
Staples C4
Stewartville E7
Stillwater E5
Thief River Falls A2
Tracy B6
Truman C7
Two Harbors F3
Tyler A6
Virginia E3
Wabasha E6
Wadena B4
Waite Park C5
Walker C3
Warren A2
Warroad B2
Waseca D6
Waterville D6
Wells D7
Wheaton A5
White Bear Lake F5
Willmar B5
Windom B7
Winnebago C7
Winona F6
Winsted C6
Winthrop C6
Worthington B7
Wyoming E5
Young America D6
Zimmerman D5
Zumbrota E6

Other Features

Big Fork, *river* D2
Brule, *lake* E4
Buffalo, *river* A4
Chippewa, *river* B5
Clearwater, *river* B3
Cloquet, *river* F3
Des Moines, *river* B6
Eagle, *mt.* F4
Grand Portage Natl. Monument F4
Gull, *lake* C4
Lake of the Woods, *lake* C1
Leech, *lake* C3
Little Fork, *river* D2
Lower Red, *lake* B3
Lower Whitefish, *lake* C4
Mall of America F6
Mesabi, *range* D3
Mille Lacs, *lake* D4
Minnesota, *river* B6
Mississippi, *river* D5
Mud, *lake* B2
Namakan, *lake* E2
Pipestone Natl. Monument A6
Pokegama, *lake* D3
Rainy, *river* C2
Red River of the North, *river* A3
Root, *river* E7
Rum, *river* D5
St. Croix, *river* E5
St. Louis, *river* E3
Superior, *lake* F3
Upper Red, *lake* C2
Vermilion, *range* F3
Voyageurs Natl. Park E2
Winnibigoshish, *lake* D3

Mississippi ....page 151

Cities and Towns

Aberdeen D2
Ackerman C2
Alligator B1
Amory D2
Ashland C1
Baldwyn D1
Bassfield C4
Batesville C1
Bay St. Louis C5
Bay Springs C4
Beauregard B4
Belmont D1
Belzoni B2
Biloxi D5
Blue Springs D1
Booneville D1
Brandon C3
Braxton C3
Brookhaven B4
Bruce C2
Calhoun City C2
Canton B3

Key
Carrollton C2
Carthage C3
Centreville B4
Charleston B1
Clarksdale B1
Cleveland B2
Clinton B3
Coahoma B1
Coffeeville C2
Coldwater C1
Collins C4
Collinsville D3
Columbia C4
Columbus D2
Como C1
Corinth D1
Crystal Springs B4
Decatur C3
De Kalb D3
Diamondhead C5
D'Iberville D5
Doddsville B2
Drew B2
Durant C2
Eden B3
Edwards B3
Ellisville C4
Eupora C2
Falcon B1
Falkner D1
Fayette A4
Flora B3
Florence B3
Forest C3
Friars Point B1
Fulton D1
Gautier D5
Glendora B2
Gloster A4
Golden D1
Goodman C3
Greenville A2
Greenwood B2
Grenada C2
Gulfport C5
Hattiesburg C4
Hazlehurst B4
Hernando C1
Hollandale B2
Holly Springs C1
Horn Lake B1
Houston D2
Indianola B2
Itta Bena B2
Iuka D1
Jackson, *capital* B3
Jonestown B1
Kiln C5
Kosciusko C2
Kossuth D1
Laurel C4
Leakesville D4
Learned B3
Leland B2
Lena C3
Lexington B2
Liberty B4
Long Beach C5
Louisville C2
Lucedale D5
Lula B1
Lumberton C4
Lyman C5
McComb B4
McCool C2
Macon D2
Madison B3
Magee C4
Magnolia B4
Mantee C2
Marion D3
Marks B1
Mayersville A3
Meadville B4
Mendenhall C4
Meridian D3
Monticello B4
Montrose C3
Moorhead B2
Morton C3
Moss Point D5
Mound Bayou B2
Natchez A4
Nettleton D1
New Albany D1
New Augusta C4
Newton C3
Ocean Springs D5
Okolona D1
Olive Branch C1
Oxford C1
Paden D1
Pascagoula D5
Pass Christian C5
Paulding C3
Pearl B3
Pearlington C5
Pelahatchie C3
Petal C4
Philadelphia C3
Picayune C5
Pickens C3
Pittsboro C2
Polkville C3
Pontotoc D1
Pope C1
Poplarville C5
Port Gibson B4
Prentiss C4
Purvis C4
Quitman D3
Raleigh C3
Raymond B3
Richland B3
Ridgeland B3
Ripley D1
Rolling Fork B3
Rosedale A2
Ruleville B2
Sallis C2
Saltillo D1
Sardis C1
Satartia B3
Seminary C4
Senatobia C1
Shannon D1
Shaw B2
Shelby B2
Shubuta D4
Silver Creek B4
Slate Spring C2

Key
Southaven B1
Starkville D2
Summit B4
Sumner B2
Sylvarena C3
Taylorsville C4
Tchula B2
Tillatoba C2
Toccopola C1
Tunica B1
Tupelo D1
Tutwiler B1
Tylertown B4
Union C3
Vaiden C2
Vancleave D5
Verona D1
Vicksburg B3
Walthall C2
Water Valley C1
Waveland C5
Waynesboro D4
Wesson B4
West C2
West Point D2
Wiggins C3
Winona C2
Woodland C2
Woodville A4
Yazoo City B3

Other Features

Arkabatula, *lake* B1
Big Black, *river* B3
Big Springs, *lake* D1
Big Sunflower, *river* B2
Bogue Chitto, *river* B4
Buttahatchee, *river* D2
Cat, *island* C5
Chickasawhay, *river* D4
Coldwater, *river* B1
Columbus, *lake* D2
Enid, *lake* C1
Grenada, *lake* C2
Gulf Island Natl. Seashore D5
Homochitto, *river* A4
Horn, *island* D5
Leaf, *river* C4
Mississippi, *river* B1
Mississippi, *sound* D5
Natchez Natl. Hist. Park A4
Noxubee, *river* D2
Okatibbee, *lake* D3
Pascagoula, *river* D5
Pearl, *river* C3
Petit Bois, *island* D5
Pickwick, *lake* D1
Pontotoc, *mt. ridge* D1
Ross Barnett, *reservoir* C3
Sardis, *lake* C1
Ship, *island* D5
Tallahatchie, *river* B1
Tombigbee, *river* D1
Tupelo Natl. Battlefield D1
Vicksburg Natl. Mil. Park B3
Woodall, *mt* D1
Yazoo, *river* B2

Missouri ....page 152

Cities and Towns

Adrian B3
Affton H3
Albany B1
Alton E5
Anderson B5
Appleton City B3
Ashland D3
Atherton J4
Aurora C5
Ava D5
Barnett D3
Belton B3
Benton G4
Bernie G5
Bethany B1
Birmingham J4
Bloomfield G5
Blue Springs J4
Bolivar C4
Bonne Terre F4
Boonville D3
Bowling Green E2
Branson C5
Brentwood H2
Bridgeton H2
Brookfield C2
Buckner J4
Buffalo C4
Butler B3
Cabool D4
California D3
Calverton Park H2
Camdenton D4
Cameron B2
Campbell F5
Canton E1
Cape Girardeau G4
Carrollton C2
Carthage B4
Caruthersville G5
Cassville C5
Cedar Hill F3
Centerville F4
Centralia D2
Chaffee G4
Charleston G5
Chesterfield F3
Chillicothe C2
Claycomo J4
Clayton F3, H2
Clinton C3
Columbia D3
Concord H3
Concordia C3
Crestwood H3
Creve Coeur H2
Cuba E3
Dellwood H2
Desloge F4
De Soto F3
Des Peres G2
Dexter G5
Dixon D3
Doniphan F5
East Prairie G5
Edina D1
Eldon D3
El Dorado Springs B4
Elsberry F2

Key
Eminence E4
Eureka F3
Excelsior Springs B2, J3
Farley H3
Farmington F4
Fayette D2
Fenton G3
Ferguson H2
Festus F3
Florissant H2
Forsyth C5
Fredericktown F4
Fulton E3
Gainesville D5
Galena C5
Gallatin C2
Gladstone B2, J3
Glasgow D2
Glasgow Village H2
Glendale H3
Grain Valley J4
Granby B5
Grandview J4
Grant City B1
Greenfield C4
Greenville F4
Hamilton C2
Hannibal E2
Harrisonville B3
Hartville D4
Hayti G5
Hazelwood H2
Hermann E3
Hermitage C4
Higginsville C2
Hillsboro F3
Holden C3
Hollister C5
Houston E4
Huntsville D2
Independence B2, J4
Ironton F4
Jackson G4
Jefferson City, *capital* D3
Jennings H2
Joplin B4
Kahoka E1
Kansas City B2, H4
Kennett F5
Keytesville D2
Kingston B2
Kinloch H2
Kirksville D1
Kirkwood H3
Knob Noster C3
Ladue H2
Lake Lotawana J4
Lake St. Louis F3
Lamar B4
Lancaster D1
La Plata D1
Lathrop B2
Lawson B2
Lebanon D4
Lee's Summit B3, J4
Lemay H3
Lexington C2
Liberty B2, J3
Licking E4
Lilbourn G5
Linn Creek D3
Linneus C2
Louisiana E2
Mackenzie H3
Macon D2
Malden G5
Manchester G3
Mansfield D4
Maplewood H3
Marble Hill G4
Marceline D2
Marionville C5
Marshall C2
Marshfield D4
Maryland Heights H2
Maryville B1
Mattese H3
Maysville B2
Mehlville H3
Memphis D1
Mexico E2
Milan C1
Millard D1
Moberly D2
Monett C5
Monroe City E2
Montgomery City E3
Monticello E1
Mosby J3
Mound City A1
Mountain Grove D4
Mountain View E4
Mt. Vernon C4
Murphy G3
Neosho B5
Nevada B4
New Haven E3
New London E2
New Madrid G5
Nixa C4
North Kansas City H4
Northwoods H2
Oaks J4
O'Fallon F3
Olivette H2
Oregon A2
Osage Beach D3
Osceola C3
Overland H2
Owensville E3
Ozark C4
Pacific F3
Pagedale H2
Palmyra E2
Paris D2
Park Hills F4
Parkville H4
Peculiar B3
Peerless Park G3
Perryville G4
Pevely F3
Piedmont F4
Pierce City C5
Pine Lawn H2
Pineville B5
Platte City B2, H3
Plattsburg B2
Pleasant Hill B3
Poplar Bluff F5
Portageville G5
Potosi F4

Key
Princeton C1
Randolph J4
Raymore B3
Raytown J4
Republic C4
Rich Hill B3
Richland D4
Richmond C2
Richmond Heights H2
Riverside H4
Rock Hill H2
Rock Port A1
Rolla E4
St. Ann H2
St. Charles F3, G2
St. Clair F3
Ste. Genevieve F4
St. James E3
St. John H2
St. Joseph B2
St. Louis F3, H2
St. Peters F3
St. Robert D4
Salem E4
Salisbury D2
Sappington H3
Sarcoxie B4
Savannah B2
Scott City G4
Sedalia C3
Senath F5
Seymour D4
Shelbina D2
Shelbyville D2
Shirley F4
Sikeston G5
Slater C2
Smithville B2
Springfield C4
Stanberry B1
Steele G5
Steelville E4
Stockton C4
Stoutsville E2
Sugar Creek J4
Sullivan E3
Sweet Springs C3
Tarkio A1
Thayer E5
Town and Country G2
Trenton C1
Troy F3
Tuscumbia D3
Union F3
Unionville C1
Unity Village J4
University City H2
Van Buren E5
Vandalia E2
Versailles D3
Vienna E3
Villa Ridge F3
Waldron H3
Warrensburg C3
Warrenton E3
Warsaw C3
Washington E3
Watson A1
Waynesville D4
Weatherby Lake H3
Webb City B4
Webster Groves H3
Wellsville E2
Wentzville F3
West Plains E5
Weston B2
Willard C4
Willow Springs E4
Windsor C3

Other Features

Bull Shoals, *lake* D5
Eleven Point, *river* E5
Fox, *river* E1
G.W. Carver Natl. Monument B5
Grand, *river* B1
Harry S. Truman, *reservoir* C3
Lake of the Ozarks, *lake* D3
Mark Twain, *lake* E2
Meramec, *river* E4
Mississippi, *river* G4
Missouri, *river* C2
Osage, *river* B4, D3
Ozark Natl. Scenic Riverways E4
Platte, *river* B2
St. Francis, *river* F4
Stockton, *lake* C4
Table Rock, *lake* C5
Taum Sauk, *mt.* F4
Thomas Hill, *reservoir* D2
Weldon, *river* C2

Montana..................page 153

Cities and Towns

Anaconda D3
Baker M3
Belgrade E4
Big Timber F4
Billings H4
Boulder D3
Bozeman E4
Bridger H4
Broadus L4
Butte D3
Chester F1
Chinook G1
Choteau D2
Circle L2
Columbus G4
Conrad E1
Crow Agency J4
Cut Bank D1
Deer Lodge D3
Dell D5
Dillon D4
East Helena E3
Ekalaka M4
Evergreen B1
Forsyth K3
Fort Benton F2
Gardiner F4
Glasgow K1
Glendive M2
Great Falls E2
Hamilton B3
Hardin J4
Harlowton G3
Hathaway K3
Havre G1

186 MONTANA–NEW JERSEY

Key

- Helena, *capital* … D3
- Kalispell … B1
- Lame Deer … K4
- Laurel … H4
- Lewistown … G2
- Libby … A1
- Lincoln … D3
- Livingston … F4
- Lolo Hot Springs … B3
- Malta … J1
- Miles City … L3
- Missoula … C3
- Orchard Homes … B3
- Philipsburg … C3
- Plentywood … M1
- Polson … B2
- Pony … E4
- Red Lodge … G4
- Ronan … B2
- Roundup … H3
- Rudyard … F1
- St. Regis … A2
- Scobey … L1
- Shelby … E1
- Sidney … M2
- Somers … B1
- Stanford … F2
- Superior … B2
- Terry … L3
- Thompson Falls … A2
- Townsend … E3
- West Yellowstone … E5
- Whitefish … B1
- Wibaux … M3
- Wolf Point … L1

Other Features

- Bighorn, *river* … J4
- Bighorn Canyon Natl. Rec. Area … H4
- Bitterroot, *river* … B3
- Bull, *mts.* … H3
- Canyon Ferry *lake* … E3
- Clark Fork, *river* … D3
- Cleveland, *mt.* … C1
- Custer Battlefield Natl. Monument … J4
- Elwell, *lake* … E1
- Flathead, *lake* … B2
- Flathead *river* … B1
- Fort Peck, *lake* … K2
- Fresno, *reservoir* … F1
- Glacier Natl. Park … C1
- Granite Peak, *mt.* … D4
- Granite Peak, *mt.* … G4
- Grant-Kohrs Ranch N.H.S. … D3
- Homer Youngs Peak, *mt.* … C4
- Hungry Horse, *reservoir* … C1
- Koocanusa, *lake* … A1
- Kootenai, *river* … A1
- Little Missouri, *river* … M5
- Madison, *river* … E4
- Marias, *river* … E1
- Middle Fork, *river* … C1
- Milk, *river* … D1
- Missouri, *river* … G2
- Musselshell, *river* … H3
- Northwest Peak, *mt.* … A1
- Powder, *river* … L3
- Rocky, *mts.* … C2
- St. Mary, *river* … C1
- St. Regis, *river* … B2
- Scarface Peak, *mt.* … C2
- South Fork, *river* … C2
- Swan, *river* … C2
- Teton, *river* … E2
- Tongue, *river* … K4
- Warren Peak, *mt.* … C4
- Yellowstone, *river* … L3
- Yellowstone Natl. Park … F5

Nebraska … page 154

Cities and Towns

- Ainsworth … E2
- Albion … G3
- Alliance … B2
- Alma … E4
- Ashland … H3
- Atkinson … F2
- Auburn … J4
- Aurora … F4
- Bartlett … F3
- Bassett … E2
- Beatrice … H4
- Beaver City … E4
- Bellevue … J3
- Benkelman … C4
- Blair … H3
- Brewster … E3
- Bridgeport … A3
- Broken Bow … E3
- Burwell … E3
- Butte … F2
- Center … G2
- Central City … F3
- Chadron … B2
- Chapman … F3
- Chappell … B3
- Clay Center … F4
- Columbus … G3
- Cozad … E4
- Crete … H4
- Dakota City … H2
- David City … G3
- Elkhorn … H3
- Elwood … E4
- Exeter … G4
- Fairbury … G4
- Falls City … J4
- Franklin … F4
- Fremont … H3
- Fullerton … G3
- Geneva … G4
- Gering … A3
- Gibbon … F4
- Gordon … B2
- Gothenburg … D4
- Grand Island … F4
- Grant … C4
- Greeley … F3
- Gretna … H3
- Guide Rock … F4
- Harrisburg … A3
- Harrison … A2
- Hartington … G2
- Hastings … F4
- Hayes Center … C4
- Hebron … G4
- Holdrege … E4
- Hyannis … C3
- Imperial … C4
- Kearney … F4
- Kimball … A3
- La Vista … A3
- Leigh … G3
- Lexington … E4
- Lincoln, *capital* … H4
- Loomis … E4
- Loup City … F3
- McCook … D4
- Madison … G3
- Milford … G4
- Minden … F4
- Mitchell … A3
- Mullen … C2
- Nebraska City … J4
- Neligh … F2
- Nelson … F4
- Norfolk … G2
- North Platte … D3
- Oakland … H3
- Ogallala … C3
- Omaha … J3
- O'Neill … F2
- Ord … F3
- Osceola … G3
- Oshkosh … B3
- Papillion … H3
- Pawnee City … H4
- Paxton … C3
- Pender … H2
- Pierce … G2
- Plainview … G2
- Plattsmouth … J3
- Plymouth … H4
- Ponca … H2
- Prague … H3
- Ravenna … F3
- Red Cloud … F4
- Rushville … B2
- St. Paul … F3
- Schuyler … G3
- Scottsbluff … A3
- Seward … G4
- Sidney … B3
- South Sioux City … H2
- Springfield … H3
- Springview … E2
- Stanton … G3
- Stapleton … D3
- Stockville … D4
- Superior … F4
- Sutton … G4
- Syracuse … H4
- Taylor … E3
- Tecumseh … H4
- Tekamah … H3
- Thedford … D3
- Trenton … C4
- Tryon … D3
- Valentine … D2
- Valley … H3
- Wahoo … H3
- Waverly … H4
- Wayne … G2
- West Point … H3
- Wilber … H4
- Wisner … H3
- Wymore … H4
- York … G4

Other Features

- Agate Fossil Beds N.M. … A2
- Arikee, *river* … B5
- Big Blue, *river* … G3
- C.W. McConaughy, *lake* … C3
- Calamus, *reservoir* … E3
- Calamus, *river* … E2
- Cedar, *river* … F3
- Chimney Rock Natl. Hist. Site … A3
- Elkhorn, *river* … E2, G3
- Harlan Co., *lake* … E4
- Homestead Natl. Monument … H4
- Lewis and Clark, *lake* … G2
- Little Blue, *river* … G4
- Loup, *river* … F3
- Middle Loup, *river* … D3
- Missouri, *river* … J4
- Niobrara, *river* … B2, E2
- North Loup, *river* … C2, E3
- North Platte, *river* … B3
- Pine, *mt. ridge* … B2
- Platte, *river* … D4, G3
- Republican, *river* … D4
- Sand, *hills* … C3
- Scotts Bluff Natl. Monument … A3
- South Fork Republican, *river* … B5
- South Loup, *river* … E3

Nevada … page 155

Cities and Towns

- Alamo … C3
- Battle Mountain … B1
- Beatty … B3
- Boulder City … C4
- Carlin … B1
- Carson City, *capital* … A2
- Elko … C1
- Ely … C2
- Eureka … C2
- Fallon … A2
- Fernley … A2
- Gardnerville … A2
- Goldfield … B3
- Hawthorne … A2
- Henderson … C3
- Incline Village … A2
- Las Vegas … C3
- Laughlin … C4
- Lovelock … A1
- McGill … C2
- Mesquite … C3
- Minden … A2
- North Fork … C1
- North Las Vegas … C3
- Pahrump … C3
- Paradise … C3
- Pioche … C3
- Reno … A2
- Silver Peak … B3
- Sparks … A2
- Spring Creek … C1
- Spring Valley … C3
- Sun Valley … A2
- Tonopah … B2
- Virginia City … A2
- Wells … C1
- West Wendover … C1
- Winnemucca … B1
- Yerington … A2
- Zephyr Cove … A2

Other Features

- Arc Dome, *mt.* … B2
- Black Rock, *desert* … A1
- Boundary Peak, *mt.* … A3
- Colorado, *river* … C4
- Desert, *valley* … A1
- Egan, *range* … C2
- Goshute, *lake* … C1
- Grant, *mts.* … C2
- Grant, *mt.* … A2
- Great Basin … B2
- Great Basin Natl. Park … C2
- Hoover Dam … C3
- Hot Creek, *range* … B2
- Independence, *mts.* … C1
- Jefferson, *mt.* … B2
- Lake Mead Natl. Rec. Area … C3
- Marys, *river* … C1
- Matterhorn, *mt.* … C1
- Mead, *lake* … C3
- Mohave, *lake* … C4
- Monitor, *range* … B2
- Moriah, *mt.* … C2
- North Toiyabe Peak, *mt.* … B2
- Owyhee, *desert* … B1
- Owyhee, *river* … B1
- Pilot Peak, *mt.* … C1
- Pyramid, *lake* … A1
- Quinn, *river* … B1
- Ruby, *mts.* … C1
- Ruby Dome, *mt.* … C1
- Rye Patch, *reservoir* … A1
- Schell Creek, *range* … C2
- Shoshone, *mts.* … B2
- Shoshone, *range* … B1
- Smoky, *valley* … B2
- Snake, *range* … C2
- Summit, *mt.* … B2
- Tahoe, *lake* … A2
- Tobin, *mt.* … B1
- Toiyabe, *range* … B2
- Toquima, *range* … B2
- Tuscarora, *mts.* … B1
- Virgin, *river* … C3
- Walker, *lake* … A2
- Wheeler Peak, *mt.* … C2
- White, *river* … C3

New Hampshire … page 156

Cities and Towns

- Albany … B3
- Amherst … B4
- Antrim … B3
- Barnstead … B3
- Bartlett … B2
- Benton … B2
- Berlin … B2
- Blair … B3
- Bradford … B3
- Bretton Woods … B2
- Bristol … B3
- Candia … B3
- Cascade … B2
- Claremont … A3
- Concord, *capital* … B3
- Contoocook … B3
- Conway … B3
- Cornish City … A3
- Dalton … B2
- Deerfield … B3
- Deering … B3
- Derry … B4
- Dixville Notch … B2
- Dover … C3
- Dunbarton Center … B3
- Durham … C3
- Easton … B2
- Enfield … A3
- Epping … B3
- Exeter … C4
- Farmington … B3
- Franklin … B3
- Gilmanton … B3
- Glencliff … B3
- Gorham … B2
- Groveton … B2
- Hampstead … B4
- Hampton … C4
- Hanover … A3
- Haverhill … A2
- Henniker … B3
- Hillsboro … B3
- Hinsdale … A4
- Hollis … B4
- Hooksett … B3
- Hudson … B4
- Jackson … B2
- Jaffrey … A4
- Jefferson … B2
- Keene … A4
- Laconia … B3
- Lancaster … B2
- Lebanon … A3
- Littleton … B2
- Loudon … B3
- Lyman … B2
- Manchester … B4
- Meredith … B3
- Merrimack … B4
- Milan … B2
- Milford … B4
- Monroe … A2
- Munsonville … A3
- Nashua … B4
- Newbury … A3
- New Castle … C3
- New London … B3
- Newmarket … C3
- Newport … A3
- North Conway … B2
- Northfield … B3
- North Haverhill … A2
- North Walpole … A3
- North Woodstock … B2
- Orford … A3
- Ossipee … B3
- Pelham … B4
- Percy … B2
- Peterborough … B4
- Pinardville … B4
- Pittsfield … B3
- Plymouth … B3
- Portsmouth … C3
- Quaker City … A3
- Randolph … B2
- Raymond … B3
- Rochester … C3
- Rumney … B3
- Rye … C4
- Sandwich … B3
- Sharon … B4
- Shelburne … B2
- Silver Lake … B3
- Somersworth … C3
- South Hooksett … B3
- Springfield … A3
- Stewartstown Hollow … B2
- Strafford … B3
- Stratford … B2
- Suncook … B3
- Sutton … B3
- Tilton … B3
- Warner … B3
- Waterville Valley … B3
- Westport … A4
- West Rindge … A4
- West Stewardstown … B2
- Whittier … B3
- Willey House … B2
- Winchester … A4
- Wolfeboro … B3
- Woodsville … A2

Other Features

- Appalachian Natl. Scenic Trail … A3
- Blackwater, *reservoir* … B3
- Blue, *mt.* … B2
- Cabot, *mt.* … B2
- Cardigan, *mt.* … B3
- Connecticut, *river* … A3
- First Connecticut, *lake* … B1
- Franconia, *notch* … B2
- Great, *bay* … C3
- Indian, *river* … B1
- Kearsarge, *mt.* … B3
- Merrimack, *river* … B4
- Monadnock, *mt.* … A4
- Newfound, *lake* … B3
- Ossipee, *lake* … B3
- Presidential, *mt. range* … B2
- Saint-Gaudens Natl. Hist. Site … A3
- Second Connecticut, *lake* … B1
- Smarts, *mt.* … A3
- Squam, *lake* … B3
- Sunapee, *lake* … A3
- Swift, *river* … B3
- Umbagog, *lake* … B2
- Washington, *mt.* … B2
- White, *mts.* … B2
- Winnipesaukee, *lake* … B3
- Winnisquam, *lake* … B3

New Jersey … page 157

Cities and Towns

- Absecon … E5
- Allendale … E1
- Allentown … D3
- Alloway … C4
- Alpine … C1
- Asbury Park … E3
- Atlantic City … E5
- Atlantic Highlands … E3
- Atsion … D4
- Avalon … D5
- Barrington … B3
- Basking Ridge … D2
- Batsto … D4
- Bay Point … C5
- Bayonne … E2
- Bayside … C5
- Beachwood … E4
- Beattyestown … D2
- Beckett … C4
- Belle Mead … D3
- Belleville … B2
- Bellmawr … B3, C4
- Belmar … E3
- Belvidere … C2
- Bergenfield … B1
- Berkeley Heights … E2
- Berlin … D4
- Bernardsville … D2
- Blackwood … C4
- Blairstown … D2
- Bloomfield … E2
- Bogota … B1
- Boonton … E2
- Bordentown … D3
- Bound Brook … D2
- Bradley Beach … E2
- Brass Castle … C2
- Brick … E3
- Bridgeboro … C3
- Bridgeton … C5
- Brielle … E3
- Brigantine … E5
- Brookdale … B1
- Browns Mills … D4
- Budd Lake … D2
- Buena … D4
- Burlington … D3
- Butler … E1
- Caldwell … A1
- Camden … B3, C4
- Cape May … D6
- Cape May Court House … D5
- Carlstadt … B1
- Carneys Point … C4
- Carteret … B2
- Carteret … E2
- Cedar Grove … B1
- Centerton … C4
- Centerville … D2
- Chatham … E2
- Cherry Hill … B3, C4
- Chesilhurst … D4
- Chesterfield … D3
- Cinnaminson … B3, D4
- Clark … A2
- Clayton … C4
- Cliffside Park … C2
- Clifton … B1
- Clinton … D2
- Closter … F2
- Colesville … D1
- Collings Lakes … D4
- Collingswood … B3
- Colonia … E2
- Cranford … E2
- Deerfield … C4
- Delanco … D3
- Denville … E2
- Deptford … B4
- Dover … D2
- Dumont … C1
- Dunellen … E2
- East Brunswick … E3
- East Orange … E2
- East Rutherford … B1
- Eatontown … E3
- Edgewater … F2
- Edison … E2
- Egg Harbor City … D4
- Elizabeth … E2
- Elmer … C4
- Elmwood Park … B1
- Elwood … D4
- Emerson … E2
- Englewood … C1
- Englewood Cliffs … C1
- Englishtown … E3
- Erma … D6
- Estell Manor … D5
- Evesboro … C3
- Ewing … D3
- Fair Lawn … B1, E2
- Fairfield … E2
- Fairton … C5
- Fairview … F2
- Fanwood … E2
- Farmingdale … E3
- Fellowship … C3
- Fieldsboro … D3
- Flemington … D3
- Folsom … D4
- Fords … E2
- Forked River … E4
- Fort Lee … F2
- Franklin … D1
- Franklinville … C4
- Freehold … E3
- Frenchtown … C2
- Garfield … E2
- Gilford Park … E4
- Glassboro … C4
- Glen Gardner … D2
- Glen Ridge … B2
- Glendora … B4
- Gloucester City … B3, C4
- Goshen … D5
- Great Notch … B1
- Green Bank … D4
- Greenwich … C5
- Guttenberg … F2
- Hackensack … E2
- Hackettstown … D2
- Haddon Heights … B3
- Haddonfield … B3
- Hainesville … D1
- Haledon … B1
- Hamburg … D1
- Hammonton … D4
- Hampton … D2
- Harrison … B2
- Haworth … C1
- Hawthorne … B1
- Hedger House … D4
- High Bridge … D2
- Highland Lakes … E1
- Highland Park … E3
- Highlands … F3
- Hightstown … D3
- Hillsdale … E1
- Hillside … B2
- Hoboken … E2
- Hopatcong … D2
- Hopewell … D3
- Howardsville … E4
- Indian Mills … D4
- Irvington … B2
- Jamesburg … E3
- Jenkins Neck … D4
- Jersey City … E2
- Keansburg … E3
- Kearny … B2
- Kendall Park … D3
- Kenilworth … E2
- Kinnelon … E2
- Lakehurst … E3
- Lakewood … E3
- Lambertville … D3
- Lavallette … E4
- Lawnside … B3
- Lawrenceville … D3
- Leeds Point … E5
- Leisure Village … E3
- Leisuretowne … D4
- Leonardo … E3
- Lincroft … E3
- Linden … E2
- Lindenwold … B4, C4
- Linwood … D5
- Little Falls … B1
- Livingston … E2
- Lodi … B1
- Long Branch … F3
- Long Valley … D2
- Lyndhurst … B2
- Madison … E2
- Mahwah … E1
- Manahawkin … E4
- Manalapan … E3
- Manasquan … E3
- Manumuskin … D5
- Manville … D2
- Maple Shade … B3, D4
- Maplewood … E2
- Marcella … E2
- Margate City … E5
- Marlboro … E3
- Marlton … C3, D4
- Matawan … E3
- Mays Landing … D5
- Maywood … B1
- Medford Lakes … D4
- Mendham … D2
- Menlo Park … E2
- Merchantville … B3
- Metuchen … E2
- Middlesex … E2
- Middletown … E3
- Midland Park … E2
- Milford … C2
- Millburn … E2
- Millville … C5
- Monmouth Beach … F3
- Montclair … E2
- Montvale … E1
- Moorestown … C3, D4
- Morris Plains … E2
- Morristown … E2
- Mountain Lakes … E2
- Mount Holly … D4
- Mount Laurel … D4
- Mystic Islands … E4
- National Park … B3
- Neptune City … E3
- Netcong … D2
- Newark … E2
- New Brunswick
- New Egypt
- Newfield
- New Gretna
- Newfoundland
- New Providence
- Newton
- Normandy Beach
- North Arlington
- North Bergen
- North Cape May
- Northfield
- North Wildwood
- Nutley
- Oakland
- Oaklyn
- Ocean City
- Oceanport
- Ogdensburg
- Olivet
- Oradell
- Orange
- Othello
- Oxford
- Palisades Park
- Palmyra … B3
- Paramus … B
- Park Ridge
- Passaic
- Paterson
- Paulsboro … A4
- Pemberton
- Pennington
- Penns Grove
- Pennsauken
- Pennsville
- Perth Amboy
- Phillipsburg
- Piscataway
- Pine Hill
- Pitman
- Pittstown
- Plainfield
- Pleasant Plains
- Pleasantville
- Point Pleasant
- Pomona
- Port Monmouth
- Port Norris
- Princeton
- Princeton Junction
- Prospect Park
- Quinton
- Rahway
- Ramblewood
- Ramsey
- Raritan
- Red Bank
- Ridgefield
- Ridgefield Park … B1
- Ridgewood
- Ringoes
- Ringwood
- Rio Grande
- River Edge
- Riverside … C3,
- Riverton … B3
- Robertsville
- Rochelle Park
- Rocktown
- Roselle
- Roselle Park
- Rumson
- Runnemede … B4,
- Rutherford
- Salem
- Sayreville
- Seabrook
- Sea Girt
- Sea Isle City
- Seaside Heights
- Seaside Park
- Secaucus
- Ship Bottom
- Shrewsbury
- Silverton
- Smithville
- Somerdale
- Somers Point
- Somerset
- Somerville
- South Amboy
- South Orange
- South River
- Sparta
- Spotswood
- Spring Lake Heights
- Stanhope
- Stillwater
- Stockholm
- Stratford … B4,
- Strathmere
- Summit
- Surf City
- Sussex
- Swedesboro
- Teaneck
- Tenafly
- Tinton Falls
- Toms River
- Totowa
- Trenton, *capital*
- Tuckahoe
- Tuckerton
- Turnersville
- Twin Rivers
- Union
- Union Beach
- Union City
- Upton
- Vauxhall
- Ventnor City
- Vernon
- Verona
- Villas
- Vineland
- Voorhees
- Waldwick
- Wanamassa
- Wanaque
- Waretown
- Warren Glen
- Warren Grove
- Washington
- Washington Crossing
- Watchung
- Wayne … A1,
- Weehawken
- Welchville
- Wenonah
- Westfield

	Key
Milford	E1
mont	B3
New York	C2
Orange	E2
Paterson	B1
lle	B3
ood	B1
on	D2
Horse	D3
House Station	D2
Meadow Lake	D2
ng	E4
ood	D6
ood Crest	D6
nstown	D4
sboro	D5
bine	E2
bridge	
bury	B4, C4
lynne	B3
Ridge	B1
stown	C4
stream	C3
stown	D3
off	E1

Features
	Key
May, point	D6
and river	B4
are, bay	C5
are, river	D3
are Water Gap N.R.A.	D1
Natl. Hist. Site	B2
way Natl. Rec. Area	F3
bay	E5
on, river	C2
stown Nat. Hist. Park	D2
lake	
n, bay	E3
of Liberty N.M.	B2

Mexico .... page 158

s and Towns
	Key
a Pueblo	B2
ita	B2
eda	B2
ogro	C3
uerque	B2
ony	B4
a	C3
d	B1
	A3
	B2
alillo	B2
nfield	B1
ue Farms	C3
ozo	C3
al	A3
arral	B3
ayo	C1
on	D1
	D2
les	B2
ng	B3
	B1
	D3
iola	C3
cia	C3
	B2
cres	D3
ington	A1
	D2
Sumner	C2
es	A2
	B2
nfield	C3
ts	D3
y	A3
	D3
Pueblo	B2
nd	A1
z	C3
uces	B3
egas	C2
sburg	A3
lamos	B2
havez	B2
unas	B2
adillas	B2
dgton	D3
r Colonias	C2
r San Francisco Plaza	C1
well	C1
hill	C3
oso	C3
lla	B3
	B2
arty	B2
quero	D2
ojo	A2
dera	A2
ales	D2
sta	C1
hos De Taos	C1
rve	A3
ancho	C2
vell	B2
oso	C3
noso	C2
Felipe Pueblo	B2
Miguel	B1
Miguel	B2
Fe, capital	C2
a Rosa	C2
o Domingo Pueblo	B2
rock	A1
er City	A3
rro	C1
ager	C2
Park	B4
que	C2
a Amarilla	B1
or Consequences	B3
cari	D2
osa	C2
rsity Park	B3
ncia	B2
Park	C2
erflow	A1
Pueblo	A2

r Features
	Key
uiu, reservoir	B1
are	B2
	A2

	Key
Aztec Ruins Natl. Monument	B1
Baldy, mt.	C1
Bandelier Natl. Monument	B2
Black, mt. range	B3
Burro, mt.	A3
Caballo, reservoir	B3
Canadian, river	C1
Capulin Volcano N.M.	D1
Carlsbad Caverns Natl. Park	C3
Cebolleta, mt.	B2
Cerro Vista, mt.	C1
Chaco Culture Natl. Hist. Park	D1
Cimarron, river	C1
Conchas, lake	C2
Contintal Divide, mt. ridge	B3
Cooke's, mt.	B3
Elephant Butte, res.	B3
El Malpais Natl. Monument	B2
El Morro Natl. Monument	A2
Fort Union Natl. Monument	C2
Gallinas, mts.	C2
Gila, river	A3
Gila Cliff Dwellings N.M.	A3
Guadalupe, mts.	C3
Jornada Del Muerto	B3
Llano Estacado, plateau	D3
Navajo, reservoir	B1
Navajo Indian Res.	A1
Pecos, river	C2, C3
Pecos, plains	C3
Pecos N.H.P.	C2
Petroglyph Natl. Monument	B2
Playas, lake	A4
Reeds, mt.	B3
Rio Grande, river	C1
Rio Hondo, river	C3
Rio Puerco, river	B2
Salinas Pueblo Missions N.M.	B2
San Andres, mts.	B3
San Juan, river	A1
Sangre De Cristo, mts.	C1
Shiprock, mt.	A1
Sierra Blanca, mt.	C3
South Baldy, mt.	B3
Sumner, lake	C2
Taylor, mt.	B2
Wheeler, mt.	C1
White Sands Natl. Monument.	B3
Whitewater Baldy, mt.	A3
Withington, mt.	B3
Zuni, mts.	A2

New York .... page 159

Cities and Towns
	Key
Adams	H3
Adams Center	H3
Akron	C4
Albany, capital	N5
Albion	D4
Alden	D5
Alfred	E6
Allegany	D6
Altamont	M5
Amsterdam	M5
Angola	B5
Arcade	D5
Astoria	A3
Athens	N6
Attica	D5
Auburn	G5
Avon	E5
Bainbridge	J6
Baldwinsville	H4
Ballston Spa	N4
Batavia	D5
Bath	F6
Beacon	N7
Bedford-Stuyvesant	A4
Belle Harbor	A4
Belmont	D6
Bensonhurst	A4
Big Flats	G6
Binghamton	J6
Bloomfield	F5
Bolivar	D6
Boonville	K4
Breezy Point	A4
Brewerton	H4
Bridgehampton	E1
Brighton Beach	A4
Broadalbin	M4
Brockport	E4
Brocton	B6
Bronx	A3, B1
Bronxville	A2
Brooklyn	A4, B1
Buffalo	C5
Cairo	M6
Calcium	J2
Caledonia	E5
Cambridge	P4
Camden	J4
Canajoharie	L5
Canandaigua	F5
Canarsie	A4
Canastota	J4
Canisteo	E6
Canton	K1
Carmel	N7
Carthage	J3
Castleton-on-Hudson	N5
Catskill	N6
Cayuga Heights	H6
Cazenovia	J5
Cedarhurst	B4
Central Square	H4
Chatham	N6
Cheektowaga	C5
Chittenango	J4
Churchville	E4
Clayton	H2
Clinton	K4
Clyde	G4
Cobleskill	L5
Cohoes	N5
College Point	A3
Colonie	N5
Coney Island	A4
Cooperstown	L5
Corinth	N4
Corning	F6
Cortland	H5
Coxsackie	N6
Cuba	D6
Dannemora	N1
Dansville	E5
Delhi	L6
De Ruyter	J5

	Key
Deposit	K6
Dolgeville	L4
Dover Plains	N7
Dryden	H6
Dundee	G6
Dunkirk	B6
East Atlantic Beach	B4
Eastchester	A2
East Hampton	E1
East Islip	C2
East New York	A4
East Northport	D1
East Patchogue	C5
Eden	C5
Elizabethtown	N2
Ellenville	M7
Elmira	G6
Elmira Heights	G6
Elmont	B4
Endicott	H6
Endwell	H6
Fairmount	H4
Far Rockaway	A4
Fayette	G5
Fine	K2
Flatbush	A4
Flushing	A3
Fonda	M5
Fort Edward	N4
Fort Plain	L5
Franklin Sq.	B4
Franklinville	D6
Fredonia	B6
Freeport	C2
Frewsburg	B6
Friendship	D6
Fulton	H4
Geneseo	E5
Geneva	G5
Glen Cove	B2
Glens Falls	N4
Gloversville	M4
Goshen	M7
Gouverneur	K2
Gowanda	C6
Granville	P4
Gravesend	A4
Great Neck	B2
Greece	E4
Greene	J6
Greenport	E1
Greenwich	P4
Groton	H5
Hamburg	C5
Hamilton	J5
Hampton Bays	E1
Hancock	K7
Harlem	A3
Hempstead	B2
Herkimer	L4
Hicksville	C1
Highland	N7
Hilton	E4
Holbrook	C1
Holland	C5
Holley	D4
Homer	H5
Hoosick Falls	P5
Hornell	E6
Horseheads	G6
Houghton	D6
Howard Beach	A4
Hudson	N6
Hudson Falls	N4
Huntington Station	C1
Hurley	M7
Ilion	K4
Inwood	B4
Irondequoit	E4
Ithaca	H6
Jamaica	B4
Jamestown	B6
Johnson City	J6
Johnstown	M4
Keeseville	P1
Kew Gardens	A4
Kinderhook	N6
Kingston	N7
Lake George	N4
Lake Placid	M2
Lake Pleasant	M4
Lakewood	B6
Lansing	H5
Larchmont	B2
Lawrence	B4
Le Roy	D5
Levittown	C1
Liberty	L7
Lima	E5
Lindenhurst	C2
Little Falls	L4
Little Valley	C6
Livingston Manor	L7
Livonia	E5
Lockport	C4
Long Beach	B2
Long Eddy	K7
Long Island City	A3
Long Lake	M3
Loon Lake	M1
Lowville	K3
Lynbrook	B4
Lyons	G4
Malone	M1
Mamaroneck	B2
Manhasset Hills	B3
Manhattan	A3
Manlius	J4
Manorhaven	B3
Massapequa	C2
Massena	L1
Mastic	D1
Mastic Beach	D1
Mattituck	E1
Mayville	A6
Mechanicville	N5
Medina	D4
Mexico	H4
Middleburgh	M5
Middleport	D4
Middletown	M7
Millbrook	N7
Mineola	B2
Mohawk	K5
Monroe	M7
Montauk	F1
Monticello	L7
Montour Falls	G6
Moravia	H5
Mount Kisco	B1
Mount Morris	E5

	Key
Mount Vernon	B1, C5
Munnsville	J5
Nassau	N5
Newark	F4
Newburgh	M7
New City	B1
Newfane	C4
New Hartford	K4
New Hyde Park	B4
New Paltz	M7
New Rochelle	B2
New York	B4
Niagara Falls	B4
Norfolk	L1
North Collins	C5
North Hills	B3
North Syracuse	H4
North Tonawanda	C4
Norwich	J5
Norwood	L1
Nunda	E5
Nyack	B1
Oakfield	D4
Ogdensburg	K1
Olcott	C4
Olean	D6
Oneida	J4
Oneonta	K6
Ossining	B1
Oswego	H4
Owego	J6
Oxford	J5
Ozone Park	A4
Painted Post	F6
Palmyra	F4
Pawling	N7
Peekskill	B1
Pelham	A3
Pelham Manor	A3
Penn Yan	F5
Perry	D5
Peru	N1
Philadelphia	J2
Philmont	N6
Phoenix	H4
Pine Bush	M7
Plattsburgh	P1
Port Henry	P2
Port Jefferson	D1
Port Morris	A3
Port Washington	B3
Potsdam	K1
Poughkeepsie	N7
Pulaski	H3
Queens	B4
Randolph	C6
Ransomville	C4
Ravena	N6
Red Hook	N7
Rensselaer	N5
Rhinebeck	N7
Richfield Springs	L5
Riverhead	D1
Rochester	E4
Rockaway Point	A4
Rocky Point	D1
Rome	K4
Rosendale	M7
Rouses Point	P1
Rye	B2
Sackets Harbor	H3
Sag Harbor	E1
St. George	L4
St. Johnsville	L4
Salamanca	C6
Sands Point	M2
Saranac Lake	M2
Saratoga Springs	N6
Saugerties	N6
Sayville	C2
Schenectady	M5
Schoharie	M5
Scotia	N5
Seneca Falls	G5
Sherburne	K5
Shortsville	F5
Sidney	K6
Silver Creek	B5
Skaneateles	H5
Sodus	F4
Southampton	E1
South Fallsburg	L7
Southold	E1
Southport	G6
Spencerport	E4
Springville	C5
Stillwater	N5
Stony Brook	C1
Suffern	A1
Syracuse	H4
Throgs Neck	A3
Ticonderoga	P3
Troy	N5
Trumansburg	G5
Tupper Lake	M3
Unadilla	K6
Utica	K4
Valley Stream	B2
Victory Mills	N4
Voorheesville	N5
Walden	M7
Walton	K6
Wampsville	J4
Wappingers Falls	N7
Warrensburg	N4
Warsaw	D5
Warwick	M7
Waterloo	G5
Watertown	J3
Waterville	K5
Watkins Glen	G6
Waverly	G6
Wayland	E5
Weedsport	G4
Wellsville	E6
West Carthage	J3
Westfield	A6
West Point	N7
West Seneca	C5
Whitehall	P4
White Plains	B1
Whitesboro	K4
Whitestone	A3
Williamsburg	A4
Wilson	C4
Wolcott	G4
Woodmere	B4
Woodstock	M6
Yonkers	B1
Yorktown Heights	B1

Other Features
	Key
Adirondack, mts.	L2
Adirondack Park	M2
Appalachian Natl. Scenic Trail	A1
Black, lake	J2
Black, river	K3
Cannonsville, reservoir	K6
Catskill, mts.	L6
Catskill Park	L6
Cayuga, lake	G5
Champlain, lake	P1
Chenango, river	J6
Cranberry, lake	L2
Delaware, river	K7
Erie, canal	J4
Erie, lake	A5
Fire Island Natl. Seashore	D2
Fishers, island	F1
Fort Stanwix Natl. Monument	K4
Galloo, island	H3
Gardiners, island	F1
Gateway Natl. Rec. Area	B2
Genesee, river	D6
George, lake	N3
Great Sacandaga, lake	M4
Hinckley, reservoir	K4
Home of F.D.R. Natl. Hist Site	N7
Hudson, river	M3
Indian, lake	M3
J.F.K. Int'l Airport	A4
Keuka, lake	F5
Long, island	E1
Long, lake	M3
Long Island, sound	C1
Marcy, mt.	M2
Martin Van Buren Natl. Hist. Site	N6
Mettawee, river	P3
Mohawk, river	L5
Oneida, lake	J4
Ontario, lake	E3
Pepacton, reservoir	L6
Piseco, lake	L4
St. Lawrence, river	K1
Salmon River, reservoir	J3
Saratoga, lake	N4
Saratoga Natl. Hist. Park	N4
Schoharie, reservoir	M6
Schroon, lake	N3
Slide, mt.	M7
Staten, island	A2
Stony, island	H3
Susquehanna, river	H2
Thousand, islands	H2
Tupper, lake	L2
Unadilla, river	K5
Upper Saranac, lake	M2
West Point Military Academy	A1

North Carolina .... page 160

Cities and Towns
	Key
Aberdeen	G4
Ahoskie	L2
Albemarle	E4
Andrews	C8
Angier	H3
Apex	H3
Archdale	F3
Asheboro	F3
Asheville	E7
Atlantic Beach	M5
Ayden	K4
Badin	E4
Bakersville	A2
Bayboro	M4
Beaufort	M5
Belhaven	M3
Belmont	C4
Benson	H4
Bessemer City	C4
Bethel	L3
Biscoe	F4
Black Mt.	A3
Bladenboro	H5
Blowing Rock	B2
Boiling Spring Lakes	J6
Boiling Springs	B4
Bolivia	J6
Boone	B2
Brevard	E8
Bryson City	C8
Buies Creek	H4
Burgaw	K5
Burlington	G2
Burnsville	A3
Butner	H2
Camden	N2
Canton	E7
Carolina Beach	K6
Carthage	G4
Cary	H3
Chadbourn	H6
Chapel Hill	G3
Charlotte	D4
Cherryville	C4
China Grove	D3
Clayton	J3
Clemmons	E3
Clinton	J5
Coats	H4
Columbia	N3
Columbus	A4
Concord	D4
Conover	C3
Cornelius	D4
Creedmoor	H2
Cullowhee	D8
Currituck	N2
Dallas	C4
Danbury	E2
Davidson	D3
Denton	E3
Dobson	D2
Drexel	B3
Dunn	H4
Durham	H2
E. Flat Rock	E8
Eden	F2
Edenton	M2
Elizabeth City	N2
Elizabethtown	H5
Elkin	D2
Elm City	K3
Emerald Isle	M5
Enfield	K2
Erwin	H4
Fairmont	G5
Farmville	K3
Fayetteville	H4
Fletcher	E8

	Key
Forest City	B4
Four Oaks	J4
Franklin	C8
Franklinton	J2
Fremont	K3
Fuquay-Varina	H3
Gamewell	B3
Garner	H3
Gastonia	C4
Gatesville	M2
Gibsonville	F3
Goldsboro	K4
Graham	G2
Granite Falls	C3
Granite Quarry	E3
Greensboro	F2
Greenville	L3
Grifton	L4
Halifax	K2
Hamlet	F5
Harkers Island	M5
Harrisburg	D4
Havelock	M5
Hayesville	C8
Hays	C2
Henderson	J2
Hendersonville	E8
Hertford	N2
Hickory	C3
High Point	E3
Hillsborough	G2
Hope Mills	H5
Hudson	C3
Huntersville	C3
Icard	B3
Indian Trail	D4
Jackson	L2
Jacksonville	L5
Jamestown	F3
Jefferson	C2
Jonesville	D2
Kannapolis	D4
Kenansville	K5
Kenly	J3
Kernersville	E2
Kill Devil Hills	P2
King	E2
Kings Mt.	C4
Kinston	K4
Kitty Hawk	P2
La Grange	K4
Laurinburg	G5
Leland	J6
Lenoir	B3
Lewisville	E3
Lexington	E3
Liberty	F3
Lillington	H4
Lincolnton	C3
Locust	E4
Long Beach	J7
Long View	C3
Louisburg	J2
Lumberton	G5
Madison	F2
Maiden	C3
Manteo	P3
Marion	A3
Marshall	E7
Marshville	E4
Matthews	D4
Maxton	G5
Maysdan	F2
Mebane	G2
Mint Hill	D4
Mocksville	D3
Monroe	D5
Mooresville	D3
Moravian Falls	C3
Morehead City	M5
Morganton	B3
Mt. Airy	E2
Mt. Gilead	F4
Mt. Holly	C4
Mt. Olive	J4
Mulberry	B3
Murfreesboro	L2
Murphy	B8
Nags Head	P3
Nashville	K3
New Bern	L4
Newland	B2
Newport	M5
Newton	C3
Norwood	E4
North Wilkesboro	C2
Oxford	H2
Pembroke	G5
Pinehurst	G4
Pinetops	K3
Pineville	D4
Piney Green	L5
Pittsboro	G3
Plymouth	M3
Polkville	B4
Raeford	G5
Raleigh, capital	H3
Randleman	F3
Red Springs	G5
Reidsville	F2
River Bend	L4
Roanoke Rapids	K2
Robbinsville	C8
Robersonville	L3
Rockingham	F5
Rockwell	E3
Rocky Mount	K3
Rolesville	J3
Rose Hill	J5
Roseboro	H5
Roxboro	H2
Rural Hall	E2
Rutherfordton	B4
Salisbury	D3
Sanford	G4
Sawmills	C3
Scotland Neck	L2
Selma	J3
Seven Lakes	F4
Sharpsburg	K3
Shelby	B4
Siler City	F3
Smithfield	J3
Sneads Ferry	L5
Snow Hill	K4
Southern Pines	G4
Southern Shores	P2
Southport	J7
Sparta	C1
Spencer	E3
Spindale	B4

188 NORTH CAROLINA–OREGON

Key
Spring Lake H4
Spruce Pine A3
St. Pauls H5
Stanley C4
Stanleyville E2
Statesville D3
Stokesdale F2
Stony Point C3
Summerfield F2
Swan Quarter N4
Sylva D8
Tabor City H6
Tarboro K3
Taylorsville C3
Thomasville E3
Toast D2
Trenton L4
Troutman D3
Troy F4
Valdese B3
Wadesboro E5
Wake Forest H3
Wallace K5
Wanchese P3
Warrenton J2
Warsaw J5
Washington L3
Waxhaw D5
Waynesville D7
Weddington D4
Welcome E3
Weldon K2
Wendell J3
Wentworth F2
W. Jefferson C2
Whiteville H6
Wilkesboro C2
Williamston L3
Wilmington K6
Wilson K3
Windsor M2
Winfall N2
Wingate E5
Winston-Salem E2
Winterville L3
Winton M2
Woodfin E7
Wrightsville Beach K6
Yadkinville D2
Yanceyville G2
Zebulon J3

Other Features
Albemarle, *sound* N3
Alligator, *lake* N3
Alligator, *river* N3
B. Everett Jordan, *lake* G3
Bodie, *island* P3
Cape Fear, *river* H5
Cape Hatteras Natl. Seashore P4
Cape Lookout Natl. Seashore N5
Chatuga, *lake* C8
Clingmans Dome, *mt.* C7
Dan, *river* F2
Deep, *river* F3
Falls Lake, *reservoir* H3
Fear, *cape* K7
Fontana, *lake* C7
Fort Raleigh Natl. Hist. Site P3
Gaston, *lake* K1
Great, *lake* L5
Great Smoky Mts. Natl. Park C7
Hatteras, *cape* P4
Hatteras, *inlet* P4
Highrock, *lake* E3
Hiwassee, *lake* B8
Hyco, *lake* G2
John H. Kerr, *reservoir* H1
Lookout, *cape* M5
Mattamuskeat, *lake* N3
Mitchell, *mt.* A3
Nantahala, *lake* C8
Neuse, *river* J4
Norman, *lake* D3
Ocracoke, *inlet* N4
Oregon, *inlet* P3
Pamlico, *river* M4
Pamlico, *sound* P4
Phelps, *lake* N3
Roan, *mt.* A2
Roanoke, *river* K2
Rocky, *river* E4
Smith, *island* K7
Standing Indian, *mt.* C8
Tar, *river* J2
Waccamaw, *lake* J6
Wright Brothers Natl. Memorial P2
Yadkin, *river* D2

North Dakota ....page 161

Cities and Towns
Ashley F3
Beach A3
Belcourt F1
Beulah D2
Bismarck, *capital* E3
Bowman B3
Cando F1
Carrington F2
Casselton H3
Cavalier H1
Center D2
Cooperstown G2
Crosby B1
Devils Lake G1
Dickinson C3
Ellendale G3
Fargo J3
Fessenden F2
Finley H2
Forman H3
Fort Yates E3
Garrison D2
Grafton H1
Grand Forks H2
Harvey F2
Hazen D2
Hettinger C3
Hillsboro H2
Jamestown G3
Lakota G1
La Moure G3
Langdon G1
Larimore H2
Linton E3
Lisbon H3
McClusky E2
Mandan E3
Mayville H2
Mohall D1
Mott C3
Napoleon F3
New Rockford F2
New Town C1
Oakes G3
Park River H1
Rolla F1
Rugby F1
Stanley C1
Stanton D2
Steele F3
Tioga C1
Towner E1
Valley City H3
Wahpeton J3
Washburn D2
Watford City B2
West Fargo J3
Williston B1

Other Features
Cannonball, *river* D3
Devils, *lake* G1
Fort Union Trading Post N.H.S. A1
Green, *river* B2
Heart, *river* D3
Intl. Peace Garden E1
James, *river* F2
Jamestown, *reservoir* G2
Knife, *river* C2
Knife River Indian Villages N.H.S. D2
Little Missouri, *river* B3
Long, *lake* E3
Maple, *river* G3, H2
Missouri, *river* D2
Oahe, *lake* E3
Pembina, *river* G1
Sakakawea, *lake* C2
Sheyenne, *river* E2, G2, H3
Souris, *river* D1
Theodore Roosevelt N.P. B2, B3
White Butte, *mt.* B3
Wild Rice, *river* H3

Ohio ....page 162

Cities and Towns
Aberdeen C8
Ada C4
Akron G3
Alliance H4
Ansonia A5
Antrim H5
Antwerp A3
Arabia F8
Arcanum A6
Archbold B2
Arlington C4
Ashland F4
Ashtabula J2
Athens F7
Aurora H3
Avon Lake F2
Baltimore E6
Barberton G3
Barnesville H6
Batavia B7
Bay Village G9
Beachwood J9
Bedford J9
Bedford Heights J9
Bellaire J5
Bellefontaine C5
Bellevue E3
Bellville E4
Berea G9
Berlin Heights F3
Bethel B8
Beverly G6
Blanchester C7
Blissfield G5
Blue Ash C9
Bluffton C4
Boardman J3
Bowling Green C3
Bradford B5
Bremen F6
Brewster G4
Bridgetown B9
Broadview Heights H10
Brook Park G9
Brooklyn H9
Brookville B6
Brunswick G3
Bryan A3
Bucyrus E4
Burton H3
Cadiz J5
Caldwell G6
Cambridge G5
Camden A6
Canal Fulton G4
Canal Winchester E6
Canfield J3
Canton H4
Cardington E5
Carey D4
Carrollton H4
Cedarville C6
Celina A4
Centerburg E5
Chagrin Falls H3
Chardon H2
Chesterhill G7
Cheviot B9
Chillicothe E7
Cincinnati A7
Circleville E6
Cleveland G2
Cleveland Heights G2
Cleves A9
Clyde E3
Coldwater A5
Columbiana J4
Columbus, *capital* D6
Columbus Grove B4
Congress F4
Conneaut J2
Cortland J3
Coshocton G5
Covington B5
Crestline E4
Creston G4
Crooksville F6
Cuyahoga Falls H3
Dalton G4
Dayton B6
De Graff C5
Deer Park C9
Defiance B3
Delaware D5
Delhi Hills B9
Delphos B4
Delta C2
Deshler C3
Dover H4
Dresden F5
Dublin D5
Dunkinsville D8
E. Cleveland H8
East Liverpool J4
East Palestine J4
Eaton A6
Edgerton A3
Elida B4
Elyria F3
Euclid G2
Fairborn C6
Fairfield A7
Fairport Harbor H2
Fairview Park G9
Findlay C3
Fitchville F3
Forest C4
Forest Park B8
Forestville B7
Fort Recovery A5
Fort Shawnee B4
Fostoria D3
Franklin B6
Fredericktown E5
Fremont D3
Fresno G5
Gahanna E5
Galion E4
Gallipolis F8
Gambier F5
Garfield Hts. H9
Geneva J2
Genoa D2
Georgetown C8
Germantown B6
Gibsonburg D3
Grafton F3
Granville E5
Green G4
Green Springs D3
Greenfield D7
Greenville A5
Greenwich E3
Grove City D6
Hamilton A7
Hannibal J6
Harrisburg D6
Harrison A9
Heath F5
Hebron F6
Hicksville A3
Hillsboro C7
Hiram H3
Holgate B3
Hubbard J3
Huron E3
Independence H9
Jackson E7
Jackson Center B5
Jefferson J2
Jeffersonville C6
Johnstown E5
Keene G5
Kent H3
Kenton C4
Kettering B6
Kimbolton G5
Kirtland H2
Lakewood G9
Lancaster E6
Lebanon B7
Leipsic C3
Lewisburg A6
Lexington E4
Lima B4
Lisbon J4
Lodi G3
Logan F6
London D6
Lorain F3
Loudonville F4
Louisville H4
Loveland B7
Lucasville E8
Lyndhurst J8
McArthur F7
McConnelsville G6
Macedonia J10
Macksburg H6
Madeira C9
Manchester C8
Mansfield E4
Maple Hts. J9
Marietta H7
Marion D4
Martins Ferry J5
Marysville D5
Mason B7
Massillon G4
Maumee C2
Mayfield Hts. J9
Mechanicsburg C5
Medina G3
Mentor H2
Miamitown B9
Middleburg Heights G9
Middlefield H3
Middletown B6
Milan E3
Milford B7
Millersburg G4
Minerva H4
Minster B5
Monfort Heights B9
Monroe B7
Montgomery C9
Montpelier A2
Mount Gilead E4
Mount Healthy B9
Mount Orab C7
Mount Sterling D6
Mount Vernon E5
Napoleon B3
Nelsonville F7
Newark F5
New Baltimore B9
New Boston E8
New Bremen B5
New Carlisle B6
Newcomerstown G5
New Concord G6
New Lebanon B6
New Lexington F6
New London F3
New Paris A6
New Philadelphia H5
New Richmond B8
Newtown C9
Niles J3
North Baltimore C3
North Canton H4
North College Hill B9
North Kingsville J2
North Olmsted G3
North Royalton H10
Northfield J9
Northridge C6
Norwalk E3
Norwood C9
Oak Harbor D2
Oak Hill E8
Oberlin F3
Olmsted Falls G9
Oregon D2
Orrville G4
Orwell J2
Otsego G5
Ottawa B3
Painesville H2
Parma G3
Parma Heights H9
Pataskala E6
Paulding A3
Peebles D8
Pepper Pike J9
Perrysburg C2
Pickerington E6
Piketon E7
Pioneer A2
Piqua B5
Plain City D5
Plymouth E4
Pomeroy F7
Port Clinton E2
Portsmouth E8
Powhatan Point J6
Ravenna H3
Reading B7
Reynoldsburg E6
Richmond Heights J8
Richwood D5
Ripley C8
Rittman G4
Roseville F6
Russells Point C5
Sabina C7
Sagamore Hills J9
St. Bernard C9
St. Clairsville J5
St. Henry A5
St. Louisville F5
St. Marys B4
St. Paris C5
Salem J4
Salineville J4
Sandusky E3
Selma C6
Seven Hills H9
Shadyside J6
Shaker Hts. J9
Sharonville C9
Shelby E4
Shreve F4
Sidney B5
Silverton C9
Smithville G4
Solon J9
Somerset F6
South Charleston C6
South Euclid J8
South Point E9
Springdale C9
Springfield C6
Steubenville J5
Strasburg G4
Streetsboro H3
Strongsville G3
Stryker B3
Sugarcreek G5
Sunbury E5
Sylvania C2
The Village of Indian Hill C9
Tiffin D3
Tipp City B6
Toledo C2
Troy B5
Twinsburg J10
Uhrichsville H5
University Hts. J9
Upper Sandusky D4
Urbana C5
Utica F5
Van Wert A4
Vandalia B6
Venedocia B4
Vermilion F3
Versailles B5
Wapakoneta B4
Warren J3
Warrensville Heights J9
Warsaw G5
Washington Court House D6
Waterville C2
Wauseon B2
Waverly E7
Waynesville B6
Wellington F3
Wellston E7
Wellsville J4
West Alexandria A6
West Jefferson D6
West Lafayette G5
West Liberty C5
West Milton B6
West Salem F4
West Union C8
West Unity B2
Westerville E5
Westlake G9
Weston C3
Wheelersburg E8
Wickliffe J8
Wilkesville F7
Willard E3
Williamsburg B7
Williamsport D6
Williamsport E4
Wilmington C7
Woodsfield H6
Woodville D3
Wooster G4
Wyoming C9
Xenia C6
Yellow Springs C6
Youngstown J3

Other Features
Clendening, *lake* H5
Cuyahoga Valley N.R.A. H9
Erie, *lake* G1
Hocking, *river* F7
Hopewell Culture N.H.P. E7
James A. Garfield N.H.P. H2
Kelleys, *island* E2
Mohican, *river* F4
Muskingum, *river* G6
Ohio, *river* J6
Salt Fork, *lake* H5
Sandusky, *river* D3
Scioto, *river* D4
Senecaville, *lake* H6
William H. Taft Natl. Hist. Site C9

Oklahoma ....page 163

Cities and Towns
Ada F3
Agawam E3
Altus C3
Alva D1
Anadarko D2
Antlers G3
Apache D3
Arapaho D2
Ardmore E3
Arkoma H2
Atoka F3
Barnsdall F1
Bartlesville F1
Beaver B1
Bethel Acres E2
Bixby G2
Blackwell E1
Blanchard E2
Boise City B4
Bristow F2
Broken Arrow G1
Broken Bow H3
Buffalo C1
Cache D3
Calera F4
Carnegie D2
Catoosa G1
Chandler F2
Checotah G2
Chelsea G1
Cherokee D1
Cheyenne C2
Chickasha E2
Choctaw E2
Chouteau G1
Claremore G1
Cleveland F1
Clinton D2
Coalgate F3
Collinsville G1
Comanche E3
Commerce H1
Cordell D2
Corum D3
Coweta G2
Cushing F2
Davis E3
Dewey G1
Drumright F2
Durant F4
Eagletown H3
Edmond E2
Elk City C2
Enid E1
Eufaula G2
Fairfax F1
Fairview D1
Farris G3
Fittstown F3
Floris B1
Forgan B1
Fort Gibson G2
Frederick D3
Geary D2
Glenpool G2
Granite C3
Grove H1
Guthrie E2
Guymon C4
Harmon C1
Hartshorne G3
Haskell G2
Healdton E3
Heavener H3
Hennessey E1
Henryetta F2
Hobart C2
Holdenville F2
Hollis C3
Hominy F1
Hooker A1
Hugo G3
Idabel H4
Inola G1
Jay H1
Jenks G1
Joy E3
Kingfisher E2
Konawa F3
Krebs G3
Laverne C1
Lawton D3
Lenora C1
Lindsay E3
Locust Grove G1
Lone Grove E3
Loveland D3
Lovell E1
McAlester G3
McCurtain H2
McKnight C3
Madill F3
Mangum C3
Mannford F1
Marietta E4
Marlow E3
Medford E1
Midwest City E2
Minco E2
Moore E2
Muldrow H2
Muskogee G2
Mustang E2
Newcastle E2
Newkirk E1
Norman E2
Nowata G1
Oakhurst F1
Okeene
Okemah
Oklahoma City, *capital*
Okmulgee
Owasso
Panama
Pawhuska
Pawnee
Perkins
Perry
Picher
Piedmont
Ponca City
Poteau
Prague
Pryor Creek
Purcell
Roll
Sallisaw
Sand Springs
Sapulpa
Sayre
Seminole
Shattuck
Shawnee
Skiatook
Slaughterville
Snyder
Sparks
Spiro
Stanley
Stigler
Stillwater
Stilwell
Stratford
Stroud
Sulphur
Tahlequah
Talihina
Tecumseh
Tishomingo
Tonkawa
Tulsa
Turley
Tuttle
Vian
Vinita
Wagoner
Walters
Wanette
Warner
Warren
Watonga
Watova
Waukomis
Waurika
Weatherford
Westville
Wetumka
Wewoka
Wilburton
Wilson
Woodward
Wynnewood
Yale
Yukon

Other Features
Arkansas, *river*
Black Mesa, *mt.*
Broken Bow, *lake*
Canadian, *river*
Canton, *lake*
Chickasaw Natl. Rec. Area
Cimarron, *river*
Fort Gibson, *lake*
Hugo, *lake*
Illinois , *river*
Kaw, *lake*
Keystone, *lake*
North Canadian, *river*
Oologah, *lake*
Ouachita, *mts.*
Red, *river*
Sooner, *lake*
Texoma, *lake*
Washita Battlefield N.H.S.
Winding Stair Natl. Rec. Area

Oregon ....page 1

Cities and Towns
Albany
Aloha
Altamont
Ashland
Astoria
Baker City
Bandon
Beaverton A2,
Bend
Brookings
Brownsville
Burns
Canby A2,
Canyon City
Cedar Hills
Central Point
Clatskanie
Condon
Coos Bay
Coquille
Cornelius
Corvallis
Cottage Grove
Creswell
Crowley
Dallas
Eagle Point
Elgin
Enterprise
Eugene
Florence
Forest Grove
Fossil
Four Corners A2,
Glendale
Gold Beach
Grants Pass
Green
Gresham
Harbor
Harrisburg
Hayesville A2,
Heppner
Hermiston
Hillsboro A2,
Hines
Homestead
Hood River

	Key
ard	C2
onville	C3
son	C2
Day	E2
ion City	B2
ra	E3
	A2
ath Falls	C3
ande	E2
reek	C3
Oswego	A2, C3
	B3
view	D3
non	C2
gton	D2
ln Beach	B2
anville	B2
as	C2
cham	A2
ord	C2
	A2
ger	A2
idge	C3
ario	F2
on City	A2, C2
leton	E2
math	B2
nix	E2
Rock	E2
and	A2, C2
	D2
eville	C1
mond	C2
sport	B3
	D3
ue River	B3
burg	B3
s	C2
elens	C2
field	D2
m, capital	A2, B2
a Clara	B2
poose	B2
ide	B2
ca	E2
ly Cove	C3
wood	C2
rton	A2, C2
ngfield	C2
ton	C2
	C3
erlin	C3
et Home	C3
Dalles	C2
	A2, C2
nook	B2
odo	B2
qua	B3
on	B2
	E3
eta	B2
onia	B2
sport	B2
n Springs	C2
renton	B1
erloo	C2
t Slope	A2
ate City	C3
	B2
onville	A2, C2
odburn	A2
d Village	A2

er Features

	Key
rt, lake	D3
e, mts.	E2
pooya, mts.	C3
cade, range	C3
kamas, river	B2
st, mt. ranges	B2
umbia, river	D2
er, lake	A2
er Lake Natl. Park	C3
scent, lake	C3
oked, river	D2
is, lake	C2
chutes, river	C2
mond Peak, mt.	C3
rhart Mtn., mt.	D3
en Peter, mt.	C3
ney, basin	D3
ney, lake	E3
	F2
s Canyon Natl. Rec. Area	F2
od, mt.	C2
n Day, river	D2
n Day Fossil Beds N.M.	D2
math, mts.	B3
kout, cape	B2
Loughlin house N.H.S.	A2
heur, lake	E3
heur, river	E3
alla, river	B2
tnomah, waterfalls	C2
noco, mts.	D2
gon Caves Natl. Monument	B3
gon Dunes Natl. Rec. Area	B2
yhee, lake	E3
yhee, river	E3
nd, river	A2
blo, mts.	B3
	B3
ajawea Peak, mt.	E2
slaw, river	B2
h Umpqua, river	B3
ens, mts.	E3
wberry Mt., mt.	E3
mer, lake	D3

	Key
Thielsen, mt.	C3
Tillamook, bay	B2
Trout Creek, mts.	E3
Umatilla, lake	D2
Upper Klamath, lake	C3
Waldo, lake	C3
Wallowa, mts.	E2
Willamette, river	A2

Pennsylvania ....page 165

Cities and Towns

	Key
Albion	A2
Aliquippa	A4
Allensville	F4
Allentown	L4
Allison Park	E6
Altoona	E4
Ambridge	A4
Annville	H5
Archbald	K2
Ardmore	M6
Arnot	G2
Ashland	J4
Athens	H2
Austin	E2
Avalon	D7
Avis	G3
Bala Cynwyd	M6
Baldwin	E7
Bangor	L4
Barnesboro	D4
Beaver	A4
Beaver Falls	A4
Beavertown	G4
Bedford	E5
Bellefonte	F4
Belleville	F4
Bellevue	D7
Bellwood	D6
Berlin	D6
Berwick	J3
Berwyn	L6
Bethel Park	A5, D7
Bethlehem	L4
Birdsboro	K5
Blairsville	C5
Blakely	K3
Bloomsburg	J4
Blossburg	G2
Boalsburg	F4
Boothwyn	L7
Boswell	C5
Boyertown	K5
Bradford	D2
Brentwood	E7
Bridgeville	D7
Brockport	D3
Brockway	D3
Brodheadsville	L4
Brooklyn	K2
Brookville	C3
Broomall	L6
Brownsville	B5
Bryn Mawr	L6
Burgettstown	A5
Butler	B4
California	B5
Cambridge Springs	A2
Canonsburg	A5
Canton	H2
Carbondale	K2
Carlisle	G5
Carnegie	D7
Carroll Valley	G6
Carrolltown	D4
Castle Shannon	E7
Catawissa	J4
Chambersburg	F6
Chelsea	L7
Chester	L6, L7
Clairton	B5
Clarion	C3
Clarks Summit	K2
Claysburg	E5
Clearfield	E3
Clifton Heights	L7
Clymer	C4
Coatesville	K6
Columbia	H5
Connellsville	B6
Conyngham	J4
Coopersburg	L5
Coraopolis	D7
Cornwall	J5
Corry	B2
Coudersport	E2
Crafton	D7
Cresson	D5
Crosby	E2
Cuddy	D7
Curwensville	D4
Dallas	J3
Danville	H4
Darby	M7
Delmont	B5
Denver	J5
Derry	C5
Dillsburg	G5
Dormont	D7
Dover	H5
Downingtown	K5
Doylestown	L5
Drexel Hill	M7
DuBois	D3
Duncannon	G5
Duquesne	E7
Dushore	J2
East Greenville	K5
East Lansdowne	M7
Easton	L4
East Petersburg	J5
East Stroudsburg	L3
Ebensburg	D4
Eddystone	L7
Edinboro	A2
Effinwild	E6
Elizabethtown	H5
Elizabethville	H4
Elkland	G2
Ellwood City	A4
Elysburg	H4
Emlenton	B3
Emmaus	L4
Emporium	E2
Emsworth	D7
Ephrata	J5
Erie	A1
Etna	E7
Evans City	A4

	Key
Everett	E5
Exton	K5
Fayetteville	F6
Fleetwood	K5
Ford City	B4
Forest City	L2
Forest Grove	D7
Forksville	H2
Fox Chapel	E7
Freeland	K3
Freeport	B4
Galeton	F2
Gettysburg	G6
Girard	A2
Gladden	D7
Gladwyne	M6
Glenolden	M7
Glen Riddle	L7
Glen Rock	H6
Gradyville	L7
Greencastle	F6
Greensburg	B5
Greenville	A3
Gregg	D7
Grove City	A3
Hallstead	K2
Hamburg	K4
Hanover	H6
Harmarville	E6
Harrisburg, capital	H5
Harrisville	A3
Harveys Lake	J3
Haverford	M6
Havertown	M6
Hazel Hurst	D2
Hazleton	K4
Hermitage	A3
Herndon	H4
Hershey	H5
Highland	D6
Hollidaysburg	E5
Homer City	C4
Honesdale	L2
Huntingdon	E5
Hyndman	D6
Indiana	C4
Indianola	E6
Jersey Shore	G3
Jim Thorpe	K4
Johnsonburg	D3
Johnstown	D5
Kane	D2
Kennett Square	K6
King of Prussia	L5
Kingston	K3
Kittanning	B4
Kutztown	K5
Lake City	A1
Lancaster	J5
Lansdale	L5
Lansdowne	M7
Laporte	J3
Latrobe	C5
Lebanon	J5
Leechburg	B4
Lehighton	K4
Levittown	M5
Lewisburg	H4
Lewistown	F4
Ligonier	C5
Lima	L7
Linglestown	H5
Lititz	J5
Littlestown	G6
Lock Haven	G3
Lykens	H4
McCandless	A4, D6
McConnellsburg	E6
McKees Rocks	D7
McKeesport	B5
Macungie	K4
Mahanoy City	J4
Manchester	H5
Manheim	J5
Mansfield	G2
Mars	A4
Martinsburg	E5
Marysville	H5
Masontown	B6
Matamoras	M3
Meadville	A2
Mechanicsburg	G5
Media	L6, L7
Mercer	A3
Mercersburg	F6
Meridian	B4
Merion	M6
Meyersdale	C6
Middleburg	G4
Middletown	H5
Midland	A4
Mifflinburg	G4
Mifflintown	G4
Mifflinville	J3
Milford	M3
Millersburg	H4
Millersville	J6
Millheim	G4
Millvale	E7
Milroy	F4
Milton	H3
Minersville	J4
Monessen	B5
Monroeville	B5, F7
Mont Alto	F6
Montgomery	H3
Montoursville	H3
Montrose	K2
Moon Run	D7
Moscow	K3
Mt. Carmel	J4
Mt. Holly Springs	G5
Mount Joy	J5
Mt. Lebanon	D7
Mt. Nebo	D6
Mt. Oliver	E7
Mt. Pleasant	B5
Mount Union	F5
Muncy	H3
Munhall	E7
Myerstown	J5
Nanticoke	J3
Nanty Glo	D5
Nazareth	L4
Nesquehoning	K4
New Bloomfield	G4
New Castle	A4
New Freedom	H6
New Holland	J5
New Kensington	B4, F6

	Key
New Oxford	G6
Newport	G5
Newtown	M5
Newtown Square	L6
Newville	G5
New Wilmington	A3
Norristown	L5
North East	B1
Northampton	L4
North Springfield	A1
Northumberland	H4
Oakmont	E7
Oil City	B3
Old Forge	K3
Orwigsburg	J4
Oxford	J6
Palmerton	K4
Patton	D4
Pen Argyl	L4
Penn Hills	F7
Penn Wynne	M6
Perkasie	L4
Philadelphia	L6, M7
Philipsburg	E4
Phoenixville	K5
Picture Rocks	H3
Pine Grove	J4
Pittsburgh	B5, E7
Pittston	K3
Pleasantville	B2
Pleasantville	D5
Point Marion	B6
Polk	B3
Port Allegany	E2
Port Matilda	E4
Portage	D5
Portland Mills	D3
Pottstown	K5
Pottsville	J4
Powell	H2
Prospect Park	L7
Punxsutawney	C4
Quakertown	L5
Quarryville	J6
Radnor	L6
Rainsburg	D6
Reading	K5
Red Lion	H6
Renovo	F3
Reynoldsville	D3
Ridgway	D3
Ridley Park	L7
Roaring Spring	D5
St. Marys	D3
Saxonburg	B4
Sayre	H2
Schnecksville	K4
Schuylkill Haven	J4
Scottdale	B5
Scranton	K3
Selinsgrove	H4
Shamokin	H4
Sharon	A3
Sharon Hill	M7
Sharpsville	A3
Sheffield	C2
Shenandoah	J4
Shippensburg	F5
Shoemakersville	K4
Shrewsbury	H6
Sinking Spring	J5
Slatington	K4
Slippery Rock	A3
Smethport	E2
Somerset	C5
Souderton	L5
South Williamsport	G3
Spring Grove	H6
Springdale	F6
Springfield	L7
State College	F4
Stewartstown	H6
Strasburg	J6
Stroudsburg	L4
Sugarcreek	B3
Sunbury	H4
Susquehanna	K2
Swarthmore	L7
Sykesville	D3
Tamaqua	K4
Tionesta	B2
Titusville	B2
Tobyhanna	L3
Towanda	J2
Tower City	H4
Tremont	H4
Trevorton	H4
Troy	H2
Tunkhannock	K2
Tyrone	E4
Union City	B2
Uniontown	B6
Upland	L7
Valley View	H4
Vandergrift	B4
Verona	E7
Village Green	L7
Villanova	L6
Warren	C2
Washington	A5
Waterford	B2
Watsontown	H3
Waymart	L2
Wayne	L6
Waynesboro	F6
Waynesburg	A6
Weatherly	K4
Wellsboro	G2
Wesleyville	A1
West Chester	K6
West Grove	K6
West Mifflin	E7
Westmont	D5
West Pike	F2
West View	D7
Whitehall	L6
White Horse	L6
Wilcox	D2
Wilkes-Barre	K3
Wilkinsburg	E7
Williamsport	H3
Willow Grove	L5
Windber	D5
Womelsdorf	J5
York	H6
York Springs	G5
Youngsville	B2
Zelienople	A4

Other Features

	Key
Allegheny, reservoir	D2
Allegheny, river	B3
Allegheny Natl. Rec. Area	D2
Allegheny Portage Railroad N.H.S.	D5
Appalachian, mts.	F5
Clarion, river	C3
Conemaugh, river	C4
Davis, mt.	C6
Delaware, river	L2
Delaware Water Gap N.R.A.	M3
Erie, lake	A1
Friendship Hill Natl. Hist. Site	B6
Gettysburg Natl. Mil. Park	G6
Johnstown Flood Natl. Memorial	D5
Juniata, river	K3
Lehigh, river	K3
Ohio, river	A4
Presque Isle, island	A1
Raystown, lake	E5
Schuylkill, river	K5
Susquehanna, river	J2
Tioga, river	G2
Valley Forge Natl. Hist. Park	L5

Rhode Island ....page 166

Cities and Towns

	Key
Adamsville	F4
Allenton	D4
Alton	B5
Anthony	C3
Arcadia	B4
Ashaway	A5
Ashton	D2
Avondale	A6
Barrington	E3
Berkeley	D2
Bradford	B5
Bristol	E3
Carolina	C5
Central Falls	D2
Charlestown	C5
Chepachet	B2
Clayville	B3
Coventry Center	C3
Cranston	D3
Cumberland Hill	D2
Diamond Hill	D2
Dunn Corner	B5
East Greenwich	D4
East Providence	D3
Exeter	C4
Fiskeville	C3
Foster Center	B3
Galilee	C5
Glendale	C2
Green Hill	C5
Greenville	C2
Hamilton	D4
Harmony	C2
Harrisville	B2
Hope	C3
Hope Valley	B5
Hopkinton	B5
Jamestown	D5
Jerusalem	C5
Kingston	C5
Little Compton	E4
Lonsdale	D2
Matunuck	C5
Middletown	E4
Moosup Valley	B3
Narragansett Pier	D5
Newport	E4
Nooseneck	C4
North Foster	B2
North Providence	D2
North Scituate	C3
Pascoag	B2
Pawtucket	D2
Pawtuxet	D3
Perryville	C5
Plum Point	D4
Point Judith	D5
Portsmouth	E4
Providence, capital	D3
Prudence	E4
Quidnick	C3
Quonochontaug	B6
Rice City	B3
Riverside	D3
Rockville	B4
Rumford	D2
Sakonnet	E5
Saunderstown	D4
Saylesville	D2
Shannock	C5
Slatersville	C1
Slocum	C4
South Foster	B3
Spragueville	B2
Tarkiln	B2
Tiverton	E4
Usquepaug	C4
Valley Falls	D2
Wakefield	D5
Wallum Lake	B2
Warren	E3
Warwick	D3
Washington	C3
Watch Hill	A6
Weekapaug	B6
West Barrington	D3
Westerly	A6
West Glocester	B2
West Kingston	C5
West Warwick	C3
Woonsocket	C1
Wyoming	B4

Other Features

	Key
Block, island	C7
Block Island, sound	B6
Mt. Hope, bay	E4
Narragansett, bay	D4
Rhode Island, sound	E5
Roger Williams Natl. Mem.	D3
Sakonnet, river	E4
Scituate, reservoir	C3
Touro Synagogue N.H.S.	E5

South Carolina ....page 167

Cities and Towns

	Key
Abbeville	B2
Aiken	C3
Allendale	C3
Anderson	B2
Andrews	E3
Bamberg	C3
Barnwell	C3
Batesburg-Leesville	C3
Beaufort	D4
Belton	B2
Belvedere	C3
Bennettsville	D2
Bishopville	D2
Blacksburg	C1
Blackville	C3
Boiling Springs	C1
Brownsville	E2
Buffalo	D4
Burton	D4
Calhoun Falls	B2
Camden	D2
Cayce	C3
Central	B2
Charleston	E4
Cheraw	E2
Chester	C2
Chesterfield	D2
Clemson	B2
Clinton	C2
Clover	C1
Columbia, capital	C2
Conway	E3
Cowpens	C1
Darlington	E2
Denmark	C3
Dentsville	D2
Dillon	E2
Easley	B2
Edgefield	C3
Elgin	D2
Enoree	C2
Estill	C4
Fairfax	C4
Florence	E2
Folly Beach	E4
Forest Acres	D2
Foreston	D3
Fort Mill	D1
Fountain Inn	B2
Furman	C4
Gaffney	C1
Garden City	F3
Georgetown	E3
Gifford	C4
Gloverville	C3
Goose Creek	D3
Great Falls	D2
Greeleyville	E3
Greenville	B2
Greenwood	B2
Greer	B2
Hampton	C4
Hanahan	D4
Hardeeville	C4
Harleyville	D3
Hartsville	D2
Hickory Grove	C2
Hickory Grove	F3
Hilda	C3
Hilton Head Island	D4
Holly Hill	D3
Hollywood	D4
Honea Path	B2
Horrel Hill	D3
Inman	B1
Irmo	C2
Isle of Palms	E4
Jackson	C3
Jefferson	D2
Joanna	C2
Johnsonville	E3
Johnston	C3
Kershaw	D2
Kiawah Island	D4
Kingstree	E3
Kline	C3
Ladson	D4
Lake City	E3
Lancaster	D2
Landrum	B1
Lane	E3
Latta	E2
Laurel Bay	D4
Laurens	B2
Lexington	C3
Liberty	B2
Little River	F3
Little Rock	E2
Loris	F2
Lugoff	D2
Lyman	B1
Lynchburg	D2
McBee	D2
McClellanville	E3
McColl	D2
McCormick	B3
Manning	D3
Marion	E2
Mauldin	B2
Mayesville	D3
Mayo	C1
Moncks Corner	D3
Mt. Pleasant	E4
Mullins	E2
Murrells Inlet	F3
Myrtle Beach	F3
Neeses	C3
New Ellenton	C3
Newberry	C2
Nichols	E2
Ninety Six	B2
North Augusta	C3
North Charleston	E4
North Myrtle Beach	F3
Norway	C3
Olanta	E3
Olar	C3
Orangeburg	D3
Pacolet	C2
Pacolet Mills	C2
Pageland	D2
Pamplico	E3
Patrick	D2
Pelion	C3
Pendleton	B2
Pickens	B2
Piedmont	B2
Pinewood	D3
Pomaria	C2
Port Royal	D4
Ravenel	D4
Red Bank	C3
Ridgeland	D4
Ridgeville	D3
Ridgeway	D2
Rock Hill	D1
Roebuck	C2
Rowesville	D3

	Key
Ruby	D2
St. George	D3
St. Matthews	D3
St. Stephen	E3
Salley	C3
Salters	C3
Saluda	C3
Santee	D3
Sellers	E2
Seneca	B2
Simpsonville	B2
Socastee	E3
Society Hill	E2
South Congaree	C3
Spartanburg	C2
Springfield	C3
Starr	B2
Stuckey	E3
Summerville	D3
Sumter	D3
Surfside Beach	F3
Swansea	C3
Sycamore	C3
Taylors	B2
Timmonsville	E2
Travelers Rest	B2
Trenton	C3
Turbeville	D3
Union	C2
Varnville	C4
Wagener	C3
Walhalla	A2
Walterboro	D4
Ware Shoals	B2
Westminster	A2
Whitmire	C2
Williamston	B2
Williston	C3
Winnsboro	C2
Woodruff	B2
Yemassee	D4
York	C2

Other Features

	Key
Bull, island	E4
Bulls, bay	E4
Cape, island	E3
Congaree Swamp N.M.	D3
Cowpens Natl. Bfld.	C1
Edisto, river	D3
Fort Sumter Natl. Monument	E4
Greenwood, lake	C2
Hartwell, lake	B2
J. Strom Thurmond, lake	B3
Keowee, lake	B2
Kings Mt. Natl. Mil. Park	C1
Long, bay	F3
Lynches, river	D2
Marion, reservoir	C2
Monticello, reservoir	C2
Moultrie, lake	D3
Murray, lake	C2
Ninety Six Natl. Hist. Site	B2
North, island	E3
Port Royal, sound	D4
Russell, lake	B2
St. Helena, sound	D4
Saluda, river	C2
Santee, river	C3
Savannah, river	C3
South, island	E3
The Grand Strand	F3
Wateree, lake	D2
Wateree, river	D2

South Dakota .... page 168

Cities and Towns

	Key
Aberdeen	F1
Alexandria	G3
Armour	F3
Belle Fourche	A2
Beresford	H3
Black Hawk	A2
Box Elder	A2
Britton	G1
Brookings	H2
Burke	E3
Canton	H3
Chamberlain	E3
Cherry Creek	C2
Clark	G2
Clear Lake	H2
Custer	A3
Deadwood	A2
Dell Rapids	H3
De Smet	G2
Dupree	C1
Elk Point	H4
Faulkton	E1
Flandreau	H2
Fort Pierre	D2
Freeman	G3
Gettysburg	E1
Hartford	H3
Highmore	E2
Hot Springs	A3
Howard	G2
Huron	F2
Ipswich	E1
Kadoka	C3
Lake Andes	F3
Lead	A2
Lemmon	B1
Lennox	G3
Leola	F1
Madison	G2
Martin	C3
Milbank	H1
Miller	E2
Mitchell	G3
Mobridge	D1
Murdo	D3
Onida	D2
Parker	G3
Parkston	G3
Philip	C2
Pierre, capital	D2
Pine Ridge	B3
Plankinton	F3
Platte	F3
Rapid City	A2
Redfield	F2
Rosebud	D3
Salem	G3
Selby	D1
Sioux Falls	H3
Sisseton	G1
Spearfish	A2
Sturgis	A2

	Key
Timber Lake	C1
Tyndall	G4
Vermillion	H4
Volga	H2
Wagner	F3
Watertown	G2
Webster	G1
Wessington Springs	F2
White River	D3
Winner	E3
Woonsocket	F2
Wounded Knee	B3
Yankton	G4

Other Features

	Key
Andes, lake	F3
Angostura, reservoir	A3
Bad, river	C2
Badlands Natl. Park	B3
Belle Fourche, reservoir	A2
Belle Fourche, river	A2
Big Sioux, river	G2
Big Stone, lake	H1
Black, hills	A2
Bois de Sioux, river	H1
Cheyenne, river	C2
Francis Case, lake	F3
Grand, river	C1
Harney Peak, mt.	A3
James, river	F1
Jewel Cave Natl. Monument	A3
Keya Paha, river	D3
Lewis and Clark, lake	G4
Little Missouri, river	A1
Little White, river	D3
Missouri, river	F3
Moreau, river	B1
Mount Rushmore Natl. Memorial	A3
North Fork Grand, river	B1
Oahe, lake	D2
Pine, ridge	B3
Sharpe, lake	D2
South Fork Grand, river	A1
Traverse, lake	H1
Vermillion, river	G3
Waubay, lake	G1
White, river	C3
Whitewood, river	G2
Wind Cave Natl. Park	A3

Tennessee .... page 169

Cities and Towns

	Key
Adamsville	E4
Alamo	C3
Alcoa	P3
Algood	L2
Altamont	K4
Arlington	B4
Ashland City	G2
Athens	M4
Bartlett	B4
Baxter	K2
Bells	C3
Benton	M4
Bethel Springs	D4
Bethpage	J2
Blaine	P2
Blountville	S1
Bluff City	S2
Bolivar	D4
Brentwood	H2
Bristol	S1
Brownsville	C3
Bruceton	D2
Buffalo Valley	K2
Byrdstown	L1
Camden	E2
Campaign	K3
Carthage	K2
Caryville	N2
Celina	K1
Centerville	G3
Charlotte	G2
Chattanooga	L4
Church Hill	R1
Clarksville	G1
Cleveland	M4
Clinton	N2
Collegedale	L4
Collierville	B4
Columbia	G3
Conasauga	M4
Cookeville	L2
Covington	B3
Cowan	J4
Crossville	L3
Dandridge	Q2
Dayton	L4
Decatur	M3
Decaturville	E3
Decherd	J4
Dickson	G2
Dover	F2
Dresden	D2
Dunlap	L4
Dyer	C2
Dyersburg	C2
East Ridge	L4
Elizabethton	S2
Englewood	N4
Erin	F2
Erwin	S2
Estill Springs	J4
Etowah	M4
Fairfield Glade	M2
Farragut	N3
Fayetteville	H4
Forest Hills	H3
Frankewing	H4
Franklin	H3
Gainesboro	K2
Gallatin	J2
Gatlinburg	P3
Germantown	B4
Gleason	D2
Goodlettsville	H2
Granville	K2
Graysville	L4
Greeneville	R2
Greenfield	D2
Grimsley	L2
Gruetli-Laager	K4
Halls	C3
Halls Crossroads	N3
Hampshire	G3
Harriman	M3
Hartsville	J2
Henderson	D4
Hendersonville	H2

	Key
Humboldt	D3
Huntingdon	E3
Huntsville	N2
Jacksboro	N2
Jackson	D3
Jamestown	M2
Jasper	K4
Jefferson City	Q2
Jellico	N1
Johnson City	S2
Jonesborough	S2
Karns	N3
Kenton	C2
Kingsport	R1
Kingston	M3
Kingston Springs	G2
Knoxville	P3
La Follette	N2
Lake City	N2
Lakewood	H2
La Vergne	H2
Lawrenceburg	G4
Lebanon	J2
Lenoir City	N3
Lewisburg	H4
Lexington	E3
Linden	F3
Livingston	L2
Loretto	G4
Loudon	N3
Lynchburg	J4
McEwen	F2
McKenzie	D2
McKinnon	F2
McMinnville	K3
Madisonville	N3
Manchester	J4
Martin	D2
Maryville	P3
Mascot	P2
Maynardville	P2
Medon	D4
Memphis	A4
Middleton	D4
Milan	D3
Millersville	H2
Milligan College	S2
Millington	B4
Monterey	L2
Morristown	Q2
Mosheim	R2
Mountain City	T1
Mount Juliet	H2
Mount Pleasant	G3
Munford	B4
Murfreesboro	J3
Nashville, capital	H2
Newbern	C2
New Johnsonville	F2
New Tazewell	P2
Nolensville	H3
Norris	N2
Oak Hill	H2
Oak Ridge	N2
Oliver Springs	N2
Oneida	M2
Overall	J3
Paris	E2
Parsons	E3
Pegram	G2
Pigeon Forge	P3
Pikeville	L3
Portland	H1
Powell	N2
Pulaski	G4
Reagan	E3
Red Bank	L4
Ridgely	B3
Ripley	B3
Rockwood	M3
Rogersville	R2
Rutherford	C2
Rutledge	Q2
Savannah	E4
Selmer	D4
Sevierville	P3
Sewanee	K4
Shelbyville	J4
Signal Mountain	L4
Smithville	K3
Smyrna	H3
Sneedville	Q1
Soddy-Daisy	L4
Somerville	C4
South Fulton	D2
South Pittsburg	K4
Sparta	L3
Spencer	L3
Spring City	L3
Spring Hill	H3
Springfield	H1
Stanton	C4
Surgoinsville	R2
Sweetwater	N3
Taft	H4
Tazewell	P2
Tellico Plains	N4
Tennessee Ridge	F2
Tiptonville	C2
Tracy City	K4
Trenton	D3
Trimble	C2
Tullahoma	J4
Tusculum	R2
Union City	M2
Wartburg	M2
Waverly	F2
Waynesboro	F4
Westmoreland	J1
White House	H2
White Pine	Q2
Whitwell	K4
Winchester	J4
Woodbury	J3

Other Features

	Key
Andrew Johnson Natl. Hist. Site	R2
Appalachian, mts.	N4
Appalachian Natl. Scenic Trail	Q3
Barkley, lake	F1
Big South Fork Natl. River and Rec. Area	M1
Center Hill, lake	K3
Cherokee, lake	Q2
Chickamauga & Chattanooga Natl. Mil. Park	L5
Chickamauga, lake	M3
Clinch, river	Q2
Clingmans Dome, mt.	Q3
Cumberland, river	G2

	Key
Dale Hollow, lake	L1
Douglas, lake	Q3
Duck, river	H3
Great Smoky, mts.	P3
Great Smoky Mts. Natl. Park	Q3
Holston, river	R2
Kentucky, lake	F2
Mississippi, river	B3
Norris, lake	P2
Roan, mt.	S2
Shiloh Natl. Mil. Park	E4
Tennessee, river	E5, K5
Watts Bar, lake	M3
Woods, reservoir	J4

Texas .... page 170

Cities and Towns

	Key
Abernathy	F2
Abilene	H3
Addison	C1
Alamo Heights	B7
Albany	H3
Algoa	F9
Alice	J8
Alpine	D5
Alvin	M6
Amarillo	B9
Anahuac	N6
Anderson	M5
Andrews	E3
Angleton	M6
Anson	H3
Anthony	A3
Aransas Pass	K8
Archer City	J2
Arlington	L3
Asherton	H7
Aspermont	G2
Atascosa	A7
Athens	M3
Atlanta	N2
Austin, capital	K5
Avondale	A1
Azle	K3
Bacliff	G9
Baird	H3
Balch Springs	C2
Balcones Heights	A7
Ballinger	H4
Bandera	H6
Barrett	F8
Bastrop	K5
Batesville	H7
Bay City	M7
Bayou Vista	G10
Baytown	N6
Beaumont	N5
Beaumont Place	F8
Beaver	C8
Bedford	B2
Beeville	K7
Bellaire	E8
Bellmead	K4
Belton	K4
Benavides	J8
Benbrook	A2
Benjamin	H2
Bergheim	A6
Big Lake	F4
Big Spring	F3
Bishop	K8
Boerne	J6
Bogata	M2
Bonham	L2
Borger	C9
Bovina	E1
Bowie	K2
Bracken	B6
Brackettville	G6
Brady	H4
Breckenridge	J3
Brenham	L5
Briar	A1
Bridge City	P5
Bridgeport	K2
Brookshire	M6
Brookside Village	F9
Brownfield	E2
Brownsville	K10
Brownwood	J4
Bryan	L5
Buckingham	C1
Buena Vista	B7
Buffalo	L4
Bulverde	A6
Buna	P5
Bunker Hill Village	E8
Burkburnett	J1
Burleson	A3
Burleson	K3
Burnet	J5
Caldwell	L5
Cameron	L5
Canadian	D9
Canton	M3
Canutillo	A4
Canyon	B9
Carrizo Springs	H7
Carrollton	B1
Carthage	N3
Castle Hills	A6
Castle Hills	J6
Cedar Hill	B3
Cedar Park	K5
Center	N4
Centerville	M4
Chandler	M3
Channelview	F8
Channing	B9
Childress	G1
Chocolate Bayou	F10
Cisco	J3
Clarendon	C10
Clarksville	M2
Claude	C9
Cleburne	K3
Cleveland	M5
Clifton	K4
Cloverleaf	F8
Clute	M6
Cockrell Hill	B2
Coldspring	M5
Coleman	H4
College Station	L5
Colleyville	A1
Colorado City	G3
Columbus	L6
Comanche	J4
Combine	D2

	Key
Commerce	L2
Conroe	M5
Converse	B6
Cooper	M2
Copperas Cove	K4
Corpus Christi	K8
Corsicana	L3
Cotulla	H7
Crane	E4
Crockett	M4
Crosby	F8
Crosbyton	F2
Crowell	H2
Crowley	A3
Crystal City	H7
Cuero	K6
Daingerfield	N2
Dalhart	B8
Dallas	L3
Dalworthington Gardens	B2
Danbury	F10
Dayton	N5
Decatur	K2
Deer Park	F8
Del Rio	G6
Denison	L2
Denton	K2
Denver City	E3
De Soto	L3
Devine	J6
Diboll	N4
Dickens	G2
Dickinson	F9
Dilley	H7
Dimmitt	E1
Dublin	J4
Dumas	B9
Duncanville	B2
Eagle Lake	L6
Eagle Pass	G7
Eastland	J3
Eden	H4
Edgecliff	A3
Edinburg	J9
Edna	L7
El Campo	L6
Eldorado	G5
El Paso	A4
Electra	J1
Elgin	K5
Elsa	J9
Emory	M3
Ennis	L3
Euless	B2
Everman	A3
Fabens	A4
Fair Oaks Ranch	A6
Fairfield	L4
Falfurrias	J8
Farmers Branch	B1
Farwell	D1
Ferris	L3
Flatonia	K6
Floresville	J6
Floydada	F2
Forest Hill	A2
Fort Davis	D5
Fort Stockton	E5
Fort Worth	K3
Franklin	L4
Fredericksburg	J5
Freeport	M7
Freer	J8
Friendswood	F9
Gail	F3
Gainesville	L2
Galena Park	F8
Galveston	N6
Ganado	L6
Garden City	F4
Garden Ridge	B6
Gardendale	B7
Garland	C2
Gatesville	K4
George West	J7
Georgetown	K5
Germann	C3
Giddings	L5
Gilmer	N3
Gladewater	N3
Glen Rose	K3
Glenn Heights	B3
Goldthwaite	J4
Goliad	K6
Gonzales	K6
Gorman	J3
Graham	K3
Granbury	K3
Grand Prairie	B2
Grand Saline	M3
Grapeland	M4
Grapevine	B1
Grapevine	A1
Greenville	L2
Groesbeck	L4
Groves	P6
Groveton	M4
Guthrie	G2
Hallettsville	L6
Haltom City	A2
Hamilton	J4
Hamlin	H3
Harker Heights	K4
Harlingen	K9
Haskell	H2
Hearne	L5
Hebbronville	J8
Helotes	A6
Hemphill	P4
Hempstead	M5
Henderson	N3
Henrietta	J2
Hereford	B10
Hewitt	K4
Hico	J4
Hidalgo	J9
Highland Park	C2
Highlands	F8
Hillsboro	K3
Hitchcock	F9
Hollywood Park	A6
Hondo	H6
Houston	M6
Hubbard	L4
Huntsville	M5
Hutchins	C2
Idalou	F2
India	C3
Ingleside	K8

	Key
Iowa Park	J2
Irving	C2
Jacinto City	E8
Jacksboro	J2
Jacksonville	M3
Jasper	P4
Jayton	G2
Jefferson	N2
Jersey Village	E8
Johnson City	J5
Jourdanton	J7
Juliff	F9
Junction	H5
Karnes City	K7
Katy	M6
Kaufman	L3
Keller	A1
Kermit	D4
Kerrville	H5
Kilgore	N3
Killeen	K4
Kingsland	J5
Kingsville	K8
Kirby	B7
Kirbyville	P5
Knox City	H2
Kountze	N5
La Grange	L6
Lake Jackson	M7
Lakehills	H6
La Marque	F9
Lamesa	F3
Lampasas	J5
Lancaster	B3
La Porte	F8
La Pryor	H7
Laredo	H8
League City	F9
Leakey	H6
Leon Springs	A6
Leon Valley	A7
Levelland	E2
Lewisville	L2
Liberty	N5
Linden	N2
Lipscomb	D9
Littlefield	E2
Live Oak	B6
Livingston	N4
Llano	J5
Lockhart	K5
Lockney	F2
Longview	N3
Lubbock	F2
Lufkin	N4
Luling	K6
Mabank	M3
McAllen	J9
McCamey	E4
Macdona	A7
McKinney	L2
Mangus Corner	J6
Mansfield	A2
Manvel	F9
Marble Falls	J5
Marfa	C5
Marlin	L4
Marshall	N3
Mason	H5
Matador	F2
Mathis	K7
Memphis	C10
Menard	H5
Mentone	D4
Meridian	K4
Merkel	H3
Mertzon	G4
Mesquite	C2
Mesquite	L3
Mexia	L4
Miami	C9
Midland	E4
Midlothian	K3
Mineola	M3
Mineral Wells	K3
Mission	J9
Missouri City	F9
Monahans	E4
Mont Belvieu	N6
Montague	K2
Morgans Point	F9
Morton	E2
Moss Bluff	N6
Mt. Houston	E8
Mt. Pleasant	N2
Mt. Vernon	M2
Muleshoe	E1
Munday	H2
Murphy	C1
Nacogdoches	N4
Nassau Bay	F9
Navasota	L5
Nederland	P5
New Berlin	B7
New Boston	N2
New Braunfels	J6
Newton	P5
Nixon	K6
Nocona	K2
North Houston	E8
North Richland Hills	A1
Odessa	E4
Olmos Park	B7
Olney	J2
Olton	E1
Orange	P5
Ovilla	B3
Ozona	F5
Paducah	G1
Paint Rock	H4
Palacios	L7
Palestine	M3
Palo Pinto	K3
Pampa	C10
Panhandle	C9
Pantego	B2
Paris	M2
Parita	A2
Parker	C1
Pasadena	F8
Pearland	F9
Pearsall	H7
Pecos	D4
Pelican Bay	A1
Perryton	C9
Pharr	J9
Pilot Point	L2
Pittsburg	N2

	Key
...Columbia	E2
...ew	F1
...ton	J7
...P6
...livar	G9
...bel	K9
...ael	K8
...vaca	L7
...F2
...j6
...j8
...O6
...nt	H1
...sh	M3
...an	J3
...F4
...ondville	K9
...oak	C3
...K7
...A2
...dson	C1
...nd Hills	A2
...ond	M6
...ande City	A1
...ke	J9
...Lee	G4
...own	K4
...G3
...ale	L5
...ort	K7
...prings	G5
...all	L3
...H9
...G3
...berg	M6
...ron	E9
...G3
... Rock	K5
...t	C2
...M4
...H6
...al	K1
...dwig	A7
...ngelo	G4
...ntonio	J6
...ugustine	N4
...enito	L7
...rson	E5
...iego	J8
... Point	E9
...K2
...eronimo	A6
...ion	G9
...arcos	K6
...aba	J4
...m Park	A2
...K8
...na	E8
...B7
...z	B6
...hansville	C6
...ook	F9
...ft	L7
...ville	C2
...aves	L6
...K6
...B6
...ole	E3
...our	H2
...water	E2
...no Park	A6
...ake	L2
...acres	G9
... Blanca	B4
...e	N5
...on	F1
...K7
... Point	G9
...ville	K5
...C3
...ro	A4
...a	G5
...Houston	F9
...lake	A1
...side Place	E8
...B7
...man	A1
... Valley	E8
...rd	G2
...ord	E9
...ord	H3
...on	F3
...enville	J3
...ng City	G4
...ord	B8
... Land	E9
...ur Springs	M2
...own	E2
...yvale	C2
...water	G3
...a	F2
...K5
...xana	N2
... City	N6
...Woodlands	E9
...psons	J7
... Rivers	H2
...kmorton	J7
...M5
...all	M5
...y Club	A1
...F1
...M3
...rsal City	J6
...rsity Park	C2
...H6
...alstyne	L2
...orn	C4
...B9
...ia	A1
...H1
...L7
...N5
...Ormy	A7
...om	N3
...uga	J4
...achie	L3
...herford	K3
...ter	F9
...gton	D10
...aco	K9
...Columbia	M6
...Odessa	E4
...er Hills	A2

	Key
West University Place	E8
Westworth	A2
Wharton	L6
Wheatland	A3
Wheeler	D9
White Settlement	A2
Whitesboro	L2
Wichita Falls	J2
Willis	M5
Wills Point	L3
Wilmer	C3
Windcrest	B6
Winnie	N6
Winnsboro	M3
Winters	H4
Wolfforth	F2
Woodville	N5
Woodway	K4
Wylie	D1
Yoakum	K6
Zapata	H9
Zuehl	B7

Other Features

Alibates Flint Quarries N.M.	B9
Amistad, reservoir	F6
Amistad Natl. Rec. Area	G6
Balcones, escarpment	A6
Big Bend Natl. Park	D6
Big Thicket Natl. Preserve	N5
Black, mt.	G6
Canadian, river	C9
Cathedral, mt.	D5
Chamizal Natl. Mem.	A4
Chinati Peak, mt.	C6
Dallas-Fort Worth Intl. Airport	B2
Davis, mts.	C5
Eagle Peak, mt.	B5
Edwards, plateau	G5
Emory Peak, mt.	D6
Falcon, reservoir	H9
Fort Davis Natl. Hist. Site	D5
Galveston, bay	N6
Galveston, island	N6
Guadalupe, mts.	C4
Guadalupe Mts. Natl. Park	C4
Guadalupe Peak, mt.	C4
Kemp, lake	H2
Livermore, mt.	C5
Livingston, lake	M5
Lyndon B. Johnson N.H.P.	J5
Meredith, lake	C9
Nueces, river	J7
O.H. Ivie, lake	H4
Padre Island Natl. Seashore	K8
Pecos, river	E4
Pelican, island	G9
Red, river	H1
Red Bluff, lake	D4
Rio Grande, river	F6
Sabine, pass	P6
Sabine, river	P5
Sam Rayburn, reservoir	N4
Santiago Peak, mt.	D6
Sierra Del Carmen, mt.	D6
Stockton, plateau	E5
Toledo Bend, reservoir	P4

Utah .... page 171

Cities and Towns

American Fork	C3
Beaver	B5
Bicknell	C5
Blanding	E6
Bluffdale	C3
Bountiful	C3
Brigham City	C2
Castle Dale	C4
Cedar City	A6
Centerville	C3
Clearfield	B2
Coalville	C3
Cottonwood Heights	C3
Delta	B4
Draper	C3
Duchesne	D3
East Carbon	D4
Enoch	A6
Ephraim	C4
Farmington	C3
Ferron	C4
Fillmore	B5
Garland	B2
Grantsville	B3
Gunnison	C4
Heber City	C3
Helper	D4
Hildale	A6
Huntington	D4
Hurricane	A6
Hyrum	C2
Ivins	A6
Junction	B5
Kanab	A6
Lapoint	E3
Layton	C3
Lehi	C3
Lewiston	C2
Loa	C5
Logan	C2
Long Valley Junction	B6
Maeser	E3
Magna	B3
Manila	E3
Manti	C4
Mapleton	C3
Moab	E5
Monroe	B5
Monticello	E6
Morgan	C2
Mount Pleasant	C4
Murray	C3
Myton	D3
N. Salt Lake	C3
Nephi	C4
North Ogden	C2
Ogden	C2
Orangeville	C4
Orem	C3
Panguitch	B6
Parowan	B6
Payson	C3
Plain City	B2
Pleasant Grove	C3
Price	D4
Provo	C3
Randolph	C2
Richfield	B5
Richmond	C2

	Key
Riverton	C3
Roosevelt	D3
Roy	B2
St. George	A6
Salem	C3
Salina	C5
Salt Lake City, capital	C3
Sandy	C3
Santa Clara	A6
Santaquin	C4
Smithfield	C2
South Jordan	C3
Spanish Fork	C3
Springville	C3
Sugarville	B4
Tooele	B3
Tremonton	B2
Vernal	E3
Washington	A6
Wellington	D4
West Jordan	C3
West Valley City	C3
Willard	B2

Other Features

Abajo Peak, mt.	E6
Arches Natl. Park	E5
Bear, lake	C2
Bear, river	B5
Beaver, river	B5
Bonneville Salt Flats	A3
Bruin Point, mt.	D4
Bryce Canyon Natl. Park	B6
Canyonlands Natl. Park	E5
Capitol Reef Natl. Park	C5
Cedar Breaks Natl. Monument	B6
Colorado, river	E5
Delano Peak, mt.	B5
Deseret Peak, mt.	B3
Dinosaur Natl. Monument	E3
Dutton, mt.	B5
Escalante, river	C6
Flaming Gorge, reservoir	E2
Flaming Gorge Natl. Rec. Area	E2
Frisco Peak, mt.	A5
Glen Canyon Natl. Rec. Area	D6
Golden Spike Natl. Hist. Site	B2
Great, basin	A4
Great Salt, lake	B2
Great Salt Lake, desert	A3
Green, river	D4
Heliotrope, mt.	D6
Henry, mts.	D6
Ibapah Peak, mt.	A4
Kings Peak, mt.	D3
Marsh Peak, mt.	E3
Marvine, mt.	C5
Monument, valley	D6
Natural Bridges Natl. Monument	E6
Navajo, river	D6
Navajo Indian Res.	E6
Nebo, mt.	C4
Paria, river	C6
Pavant, range	B5
Peale, mt.	E5
Pennell, mt.	D6
Powell, lake	D6
Price, river	D4
Rainbow Bridge Natl. Monument	D6
Salt Marsh, lake	A4
San Juan, river	D6
San Rafael, river	D4
Sevier, desert	B4
Sevier, lake	A5
Strawberry, river	D3
Swasey Peak, mt.	A4
Timpanogos Cave N.M.	C3
Uinta, mts.	D3
Utah, lake	C3
Wasatch, plateau	C4
White, river	E3
Zion Natl. Park	A6

Vermont .... page 172

Cities and Towns

Addison	A2
Albany	C1
Ascutney	C4
Averill	D1
Bakersfield	B1
Barnard	B3
Barnet	C2
Barre	C2
Basin Harbor	A2
Beecher Falls	D1
Bellows Falls	C4
Bennington	A5
Benson	A3
Berlin	B2
Bethel	B3
Bloomfield	D1
Bradford	C3
Brandon	A3
Brattleboro	B5
Bristol	A2
Brookfield	B2
Burlington	A2
Cabot	C2
Cambridge	B1
Castleton	A3
Cavendish	B4
Charlotte	A2
Chelsea	C3
Colchester	A1
Concord	D2
Danby	B4
Dorset	A4
East Burke	D1
East Haven	D1
East Middlebury	A3
East Randolph	B3
Eden	B1
Enosburg Falls	B1
Essex	A1
Essex Junction	A1
Evansville	D1
Fair Haven	A3
Fairfax	B1
Fairfield	B1
Fairlee	C3
Franklin	B1
Gallup Mills	D1
Gaysville	B3
Georgia Center	A1
Grafton	B4
Granby	D1
Grand Isle	A1
Groton	C2

	Key
Guildhall	D1
Guilford	B5
Hancock	B3
Hanover	C3
Hardwick	C2
Hartford	C3
Hartland	C3
Hartwellville	D1
Heartwellville	A5
Highgate Center	A1
Hinesburg	A2
Hortonia	A3
Hubbardton	A3
Hyde Park	B1
Irasburg	C1
Irasville	B2
Jacksonville	B5
Jamaica	B4
Jeffersonville	B1
Johnson	B1
Keeler Bay	A1
Larrabees Point	A3
Lemington	D1
Londonderry	B4
Lowell	C1
Lyndon	C1
Lyndonville	C1
McIndoe Falls	C2
Marlboro	B5
Mendon	B3
Middlebury	A2
Middlesex	B2
Milton	A1
Monkton	A2
Montgomery	B1
Montgomery Center	B1
Montpelier, capital	B2
Morgan	C1
Morrisville	B1
Moscow	B1
Newbury	C2
Newfane	B4
New Haven	A2
Newport	C1
North Bennington	A5
Northfield	B2
North Hero	A1
North Wolcott	C1
Norton	D1
Orange	C2
Panton	A2
Peacham	C2
Pittsfield	B3
Pittsford	A3
Plainfield	C2
Plymouth	B3
Pompanoosuc	C3
Post Mills	C3
Poultney	A3
Pownal	A5
Proctor	A3
Putney	B5
Randolph	B3
Readsboro	B5
Richford	B1
Richmond	B2
Rochester	B3
Roxbury	B2
Rutland	B3
St. Albans	A1
St. Johnsbury	C2
Searsburg	B5
Shaftsbury	A4
Sharon	C3
Shelburne	A2
Sheldon	B1
Shoreham	A3
South Burlington	A2
South Hero	A1
Springfield	C4
Stamford	A5
Starksboro	A2
Swanton	A1
Timmouth	A4
Troy	C1
Tunbridge	C3
Tyson	B4
Underhill	B1
Vergennes	A2
Vernon	B5
Warren	B2
Washington	C2
Waterbury	B2
Waterville	B1
Wells River	C2
West Burke	D1
West Dover	B5
West Haven	A3
Westminster	C4
Weston	B4
West Pawlet	A4
West Topsham	C2
Wheelock	C2
White River Junction	C3
Williamsville	B5
Wilmington	B5
Windsor	C4
Winooski	A1
Wolcott	C1
Woodford	A5
Woodstock	B3
Worcester	B2

Other Features

Appalachian Natl. Scenic Trail	A5
Black, river	C1
Bomoseen, lake	A3
Bread Loaf, mt.	B3
Bromley, mt.	B4
Camels Hump, mt.	B2
Champlain, lake	A1
Connecticut, river	C3
Ellen, mt.	B2
Green, mts.	B4
Harriman, reservoir	B5
Jay Peak, mt.	B1
Killington Peak, mt.	B3
Lamoille, river	B1
Mansfield, mt.	B1
Mettawee, river	A3
Missisquoi, river	C1
Seymour, lake	C1
Smugglers Notch, pass	B1
Snow, mt.	B5
Somerset, reservoir	B4
Waterbury, reservoir	B2
West, river	B4
White, river	B3
White Rocks N.R.A.	B4

	Key
Willoughby, lake	C1

Virginia .... page 173

Cities and Towns

Abingdon	D1
Accomac	M4
Achilles	L5
Alberta	H6
Alexandria	J2
Allison Gap	D1
Altavista	E5
Amelia Court House	H5
Amherst	E4
Annandale	M2
Appalachia	B1
Appomattox	F5
Arlington	J2
Ashland	H4
Baileys Crossroads	M2
Bassett	C6
Basye	F2
Bedford	D5
Belleair	L2
Belle Haven	M4
Belle View	M2
Bensley	J5
Berryville	H1
Big Stone Gap	B1
Blacksburg	B5
Blackstone	H5
Bland	A5
Bloxom	M4
Bluefield	A5
Bon Air	H4
Bowling Green	J3
Boyce	G1
Boydton	G6
Boykins	J6
Bridgewater	F3
Bristol	D2
Brodnax	G6
Brookneal	F5
Brunswick	H6
Buckingham	F4
Buena Vista	E4
Burke	L2
Burkeville	G5
Callands	D6
Cape Charles	L5
Castlewood	C1
Centreville	J2
Charles City	J5
Charlotte Court House	F5
Charlottesville	F4
Chase City	G6
Chatham	E6
Cheriton	M5
Chesapeake	L6
Chester	J5
Chesterfield	H5
Chilhowie	E1
Chincoteague	M4
Christiansburg	C5
Chula	H5
Claremont	K5
Clifton Forge	D4
Clinchco	C1
Clintwood	C1
Coeburn	C1
Collinsville	D6
Colonial Beach	K3
Colonial Hts.	J5
Concord	E5
Courtland	J6
Covington	C4
Crewe	G5
Crimora	F3
Crystal City	M2
Crystal Hill	F6
Culpeper	G3
Cumberland	G4
Dale City	J2
Danville	E6
Dendron	K5
Dillwyn	G4
Dinwiddie	H5
Drakes Branch	F6
Dublin	B5
Dumfries	J2
Dungannon	C1
Eastville	M5
Elkton	F3
Emory	D1
Emporia	H6
Ewing	A1
Fairfax	J2
Fairfax Station	L2
Falls Church	M2
Falmouth	J3
Farmville	G5
Ferrum	D6
Figsboro	D6
Fincastle	D4
Fishersville	F3
Flint Hill	G2
Floyd	C6
Forest	E5
Fort Mitchell	G6
Franconia	M2
Franklin	K6
Fredericksburg	J3
Fries	B6
Front Royal	G2
Galax	B6
Gate City	C1
Glade Spring	D1
Gloucester	K5
Gloucester Point	L5
Goochland	H4
Gordonsville	G3
Goshen	E3
Gretna	E6
Grottoes	F3
Groveton	M2
Grundy	D1
Halifax	F6
Hampton	L5
Hanover	J4
Harrisonburg	F3
Harrogate	A1
Heathsville	L4
Hollins	D5
Hopewell	J5
Horse Pasture	D6
Huntington	M2
Hurt	E5
Independence	A6
Isle of Wight	K6
Jetersville	G5

	Key
Jonesville	B1
Kenbridge	G6
King and Queen Courthouse	K4
King George	J3
Kings Park	L2
King William	J4
Lancaster	L4
Lawrenceville	H6
Lebanon	D1
Leesburg	H1
Lexington	E4
Lincolnia	M2
Louisa	G3
Lovingston	F4
Lunenburg	G6
Luray	G2
Lynchburg	E5
McLean	M1
Madison	G3
Manakin	H4
Manassas	J2
Manassas Park	J2
Mantua	M2
Marion	A6
Martinsville	D6
Mathews	L5
Mechanicsburg	J4
Mechanicsville	J4
Meherrin	G5
Millboro	D4
Monterey	D3
Montross	K3
Mount Jackson	F2
Narrows	B5
New Castle	C4
New Kent	K4
New Market	F2
Newport News	L5
Newsoms	J6
Norfolk	L6
North Springfield	M2
Norton	C1
Nottoway Court House	G5
Oakton	L2
Onancock	M4
Orange	G3
Palmyra	G4
Pearisburg	B5
Petersburg	J5
Peterstown	B5
Pimmit Hills	M1
Poquoson	L5
Portsmouth	L6
Powhatan	H4
Prince George	J5
Pulaski	B5
Purcellville	H1
Radford	B5
Raven	D1
Reston	J2
Richlands	D1
Richmond, capital	J4
Ridgeway	D6
Roanoke	D5
Rocky Mount	D6
Rustburg	E5
Ruther Glen	J4
Salem	D5
Saltville	D1
Saluda	K4
Shenandoah	F3
Smithfield	K6
South Boston	F6
South Hill	G6
Spotsylvania	H3
Springfield	M2
Spring Hill	M1
Stafford	J3
Stanardsville	G3
Staunton	E3
Sterling	J1
Stony Creek	J6
Strasburg	G2
Stuart	C6
Stuarts Draft	E3
Suffolk	K5
Surry	K5
Sussex	J6
Tappahannock	K4
Tazewell	D1
Timberville	F2
Triangle	J2
Tysons Corner	M1
Vale	L1
Verona	E3
Victoria	G5
Vienna	L1
Virginia Beach	M6
Warm Springs	D3
Warrenton	H2
Warsaw	K4
Washington	G2
Waverly	J5
Waynesboro	F3
Weber City	C1
Wellington	M3
West Point	K4
West Springfield	M2
Williamsburg	K5
Winchester	G1
Wise	C1
Woodbridge	J2
Woodstock	F2
Wytheville	A5
Yorktown	K5

Other Features

Allegheny, mts.	D3
Anna, lake	H3
Appalachian, mts.	C5
Appomattox Court House N.H.P.	F5
Arlington Natl. Cem.	M2
Assateague Island Natl. Seashore	M4
Booker T. Washington N.M.	D5
Charles, cape	M5
Chesapeake, bay	L5
Colonial Natl. Hist. Park	K5
Fredericksburg & Spotsylvania Natl. Mil. Park	H3
Gaston, lake	G6
George Washington Birthplace N.M.	K3
Henry, cape	M6
Iron, mts.	A6
James, river	E5
John H. Kerr, reservoir	F6
Manassas Natl. Battlefield Park	H2
Mount Rogers Natl. Rec. Area	A6
Petersburg Natl. Battlefield	J5
Potomac, river	K3
Rappahannock, river	J3
Rogers, mt.	A6

192 VIRGINIA–WYOMING

Name	Key
Shenandoah, *mts.*	E3
Shenandoah, *river*	F3
Shenandoah Natl. Park	G2
Smith Mtn., *lake*	D5
York, *river*	K5

Washington ....page 174

Cities and Towns

Name	Key
Aberdeen	C4
Amboy	D5
Anacortes	D2
Arlington	D2
Asotin	J4
Auburn	D3
Bangor	A1
Battle Ground	D5
Bellingham	D2
Belvedere	H2
Benton City	G4
Bethel	A2
Birch Bay	D2
Blaine	D2
Boardman	G5
Bothel	D3
Bremerton	D3
Brewster	G2
Bridgeport	G3
Bucoda	D4
Burien	B2
Burlington	D2
Camas	D5
Cashmere	F3
Castle Rock	D4
Cathlamet	C4
Central Park	C3
Centralia	D4
Chehalis	D4
Chelan	F3
Cheney	J4
Chewelah	J2
Clarkston	J4
Cle Elum	F3
Clinton	D3
Colfax	J4
College Place	H4
Colville	J2
Connell	H4
Cosmopolis	C4
Country Homes	J3
Coupeville	D2
Davenport	H3
Dayton	J4
Deer Park	J3
Dusty	J4
Eastgate	B2
Easton	E3
Eastsound	D2
East Wenatchee	F3
Eatonville	D4
Edmonds	D3
Ellensburg	F3
Elma	C3
Elmer City	H3
Enumclaw	E3
Ephrata	G3
Everett	D2
Everson	D2
Fall City	E3
Federal Way	D3
Ferndale	D2
Fords Prairie	C4
Forks	B3
Four Lakes	J3
Friday Harbor	C2
Fruitvale	F4
Goldendale	F5
Gorst	A2
Grandview	G4
Granger	F4
Hoquiam	C3
Inglewood	C2
Kelso	D4
Kenmore	B1
Kennewick	G4
Kent	D3
Kettle Falls	H2
Kirkland	D3
Lacey	D3
La Grande	D4
Lake Stevens	D2
Leavenworth	F3
Lexington	D4
Longmire	E4
Longview	D4
Lynden	D2
Mabton	G4
McKenna	D4
McMurray	D2
Markham	C4
Marysville	D2
Medical Lake	J3
Medina	B2
Mercer Island	D3
Merritt	F3
Monroe	D3
Montesano	C4
Moses Lake	G3
Mount Vernon	D2
Mukilteo	D3
Newhalem	E2
Newport	J2
Newport Hills	B2
Normandy Park	B2
North Bend	E3
Oak Harbor	D2
Ocean Park	B4
Ocean Shores	B3
Okanogan	G2
Olalla	B2
Olympia, *capital*	D3
Omak	G2
Opportunity	J3
Orchards	D5
Oroville	G2
Othello	G4
Oysterville	B4
Pasco	G4
Plymouth	G5
Pomeroy	J4
Port Angeles	C2
Porter	C3
Port Hadlock	D2
Port Ludlow	D3
Port Orchard	D3
Port Townsend	D2
Poulsbo	D3
Prosser	G4
Pullman	J4
Puyallup	D3

Name	Key
Quincy	G3
Raymond	C4
Redmond	D3
Renton	D3
Republic	H2
Richland	G4
Richmond Highlands	B1
Ridgefield	D5
Ritzville	H3
St. John	J3
Seabeck	A2
Sea-Tac	D3
Seattle	D3
Sedro Woolley	D2
Selah	F4
Sequim	C2
Shelton	C3
Silverton	E2
Skyway	B2
Smokey Point	D3
Snohomish	D3
Snoqualmie	E3
South Bend	C4
Southworth	B2
Spanaway	D3
Spokane	J3
Stanwood	D2
Stevenson	E5
Sultan	E3
Sumas	D2
Sumner	D3
Sunnyside	F4
Suquamish	A1
Tacoma	D3
Tekoa	J3
Tenino	D4
Tiger	J2
Toppenish	F4
Tracyton	A2
Trentwood	J3
Tukwila	B2
Tumwater	D4
Union Gap	F4
University Place	D3
Vancouver	D5
Vashon	B2
Walla Walla	H4
Wapato	F4
Warden	G4
Washougal	D5
Waterville	F3
Wenatchee	F3
Westport	B4
West Richland	G4
White Center	B2
White Salmon	E5
Winslow	D3
Woodinville	B1
Woodland	D5
Yakima	F4
Yelm	D4
Zillah	F4

Other Features

Name	Key
Adams, *mt.*	E4
Bainbridge, *island*	B2
Baker, *mt.*	E2
Banks, *lake*	G3
Cascade, *range*	E4
Chelan, *lake*	F2
Chewuch, *river*	F2
Columbia, *river*	G2
Copper Butte, *mt.*	H2
Cowlitz, *river*	E4
Disappointment, *cape*	A4
Elliott, *bay*	B2
Flattery, *cape*	B2
Franklin D. Roosevelt, *lake*	H2
Glacier Peak, *mt.*	E2
Grays, *harbor*	B4
Green, *river*	E3
Hood, *canal*	C3
Kettle River, *range*	H2
Klickitat, *river*	E4
Lake Chelan Natl. Rec. Area	F2
Lake Roosevelt Natl. Rec. Area	H2
Lewis, *river*	E4
Mt. Baker Natl. Rec. Area	E2
Mount Rainier Natl. Park	E4
Mt. St. Helens Natl. Vol. Mon.	D4
North Cascades Natl. Park	E2
Okanogan, *river*	G2
Olympic, *mts.*	C3
Olympic Natl. Park	C3
Olympus, *mt.*	C3
Omak, *mt.*	G2
Orcas, *island*	D2
Oregon Butte, *mt.*	J4
Ozette, *lake*	B2
Pasayten, *river*	F2
Pend Oreille, *river*	J2
Potholes, *reservoir*	G3
Priest Rapids, *lake*	G4
Puget, *sound*	B1, D2
Rainier, *mt.*	E4
Riffe, *lake*	D4
Rimrock, *lake*	E4
Ross, *lake*	E2
Ross Lake Natl. Rec. Area	F2
Sacajawea, *lake*	H4
St. Helens, *mt.*	D4
San Juan, *island*	C2
Sanpoil, *river*	H2
Selkirk, *mts.*	J2
Skagit, *river*	E2
Skykomish, *river*	E3
Snake, *river*	H4
Spokane, *river*	H3
Strait of Juan de Fuca	B2
Stuart, *river*	F3
Umatilla, *lake*	G5
Vashon, *island*	B2
Wallula, *lake*	H4
Washington, *lake*	B1
Wenatchee, *lake*	F3
Wenatchee, *mts.*	F3
Wenatchee, *river*	F3
White, *pass*	E4
Whitman Mission Natl. Hist. Site	H4
Willapa, *bay*	B4
Yakima, *river*	F4
Yale, *lake*	D5

West Virginia ....page 175

Cities and Towns

Name	Key
Ansted	D4
Barboursville	B4
Beckley	D5

Name	Key
Belington	G2
Berkeley Springs	K1
Bluefield	D6
Bradley	D5
Bridgeport	F2
Buckhannon	F2
Charles Town	L2
Charleston, *capital*	C4
Chester	K4
Circleville	G3
Clarksburg	F2
Clay	D3
Clendenin	D3
Craigsville	E4
Davis	H2
East Liverpool	K4
Edray	F4
Eleanor	C3
Elizabeth	D2
Elkins	G3
Fairmont	F2
Fayetteville	D4
Fort Ashby	H3
Franklin	H3
Gary	C6
Glenville	E3
Grafton	F2
Grantsville	D3
Hamlin	B4
Harpers Ferry	L2
Harrisville	E2
Hinton	E5
Huntington	B4
Hurricane	B4
Inwood	K2
Kenova	A4
Keyser	J2
Kingwood	G2
Lewisburg	F5
Logan	C5
Madison	C4
Mannington	F1
Marlinton	F4
Marmet	C4
Martinsburg	L2
Matewan	B5
Middlebourne	E2
Milton	C4
Montgomery	D4
Moorefield	J2
Morgantown	G1
Moundsville	K6
Mt. Hope	D5
Mullens	D5
Newburg	G2
New Cumberland	K4
New Haven	C3
New Martinsville	E1
New Milton	E2
Nitro	C4
Oak Hill	D5
Oceana	C5
Orma	D3
Paden City	E1
Parkersburg	C2
Parsons	G2
Pennsboro	E2
Petersburg	H3
Peterstown	E6
Philippi	F2
Pineville	C5
Point Pleasant	B3
Princeton	D6
Rainelle	E5
Ravenswood	C3
Reedy	D3
Richwood	E4
Ripley	C3
Romney	J2
Ronceverte	E5
Rupert	E5
St. Albans	C4
St. Marys	D2
Salem	E2
Shady Spring	D5
Shepherdstown	L2
Shinnston	F2
Sistersville	E1
Slanesville	J2
South Charleston	C4
Spencer	D3
Summersville	E4
Sutton	E4
Terra Alta	G2
Union	E5
Vienna	C2
Wayne	B4
Webster Springs	F4
Weirton	K5
Welch	C6
Wellsburg	K5
Wellston	K4
West Milford	F2
Weston	F2
West Union	E2
Wheeling	K5
White Sulphur Springs	F5
Whitesville	D5
Williamson	B5
Williamstown	D2
Winfield	C3

Other Features

Name	Key
Allegheny, *mts.*	G4
Big Sandy, *river*	B5
Bluestone, *lake*	E5
Bluestone Natl. Scenic River	E5
Gauley River Natl. Rec. Area	D4
Greenbrier, *river*	F4
Harpers Ferry Natl. Hist. Park	L2
Kanawha, *river*	B3
New River Gorge Natl. River	D5
Ohio, *river*	E1
Potomac, *river*	J2
Shenandoah, *mts.*	H4
Spruce Knob, *mt.*	H3
Spruce Knob Seneca Rocks N.R.A.	H3
Sutton, *lake*	E3

Wisconsin ....page 176

Cities and Towns

Name	Key
Abbotsford	C4
Adams	D5
Algoma	F4
Alma	B4
Altoona	B4
Amery	A3
Antigo	D3
Appleton	E4

Name	Key
Arcadia	B4
Ashland	C2
Augusta	B4
Baldwin	A4
Balsam Lake	A3
Baraboo	D5
Barronett	A3
Bayside	F1
Beaver Dam	E5
Belleville	D6
Bellevue	F4
Beloit	D6
Bennett	B2
Berlin	E5
Bethesda	D6
Big Bend	E2
Black River Falls	C4
Bloomer	B3
Bloomville	D3
Boscobel	C5
Breed	E4
Brillion	E4
Brodhead	D6
Brookfield	E1
Brown Deer	F1
Bryant	D3
Buena Vista	D1
Burlington	E6
Butler	E1
Cadott	B4
Cameron	B3
Canton	B3
Carlsville	F4
Cedarburg	F5
Cedar Grove	F5
Chelsea	C3
Chetek	B3
Chili	C4
Chilton	E4
Chippewa Falls	B4
Cleveland	F5
Clinton	E6
Clintonville	E4
Colby	C4
Coloma	D5
Columbus	D5
Conrath	B3
Cornell	B3
Cornucopia	B2
Crandon	E3
Crestview	F2
Cuba City	C6
Cudahy	F2
Cumberland	A3
Darlington	C6
De Forest	D5
De Pere	E4
Delafield	D1
Delavan	E6
Denmark	F4
Dodgeville	C6
Duplainville	E1
Durand	B4
Eagle River	D3
Easton	D5
East Troy	E6
Eau Claire	B4
Edgar	C4
Edgerton	D6
Elkhorn	E6
Ellsworth	A4
Elm Grove	E1
Elroy	C5
Evansville	D6
Fennimore	C6
Florence	E3
Fond du Lac	E5
Forestville	F4
Fort Atkinson	E6
Fox Lake	E5
Fox Point	F1
Fredonia	F5
Friendship	D5
Galesville	B4
Genesee	D2
Genesee Depot	E5
Germantown	E5
Gillett	E4
Glendale	F1
Grafton	F5
Green Bay	F4
Greendale	F2
Greenfield	F2
Green Lake	E5
Greenleaf	E4
Hales Corners	E2
Hamburg	D3
Harrison	E5
Hartford	E5
Hartland	D1
Hayward	B2
Hillsboro	C5
Hollister	E3
Holmen	B5
Horicon	E5
Hortonville	E4
Howard	E4
Howards Grove	F5
Hudson	A4
Hurley	C2
Husher	F2
Jackson	E5
Janesville	D6
Jefferson	E6
Juda	D6
Jump River	C3
Juneau	E5
Kaukauna	E4
Kenosha	F6
Keshena	E4
Kewaskum	E5
Kewaunee	F4
Kiel	E5
Kneeland	F2
Lac du Flambeau	D3
La Crosse	B5
Ladysmith	B3
Lake Delton	D5
Lake Geneva	E6
Lake Mills	E5
Lampson	B3
Lancaster	C6
La Pointe	C2
Little Chute	E4
Lodi	D5
Lomira	E5
McFarland	D6
Madison, *capital*	D5
Maiden Rock	A4
Manitowish	C2
Manitowoc	F4

Name	Key
Marathon City	D4
Marinette	F3
Markesan	E5
Marshfield	C4
Mason	B2
Mattoon	D3
Mauston	D5
Mayville	E5
Medford	C3
Menasha	E4
Menomonee Falls	E5
Menomonie	B4
Mequon	F5
Merrill	D3
Middleton	D5
Milton	E6
Milwaukee	F5
Mineral Point	C6
Mishicot	F4
Modena	B4
Mole Lake	E3
Mondovi	B4
Monona	D5
Monroe	D6
Montello	D5
Montfort	C6
Mosinee	D4
Muscoda	C5
Muskego	E6
Neenah	E4
Neillsville	C4
Nekoosa	D4
New Berlin	E6
New Glarus	D6
New Holstein	E5
New Lisbon	C5
New London	E4
New Richmond	A3
Newton	F5
Niagara	F3
North Fond du Lac	E5
North Lake	D1
North Prairie	D2
Oak Creek	F6
Oconto	F4
Oconto Falls	E4
Odanah	C2
Omro	E5
Onalaska	B5
Oostburg	F5
Oregon	D6
Osceola	A3
Oshkosh	E4
Paddock Lake	E6
Palmyra	E6
Park Falls	C3
Pell Lake	E6
Peshtigo	F3
Pewaukee	E1
Phillips	C3
Platteville	C6
Pleasant Prairie	F6
Plover	D4
Plymouth	F5
Polonia	D4
Portage	D5
Port Edwards	D4
Porterfield	F3
Port Washington	F5
Port Wing	B2
Poynette	D5
Prairie du Chien	B5
Prairie du Sac	D5
Prescott	A4
Princeton	D5
Pulaski	E4
Racine	F6
Randolph	E5
Random Lake	F5
Raymond	F2
Reedsburg	D5
Rhinelander	D3
Rice Lake	B3
Richland Center	C5
Ridgeway	C5
Ripon	E5
River Falls	A4
River Hills	F1
Rothschild	D4
St. Croix Falls	A3
St. Francis	F2
Sauk City	D5
Saukville	F5
Saylesville	D2
Schofield	D4
Shawano	E4
Sheboygan	F5
Sheboygan Falls	F5
Shell Lake	B3
Shorewood	F1
Slinger	E5
South Milwaukee	F2
Sparta	C5
Spencer	C4
Spooner	B3
Spread Eagle	F3
Spring Green	C5
Stanley	C4
Stevens Point	D4
Stonebank	D6
Stoughton	D6
Sturgeon Bay	F4
Sturtevant	F6
Summit Lake	D3
Sun Prairie	D5
Superior	A2
Sussex	E1
Tabor	F2
Thompsonville	F2
Thorp	C4
Tomah	C5
Tomahawk	D3
Tony	C4
Two Rivers	F4
Verona	C5
Viroqua	C5
Wales	A3
Wanderoos	A3
Washburn	B2
Watertown	E5
Waukesha	E6
Waunakee	D5
Waupaca	E4
Waupun	E5
Wausau	D4
Wautoma	E1
Wauwatosa	F2
Wauzeka	C5
West Allis	F6
West Bend	E5
Westby	C5

Name	Key
West Milwaukee	F2
Weyauwega	E5
Whitehall	B4
Whitewater	E6
Williams Bay	E6
Wind Lake	D5
Wind Point	F6
Winneconne	E4
Wisconsin Dells	C3
Wisconsin Rapids	E5
Wrightstown	E5

Other Features

Name	Key
Apostle Islands Natl. Lakeshore	C2
Big Muskego, *lake*	D5
Castle Rock, *lake*	E6
Chetek, *lake*	F5
Chippewa, *lake*	C6
Door, *peninsula*	F4
Dubay, *lake*	B4
Flambeau, *river*	E3
Green, *bay*	B4
Madeline, *island*	D5
Michigan, *lake*	D6
Mississippi, *river*	D5
Outer, *island*	C6
Peshtigo, *river*	C5
Petenwell, *lake*	E6
Pewaukee, *lake*	E4
Poygan, *lake*	E4
St. Croix Natl. Scenic Riverway	C4
Sand, *island*	D4
Spring, *lake*	D6
Stockton, *island*	C5
Superior, *lake*	C5
Timms Hill, *mt.*	C5
Winnebago, *lake*	E4
Wisconsin, *river*	A3
Wolf, *river*	F3
Yellow, *river*	C5

Wyoming ....page

Cities and Towns

Name	Key
Afton	
Basin	
Boxelder	
Buffalo	
Byron	
Casper	
Cheyenne, *capital*	
Cody	
Cokeville	
Deaver	
Douglas	
Evanston	
Gillette	
Glenrock	
Green River	
Greybull	
Jackson	
Kemmerer	
Lander	
Laramie	
Lovell	
Lusk	
Lyman	
Medicine Bow	
Mills	
Newcastle	
Pinedale	
Powell	
Rawlins	
Reliance	
Riverton	
Rock Springs	
Saratoga	
Sheridan	
Sundance	
Thermopolis	
Torrington	
Wamsutter	
Wheatland	
Worland	

Other Features

Name	Key
Absaroka, *range*	A3
Belle Fourche, *river*	F2
Big Sandy, *river*	D5
Bighorn, *lake*	D2
Bighorn, *mts.*	D2
Bighorn, *river*	D4
Bighorn Canyon Natl. Rec. Area	
Bridger Peak, *mt.*	F5
Clarks Fork Yellowstone, *river*	
Cloud Peak, *mt.*	B3
Colter Peak, *mt.*	
Continental Divide, *mt. ridge*	E5
Devils Tower Natl. Monument	
Elk, *mt.*	C5
Flaming Gorge, *reservoir*	C4
Flaming Gorge Natl. Rec. Area	
Fort Laramie Natl. Hist. Site	
Fossil Butte Natl. Monument	
Francs Peak, *mt.*	
Gannett Peak, *mt.*	D1
Grand Teton, *mt.*	
Grand Teton Natl. Park	
Great Divide, *basin*	
Green, *river*	F6
Greybull, *river*	
Jackson, *lake*	
Laramie, *mts.*	
Laramie, *river*	F2
Laramie Peak, *mt.*	
Little Bighorn, *river*	
Little Missouri, *river*	
Little Powder, *river*	
Little Snake, *river*	
Medicine Bow, *river*	
North Platte, *river*	
Nowood, *river*	
Owl Creek, *mts.*	
Pathfinder, *reservoir*	
Powder, *river*	
Rocky, *mts.*	
Seminoe, *reservoir*	
South Fork Cheyenne, *river*	
South Fork Powder, *river*	
Sweetwater, *river*	
Teton, *mts.*	
Tongue, *river*	
Trout Peak, *mt.*	
Whiskey Peak, *mt.*	
Wind, *river*	
Wind River, *range*	
Yellowstone, *lake*	
Yellowstone Natl. Park	